BHAGAVAD GITA

Bhagavad Gita

its feeling and philosophy

SWAMI B. V. TRIPURARI

MANDALA
PUBLISHING

Other books by Swāmī B. V. Tripurāri:

Aesthetic Vedānta
Ancient Wisdom for Modern Ignorance
Form of Beauty
Gopāla-tāpanī Upaniṣad
Joy of Self
Rasa: Love Relationships in Transcendence
Śikṣāṣṭakam of Śrī Caitanya
Śrī Guru-Paramparā
Tattva-sandarbha

For philosophical inquires contact:

Sri Caitanya Sangha

e-mail: sricaitanyasangha@swami.org
website: www.swamitripurari.com

To order this and other books contact:

Mandala Publishing
10 Paul Drive
San Rafael, CA 94903

phone: 415–526–1370
e-mail: info@mandalapublishing.com
website: www.mandalapublishing.com

12 11 4 5 6 7

ISBN: 978-1-88606-953-4
Printed in the United States of America

In the service of my divine guardians, Śrīla A. C. Bhaktivedanta Swami Prabhupāda and Śrīla B. R. Śrīdhara Deva Goswāmī Mahārāja, this book is dedicated to Śrīla Bhaktisiddhānta Saraswatī Ṭhākura's spiritual great grandchildren, who are scattered throughout the globe. May they bring dignity and new light to his divine mission.

Contents

abbreviations .... *x*
foreword .... *xi*
preface .... *xv*
introduction .... *xix*

CHAPTER ONE
विषादयोगः
Viṣāda-yoga: YOGA OF DESPAIR 1

CHAPTER TWO
सांख्ययोगः
Sāṅkhya-yoga: YOGA OF ANALYSIS 31

CHAPTER THREE
कर्मयोगः
Karma-yoga: YOGA OF ACTION 93

CHAPTER FOUR
ज्ञानयोगः
Jñāna-yoga: YOGA OF KNOWLEDGE 129

CHAPTER FIVE
कर्मसन्न्यासयोगः
Karma-Sannyāsa-yoga:
YOGA OF RENUNCIATION OF ACTION 169

CHAPTER SIX
ध्यानयोगः
Dhyāna-yoga: YOGA OF MEDITATION 193

CHAPTER SEVEN
ज्ञानविज्ञानयोगाः
Jñāna-Vijñāna-yoga:
YOGA OF KNOWLEDGE AND REALIZATION 225

CHAPTER EIGHT
तारकब्रह्मयोगः
Tāraka-Brahma-yoga: YOGA OF ATTAINING THE ABSOLUTE 255

CHAPTER NINE
राजगुह्ययोगः
Rāja-Guhya-yoga: YOGA OF HIDDEN TREASURE 283

CHAPTER TEN
विभूतियोगः
Vibhūti-yoga: YOGA OF DIVINE MANIFESTATION 323

CHAPTER ELEVEN
विश्वरूपदर्शनयोगः
Viśva-rūpa-Darśana-yoga: YOGA OF THEOPHANY 357

CHAPTER TWELVE
भक्तियोगः
Bhakti-yoga: YOGA OF DEVOTION 395

CHAPTER THIRTEEN
प्रकृतिपुरुषविवेकयोगः
Prakṛti-Puruṣa-Viveka-yoga:
YOGA OF DELIBERATION ON MATTER AND SPIRIT 415

CHAPTER FOURTEEN
गुणत्रयविभागयोगः
Guṇa-Traya-Vibhāga-yoga:
YOGA OF DISTINGUISHING THE THREE MODES OF NATURE 441

CHAPTER FIFTEEN
पुरुषोत्तमयोगः
Puruṣottama-yoga: YOGA OF THE HIGHEST PERSON 465

CHAPTER SIXTEEN
दैवासुरसम्पद्योगः
Daivāsura-Sampada-yoga:
YOGA OF DISCERNING GODLY AND UNGODLY NATURES 485

CHAPTER SEVENTEEN
श्रद्धत्रयविभागयोगः
Śraddha-Traya-Vibhāga-yoga:
YOGA OF DISCERNING THREEFOLD FAITH 503

CHAPTER EIGHTEEN
मोक्षयोगः
Mokṣa-yoga: YOGA OF FREEDOM 521

glossary.............................581
index of verses 585
general index.....................597

Abbreviations

Ai. Ā.	*Aitareya-āraṇyaka*
Bg.	*Bhagavad-gītā*
Bṛ.	*Bṛhadāranyaka Upaniṣad*
Brs.	*Bhakti-rasāmṛta-sindhu*
Br. Sm.	*Brahma-saṁhitā*
Bs.	*Bhakti-sandarbha*
Cc.	*Caitanya-caritāmṛta*
Ch. Up.	*Chāndogya Upaniṣad*
Gt. Up.	*Gopāla-tāpanī Upaniṣad*
Ka. Up.	*Kaṭha Upaniṣad*
Kk.	*Kṛṣṇa-karṇāmṛta*
Ks.	*Kṛṣṇa-sandarbha*
MB.	*Mahābhārata*
Pp.	*Padma Pūrāṇa*
Ps.	*Paramātmā-sandarbha*
Ṛg	*Ṛg Veda*
ŚB.	*Śrīmad-Bhāgavatam*
Śve. Up.	*Śvetāsvatara Upaniṣad*
Tai. Br.	*Taittirīya-brāhmaṇa*
Tai. Up.	*Taittirīya Upaniṣad*
Ts.	*Tattva-sandarbha*
Un.	*Ujjvala-nīlamaṇi*
Vs.	*Vedānta-sūtra*
Ya. Sm.	*Yājñavalkya-smṛti*
Ys.	*Yoga-sūtra*

Foreword

THE BHAGAVAD-GITA is one of the great classics not only of world religion but of world philosophy and the great tradition of *yoga*. If we had to choose a single book to represent the spiritual and cultural traditions of India, we would certainly have to choose the *Gītā*. A person who has not studied the *Gītā* has missed something significant in our global wisdom heritage. In fact, if we were to put together the monotheism of the Western world with the nontheistic *karma*-based meditation traditions of Buddhism and the Far East, we would come up with something like the *Bhagavad-gītā*, which combines theism with *karma*, rebirth, and self-realization and encompasses global religion and experiential spirituality.

The scope of the *Gītā* is enormous. It covers devotional mysticism, meditative insight, cosmic vision, practical psychology, and even social activism: the keys to all aspects of life, mind, and consciousness. In every generation over thousands of years, it has provided inspiration for thinkers, leaders, and *yogīs* in India. Much of the inspiration for India's independence movement came from the study of the *Gītā* by such prominent figures as Gandhi, Tilak, and Aurobindo. The *Gītā* has been a key text for the great gurus of *yoga* who have come to the West, such as Paramahansa Yogananda and Śrīla Prabhupāda. Through gurus like these, the *Gītā* has provided unceasing and undiminishing inspiration to people all over the world.

The *Gītā* remains relevant today even though it was written before the time of Christ. Its instructions are clear, concise, logical, and scientific—not just appeals to faith, belief, personality, or culture. If you study the *Gītā* deeply and sincerely, its teachings can transform your life and awareness. That is why the *Bhagavad-gītā* remains one of the most popular books in the world today—a perennial bestseller.

A number of translations and interpretations of the *Gītā* exist. In India alone, literally thousands of commentaries on the text circulate. Because of the multi-faceted nature of its approach, the *Gītā* can be viewed from various angles, much like a brilliant gemstone. It can reflect, magnify, and enhance the light within us. Many great thinkers have looked to the *Gītā* for guidance and consolation, even though their worldviews or conceptions of divinity may differ from one another. Each philosophical system in the Hindu tradition has looked to the *Gītā* for light and produced a number of commentaries that bring out the richness of the *Gītā* for people of diverse temperaments and inclinations.

Despite its broad appeal, the *Gītā* is not just a general work of practical wisdom for all of humanity; it contains specific teachings for followers of particular *yoga* paths, as many in the West are discovering through their study of the *yoga* tradition. These teachings focus on the relevance of the *Gītā*'s message for *sādhana*, or individual spiritual practice. The *Gītā* is a manual of self-realization and God-realization for those who are on the path, covering all the main *yoga* approaches: knowledge *(jñāna)*, devotion *(bhakti)*, and service *(karma)*. The *Gītā* is arguably the prime textbook of the *yoga* tradition, being longer and more detailed than the *Yoga-sūtras*. In fact, to understand the *Sūtras*, which are often brief and obscure, one should study them along with the *Gītā*. Those wishing to become *yoga* teachers in the traditional sense of the term should avail themselves of the yogic insights of the *Gītā*.

Some traditions in India consider that Patañjali, the compiler of the *Yoga-sūtras*, was himself a follower of Kṛṣṇa. Patañjali is identified with Ananta, the great serpent of potential creative energy, on whom Viṣṇu reclines. Kṛṣṇa, the speaker of the *Gītā*, is the fullest expression of Viṣṇu manifest on earth—the *pūrṇa avatārā*. The *Gītā* addresses all the main topics of classical *yoga*, including the *yamas* and *niyamas*, *samādhi*, meditation, concentration, *pratyāhāra*, and even a brief mention of *āsana*. The *Gītā* is said to be a *yoga-śāstra* and each of its chapters is said to relate to a particular *yoga* approach. Looking at the *Gītā* in light of *yoga* helps us to uncover the depths of its teachings.

Yet despite the growing popularity of the *Gītā* through the expansion of *yoga* in the West, including the many versions of the *Gītā* in the English language, few are able to probe the depth of its teaching or consider the original Sanskrit and its many traditional commentaries. Swāmī B. V. Tripurāri is one of the few writers to do so, and his version of the *Gītā* is an excellent vehicle for readers in the West to explore these roots. His translation and interpretation of the *Gītā* is clear, detailed, and true to the original meaning of the text. By explaining the Sanskrit, Swāmī Tripurāri helps readers understand the original text. Swami's study of the *Gītā* is no mere quick analysis. It goes into depth, reflecting on the meaning of each word used and its subtle implications. He also brings in references to important Vaiṣṇava teachers and a great tradition of *Gītā* analysis that is seldom given its proper due.

I have known Swāmī Tripurāri for more than twenty years. I used to write for his *Clarion Call* magazine, which was one of the most insightful and innovative publications of its time on Vedic issues. Strangely, however, it was only a year or two ago that I actually met him in person. Swāmī Tripurāri, though born an American, has the appearance, expression, and even mannerism of a seasoned Swāmī from India. He has been able to bridge both East and West in his own life and teachings. His *Gītā* reflects this sensitivity and attention as well.

Swāmī Tripurāri speaks of the *Gītā* as both philosophy and feeling. Today, philosophy is largely a bad word in the West, particularly in the United States. We don't want theories. We want something practical, something to experience quickly—not something to contemplate over time. And most of what we call philosophy in our educational system has little relevance to our lives, reflecting rather the obscurities of science, linguistics, economics, or politics.

In the spiritual traditions of India, however, the term generally rendered as "philosophy" is *darśana*, which means a way of seeing. It is something someone has actually experienced, rather than simply a matter of speculation or conjecture. The ability to arrive at such an experience rests on a particular lifestyle, discipline, and spiritual practice. Such a philosophy is a distillation of wisdom that can guide us forward like a ray of light. We all need such philosophies to make our thought and perception meaningful and linked to the transcendent. In the philosophies, or *darśanas*, of India, feeling has always had an important role. Deep insight is not possible without a depth of feeling to sustain it. Truth, after all, is a matter of conviction and has a certain passion to it. Even the most abstract of India's philosophers, the great nondualist Śaṅkara, composed some of the most beautiful Sanskrit devotional poetry.

Our higher mind (what is called *buddhi* in Sanskrit), which the *Gītā* emphasizes, is key to the practice of *yoga*. It brings together deep feeling and direct knowing like the two wings of a bird, lifting the mind to new levels. To grasp the real philosophy of the *Gītā* requires a consummate sense of feeling—the ability to feel the divine presence both in oneself and in the world as directly as one would feel the presence of a lover. Current academic approaches to the *Gītā* downplay the vitality and passion of the *Gītā* and turn it into little more than a fossil or museum piece. Attempts to secularize the *Gītā* by removing religion from it and making it into a kind of life-management strategy miss the deep devotion that the *Gītā* honors and requires (though such attempts can make the *Gītā* accessible to the nonreligious mind). Swāmī Tripurāri deftly navigates both of these poles and provides an alternative that shows both the rational and the devotional side of the text, which support, rather than contradict, one another.

Some people have the impression that the devotional traditions of India, the *bhakti-yoga* paths, are a kind of mindless emotionalism punctuated by unintelligible chants that brainwash people. Nothing could be further from the truth. The followers of *bhakti-yoga* have produced a vast tradition of philosophical texts, commentaries, and painstaking textual and logical analysis; clear principles of cosmology, psychology, and human behavior; and poignant comments on current affairs. This intellectually rigorous *bhakti* is what we find in the work of Swāmī Tripurāri. Besides a necessary commentary on the *Gītā*, his work is also a good introduction to the broader tradition of *bhakti* philosophy, showing that it is alive and well not only in India but also in the West. He quotes from and brings in the great tradition of Vaiṣṇava philosophy, particularly as it is represented in the works of Śrīla Prabhupāda, India's main teacher who brought this tradition to the West some decades ago, from whom Swāmī Tripurāri received special instruction. Both Śrīla Prabhupāda and Swāmī Tripurāri belong to the tradition of Caitanya Mahāprabhu (perhaps the greatest of all the devotional philosophers of the *Gītā*) and the great lineages of thinkers that have arisen from him.

Swāmī Tripurāri has published many books and articles on all aspects of the spiritual life over the last twenty-five years while directing a spiritual organization with global affiliations. His work deserves more attention, particularly as the subject of *bhakti-yoga* again emerges into the *yoga* community. His *Gītā* is probably his most important book. Swāmī Tripurāri's commentary on the *Gītā* is an extensive and monumental work, an important addition to the literature on the *Gītā*. It opens ground for much new study and research, particularly in the realm of spiritual practice and *yoga*. Through Swāmī Tripurāri's commentary, we can gain access not only to the *Gītā* but also to a vast tradition of devotional thought and practice that is based upon it. This can change our view of self, world, and divinity in fundamental and transformative ways.

—David Frawley
Santa Fe, New Mexico, March 2008

PREFACE

EARLY ONE MORNING in the spring of 1973, I was invited for the first time to accompany my spiritual master on a morning walk. As the sun rose on a sleeping Los Angeles, I climbed, wide-eyed at the prospect of intimate association with my guru, into a small white Toyota station wagon along with two of my Godbrothers and our Prabhupāda.

We drove to Cheviot Hills, one of two places where Prabhupāda would take his morning walk when in Los Angeles. He preferred Venice Beach, but variety has value. On this particular morning, the park was damp and the ground had just been aerated. After Prabhupāda indirectly let us know his preference for Venice Beach through his critique of the park, he spoke to us about the shortcomings of modern science. In the course of questioning the possibility of something arising out of nothing, the conversation itself dissipated and we walked in silence.

The little clumps of earth scattered all about appeared like stools to the uninformed, and I found myself questioning why we had brought Prabhupāda to this place. Were they stools? Prabhupāda broke the silence to ask this very question. Too embarrassed and ignorant to answer, I left it to the others, one of whom explained in brief the art of aerating the earth.

The silence continued, and I felt the need to absorb my mind in spiritual thoughts, lest it not take full advantage of the opportunity at hand. Crossing the field, as if influenced by a force beyond myself, I thought spontaneously of Vṛndāvana, Kṛṣṇa, and his cowherds and cows. Almost effortlessly my mind became absorbed in a sense of the pastoral setting of Vṛndāvana and Kṛṣṇa's *līlās* of cowherding with his friends. Where were we really?

Clad in saffron robes, an elderly man of five feet four, no more, walked with an eternal youthfulness that questioned the apparent youth of those who walked beside him. With his head held high in absolute confidence, he challenged the metanarrative of modern science, making it seem as if scientific materialism could be crushed by a mere poke from his cane. His glance so captivating, benedicting, his eyes tinged with the ointment of love of Kṛṣṇa, our beloved Prabhupāda wanted the world to stop and just love Kṛṣṇa. He wanted us to be his instruments through which this would be accomplished.

Prabhupāda compellingly told us to write articles, publish them, and replace the prevailing paradigm with Kṛṣṇa's message. Then someone mentioned my name and success in the field of distributing his books. Prabhupāda turned to me and said, "By distributing these books, you are doing a great service to Kṛṣṇa. He [Kṛṣṇa] wanted to say to everyone: *sarva-dharmān parityajya mām ekaṁ śaraṇaṁ vraja.* He comes, therefore. So anyone who is doing the same service, he is recognized by Kṛṣṇa very nicely. That is stated in the *Bhagavad-gītā: na ca tasmān manuṣyeṣu.* In the human society, nobody is dearer than he who is helping preaching work."

In the first words he ever spoke to me, Prabhupāda cited three verses from the *Bhagavad-gītā*, all from the eighteenth chapter. First he cited the conclusion of the *Gītā*: "Forgoing all religious injunctions, take exclusive refuge in me." Then he cited Kṛṣṇa's two verses of praise for those involved in disseminating this conclusion. The actual verses run thus: "One who explains this supreme secret to my devotees engages in the highest devotion to me. He will undoubtedly come to me. No one in this world is more dear to me than he is, nor will there ever be anyone on earth more dear to me."

In his *Gītā* commentary, Prabhupāda elaborates on Kṛṣṇa's words regarding those who explain his message: "Anyone, however, who tries sincerely to present *Bhagavad-gītā* as it is will advance in devotional activities and reach the pure devotional state of life. As a result of such pure devotion, he is sure to go back home, back to Godhead." By the phrase "as it is," which became the subtitle for Prabhupāda's edition of the *Gītā*, Prabhupāda meant explaining the *Bhagavad-gītā* from a devotional perspective. Only one who loves Kṛṣṇa is privy to the deepest implications of his eloquent speech.

After Prabhupāda encouraged all of us to write and distribute books about Kṛṣṇa, one of my Godbrothers commented, "We are simply your puppets, Śrīla Prabhupāda. You're giving us the books." This did not seem to satisfy Śrīla Prabhupāda, and he made the following reference to the *guru-paramparā:* "No. We are all puppets of Kṛṣṇa. I am also a puppet. This is disciplic succession." While he humbly gave all credit to his own guru and Kṛṣṇa for anything he had accomplished, he implied that becoming the instrument of guru and Kṛṣṇa had a dynamic application: it involved not merely circulating the books of one's guru but writing books oneself as he had done. This was the example he set. While writing his own books, he considered that he was merely acting as a puppet of guru and Kṛṣṇa.

Becoming the puppet of one's guru is about getting a spiritual life and thinking for oneself within the parameters of what is actually spiritual.

Looking back at that spring morning in Los Angeles' Cheviot Hills as I myself turned fifty, I felt that my life would be incomplete if I did not author an edition of *Bhagavad-gītā* in contemporary language. Faithfully distributing that which another has drawn down from the infinite should in time bear the fruit of enabling such a distributor to draw down something himself. This is the fruit of the seed that Śrī Guru plants in the heart of the disciple. In the form of this edition of *Bhagavad-gītā*, I have been able to taste this fruit to some extent only by my spiritual master's grace, and he sent several persons to assist me in this effort. I am grateful to all of them. May he bless them, and may Śrī Caitanya, who is none other than Rādhā-Kṛṣṇa combined, continue to bless the world with his doctrine of love of Godhead. May that blessing come in the form of devotional literature written from within the cultural context of devotees of Kṛṣṇa who are now taking birth all over the world.

Swāmī B. V. Tripurāri

Introduction

"Yet another edition of the *Bhagavad-gītā*, and yet another accompanying introduction that strains to justify it!" Let us deal with this world-weary sigh by doing nothing more than quoting the concluding words of Sañjaya, the *Gītā*'s narrator: "O King, recalling again and again this wonderful and sacred conversation between Kṛṣṇa and Arjuna, I am thrilled at every moment." (Bg. 18.76) New insights into this unfathomable, divine conversation are always welcome.

The *Song of God* has been studied for centuries, lending itself to interpretations of all kinds: academic, ecological, psychological, sociological, political, and popular. Though its wisdom has been identified with the perennial philosophy, it speaks on many levels to its varied congregation, primarily about life's ultimate necessity: self-realization within the context of God-realization.

Kṛṣṇa's speech is said to be *vāvadūka*, which means that it is ambrosial and pleasing to the ears. Kṛṣṇa himself is described as *satyavāk*, because his words never prove to be false. In his conversation with Arjuna in the *Bhagavad-gītā*, Kṛṣṇa's ambrosial speech and the truth of his message are apparent. It is no wonder that his words have been immortalized in human society, where he descends to express himself in the fullness of love.

Although some devotees have tried to establish the historicity of Kṛṣṇa's appearance five thousand years ago, as well as events that are said to have taken place at that time—such as the *Gītā*'s Kurukṣetra War—they have not made much progress in documenting physical evidence. Where devotees have succeeded is in recording their own extraordinary mystical experiences of Kṛṣṇa, and the theological and philosophical ramifications of these experiences are a spiritual reality that human society must reckon with.

Kṛṣṇa represents the love life of the Absolute. While Buddha taught wisdom leading to the cessation of suffering and Christ salvation through love, Kṛṣṇa is God in love, living in eternity with his devotees. Devotees of Kṛṣṇa embody five basic types of love: passive adoration *(śānta-rasa)*, servitude *(dāsya-rasa)*, friendship *(sakhya-rasa)*, parental affection *(vātsalya-rasa)*, and romantic love *(mādhurya-rasa)*. These five basic expressions of devotional love *(bhakti-rasa)* may also overlap, and each has its own subdivisions. Arjuna of the *Gītā* loves Kṛṣṇa as a friend with an admixture of servitude. His friendly relationship with Kṛṣṇa is called *pura-sambandhi* and is specific to Kṛṣṇa's city *līlā* (divine play), as opposed to Kṛṣṇa's more intimate, pastoral Vraja *līlā*. Among all of Kṛṣṇa's city friends, Arjuna is most prominent.

Before coming to the big city of Mathurā and later establishing his capital at Dwārakā, Kṛṣṇa was raised in Vraja. The setting of Vraja represents the beauty of simplicity, the beauty of the natural environment. Kṛṣṇa's father was a herdsman, and Kṛṣṇa himself a cowherder. Decorated with ornaments from the forest—its flowers, leaves, and multicolored clays—and crowned with the conjuror's peacock plume, this Kṛṣṇa, his only weapon the flute, is said to be Kṛṣṇa in his fullness, *svayaṁ bhagavān*. He is God when God wants to be himself, relaxing in the company of his intimate devotees, forgetful of even his own Godhood to facilitate this intimacy. This Kṛṣṇa is the connoisseur of love yet subjugated by his lover Rādhā.[1] In the language of India's aestheticians, Vraja Kṛṣṇa, subjugated by Rādhā's love, is the most perfect *(pūrṇatama) dhīra-lalita nāyaka*[2] and, as such, is in no mood to speak Upaniṣadic wisdom.

Kṛṣṇa of the *Gītā*, while the same person as Kṛṣṇa of Vraja, is in a very different mood. As is the case with all of his moods, his emotional makeup in his *Bhagavad-gītā līlā* is relative to the nature of his accompanying devotees' love. Once he leaves Vraja on his mission to establish *dharma*,[3] Kṛṣṇa is surrounded by devotees who have a greater awareness of his Godhood. This sense distances them from him slightly, introducing formalities into their dealings not found in his relationships with the devotees of Vraja. In the city, Kṛṣṇa, the village adolescent, matures into eternal youthfulness. He becomes a judicious prince—peaceful, humble, and wise. In the aesthetic language of Bharata Muni,[4] he is the perfect

1. Rādhā is Kṛṣṇa's primal *śakti*. She is the shine of the Kṛṣṇa sun. He is the supreme object of love and she is the abode of supreme love. As all *avatāras* of Godhead issue from Kṛṣṇa, similarly all of their counterwhole consorts emanate from Rādhā and partially represent her.

2. There are four basic hero *(nāyaka)* types in classical Indian drama and poetry. The *dhīra-lalita nāyaka* is described in Brs. (2.1.230) thus: "a person who is very cunning and always youthful, expert in joking and without anxiety, and always subjugated by his girlfriends is called *dhīra-lalita nāyaka*." In secular drama and poetry, Cupid is considered the ideal *dhīra-lalita nāyaka*.

3. Here *dharma* refers to the *avatāra*'s mission to establish scriptural codes. See Bg. 4.7–8.

4. Bharata Muni is considered to be the founder of Indian aesthetic theory, the legendary author of Nāṭya-śāstra.

(pūrṇa) dhīra-praśānta nāyaka.[5] It is this Kṛṣṇa who speaks *Gītopaniṣad*, the *Bhagavad-gītā*.

From the *Bhagavad-gītā*, we come to know of Kṛṣṇa's divinity. In the light of this knowledge, his village life takes on new meaning. The informal simplicity of the Vraja *līlā* is like a black backdrop that causes the valuable jewel of Kṛṣṇa to shine that much more. God's acting like a human to the extent that he falls in love, as does Kṛṣṇa with Rādhā, is indeed a sweet and charming expression of his divinity, one that gives us a clue as to how to approach him such that he becomes easily accessible to us. When the Absolute is overcome by love, he manifests a transcendental need that arises not from inadequacy but from the fullness of love. The nature of love is such that it causes one to feel both full and in need of sharing one's fullness. Kṛṣṇa becomes most accessible to anyone acquainted with his inner necessity to share his love. This is the sacred secret of the *Upaniṣads* to which *Śrī Gītā* ultimately points. While establishing the general principles of *dharma*, Kṛṣṇa reveals the glory of *prema-dharma*,[6] the *dharma* of love itself.

This edition of the *Bhagavad-gītā* follows the tradition of Gauḍīya Vedānta. It is the Gauḍīyas, disciples of Śrī Caitanya, who first conceived of explaining the Upaniṣadic subject matter in the language of aesthetics. Drawing on the *Taittirīya Upaniṣad*'s dictum *raso vai saḥ* (the Absolute is aesthetic rapture), Rūpa Goswāmī proceeded to elaborate on the heart of the Absolute, indeed, on its love life. He envisioned the Absolute as the perfect lover, the irresistible Kṛṣṇa of the sacred literature, and explained Kṛṣṇa's complexities with startling insight. To date, no one has even attempted to tell us more about the personality of Godhead.

Since Kṛṣṇa of Vraja is the origin of God's incarnations, the feature of Godhead in which all others are included, the Gauḍīyas have mostly written about him. Their commentaries on the *Śrīmad-Bhāgavatam* are well known, as are many of their original compositions. However, they have also written on the *Upaniṣads*, where the love sports of Kṛṣṇa are, if at all present, well concealed.

Baladeva Vidyābhūṣaṇa wrote *Govinda-bhāṣya*, the Gauḍīya commentary on the *Vedānta-sūtras* of Bādarāyaṇa Vyāsa, in which he seeks to demonstrate the concordance of *śruti*—the *Upaniṣads*—with Gauḍīya

5. The *dhīra-praśānta nāyaka* is described in Brs. 2.1.232 thus: "Peaceful, tolerant of miseries, judicious, and humble, such is the *dhīra-praśānta nāyaka*."

6. This term refers to the love exhibited in Kṛṣṇa's Vraja *līlā*.

theology. He also wrote a commentary on the *Bhagavad-gītā*, as did his predecessor, Viśvanātha Cakravartī Ṭhākura. Before them, Kṛṣṇadāsa Kavirāja Goswāmī cited the *Gītā* more than thirty times in his classic, *Caitanya-caritāmṛta*, and his predecessor Jīva Goswāmī cited it profusely in his seminal *Ṣaṭ-sandarbha*. Evidently, *dhīra-praśānta* Kṛṣṇa of the *Gītā* is quite relevant to devotees of *dhīra-lalita* Kṛṣṇa!

Viśvanātha Cakravartī was the first in the Gauḍīya lineage to write an entire commentary on the *Gītā*. He is most well known for his highly esoteric explanations of the inner significance of Kṛṣṇa's *līlās* of love with the *gopīs* of Vraja. Yet it would seem that he found it important to remind us that *gopī*-Kṛṣṇa is, after all, God, even when suppressing this aspect of himself for the sake of his intimate *līlās*. We must first understand the metaphysical truth *(tattva)* concerning Kṛṣṇa as the source of the world and all souls before we forget the world and lose ourselves in divine love of Kṛṣṇa. Among the sacred texts of the Hindus, no book is better suited to give this teaching than the *Bhagavad-gītā*.

Known also as *Gītopaniṣad* due to its having been spoken directly by God himself,[7] *Bhagavad-gītā* is the essence of the *Upaniṣads*. If one wants to understand the entirety of the thousands of verses in the Upaniṣadic canon, one need only understand the seven hundred verses of the *Bhagavad-gītā*. While the *Upaniṣads* are often thought to be more philosophical than religious, it is significant that this balance is reversed in the *Gītopaniṣad*. It posits a religio-philosophical metanarrative in which a mystical life of direct spiritual experience emerges. Perhaps the most significant thing about the *Gītā* is its inclusive nature, in which no particular doctrine is condemned but each finds its place in a hierarchy of spiritual practices and transcendence. Worship of God is never transcended in the *Gītā*. It takes the form of unalloyed devotion, surpassing even knowledge of both the soul and the Godhood of Godhead. It thus brings us to the door of Vraja *bhakti*.

Popular understanding holds that the *Upaniṣads* reveal a formless, impersonal Absolute, approached through the wisdom of introspection, as opposed to religious ritual. In this view, devotion can be useful, but it is ultimately dispensed with. By popular understanding, I am referring to the Adwaita Vedānta of Śaṅkara and those who hold neo-Adwaitin views. Acceptance of Śaṅkara's basic understanding of Hindu sacred literature is so widespread that many make no distinction between the two. They think

7. The *Upaniṣads* are thought to have issued directly from God.

that the Adwaitin doctrine of Śaṅkara *is* Vedānta, unaware of the fact that Adwaita Vedānta is only one strand of Vedānta philosophy, one that differs radically from the other principal schools.[8]

Of the five devotional schools, that of the Gauḍīyas is the most recent, and thus has the distinct advantage of being able to draw on the devotional wealth that came before it. The host of commentators in the devotional schools of Vedānta that followed Śaṅkara have all vociferously refuted his doctrines—doctrines that include dispensing with God, the individual soul, and the world, as well as subjugating devotion to knowledge, all in the name of nonduality. While the devotional commentators may have subtle theological differences that demarcate their particular schools of Vedānta, they are in sufficient agreement with one another to unanimously oppose these doctrines of Śaṅkara.

Among the devotional commentaries of the *Gītā*, Rāmānuja's is the first and thus the most influential. It has made significant inroads in academic circles. Rāmānuja's commentary is brilliant in its demonstration of the congruity of the *Gītā*'s many paths and the post-liberated nature of devotion. In some places I have cited Rāmānuja's commentary or followed his sense of the text. This is in keeping with Jīva Goswāmī's policy of acknowledging venerable Vaiṣṇavas, as discussed in his *Tattva-sandarbha*. I have cited Śrīdhara Swāmī's *Subodhinī* in the same spirit.

Viśvanātha Cakravartī Ṭhākura and Baladeva Vidyābhūṣaṇa have referred to Rāmānuja but seem more influenced by Śrīdhara Swāmī, whose commentary they often follow closely. This attests to the influence of Śrīdhara Swāmī on the Gauḍīya school, already well documented in the case of *Śrīmad-Bhāgavatam*.[9]

Also relevant to the present work is Adwaitin Madhusūdana Saraswatī's *Gūḍhārtha-dīpikā* commentary on *Bhagavad-gītā*,[10] which Viśvanātha Cakravartī cites numerous times. In the interest of substantiating the plausibility of the Gauḍīya understanding of the *Gītā*, I have cited Madhusūdana Saraswatī's commentary in places. As neo-Adwaitins may think the Gauḍīya rendering forced in places, it will be useful for them to know that such a highly renowned scholar and guru of the Adwaita lineage is often

8. *Viśiṣṭādvaita*, *Dvaita*, *Dvaitādvaita*, *Suddhādvaita*, and *Acintya-bhedābheda*.

9. See Cc. Antya 7.133.

10. Madhusūdana Saraswatī was a junior contemporary of Śrī Caitanya yet never met him. It is apparent that he was influenced by Gauḍīya Vedānta enough to regard it as a viable alternative to Adwaita, the doctrine of his own choice.

supportive of the Gauḍīya interpretations of the flow of *Śrī Gītā*'s verse and its emphasis on devotion.

The commentaries of Viśvanātha Cakravartī Ṭhākura and Baladeva Vidyābhūṣaṇa in the Gauḍīya lineage are, in comparison to Rāmānuja's commentary, far less known. True to their devotion to the sweet Kṛṣṇa of Vraja, their explanation of the *Gītā* brings a charm to the text that Rāmānuja's does not; moreover, they place greater emphasis on devotion, both in terms of its power to afford the highest salvation and in its magnanimity in extending itself to the lowest section of society. I have cited these two principal Gauḍīya commentators throughout, and naturally I am primarily indebted to them. Although Śrī Viśvanātha and Baladeva Vidyābhūṣaṇa occasionally differ, their differences remain within the parameters of the lineage's devotional conclusions *(siddhānta)*. These two have elaborately demonstrated from their knowledge of Sanskrit and the entire corpus of sacred literature instances in which some verses can take on a special meaning that is hidden from the vision of those whose eyes have not been tinged with the salve of love of Kṛṣṇa.

Perhaps Gauḍīya commentators appear to go out on a limb more than anywhere else when they find Vraja Kṛṣṇa speaking in the *Gītā*.[11] According to Gauḍīya theology, the *dhīra-praśānta* Kṛṣṇa of the *Gītā* is not preoccupied with Vraja and the love of the *gopīs*. As much as the *dhīra-lalita* Kṛṣṇa of Vraja is in no mood for an Upaniṣadic discourse, *dhīra-praśānta* Kṛṣṇa of Dwārakā is typically not in the mood of Vraja *bhakti*. However, careful study of the *Śrīmad-Bhāgavatam* in conjunction with the *Padma* and *Harivaṁśa Purāṇas* reveals that the prince of the *Gītā* does occasionally think of Vraja, as he did in Kurukṣetra during his first visit to this sacred place.

According to *Śrīmad-Bhāgavatam* (1.11.9), Kṛṣṇa returned to Mathurā to kill Dantavakra before the *Gītā* was spoken. *Padma Purāṇa* reveals that he then went from Mathurā to Vraja Dhāma.[12] After remaining in Vraja for two months, he transferred all of his Vraja devotees to his unmanifest eternal *līlā* of Goloka. According to Viśvanātha Cakravartī's comments on the *Padma Purāṇa*, Kṛṣṇa himself went in a nearly complete *(pūrṇa-kalpa-prakāśa)* manifestation to Goloka. In another, most complete *(pūrṇatama-prakāśa)* plenary manifestation, he remained per-

11. Viśvanātha Cakravartī hears Kṛṣṇa speaking of *rāgānuga-bhakti* in Bg. 10.9. Bhaktivinoda Ṭhākura and several other modern commentators follow his lead in their commentaries.

12. Pp., *Uttara-khaṇḍa*, 279.

petually enjoying in Vraja, invisible to material eyes. In yet another plenary manifestation *(pūrṇa-prakāśa)*, he mounted his chariot and returned alone to Dwārakā.

Following his return, Kṛṣṇa spoke *Bhagavad-gītā*. This prince of Dwārakā no doubt thought of the highest devotion of his Vraja devotees from time to time while speaking of devotion to Arjuna. Indeed, as mentioned earlier, the entire *līlā* of Dwārakā is not unrelated to Vraja. Kṛṣṇa went to Dwārakā for the sake of protecting his Vraja devotees. As Sanātana Goswāmī finds Dwārakā's prince calling out Rādhā's name in his sleep in his *Bṛhad-Bhāgavatāmṛta* (1.6.51–52), Gauḍīya commentators have heard him speak of Vraja *bhakti* by reading between the lines of his song to Arjuna. Indeed, even within the embrace of his principal queen of Dwārakā, prince Kṛṣṇa thinks of Vraja and Rādhā's love. Umāpati Dhara, quoted in Rūpa Goswāmī's *Padyāvalī* (371) and *Ujjvala-nīlamaṇi* (14.184), prays thus: "In his palace in Dwārakā, on the sparkling, gem-strewn shores of the ocean, Kṛṣṇa's body shivered with ecstasy in the tight embrace of none other than Rukmiṇī. Yet his mind recalled the fragrance of the love he had enjoyed with Rādhā in the reeds by the banks of the black Yamunā waters, and he fainted. May that faint protect you always."

Ultimately, the theological resolution to the apparent contradiction in which Vraja *bhakti* issues from the lips of the prince of Dwārakā lies in the power of *bhakti* itself. Devotees see Kṛṣṇa in everyone and everything by the force of their love for him. Śrī Caitanya is said to have made the statement, *mora mana vṛndāvana*: "My mind is Vṛndāvana (Vraja)." He saw all rivers as the Vraja's Yamunā, all mountains as its Govardhana. In the majestic Jagannātha Deity of Śrīdhāma Puri, he saw Vraja's sweet *dhīra-lalita* Kṛṣṇa, flute in hands, head adorned with peacock feather.[13] In consideration of this, it is hardly a stretch for his devotees to hear Vraja Kṛṣṇa, the *dhīra-lalita* of Rādhā, in princely Kṛṣṇa's words. The gap is further narrowed by the fact that on the battleground of sacred Kurukṣetra, long before he spoke the *Gīta* to Arjuna, Kṛṣṇa met with Rādhā and the *gopīs* after a long and painful period of separation.[14] Setting foot again in that holy place for the purpose of instructing Arjuna, prince Kṛṣṇa was no doubt influenced by that memory. Thus in the midst of his discourse to Arjuna on comparative religion, in which *bhakti* effortlessly rises to the top as the cream of the milk

13. See Cc. Antya 16.85.
14. See ŚB. 10.78.

of religion, it is natural for Arjuna's charioteer to steer the conversation in the direction of Vraja and the highest expression of devotion.

The idea that the spiritual emotion *(bhāva)* of the Gauḍīya commentators brings their interpretation of the *Gītā* to the pitch of Vraja *bhakti* is charming. The feeling that prejudices their vision is by no means a blemish. After all, it is feeling for the *Gītā* and love of Kṛṣṇa that the text seeks to arouse in its reader. Their feeling for Kṛṣṇa, arising out of a firm philosophical and scriptural foundation, is the most valuable thing one can hope to experience in the course of studying *Bhagavad-gītā*. In feeling their emotion, readers will also get the feel of the *Gītā*, and thus feeling for Kṛṣṇa.

After the time of Baladeva Vidyābhūṣaṇa, who passed from the world in the mid-eighteenth century, the *Bhagavad-gītā* became somewhat neglected in the Gauḍīya school until the time of Bhaktivinoda Ṭhākura, the great revivalist of the tradition in the late nineteenth century. Ṭhākura Bhaktivinoda published two different Bengali editions of the *Gītā* based on the two great Sanskrit commentaries that came before him.

Bhaktivinoda Ṭhākura's son and successor, Śrīla Bhaktisiddhānta Saraswatī, continued the Ṭhākura's preaching mission and recognized the necessity of translating the *Gītā* into English. Of his disciples, Bhakti Hridoy Bon Mahārāja was the first to publish a translation and commentary in the Gauḍīya spirit. His translation, *The Geeta as a Chaitanyaite Reads It*, is based on Viśvanātha Cakravartī's commentary. Bon Mahārāja's commentary was followed by Bhakti Pradīpa Tīrtha Mahārāja's English edition. The most influential Gauḍīya Vaiṣṇava edition was written by my own spiritual master, Śrīla A.C. Bhaktivedanta Swami Prabhupāda, whose *Bhagavad-gītā As It Is* has sold more copies than any other edition to date. Śrīla Prabhupāda's translation is dedicated to Baladeva Vidyābhūṣaṇa. His indebtedness to Baladeva is clear throughout his English purports. My *śikṣā-guru*, B.R. Śrīdhara Deva Goswāmī, also published a translation of the *Gītā* based on Viśvanātha Cakravartī's commentary, in which he reveals the underlying esoteric understanding of Vraja *bhakti*.

In the present edition, I have adopted a more literal translation of the original Sanskrit text, keeping the Gauḍīya purport confined to the commentary. I have also taken pains to demonstrate the congruity of the *Gītā*, its natural flow from verse to verse, which has not been a focus of other modern Gauḍīya commentators. I have occasionally cited references to the *Gītā* from the *Ṣaṭ-sandarbha* of Jīva Goswāmī and *Caitanya-caritāmṛta* of Kṛṣṇadāsa Kavirāja Goswāmī, both of which precede the earliest Gauḍīya

Bhagavad-gītā commentary, and I have also cited a number of Baladeva Vidyābhūṣaṇa's references to the *Gītā* in his *Govinda-bhāṣya* commentary on *Vedānta-sūtra*. The language is contemporary, and as much as possible I have tried to bring home the relevance of the *Gītā*, and the Gauḍīya import in particular, for the times in which we live. In all of this, I hope that this edition will serve as a meaningful contribution for the Gauḍīya lineage, an indicator of its vitality at the beginning of the twenty-first century.

While I am hopeful that both practitioners and casual readers will find this edition helpful, I initially undertook this work for my own edification and purification. In this, I feel that my work has been a success, as it has given rise in me to real feeling for the *Gītā*, Kṛṣṇa, and Arjuna. It is this feeling that I have attempted to weave into the text. May its careful study awaken spiritual sentiment in its readers as well, for it is this feeling that does not allow one to tire from hearing Kṛṣṇa's ambrosial words, edition after edition, thrilled at every moment.

CHAPTER ONE

विषादयोगः

Viṣāda-yoga

YOGA OF DESPAIR

Text 1

धृतराष्ट्र उवाच
धर्मक्षेत्रे कुरुक्षेत्रे समवेता युयुत्सवः ।
मामकाः पाण्डवाश्चैव किमकुर्वत सञ्जय ॥१॥

dhṛtarāṣṭra uvāca
dharma-kṣetre kuru-kṣetre samavetā yuyutsavaḥ/
māmakāḥ pāṇḍavāś caiva kim akurvata sañjaya//

dhṛtarāṣṭraḥ uvāca—Dhṛtarāṣṭra said; *dharma-kṣetre*—in the sacred field; *kuru-kṣetre*—at Kurukṣetra; *samavetāḥ*—assembled; *yuyutsavaḥ*—eager to fight; *māmakāḥ*—mine (my sons); *pāṇḍavāḥ*—the sons of Pāṇḍu; *ca*—and; *eva*—certainly; *kim*—what; *akurvata*—they did; *sañjaya*—O Sañjaya.

Dhṛtarāṣṭra said: O Sañjaya, what did my sons and the sons of Pāṇḍu do as they assembled at sacred Kurukṣetra, eager to fight?

The *Bhagavad-gītā* appears in the "Bhīṣma-parva" of the Hindu scripture *Mahābhārata*. Its seven hundred verses make up only one chapter in the world's longest epic. Amid romance, political intrigue, and war, *dharma*, the path of righteousness, is woven throughout the fabric of *Mahābhārata*. The *Bhagavad-gītā* brings to light the very essence of this *dharma: prema-dharma*, the *dharma* of love.

The first chapter of the *Gītā* introduces the reader to the historical setting in which Kṛṣṇa and Arjuna's sacred conversation, which constitutes the balance of the *Gītā*, will take place. Chariots are drawn in military array and war is now inevitable. The fratricidal clash that the *Mahābhārata* has been leading to is beyond stopping—the sons of Dhṛtarāṣṭra led by

Duryodhana are on one side, the sons of Dhṛtarāṣṭra's deceased brother, Pāṇḍu, led by Yudhiṣṭhira on the other. Dhṛtarāṣṭra was blind from birth, yet the sage Vyāsa offered to give him eyes to witness the battle. How unsightly the battle was to be is clear from Dhṛtarāṣṭra's refusal of Vyāsa's offer. Indeed, Dhṛtarāṣṭra, his attachment for Duryodhana blinding him to justice, was instrumental in this unfortunate turn of events. Had his sense of justice not been overruled by material attachment for his son, the battle might have been avoided. As overtly unbecoming as Dhṛtarāṣṭra's role was, it gave Kṛṣṇa the opportunity to speak about the nature of attachment, its consequences, detachment, knowledge, and ultimately love of God.

From the great evil of a fratricidal war based on selfish desire, the greatest good emerges. The *Bhagavad-gītā* takes us on a religious and spiritual journey from selfishness to selflessness in love of God. Through an exhaustive comparative analysis, Kṛṣṇa brings his disciple and dear friend Arjuna, one of the sons of Mahārāja Pāṇḍu, to the path of devotion.

Pāṇḍu's eldest son, Yudhiṣṭhira, was the rightful heir to the throne. Because Dhṛtarāṣṭra was blind, he was not chosen to be the king. It is said that the father is born again as his son. Accordingly, Dhṛtarāṣṭra desired that his son Duryodhana assume the throne, rather than the eldest son of Pāṇḍu. One meaning of the name Dhṛtarāṣṭra is "he by whom the kingdom is held." As this name indicates, Dhṛtarāṣṭra tried to hold the kingdom for himself. His attachment to his son fueled Duryodhana's enmity toward the Pāṇḍavas, by which Duryodhana lived up to his infamous name.[1] In this verse, the fire of Duryodhana's enmity is about to burst into the blaze of a full-scale war. Dhṛtarāṣṭra, aware of his own part in the fracas yet too attached to stop his son, is anxious to know what is happening as the armies assemble.

Vyāsa blessed his disciple, Sañjaya, that even though not personally present on the battlefield, he would mystically know every nuance of the war, including the minds of those involved.[2] At Vyāsa's request, Sañjaya, whose name indicates that he was all *(sam)* victorious *(jaya)* and thus master of his own mind and senses, agreed to narrate the events to the blind and aging Dhṛtarāṣṭra from within the palace compound.

Knowing well that *dharma* was on the side of the Pāṇḍavas, Dhṛtarāṣṭra refers to the battlefield in terms of its sacred heritage. The earliest refer-

1. One meaning of the name Duryodhana is "dirty fighter." In the *Mahābhārata, āśrama-vāsika*, chapter one, Duryodhana is described as a partial incarnation of Kali (the personification of evil who presides over the present age—Kali-yuga).

2. See MB. Bhīṣma-parva 2.4.

ences to the sacredness of Kurukṣetra are found in the *Jābāla Upaniṣad* and the *Śatapatha-śruti*. According to *Śrīmad-Bhāgavatam*, *avatāra* Paraśurāma performed sacrifices at Kurukṣetra. Its sacredness brought Kṛṣṇa's father, Vasudeva, there during the solar eclipse. Vasudeva also performed sacrifices in Kurukṣetra on that occasion. As we shall see, the extent of its sacredness exceeds these well-known histories.

In this verse Dhṛtarāṣṭra's voice is filled with doubt. He realized there was little hope that his sons would prevail. "Perhaps," he thought, "the piety of the Pāṇḍavas combined with the influence of Kurukṣetra will cause the Pāṇḍavas to walk away from the battle giving victory to Duryodhana by default." However, the Pāṇḍavas were more than pious. They were intimate devotees of Kṛṣṇa and thus transcendentalists of the highest order. Moreover, Kurukṣetra was far more sacred than Dhṛtarāṣṭra realized. Its sanctity is brought out by the devotional mystics of the Gauḍīya Vaiṣṇava tradition in their commentaries on *Śrīmad-Bhāgavatam*.

Jīva Goswāmī details the chronology of events leading to Kṛṣṇa's first coming to Kurukṣetra in his treatise on the *Bhāgavatam*, *Kṛṣṇa-sandarbha*. At the age of fifty Kṛṣṇa came to Kurukṣetra with his royal entourage from Dwārakā. The secret purpose of this pilgrimage was to meet with the villagers and in particular the cowherd girls (*gopīs*) of Vraja, the rural setting of his youth. He wanted to assure the Vraja devotees that he loved them and that, although he was living outside of Vraja in high society, he was thinking of them constantly. After Kṛṣṇa had killed the evil king Kaṁsa, he feared that those who sought to avenge his death would cause havoc in Vraja, whose residents were unequipped to deal with a military invasion. As Kṛṣṇa established *dharma* throughout the land, he did so with his Vraja devotees in mind. In separation from him for over one hundred years, with only one brief and somewhat awkward meeting here at Kurukṣetra, his devotees of Vraja never swayed in their love for him. Separation made their hearts grow fonder, in the same way that it made Kṛṣṇa's heart grow fonder for them. Now more than fifty years after his brief meeting with them at Kurukṣetra, Kṛṣṇa was once again setting foot in this holy place, and he was reminded of his previous meeting here with the *gopīs*.

When Kṛṣṇa met previously with the inhabitants of Vraja at Kurukṣetra, he had a private meeting with the *gopīs*, who loved him more than their own lives. How great must their necessity have been at that time. They were again with Kṛṣṇa, yet he was in princely dress. His peacock feather crown had been replaced with royal jewels, his sweetness covered by majesty. He invited them to join him, but owing to the circumstances they could not.

They loved Kṛṣṇa the cowherd, but now in Kurukṣetra he appeared before them as a prince. He used to herd cows barefoot in the forests of Vraja, but now he was riding an elephant. He used to hold a flute in his two hands, but as a prince he sometimes appeared four-handed. The *gopīs* could not join him in the big city of Dwārakā. Being simple village girls they did not know how to act in high society, nor were they interested in being his queens. They longed for the full-moon nights of Vraja and the Kṛṣṇa who was fully theirs in paramour love. Without the forests of Vraja, the river Yamunā, Kṛṣṇa's friends and cows, all of which created an atmosphere conducive to the highest love, the *gopīs* could not be satisfied even in Kṛṣṇa's presence. They did not go with him to be members of his royal assembly, but in effect he went with them, promising them that he would soon return to Vraja and telling them that in the meantime they should know that he was theirs alone. Although he physically returned to Dwārakā, his heart went with the *gopīs* to Vraja. Here in this place, Kurukṣetra, Kṛṣṇa admitted that Rādhā's devotion to him had conquered him.[3] This is the height of *dharma:* Śrī Rādhā's love *(prema-dharma).*

What is *dharma*? It is that by which God is pleased.[4] So pleased Kṛṣṇa was by the *gopīs'* devotion that he bowed to it. Although the paramour *(parakīya)* love of the *gopīs* for Kṛṣṇa is in reality a mystic illusion owing to the fact that they are his potencies *(śaktis)* and thus belong *(svakīya)* to him alone, it nonetheless brings the greatest rapture to Kṛṣṇa. As *dharma* consists of that which is pleasing to God and is judged by the measure of his pleasure, Rādhā's paramour love constitutes the highest *dharma*. Thus this mystic illusion of her paramour relationship with Kṛṣṇa is quite real, and the devotion of the Vraja *gopīs* is the full expression of *dharma*, the height of aesthetic rapture. The queen of this rapture is Rādhā, and accordingly, service to her is most pleasing to Kṛṣṇa. How great was her necessity at Kurukṣetra! She came so close to reuniting with Kṛṣṇa but could not. Value is determined by necessity. At the hour of Rādhā's greatest necessity, even the most insignificant service rendered to her draws immense remuneration. Such is the value of devotion to Rādhā at Kurukṣetra.

3. See ŚB. 10.82.44. This verse is cited three times in Cc., wherein its most esoteric significance is revealed. See also the *Śrīmad-Bhāgavatam* commentaries of Sanātana Goswāmī and Viśvanātha Cakravartī Ṭhākura.

4. See ŚB. 1.2.13.

As he pondered the king's question, Sañjaya collected himself to answer Dhṛtarāṣṭra. He knew that Kṛṣṇa would speak about *dharma* from beginning to end. Thus Kurukṣetra is *dharma-kṣetra*, the field of moral and spiritual values. Anyone who stands here must take a stand on matters good and evil, spiritual and material.

In replying to Dhṛtarāṣṭra's query concerning the outcome of the meeting between his son Duryodhana and the Pāṇḍavas, Sañjaya wanted to let him know that there was considerable cause for concern, even though Duryodhana was politically astute. He thus indicated that the military arrangement of the Pāṇḍavas was formidable.

Text 2

सञ्जय उवाच
दृष्ट्वा तु पाण्डवानीकं व्यूढं दुर्योधनस्तदा ।
आचार्यमुपसङ्गम्य राजा वचनमब्रवीत् ॥२॥

sañjaya uvāca
dṛṣṭvā tu pāṇḍavānīkaṁ vyūḍhaṁ duryodhanas tadā/
ācāryam upasaṅgamya rājā vacanam abravīt//

sañjayaḥ—Sañjaya; *uvāca*—said; *dṛṣṭvā*—seeing; *tu*—but; *pāṇḍava-anīkam*—the Pāṇḍavas' army; *vyūḍham*—arrayed in a battle formation; *duryodhanaḥ*—Duryodhana; *tadā*—then; *ācāryam*—the guru; *upasaṅgamya*—approaching; *rājā*—king; *vacanam*—words; *abravīt*—spoke.

Sañjaya said: After seeing the battle formation of the Pāṇḍavas' army, prince Duryodhana approached his guru and spoke the following words:

Madhusūdana Saraswatī says that the word *tu* (but) implies the superiority of the Pāṇḍavas. The words *abravīt* (spoke) and *vacanam* (words) placed together appear redundant. However, this usage indicates that Duryodhana's speech, although brief, was possessed of more than one meaning.

Text 3

पश्यैतां पाण्डुपुत्राणामाचार्य महतीं चमूम् ।
व्यूढां द्रुपदपुत्रेण तव शिष्येण धीमता ॥३॥

paśyaitāṁ pāṇḍu-putrāṇām ācārya mahatīṁ camūm/
vyūḍhāṁ drupada-putreṇa tava śiṣyeṇa dhīmatā//

paśya—behold; *etām*—this; *pāṇḍu-putrāṇām*—of the sons of Pāṇḍu; *ācārya*—O master; *mahatīm*—mighty; *camūm*—military formation; *vyūḍhām*—arranged; *drupada-putreṇa*—by the son of Drupada; *tava*—your; *śiṣyeṇa*—by the disciple; *dhī-matā*—by the wise.

Behold, O master, the strength of the Pāṇḍavas' military formation, wisely arranged by Drupada's son, your disciple.

Duryodhana was wise for approaching his martial guru, Droṇācārya, at a time of great necessity, yet more politically wise than spiritually. Here his tenor is filled with sarcasm. Although he approached his guru in form, the spirit of his approach was to instruct. He approached Droṇa to induce him to fight harder for his cause by mentioning that the Pāṇḍavas' army was arranged expertly by the son of Droṇa's old enemy. Duryodhana considered that his teacher, Droṇa, was to an extent the cause of his difficulty, for it was Droṇa who out of impartiality had instructed Dhṛṣṭadyumna in military science and now it was Dhṛṣṭadyumna who arranged the military formation of those who opposed him.

Dhṛṣṭadyumna was Drupada's son. He was born out of Drupada's desire for revenge against Droṇa. After Droṇa sent his best student, Arjuna, to capture Drupada for breaking his word of honor, Drupada performed a sacrifice to get a son who would kill Droṇa. Dhṛṣṭadyumna was that son. Droṇa knew this, yet he did not hesitate to instruct him in military science, owing to his commitment to his *dharma* as a teacher over concern for his personal safety. At the outset of the battle, Duryodhana proved himself to be well versed in politics and diplomacy. In form he was competent to lead, but he lacked spiritual substance. Substance aside, artful was his speech and its implications far-reaching. Knowing that Dhṛṣṭadyumna alone might not be considered sufficient cause for concern, he pointed out other prominent members of the opposition, mentioning those who might trouble Droṇa, who along with others was only circumstantially on the side of Duryodhana.

Text 4

अत्र शूरा महेष्वासा भीमार्जुनसमा युधि ।
युयुधानो विराटश्च द्रुपदश्च महारथः ॥४॥

atra śūrā maheṣvāsā bhīmārjuna-samā yudhi/
yuyudhāno virāṭaś ca drupadaś ca mahā-rathaḥ//

atra—here; *śūrāḥ*—heroes; *mahā-iṣu-āsāḥ*—mighty archers; *bhīma-arjuna-samāḥ*—equal to Bhīma and Arjuna; *yudhi*—in the fight; *yuyudhānaḥ*—Yuyudhāna; *virāṭaḥ*—Virāṭa; *ca*—and; *drupadaḥ*—Drupada; *ca*—also; *mahā-rathaḥ*—the great warrior.

Among the Pāṇḍavas' soldiers are heroes and archers equal in prowess to Bhīma and Arjuna and fighters like Yuyudhāna, Virāṭa, and the great warrior Drupada.

Text 5

धृष्टकेतुश्चेकितानः काशिराजश्च वीर्यवान्।
पुरुजित् कुन्तिभोजश्च शैब्यश्च नरपुङ्गवः॥५॥

dhṛṣṭaketuś cekitānaḥ kāśirājaś ca vīryavān/
purujit kuntibhojaś ca śaibyaś ca nara-puṅgavaḥ//

dhṛṣṭaketuḥ—Dhṛṣṭaketu; *cekitānaḥ*—Cekitāna; *kāśirājaḥ*—Kāśirāja; *ca*—also; *vīrya-vān*—valorous; *purujit*—Purujit; *kuntibhojaḥ*—Kuntibhoja; *ca*—and; *śaibyaḥ*—Śaibya; *ca*—and; *nara-puṅgavaḥ*—bull among men.

Dhṛṣṭaketu, Cekitāna, the valorous Kāśirāja, Purujit, Kuntibhoja, and the bull among men, Śaibya, are all here.

Text 6

युधामन्युश्च विक्रान्त उत्तमौजाश्च वीर्यवान्।
सौभद्रो द्रौपदेयाश्च सर्व एव महारथाः॥६॥

yudhāmanyuś ca vikrānta uttamaujāś ca vīryavān/
saubhadro draupadeyāś ca sarva eva mahā-rathāḥ//

yudhāmanyuḥ—Yudhāmanyu; *ca*—and; *vikrāntaḥ*—mighty; *uttamaujāḥ*—Uttamaujā; *ca*—and; *vīrya-vān*—very powerful; *saubhadraḥ*—the son of Subhadrā; *draupadeyāḥ*—the sons of Draupadī; *ca*—and; *sarve*—all; *eva*—certainly; *mahā-rathāḥ*—great warriors.

The mighty Yudhāmanyu, the valorous Uttamaujā, Subhadrā's son, and the sons of Draupadī are all great warriors.

Duryodhana's choice of words continues to be significant. Here he directly mentions Drupada in an effort to secure the allegiance of Droṇa.

He mentions Arjuna only by way of comparison, taking emphasis off him personally because he is dear to Droṇa. Droṇa will rise to fight against those of prowess like Arjuna, but fighting personally with Arjuna is nothing for Droṇa to be inspired about. Duryodhana also betrays his own fears by mentioning Bhīma. Bhīma vowed to personally kill every one of Dhṛtarāṣṭra's one hundred sons with his own hands, and he was quite capable of doing so.

After Duryodhana finishes naming prominent warriors in the Pāṇḍavas' army, he will have to bolster his own courage by naming the great warriors in his own ranks. As he does so, he will also have to address Droṇa's reaction to everything he has already said. As a *brāhmaṇa* (priest/teacher), Droṇa understands Duryodhana's underlying fear and naturally thinks, "If you are so fearful of the enemy, why not make a treaty with him and avoid the fight? What is the need for such eagerness to fight?" Droṇa did not appreciate the underlying sarcasm of his disciple, thus Duryodhana will also have to make up for his sarcasm and speak respectfully to Droṇācārya in the course of bolstering his own confidence.

Text 7

अस्माकं तु विशिष्टा ये तान्निबोध द्विजोत्तम ।
नायका मम सैन्यस्य संज्ञार्थं तान् ब्रवीमि ते ॥७॥

asmākaṁ tu viśiṣṭā ye tān nibodha dvijottama/
nāyakā mama sainyasya saṁjñārthaṁ tān bravīmi te//

asmākam—our; *tu*—but; *viśiṣṭāḥ*—distinguished; *ye*—who; *tān*—them; *nibodha*—be informed; *dvija-uttama*—O best of the twice-born; *nāyakāḥ*—leaders; *mama*—my; *sainyasya*—of the army; *saṁjñā-artham*—for information; *tān*—them; *bravīmi*—I tell; *te*—you.

O best of the twice-born, let me tell you the distinguished leaders of our army.

Texts 8–9

भवान् भीष्मश्च कर्णश्च कृपश्च समितिञ्जयः ।
अश्वत्थामा विकर्णश्च सौमदत्तिस्तथैव च ॥८॥

अन्ये च बहवः शूरा मदर्थे त्यक्तजीविताः ।
नानाशस्त्रप्रहरणाः सर्वे युद्धविशारदाः ॥९॥

bhavān bhīṣmaś ca karṇaś ca kṛpaś ca samitiñjayaḥ/
aśvatthāmā vikarṇaś ca saumadattis tathaiva ca//
anye ca bahavaḥ śūrā mad-arthe tyakta-jīvitāḥ/
nānā-śastra-praharaṇāḥ sarve yuddha-viśāradāḥ//

bhavān—your good self; *bhīṣmaḥ*—Bhīṣma; *ca*—also; *karṇaḥ*—Karṇa; *ca*—and; *kṛpaḥ*—Kṛpa; *ca*—and; *samitiñjayaḥ*—always victorious in battle; *aśvatthāmā*—Aśvatthāmā; *vikarṇaḥ*—Vikarṇa; *ca*—as well as; *saumadattiḥ*—the son of Somadatta; *tathā*—as well as; *eva*—certainly; *ca*—also; *anye*—other; *ca*—also; *bahavaḥ*—many; *śūrāḥ*—heroes; *mat-arthe*—for my sake; *tyakta-jīvitāḥ*—whose lives are risked; *nānā*—many; *śastra*—weapons; *praharaṇāḥ*—equipped with; *sarve*—all; *yuddha-viśāradāḥ*—skilled in battle.

Your good self, Bhīṣma, Karṇa, Kṛpa, who is always victorious in battle, Aśvatthāmā, Vikarṇa, the son of Somadatta, as well as many other heroes, skilled in battle and well-equipped, are all ready to lay down their lives for my sake.

Here Duryodhana says that his warriors are prepared to die for him. When someone utters the truth unwittingly, it is said that Saraswatī, the goddess of speech and wisdom, speaks through him. That is the case here, for what Duryodhana says will undoubtedly come true: his warriors will all die for him, as will he himself. Kṛṣṇa will tell Arjuna (Bg. 11.33), "They are already put to death by my arrangement," confirming the inevitability of their demise.

Duryodhana knows that Karṇa has vowed not to fight until Bhīṣma is killed. Duryodhana nevertheless mentions Karṇa after Bhīṣma to remind Karṇa that should Bhīṣma be defeated, he will be relying on Karṇa to bring him victory. Kṛpa and Aśvatthāmā are related to Droṇa as his brother-in-law and son, respectively. Mentioning them will certainly encourage Droṇācārya. Duryodhana gives Kṛpa the epithet "ever victorious in battle" *(samitiñjaya)* to make up for the fact that he mentioned him after Karṇa. As for Vikarṇa, he is not in the same class as the rest of the warriors mentioned. Duryodhana has mentioned him along with the others to flatter him. The battle has not yet begun, and he could still switch sides without deviating from the principles of a warrior. Duryodhana knows that there is a chance that he will do so, for he was the lone objector in Duryodhana's ranks to the insults hurled at the Pāṇḍavas' wife, Draupadī, insults that fueled the Pāṇḍavas' fury.

Text 10

अपर्याप्तं तदस्माकं बलं भीष्माभिरक्षितम् ।
पर्याप्तं त्विदमेतेषां बलं भीमाभिरक्षितम् ॥१०॥

aparyāptaṁ tad asmākaṁ balaṁ bhīṣmābhirakṣitam/
paryāptaṁ tv idam eteṣāṁ balaṁ bhīmābhirakṣitam//

aparyāptam—immeasurable; *tat*—that; *asmākam*—our; *balam*—strength; *bhīṣma-abhirakṣitam*—guarded by Bhīṣma; *paryāptam*—measurable; *tu*—but; *idam*—this; *eteṣām*—of the Pāṇḍavas; *balam*—strength; *bhīma-abhirakṣitam*—guarded by Bhīma.

Our strength is immeasurable, guarded as it is by Bhīṣma, whereas their force, guarded by Bhīma, is limited.

Expertise in social etiquette is the ornament of cultured people. However, just as looks can deceive, so can words for those who do not understand their intent. Duryodhana certainly has every appearance of a cultured gentleman. Although Duryodhana addressed Droṇa with flattering words, the spirit of his address is denigrating. The veiled spirit of Duryodhana's address is that Droṇa, being a *brāhmaṇa*, is not fit for battle. In text 8 Duryodhana praises Bhīṣma only after first praising Droṇa. Although Bhīṣma is senior, Droṇa is Duryodhana's guru. Droṇa is a *brāhmaṇa*, whereas Bhīṣma is of the warrior caste. Had he addressed Bhīṣma first, Droṇa might have taken offense, but Bhīṣma, although senior, would bow to the etiquette of respecting a *brāhmaṇa* over a *kṣatriya* (warrior).

While Duryodhana praises Bhīṣma, he also expresses doubts about him. Bhīṣma is certainly the greatest fighter on the battlefield, and thus Duryodhana's army has immeasurable strength when fortified by Bhīṣma's presence. However, the word *aparyāptam* (immeasurable) can be taken in two ways—immeasurably extensive or uncertain—and *ācāryas* like Viśvanātha Cakravartī Ṭhākura and Baladeva Vidyābhūṣaṇa have rendered verse 10 differently because of these two meanings. Baladeva Vidyābhūṣaṇa understands *aparyāptam* to indicate the strength of Duryodhana's army because of the military capability of Bhīṣma. Viśvanātha Cakravartī, on the other hand, understands *aparyāptam* to indicate the potential weakness of Duryodhana's army: Bhīṣma's commitment to Duryodhana is questionable owing to his affinity for the Pāṇḍavas, for whom he acted as a foster grandfather.

Outwardly Duryodhana's army is fortified by the strength of Bhīṣma, yet under scrutiny Bhīṣma is in a position of potential compromise, and this may weaken Duryodhana's army. The word *abhirakṣitam* in this verse can also imply, "Watch out for Bhīṣma; we cannot be entirely sure of his commitment." Duryodhana wants to rally Bhīṣma and at the same time alert others to the reality of the sympathies that might compromise his resolve to fight.

Bhīma is no doubt the most powerful of the Pāṇḍava warriors and in this sense their leader, although not officially so. However, he is no match for Bhīṣma, around whom Duryodhana's army must rally, both because of Bhīṣma's military might and because of his sentiment for the Pāṇḍavas. The army must both encourage Bhīṣma to express his military prowess and discourage him from expressing his parental affection.

Text 11

अयनेषु च सर्वेषु यथाभागमवस्थिताः ।
भीष्ममेवाभिरक्षन्तु भवन्तः सर्व एव हि ॥११॥

ayaneṣu ca sarveṣu yathā-bhāgam avasthitāḥ/
bhīṣmam evābhirakṣantu bhavantaḥ sarva eva hi//

ayaneṣu—in the battle stations; *ca*—also; *sarveṣu*—in all; *yathā-bhāgam*—each in his respective place; *avasthitāḥ*—situated; *bhīṣmam*—Bhīṣma; *eva*—certainly; *abhirakṣantu*—must support; *bhavantaḥ*—you; *sarve*—all; *eva hi*—certainly.

Throughout the battle all of you must support Bhīṣma from your battle stations.

Duryodhana's command that the troops rally around and protect Bhīṣma is intelligent, for it is well known that if Bhīṣma dies they will lose. After Duryodhana mentions Bhīṣma, the grandsire of the Pāṇḍavas responds.

Text 12

तस्य सञ्जनयन् हर्षं कुरुवृद्धः पितामहः ।
सिंहनादं विनद्योच्चैः शङ्खं दध्मौ प्रतापवान् ॥१२॥

tasya sañjanayan harṣaṁ kuru-vṛddhaḥ pitāmahaḥ/
siṁha-nādaṁ vinadyoccaiḥ śaṅkhaṁ dadhmau pratāpavan//

tasya—of him (Duryodhana); *sañjanayan*—bringing; *harṣam*—joy; *kuru-vṛddhaḥ*—the seasoned member of the Kuru dynasty (Bhīṣma); *pitāmahaḥ*—the grandsire; *siṁha-nādam*—lion's roar; *vinadya*—vibrating; *uccaiḥ*—loudly; *śaṅkham*—conch; *dadhmau*—blew; *pratāpa-vān*—triumphantly.

Bringing joy to Duryodhana, Bhīṣma, the seasoned grandsire of the Kurus, roaring like a lion, blew his conch triumphantly.

Text 13

ततः शङ्खाश्च भेर्यश्च पणवानकगोमुखाः ।
सहसैवाभ्यहन्यन्त स शब्दस्तुमुलोऽभवत् ॥१३॥

tataḥ śaṅkhāś ca bheryaś ca paṇavānaka-gomukhāḥ/
sahasaivābhyahanyanta sa śabdas tumulo 'bhavat//

tataḥ—thereafter; *śaṅkhāḥ*—conches; *ca*—also; *bheryaḥ*—kettledrums; *ca*—and; *paṇava-ānaka*—cymbals and drums; *go-mukhāḥ*—bugles; *sahasā*—all at once; *eva*—certainly; *abhyahanyanta*—sounded; *saḥ*—that; *śabdaḥ*—uproar; *tumulaḥ*—tumultuous; *abhavat*—became.

Thereafter the Kuru army's conches, drums, cymbals, and bugles all sounded together in a tumultuous uproar.

Bhīṣma's response encourages Duryodhana, whose guru, Droṇa, had remained silent out of indifference toward his disciple. However, although Bhīṣma's roar and bugling of the conch encourages Duryodhana, it has no effect on the confident Pāṇḍavas.

Text 14

ततः श्वेतैर्हयैर्युक्ते महति स्यन्दने स्थितौ ।
माधवः पाण्डवश्चैव दिव्यौ शङ्खौ प्रदध्मतुः ॥१४॥

tataḥ śvetair hayair yukte mahati syandane sthitau/
mādhavaḥ pāṇḍavaś caiva divyau śaṅkhau pradadhmatuḥ//

tataḥ—then; *śvetaiḥ*—with white; *hayaiḥ*—with horses; *yukte*—yoked; *mahati*—in a great; *syandane*—in a swift chariot; *sthitau*—standing; *mādhavaḥ*—Kṛṣṇa; *pāṇḍavaḥ*—the son of Pāṇḍu; *ca*—also; *eva*—certainly; *divyau*—divine; *śaṅkhau*—conches; *pradadhmatuḥ*—blew.

On the other side, Mādhava and the son of Pāṇḍu, standing on a great, swift chariot yoked to white horses, blew their divine conches.

This is the first time Kṛṣṇa is mentioned in the text of the *Gītā*. The name Mādhava carries with it the implication that Arjuna, who is also introduced in this verse, will be victorious, as Mādhava is often rendered "husband of the Goddess of fortune." The syllable *mā* indicates the Goddess and *dhava* means husband. The epithet Mādhava is particularly sweet. *Mad* is the Sanskrit root from which *madhu* (honey) is derived. It also indicates intoxicated passion and madness *(mada)*. In *Caitanya-caritāmṛta*, Kṛṣṇadāsa Kavirāja Goswāmī uses the term *mādhurya* (sweet) in characterizing *śṛṅgāra rasa*, the sacred aesthetic rapture of conjugal love that drove Śrī Caitanya to spiritual madness. Within the appellation Mādhava both Kṛṣṇa and his consort Rādhā reside, for there is no meaning to the husband of the Goddess of fortune without the Goddess herself. Mādhava also means spring. Later in chapter 10 Kṛṣṇa identifies himself with spring, the season of love. Herein Sañjaya indicates that the *Gītā* is ultimately a doctrine of divine love that reaches its zenith in Rādhā's love for Mādhava.

The chariot of Arjuna is singled out here. Although all of the warriors were also seated on chariots, Arjuna's chariot stands out in comparison because it was a gift he received from Agni, the god of fire. It is thought to be invincible in the plane of mortals. The fact that Kṛṣṇa was driving it only added to its invincibility.

Text 15

पाञ्चजन्यं हृषीकेशो देवदत्तं धनञ्जयः ।
पौण्ड्रं दध्मौ महाशङ्खं भीमकर्मा वृकोदरः ॥१५॥

pāñcajanyaṁ hṛṣīkeśo devadattaṁ dhanañjayaḥ/
pauṇḍraṁ dadhmau maha-śaṅkhaṁ bhīma-karmā vṛkodaraḥ//

pāñcajanyam—the conch named Pāñcajanya; *hṛṣīka-īśaḥ*—Hṛṣīkeśa (Lord of the senses); *devadattam*—the conch named Devadatta; *dhanam-jayaḥ*—Dhanañjaya (conqueror of wealth); *pauṇḍram*—the conch named Pauṇḍra; *dadhmau*—blew; *mahā-śaṅkham*—the great conch; *bhīma-karmā*—tremendous feats; *vṛka-udaraḥ*—wolf-bellied, of great appetite (Bhīma).

Kṛṣṇa, the Lord of the senses, blew his conch Pāñcajanya; Arjuna, the winner of treasure, blew his, the Devadatta; while Bhīma of great

appetite and prodigious accomplishments sounded forth his great conch, Pauṇḍra.

Although Kṛṣṇa himself was a powerful warrior, he had vowed not to fight in the battle. Instead he agreed to be the charioteer of Arjuna. Nonetheless, the power of his presence on the battlefield is not to be underestimated. Here Kṛṣṇa is addressed as Hṛṣīkeśa, which indicates that he is the controller of the senses and will thus factor significantly into the outcome of the battle. Conquering one's sensual appetite is a prerequisite to fully understanding and entering into the sacred conjugal love implied in the name Mādhava, which was invoked in the previous verse.

Dhanañjaya refers to the capacity to gather wealth, an ability that Arjuna demonstrated during the great sacrifice preceding Yudhiṣṭhira's coronation. The name also implies that Arjuna has the capacity to gather the wealth of love of God in the instructions he will receive from Kṛṣṇa.

Text 16

अनन्तविजयं राजा कुन्तीपुत्रो युधिष्ठिरः ।
नकुलः सहदेवश्च सुघोषमणिपुष्पकौ ॥१६॥

anantavijayaṁ rājā kuntī-putro yudhiṣṭhiraḥ/
nakulaḥ sahadevaś ca sughoṣa-maṇipuṣpakau//

ananta-vijayam—the conch named Ananta-vijaya; *rājā*—the king; *kuntī-putraḥ*—the son of Kuntī; *yudhiṣṭhiraḥ*—Yudhiṣṭhira; *nakulaḥ*—Nakula; *sahadevaḥ*—Sahadeva; *ca*—and; *sughoṣa-maṇipuṣpakau*—the conches named Sughoṣa and Maṇipuṣpaka.

Yudhiṣṭhira, son of Kuntī, blew the Ananta-vijaya; Nakula and Sahadeva blew the Sughoṣa and Maṇipuṣpaka, respectively.

Yudhiṣṭhira is the eldest of the Pāṇḍavas. His name means one who is unshaken *(sthira)* in battle *(yudhi)*.

Texts 17–18

काश्यश्च परमेष्वासः शिखण्डी च महारथः ।
धृष्टद्युम्नो विराटश्च सात्यकिश्चापराजितः ॥१७॥

द्रुपदो द्रौपदेयाश्च सर्वशः पृथिवीपते ।
सौभद्रश्च महाबाहुः शङ्खान् दध्मुः पृथक् पृथक् ॥१८॥

kāśyaś ca parameṣvāsaḥ śikhaṇḍī ca mahā-rathaḥ/
dhṛṣṭadyumno virāṭaś ca sātyakiś cāparājitaḥ//
drupado draupadeyāś ca sarvaśaḥ pṛthivī-pate/
saubhadraś ca mahā-bāhuḥ śaṅkhān dadhmuḥ pṛthak pṛthak//

kāśyaḥ—the king of Kāśī; *ca*—and; *parama-iṣu-āsaḥ*—the paramount archer; *śikhaṇḍī*—Śikhaṇḍī; *ca*—also; *mahā-rathaḥ*—the great warrior; *dhṛṣṭadyumnaḥ*—Dhṛṣṭadyumna; *virāṭaḥ*—Virāṭa; *ca*—also; *sātyakiḥ*—Sātyaki; *ca*—and; *aparājitaḥ*—who is invincible; *drupadaḥ*—Drupada; *draupadeyāḥ*—the sons of Draupadī; *ca*—also; *sarvaśaḥ*—all; *pṛthivī-pate*—O earthly lord; *saubhadraḥ*—the son of Subhadrā; *ca*—also; *mahā-bāhuḥ*—mighty-armed; *śaṅkhān*—conchshells; *dadhmuḥ*—blew; *pṛthak pṛthak*—each.

The paramount archer the king of Kāśī, the great warrior Śikhaṇḍī, Dhṛṣṭadyumna, Virāṭa, the invincible Sātyaki, Drupada, and the sons of Draupadī, together with the mighty-armed son of Subhadrā, all blew their own conchshells, O earthly lord.

Dhṛtarāṣṭra is at best an earthly king, but Kṛṣṇa and Arjuna ride a celestial chariot given by the fire god, Agni. As their conchshells are divine, so too are they. It is well known that when Kṛṣṇa went to the gates of hell to retrieve his guru's son, he blew his mighty conch and stopped all the suffering therein. The *Skanda Purāṇa, Avanti-khaṇḍa*, describes some of the details of this event thus: "The hell known as Asipatra-vana lost the sharp, sword-like leaves on its trees, and the hell named Raurava became free of its *ruru* beasts. The Bhairava hell lost its fearfulness, and all cooking (of people) stopped in the Kumbhīpāka hell. Their sinful reactions eradicated, all the inhabitants of hell attained liberation and entered the spiritual world."

Kṛṣṇa's conchshell heralds victory for the pious Pāṇḍavas. Its sound terrifies the heart of Duryodhana, whereas the Pāṇḍavas remain undisturbed after hearing the conches of Bhīṣma and his army. Pure hearts know no fear. Even the conchshells of the Pāṇḍavas are feared in battle, not to speak of the Pāṇḍavas themselves.

Text 19

स घोषो धार्तराष्ट्राणां हृदयानि व्यदारयात्।
नभश्च पृथिवीं चैव तुमुलोऽभ्यनुनादयन् ॥१९॥

sa ghoṣo dhārtartāṣṭrāṇāṁ hṛdayāni vyadārayat/
nabhaś ca pṛthivīṁ caiva tumulo 'bhyanunādayan//

saḥ—that; *ghoṣaḥ*—sound; *dhārtarāṣṭrāṅām*—of the sons of Dhṛtarāṣṭra; *hṛdayāni*—the hearts; *vyadārayat*—caused to burst; *nabhaḥ*—the sky; *ca*—also; *pṛthivīm*—the earth; *ca*—also; *eva*—certainly; *tumulaḥ*—uproarious; *abhyanunādayan*—causing to reverberate.

The uproarious sound reverberated through the sky and earth and sent fear into the hearts of Dhṛtarāṣṭra's sons.

Text 20

अथ व्यवस्थितान् दृष्ट्वा धार्तराष्ट्रान् कपिध्वजः ।
प्रवृत्ते शस्त्रसम्पाते धनुरुद्यम्य पाण्डवः ।
हृषीकेशं तदा वाक्यमिदमाह महीपते ॥२०॥

atha vyavasthitān dṛṣṭvā dhārtarāṣṭrān kapi-dhvajaḥ/
pravṛtte śastra-sampāte dhanur udyamya pāṇḍavaḥ/
hṛṣīkeśaṁ tadā vākyam idam āha mahī-pate//

atha—then; *vyavasthitān*—arrayed; *dṛṣṭvā*—having seen; *dhārtarāṣṭrān*—the sons of Dhṛtarāṣṭra; *kapi-dhvajaḥ*—he whose banner is marked with Hanumān; *pravṛtte*—in preparedness; *śastra-sampāte*—as weapons were readied; *dhanuḥ*—bow; *udyamya*—raising; *pāṇḍavaḥ*—the son of Pāṇḍu; *hṛṣīkeśam*—to Kṛṣṇa, master of the senses; *tadā*—then; *vākyam*—words; *idam*—these; *āha*—said; *mahī-pate*—O king.

Then, O king, the son of Pāṇḍu, who carries the banner of Hanumān, having looked over the army of Dhṛtarāṣṭra's sons in battle array, raised his bow in preparation as weapons were readied and spoke the following words to Kṛṣṇa, the master of the senses.

At this point the sacred conversation between Kṛṣṇa and Arjuna is about to begin. Victory is with Arjuna and with those who reach his conclusion: surrender to Hṛṣīkeśa, Kṛṣṇa, the master of the senses. The flag of Hanumān, the monkey servant of Rāma, implies his presence on Arjuna's chariot, which further insures Arjuna's victory. Sañjaya's reference to Kṛṣṇa as Hṛṣīkeśa indicates that he is the master of the senses, while the senses are the masters of this world. Thus he who is the master of the senses is the Lord of the earth, on whose side there will be victory over illusion.

Texts 21–23

अर्जुन उवाच
सेनयोरुभयोर्मध्ये रथं स्थापय मेऽच्युत ।
यावदेतन्निरीक्षेऽहं योद्धुकामानवस्थितान् ॥२१॥
कैर्मया सह योद्धव्यमस्मिन् रणसमुद्यमे ॥२२॥
योत्स्यमानानवेक्षेऽहं य एतेऽत्र समागताः ।
धार्तराष्ट्रस्य दुर्बुद्धेर्युद्धे प्रियचिकीर्षवः ॥२३॥

arjuna uvāca
senayor ubhayor madhye rathaṁ sthāpaya me 'cyuta/
yāvad etān nirīkṣe 'haṁ yoddhu-kāmān avasthitān//
kair mayā saha yoddhavyam asmin raṇa-samudyame//
yotsyamānān avekṣe 'haṁ ya ete 'tra samāgatāḥ/
dhārtarāṣṭrasya durbuddher yuddhe priya-cikīrṣavaḥ//

arjunaḥ uvāca—Arjuna said; *senayoḥ*—of the armies; *ubhayoḥ*—of the two; *madhye*—between; *ratham*—the chariot; *sthāpaya*—draw; *me*—my; *acyuta*—O infallible one; *yāvat*—so that; *etān*—these; *nirīkṣe*—may see; *aham*—I; *yoddhu-kāmān*—in fighting spirit; *avasthitān*—assembled; *kaiḥ*—with whom; *mayā*—with me; *saha*—together; *yoddhavyam*—to be fought; *asmin*—in this; *raṇa*—battle; *samudyame*—in the attempt; *yotsyamānān*—those who are about to do battle; *avekṣe*—I see; *aham*—I; *ye*—who; *ete*—those; *atra*—here; *samāgatāḥ*—have come; *dhārtarāṣṭrasya*—of the son of Dhṛtarāṣṭra; *durbuddheḥ*—evil-minded; *yuddhe*—in the fight; *priya*—well; *cikīrṣavaḥ*—wishing.

Arjuna said: O infallible one, draw my chariot between the two armies so that I may see who has assembled here in fighting spirit and with whom I must contend in this battle. Let me see those who have come here with a desire to please the evil-minded son of Dhṛtarāṣṭra.

Battle is no doubt the object of delight for a warrior like Arjuna. However, here Arjuna indicates that while he is a great warrior, he has doubts about this war. It is not bringing him joy at the onset. He raises his bow, but his hesitation betrays his reservations.

Here Arjuna addresses Kṛṣṇa as the infallible one and indeed he is so, but why is the infallible one driving the chariot of Arjuna? All are fallible in this world, however mighty they may appear. Kṛṣṇa's assuming the post of chariot driver and taking these orders from his devotee Arjuna, actions that seem contradictory to the notion that he holds a position of infallibility, imply that his infallible status is otherworldly. Chariot driver he may appear to be, but more he is Arjuna's friend, and Kṛṣṇa will never fail him. He has become Arjuna's driver out of affection for him. Of all of Kṛṣṇa's qualities, his affection for his devotees is foremost.

In the very first utterance of Arjuna, the conclusion of this sacred conversation is revealed: the infallible Godhead, Kṛṣṇa, is subordinated by the love of his devotees. Love of Kṛṣṇa conquers the source of all material benedictions and eternal life. Under its influence, the infallible becomes fallible; however, Kṛṣṇa's fallibility in relation to pure love demonstrates his infallibility for those who love him. Kṛṣṇa never fails his devotee.

Texts 24–25

सञ्जय उवाच
एवमुक्तो हृषीकेशो गुडाकेशेन भारत ।
सेनयोरुभयोर्मध्ये स्थापयित्वा रथोत्तमम् ॥२४॥
भीष्मद्रोणप्रमुखतः सर्वेषां च महीक्षिताम् ।
उवाच पार्थ पश्यैतान् समवेतान् कुरूनिति ॥२५॥

sañjaya uvāca
evam ukto hṛṣīkeśo guḍākeśena bhārata/
senayor ubhayor madhye sthāpayitvā rathottamam//
bhīṣma-droṇa-pramukhataḥ sarveṣāṁ ca mahī-kṣitām/
uvāca pārtha paśyaitān samavetān kurūn iti//

sañjayaḥ uvāca—Sañjaya said; *evam*—thus; *uktaḥ*—having been addressed; *hṛṣīkeśaḥ*—master of the senses; *guḍākeśena*—by Arjuna, the conqueror of sleep; *bhārata*—O descendant of Bharata; *senayoḥ*—of the armies; *ubhayoḥ*—of both; *madhye*—between; *sthāpayitvā*—stopping; *ratha-uttamam*—the best of chariots; *bhīṣma*—Bhīṣma; *droṇa*—Droṇa; *pramukhataṁ*—in front of; *sarveṣām*—of all; *ca*—also; *mahī-kṣitām*—of the rulers of the world; *uvāca*—said; *pārtha*—O son of Pṛthā; *paśya*—just see; *etān*—these; *samavetān*—assembled; *kurūn*—the Kurus; *iti*—thus.

Sañjaya said: O Dhṛtarāṣṭra, Hṛṣīkeśa, having been ordered by Guḍākeśa, pulled the best of chariots between the two armies, stopping it in

front of Bhīṣma and Droṇa in the midst of the other rulers of the world. Kṛṣṇa said: Just see, Pārtha, all of the Kurus assembled here.

Kṛṣṇa's irony implies in jest, "What is the use of just looking at the enemy?" Kṛṣṇa chuckled at the plight of Arjuna, detecting a reluctance in Arjuna that he himself had caused. Arjuna was known for having conquered sleep *(guḍākeśa)*, but now Kṛṣṇa begins to put him into a mystic sleep of divine illusion and apparent material attachment so that this conversation can take place. As Hṛṣīkeśa (the master of the senses), Kṛṣṇa will awaken Arjuna from the illusion of a life centered on the interaction between the senses and sense objects. He does so by teaching him how to control his senses, which gives rise to knowledge of the self and God and the dynamic union of the two in love.

Kṛṣṇa stops in front of Bhīṣma and Droṇa who personify Arjuna's attachment. He stresses this attachment by describing all of the soldiers as one family, the Kurus. Attachments must be retired if one is to conquer God in love. Thus the opening lines of Arjuna and Kṛṣṇa span the entire spectrum of spiritual life, from material attachment to love of God.

Text 26

तत्रापश्यत् स्थितान् पार्थः पितॄनथ पितामहान् ।
आचार्यान्मातुलान् भ्रातॄन् पुत्रान् पौत्रान् सखींस्तथा ।
श्वशुरान् सुहृदश्चैव सेनयोरुभयोरपि ॥२६॥

tatrāpaśyat sthitān pārthaḥ pitṛn atha pitāmahān/
ācāryān mātulān bhrātṛn putrān pautrān sakhīṁs tathā/
śvaśurān suhṛdaś caiva senayor ubhayor api//

tatra—there; *apaśyat*—he saw; *sthitān*—standing; *pārthaḥ*—Arjuna; *pitṛn*—fathers; *atha*—and then; *pitāmahān*—grandfathers; *ācāryān*—teachers; *mātulān*—maternal uncles; *bhrātṛn*—brothers; *putrān*—sons; *pautrān*—grandsons; *sakhīn*—friends; *tathā*—as well; *śvaśurān*—in-laws; *suhṛdaḥ*—companions; *ca*—also; *eva*—certainly; *senayoḥ*—of the armies; *ubhayoḥ*—of both parties; *api*—including.

There Pārtha saw among both parties fathers, grandfathers, teachers, maternal uncles, brothers, sons, grandsons, as well as friends. He saw in-laws and companions on both sides and thus thought deeply about all of his relatives assembled therein.

Text 27

तान् समीक्ष्य स कौन्तेयः सर्वान् बन्धूनवस्थितान् ।
कृपया परयाविष्टो विषीदन्निदमब्रवीत् ॥२७॥

tān samīkṣya sa kaunteyaḥ sarvān bandhūn avasthitān/
kṛpayā parayāviṣṭo viṣīdann idam abravīt//

tān—them; *samīkṣya*—seeing; *saḥ*—he; *kaunteyaḥ*—the son of Kuntī; *sarvān*—all; *bandhūn*—kinsmen; *avasthitān*—arrayed; *kṛpayā*—with compassion; *parayā*—with infinite; *āviṣṭaḥ*—filled; *viṣīdan*—saddened; *idam*—thus; *abravīt*—spoke.

When the son of Kuntī, Arjuna, saw all his kinsmen, he was overcome with great compassion. Filled with despair, he began to speak.

Texts 28–30

अर्जुन उवाच
दृष्ट्वेमं स्वजनं कृष्ण युयुत्सुं समुपस्थितम् ।
सीदन्ति मम गात्राणि मुखं च परिशुष्यति ॥२८॥
वेपथुश्च शरीरे मे रोमहर्षश्च जायते ।
गाण्डीवं स्रंसते हस्तात् त्वक् चैव परिदह्यते ॥२९॥
न च शक्नोम्यवस्थातुं भ्रमतीव च मे मनः ।
निमित्तानि च पश्यामि विपरीतानि केशव ॥३०॥

arjuna uvāca
dṛṣṭvemaṁ sva-janaṁ kṛṣṇa yuyutsuṁ samupasthitam/
sīdanti mama gātrāṇi mukhaṁ ca pariśuṣyati//
vepathuś ca śarīre me roma-harṣaś ca jāyate/
gāṇḍīvaṁ sraṁsate hastāt tvak caiva paridahyate//
na ca śaknomy avasthātuṁ bhramatīva ca me manaḥ/
nimittāni ca paśyāmi viparītāni keśava//

arjunaḥ uvāca—Arjuna said; *dṛṣṭvā*—seeing; *imam*—this; *sva-janam*—own people; *kṛṣṇa*—O Kṛṣṇa; *yuyutsum*—preparing to fight; *samupasthitam*—present; *sīdanti*—quivering; *mama*—my; *gātrāṇi*—limbs; *mukham*—mouth; *ca*—also; *pariśuṣyati*—is drying up; *vepathuḥ*—trembling; *ca*—also; *śarīre*—in the body; *me*—my; *roma-harṣaḥ*—bristling of hair; *ca*—also; *jāyate*—is taking place; *gāṇḍīvam*—the bow of Arjuna; *sraṁsate*—is slipping; *hastāt*—from the hand; *tvak*—skin; *ca*—also; *eva*—certainly; *paridahyate*—is burning; *na*—nor; *ca*—also; *śaknomi*—I am able; *avasthātum*—to stay; *bhramati*—losing; *iva*—as; *ca*—and; *me*—my; *manaḥ*—mind; *nimittāni*—signs; *ca*—also; *paśyāmi*—I see; *viparītāni*—inauspicious; *keśava*—O killer of the demon Keśī.

Arjuna said: O Kṛṣṇa, seeing my own relatives preparing to fight with one another, my limbs are quivering and my body trembles. My mouth is drying up and my hair is bristling. My bow, Gāṇḍīva, is slipping from my hand and my skin burns. I am unable to keep my composure and feel as though I am losing my mind. O Keśava, I can see only misfortune ahead.

Madhusūdana Saraswatī comments that the use of the name Kṛṣṇa here indicates that Arjuna is calling upon Kṛṣṇa as "the one who has the power to remove the sorrow of his devotees... being of the nature of eternal bliss."

Although Arjuna's love has the power to subordinate Kṛṣṇa, Kṛṣṇa's acceptance of a subordinate role does not change his position as God. The love that such devotees possess is the gift of God, bestowed upon those who desire nothing more. From within the compact of that love, Kṛṣṇa bewilders Arjuna to think in terms of lesser concepts, such as material gain, *dharma*, and liberation. Still, the good heart of Arjuna shines forth even as he exemplifies the plight of an illusioned being. Remembering the prowess of Kṛṣṇa when he killed Keśī, the last demon that Kṛṣṇa killed in Vraja before he ventured to Mathurā, Arjuna, while expressing doubts, demonstrates his confidence in Kṛṣṇa's ability to destroy them. Arjuna spoke with humility, as Keśī, the mad horse who attacked Kṛṣṇa in Vraja, represents false pride.

The great warrior Arjuna is brought to tears at the thought of fighting with his relatives. Such is the power of material attachment. Humbled, he takes shelter of his friend Kṛṣṇa. After expressing his reservations about fighting, Arjuna next makes an elaborate attempt to rationalize his material attachments in the name of *dharma*, decency, scripture, and compassion. While his arguments have value unto themselves, in the present context they are symptomatic of his delusion.

Text 31

न च श्रेयोऽनुपश्यामि हत्वा स्वजनमाहवे ।
न कांक्षे विजयं कृष्ण न च राज्यं सुखानि च ॥३१॥

na ca śreyo 'nupaśyāmi hatvā sva-janam āhave/
na kāṅkṣe vijayaṁ kṛṣṇa na ca rājyaṁ sukhāni ca//

na—not; *ca*—and; *śreyaḥ*—good; *anupaśyāmi*—I foresee; *hatvā*—killing; *sva-janam*—relatives; *āhave*—in battle; *na*—nor; *kāṅkṣe*—I desire; *vijayam*—victory; *kṛṣṇa*—O Kṛṣṇa; *na*—nor; *ca*—also; *rājyam*—kingdom; *sukhāni*—pleasures; *ca*—also.

O Kṛṣṇa, I do not see how any good can come from killing my relatives in battle. I have no desire for victory, a kingdom, or the pleasure derived from attaining these things.

Here Arjuna invokes the holy name of Kṛṣṇa as he begins to rationalize why he should not fight. Kṛṣṇa and his name are one and the same, yet the holy name of Kṛṣṇa is a more compassionate manifestation of himself. By invoking Kṛṣṇa's name in this and the previous verse, Arjuna implies that Kṛṣṇa's name alone can remove all of his sorrows arising from material attachment.

Texts 32–35

किं नो राज्येन गोविन्द किं भोगैर्जीवितेन वा ।
येषामर्थे कांक्षितं नो राज्यं भोगाः सुखानि च ॥३२॥
त इमेऽवस्थिता युद्धे प्राणांस्त्यक्त्वा धनानि च ।
आचार्याः पितरः पुत्रास्तथैव च पितामहाः ॥३३॥
मातुलाः श्वशुराः पौत्राः श्यालाः सम्बन्धिनस्तथा ।
एतान्न हन्तुमिच्छामि घ्नतोऽपि मधुसूदन ॥३४॥
अपि त्रैलोक्यराज्यस्य हेतोः किं नु महीकृते ।
निहत्य धार्तराष्ट्रान्नः का प्रीतिः स्याज्जनार्दन ॥३५॥

kiṁ no rājyena govinda kiṁ bhogair jīvitena vā/
yeṣām arthe kāṅkṣitaṁ no rājyaṁ bhogāḥ sukhāni ca//
ta ime 'vasthitā yuddhe prāṇāṁs tyaktvā dhanāni ca/
ācāryāḥ pitaraḥ putrās tathaiva ca pitāmahāḥ//
mātulāḥ śvaśurāḥ pautrāḥ śyālāḥ sambandhinas tathā/
etān na hantum icchāmi ghnato 'pi madhusūdana//
api trailokya-rājyasya hetoḥ kiṁ nu mahī-kṛte/
nihatya dhārtarāṣṭrān naḥ kā prītiḥ syāj janārdana//

kim—what; *naḥ*—by us; *rājyena*—with kingdom; *govinda*—O Govinda, Lord of the cowherds who gives pleasure to the senses; *kim*—what; *bhogaiḥ*—with pleasures; *jīvitena*—living; *vā*—either; *yeṣām*—of whom; *arthe*—for the sake; *kāṅkṣitam*—desired; *naḥ*—to us; *rājyam*—kingdom; *bhogāḥ*—material enjoyment; *sukhāni*—joys; *ca*—also; *te*—they; *ime*—these; *avasthitāḥ*—situated; *yuddhe*—in battle; *prāṇān*—lives; *tyaktvā*—sacrificing; *dhanāni*—riches; *ca*—also; *ācāryāḥ*—teachers; *pitaraḥ*—fathers; *putrāḥ*—sons; *tathā*—as well as; *eva*—certainly; *ca*—also; *pitāmahāḥ*—grandfathers; *mātulāḥ*—maternal uncles; *śvaśurāḥ*—fathers-in-law; *pautrāḥ*—grandsons; *śyālāḥ*—brothers-in-law; *sambandhinaḥ*—brethren; *tathā*—as well as; *etān*—these; *na*—not; *hantum*—to kill; *icchāmi*—I wish; *ghnataḥ*—being killed; *api*—even if; *madhusūdana*—O killer of the demon Madhu; *api*—even; *trailokya*—the three worlds; *rājyasya*—for the kingdom; *hetoḥ*—in exchange; *kim nu*—what then; *mahī-kṛte*—for the kingdom of the earth; *nihatya*—by killing; *dhārtarāṣṭrān*—the sons of Dhṛtarāṣṭra; *naḥ*—our; *kā*—what; *prītiḥ*—joy; *syāt*—will there be; *janārdana*—O caretaker of all living beings.

O Govinda, what are kingdom and happiness to us, when those with whom we might desire to enjoy these things—teachers, fathers, sons, grandfathers, maternal uncles, fathers-in-law, grandsons, brothers-in-law, and other brethren—are standing here ready to fight, risking their own kingdoms, happiness, wealth, and lives? I have no desire to kill even those bent on killing me, O Madhusūdana. O Janārdana, I am not prepared to fight with the sons of Dhṛtarāṣṭra even for the sovereignty of the three worlds, much less an earthly kingdom.

Govinda is the eternal cowherder, the pastoral friend of nature—God in his private, carefree life. Govinda is also the joy of the *Vedas*. Owing to his relationship with Govinda, Arjuna has no desire for an earthly kingdom.

Here, under the divine illusion orchestrated by Kṛṣṇa, Arjuna offers other reasons as to why he does not want a kingdom, either for himself or for those dear to him, who would not live through the battle to enjoy one. As Madhusūdana, Kṛṣṇa is the slayer of the illusion of material happiness. Arjuna fears karmic reactions for killing relatives, and in ordinary circumstances he would be correct. He wants Kṛṣṇa to take responsibility, for he is Janārdana, the caretaker and killer of everyone. Furthermore, Arjuna implores Kṛṣṇa as Madhusūdana not to engage him in a war that he perceives to be contrary to the Vedic law, for Madhusūdana is the killer of the demon Madhu, from whom the Lord recovered the *Vedas*, reinstating the Vedic path.

Here Kṛṣṇa thinks, "But these people are aggressors, and there is no reaction from killing them," to which Arjuna responds in the following verse.

Text 36

पापमेवाश्रयेदस्मान् हत्वैतानाततायिनः ।
तस्मान्नार्हा वयं हन्तुं धार्तराष्ट्रान् सबान्धवान् ।
स्वजनं हि कथं हत्वा सुखिनः स्याम माधव ॥३६॥

pāpam evāśrayed asmān hatvaitān ātatāyinaḥ/
tasmān nārhā vayaṁ hantuṁ dhārtarāṣṭrān sa-bāndhavān/
sva-janaṁ hi kathaṁ hatvā sukhinaḥ syāma mādhava//

pāpam—sin; *eva*—certainly; *āśrayet*—should come upon; *asmān*—us; *hatvā*—by killing; *etān*—these; *ātatāyinaḥ*—aggressors; *tasmāt*—therefore; *na*—not; *arhāḥ*—justified; *vayam*—we; *hantum*—to kill; *dhārtarāṣṭrān*—the sons of Dhṛtarāṣṭra; *sa-bāndhavān*—along with friends; *sva-janam*—one's own family; *hi*—certainly; *katham*—how; *hatvā*—after destroying; *sukhinaḥ*—happy; *syāma*—we should become; *mādhava*—O Mādhava.

O Mādhava, by killing these aggressors we will incur only sin. It is not appropriate for us to kill Dhṛtarāṣṭra's sons along with our friends. How can one be happy after destroying one's family?

Although according to *artha-śāstra*, the Vedic political science, one can kill aggressors without incurring a reaction, this does not apply in this situation, for it is against the *dharma-śāstra*, or religious codes, to kill one's guru or elders. If in legal decisions the political and religious codes differ, the religious codes are to be given preference. The rule is that when two *smṛtis* conflict in worldly matters, reason prevails. However, the moral and religious code *(dharma-śāstra)* is more authoritative than that of political science *(artha-śāstra)*.[5]

Arjuna is certainly well versed in *dharma*. He also knows that in the battle not only will the aggressors, the sons of Dhṛtarāṣṭra, be killed, but others will as well. Thus he asks Mādhava, the bringer of good fortune, not to bring him misfortune by encouraging him in acts he understands to be irreligious.

Before Kṛṣṇa can question Arjuna as to why Bhīṣma and Droṇa, who certainly understood *dharma*, were nonetheless willing to fight, Arjuna answers him in the next verse. In doing so he stresses the importance of taking pride in family tradition, as this helps one to avoid capriciousness.

5. See Yā. Sm. 2.21.

Texts 37–38

यद्यप्येते न पश्यन्ति लोभोपहतचेतसः ।
कुलक्षयकृतं दोषं मित्रद्रोहे च पातकम् ॥३७॥
कथं न ज्ञेयमस्माभिः पापादस्मान्निवर्तितुम् ।
कुलक्षयकृतं दोषं प्रपश्यद्भिर्जनार्दन ॥३८॥

yady apy ete na paśyanti lobhopahata-cetasaḥ/
kula-kṣaya-kṛtaṁ doṣaṁ mitra-drohe ca pātakam//
kathaṁ na jñeyam asmābhiḥ pāpād asmān nivartitum/
kula-kṣaya-kṛtaṁ doṣaṁ prapaśyadbhir janārdana//

yadi—if; *api*—even; *ete*—they; *na*—not; *paśyanti*—see; *lobha*—greed; *upahata*—overwhelmed; *cetasaḥ*—their hearts; *kula-kṣaya*—destroying the family; *kṛtam*—done; *doṣam*—fault; *mitra-drohe*—in deceiving friends; *ca*—also; *pātakam*—sinful reactions; *katham*—why; *na*—not; *jñeyam*—should be known; *asmābhiḥ*—by us; *pāpāt*—from sin; *asmāt*—from this; *nivartitum*—to cease; *kula-kṣaya*—in the destruction of a dynasty; *kṛtam*—done; *doṣam*—crime; *prapaśyadbhiḥ*—by those who can see; *janārdana*—O Janārdana.

O Janārdana, although others gathered here, being overwhelmed by greed for a kingdom, are blind to the faults of destroying the dynasty or deceiving friends, why should we, who know better, engage in this battle?

Text 39

कुलक्षये प्रणश्यन्ति कुलधर्माः सनातनाः ।
धर्मे नष्टे कुलं कृत्स्नमधर्मोऽभिभवत्युत ॥३९॥

kula-kṣaye praṇaśyanti kula-dharmāḥ sanātanāḥ/
dharme naṣṭe kulaṁ kṛtsnam adharmo 'bhibhavaty uta//

kula-kṣaye—with the destruction of the dynasty; *praṇaśyanti*—are lost; *kula-dharmāḥ*—the family traditions; *sanātanāḥ*—eternal; *dharme-naṣṭe*—religion being destroyed; *kulam*—family; *kṛtsnam*—whole; *adharmaḥ*—irreligion; *abhibhavati*—overpowers; *uta*—also.

With the destruction of the dynasty, tradition is destroyed and remaining family members will be overpowered by irreligious practice.

Text 40

अधर्माभिभवात्कृष्ण प्रदुष्यन्ति कुलस्त्रियः ।
स्त्रीषु दुष्टासु वार्ष्णेय जायते वर्णसङ्करः ॥४०॥

adharmābhibhavāt kṛṣṇa praduṣyanti kula-striyaḥ/
strīṣu duṣṭāsu vārṣṇeya jāyate varṇa-saṅkaraḥ//

adharma—irreligion; *abhibhavāt*—having increased; *kṛṣṇa*—O Kṛṣṇa; *praduṣyanti*—become corrupted; *kula-striyaḥ*—women of the family; *strīṣu duṣṭāsu*—women being corrupted; *vārṣṇeya*—O descendant of Vṛṣṇi; *jāyate*—is produced; *varṇa-saṅkaraḥ*—unwanted children.

O Kṛṣṇa, when irreligion increases, women are taken advantage of. From the corruption of women, O descendant of Vṛṣṇi, arises inappropriate mixing, producing unwanted children.

Although it is certainly true that when irreligion increases women can be taken advantage of, it is also true women can take advantage of men. Inappropriate mixing between men and women often does produce unwanted children. This section of the *Gītā* extols the virtues of family life, which is a vital component of a healthy society.

The argument raised here by Arjuna is one of many arguments he raises in this chapter based on religious—but nonetheless material—considerations. He raises them to justify not doing Kṛṣṇa's bidding. Kṛṣṇa refutes all of these arguments when he takes the discussion to the level of the soul in the second chapter. However, Kṛṣṇa expresses his own concern for family values in chapter 3 (Bg. 3.24).

Text 41

सङ्करो नरकायैव कुलघ्नानां कुलस्य च ।
पतन्ति पितरो ह्येषां लुप्तपिण्डोदकक्रियाः ॥४१॥

saṅkaro narakāyaiva kula-ghnānāṁ kulasya ca/
patanti pitaro hy eṣāṁ lupta-piṇḍodaka-kriyāḥ//

saṅkaraḥ—mixing; *narakāya*—to hell; *eva*—certainly; *kula-ghnānām*—of those who are killers of the family; *kulasya*—of the family; *ca*—also; *patanti*—fall; *pitaraḥ*—forefathers; *hi*—certainly; *eṣām*—of them; *lupta*—stopped; *piṇḍa*—mouthful of rice; *udaka*—water; *kriyāḥ*—oblations.

Such inappropriate mixing sends the dynasty and its destroyers to hell. Even the ancestors fall, being deprived of oblations of rice and water.

Text 42

दोषैरेतैः कुलघ्नानां वर्णसङ्करकारकैः ।
उत्साद्यन्ते जातिधर्माः कुलधर्माश्च शाश्वताः ॥४२॥

doṣair etaiḥ kula-ghnānāṁ varṇa-saṅkara-kārakaiḥ/
utsādyante jāti-dharmāḥ kula-dharmāś ca śāśvatāḥ//

doṣaiḥ—by such faults; *etaiḥ*—by these; *kula-ghnānām*—of the destroyers of the family; *varṇa-saṅkara*—unwanted children; *kārakaiḥ*—which are causes; *utsādyante*—are destroyed; *jāti-dharmāḥ*—caste duties; *kula-dharmāḥ*—family traditions; *ca*—also; *śāśvatāḥ*—long-standing.

Inappropriate mixing destroys social norms and long-standing family traditions.

Text 43

उत्सन्नकुलधर्माणां मनुष्याणां जनार्दन ।
नरके नियतं वासो भवतीत्यनुशुश्रुम ॥४३॥

utsanna-kula-dharmāṇāṁ manuṣyāṇāṁ janārdana/
narake niyataṁ vāso bhavatīty anuśuśruma//

utsanna-kula-dharmāṇām—of those whose family traditions have been destroyed; *manuṣyāṇām*—of men; *janārdana*—O Janārdana; *narake*—in hell; *niyatam*—always; *vāsaḥ*—residence; *bhavati*—it is; *iti*—thus; *anuśuśruma*—we have heard from reliable sources.

O Janārdana, I have heard from reliable sources that those whose family traditions and values have been lost live indefinitely in hell.

Text 44

अहो बत महत्पापं कर्तुं व्यवसिता वयम् ।
यद्राज्यसुखलोभेन हन्तुं स्वजनमुद्यताः ॥४४॥

aho bata mahat-pāpaṁ kartuṁ vyavasitā vayam/
yad rājya-sukha-lobhena hantuṁ sva-janam udyatāḥ//

aho—alas; *bata*—how has it happened; *mahat*—great; *pāpam*—evil; *kartum*—to perform; *vyavasitāḥ*—prepared; *vayam*—we; *yat*—that; *rājya-sukha-lobhena*—out of greed for royal pleasures; *hantum*—to kill; *sva-janam*—one's own people; *udyatāḥ*—trying.

Alas! How has it happened that we are prepared to commit such a great evil as killing our own kinsmen out of greed for royal pleasures?

Text 45

यदि मामप्रतीकारमशस्त्रं शस्त्रपाणयः ।
धार्तराष्ट्रा रणे हन्युस्तन्मे क्षेमतरं भवेत् ॥४५॥

yadi mām apratikāram aśastraṁ śastra-pāṇayaḥ/
dhārtarāṣṭrā raṇe hanyus tan me kṣemataraṁ bhavet//

yadi—if; *mām*—me; *apratikāram*—without resisting; *aśastram*—unarmed; *śastra-pāṇayaḥ*—those with weapons in hand; *dhārtarāṣṭrāḥ*—the sons of Dhṛtarāṣṭra; *raṇe*—in battle; *hanyuḥ*—should kill; *tat*—that; *me*—for me; *kṣemataram*—weapons in hand; *bhavet*—would be.

It would be better for the sons of Dhṛtarāṣṭra, weapons in hand, to kill me in battle unarmed and unresisting.

Although Arjuna reasons that shunning the war would not stop the opposition from fighting, his conviction to avoid the battle remains firm.

Text 46

सञ्जय उवाच
एवमुक्त्वार्जुनः संख्ये रथोपस्थ उपाविशत् ।
विसृज्य सशरं चापं शोकसंविग्नमानसः ॥४६॥

sañjaya uvāca
evam uktvārjunaḥ saṅkhye rathopastha upāviśat/
visṛjya sa-śaraṁ cāpaṁ śoka-saṁvigna-mānasaḥ//

sañjayaḥ uvāca—Sañjaya said; *evam*—thus; *uktvā*—having spoken; *arjunaḥ*—Arjuna; *saṅkhye*—in the battlefield; *ratha*—of the chariot; *upasthe*—on the seat; *upāviśat*—sat down; *visṛjya*—casting aside; *sa-śaram*—along with arrows; *cāpam*—the bow; *śoka*—grief; *saṁvigna*—overcome; *mānasaḥ*—mind.

Sañjaya said: Having spoken thus, Arjuna sat down on his chariot and cast aside his bow and arrows, his heart overcome with grief.

Arjuna's grief is rooted in material attachment. His rationale for not fighting, which begins with verse 28 and concludes with verse 45, is a product of his attachment, and this attachment is what Kṛṣṇa wants him to slay. Arjuna's attachment is so powerful that it has caused this otherwise great warrior to cast aside his weapons.

Arjuna's material identity is a product of his attachment to his family members. Slaying them, he sees no prospect in life because his sense of self is dependent on their existence. Because this fleeting superficial identity changes as the people and things one considers one's own prove to be otherwise, the material ego must be dismantled for one's authentic self to emerge. Kṛṣṇa wants Arjuna to know his eternal self that outlives his identity based on his present attachments. All spiritual practitioners are first and foremost faced with this challenge. Thus the importance of dismantling the material ego is brought to light here in the first chapter. Although the *Bhagavad-gītā* is about slaying one's material attachments, most people who read it skip over this important step and argue about the significance of the balance of the text. It should be understood, however, that spiritual life requires that we slay our material ego. From then on, like a boat that has pulled up its anchor, we can successfully sail the sea of our spiritual potential.

CHAPTER TWO

सांख्ययोगः

Sāṅkhya-yoga

YOGA OF ANALYSIS

Text 1

सञ्जय उवाच
तं तथा कृपयाविष्टमश्रुपूर्णाकुलेक्षणम् ।
विषीदन्तमिदं वाक्यमुवाच मधुसूदनः ॥१॥

sañjaya uvāca
taṁ tathā kṛpayāviṣṭam aśru-pūrṇākulekṣaṇam/
viṣīdantam idaṁ vākyam uvāca madhusūdanaḥ//

sañjayaḥ uvāca—Sañjaya said; *tam*—to him; *tathā*—thus; *kṛpayā*—by compassion; *āviṣṭam*—overwhelmed; *aśru*—tear; *pūrṇa*—full; *ākula*—downcast; *īkṣaṇam*—eye; *viṣīdantam*—grieving; *idam*—this; *vākyam*—word; *uvāca*—said; *madhu-sūdanaḥ*—Madhusūdana.

Sañjaya said: To Arjuna, who was thus overcome with pity and had tears filling his downcast eyes in despair, Madhusūdana began to speak.

The previous chapter is called *viṣāda-yoga. Viṣāda* is the condition of distress. The symptoms of Arjuna's distress *(viṣīdantam)* in the form of downcast eyes filled with tears *(aśrū-pūrṇākulekṣaṇam)* are described in this verse in the course of introducing Kṛṣṇa's speech. The grammatical arrangement in this verse indicates that Arjuna's despair is external and thus possible to remove. Kṛṣṇa's instructions in this chapter, by which he seeks to remove Arjuna's despair, constitute a *sūtra*-like summary of the *Gītā*'s contents.

When Arjuna dropped his bow at the end of the previous chapter, Dhṛtarāṣṭra's heart leaped. The old king thought, "Despite Sañjaya's subtle inferences to the contrary, it appears that I was right. The piety of the Pāṇḍavas and that of Kurukṣetra have combined to grant victory to my son by default. Arjuna will not fight, and Duryodhana will be the king without shooting an arrow!" Sensing his false hopes, Sañjaya continues his narration, relating how Kṛṣṇa, whom he addresses here as Madhusūdana, begins to speak. He refers to Kṛṣṇa by this name to indicate to Dhṛtarāṣṭra that just as Kṛṣṇa had long before slain the demon Madhu, so now he would slay the demonlike doubts of Arjuna. Free from doubt, Arjuna will fight and be victorious. Although Arjuna's reluctance to fight appears to be supported by valid and even religious concerns, Kṛṣṇa thinks otherwise, as does Sañjaya, comparing Arjuna's doubts to demons.

Text 2

श्रीभगवानुवाच
कुतस्त्वा कश्मलमिदं विषमे समुपस्थितम् ।
अनार्यजुष्टमस्वर्ग्यमकीर्तिकरमर्जुन ॥२॥

śrī-bhagavān uvāca
kutas tvā kaśmalam idaṁ viṣame samupasthitam/
anārya-juṣṭam asvargyam akīrti-karam arjuna//

śrī-bhagavān uvāca—the Lord of Śrī said; *kutaḥ*—from where; *tvā*—to you; *kaśmalam*—faintheartedness; *idam*—this; *viṣame*—at the hour of danger; *samupasthitam*—arrived; *anārya*—not Aryan; *juṣṭam*—befitting; *asvargyam*—which does not lead to heaven; *akīrti*—infamy; *karam*—the cause of; *arjuna*—O Arjuna.

The Lord of Śrī said: Arjuna, from where has this faintheartedness come at the hour of fighting? It is not befitting a man of your character, an Āryan. It does not lead to heaven or a good reputation.

As Kṛṣṇa utters his first words of this chapter, the *Gītā* refers to him as Śrī Bhagavān. *Śrī* indicates the Goddess of fortune, and *Bhagavān* the Supreme God who is possessed of all opulence. There is no meaning to Bhagavān without Śrī, for the Absolute devoid of *śakti* is not Bhagavān but *nirviśeṣa brahman*, pure undifferentiated consciousness devoid of form, *līlā*, and so on—the spiritual halo of Bhagavān.

Śrī indicates the *śakti* of Godhead, in relation with which Brahman, the Absolute, is known as *paraṁ brahman*, or Bhagavān, the Supreme Person. According to the *Upaniṣads*, Brahman is possessed of innumerable *śaktis*: *parāsya śaktir vividhaiva śrūyate* (Śve. Up. 6.8). The *śaktis*, or potencies, of

Brahman are simultaneously one and different from him, as light and heat are one with and different from fire. Gauḍīya Vedānta posits three principal potencies of the Absolute: primary *(svarūpa-śakti)*, intermediate *(taṭastha* or *jīva-śakti)*, and secondary *(māyā-śakti)*. The primary *śakti* of God is that by which he conducts his personal affairs. This *śakti* is alluded to in the fourth chapter of the *Gītā* in relation to the descent of Godhead to the world of our experience (Bg. 4.6). The predominant manifestation of this *śakti* is Śrī, who is the fountainhead of all of Bhagavān's innumerable *śaktis*. She is the *śakti* by which he himself feels blessed—the Blessed Lord. The intermediate *śakti* consists of the individual souls, and the secondary *śakti* is the material influence. These two *śaktis* are introduced in chapter 7 and discussed in greater detail in chapter 13.[1]

Jīva Goswāmī has defined Bhagavān as *bhajanīya-guṇa-viśiṣṭa*, "He whose nature is such that whoever comes in touch with him cannot resist feeling moved to worship and adore his charming personality."[2] This explanation is in line with Parāśara Muni's definition, but it emphasizes Kṛṣṇa himself, as opposed to a general conception of Bhagavān. Parāśara Muni says that he who possesses all opulences in full—wealth, strength, beauty, fame, knowledge, and renunciation—is known as Bhagavān.[3]

According to Jīva Goswāmī, the word Bhagavān is derived from "Bhagavavān." Śrī Jīva says that the *a* in the syllable *va* is elided enabling the two *v*'s to join and become a single letter. Thus Bhagavavān becomes Bhagavān. It means he who possesses *(van) bha*, *ga*, and *va*. *Bha* represents *bhartā*, which implies the power to nourish or maintain. Kṛṣṇa possesses the power to maintain and nourish his devotees. *Ga* stands for *gamayayitā*. It means he who has the power to grant love of God or bring God's devotees to his abode. *Va* stands for the verb *vas*, which means to reside. Bhagavān is he in whom everything resides, and he who resides in the hearts of his devotees.[4]

Here Kṛṣṇa addresses Arjuna by his given name. The name Arjuna means white, spotless, or pure. Kṛṣṇa addresses his friend and disciple-to-be by name to further emphasize that his reservation to fight is unbecoming for one so pure as to go by the name Arjuna.

1. See Bg. 7.4–5 and 13.1.

2. This is the explanation/translation of Swāmī B. R. Śrīdhara.

3. This verse can be found in Veda Vyāsa's *Viṣṇu Purāṇa* (6.5.47), although it has been attributed to Parāśara Muni, the father of Vyāsa.

4. See Bs. 3.

In this verse Kṛṣṇa dismisses all of Arjuna's reservations thus far. Sañjaya described the basis of Arjuna's reservations as "brimming with compassion." (Bg. 1.27) Here Kṛṣṇa dismisses this entire basis, asking Arjuna, "from where has this faintheartedness come?" Kṛṣṇa calls Arjuna's symptoms of fear "faintheartedness" *(kaśmalam)*. In response to Arjuna's five-verse speech about winning and losing kingdoms and nobility (Bg. 1.31–35), Kṛṣṇa tells Arjuna that while speaking about that which is noble, his speech is not befitting a noble person *(anāryam)*. To Arjuna's five verses concerning not acting disgracefully (Bg. 1.36–40), Kṛṣṇa replies that he has attracted infamy *(akīrtikaram)*, and to Arjuna's concerns about attaining heaven (Bg. 1.41–45), Kṛṣṇa tells him his speech will not lead him there *(asvargyam)*. Arjuna is thus shattered by Kṛṣṇa's opening remarks, which are followed by Kṛṣṇa's remedial measures.

Text 3

क्लैब्यं मा स्म गमः पार्थ नैतत्त्वय्युपपद्यते ।
क्षुद्रं हृदयदौर्बल्यं त्यक्त्वोत्तिष्ठ परन्तप ॥३॥

klaibyaṁ mā sma gamaḥ pārtha naitat tvayy upapadyate/
kṣudraṁ hṛdaya-daurbalyaṁ tyaktvottiṣṭha parantapa//

klaibyam—impotency; *mā sma*—do not; *gamaḥ*—undergo; *pārtha*—O son of Pṛthā; *na*—not; *etat*—this; *tvayi*—in you; *upapadyate*—is becoming; *kṣudram*—petty; *hṛdaya*—heart; *daurbalyam*—weakness; *tyaktvā*—giving up; *uttiṣṭha*—stand up; *param-tapa*—O chastiser of enemies.

Therefore, O son of Pṛthā, do not yield to impotency for it is not becoming. O chastiser of enemies, cast off this petty weakness of heart. Stand up and fight.

Kṛṣṇa began speaking to Arjuna by reminding him of his maternal family in order to draw out family affection from him so that his instructions for all souls could be revealed through the instrument of his devotee. Here Kṛṣṇa again reminds Arjuna that he is the son of Pṛthā, but this time with the purpose of drawing his attention to the fact that as Pṛthā's son his father is Indra, the king of heaven and a powerful warrior. A great warrior like Arjuna should not yield to impotency, which is superficial and springs from weakness of heart. Material conditioning has no roots. The foundation of existence is consciousness. Casting off the weakheartedness of material conditioning, one treads the path of *dharma*. Although Arjuna is crushed, owing to his warrior spirit he makes a feeble attempt to rebut Kṛṣṇa in the following verse.

Text 4

अर्जुन उवाच
कथं भीष्ममहं संख्ये द्रोणं च मधुसूदन ।
इषुभिः प्रतियोत्स्यामि पूजार्हावरिसूदन ॥४॥

arjuna uvāca
kathaṁ bhīṣmam ahaṁ saṅkhye droṇaṁ ca madhusūdana/
iṣubhiḥ pratiyotsyāmi pūjārhāv ari-sūdana//

arjunaḥ uvāca—Arjuna said; *katham*—how; *bhīṣmam*—Bhīṣma; *aham*—I; *saṅkhye*—in battle; *droṇam*—Droṇa; *ca*—also; *madhu-sūdana*—O killer of Madhu; *iṣubhiḥ*—with arrows; *pratiyotsyāmi*—shall attack; *pūjā-arhau*—those who are worshippable; *ari-sūdana*—O killer of the enemies.

Arjuna said: O killer of the Madhu demon, how can I kill in battle Bhīṣma and Droṇa? How can I use arrows against these two worshippable men, O killer of enemies?

Here two names of Kṛṣṇa are used which seem redundant. Madhusūdana indicates that Kṛṣṇa is a killer of enemies, such as the Madhu demon. The name Arisūdana at the end of the verse also means killer of enemies. However, Madhu in Madhusūdana could be confused with the Madhu patriarch of the Yadu dynasty. Thus Arisūdana is used to clear any confusion.

Arjuna addresses Kṛṣṇa in terms of Kṛṣṇa's wrath against his own enemies. By doing so, Arjuna contrasts Kṛṣṇa's own actions with that which Kṛṣṇa expects of him: killing his gurus! Droṇa and Bhīṣma are worthy of Arjuna's worship, yet Arjuna is expected to throw arrows at them rather than flowers? "You kill your enemies," reasoned Arjuna, "but when have you killed your friends and teachers? Would you ever think of doing so? You call my reluctance weakness of heart?"

Kṛṣṇa thought, "Well, if you don't kill them, how will you live? After all you are a warrior and this battle, welcome or not, has come to your doorstep. What else are you going to do?"

Arjuna demonstrates just how opposed to fighting his relatives he is. He tells Kṛṣṇa he would rather live the life of a beggar than fight. Begging is not the prescribed duty of a warrior. According to the socioreligious system of the *Gītā*, a warrior's begging for his sustenance would be contrary to *dharma*. Warriors are to give in charity, never beg. However, Arjuna preferred begging over killing his relatives. He reasoned, "Should I maintain my body by killing my guru (Droṇa)?"

Text 5

गुरूनहत्वा हि महानुभावान्
श्रेयो भोक्तुं भैक्ष्यमपीह लोके ।
हत्वार्थकामांस्तु गुरूनिहैव
भुञ्जीय भोगान् रुधिरप्रदिग्धान् ॥५॥

gurūn ahatvā hi mahānubhāvān
śreyo bhoktuṁ bhaikṣyam apīha loke/
hatvārtha-kāmāṁs tu gurūn ihaiva
bhuñjīya bhogān rudhira-pradigdhān//

gurūn—the superiors; *ahatvā*—not killing; *hi*—certainly; *mahā-anubhāvān*—venerable; *śreyaḥ*—better; *bhoktum*—to enjoy; *bhaikṣyam*—by begging; *api*—even; *iha*—here; *loke*—in the world; *hatvā*—killing; *artha-kāmān*—desirous of gain; *tu*—but; *gurūn*—superiors; *iha*—here; *eva*—certainly; *bhuñjīya*—I should enjoy; *bhogān*—enjoyable things; *rudhira*—blood; *pradigdhān*—tainted.

It is better to live in this world as a beggar than to live at the cost of the lives of my venerable elders. If these respectable elders are killed, the spoils will be tainted with blood.

Great souls are to be excused for apparent flaws in character.[5] Here Arjuna has compared Bhīṣma and Droṇa to the sun, which remains pure even after touching impure things. Indeed, the sun purifies even urine. Combining *hi* with *mahānubhāvān (himahānubhāvān)* we get: "those who have power *(anubhāva)* like that of the destroyer *(hi)* of the cold *(mahā)*." Adding *hi* to *mahā* we get *himahā* (the sun).

In this verse the meter of the *Gītā* changes for the first time from *anuṣṭubh* to *triṣṭubh*, also known commonly as the *kṣatriya* meter. This change of meter, which lasts for four verses, indicates the heightened emotion of Arjuna.

5. See ŚB. 10.33.29.

Text 6

न चैतद्विद्मः कतरन्नो गरीयो
यद्वा जयेम यदि वा नो जयेयुः ।
यानेव हत्वा न जिजीविषाम-
स्तेऽवस्थिताः प्रमुखे धार्तराष्ट्राः ॥६॥

na caitad vidmaḥ kataran no garīyo
yad vā jayema yadi vā no jayeyuḥ/
yān eva hatvā na jijīviṣāmas
te 'vasthitāḥ pramukhe dhārtarāṣṭrāḥ//

na—not; *ca*—also; *etat*—this; *vidmaḥ*—we know; *katarat*—which; *naḥ*—for us; *garīyaḥ*—better; *yat vā*—whether; *jayema*—we should conquer; *yadi*—if; *vā*—or; *naḥ*—us; *jayeyuḥ*—they should conquer; *yān*—whom; *eva*—certainly; *hatvā*—by killing; *na*—not; *jijīviṣāmaḥ*—we would want to live; *te*—they; *avasthitāḥ*—are situated; *pramukhe*—in the front; *dhārtarāṣṭrāḥ*—the sons of Dhṛtarāṣṭra.

I no longer know which is better, conquering or being conquered. If I kill the sons of Dhṛtarāṣṭra, who are standing before me, I shall not care to live.

Here Arjuna's bewilderment peaks. He does not know what to do. However, in the midst of this bewilderment, he expresses a conviction that material life is futile. Whether he wins or loses, he sees no prospect. Thus he demonstrates his eligibility *(adhikāra)* for approaching a guru.

In the first chapter, Arjuna also demonstrates his qualification for sitting at the feet of the guru. In verse 31 Arjuna exhibits knowledge of difference between the permanent and the impermanent by stating that he sees no ultimate good *(śreyaḥ)* in killing; in verses 32 and 35 he demonstrates dispassion for material gain, both in this life and in the next; in verse 43 he shows an understanding of the difference between the body and soul when he acknowledges the soul's potential plight in hell; in verse 32 he displays both internal *(śama)* and external *(dama)* control; he exhibits an absence of greed in verse 38 and shows tolerance in verse 46. Tracing the underlying eligibility of Arjuna, Madhusūdana Saraswatī sees the first chapter's purpose as indicating the discipline necessary for discipleship.

Appropriately, Arjuna submits to his extraordinary friend, Kṛṣṇa, asking for God's intervention in the form of Śrī Guru. Thus he lays the foundation for Kṛṣṇa's speech, for God speaks directly only to those who realize that if we are to make a comprehensive solution to the material predicament, there is no other real shelter in this world than him.

Text 7

कार्पण्यदोषोपहतस्वभावः
  पृच्छामि त्वां धर्मसम्मूढचेताः ।
यच्छ्रेयः स्यान्निश्चितं ब्रूहि तन्मे
  शिष्यस्तेऽहं शाधि मां त्वां प्रपन्नम् ॥७॥

kārpaṇya-doṣopahata-svabhāvaḥ
  pṛcchāmi tvāṁ dharma-sammūḍha-cetāḥ/
yac chreyaḥ syān niścitaṁ brūhi tan me
  śiṣyas te 'haṁ śādhi māṁ tvāṁ prapannam//

kārpaṇya—miserliness; *doṣa*—weakness; *upahata*—overcome; *sva-bhāvaḥ*—characteristics; *pṛcchāmi*—I ask; *tvām*—you; *dharma*—duty; *sammūḍha*—confused; *cetāḥ*—heart; *yat*—what; *śreyaḥ*—better; *syāt*—should be; *niścitam*—confidently; *brūhi*—tell; *tat*—that; *me*—to me; *śiṣyaḥ*—disciple; *te*—your; *aham*—I; *śādhi*—instruct; *mām*—me; *tvām*—unto you; *prapannam*—surrendered.

I am confused about my duty due to miserly weakness. Therefore please tell me what is best for me. I am your disciple, a soul surrendered unto you. Please instruct me.

The word *kārpaṇyam*, "covered by the material ego," in this verse is the abstract form of *kṛpaṇa*. One who leaves the world mentally unable to part with his possessions is considered a miser who remains falsely identified with matter.

In the midst of his confusion, Arjuna himself understands the reality of what Kṛṣṇa has indicated. He admits his weakness of heart. He knows that as long as a person thinks he knows, he cannot know the truth. Yet as qualified as Arjuna is, manifesting the disposition of an ideal disciple, Kṛṣṇa does not reply right away. He tests Arjuna's resolve rather than immediately accepting him as his disciple. Kṛṣṇa hesitates as if to say, "What can I say? You have already given so many logical arguments and have cited the scripture as well. What need does such a learned person have for a guru? What will a guru do for you on the battlefield? Furthermore, we are just friends. If you want a guru, you should approach someone else. If you want to remove your distress, just fight." Sensing this, Arjuna speaks strongly as to the futility of fighting, reiterating his conviction to accept Kṛṣṇa as his guru.

Text 8

न हि प्रपश्यामि ममापनुद्या-
द्यच्छोकमुच्छोषणमिन्द्रियाणाम् ।
अवाप्य भूमावसपत्नमृद्धं
राज्यं सुराणामपि चाधिपत्यम् ॥८॥

na hi prapaśyāmi mamāpanudyād
yac chokam ucchoṣaṇam indriyāṇām/
avāpya bhūmāv asapatnam ṛddhaṁ
rājyaṁ surāṇām api cādhipatyam//

na—not; *hi*—certainly; *prapaśyāmi*—I see; *mama*—my; *apanudyāt*—it could remove; *yat*—which; *śokam*—grief; *ucchoṣaṇam*—drying up; *indriyāṇām*—of the senses; *avāpya*—gaining; *bhūmau*—on the earth; *asapatnam*—uncontested; *ṛddham*—prosperous; *rājyam*—kingdom; *surāṇām*—of the gods; *api*—even; *ca*—also; *ādhipatyam*—sovereignty.

Even if I were to gain the entire earth as an uncontested kingdom or sovereignty in heaven, I do not see how I could remove the grief that is drying up the power of my senses.

Text 9

सञ्जय उवाच
एवमुक्त्वा हृषीकेशं गुडाकेशः परन्तपः ।
न योत्स्य इति गोविन्दमुक्त्वा तूष्णीं बभूव ह ॥९॥

sañjaya uvāca
evam uktvā hṛṣīkeśaṁ guḍākeśaḥ parantapaḥ/
na yotsya iti govindam uktvā tūṣṇīṁ babhūva ha//

sañjayaḥ uvāca—Sañjaya said; *evam*—thus; *uktvā*—speaking; *hṛṣīkeśam*—to Hṛṣīkeśa; *guḍākeśaḥ*—Arjuna, the conqueror of sleep; *parantapaḥ*—the chastiser of the enemies; *na yotsye*—I shall not fight; *iti*—thus; *govindam*—to Govinda; *uktva*—speaking; *tūṣṇīm*—silent; *babhūva*—became; *ha*—certainly.

Sañjaya said: Then Guḍākeśa said to Hṛṣīkeśa, "O Govinda! I shall not fight," and fell silent.

In Arjuna's refusal to fight, he further places himself in Kṛṣṇa's hands. Having accepted Kṛṣṇa as his guru, he unknowingly speaks the truth when he says he will not fight. Although he will ultimately engage in the battle, he will do so only as an instrument in the hands of Kṛṣṇa, who is known as Hṛṣīkeśa, controller of the senses. In consideration of this, Arjuna himself will not fight. Thus Guḍākeśa, the conqueror of sleep (Arjuna), put himself in the hands of Govinda, who being the source of the *Vedas (vindati gam)* is omniscient and thereby capable of awakening all souls to their highest prospect. Through all of these epithets, Sañjaya is hinting to Dhṛtarāṣṭra that Kṛṣṇa will inspire Arjuna to fight, and thus there is no hope for Dhṛtarāṣṭra's sons.

Text 10

तमुवाच हृषीकेशः प्रहसन्निव भारत ।
सेनयोरुभयोर्मध्ये विषीदन्तमिदं वचः ॥१०॥

tam uvāca hṛṣīkeśaḥ prahasann iva bhārata/
senayor ubhayor madhye viṣīdantam idaṁ vacaḥ//

tam—to him; *uvāca*—said; *hṛṣīkeśaḥ*—Hṛṣīkeśa; *prahasan*—smiling; *iva*—like that; *bhārata*—O Dhṛtarāṣṭra, descendant of Bharata; *senayoḥ*—of the armies; *ubhayoḥ*—of both; *madhye*—in the middle; *viṣīdantam*—to the sorrowful one; *idam*—this; *vacaḥ*—word.

O King, in the midst of both armies, Hṛṣīkeśa, smiling, spoke these words to the sorrowful Arjuna.

Kṛṣṇa smiles to encourage Arjuna. As Kṛṣṇa prepared to speak grave topics, he sought to make light of the situation that so overwhelmed Arjuna. The preceptor similarly makes light of the task at hand in the beginning by allowing us to believe that perfection is almost within our grasp, when in fact it may be lifetimes away. Kṛṣṇa's smile further indicates his affection for Arjuna, who remains his friend even as he becomes his disciple. In the Gauḍīya tradition, the disciple sees the guru as a dearmost friend. The guru teaches the disciple like a friendly elder. Here Kṛṣṇa's smile indicates the union of friendship and servitude that characterizes Arjuna's love for him.

Viśvanātha Cakravartī comments that because Arjuna has at this point become Kṛṣṇa's disciple, Kṛṣṇa merely smiles and refrains from chiding him as he did earlier.

Although Kṛṣṇa's speech is directed to Arjuna, it is spoken in the midst of everyone assembled *(senayor ubhayor madhye)*, and is therefore a universal message for all to hear. Responding to Arjuna's appeal, Kṛṣṇa begins to speak to him in Upaniṣadic language, which is appropriate when speaking to those who have understood the conclusion of religious injunctions. Arjuna has demonstrated even in his apparent confusion that he is well versed in the religious codes. He has surpassed inquiry into religious life *(dharma-jijñāsā)* and is now at least ready to hear about spiritual life *(brahma-jijñāsā)*. He knows well the futility of pursuing enduring happiness in this world even when one's efforts are in concert with the religious injunctions. If one somehow or other, either by religious adherence or association with a saint, reaches this point in life, one is qualified to hear Vedānta, the conclusion of the sacred literature, through which one can touch the soul.

The *Upaniṣads* are known as *śruti*, that which is to be heard, having been spoken by God himself for our benefit. As Kṛṣṇa begins to speak, Sañjaya refers to him as Bhagavān, God, and thus the song of God, *Śrī Gītopaniṣad*, begins.

Text 11

श्रीभगवानुवाच
अशोच्यानन्वशोचस्त्वं प्रज्ञावादांश्च भाषसे ।
गतासूनगतासूंश्च नानुशोचन्ति पण्डिताः ॥११॥

śrī-bhagavān uvāca
aśocyān anvaśocas tvaṁ prajñā-vādāṁś ca bhāṣase/
gatāsūn agatāsūṁś ca nānuśocanti paṇḍitāḥ//

śrī-bhagavān uvāca—the Lord of Śrī said; *aśocyān*—not worthy of lamentation; *anvaśocaḥ*—you have lamented; *tvam*—you; *prajñā-vādān*—learned words; *ca*—also; *bhāṣase*—you speak; *gata*—lost; *asūn*—life; *agata*—not lost; *asūn*—life; *ca*—also; *na*—never; *anuśocanti*—lament; *paṇḍitāḥ*—the wise.

The Lord of Śrī said: While speaking learned words, you lament for those not worthy of lamentation. The wise lament neither for the living nor the dead.

In *Paramātma-sandarbha*, Jīva Goswāmī points out the parallelism between this verse and Kṛṣṇa's concluding verse in chapter 18 (Bg. 18.66). These two verses mark the beginning and end of Kṛṣṇa's instructions to Arjuna, and thus one can surmise the essence of the entire text from them. In both verses Kṛṣṇa instructs, "Don't lament, don't worry" *(na anuśocanti/mā śucaḥ)*. Mental energy expended on worrying would be better spent in remembering Bhagavān, our maintainer and protector and the perfect object of love.

One may question why remorse for the loss of loved ones is not deemed appropriate, for such behavior is seen even in great souls. Kṛṣṇa anticipates that Arjuna might argue in this direction in the face of the strong possibility that his dear ones will depart, and he says they should not be lamented for. Knowledgeable persons *(paṇḍitāḥ)* know that the departed have merely gone elsewhere, as they do even in embodied life. Although great persons are seen to lament at times, this is merely the expression of their manifest *(prārabdha) karma* exhausting itself, while they themselves know better and remain situated in knowledge of the nature of the self. The manifest *karma* of great souls expires without diminishing their greatness. Although lamentation may be unavoidable, great souls teach us to pass through it without identifying with it. When we witness the passing of our good and bad *karma* without reacting to it, we progress in spiritual life.

In this verse spiritual education begins appropriately with the first letter in the Sanskrit alphabet, *a (aśocyān)*, requiring Kṛṣṇa to contract his smile in pronouncing it as he sobers to explain the ABCs of spiritual life. He tells Arjuna that he should not lament for the gross or subtle body, as they have no life or permanence, nor should he lament for the soul, which although worthy of affection, does not die. Kṛṣṇa will refute Arjuna's arguments from the religious scriptures *(dharma-śāstra)* by citing scripture dealing with experiential spiritual life *(jñāna-śāstra*, the *Upaniṣads)*. Thus after first dismissing Arjuna's questions, Kṛṣṇa brings the discussion to a higher level in the next nineteen verses, after which he will digress and actually address Arjuna's socioreligious concerns.

Text 12

न त्वेवाहं जातु नासं न त्वं नेमे जनाधिपाः ।
न चैव न भविष्यामः सर्वे वयमतः परम् ॥१२॥

na tv evāhaṁ jātu nāsaṁ na tvaṁ neme janādhipāḥ/
na caiva na bhaviṣyāmaḥ sarve vayam ataḥ param//

na—never; *tu*—but; *eva*—certainly; *aham*—I; *jātu*—at any time; *na*—not; *āsam*—exist; *na*—not; *tvam*—you; *na*—not; *ime*—these; *jana-adhipāḥ*—kings; *na*—never; *ca*—also; *eva*—certainly; *na*—not; *bhaviṣyāmaḥ*—shall exist; *sarve vayam*—all of us; *ataḥ param*—in the future.

Never was there a time when I did not exist, nor you, nor all these kings. Nor shall any of us cease to exist in the future.

Here Kṛṣṇa implies that there are two types of souls: God himself and the living beings, such as Arjuna and the other kings assembled. Kṛṣṇa informs us that the soul's individuality exists in all three phases of time—past, present, and future—as well as in the liberated status beyond the influence of time. Employing the technique of Nyāya, Kṛṣṇa says that the self is not a product of time. It has no *prāg-abhāva*, or nonexistence prior to its manifestation. Conversely, Kṛṣṇa declares that the soul is not subject to the nonexistence brought about by destruction.

Bhaktivedanta Swami Prabhupāda comments that the individuality stressed in this verse is not relative to material embodiment. Previous to this verse Kṛṣṇa told Arjuna about the shortcomings of embodied material life, whereas in this verse he begins his discourse on the soul. Furthermore, were Kṛṣṇa merely speaking about an apparent individuality resulting from material embodiment, he would not have mentioned himself along with Arjuna and the other assembled kings. Here Kṛṣṇa affirms his own individuality, and he is not a materially conditioned soul. Thus in his opening words regarding the soul, Kṛṣṇa begins to lay the foundation for eternal devotion, for the eternal individuality of the self and God is required for reciprocal dealings in loving devotional union.

Arjuna might question how it is that the self can be different from the body when experience appears to indicate that when the body dies, so too does the soul. Kṛṣṇa addresses this misperception with the following example from our common experience.

Text 13

देहिनोऽस्मिन्यथा देहे कौमारं यौवनं जरा ।
तथा देहान्तरप्राप्तिर्धीरस्तत्र न मुह्यति ॥१३॥

dehino 'smin yathā dehe kaumāraṁ yauvanaṁ jarā/
tathā dehāntara-prāptir dhīras tatra na muhyati//

dehinaḥ—the embodied soul; *asmin*—in this; *yathā*—as; *dehe*—in the body; *kaumāram*—childhood; *yauvanam*—adulthood; *jarā*—old age; *tathā*—similarly; *deha-antara*—another body; *prāptiḥ*—acquiring; *dhīraḥ*—the wise; *tatra*—about this; *na*—never; *muhyati*—is deluded.

Just as the embodied soul experiences changes of body, such as childhood, adulthood, and old age, so similarly it will acquire another body after death. Wise persons are not deluded about this change.

In this verse, the word *dehinaḥ* is singular. However, Kṛṣṇa is not saying that there is only one soul appearing to be embodied as many, but rather a particular class of souls, those presently deluded in material life. Were this not so, it would contradict the plural usage in the previous verse (*sarve vayam*). Although Kṛṣṇa is clearly speaking about the soul in these verses, Madhusūdana Saraswatī offers an interpretation in an effort to establish Adwaita Vedānta, in which he says that *sarve vayam* (all of us) in verse 12 refers to the "multiplicity of [material] bodies previously mentioned (Kṛṣṇa, Arjuna, and the other kings—*aham, tvam, janādhipāḥ*)." This forced reading contradicts the explicit teaching in the *Gītā* as to the eternality of Kṛṣṇa's form.

It is the individual soul in every body that remains constant amidst changing bodies. Were the self the body, it would not remember the changes from childhood to youth to old age mentioned in this verse, for each of these bodies is different, and an impression formed in one person cannot produce recollection in another. Thus the recollection of different bodies that we experience is a result of being different from them and changeless ourselves.

Kṛṣṇa implies that no one laments when a child's body is replaced by an adult body. Nor do they cry when an adult body changes into an old-age body. Even if some do lament in this latter case, Bhīṣma and Droṇa, upon dying in battle, will get young bodies. Therefore, either from the material or spiritual point of view, Arjuna has no cause to lament. Even so, Arjuna's mind *is* disturbed due to its being attached to sense objects in the form of his relatives' bodies. Thus Kṛṣṇa next distinguishes the self from the subtle mental/emotional body.

Text 14

मात्रास्पर्शस्तु कौन्तेय शितोष्णसुखदुःखदाः ।
आगमापायिनोऽनित्यास्तांस्तितिक्षस्व भारत ॥१४॥

mātrā-sparśās tu kaunteya śītoṣṇa-sukha-duḥkha-dāḥ/
āgamāpāyino 'nityās tāṁs titikṣasva bhārata//

mātrā-sparśāḥ—contact with sense objects; *tu*—only; *kaunteya*—O son of Kuntī; *śīta*—cold; *uṣṇa*—heat; *sukha*—happiness; *duḥkha*—pain; *dāḥ*—giving; *āgama*—coming; *apāyinaḥ*—going; *anityāḥ*—temporary; *tān*—them; *titikṣasva*—must learn to tolerate; *bhārata*—O descendant of Bharata.

O son of Kuntī, happiness and distress are temporary experiences that arise from sense perception. Heat, cold, pleasure, and pain come and go, and you must learn to tolerate them, O descendant of Bharata.

Because the self is the witness of the many changes of the mind, such as happiness and distress, it must be different from them and changeless, for an entity subject to change cannot be a witness of that change. As the self is different from the gross body, so too is it different from the subtle body, which consists of various fluctuating states of the mind.

The experiences of happiness and distress differ from those of heat and cold inasmuch as heat and cold can be either enjoyable or distressful, whereas happiness and distress remain the same. First Kṛṣṇa speaks regarding the macrocosmic and then the microcosmic level of experience. All of these experiences are relative to the mind's marriage to the senses and their perception of sense objects. That which is at one time hot may be cold at another. That which brings happiness may later be the cause of distress. These mental perceptions create a world in which the self lives without knowledge of itself, the world of the mind. The first step out of this small world is theoretical knowledge followed by the cultivation of stoic tolerance.

Tolerance is a virtue that is required no matter how one lives, yet its virtues are certainly greater when based on the bigger picture of life described in the sacred literature. The world of the mind is a small world. What is good for one may be experienced as bad for another; one person's happiness is another's sadness. Ultimate reality is bigger than the mind, and this is what the sacred literature informs us about. The beginning of realizing and living in this bigger picture beyond the duality of sense perception is tolerance. By addressing Arjuna in terms of both sides of his noble family heritage (Kaunteya and Bhārata), Kṛṣṇa strongly suggested that Arjuna should take the noble path of tolerance in relation to dualities, knowing them to be mere fluctuations of the mind. Kṛṣṇa goes on to describe tolerance in greater detail.

Text 15

यं हि न व्यथयन्त्येते पुरुषं पुरुषर्षभ ।
समदुःखसुखं धीरं सोऽमृतत्वाय कल्पते ॥१५॥

yaṁ hi na vyathayanty ete puruṣaṁ puruṣarṣabha/
sama-duḥkha-sukhaṁ dhīraṁ so 'mṛtatvāya kalpate//

yam—who; *hi*—certainly; *na*—never; *vyathayanti*—afflict; *ete*—these [dualities of sense perception]; *puruṣam*—to a person; *puruṣa-ṛṣabha*—O best among men; *sama*—same; *duḥkha*—unhappiness; *sukham*—happiness; *dhīram*—wise; *saḥ*—he; *amṛtatvāya*—for eternal life; *kalpate*—is eligible.

Indeed, one who tolerates these dualities of sense perception, such a wise person to whom happiness and unhappiness are thus the same, is eligible for eternal life of self-realization, O best among men.

For the first time in this great treatise Kṛṣṇa mentions self-realization, which takes one beyond material happiness and distress. Material happiness invariably turns to unhappiness in its absence. Thus one should tolerate both happiness and distress knowing them ultimately to be one and the same. From a world of apparent variety one must learn to identify with the underlying unity.

Text 16

नासतो विद्यते भावो नाभावो विद्यते सतः ।
उभयोरपि दृष्टोऽन्तस्त्वनयोस्तत्त्वदर्शिभिः ॥१६॥

nāsato vidyate bhāvo nābhāvo vidyate sataḥ/
ubhayor api dṛṣṭo 'ntas tv anayos tattva-darśibhiḥ//

na—never; *asataḥ*—of the nonexistent; *vidyate*—there is; *bhāvaḥ*—coming to be; *na*—never; *abhāvaḥ*—absence; *vidyate*—there is; *sataḥ*—of the eternal; *ubhayoḥ*—of the two; *api*—verily; *dṛṣṭaḥ*—observed; *antaḥ*—conclusion; *tu*—indeed; *anayoḥ*—of them; *tattva*—the truth; *darśibhiḥ*—by the seers.

That which is subject to change is not eternal or ultimately real. That which is real is neither temporary nor subject to change. It cannot be destroyed. This is the conclusion the seers of truth reached after deliberating on both.

Here Kṛṣṇa cites the vision of the seers (*tattva-darśī*). He does so in appropriately abstract Upaniṣadic language. Their vision is revelation concerning that which is real and that which is unreal.

The spirit of this verse is that Kṛṣṇa is chiding Arjuna for not being a seer himself. Indeed, Arjuna is confused by this verse. Thus in the following verse Kṛṣṇa gives him practical examples of what he means by the real and unreal. First in verse 17, Kṛṣṇa explains that the self that pervades the body is real and not subject to change. Then in text 18, Kṛṣṇa explains that the destructible material body is an example of what is not ultimately real.

Text 17

अविनाशि तु तद्विद्धि येन सर्वमिदं ततम् ।
विनाशमव्ययस्यास्य न कश्चित् कर्तुमर्हति ॥१७॥

avināśi tu tad viddhi yena sarvam idaṁ tatam/
vināśam avyayasyāsya na kaścit kartum arhati//

avināśi—imperishable; *tu*—but; *tat*—that; *viddhi*—know; *yena*—by which; *sarvam*—all; *idam*—this [body]; *tatam*—pervaded; *vināśam*—destruction; *avyayasya*—of the imperishable; *asya*—of it; *kaścit*—anyone; *kartum*—to do; *na arhati*—is not able.

You should know that which pervades all to be indestructible. No one can bring about the destruction of the imperishable being.

In this verse, Kṛṣṇa rejects the idea that consciousness is momentary. It is not here today and gone tomorrow. Thus it cannot be denied, for denial itself is an act of consciousness. The self is of the nature of consciousness, and it pervades the entire body. It also projects itself beyond the body and into other material objects with which it identifies. Thus one develops attachment to the body and its extensions in the form of material objects and other embodied persons. When we project ourselves into a material object, we then identify with it, considering it to be ours. The sense that something is ours is a result of our soul, our actual self, projecting itself into that object. Being unaware of the nature of the self, we misconstrue our material possessions, into which we have projected ourselves, to be of value without realizing that their value lies in the fact that we ourselves are within them. Thus it is the self that holds enduring value. It is the self that is dear to one in all circumstances, while material objects and our destructible bodies only appear to be so.

Text 18

अन्तवन्त इमे देहा नित्यस्योक्ताः शरीरिणः ।
अनाशिनोऽप्रमेयस्य तस्माद्युध्यस्व भारत ॥१८॥

antavanta ime dehā nityasyoktāḥ śarīriṇaḥ/
anāśino 'prameyasya tasmād yudhyasva bhārata//

anta-vantaḥ—perishable; *ime*—all these; *dehāḥ*—bodies; *nityasya*—eternal; *uktāḥ*—are said; *śarīriṇaḥ*—of the soul; *anāśinaḥ*—indestructible; *aprameyasya*—immeasurable; *tasmāt*—therefore; *yudhyasva*—fight; *bhārata*—O descendant of Bharata.

Only the bodies inhabited by the eternal, indestructible, and immeasurable soul are said to be subject to destruction. Therefore get up and fight, O descendant of Bharata!

The plural bodies *(ime dehāḥ)* in this verse refer to the physical and subtle mental bodies mentioned in verses 13 and 14, respectively. According to the *śruti (uktāḥ)*, both of these are subject to destruction *(antavantaḥ)*. The embodied soul, on the other hand, is indestructible *(anāśinaḥ)*.

Kṛṣṇa describes the soul as immeasurable *(aprameyasya)*, yet it is mentioned elsewhere that the individual soul is one ten-thousandth the size of the tip of a hair (Śve. Up. 5.9). However, these two statements are not contradictory, for no one can measure one ten-thousandth of the tip of a hair. The Upaniṣadic measurement of the soul is not to be taken literally. Furthermore, *aprameyasya* refers to the soul's being incomprehensible. It cannot be measured in our mind due to its being beyond mind rather than a product of it. *Māyā* (illusion) also means to measure. The soul cannot be measured with the limited instrument of the mind. Thus it is implied here that it can only be known through scripture or revelation.

The soul being immeasurable and indestructible, Arjuna has nothing to fear. Therefore *(tasmād)* he should not desist from battle, but rather follow his *dharma*. Without performing one's *dharma*, the difficult subject matter Kṛṣṇa is explaining cannot be easily understood. Commitment to performing one's *dharma* is also a form of knowledge. It purifies the heart, enabling one to understand practically the nature of the self. In general terms, Kṛṣṇa's order to fight here means to perform one's own *dharma*, which for Arjuna was to act as a warrior.

At this point Arjuna is left with the thought that although he should not grieve for anyone lost in the battle, the sins arising from killing others will still be his. There is no rule that says one will be free from the sin of killing another as long as he does not grieve for their loss. Thus Kṛṣṇa addresses this issue in the next verse, echoing the *Kaṭha Upaniṣad* (2.19).

Text 19

य एनं वेत्ति हन्तारं यश्चैनं मन्यते हतम् ।
उभौ तौ न विजानीतो नायं हन्ति न हन्यते ॥१९॥

ya enaṁ vetti hantāraṁ yaś cainaṁ manyate hatam/
ubhau tau na vijānīto nāyaṁ hanti na hanyate//

yaḥ—one who; *enam*—this; *vetti*—knows; *hantāram*—slayer; *yaḥ*—one who; *ca*—and; *enam*—this; *manyate*—thinks; *hatam*—slain; *ubhau*—both; *tau*—they; *na*—never; *vijānītaḥ*—are in knowledge; *na*—never; *ayam*—this; *hanti*—slays; *na*—nor; *hanyate*—is slain.

Both one who thinks that the soul is the slayer and one who thinks that the soul is slain are confused. The soul neither slays nor is slain.

As Kṛṣṇa instructs Arjuna, he addresses the erroneous notion that the self is an independent doer, as well as the idea that the self is destructible, which are held by the Nyāya schools of Gautama and Carvaka Muni's materialism, respectively.

Next Kṛṣṇa states *why* the soul is neither the agent nor object of killing. He does so by restating another *mantra* from the *Kaṭha Upaniṣad* (1.2.18).

Text 20

न जायते म्रियते वा कदाचि-
न्नायं भूत्वा भविता वा न भूयः ।
अजो नित्यः शाश्वतोऽयं पुराणो
न हन्यते हन्यमाने शरीरे ॥२०॥

na jāyate mriyate vā kadācin
nāyaṁ bhūtvā bhavitā vā na bhūyaḥ/
ajo nityaḥ śāśvato 'yaṁ purāṇo
na hanyate hanyamāne śarīre//

na—never; *jāyate*—is born; *mriyate*—dies; *vā*—either; *kadācit*—at any time; *na*—never; *ayam*—this; *bhūtvā*—having come into being; *bhavitā*—will come to be; *vā*—or; *na*—not; *bhūyaḥ*—again; *ajaḥ*—unborn; *nityaḥ*—eternal; *śāśvataḥ*—permanent; *ayam*—this; *purāṇaḥ*—primeval; *na*—never; *hanyate*—is slain; *hanyamāne*—on being slain; *śarīre*—in the body.

The soul neither is born nor does it ever die. Nor being will it ever cease to be. Unborn, eternal, not subject to decay, primeval, it is not slain when the body is slain.

The soul can be neither the agent nor the object of the act of killing, for it is changeless. It does not undergo the sixfold transformations of birth, growth, maturation, mutation, decay, and death. The logic of this verse is as follows: The soul is not born and does not die. This is so because the soul has never been nonexistent, nor has it become existent at some point in time. Therefore, the soul is eternal.

This idea that the soul does not undergo transformation is indicated by the words *purāṇaḥ* and *śāśvataḥ*. Because the soul exists forever *(śāśvataḥ)* it never decays, and because it is primeval *(purāṇaḥ)* it has not grown into a new state, nor has it matured or mutated.

Having advanced his proposition, Kṛṣṇa next seeks to prove it.

Text 21

वेदाविनाशिनं नित्यं य एनमजमव्ययम् ।
कथं स पुरुषः पार्थ कं घातयति हन्ति कम् ॥२१॥

vedāvināśinaṁ nityaṁ ya enam ajam avyayam/
kathaṁ sa puruṣaḥ pārtha kaṁ ghātayati hanti kam//

veda—knows; *avināśinam*—indestructible; *nityam*—eternal; *yaḥ*—one who; *enam*—this; *ajam*—birthless; *avyayam*—imperishable; *katham*—how; *saḥ*—that; *puruṣaḥ*—person; *pārtha*—O Pārtha (Arjuna); *kam*—whom; *ghātayati*—causes to be slain; *hanti*—slays; *kam*—whom.

How can one who knows this indestructible, eternal, birthless, imperishable nature of the self cause anyone to be slain? Whom does he slay?

In spite of Kṛṣṇa's logic, Arjuna fears that although he may not be the cause of anyone's death, he will be the cause of others changing their bodies. Kṛṣṇa replies to this doubt in the next verse.

Text 22

वासांसि जीर्णानि यथा विहाय
नवानि गृह्णाति नरोऽपराणि ।
तथा शरीराणि विहाय जीर्णा-
न्यन्यानि संयाति नवानि देही ॥२२॥

vāsāṁsi jīrṇāni yathā vihāya
navāni gṛhṇāti naro 'parāṇi/
tathā śarīrāṇi vihāya jīrṇāny
anyāni saṁyāti navāni dehī//

vāsāṁsi—clothes; *jīrṇāni*—old; *yathā*—just as; *vihāya*—discarding; *navāni*—new ones; *gṛhṇāti*—takes; *naraḥ*—a man; *aparāṇi*—others; *tathā*—similarly; *śarīrāṇi*—bodies; *vihāya*—discarding; *jīrṇāni*—old; *anyāni*—different; *saṁyāti*—meets; *navāni*—new; *dehī*—the embodied.

Just as one dons new garments after discarding old ones, similarly, the self in embodied consciousness accepts new bodies after discarding the worn-out ones.

Kṛṣṇa replies to Arjuna that the changing of bodies is inevitable in this world. Moreover, he indicates that for elders such as Bhīṣma this may be a cause of rejoicing rather than sorrow, for no one laments on giving up an old garment in exchange for a new one. The word *aparāṇi* (others) implies an improvement, whereas *jīrṇāni* (worn out) indicates something that has passed its usefulness. The word *saṁyāti* indicates an attainment such as that which Bhīṣma is due: a heavenly body resulting from his righteous life, now that the current one had been worn out in the discharge of his religious duty.

Arjuna next wonders how the soul within the body is not affected by the destruction of the body, as one within a burning house is injured when the house burns. Kṛṣṇa answers his doubt in the following verse.

Text 23

नैनं छिन्दन्ति शस्त्राणि नैनं दहति पावकः ।
न चैनं क्लेदयन्त्यापो न शोषयति मारुतः ॥२३॥

nainaṁ chindanti śastrāṇi nainaṁ dahati pāvakaḥ/
na cainaṁ kledayanty āpo na śoṣayati mārutaḥ//

na—never; *enam*—this; *chindanti*—can pierce; *śastrāṇi*—weapons; *na*—never; *enam*—this; *dahati*—burns; *pāvakaḥ*—fire; *na*—never; *ca*—also; *enam*—this; *kledayanti*—moisten; *āpaḥ*—waters; *na*—never; *śoṣayati*—dries; *mārutaḥ*—wind.

The self cannot be pierced by weapons, burned by fire, moistened by water, or withered by wind.

As Kṛṣṇa speaks he gestures to Arjuna's arsenal of arrows, which include not only sharp arrows that cut, but others that harness the powers of fire, water, and wind through the use of *mantra*. None of these weapons can harm the soul, nor protect the body from its destiny of destruction. Kṛṣṇa next states why these weapons cannot destroy the soul and how it is that the soul is not susceptible to destruction by them.

Text 24

अच्छेद्योऽयमदाह्योऽयमक्लेद्योऽशोष्य एव च ।
नित्यः सर्वगतः स्थानुरचलोऽयं सनातनः ॥२४॥

acchedyo 'yam adāhyo 'yam akledyo 'śoṣya eva ca/
nityaḥ sarva-gataḥ sthāṇur acalo 'yaṁ sanātanaḥ//

acchedyaḥ—indivisible; *ayam*—this; *adāhyaḥ*—unburnable; *ayam*—this; *akledyaḥ*—insoluble; *aśoṣyaḥ*—not able to be dried; *eva*—certainly; *ca*—and; *nityaḥ*—eternal; *sarva-gataḥ*—all-pervading; *sthāṇuḥ*—changeless; *acalaḥ*—unmoving; *ayam*—this; *sanātanaḥ*—primeval.

Surely the self is indivisible, unburnable, insoluble, and cannot be dried up. It is eternal, all-pervading, changeless, unmoving, and primeval.

Since the soul is indivisible *(acchedyaḥ)*, it cannot be cut. It cannot be burnt because it is unburnable *(adāhyaḥ)*. The soul cannot be moistened by water because it is insoluble *(akledyaḥ)*, nor can it be withered by wind because it cannot be dried up *(aśoṣyaḥ)*. Thus the effects stated in the previous verse are by-products of the soul's qualities mentioned in this one.

The second half of this verse explains why the soul is not subject to the effects of the above-mentioned weapons. Because it is eternal *(nityaḥ)*, all-pervading *(sarva-gataḥ)*, changeless *(sthāṇuḥ)*, unmoving *(acalaḥ)*, and primeval *(sanātanaḥ)*, it is not subject to any transformation whatsoever. Something subject to action causes a result of that action, such as production, acquisition, transformation, and change of condition. Being eternal the soul is not produced. Since it is all-pervading it cannot be acquired. Being changeless it is not transformed, and being unmoving it is not subject to any change of condition. For emphasis, the word *eva* (surely) is intended to modify all of the soul's qualities mentioned in this verse.

Jīva Goswāmī explains the word *sarva-gataḥ* as meaning "dependent *(gataḥ)* on God, who is everything *(sarva)*." (Ps. 34) Everything is but God and his energies. One who is aware of this and thus depends exclusively on God in all circumstances experiences all-pervasiveness through dependence on the person who is all-pervasive.

Text 25

अव्यक्तोऽयमचिन्त्योऽयमविकार्योऽयमुच्यते ।
तस्मादेवं विदित्वैनं नानुशोचितुमर्हसि ॥२५॥

avyakto 'yam acintyo 'yam avikāryo 'yam ucyate/
tasmād evaṁ viditvainaṁ nānuśocitum arhasi//

avyaktaḥ—invisible; *ayam*—this; *acintyaḥ*—inconceivable; *ayam*—this; *avikāryaḥ*—immutable; *ayam*—this; *ucyate*—is said; *tasmāt*—therefore; *evam*—like this; *viditvā*—knowing; *enam*—this; *na*—not; *anuśocitum*—to mourn; *arhasi*—should.

It is said that the self is invisible, inconceivable, and unchangeable. Knowing this, you should not mourn for the body.

Here Kṛṣṇa repeats himself for emphasis. The subject of the soul is difficult to comprehend, and thus Kṛṣṇa speaks of its nature again and again invoking various words to describe it. This time he supports what he has said thus far referring to scriptural authority, as implied by the use of the word *ucyate*.

This verse concludes Kṛṣṇa's description of the soul with the word *tasmāt* (therefore). Because the soul is as Kṛṣṇa has described, Arjuna's lamentation is not appropriate once he understands its nature *(viditvā)*. Next Kṛṣṇa states that even if for argument's sake one accepts the soul to be noneternal, still one should not lament for it.

Text 26

अथ चैनं नित्यजातं नित्यं वा मन्यसे मृतम् ।
तथापि त्वं महाबाहो नैनं शोचितुमर्हसि ॥२६॥

atha cainaṁ nitya-jātaṁ nityaṁ vā manyase mṛtam/
tathāpi tvaṁ mahā-bāho nainaṁ śocitum arhasi//

atha—if; *ca*—and; *enam*—this; *nitya-jātam*—continually born; *nityam*—continually; *vā*—either; *manyase*—you think; *mṛtam*—dead; *tathā api*—still; *tvam*—you; *mahā-bāho*—O mighty-armed one; *na*—not; *enam*—this; *śocitum*—to mourn; *arhasi*—should.

O mighty-armed one, even if you think that the self is continually born and continually dies, you still have no reason to lament for it.

Having spoken strongly about the ultimacy of consciousness in accordance with the sacred literature, here Kṛṣṇa changes direction *(atha ca)*, accepting for argument's sake the notion that consciousness itself is ephemeral. Kṛṣṇa cites atheistic and Buddhist philosophy, in which consciousness is considered noneternal. Buddhists do not believe in the existence of a self. They believe that consciousness is a product of conditions and thus changes from moment to moment. Materialists such as Carvaka Muni consider the self to be the body, which, though enduring for some time, is born, dies, and changes at every moment. In a cynical tone, Kṛṣṇa reasons that even if the noble and mighty Arjuna is so foolish as to succumb to such understandings, still he should fight.

Text 27

जातस्य हि ध्रुवो मृत्युर्ध्रुवं जन्म मृतस्य च ।
तस्मादपरिहार्येऽर्थे न त्वं शोचितुमर्हसि ॥२७॥

jātasya hi dhruvo mṛtyur dhruvaṁ janma mṛtasya ca/
tasmād aparihārye 'rthe na tvaṁ śocitum arhasi//

jātasya—of the born; *hi*—certainly; *dhruvaḥ*—certain; *mṛtyuḥ*—death; *dhruvam*—certain; *janma*—birth; *mṛtasya*—of the dead; *ca*—also; *tasmāt*—therefore; *aparihārye*—of that which is inevitable; *arthe*—in a matter; *na*—not; *tvam*—you; *śocitum*—to lament; *arhasi*—should.

Death is certain for all who take birth. Birth is just as certain for all who die. Therefore, do not lament in matters like this, which are unavoidable.

Text 28

अव्यक्तादीनि भूतानि व्यक्तमध्यानि भारत ।
अव्यक्तनिधनान्येव तत्र का परिदेवना ॥२८॥

avyaktādīni bhūtāni vyakta-madhyāni bhārata/
avyakta-nidhanāny eva tatra kā paridevanā//

avyakta-ādīni—in the beginning unmanifested; *bhūtāni*—beings; *vyakta*—manifested; *madhyāni*—in the middle; *bhārata*—O descendant of Bharata; *avyakta*—nonmanifested; *nidhanāni*—ends; *eva*—again; *tatra*—so; *kā*—what; *paridevanā*—lamentation.

O descendant of Bharata, all beings are unmanifest in their beginning, manifest in their middle period, and again unmanifest at their end. Thus there is no cause for lamentation.

Previous to the last two verses, Kṛṣṇa argues that one should not lament for the imperishable soul. Here he argues that one should not lament for the loss of the body either, for it is always existing in terms of its elemental constituents, although in an unmanifest condition before and after the body actually manifests during the period of a lifetime. Thus the body has a name and form only in the middle stage during its connection with the soul.

Text 29

आश्चर्यवत् पश्यति कश्चिदेन-
माश्चर्यवद् वदति तथैव चान्यः ।
आश्चर्यवच्चैनमन्यः शृणोति
श्रुत्वाप्येनं वेद न चैव कश्चित् ॥२९॥

āścarya-vat paśyati kaścid enam
āścarya-vad vadati tathaiva cānyaḥ/
āścarya-vac cainam anyaḥ śṛṇoti
śrutvāpy enaṁ veda na caiva kaścit//

āścarya-vat—as awesome; *paśyati*—sees; *kaścit*—someone; *enam*—this; *āścarya-vat*—as awesome; *vadati*—speaks; *tathā*—thus; *eva*—certainly; *ca*—also; *anyaḥ*—another; *āścarya-vat*—as awesome; *ca*—also; *enam*—this; *anyaḥ*—another; *śṛṇoti*—hears; *śrutvā*—having heard; *api*—even; *enam*—this; *veda*—knows; *na*—never; *ca*—and; *eva*—certainly; *kaścit*—someone.

Some see the self as being a wonder, others proclaim it to be a wonder, while still others hear of it as a wonder. Yet even after hearing about it, none can fathom it.

In this verse Kṛṣṇa explains the difficulty in understanding the position of the soul. In doing so he sympathizes to some extent with Arjuna's plight. Beginning with verse 31, he will shift his emphasis from the wisdom of the soul to the proper understanding of *dharma*.

Text 30

देही नित्यमवध्योऽयं देहे सर्वस्य भारत ।
तस्मात्सर्वाणि भूतानि न त्वं शोचितुमर्हसि ॥३०॥

dehī nityam avadhyo 'yaṁ dehe sarvasya bhārata/
tasmāt sarvāṇi bhūtāni na tvaṁ śocitum arhasi//

dehī—the embodied; *nityam*—eternal; *avadhyaḥ*—indestructible; *ayam*—this; *dehe*—in the body; *sarvasya*—of everyone; *bhārata*—O descendant of Bharata; *tasmāt*—therefore; *sarvāṇi*—all; *bhūtāni*—beings; *na*—not; *tvam*—you; *śocitum*—to lament; *arhasi*—should.

O descendant of Bharata, this self embodied in every being is eternal and indestructible. Therefore you should not lament for anyone.

Having analyzed the nature of the self in relation to the body by contrasting the two, Kṛṣṇa concludes his Upaniṣadic discourse, which was intended to give Arjuna a spiritual conceptual framework from which to view his dilemma. Although he did so, he knew that Arjuna was not capable at this point of fully digesting this knowledge and its implications. Furthermore, although Kṛṣṇa insisted that Arjuna fight on the basis of insights into the nature of the self, knowledge of the eternal self curbs the impetus to act in a world that does not endure. Desiring to take Arjuna back to his practical reality, Kṛṣṇa directly addresses the concerns Arjuna had voiced earlier and argues that he should engage in battle despite his attachments and reservations.

Text 31

स्वधर्ममपि चावेक्ष्य न विकम्पितुमर्हसि ।
धर्म्याद्धि युद्धाच्छ्रेयोऽन्यत् क्षत्रियस्य न विद्यते ॥३१॥

sva-dharmam api cāvekṣya na vikampitum arhasi/
dharmyād dhi yuddhāc chreyo 'nyat kṣatriyasya na vidyate//

sva-dharmam—one's own *dharma*; *api*—also; *ca*—indeed; *avekṣya*—considering; *na*—never; *vikampitum*—to hesitate; *arhasi*—you should; *dharmyāt*—for *dharma*; *hi*—indeed; *yuddhāt*—than fighting; *śreyaḥ*—better; *anyat*—any other; *kṣatriyasya*—of the warrior; *na*—not; *vidyate*—exist.

In consideration of your dharma as a warrior, you should not hesitate, for there is nothing more righteous for a warrior than to fight for dharma itself.

Here Kṛṣṇa is replying to Arjuna's earlier plea that *dharma-śāstra* supersedes *artha-śāstra*, and thus he should not kill his superiors even though they are aggressors. Kṛṣṇa says that although superiors should not be killed, if they are killed in the course of fighting for *dharma*, there is no fault.

Text 32

यदृच्छया चोपपन्नं स्वर्गद्वारमपावृतम् ।
सुखिनः क्षत्रियाः पार्थ लभन्ते युद्धमीदृशम् ॥३२॥

yadṛcchayā copapannaṁ svarga-dvāram apāvṛtam/
sukhinaḥ kṣatriyāḥ pārtha labhante yuddham īdṛśam//

yadṛcchayā—by good fortune; *ca*—also; *upapannam*—happened; *svarga*—heaven; *dvāram*—door; *apāvṛtam*—wide open; *sukhinaḥ*—very happy; *kṣatriyāḥ*—the warriors; *pārtha*—O Pārtha; *labhante*—they achieve; *yuddham*—war; *īdṛśam*—like this.

O Pārtha, warriors who get such an opportunity for battle by good fortune rejoice, for this opens the gates of heaven for them.

With this and the previous verse, Kṛṣṇa intimates to Arjuna that not only those interested in eternal life and love of God should follow his guidance but even those who desire material benefit or heaven.

Although previously Arjuna had thought that by fighting he would be engaged in an unrighteous activity, here Kṛṣṇa acting in the capacity of his guru tells him otherwise. He tells him he would incur an unrighteous reaction by not fighting. After telling Arjuna why he should fight from the angle of religious life, Kṛṣṇa tells him what will happen if he desists.

Text 33

अथ चेत्त्वमिमं धर्म्यं संग्रामं न करिष्यसि ।
ततः स्वधर्मं कीर्तिं च हित्वा पापमवाप्स्यसि ॥३३॥

atha cet tvam imaṁ dharmyaṁ saṅgrāmaṁ na kariṣyasi/
tataḥ sva-dharmaṁ kīrtiṁ ca hitvā pāpam avāpsyasi//

atha cet—however, if; *tvam*—you; *imam*—this; *dharmyam*—religious; *saṅgrāmam*—fight; *na*—not; *kariṣyasi*—perform; *tataḥ*—then; *sva-dharmam*—own *dharma; kīrtim*—reputation; *ca*—also; *hitvā*—losing; *pāpam*—evil; *avāpsyasi*—will incur.

However, if you do not fight this righteous war, having avoided your own dharma as a warrior, you will incur evil and lose your good reputation.

Well aware of Arjuna's warrior ego, Kṛṣṇa pinches his pride. Here he tells him that Bhīṣma and Droṇa will not think that he had left the battle out of compassion, but rather out of cowardice. Should Arjuna think that even if great people like Bhīṣma and Droṇa belittled him, at least his direct enemies, the sons of Dhṛtarāṣṭra, would appreciate his compassion, Kṛṣṇa addresses this misconception in the next three verses.

Text 34

अकीर्तिं चापि भूतानि कथयिष्यन्ति तेऽव्ययम् ।
सम्भावितस्य चाकीर्तिर्मरणादतिरिच्यते ॥३४॥

akīrtiṁ cāpi bhūtāni kathayiṣyanti te 'vyayām/
sambhāvitasya cākīrtir maraṇād atiricyate//

akīrtim—infamy; *ca*—and; *api*—also; *bhūtāni*—people; *kathayiṣyanti*—will speak; *te*—of you; *avyayām*—always; *sambhāvitasya*—of a respectable person; *ca*—also; *akīrtiḥ*—dishonor; *maraṇāt*—than death; *atiricyate*—becomes more.

People will always speak of your infamy, and for a respectable person, dishonor is worse than death.

Text 35

भयाद्रणादुपरतं मंस्यन्ते त्वां महारथाः ।
येषां च त्वं बहुमतो भूत्वा यास्यसि लाघवम् ॥३५॥

bhayād raṇād uparataṁ maṁsyante tvāṁ mahā-rathāḥ/
yeṣāṁ ca tvaṁ bahu-mato bhūtvā yāsyasi lāghavam//

bhayāt—out of fear; *raṇāt*—from the battle; *uparatam*—ceased; *maṁsyante*—they will consider; *tvam*—you; *mahā-rathāḥ*—the great warriors; *yeṣām*—of whom; *ca*—also; *tvām*—you; *bahu-mataḥ*—in high esteem; *bhūtvā*—having been; *yāsyasi*—you will go; *lāghavam*—decreased in value.

The great warriors will think that you have left the battle out of fear and thus those who once held you in high esteem will no longer take you seriously.

Text 36

अवाच्यवादांश्च बहून्वदिष्यन्ति तवाहिताः ।
निन्दन्तस्तव सामर्थ्यं ततो दुःखतरं नु किम् ॥३६॥

avācya-vādāṁś ca bahūn vadiṣyanti tavāhitāḥ/
nindantas tava sāmarthyaṁ tato duḥkhataraṁ nu kim//

avācya—not to be spoken; *vādān*—words; *ca*—also; *bahūn*—many; *vadiṣyanti*—will speak; *tava*—your; *ahitāḥ*—enemies; *nindantaḥ*—while decrying; *tava*—your; *sāmarthyam*—ability; *tataḥ*—than that; *duḥkha-taram*—more painful; *nu*—indeed; *kim*—what.

Your enemies will speak the unspeakable of you, decrying your ability. What could be more painful than that?

Here Kṛṣṇa informs Arjuna that not even his enemies will praise him for not fighting. In verses 31 through 36 Kṛṣṇa has explained the words *akīrti* and *asvargya* ("infamy" and "not leading to heaven"), with which he had characterized Arjuna's reluctance to fight in the second verse of this chapter.

Text 37

हतो वा प्राप्स्यसि स्वर्गं जित्वा वा भोक्ष्यसे महीम् ।
तस्मादुत्तिष्ठ कौन्तेय युद्धाय कृतनिश्चयः ॥३७॥

hato vā prāpsyasi svargaṁ jitvā vā bhokṣyase mahīm/
tasmād uttiṣṭha kaunteya yuddhāya kṛta-niścayaḥ//

hataḥ—being killed; *vā*—either; *prāpsyasi*—you will gain; *svargam*—heaven; *jitvā*—by conquering; *vā*—or; *bhokṣyase*—you will enjoy; *mahīm*—the earth; *tasmāt*—therefore; *uttiṣṭha*—get up; *kaunteya*—O son of Kuntī; *yuddhāya*—to fight; *kṛta-niścayaḥ*—with resolve.

O son of Kuntī, either you will die in battle and go to heaven, or having won the battle you will enjoy the earth. Therefore stand with resolve and fight.

Kṛṣṇa declares that even if Arjuna loses the battle he will gain through fighting. In other words, heavenly gain in the case of defeat and earthly kingdom in the case of victory are side benefits of desireless adherence to *dharma*. This is also stated in the *Āpastamba-dharma-sūtras* (1.20.3), "Just as when a mango tree is grown for fruit, shade and fragrance follow naturally, so too when *dharma* is practiced for its own sake, other desirable ends follow as a consequence."

Text 38

सुखदुःखे समे कृत्वा लाभालाभौ जयाजयौ ।
ततो युद्धाय युज्यस्व नैवं पापमवाप्स्यसि ॥३८॥

sukha-duḥkhe same kṛtvā lābhālābhau jayājayau/
tato yuddhāya yujyasva naivaṁ pāpam avāpsyasi//

sukha-duḥkhe—in pleasure and pain; *same*—to be equal; *kṛtvā*—doing so; *lābha-alābhau*—both gain and loss; *jaya-ajayau*—both victory and defeat; *tataḥ*—thereafter; *yuddhāya*—for battle; *yujyasva*—fight; *na*—never; *evam*—in this way; *pāpam*—unrighteousness; *avāpsyasi*—you will incur.

Considering pleasure and pain, gain and loss, victory and defeat to be equal, prepare yourself for battle without fear of incurring sin.

The equanimity stressed in this verse (*same kṛtvā*) is the same as that which is used in verse 48 to define *yoga* (*samaḥ*, *samatvam*). Thus by encouraging Arjuna to fight, Kṛṣṇa is actually instructing Arjuna in *yoga*.

Having dismissed Arjuna's arguments at the beginning of his speech, Kṛṣṇa now addresses them directly. Yet his confused disciple is thinking,

"Even if no sin will be incurred from righteous action, how can you advise me to fight after telling me that enlightened persons are nondoers? Indeed, your instruction appears contradictory. You simultaneously advocate that I become a nondoer, stressing that only the ignorant think that one slays or is slain (Bg. 2.19), and that I fight and reap the fruit of righteous action" (Bg. 2.37). This is the seed of Arjuna's doubt regarding Kṛṣṇa's simultaneous advocacy of knowledge and action that flowers at the onset of the next chapter.

After a moment of silence Kṛṣṇa continues to explain the notion of enlightened work, without which Arjuna is neither able to realize the self nor the relationship between knowledge and action on the spiritual path. In the midst of doing so, Kṛṣṇa also indirectly speaks of the virtue of *bhakti*, which he ultimately wants Arjuna to embrace.

Text 39

एषा तेऽभिहिता सांख्ये बुद्धिर्योगे त्विमां शृणु ।
बुद्ध्या युक्तो यया पार्थ कर्मबन्धं प्रहास्यसि ॥३९॥

eṣā te 'bhihitā sāṅkhye buddhir yoge tv imāṁ śṛṇu/
buddhyā yukto yayā pārtha karma-bandhaṁ prahāsyasi//

eṣā—this; *te*—to you; *abhihitā*—spoken; *sāṅkhye*—in *sāṅkhya; buddhiḥ*—wisdom; *yoge*—in *yoga*; *tu*—but; *imām*—this; *śṛṇu*—hear; *buddhyā*—by wisdom; *yuktaḥ*—disciplined; *yayā*—by which; *pārtha*—O son of Pṛthā; *karma-bandhaṁ*—bondage of *karma*; *prahāsyasi*—you can be released.

I have spoken to you of how to use wisdom in sāṅkhya, now hear about wisdom in yoga. With this wisdom, Arjuna, you will free yourself from the bondage resulting from karma.

Sāṅkhya has been explained in verses 12 through 30. Here it does not refer to the Sāṅkhya philosophy of Kapila, one of the six *darśanas* of India. It is used in a generic sense in reference to the analytical study of phenomena and the introspection that sheds light on the soul. Madhusūdana Saraswatī says that *sāṅkhya* means "that in which the reality of the Supreme Self is fully presented." Viśvanātha Cakravartī Ṭhākura defines *sāṅkhya* as that which perfectly *(sam)* explains *(khyā)* or illuminates the nature of an object.

However, there is similarity between the Sāṅkhya philosophy of Kapila and that which is introduced by Kṛṣṇa in this verse. Kapila's Sāṅkhya begins with an analysis of matter, but with the goal of discriminating between matter and spirit. Such discrimination is at the heart of what Kṛṣṇa intends here by the use of the word *sāṅkhya.*

Just as it is important to distinguish the word *sāṅkhya* in this verse from Kapila's philosophical system, it is also important to distinguish the word *yoga* in this verse from the *yoga* system of Patañjali. Both of these two schools of thought are distinct from that which Kṛṣṇa teaches in the *Bhagavad-gītā.* There is, however, considerable overlap between the systems of Patañjali and that which is considered *yoga* in the schools of Vedānta represented in the *Gītā.*

Later in the *Gītā* the word *sāṅkhya* is associated with knowledge *(jñāna),* while *yoga* is associated with *karma. Jñāna* is further associated with renunciation, and *yoga* with *bhakti.* This is how *bhakti, karma,* and *yoga* are connected as if in a continuum. *Yoga* in this sense can be translated as "engagement." It implies the positive notion of union, whereas *sāṅkhya* denotes separation and discrimination, which bear negative connotations. Kṛṣṇa has encouraged Arjuna to separate himself from the negativity of material identification through proper discrimination. Now he begins to encourage him to engage in the positive action of uniting himself with God.

One who knows the self to be of the same nature as that of the Absolute is not bound to perform any duty. This will be further explained later (Bg. 3.17). However, here Kṛṣṇa realizes that Arjuna is not capable of assimilating knowledge of the self without undergoing actions that will purify his heart, for he is absorbed in worldly concerns, even though religious in nature. Thus he advises him to engage in *yoga.* Here the word *yoga* implies the spirit of *yoga:* selflessness and sacrifice, the mother of love. While action in relation to sense objects with a view to enjoy them gives rise to karmic bondage, one cannot artificially divorce oneself from action itself. Indeed, as we shall see, such artificiality in *yoga* is condemned. In its stead Kṛṣṇa recommends proper action in the spirit of detachment. He tells Arjuna that by acting in *yoga* he will free himself from the bondage of *karma* and realize the self that is intellectually understood through the introspection involved in *sāṅkhya.* The detached spirit of this *yoga* was characterized in the previous verse.

With the introduction of *yoga* in this verse, the *Gītā* begins to speak about experiential spiritual life in practice. Beginning here and extending over the next four chapters, Kṛṣṇa explains gradual steps on the ladder of *yoga,* from the *yoga* of selfless action *(niṣkāma-karma-yoga),* to the *yoga* of knowledge *(jñāna-yoga)*,[6] to the *yoga* of meditation *(dhyāna/aṣṭāṅga-yoga)*, and culminating in the *yoga* of love *(bhakti-yoga)*.

From this point until the end of chapter 6, Kṛṣṇa instructs Arjuna about the ideal, well-integrated, enlightened person he wants him to be: a dutiful person whose action is informed by knowledge, who realizes the fruit of such action in the form of inner wisdom and develops spiritual emotions for God—a devotee of Kṛṣṇa. As this section begins, Kṛṣṇa speaks covertly about *bhakti* and overtly about *niṣkāma-karma-yoga*. He then informs Arjuna that at this time he is only eligible for *niṣkāma-karma-yoga*. In this way, Kṛṣṇa instructs us through Arjuna that what is achieved through *niṣkāma-karma-yoga* is concomitant to *bhakti-yoga* proper. Through the practice of the *yoga* of selfless action, one's heart is purified and knowledge begins to manifest. Knowledge of the self will not manifest in a heart cluttered by material attachment, and inner wisdom in which the spiritual self is realized is included within mature *bhakti-yoga*.

Kṛṣṇa repeatedly advises Arjuna that *niṣkāma-karma-yoga* is the best course of action for him at this time, and eventually he declares its mature stage to be synonymous with *jñāna-yoga*. As knowledge manifests through *niṣkāma-karma-yoga*, one situated in knowledge becomes qualified to practice meditation. While the fruit of *niṣkāma-karma-yoga* is knowledge of the Brahman feature of the Absolute, the focus of meditation in *dhyāna-yoga* is the Paramātmā feature of God. As one realizes this feature of God one can progress to worship of the Bhagavān feature of the Absolute. This worship in *yoga* is *bhakti*, the final step on the ladder of *yoga* discussed in the first six chapters of the *Gītā*.

Although Kṛṣṇa advises Arjuna to practice *niṣkāma-karma-yoga* throughout the first six chapters, he also implies that he ultimately wants Arjuna to practice *bhakti-yoga*. Kṛṣṇa makes this abundantly clear at the end of the sixth chapter. Kṛṣṇa takes Arjuna up the ladder of *yoga* to illustrate the glory of *bhakti*. This glory of *bhakti* is twofold. *Bhakti* continues after one is liberated from material existence, whereas the other forms of *yoga* do not. Only when the heart has been purified, knowledge of the self has manifested, and one attains perfection in meditation does mature *bhakti* manifest. This glory of *bhakti* is brought out in the *Gītā*'s first six chapters. The second glory of *bhakti* is the generosity and independence by which she extends herself to whomever she chooses, even those whose hearts are

6. In the *Gītā* the *yoga* of knowledge is referred to variously as *sāṅkhya-yoga*, *karma-sannyāsa*, and *jñāna-yoga*.

cluttered with material desire. She does so through the medium of Kṛṣṇa's realized devotees, who awaken faith in her efficacy. Those who tread the path of *bhakti* as a result of her generosity will gradually develop detachment, knowledge, and mental absorption in God, maturing gradually into *bhakti* proper, the liberated *yoga*.

Here Kṛṣṇa eulogizes the practice of *yoga* in general by stating its fruit: *karma-bandhaṁ prahāsyasi*. Viśvanātha Cakravartī Ṭhākura comments that while the word *yoga* in this verse refers to selfless action in which the fruit of one's efforts are offered to God, a stage prior to *bhakti*, *yoga* also implies *bhakti* itself consisting of hearing and chanting about God. Viśvanātha Cakravartī senses that *bhakti* is implied here because *bhakti* is both the means to transcendental life as well as continued engagement in devotional life beyond the influence of material nature. Later in verse 45 of this chapter Kṛṣṇa implores Arjuna to attain this condition *(nistraiguṇya)* through the *yoga* practice that he is encouraging him to engage in here.

Text 40

नेहाभिक्रमनाशोऽस्ति प्रत्यवायो न विद्यते ।
स्वल्पमप्यस्य धर्मस्य त्रायते महतो भयात् ॥४०॥

nehābhikrama-nāśo 'sti pratyavāyo na vidyate/
sv-alpam apy asya dharmasya trāyate mahato bhayāt//

na—not; *iha*—this; *abhikrama*—endeavor; *nāśaḥ*—loss; *asti*—there is; *pratyavāyaḥ*—diminution; *na*—never; *vidyate*—there is; *su-alpam*—a very little; *api*—although; *asya*—of this; *dharmasya*—of *dharma*; *trāyate*—protects; *mahataḥ*—from great; *bhayāt*—from danger.

In the practice of this dharma no effort is wasted, nor is one's progress ever diminished. Even the slightest practice of this discipline protects one from great danger.

Kṛṣṇa secures Arjuna's attention by first glorifying that which he wants him to ultimately engage in, *bhakti*. Kṛṣṇa also wants Arjuna to fight. At this point he wants him to do so because he is by nature a warrior, but he wants him to fight with knowledge of the self and thus detached from the fruits of his effort, offering them to God. This type of *niṣkāma-karma-yoga* will lead him to *bhakti*.

Acting with the wisdom of *yoga* in devotion may look like ordinary religious action *(dharma)* that is enjoined in the *Vedas* as a means for material advancement, but it is quite different in terms of its motive and result. When one works according to the scripture, motivated by the prospect of enjoying the fruit of one's labor, such work is troublesome. If even one small item is neglected in such ritualistic performance, one will not get the desired result. If everything is done correctly, the resulting gain will be lost in time. Even if one works selflessly within the realm of *karma*, one may not get the desired result if something is left undone or the work is improperly performed. There is also the possibility of incurring unwanted reactions within the execution of *niṣkāma-karma-yoga*, should one's duties be improperly performed. In contrast, *bhakti-yoga-dharma* even if imperfectly performed produces a positive result that is never lost under the influence of time. This is discussed further in the thirty-first verse of chapter 9.

Text 41

व्यवसायात्मिका बुद्धिरेकेह कुरुनन्दन ।
बहुशाखा ह्यनन्ताश्च बुद्धयोऽव्यवसायिनाम् ॥४१॥

vyavasāyātmikā buddhir ekeha kuru-nandana/
bahu-śākhā hy anantāś ca buddhayo 'vyavasāyinām//

vyavasāya-ātmikā—resolute in purpose; *buddhiḥ*—intelligence; *ekā*—only one; *iha*—here; *kuru-nandana*—O joy of the Kuru dynasty; *bahu-śākhāḥ*—having various branches; *hi*—indeed; *anantāḥ*—unlimited; *ca*—also; *buddhayaḥ*—intelligence; *avyavasāyinām*—of those who are irresolute.

O joy of the Kuru dynasty, on this path one must be resolute in purpose with one's intelligence fixed. Indeed, those who are irresolute are endlessly distracted by other thoughts.

Here Kṛṣṇa chastens Arjuna's mind to do his bidding alone, speaking affectionately to his disciple. As a reference to *bhakti* this verse points to the stage of *niṣṭhā*, in which one's intelligence is fixed in spiritual pursuit as a result of hearing about God regularly and serving his devotees.[7] At this stage one is fixed in consideration of his *iṣṭa devata* (personal Deity). Viśvanātha Cakravartī Ṭhākura says that intelligence fixed on the advice of

7. See ŚB. 1.2.18.

one's guru regarding the cultivation of *bhakti* is *vyavasāyātmikā buddhi*. He has equated attaining the grace of the guru with adherence to the spiritual practices he outlines.

The word *hi* (indeed) conveys the sense that it is well known that those troubled by worldly thoughts are not peaceful, for their thoughts lack the certainty that arises from self-realization and its pursuit. Kṛṣṇa speaks further about such people in the following three verses to stress *bhakti* by way of contrast.

Texts 42–43

यामिमां पुष्पितां वाचं प्रवदन्त्यविपश्चितः ।
वेदवादरताः पार्थ नान्यदस्तीति वादिनः ॥४२॥
कामात्मानः स्वर्गपरा जन्मकर्मफलप्रदाम् ।
क्रियाविशेषबहुलां भोगैश्वर्यगतिं प्रति ॥४३॥

yām imāṁ puṣpitāṁ vācaṁ pravadanty avipaścitaḥ/
veda-vāda-ratāḥ pārtha nānyad astīti vādinaḥ//
kāmātmānaḥ svarga-parā janma-karma-phala-pradām/
kriyā-viśeṣa-bahulāṁ bhogaiśvarya-gatiṁ prati//

yām imām—which this; *puṣpitām*—flowery; *vācam*—words; *pravadanti*—say; *avipaścitaḥ*—people of meager intelligence; *veda-vāda-ratāḥ*—take delight in the letter of the *Vedas*; *pārtha*—O son of Pṛthā; *na*—never; *anyat*—anything else; *asti*—there is; *iti*—thus; *vādinaḥ*—saying; *kāma-ātmānaḥ*—desirous of sense gratification; *svarga-parāḥ*—aiming to achieve heaven; *janma-karma-phala-pradām*—resulting in good birth and other fruitive reactions; *kriyā-viśeṣa*—ritualistic performance; *bahulām*—various; *bhoga*—sense enjoyment; *aiśvarya*—opulence; *gatim*—progress; *prati*—toward.

Such people of meager intelligence proclaim that the flowery words of the Vedas are all in all. They take delight in the letter of the Vedic law, saying there is nothing more than this. They are full of desires for opulence and material enjoyment and think that attaining heaven or a good birth in the next life is desirable. Thus they remain attached to ritualistic performance.

Text 44

भोगैश्वर्यप्रसक्तानां तयापहृतचेतसाम् ।
व्यवसायात्मिका बुद्धिः समाधौ न विधीयते ॥४४॥

bhogaiśvarya-prasaktānāṁ tayāpahṛta-cetasām/
vyavasāyātmikā buddhiḥ samādhau na vidhīyate//

bhoga—sense enjoyment; *aiśvarya*—opulence; *prasaktānām*—of those who are attached; *tayā*—by them; *apahṛta-cetasām*—whose mind is stolen away; *vyavasāya-ātmikā*—resolute; *buddhiḥ*—insight; *samādhau*—in *samādhi; na*—never; *vidhīyate*—is forthcoming.

Too attached to material opulence and sense enjoyment, their minds are stolen away, and resolute insight in samādhi is not forthcoming.

Śrīdhara Swāmī comments that *samādhi* is single-minded concentration leading to consciousness of God. Baladeva Vidyābhūṣaṇa defines *samādhi* as that condition in which correct understanding of the self is perfectly achieved. Arjuna asks Kṛṣṇa about the state of *samādhi* later in this chapter (Bg. 2.54). Kṛṣṇa answers him in the concluding section of this chapter (Bg. 2.55–72). Absorption *(samādhi)* in sacrifices leading to Brahman are discussed in chapter 4 (Bg. 4.24–29), and *yoga-samādhi* and its basic varieties are discussed at length in chapter 6.

Text 45

त्रैगुण्यविषया वेदा निस्त्रैगुण्यो भवार्जुन ।
निर्द्वन्द्वो नित्यसत्त्वस्थो निर्योगक्षेम आत्मवान् ॥४५॥

trai-guṇya-viṣayā vedā nistraiguṇyo bhavārjuna/
nirdvandvo nitya-sattva-stho niryoga-kṣema ātmavān//

trai-guṇya—pertaining to the three modes of material nature; *viṣayāḥ*—jurisdictions; *vedāḥ*—the *Vedas*; *nistraiguṇyaḥ*—transcendental to the three *guṇas*; *bhava*—be; *arjuna*—Arjuna; *nirdvandvaḥ*—without duality; *nitya-sattva-sthaḥ*—fixed in truth; *niryoga-kṣemaḥ*—free from concerns for acquisition and comfort; *ātma-vān*—established in the self.

The Vedas deal mainly with life within the jurisdiction of the three guṇas. Arjuna, you should transcend these guṇas, becoming indifferent to material dualities, fixed in truth, free from concerns for acquisition and comfort, and established in the self.

Kṛṣṇa's secondary potency, known variously as *prakṛti*, *māyā-śakti*, and so on, is discussed throughout the *Gītā*. It consists of the three influences known as the *guṇas*.[8] The vast majority of the *Vedas* deal with fruitive action under the influence of the *guṇas* in the pursuit of religious life and heavenly attainment. The smaller and concluding portion deals with self-realization and experiential spiritual life, which involves transcending material dualities and freedom from concerns for one's maintenance through acquaintance with the self-sustaining nature of the soul in the self-surrender of devotion.

Kṛṣṇa's use of the word *sattva* does not indicate that one should become situated in *sattva-guṇa* (the material influence of goodness), for in the first line of this verse he speaks of transcending all three *guṇas*. *Sattva-guṇa* begets knowledge, whereas *bhakti* gives birth to transcendental experience. The words *nitya-sattva-sthaḥ* imply remaining always in the association of devotees, who have been characterized in the *Bhāgavata* as truthful *(sat)*.

In his comments on this verse, Viśvanātha Cakravartī Ṭhākura stresses the futility of the paths of *jñāna* and *karma* in terms of transcending the *guṇas*. Citing numerous verses from the *Śrīmad-Bhāgavatam*'s *Uddhava-gītā* that correspond with this verse, Cakravartī Ṭhākura offers considerable evidence that only *bhakti* has the power to deliver one from the *guṇas* and situate one in transcendence. Such *bhakti* is *niryoga-kṣema*, free from the concerns for acquisition *(yoga)* and maintenance *(kṣema)*. The full sense of what it means to be free from concerns for acquisition and comfort is related in the twenty-second verse of chapter 9 in reference to *bhakti-yoga*. Any necessity Kṛṣṇa's devotees might have for these two is seen to by Kṛṣṇa himself.

Text 46

यावानर्थ उदपाने सर्वतः सम्प्लुतोदके ।
तावान् सर्वेषु वेदेषु ब्राह्मणस्य विजानतः ॥४६॥

yāvān artha udapāne sarvataḥ samplutodake/
tāvān sarveṣu vedeṣu brāhmaṇasya vijānataḥ//

yāvān—as much; *arthaḥ*—purpose; *uda-pāne*—in a well of water; *sarvataḥ*—in all respects; *sampluta-udake*—in a great reservoir of water; *tāvān*—similarly; *sarveṣu*—in all; *vedeṣu*—scriptures; *brāhmaṇasya*—of the *brāhmaṇa*; *vijānataḥ*—who knows.

8. See Bg. 14.5 for an explanation of the *guṇas*.

All purposes that are fulfilled by a well and more can be served by a reservoir of water. Similarly, all the purposes of the scripture can be served by a brāhmaṇa who knows their purpose.

In the preceding verses Kṛṣṇa differentiates between those sections of the scripture that advocate material advancement and those that advocate spiritual progress. He also criticizes those who do not understand the purpose of the *Vedas* and thus take their statements about material advancement out of context. The sections of the *Vedas* dealing with material advancement, which make up the greater balance of the text, are for the general populace who are full of material desires. The rituals prescribed therein seek to regulate desires bringing about religious life. Furthermore, they awaken faith in their words in those who practice the enjoined rituals. The real fruit of this subsequent faith in the scripture is that in time it causes people to look more deeply into the scripture, wherein they will learn about experiential spiritual life, as opposed to religious life. Kṛṣṇa wants Arjuna to come to experiential spiritual life.

In encouraging him along the lines of experiential spiritual life in devotion, Kṛṣṇa also prepares him for that which he (representing a beginner on the spiritual path) is presently eligible to practice: *niṣkāma-karma-yoga.* Kṛṣṇa indirectly informs Arjuna in this verse that such pursuit will not leave him bereft of the fruit of his action, even though it involves sacrificing this fruit. Thus he offers an example to help Arjuna understand. Arjuna will gain the fruits of his work even while sacrificing them, for that which he will gain by this course includes within it that which is sacrificed, just as the amount of water in a small pond is contained within a large lake. One who realizes God experiences all the bliss available through Vedic ritual and more.

Although the *Vedas* offer many things to their adherents, their real fruit is *bhakti*. Kṛṣṇa indicates this here. A well may dry up and its water may not be sweet. To drink from it one must hoist up the water with considerable effort after having labored to find the well in the first place. Paths other than *bhakti* are compared to wells. *Bhakti* on the other hand is oceanic in its outreach and depth of spiritual possibility, and whatever one can attain through other paths can be attained on the path of *bhakti* with less effort.

In the next verse Kṛṣṇa abruptly informs Arjuna of his level of eligibility for spiritual practice, telling him to act in battle in accordance with his acquired nature. The apparent lack of connection between this verse and the next causes some confusion in Arjuna, giving rise to his question in the beginning of the next chapter.

Text 47

कर्मण्येवाधिकारस्ते मा फलेषु कदाचन ।
मा कर्मफलहेतुर्भूर्मा ते सङ्गोऽस्त्वकर्मणि ॥४७॥

karmaṇy evādhikāras te mā phaleṣu kadācana/
mā karma-phala-hetur bhūr mā te saṅgo 'stv akarmaṇi//

karmaṇi—in prescribed duties; *eva*—only; *adhikāraḥ*—eligibility; *te*—of you; *mā*—never; *phaleṣu*—in the fruits; *kadācana*—at any time; *mā*—never; *karma-phala*—fruit of action; *hetuḥ*—cause; *bhūḥ*—become; *mā*—never; *te*—of you; *saṅgaḥ*—attachment; *astu*—there should be; *akarmaṇi*—in not doing prescribed duties.

You are only eligible to act in terms of your acquired nature as a warrior. You are not entitled to the fruits of your action. You should neither be motivated to act by the hope of enjoying the fruits of your action, nor become attached to not acting at all!

In *Śrīmad-Bhāgavatam* (11.21.2) it is mentioned that "virtue constitutes acting in accordance with one's level of eligibility and acting beyond that which one is qualified for is vice." Much of the *Gītā* is contingent on this point. Here Kṛṣṇa says that those who are not eligible for *bhakti* or *jñāna* should engage in *niṣkāma-karma-yoga*. Should Arjuna question the value of work performed for which there is no fruit to be enjoyed and thus lean towards inaction, Kṛṣṇa tells him that attachment to inaction is also inappropriate. He stresses this point to underscore the importance of action. Arjuna is to act within the socioreligious structure of society with the spirit of detachment, offering the fruits of his work to God.

The practice of *niṣkāma-karma-yoga* in the strict sense advocated in the *Gītā* would be practically impossible to implement in the modern world. It arises out of a socioreligious culture governed by scriptural canon in which society is divided fourfold in terms of both occupational and religious orders. Men and women are further divided, and numerous rules governing all spheres of human activity are mandated for all sections of society. The practice of *niṣkāma-karma-yoga* involves strictly adhering to the rules and duties governing one's particular socioreligious classification while cultivating detachment from the fruit of one's work. Thus the *Gītā* speaks of prescribed duties and Arjuna's warrior status is repeatedly mentioned.

However, the spirit of *niṣkāma-karma-yoga* is selfless action in the spirit of sacrifice. Many have adopted this principle in an attempt to apply *niṣkāma-karma-yoga* to the modern world. Although the modern world does not prescribe social and religious duties for everyone from birth, we nonetheless do have duties to perform, and these duties will likely conform with our status within the *guṇas*. Such duties should be performed responsibly, without attachment to the results. This no doubt has merit. However, one can remain in stride with the *Gītā* both in spirit and in terms of the letter of its law of love by embracing the generosity of *bhakti*. Faith in the efficacy of *bhakti* leads to mature *bhakti*, and this relieves one from obligations to the socioreligious order the *Gītā* speaks of, as well as any other social order.

Text 48

योगस्थः कुरु कर्माणि सङ्गं त्यक्त्वा धनञ्जय ।
सिद्ध्यासिद्ध्योः समो भूत्वा समत्वं योग उच्यते ॥४८॥

yoga-sthaḥ kuru karmāṇi saṅgaṁ tyaktvā dhanañjaya/
siddhy-asiddhyoḥ samo bhūtvā samatvaṁ yoga ucyate//

yoga-sthaḥ—fixed in *yoga*; *kuru*—perform; *karmāṇi*—duty; *saṅgam*—attachment; *tyaktvā*—abandoning; *dhanañjaya*—O winner of wealth; *siddhi-asiddhyoḥ*—in success and failure; *samaḥ*—equipoised; *bhūtvā*—becoming; *samatvam*—equanimity; *yogaḥ*—*yoga*; *ucyate*—is called.

Perform your duty fixed in the yoga of action, abandoning all attachment to success or failure, O winner of wealth. Such equanimity of mind is what is meant by yoga.

Here Kṛṣṇa helps Arjuna to understand the practical application of his instructions. While working in the spirit of glorifying God, one should be equipoised (*samo bhūtvā*), neither overly elated upon acquiring success nor dejected in failure. Kṛṣṇa defines *yoga* in this verse as equanimity of mind (*samatvam*). It is this spirit of action that he means by *yoga*, not merely action. Thus there is no contradiction when he describes *yoga* as action and *yoga* as being equipoised. While previously in verse 38 Kṛṣṇa spoke of equanimity in the midst of battle, here he speaks in a broader sense of performing all actions with equanimity of mind.

Text 49

दूरेण ह्यवरं कर्म बुद्धियोगाद्धनञ्जय ।
बुद्धौ शरणमन्विच्छ कृपणाः फलहेतवः ॥४९॥

dūreṇa hy avaraṁ karma buddhi-yogād dhanañjaya/
buddhau śaraṇam anviccha kṛpaṇāḥ phala-hetavaḥ//

dūreṇa—by far; *hi*—certainly; *avaram*—inferior; *karma*—action; *buddhi-yogāt*—to disciplined intelligence; *dhanañjaya*—O conqueror of wealth; *buddhau*—in wisdom; *śaraṇam*—refuge; *anviccha*—seek; *kṛpaṇāḥ*—misers; *phala-hetavaḥ*—those motivated by the fruit.

O winner of wealth, action motivated by the desire to enjoy the results of one's work is far inferior to disciplined intelligence. Take refuge in wisdom. Those whose actions are motivated by the desire to enjoy the fruits of action for themselves are miserly.

With a hint of sarcasm Kṛṣṇa addresses Arjuna as Dhanañjaya, winner of wealth. In doing so he appeals to his wealth of heart and implores him not to be miserly. The *śruti* (Bṛ. 3.8.10) defines a miser as one who departs from this world without knowing the Absolute, thus remaining in *saṁsāra*. Arjuna was well known for having acquired vast wealth. Here Kṛṣṇa says that such acquisition is by far inferior *(dūreṇa hy āvaram)* to the acquisition of inner wealth. Kṛṣṇa tells Arjuna to take shelter of wisdom.

Here *buddhi-yoga* refers to the disciplined intelligence required for the execution of *niṣkāma-karma-yoga*. Having spoken of the inferiority and foolishness of action devoid of yogic wisdom, Kṛṣṇa speaks next of the power in the wisdom of *yoga*.

Text 50

बुद्धियुक्तो जहातीह उभे सुकृतदुष्कृते ।
तस्माद्योगाय युज्यस्व योगः कर्मसु कौशलम् ॥५०॥

buddhi-yukto jahātīha ubhe sukṛta-duṣkṛte/
tasmād yogāya yujyasva yogaḥ karmasu kauśalam//

buddhi-yuktaḥ—one who is disciplined by wisdom; *jahāti*—rids himself; *iha*—here; *ubhe*—both; *sukṛta-duṣkṛte*—good and bad *karma*; *tasmāt*—therefore; *yogāya*—to *yoga*; *yujyasva*—devote yourself; *yogaḥ*—*yoga*; *karmasu*—in actions; *kauśalam*—art.

One whose intelligence is disciplined to act in this way rids himself of both good and bad karma. Therefore devote yourself to yoga, the art of work.

In this verse Kṛṣṇa chides Arjuna for his reluctance to fight with his relatives. Arjuna is not adroit in his reticence to fight. *Yoga* is the art of work because although it is action, it destroys the results of both evil and pious action. Good *karma* does not destroy bad *karma*, but the act of *yoga* destroys good and bad *karma*.

In verse 39 of this chapter Kṛṣṇa began speaking about *yoga*. Therein he spoke of it in terms of practice as opposed to theory. He taught that *yoga* is a spiritual exercise that involves control and integration. In verses 48 through 50 he also spoke of *yoga* in terms of its involving control and the integration of intelligence or introspection and action. In verse 48 he also defined *yoga* as equanimity of mind, and here in this verse he further defines it as the art of or skill in performing work that results in freedom from karmic reaction.

Should Arjuna question the value of forgoing pious acts, Kṛṣṇa next speaks of the attainment of *yoga*, by which piety and impiety are transcended.

Text 51

कर्मजं बुद्धियुक्ता हि फलं त्यक्त्वा मनीषिणः ।
जन्मबन्धविनिर्मुक्ताः पदं गच्छन्त्यनामयम् ॥५१॥

karma-jaṁ buddhi-yuktā hi phalaṁ tyaktvā manīṣiṇaḥ/
janma-bandha-vinirmuktāḥ padaṁ gacchanty anāmayam//

karma-jam—born of action; *buddhi-yuktāḥ*—those established in yogic wisdom; *hi*—certainly; *phalam*—fruit; *tyaktvā*—renouncing; *manīṣiṇaḥ*—the wise; *janma-bandha*—from the bondage of rebirth; *vinirmuktāḥ*—released; *padam*—abode; *gacchanti*—they attain; *anāmayam*—without anxiety.

Those established in yogic wisdom, the wise who have renounced the fruits of action and are thus released from the bondage of rebirth, attain that abode that is without anxiety.

Here Kṛṣṇa answers the question Arjuna raised in verse 7, wherein he asks what is best for him (*śreyaḥ*). After release from *saṁsāra* there is still something to attain: Kṛṣṇa's abode. It will be attained through devotion after one is free from distraction, both worldly and scriptural. Through *karma-yoga* one attains self-knowledge *(jñāna)* and then through *bhakti* one attains the abode of God. Here Kṛṣṇa, while speaking overtly about attaining spiritual knowledge of the self through *karma-yoga*, also hints at *bhakti*. Knowledge of the soul leads to knowledge of God, which determines the function of the soul in eternity.

Winthrop Sargeant renders the last two *padas* of this verse as "free from the bondage of rebirth, [they] go to that place that is free from pain." *Janma-bandha-vinirmuktāḥ* (liberated from repeated birth) and *padaṁ gacchanty anāmayam* (they go to the place of no anxiety) indicate two distinct aspects of devotional liberation: release from the negative influence of *saṁsāra* and attainment of positive standing in the liberated realm of devotion (Vaikuṇṭha), *muktir hitvānyathā-rūpaṁ svarūpeṇa vyavasthitiḥ*.[9] As Arjuna wonders when he will attain the goal mentioned in this verse, Kṛṣṇa answers.

Text 52–53

यदा ते मोहकलिलं बुद्धिर्व्यतितरिष्यति ।
तदा गन्तासि निर्वेदं श्रोतव्यस्य श्रुतस्य च ॥५२॥
श्रुतिविप्रतिपन्ना ते यदा स्थास्यति निश्चला ।
समाधावचला बुद्धिस्तदा योगमवाप्स्यसि ॥५३॥

yadā te moha-kalilaṁ buddhir vyatitariṣyati/
tadā gantāsi nirvedaṁ śrotavyasya śrutasya ca//
śruti-vipratipannā te yadā sthāsyati niścalā/
samādhāv acalā buddhis tadā yogam avāpsyasi//

yadā—when; *te*—your; *moha*—illusion; *kalilam*—thicket; *buddhiḥ*—intellect; *vyatitariṣyati*—surpasses; *tadā*—at that time; *gantā asi*—you shall go; *nirvedam*—disgusted; *śrotavyasya*—toward all that is to be heard; *śrutasya*—all that is already heard; *ca*—also; *śruti*—scriptural injunctions; *vipratipannā*—perplexed; *te*—your; *yadā*—when; *sthāsyati*—remains; *niścalā*—fixed; *samādhau*—in *samādhi*; *acalā*—unflinching; *buddhiḥ*—intellect; *tadā*—at that time; *yogam*—*yoga*; *avāpsyasi*—you will attain.

When your intellect emerges from the thicket of delusion, you shall become disgusted with all that has been heard and all that is to be heard. Thereafter, when your intellect is fixed and not perplexed by scriptural injunctions, you shall attain yoga-samādhi.

9. See ŚB. 2.10.6.

In *Bhāgavata-sandarbha* (82), Jīva Goswāmī cites verse 52 as an explanation of the word *nirgrantha* (beyond scripture) found in the famous *ātmārāma* verse of the *Śrīmad-Bhāgavatam* (1.7.10). This *Bhāgavata* verse describes why the liberated Śukadeva was attracted to serve Kṛṣṇa in a post-liberated status—why he studied the *Bhāgavata* even though he was beyond scripture. The *Bhāgavata* explains that "such is the nature of the qualities of Hari." It is Hari's [Kṛṣṇa's] qualities and *līlās* that the *Bhāgavata* is centered on. Their nature is such that liberated souls become attracted to them and thus to the study, and more, the relishing of *Śrīmad-Bhāgavatam*.

Relative to the flow of the *Gītā*, Kṛṣṇa speaks of not being perplexed by the Vedic doctrine of fruitive work *(karma-kāṇḍa)*. He stresses that fixing one's intelligence in spiritual pursuit will only come about when one is no longer bewildered by this doctrine, thinking it to be the sum and substance of the Vedic advocacy. Only by such fixed intelligence can one realize *yoga*.

Having heard about that abode that lies beyond religious life, the spirit of the scripture that underlies the scripture's words, Arjuna thoughtfully inquired about those in this world who have attained that destination. Herein Arjuna asks a fourfold question to which Kṛṣṇa replies by describing overtly those in knowledge and covertly his devotees.

Text 54

अर्जुन उवाच
स्थितप्रज्ञस्य का भाषा समाधिस्थस्य केशव ।
स्थितधीः किं प्रभाषेत किमासीत व्रजेत किम् ॥५४॥

arjuna uvāca
sthita-prajñasya kā bhāṣā samādhi-sthasya keśava/
sthita-dhīḥ kiṁ prabhāṣeta kim āsīta vrajeta kim//

arjunaḥ uvāca—Arjuna said; *sthita-prajñasya*—of one who is steady of insight; *kā*—what; *bhāṣā*—language; *samādhi-sthasya*—of one accomplished in meditation; *keśava*—O Keśava; *sthita-dhīḥ*—one steady in intelligence; *kim*—what; *prabhāṣeta*—speaks; *kim*—how; *āsīta*—sits; *vrajeta*—moves; *kim*—how.

Arjuna asked: What, O Keśava, are the characteristics of one who is accomplished in meditation and steady in intelligence? How does such a steady person speak? How does he sit? How does he move?

In asking Kṛṣṇa how the realized soul speaks *(prabhāṣeta)*, Arjuna wants to know how he reacts to others. Sitting *(āsīta)* implies how the realized soul withdraws from worldliness, while his movement *(vrajeta)* involves the manner in which he interacts with the world.

As Kṛṣṇa answers Arjuna's first question concerning the symptoms of a self-realized soul, he speaks in general about the nature of those aloof from worldly responsibilities, the pure-hearted devotees he alluded to earlier in verse 51. Such persons of inner attainment experience the fruit of the *yoga* of action in devotion to God. Outwardly, however, Kṛṣṇa speaks of realization of Brahman,[10] that aspect of himself attained by *karma-yogīs* who have awakened self-knowledge.

The section of the *Gītā* beginning with the next verse continues through the end of this chapter. In this important division of the text Kṛṣṇa describes the ideal person he ultimately wants Arjuna to become. He will elaborate on this section throughout the next four chapters, unpacking all that is contained herein.

Text 55

श्रीभगवानुवाच
प्रजहाति यदा कामान् सर्वान् पार्थ मनोगतान् ।
आत्मन्येवात्मना तुष्टः स्थितप्रज्ञस्तदोच्यते ॥५५॥

śrī-bhagavān uvāca
prajahāti yadā kāmān sarvān pārtha mano-gatān/
ātmany evātmanā tuṣṭaḥ sthita-prajñas tadocyate//

śrī-bhagavān uvāca—the Lord of Śrī said; *prajahāti*—renounces; *yadā*—when; *kāmān*—desires; *sarvān*—all; *pārtha*—O Pārtha; *manaḥ-gatān*—born of the mind; *ātmani*—in the self; *eva*—certainly; *ātmanā*—by the self; *tuṣṭaḥ*—satisfied; *sthita-prajñaḥ*—of steady insight; *tadā*—at that time; *ucyate*—is said.

The Lord of Śrī said: O Pārtha, one who, having renounced all desires born of the mind, is satisfied in the self and by the self, is said to be one whose insight is steady.

10. Brahman refers to undifferentiated consciousness, which is compared to the halo of God. Both this feature of Godhead and that of the indwelling guide, Paramātmā, are aspects of Bhagavān, God himself.

Kṛṣṇa answers Arjuna's questions by explaining the status of the *jīvanmukta*, one who is liberated in this life. *Jīvanmukti* is the penultimate stage of realization. It is followed by *videha-mukti*, or the liberation that occurs upon the demise of the realized soul's body.

According to Rāmānujācārya, Kṛṣṇa's answers appear to be a description of four stages of inner development, beginning with the highest stage and descending to the beginning stage—from *samādhi* (trance) to *pratyāhāra* (withdrawal of the senses from their objects). In the highest stage of *samādhi* all material desires have been uprooted with no possibility of revival. In the next to highest stage, the seeds of one's material tendencies have not yet been destroyed. They exist in the form of subtle hankerings and unconscious predispositions. The sage in this stage engages in eliminating them through repeated contemplation of the self and God. In doing so, he consciously controls anger, attachment, fear, and the like. Beneath this stage the sage's mind is not yet mastered. He must practice indifference to the elation and depression of the mind. Lastly, the entry level to enlightened life involves controlling one's senses, even when the mind is uncontrolled. While the two stages above this one involve a mental culture, this beginning stage involves merely the outward control of the senses.

Madhusūdana Saraswatī sees this section as a description of *samādhi* and coming out of *samādhi* owing to the influence of one's manifest *(prārabdha) karma*. In his understanding, the subsequent verses that describe the sage's talking, sitting, and walking represent his coming out of *samādhi*.

In this verse Kṛṣṇa speaks of contentment *(tuṣṭaḥ)* in the midst of renouncing desire. When desire born of the mind is renounced, the fact that one exhibits contentment is not contradictory because in this state the self finds contentment not in the mind but in the self itself. Mental desires can be renounced because they are not intrinsic to the self, whereas desire itself cannot be, being the very makeup of the self, which is a unit of will.

Kṛṣṇa next describes how a *jīvanmukta* speaks, or responds to the world, answering the second part of Arjuna's question.

Text 56

दुःखेष्वनुद्विग्नमनाः सुखेषु विगतस्पृहः ।
वीतरागभयक्रोधः स्थितधीर्मुनिरुच्यते ॥५६॥

duḥkheṣv anudvigna-manāḥ sukheṣu vigata-spṛhaḥ/
vīta-rāga-bhaya-krodhaḥ sthita-dhīr munir ucyate//

duḥkheṣu—in miseries; *anudvigna-manāḥ*—without being agitated in mind; *sukheṣu*—in joy; *vigata-spṛhaḥ*—without being deluded; *vīta*—departed; *rāga*—passion; *bhaya*—fear; *krodhaḥ*—anger; *sthita-dhīḥ*—whose mind is steady; *muniḥ*—a sage; *ucyate*—is called.

Amid suffering and happiness his mind is neither deluded nor delighted. He who is free from desire and whose passion, fear, and anger have subsided is said to be a sage of steady mind.

Here suffering *(duḥkheṣu)* refers to the three miseries: *ādhyātmika* (miseries arising from one's own body or mind), *ādhibhautika* (miseries arising from others), and *ādhidaivika* (miseries from natural disturbances). The *jñānī*'s experience of both sorrow and happiness are a result of his *prārabdha-karma*. In the case of the unalloyed devotee, however, it is due to God's special arrangement.

According to the *Padma Purāṇa*, *karma* appears in various stages of development. *Karma* acquired over lifetimes is stored in an unmanifest stage known as *aprārabdha-karma*. When this stock of karmic reactions begins to manifest is it called *kūṭa*. From the stage of *kūṭa*, *karma* develops into a seedlike stage known as *bīja*. This seed stage of *karma* appears as one's predisposition and desire. When the seed stage of *karma* blossoms and actually manifests in our life, this is called *prārabdha-karma*. Once this *karma* has blossomed, it must bear its fruit. Although *karma* in its earlier stages of development can be destroyed by spiritual practice, one's *prārabdha-karma* must play itself out. One who has attained knowledge of the self witnesses the expiration of his *prārabdha-karma*, remaining unattached in the midst of the happiness and distress that it brings about.

In this verse we learn that the *prārabdha-karma* experiences of sorrow and happiness continue for the realized soul. However, we also learn that the realized soul is not overwhelmed by delusion arising from sorrow that produces lamentation, nor is he overwhelmed by a sense of delight arising from happiness causing him to hanker for its recurrence. Both the experiences of sorrow and happiness alone are the result of *prārabdha-karma*, not the indulgence in lamentation and hankering that unenlightened souls are involved with. This indulgence on the part of the unenlightened is what perpetuates their karmic involvement. It is their unenlightened response to their *prārabdha-karma*. Because the realized soul is merely witnessing the expiration of his *prārabdha-karma*, he does not indulge in lamentation and hankering and further implicate himself in the karmic circle. His ability to forgo such indulgence is not a mental adjustment, but a result of his realized knowledge of the true position of the self.

The devotee's status with regard to *prārabdha-karma* is slightly different from that of the self-realized *jñānī*. *Bhakti* has the power to change one's *prārabdha-karma* in this life.[11] It uproots the foundation of ignorance that underlies all *karma*, but it also places one under the charge of God for the purpose of doing his bidding in this world. The unalloyed devotee is not concerned with liberation. His concern lies only in God's service. Having destroyed his *karma* in the order of *aprārabdha*, *kūṭa*, and *bīja*, God arranges for him to remain in this world as long as he sees fit, be it for the remainder of this life or for several lives. He does so by preserving his devotee's *prārabdha-karma* and infusing him with divine *śakti*. When God desires to take his devotee from the world, no longer able to bear the pain of separation from him, he distributes his devotee's pious *prārabdha-karma* to those who love him and any impious *prārabdha-karma* to those who oppose him. This is the opinion of Baladeva Vidyābhūṣaṇa, as explained in his *Vedānta-sūtra* commentary (4.1.15–18).

Baladeva Vidyābhūṣaṇa's remarks are in keeping with the *sūtras*. They do not, however, stress the efficacy of *bhakti* in removing *prārabdha-karma*, as other *ācāryas'* comments have. Baladeva speaks more of the power of knowledge born of *bhakti* than he does the power of *bhakti* itself.

The Gauḍīya position on the bodily status of a devotee is stated by Śrī Caitanya himself thus: "A devotee's body should never be thought of as material. It is transcendental and made of spiritual substance. At the time of initiation, when the devotee offers himself to God, God makes the devotee equal to himself. He makes the devotee's body spiritual like his own so that the devotee can engage in the service of his lotus feet." (Cc. Antya 4.191–193)

Speaking of the spiritual nature of the devotee's body, Sanātana Goswāmī recounts Śiva's explanation to Nārada in *Bṛhad-bhāgavatāmṛta* (1.3.60–61). Therein, Śiva speaks of his own experience, stating that he feels no necessity of citing scriptural evidence in support of his opinion. Śiva says that owing to their drinking the nectar of devotion to Kṛṣṇa, devotees' bodies become transformed into something spiritual, just as when drinking certain potions one's body becomes transformed.

11. See Brs. 1.1.17–26.

The scriptural example of Dhruva Mahārāja is noteworthy. In the *Bhāgavatam* it is described how Dhruva left the material world and entered the spiritual abode of Viṣṇu in his selfsame body. Viśvanātha Cakravartī comments that this pastime of Dhruva was revealed by God just to stress the spiritual position of the devotee's body. Although this is not the norm, we should nevertheless learn to appreciate that even the bodies of practicing devotees take on a spiritual quality in proportion to their absorption in devotional practice. The practitioner's body is thus both material and spiritual at the same time, and eventually it is completely spiritualized—its apparent death a divine illusion. As such, the form of the departed devotee who has attained *prema* is itself an eternal object of veneration. Other than the devotee, no one—not the *jñānī*, *yogī*, or any other transcendentalist's body—is completely free from material qualities. This is the opinion of Viśvanātha Cakravartī,[12] who supports his position with Kṛṣṇa's words to Uddhava in *Śrīmad-Bhāgavatam* (11.25.26). Therein Kṛṣṇa tells Uddhava that one who has taken shelter of him in devotion is free from all material qualities, *nirguṇo mad-apāśrayaḥ*.

Text 57

यः सर्वत्रानभिस्नेहस्तत्तत्प्राप्य शुभाशुभम् ।
नाभिनन्दति न द्वेष्टि तस्य प्रज्ञा प्रतिष्ठिता ॥५७॥

yaḥ sarvatrānabhisnehas tat tat prāpya śubhāśubham/
nābhinandati na dveṣṭi tasya prajñā pratiṣṭhitā//

yaḥ—one who; *sarvatra*—everywhere; *anabhisnehaḥ*—without affection; *tat*—that; *tat*—that; *prāpya*—upon attaining; *śubha*—pleasant; *aśubham*—unpleasant; *na*—neither; *abhinandati*—praises; *na*—nor; *dveṣṭi*—dislikes; *tasya*—his; *prajñā*—wisdom; *pratiṣṭhitā*—firm.

One who is free from all material affection, who upon attaining that which is pleasant or unpleasant neither praises nor disapproves, stands firm in wisdom.

Here Kṛṣṇa describes the *jīvanmukta*'s speech. Free from all material affection *(anabhisnehaḥ)*, he is full with love of God. His praise is for God alone, and he does not hate anything.

12. See his commentary on ŚB. 10.29.10.

Next Kṛṣṇa addresses the third part of Arjuna's question, regarding the manner in which a person of steady wisdom sits, or withdraws from the world.

Text 58

यदा संहरते चायं कूर्मोऽङ्गानीव सर्वशः ।
इन्द्रियाणीन्द्रियार्थेभ्यस्तस्य प्रज्ञा प्रतिष्ठिता ॥५८॥

yadā saṁharate cāyaṁ kūrmo 'ṅgānīva sarvaśaḥ/
indriyāṇīndriyārthebhyas tasya prajñā pratiṣṭhitā//

yadā—when; *saṁharate*—withdraws; *ca*—and; *ayam*—he; *kūrmaḥ*—tortoise; *aṅgāni*—limbs; *iva*—like; *sarvaśaḥ*—altogether; *indriyāṇi*—senses; *indriya-arthebhyaḥ*—from the sense objects; *tasya*—his; *prajñā*—wisdom; *pratiṣṭhitā*—firm.

And when he completely withdraws his senses from their objects, like a tortoise draws its limbs within its shell, his wisdom stands firm.

While informing Arjuna of the nature of the enlightened, Kṛṣṇa simultaneously articulates the proper course of action to reach enlightened life. Thus he continues in the following verse in response to Arjuna's mental question: "What is the difference between one who withdraws his senses from their objects out of sickness or even out of laziness and one who does so in pursuit of enlightened consciousness?"

Text 59

विषया विनिवर्तन्ते निराहारस्य देहिनः ।
रसवर्जं रसोऽप्यस्य परं दृष्ट्वा निवर्तते ॥५९॥

viṣayā vinivartante nirāhārasya dehinaḥ/
rasa-varjaṁ raso 'py asya paraṁ dṛṣṭvā nivartate//

viṣayāḥ—sense objects; *vinivartante*—they turn away; *nirāhārasya*—of one who is fasting; *dehinaḥ*—the embodied; *rasa-varjam*—except for the taste; *rasaḥ*—the taste; *api*—however; *asya*—his; *param*—the Supreme; *dṛṣṭvā*—by seeing; *nivartate*—loses.

One embodied may fast from feeding the senses, turning away from their objects, but the taste for those objects remains. However, one who does

the same in the course of experiencing a higher taste derived from seeing God loses the very taste for sense objects as well. Thus he remains fixed.

Here Kṛṣṇa advocates the *pramāṇa*, or valid evidence, of experience above all other forms of evidence. Feeling rules our life. This is both our misfortune and good fortune. When this feeling or taste takes one in the direction of animality, one's spiritual life is spoiled. One should be guided by evidence from scripture away from the bestial life of sense indulgence. While scripture sheds light on reality, applying oneself in accordance with its dictates affords one experience. One drop of such experience is more confirming than an ocean of scriptural mandates. At the same time, spiritual experience conforms with that which is described in the scripture, limited though scriptural language is in terms of describing it. Indeed, it is said that spiritual feeling, *bhāva* or *rasa*, in the school of Vraja *bhakti* takes one beyond the reach of scripture.[13]

The word *param* in this verse indicates the Supreme. One who develops a taste *(dṛṣṭvā)* for the Supreme *(param)* is able to forgo the taste for sense indulgence. Viśvanātha Cakravartī comments that here Kṛṣṇa is saying that the experience of the self alone is not sufficient to retire the taste for material life. Direct experience of God is required.

As for the power of the senses, Kṛṣṇa next advises Arjuna not to underestimate them.

Text 60

यततो ह्यपि कौन्तेय पुरुषस्य विपश्चितः ।
इन्द्रियाणि प्रमाथीनि हरन्ति प्रसभं मनः ॥६०॥

yatato hy api kaunteya puruṣasya vipaścitaḥ/
indriyāṇi pramāthīni haranti prasabhaṁ manaḥ//

yatataḥ—of the striving; *hi*—certainly; *api*—even; *kaunteya*—O son of Kuntī; *puruṣasya*—of a man; *vipaścitaḥ*—of discrimination; *indriyāṇi*—the senses; *pramāthīni*—disturbing; *haranti*—carry away; *prasabham*—forcibly; *manaḥ*—the mind.

Indeed, O son of Kuntī, the senses are so strong that they can forcibly carry away the mind of even a discriminating person.

13. See ŚB. 10.47.61.

In this verse Kṛṣṇa hints at the weakness of the path of *jñāna-yoga* when it lacks the support of *bhakti*. *Bhakti* offers spiritual engagement for the senses, whereas the *jñānī* must forgo all sensual activity.

Next Kṛṣṇa underscores that which he has implied all along *(bhakti)* by mentioning himself as the appropriate focal point of *yoga*. In doing so, he identifies himself with the Brahman and Paramātmā features of the Absolute.

Text 61

तानि सर्वाणि संयम्य युक्त आसीत मत्परः ।
वशे हि यस्येन्द्रियाणि तस्य प्रज्ञा प्रतिष्ठिता ॥६१॥

tāni sarvāṇi saṁyamya yukta āsīta mat-paraḥ/
vaśe hi yasyendriyāṇi tasya prajñā pratiṣṭhitā//

tāni—these; *sarvāṇi*—all; *saṁyamya*—restraining; *yuktaḥ*—disciplined; *āsīta*—should sit; *mat-paraḥ*—with me as the highest object; *vaśe*—in subjugation; *hi*—certainly; *yasya*—one whose; *indriyāṇi*—senses; *tasya*—his; *prajñā*—wisdom; *pratiṣṭhitā*—steady.

Restraining the senses and disciplining oneself, one should sit fixing one's consciousness on me. Such a person is known to be steady in wisdom.

The first half of this verse speaks of practice, the second half speaks of perfection. This sitting procedure and other such attendant practices of meditation *(dhyāna)* will be elaborated on in the sixth chapter. Here Kṛṣṇa concludes his answer to Arjuna's question regarding how the enlightened sit.

Madhusūdana Saraswatī acknowledges that Kṛṣṇa says here he is "the Supreme *(paraḥ)*, the most excellent goal to be attained. That is to say, he (the enlightened one) should be absolutely devoted to me." As thieves are subdued by one who takes shelter of a powerful king and ultimately submit to the one who has come under the king's shelter, so the senses are subdued and ultimately submit to the soul who takes shelter of Kṛṣṇa. Thus in the matter of controlling the senses the most important element is fixing one's consciousness on Kṛṣṇa. Although one has to control one's senses to do this, having done so even to a limited degree one can quickly become successful due to the power of the object of devotion, Kṛṣṇa himself, on whom the senses are focused. Thus arbitrary focal points for meditation are not encouraged in the *Gītā*.

For emphasis, to restate his points regarding the path to proper discrimination and enlightened intelligence, Kṛṣṇa continues by stating the reverse sequence of events that leads to the loss of one's power of discrimination. While the *sthita-prajña* is able to control his senses because his mind is controlled, what happens when the mind is left uncontrolled is described next.

Text 62–63

ध्यायतो विषयान् पुंसः सङ्गस्तेषूपजायते ।
सङ्गात् सञ्जायते कामः कामात् क्रोधोऽभिजायते ॥६२॥

क्रोधाद्भवति सम्मोहः सम्मोहात् स्मृतिविभ्रमः ।
स्मृतिभ्रंशाद् बुद्धिनाशो बुद्धिनाशात् प्रणश्यति ॥६३॥

dhyāyato viṣayān puṁsaḥ saṅgas teṣūpajāyate/
saṅgāt sañjāyate kāmaḥ kāmāt krodho 'bhijāyate//
krodhād bhavati sammohaḥ sammohāt smṛti-vibhramaḥ/
smṛti-bhraṁśād buddhi-nāśo buddhi-nāśāt praṇaśyati//

dhyāyataḥ—of contemplating; *viṣayān*—sense objects; *puṁsaḥ*—of a person; *saṅgaḥ*—attachment; *teṣu*—in them; *upajāyate*—is born; *saṅgāt*—from attachment; *sañjāyate*—is born; *kāmaḥ*—desire; *kāmāt*—from desire; *krodhaḥ*—anger; *abhijāyate*—is born; *krodhāt*—from anger; *bhavati*—arises; *sammohaḥ*—illusion; *sammohāt*—from illusion; *smṛti*—memory; *vibhramaḥ*—wandering; *smṛti-bhraṁśāt*—from wandering of memory; *buddhi-nāśaḥ*—destruction of discrimination; *buddhi-nāśāt*—and from loss of discrimination; *praṇaśyati*—one is lost.

When one contemplates the sense objects, attachment for them is born. From attachment, desire is born; from desire, frustration; and from frustration, delusion. When one is deluded, memory is lost; with the loss of memory, the power of discrimination is destroyed; with the destruction of discrimination, one's own self is lost.

The self is lost for one who succumbs to the contemplation of sense objects. The real work of *yoga* is in curbing the mind from such contemplation. If the mind is controlled, one can be peaceful, even when physical circumstances are disturbing. If the physical circumstances are in order but the mind is not peaceful, one cannot be happy.

When the mind contemplates sense objects *(dhyāyato viṣayān)*, fondness for them and attachment *(saṅgaḥ)* to them follow. Thinking the sense objects to be in our interest, we hanker *(kāmaḥ)* for them. When their acquisition is obstructed by something, frustration and anger *(krodhaḥ)* appear. This anger is directed toward that which thwarts our efforts to acquire sense objects. From anger, delusion *(sammohaḥ)* develops, and under its influence one does not know what is to be done and what is not to be done. This is followed by loss of memory *(smṛti-vibhramaḥ)*, in which condition one goes astray from that which is taught in the scripture and instructed by the spiritual preceptor. Thus naturally one does not get the proper understanding and certainty that are characteristic of *buddhi*. Certainty about the nature of ultimate reality does not arise in one who has been dragged down into the maelstrom of desire and destruction. Even if such certainty were to somehow arise, it would not remain constant and thus would not bear the fruit of liberation. Hence, one's self is lost *(praṇaśyati)*.

Kṛṣṇa next begins to answer the fourth part of Arjuna's question regarding the way in which an enlightened person "walks," or interacts with the world. Such a person's mind is controlled while his senses are interacting with sense objects.

Text 64

रागद्वेषवियुक्तैस्तु विषयानिन्द्रियैश्चरन् ।
आत्मवश्यैर्विधेयात्मा प्रसादमधिगच्छति ॥६४॥

rāga-dveṣa-viyuktais tu viṣayān indriyaiś caran/
ātma-vaśyair vidheyātmā prasādam adhigacchati//

rāga—attachment; *dveṣa*—aversion; *viyuktaiḥ*—by one who has become free; *tu*—however; *viṣayān*—sense objects; *indriyaiḥ*—by the senses; *caran*—moving; *ātma-vaśyaiḥ*—by self-control; *vidheya-ātmā*—one who is controlled by the self; *prasādam*—grace; *adhigacchati*—attains.

However, even while moving among the sense objects, the self-controlled one who is free from attachment and aversion, bringing his self under the jurisdiction of God, attains God's grace.

Kṛṣṇa differentiates the person he speaks of in this verse from the person described in the previous verse by the word *tu* (however). The enlightened soul can have healthy interaction with sense objects because his mind is controlled and thus free from attachment *(rāga)* and aversion *(dveṣa)*. When the senses are under the influence of attachment and repulsion for sense objects, interaction with sense objects is a source of misery. Attachment eventually bears the fruit of suffering at the inevitable loss of desirable sense objects, and repulsion for undesirable sense objects is directly a source of suffering when we are in touch with them. When one whose mind is controlled understands the nature of attachment and repulsion, interaction with sense objects is not a cause of suffering. The enlightened soul interacts with sense objects knowing the proprietorship of God. Thus he attains serenity *(prasādam)*, the result of attaining which is discussed in the following verse.

Text 65

प्रसादे सर्वदुःखानां हानिरस्योपजायते ।
प्रसन्नचेतसो ह्याशु बुद्धिः पर्यवतिष्ठते ॥६५॥

prasāde sarva-duḥkhānāṁ hānir asyopajāyate/
prasanna-cetaso hy āśu buddhiḥ paryavatiṣṭhate//

prasāde—in a state of grace; *sarva*—all; *duḥkhānām*—miseries; *hāniḥ*—destruction; *asya*—his; *upajāyate*—is born; *prasanna-cetasaḥ*—of the happy-minded; *hi*—certainly; *āśu*—very soon; *buddhiḥ*—intelligence; *paryavatiṣṭhate*—becomes established.

For the pure-minded, all suffering ceases. Without a doubt, he who has attained purity of mind soon develops steadfast intelligence.

Here and in the previous verse the word *prasāde* (serenity) also means "grace," which implies theistic intervention. Without the intervention of God in one's life true serenity is not possible.

Text 66

नास्ति बुद्धिरयुक्तस्य न चायुक्तस्य भावना ।
न चाभावयतः शान्तिरशान्तस्य कुतः सुखम् ॥६६॥

nāsti buddhir ayuktasya na cāyuktasya bhāvanā/
na cābhāvayataḥ śāntir aśāntasya kutaḥ sukham//

na asti—there is; *buddhiḥ*—intelligence; *ayuktasya*—of one who is not connected; *na*—not; *ca*—and; *ayuktasya*—of one who is not connected;

bhāvanā—meditation; *na*—not; *ca*—and; *abhāvayataḥ*—of one who does not meditate; *śāntiḥ*—peace; *aśāntasya*—of the unpeaceful; *kutaḥ*—where is; *sukham*—happiness.

Unless one is disciplined in yoga, one cannot have clear intelligence. Unless one is so disciplined, one cannot engage in meditation. Without meditation, there is no peace, and how can one have happiness without peace?

As we have seen in verse 61 of this chapter, here Kṛṣṇa is again speaking of fixing the mind on himself. Those whose senses are uncontrolled cannot have knowledge and thus they cannot fix their mind and intelligence on Kṛṣṇa. Such persons cannot have peace, and without peace of mind there is no question of real happiness.

People think happiness comes from sense indulgence, but it is not true. Happiness can only come after controlling the senses. When the senses are controlled, the mind becomes pure, and then one can think of God with steady intelligence and engage in meditation. Only by such meditation in devotion can one attain enlightened life and real happiness. Kṛṣṇa next illustrates his point by citing an example. He wants to demonstrate how failure to concentrate one's mind on him results in spiritual disaster.

Text 67

इन्द्रियाणां हि चरतां यन्मनोऽनुविधीयते ।
तदस्य हरति प्रज्ञां वायुर्नावमिवाम्भसि ॥६७॥

indriyāṇāṁ hi caratāṁ yan mano 'nuvidhīyate/
tad asya harati prajñāṁ vāyur nāvam ivāmbhasi//

indriyāṇām—of the senses; *hi*—certainly; *caratām*—of roving; *yat*—which; *manaḥ*—the mind; *anuvidhīyate*—is guided; *tat*—that; *asya*—his; *harati*—takes away; *prajñām*—intelligence; *vāyuḥ*—wind; *nāvam*—a ship; *iva*—like; *ambhasi*—on the water.

Whichever of the roving senses the mind runs after, that sense carries away one's intelligence, just as the wind carries away a ship on water.

This verse states that if the demands of even one of the senses is pursued, such pursuit steals away one's hopes for enlightenment. All commentators have understood it in this way. Accordingly, *yat* in this verse has been rendered "whichever." Whichever of the wandering senses the mind runs after, this one sense carries away one's intelligence. How much more is this the case if the mind runs after all of the senses! This understanding of the verse is further evidenced by the following verse in which Kṛṣṇa says that only complete withdrawal of the senses brings about enlightenment.

Text 68

तस्माद्यस्य महाबाहो निगृहीतानि सर्वशः ।
इन्द्रियाणीन्द्रियार्थेभ्यस्तस्य प्रज्ञा प्रतिष्ठिता ॥६८॥

tasmād yasya mahā-bāho nigṛhītāni sarvaśaḥ/
indriyāṇīndriyārthebhyas tasya prajñā pratiṣṭhitā//

tasmāt—therefore; *yasya*—whose; *mahā-bāho*—O mighty-armed one; *nigṛhītāni*—withdraws; *sarvaśaḥ*—completely; *indriyāṇi*—the senses; *indriya-arthebhyaḥ*—from sense objects; *tasya*—his; *prajñā*—wisdom; *pratiṣṭhitā*—fixed.

Therefore, O mighty-armed, one who completely withdraws his senses from sense objects is fixed in wisdom.

Here Kṛṣṇa reasons that he who is mighty-armed (*mahā-bāho*) in battle should also be so with regard to controlling the senses. One who completely withdraws his senses in the manner described in the preceding verses becomes spiritually powerful. *Sarvaśaḥ* (all, completely) in this verse is used to include the mind along with the senses. Here Kṛṣṇa speaks about the need of the practitioner.

In response to this verse Arjuna has a doubt. Why is it that we never see anyone in this world who fits the above description? In reply Kṛṣṇa explains the experience of the more accomplished transcendentalist.

Text 69

या निशा सर्वभूतानां तस्यां जागर्ति संयमी ।
यस्यां जाग्रति भूतानि सा निशा पश्यतो मुनेः ॥६९॥

yā niśā sarva-bhūtānāṁ tasyāṁ jāgarti saṁyamī/
yasyāṁ jāgrati bhūtāni sā niśā paśyato muneḥ//

yā—what; *niśā*—night; *sarva*—all; *bhūtānām*—of sentient beings; *tasyām*—in that; *jāgarti*—is wakeful; *saṁyamī*—the self-controlled; *yasyām*—in which; *jāgrati*—are awake; *bhūtāni*—sentient beings; *sā*—that; *niśā*—night; *paśyataḥ*—for the introspective; *muneḥ*—for the sage.

That which is night for all sentient beings is like day for one whose senses are controlled. That which is the time of awakening for a sentient being is like the night for the introspective sage who sees.

Since we never see anyone in this world whose senses are not functioning on some level, how can the complete sensual withdrawal mentioned in the previous verse be possible? Śrīdhara Swāmī raises this question in his introductory remarks to the present verse. Here Kṛṣṇa explains more clearly the experience of the enlightened soul. He sees, and so on, but his seeing is different than that of the ordinary person. Just as an owl sees during the night and is blind during the daylight hours, so also one who has realized God sees only God and his service in this world and not the objects of sense enjoyment.

Because the enlightened soul remains neutral in relation to happiness and distress he appears to be asleep. In reality he is awake to the true nature of these polar opposites, and thus he alone in this world is alert. Others, while awake to happiness and distress—their lives centered on attaining the former and avoiding the latter—are asleep to the underlying reality of life.

Text 70

आपूर्यमाणमचलप्रतिष्ठं समुद्रमापः प्रविशन्ति यद्वत् ।
तद्वत् कामा यं प्रविशन्ति सर्वे स शान्तिमाप्नोति न कामकामी ॥७०॥

āpūryamāṇam acala-pratiṣṭhaṁ samudram āpaḥ praviśanti yadvat/
tadvat kāmā yaṁ praviśanti sarve sa śāntim āpnoti na kāma-kāmī//

āpūryamāṇam—being filled; *acala-pratiṣṭham*—remaining still; *samudram*—the ocean; *āpaḥ*—waters; *praviśanti*—enter; *yadvat*—as; *tadvat*—so; *kāmāḥ*—desires; *yam*—whom; *praviśanti*—enter; *sarve*—all; *saḥ*—that person; *śāntim*—peace; *āpnoti*—achieves; *na*—not; *kāma-kāmī*—one who desires to fulfill desires.

As the ocean remains still even while rivers enter into it, he who remains unmoved in spite of all desires attains peace, not he who strives to fulfill such desires.

Text 71

विहाय कामान्यः सर्वान् पुमांश्चरति निस्पृहः ।
निर्ममो निरहंकारः स शान्तिमधिगच्छति ॥७१॥

vihāya kāmān yaḥ sarvān pumāṁś carati niḥspṛhaḥ/
nirmamo nirahaṅkāraḥ sa śāntim adhigacchati//

vihāya—abandoning; *kāmān*—desires for sense indulgence; *yaḥ*—who; *sarvān*—all; *pumān*—a person; *carati*—lives; *niḥspṛhaḥ*—free from desire; *nirmamaḥ*—without a sense of proprietorship; *nirahaṅkāraḥ*—without egotism; *saḥ*—he; *śāntim*—peace; *adhigacchati*—attains.

A person who has abandoned all desires for sense indulgence acts free from desire. Indifferent to proprietorship and free from egotism, he attains peace.

Here Kṛṣṇa concludes his answer to the fourth part of Arjuna's first principal question, as to how the enlightened move in this world. Next he makes a concluding remark indicating further the goal of spiritual life.

Text 72

एषा ब्राह्मी स्थितिः पार्थ नैनां प्राप्य विमुह्यति ।
स्थित्वास्यामन्तकालेऽपि ब्रह्मनिर्वाणमृच्छति ॥७२॥

eṣā brāhmī sthitiḥ pārtha naināṁ prāpya vimuhyati/
sthitvāsyām anta-kāle 'pi brahma-nirvāṇam ṛcchati//

eṣā—this; *brāhmī*—divine; *sthitiḥ*—state; *pārtha*—O Pārtha; *na*—never; *enām*—this; *prāpya*—having attained; *vimuhyati*—one is deluded; *sthitvā*—being situated; *asyām*—in this; *anta-kāle*—at the moment of death; *api*—even; *brahma-nirvāṇam*—the spiritual consciousness; *ṛcchati*—one attains.

O Pārtha, having attained this divine state one is not deluded; if one is fixed in this consciousness even at the moment of death, one attains Brahman and the cessation of all suffering.

Having attained enlightenment, there can be no recurrence of ignorance (*vimuhyati*). Here Kṛṣṇa describes the enlightened condition as *brahma-nirvāṇa*. The word *nirvāṇa* is distinctly Buddhist, although it is also found in some of the later *Upaniṣads*. Here Kṛṣṇa includes it within Brahman.

Literally *nirvāṇa* means to "blow out," as one does a candle to extinguish its light. The word has a negative connotation, and thus Buddhism has sometimes been considered a negative form of spirituality. It is negative, however, in a positive way. Its goal is to negate the suffering that it considers the world to consist of.

Cessation of suffering is also concomitant to the goal of the *Gītā*, and thus all that is included in *nirvāṇa* is within Kṛṣṇa's general conception of enlightenment. Brahman is, as will become apparent in later chapters, an aspect of Kṛṣṇa. It is not the complete expression of divinity, which is Bhagavān Kṛṣṇa himself. At this point in the *Gītā*, Kṛṣṇa has not entirely revealed everything that the fully enlightened state of God consciousness includes, although he has hinted at it (Bg. 2.59, 2.61, 2.64).

In the next chapter Kṛṣṇa will elaborate on dutiful action and action informed by knowledge, and in chapter 4 he will discuss the wisdom that is the fruit of such informed action. In chapter 5 Kṛṣṇa uses the word *nirvāṇa* three times (Bg. 5.24–26) in the course of elaborating on the enlightened condition of *samādhi* that he has explained in this concluding section of chapter 2 (Bg. 2.55–72). In each of these verses Kṛṣṇa calls the enlightened condition *brahma-nirvāṇa*. However, he ends chapter 5 by placing realization of himself within the equation of enlightenment (Bg. 5.29) when he says that the peace of enlightenment *(śāntiḥ)* is attained quickly by acknowledging himself as the ideal of the *jñānīs* (Brahman), the *yogīs* (Paramātmā), and his devotees (Bhagavān).

In chapter 6, which involves an extended discussion of the spiritual practices of *yoga* that lead to enlightenment, Kṛṣṇa elaborates further on the enlightened condition by including realization of the Paramātmā feature of the Absolute within it, *paramātmā samāhitaḥ* (Bg. 6.7). In the same section of chapter 6 (Bg. 6.15), he reveals that the enlightened state of yogic attainment includes the supremely peaceful cessation of material existence in Brahman *(śāntiṁ nirvāṇa-paramām)*, which is contained within realization of his person (*mat-saṁsthām*/Bhagavān). He concludes chapter 6 by calling the *yoga* of devotion *(bhakti)* the highest expression of *yoga*. This is the *yoga* that corresponds with the *Gītā*'s full sense of enlightenment—God-realization. Thus within this concluding section of chapter 2, Kṛṣṇa's description of the enlightened person refers ultimately to his devotee.

CHAPTER THREE

कर्मयोगः
Karma-yoga

YOGA OF ACTION

Text 1

अर्जुन उवाच
ज्यायसी चेत् कर्मणस्ते मता बुद्धिर्जनार्दन ।
तत् किं कर्मणि घोरे मां नियोजयसि केशव ॥१॥

arjuna uvāca
jyāyasī cet karmaṇas te matā buddhir janārdana/
tat kiṁ karmaṇi ghore māṁ niyojayasi keśava//

arjunaḥ uvāca—Arjuna said; *jyāyasī*—better; *cet*—if; *karmaṇaḥ*—than action; *te*—your; *matā*—opinion; *buddhiḥ*—intelligence; *janārdana*—O Janārdana; *tat*—then; *kim*—why; *karmaṇi*—in action; *ghore*—horrible; *mām*—me; *niyojayasi*—you are engaging; *keśava*—O Keśava.

If in your opinion, O Janārdana, knowledge is superior to action, then why, O Keśava, are you engaging me in this horrible action?

Arjuna's confusion with regard to Kṛṣṇa's apparent simultaneous advocacy of action and knowledge appears in seed form in the previous chapter. In verse 38 of chapter 2 Kṛṣṇa tells Arjuna to fight after having explained to him the wisdom of the soul and the fact that no one kills or is killed. Arjuna's doubt is addressed in the subsequent verse, but not such that it is removed. Indeed, Kṛṣṇa's apparent advocacy of *bhakti* therein only adds to Arjuna's confusion. At the onset of chapter 3 the seed of Arjuna's lingering doubt blossoms in the first two verses.

Arjuna's question arises from the fact that first and foremost he is a devotee of Kṛṣṇa, and thus has no interest in either the path of action or knowledge. Although his awareness of his status as a devotee has been somewhat suppressed by Kṛṣṇa's arrangement, giving rise to apparent ignorance, it has not been lost, and therefore it surfaces here as it does in other places throughout the *Gītā*. Thus here Arjuna addresses Kṛṣṇa as Janārdana. By this address he says to Kṛṣṇa, "O you who are petitioned *(ardana)* by all persons *(jana)* for the fulfillment of their desires, I too pray to you that I might know what is best for me." Viśvanātha Cakravartī adds that the epithet Janārdana has another meaning. Arjuna intimates that Kṛṣṇa makes his friends *(jana)* suffer *(ardana)* by giving them painful orders of this type. However, by then addressing him as Keśava, Arjuna immediately admits that no living being can ignore Kṛṣṇa's desire, for even Brahmā *(ka)* and Śiva *(īśa)* are under his thrall *(va,* from *vaśa)*.

Arjuna wonders why Kṛṣṇa has urged him to engage in such an unpalatable action as killing his relatives and even his gurus if knowledge is superior to action. He says, *tat kiṁ karmaṇi ghore mām*, "Then why are you engaging me in this horrible action?" implying through the word *mām* (me), "who am your devotee and thus not even interested in the path of knowledge, much less that of *karma*."

Madhusūdana Saraswatī also acknowledges Arjuna's underlying devotional sentiment. He hears him saying, "O Keśava, Lord of all, it does not befit you who are the fulfiller of all desires to deceive me, a devotee, who has approached you as the sole refuge." Thus Arjuna wonders that if *jñāna*, or knowledge of the self, is the ideal, and more so *bhakti*, why should he engage in battle as Kṛṣṇa has instructed him?

Kṛṣṇa's response to Arjuna's confusion beginning with the third verse of this chapter is an elaboration on the efficacy of *niṣkāma-karma-yoga*, the principal subject of this chapter.

Text 2

व्यामिश्रेणेव वाक्येन बुद्धिं मोहयसीव मे ।
तदेकं वद निश्चित्य येन श्रेयोऽहमाप्नुयाम् ॥२॥

vyāmiśreṇeva vākyena buddhiṁ mohayasīva me/
tad ekaṁ vada niścitya yena śreyo 'ham āpnuyām//

vyāmiśreṇa—by equivocal; *iva*—like; *vākyena*—with speech; *buddhim*—intelligence; *mohayasi*—you are confusing; *iva*—like; *me*—my; *tat*—therefore; *ekam*—one; *vada*—tell; *niścitya*—without doubt; *yena*—by which; *śreyaḥ*—the highest good; *aham*—I; *āpnuyām*—should attain.

With speech that seems equivocal, you have confused my intelligence. Therefore, please tell me clearly by which path I will attain the highest good.

Here Arjuna qualifies his question in the previous verse by stating that he finds no fault in Kṛṣṇa. It is not Kṛṣṇa's instructions that are faulty or confusing; they only *seem (iva)* so to Arjuna, who submissively asks for clarification.

In the previous verse we saw that Arjuna is predisposed toward devotion such that the paths of action and knowledge are unattractive to him. Here, however, his question is centered on eligibility. It seems contradictory for a person to be eligible for action and knowledge at the same time: If a person is not eligible for the path of knowledge, he must tread the path of action until he acquires the requisite purity of heart which makes him eligible for contemplative life. If a person is eligible for contemplative life, he has nothing to do with the path of action. As Kṛṣṇa will gradually reveal in this chapter, while knowledge is the goal of the path of action, it must be attained through the path of action and not prematurely adopted through an intellectual sleight of hand. The solution to Arjuna's dilemma lies in understanding the secret of inaction within action that is the heart of *karma-yoga* and ultimately in treading the path of devotion.

In speaking about action in knowledge and knowledge itself, Kṛṣṇa is subtly advocating one thing: devotion to himself as it is cultured by persons in developmental stages from *karma-yoga*, for those whose minds are not yet pure, to *jñāna-yoga*, for those whose hearts are free from material desire. However, at this point in his discourse, Kṛṣṇa overtly emphasizes only self-realization actuated through *karma-yoga* and fructifying in *jñāna-yoga*.

Kṛṣṇa looks lovingly at Arjuna, who is so pure as to be intimately involved with Kṛṣṇa as his dear friend, yet by Kṛṣṇa's arrangement has been placed in a mystical illusion so that Kṛṣṇa could speak to human society through his dearmost friend. Kṛṣṇa thought, "Arjuna is thinking that I have talked about two different things, but in fact I have spoken only about one thing approached by different persons in different stages of devotional culture. Arjuna's real interest is in pure devotion, not *karma* or *jñāna*, but I have only spoken about that indirectly, emphasizing for now detached work culminating in knowledge. Being my devotee, it is no wonder that he is hesitating."

Text 3

श्रीभगवानुवाच
लोकेऽस्मिन्द्विविधा निष्ठा पुरा प्रोक्ता मयानघ ।
ज्ञानयोगेन सांख्यानां कर्मयोगेन योगिनाम् ॥३॥

śrī-bhagavān uvāca
loke 'smin dvi-vidhā niṣṭhā purā proktā mayānagha/
jñāna-yogena sāṅkhyānāṁ karma-yogena yogināṁ//

śrī-bhagavān uvāca—the Lord of Śrī said; *loke*—in the world; *asmin*—this; *dvi-vidhā*—two kinds of; *niṣṭhā*—faith; *purā*—formerly; *proktā*—were said; *mayā*—by me; *anagha*—O sinless one; *jñāna-yogena*—by the linking process of knowledge; *sāṅkhyānām*—of the empirical philosophers; *karma-yogena*—by the linking process of action; *yoginām*—of the devotees.

The Lord of Śrī said: O sinless one, as I have explained previously, in this world there is a twofold basis of devotion, that of knowledge for contemplatives and action for yogīs.

The word *niṣṭhā* in this verse literally means steadiness, basis, or attachment. It is in the singular, for Kṛṣṇa is speaking about only one type of steadiness. This steadiness is derived from the controlled mind and knowledge of the self, which underlies a life of devotion proper. The *jñānī* achieves this through contemplation and the *karma-yogī* approaches it through detached action. Rūpa Goswāmī has used the term *niṣṭhā* to refer to steadiness in devotion, and in Winthrop Sargeant's translation of this verse, *niṣṭhā* is rendered as "twofold basis (of devotion)." This fits well with the direction in which Kṛṣṇa is taking Arjuna. One who is steady in detached action attains steadiness of mind. One who is steady in mind attains steadiness in knowledge, and one steady in knowledge can attain devotion proper. If one expects to attain devotion proper, one must in due course control the mind and acquire knowledge of the self.

Indicating that in his present condition Arjuna was not suited for a life of contemplation, Kṛṣṇa advises him further regarding the relative superiority of *karma-yoga* over *jñāna-yoga*. The sense in which the word *yoga* is joined with both *jñāna* and *karma* is this: *jñāna* is *yoga* because through knowledge one is united with the Absolute. *Karma* is *yoga* because through detached action one's mind becomes purified and thus the possibility of attaining knowledge of the self arises. Without a purified mind, one cannot assume to be qualified for contemplative life. Kṛṣṇa thus stresses that the desired purity arises out of proper action.

Text 4

न कर्मणामनारम्भान्नैष्कर्म्यं पुरुषोऽश्नुते ।
न च सन्न्यसनादेव सिद्धिं समधिगच्छति ॥४॥

na karmaṇām anārambhān naiṣkarmyaṁ puruṣo 'śnute/
na ca sannyasanād eva siddhiṁ samadhigacchati//

na—not; *karmaṇām*—of prescribed action; *anārambhāt*—by abstaining; *naiṣkarmyam*—state beyond reaction; *puruṣaḥ*—a man; *aśnute*—attains; *na*—nor; *ca*—also; *sannyasanāt*—by renunciation; *eva*—alone; *siddhim*—perfection; *samadhigacchati*—attains perfection.

Not merely by abstaining from prescribed action can one attain the state beyond action, nor by renunciation alone can one attain perfection.

There can be no result without a cause. Therefore Kṛṣṇa says that abstaining from prescribed duties *(anārambhāt)*, which are the cause of purification and subsequently the self-knowledge that delivers one from karmic action, will not bring the desired result of self-knowledge. As for renunciation *(sannyāsa)* without prior purification, such artificial renunciation is fruitless.

Beginning with this verse Kṛṣṇa elaborates over the next six verses on the necessity of purification through action. Unless one's heart is pure, one should engage in *karma-yoga*, for knowledge will not arise from artificial renunciation in an impure heart. Action in accordance with scriptural injunctions brings about purification of the heart. This is especially so when scripturally enjoined action is performed without attachment to enjoying the result for oneself—*niṣkāma-karma-yoga*.

Text 5

न हि कश्चित् क्षणमपि जातु तिष्ठत्यकर्मकृत् ।
कार्यते ह्यवशः कर्म सर्वः प्रकृतिजैर्गुणैः ॥५॥

na hi kaścit kṣaṇam api jātu tiṣṭhaty akarma-kṛt/
kāryate hy avaśaḥ karma sarvaḥ prakṛti-jair guṇaiḥ//

na—nor; *hi*—indeed; *kaścit*—anyone; *kṣaṇam*—a moment; *api*—even; *jātu*—at any time; *tiṣṭhati*—remains; *akarma-kṛt*—free from action; *kāryate*—

is forced to do; *hi*—certainly; *avaśaḥ*—against will; *karma*—work; *sarvaḥ*—all; *prakṛti-jaiḥ*—born of the material nature; *guṇaiḥ*—by the *guṇas*.

Indeed, no one, even for the twinkling of an eye, remains free from action. All people are forced to act even against their own will under the influence of the guṇas born of material nature.

Owing to lack of purification, which manifests in the form of material desire, common persons are forced to act under the influence of the *guṇas* of material nature. Such persons cannot artificially take to monastic life, for material nature will force them to act contrary to that which is appropriate for monasticism. To enter contemplative life, one must be sufficiently situated in the material *guṇa* of *sattva* through acts of purification. Although *sattva* is also a material influence, it begets knowledge (see Bg. 14.6).

Text 6

कर्मेन्द्रियाणि संयम्य य आस्ते मनसा स्मरन् ।
इन्द्रियार्थान्विमूढात्मा मिथ्याचारः स उच्यते ॥६॥

karmendriyāṇi saṁyamya ya āste manasā smaran/
indriyārthān vimūḍhātmā mithyācāraḥ sa ucyate//

karma-indriyāṇi—the five working sense organs; *saṁyamya*—restraining; *yaḥ*—one who; *āste*—sits; *manasā*—by the mind; *smaran*—remembering; *indriya-arthān*—sense objects; *vimūḍha*—deluded; *ātmā*—self; *saḥ*—he; *mithyā-ācāraḥ*—hypocrite; *ucyate*—is called.

A person who sits restraining his working senses while contemplating sense objects deludes himself and is called a hypocrite.

Should a person renounce artificially and by force restrain his senses from contact with sense objects, his mind will nevertheless continue to contemplate those sense objects.

Text 7

यस्त्विन्द्रियाणि मनसा नियम्यारभतेऽर्जुन ।
कर्मेन्द्रियैः कर्मयोगमसक्तः स विशिष्यते ॥७॥

yas tv indriyāṇi manasā niyamyārabhate 'rjuna/
karmendriyaiḥ karma-yogam asaktaḥ sa viśiṣyate//

yaḥ—one who; *tu*—however; *indriyāṇi*—the senses; *manasā*—by the mind; *niyamya*—controlling; *ārabhate*—begins; *arjuna*—O Arjuna; *karma-indriyaiḥ*—by the working senses; *karma-yogam*—*karma-yoga*; *asaktaḥ*—without attachment; *saḥ*—he; *viśiṣyate*—is superior.

However, one who begins to control the senses by the mind, O Arjuna, and without attachment engages his working senses in karma-yoga is superior.

Kṛṣṇa's advocacy of pure action over artificial renunciation should appeal to those inspired by the concept of enlightened activism. Social activism is a rudimentary form of selfless action, and although in today's world it is not embarked on in consideration of scriptural mandates, it does embrace the spirit of scriptural law. Although monasticism is superior in that it is possible only after one has been sufficiently purified from material desire, it is not superior for those unqualified for it. One person's food is another's poison. Lack of appreciation for the monastic order stems primarily from the fact that unqualified persons have adopted it as a means to circumvent the actual work involved in purifying the heart.

Text 8

नियतं कुरु कर्म त्वं कर्म ज्यायो ह्यकर्मणः ।
शरीरयात्रापि च ते न प्रसिद्ध्येदकर्मणः ॥८॥

niyataṁ kuru karma tvaṁ karma jyāyo hy akarmaṇaḥ/
śarīra-yātrāpi ca te na prasiddhyed akarmaṇaḥ//

niyatam—prescribed; *kuru*—do; *karma*—action; *tvam*—you; *karma*—work; *jyāyaḥ*—better; *hi*—certainly; *akarmaṇaḥ*—than inaction; *śarīra*—body; *yātrā*—maintenance; *api*—even; *ca*—also; *te*—your; *na*—not; *prasiddhyet*—should be accomplished; *akarmaṇaḥ*—without action.

Perform your prescribed duty, for doing so is better than inaction. One cannot even maintain one's body without action.

Even contemplatives must act to gather the needs of their bodies. In saying this, Kṛṣṇa drives his point home: Arjuna should act (in this case fight) and not withdraw to a contemplative life. He is a warrior and should not adopt begging, the ordained activity of monastics, for his livelihood.

Text 9

यज्ञार्थात् कर्मणोऽन्यत्र लोकोऽयं कर्मबन्धनः ।
तदर्थं कर्म कौन्तेय मुक्तसङ्गः समाचर ॥९॥

yajñārthāt karmaṇo 'nyatra loko 'yaṁ karma-bandhanaḥ/
tad-arthaṁ karma kaunteya mukta-saṅgaḥ samācara//

yajña-arthāt—for the purpose of sacrifice; *karmaṇaḥ*—than action; *anyatra*—other than; *lokaḥ*—world; *ayam*—this; *karma-bandhanaḥ*—binding by action; *tat*—of him; *artham*—for the sake; *karma*—action; *kaunteya*—O son of Kuntī; *mukta-saṅgaḥ*—free from attachment; *samācara*—perform.

Other than action performed for the purpose of sacrifice, all action in this world is binding. Act in sacrifice for the satisfaction of God, O son of Kuntī, without being attached to enjoying the results.

With this verse Kṛṣṇa concludes his instruction on selfless *karma-yoga*. He says that action is binding unless it is performed as an act of sacrifice. It is said, *yajño vai viṣṇuḥ*, "Viṣṇu himself is sacrifice." Baladeva Vidyābhūṣaṇa comments further, "One can only worship the Lord in sacrifice with goods that have been acquired honestly; then one's material needs can be met as a by-product of such sacrifices."

At the onset of this chapter, Arjuna considered that if knowledge is better than action, why should he act in battle? After Kṛṣṇa's emphatic answer and clear advocacy of selfless action as the prerequisite to knowledge, Arjuna, humbled, mentally questions his eligibility even for a life of *karma-yoga*. After all, even this is not for the common person. Addressing this in the following seven verses, Kṛṣṇa describes the course for those not yet qualified to engage in selfless action.

Text 10

सहयज्ञाः प्रजाः सृष्ट्वा पुरोवाच प्रजापतिः ।
अनेन प्रसविष्यध्वमेष वोऽस्त्विष्टकामधुक् ॥१०॥

saha-yajñāḥ prajāḥ sṛṣṭvā purovāca prajāpatiḥ/
anena prasaviṣyadhvam eṣa vo 'stv iṣṭa-kāma-dhuk//

saha—along with; *yajñāḥ*—sacrifices; *prajāḥ*—humanity; *sṛṣṭvā*—having created; *purā*—previously; *uvāca*—said; *prajā-patiḥ*—progenitor; *anena*—by this; *prasaviṣyadhvam*—may you go forth and prosper; *eṣaḥ*—this; *vaḥ*—your; *astu*—let it be; *iṣṭa-kāma-dhuk*—wish-fulfilling cow of plenty.

Having created humanity along with sacrifice, the progenitor said at the beginning of creation, "By this (sacrifice) you shall attain all things; may such sacrifice be your wish-fulfilling cow of plenty."

Here, as well as in the following two verses, Kṛṣṇa quotes the progenitor (*prajāpatiḥ*), whom Baladeva Vidyābhūṣaṇa identifies with Viṣṇu based on *śruti* references and Viśvanātha Cakravartī Ṭhākura identifies with Brahmā.

In this section Kṛṣṇa speaks about the duty of those who remain attached to the fruits of their work, as well as about the principle of sacrifice and its efficacy. Those who cannot live a life of *karma-yoga* should regularly perform religious sacrifices in conjunction with important events such as marriage and childbirth. In this way, their desires will be fulfilled by the cosmic arrangement, and they will have acknowledged their dependence on God and regulated their senses accordingly.

Here Kṛṣṇa speaks of the proper way to approach the Vedic rituals, the abuse of which he condemned earlier when first speaking to Arjuna of the *Vedas* and their rituals (Bg. 2.42–46). Those who are not qualified to practice *karma-yoga* must begin to regulate their senses by performing acts of sacrifice, thereby acknowledging the cosmic order. Indeed, they must embrace sacrifice itself as the way of progressive life and honor the various manifestations of the divine in nature.

Text 11

देवान् भावयतानेन ते देवा भावयन्तु वः ।
परस्परं भावयन्तः श्रेयः परमवाप्स्यथ ॥११॥

devān bhāvayatānena te devā bhāvayantu vaḥ/
parasparaṁ bhāvayantaḥ śreyaḥ param avāpsyatha//

devān—gods; *bhāvayata*—may you please; *anena*—by this; *te*—they; *devāḥ*—gods; *bhāvayantu*—will please; *vaḥ*—you; *parasparam*—mutually; *bhāvayantaḥ*—pleasing; *śreyaḥ*—good; *param*—greatest; *avāpsyatha*—you will attain.

By sacrifice you will satisfy the gods, who in turn will satisfy you. By this mutual arrangement, you shall attain the greatest good.

The gods include the deities that preside over the senses. For each of our sensual functions there is a corresponding aspect of nature that the senses' functions depend on. The personification of these aspects of nature are the gods under discussion. They represent the conscious principle behind all the functions of nature. For example, our eyes are not independent in their capacity to afford us vision. They depend on light, the source of which is the sun. The sacrifice mentioned in this verse refers to acknowledging our dependence on these presiding deities. This helps us realize that we are not independent, but rather part of an interdependent system in which humanity and nature flourish in the culture of God consciousness. This gradual culture leads to the ultimate good for all concerned.

Text 12

इष्टान् भोगान् हि वो देवा दास्यन्ते यज्ञभाविताः ।
तैर्दत्तानप्रदायैभ्यो यो भुंक्ते स्तेन एव सः ॥१२॥

iṣṭān bhogān hi vo devā dāsyante yajña-bhāvitāḥ/
tair dattān apradāyaibhyo yo bhuṅkte stena eva saḥ//

iṣṭān—desired; *bhogān*—enjoyments; *hi*—certainly; *vaḥ*—to you; *devāḥ*—the gods; *dāsyante*—will bestow; *yajña-bhāvitāḥ*—nourished by the sacrifice; *taiḥ*—by them; *dattān*—gifts; *apradāya*—without offering; *ebhyaḥ*—to them; *yaḥ*—he who; *bhuṅkte*—enjoys; *stenaḥ*—thief; *eva*—certainly; *saḥ*—he.

The gods, nourished by sacrifice, will certainly bestow the fulfillment of your desires. However, one who enjoys the gods' natural gifts without acknowledging the gods themselves is a thief.

False proprietorship is the basic misconception of our material lives. If we do not acknowledge our indebtedness to others, we are criminals. The debt incurred from enjoying the bounty of nature must be acknowledged and repaid. This is the principle of sacrifice. In our everyday modern experience we must acknowledge the municipality for our supply of heat, light, water, and so on. If we do not do so by paying our monthly bills, we break the law. Similarly, there is a cosmic order that must be acknowledged by human society.

Text 13

यज्ञशिष्टाशिनः सन्तो मुच्यन्ते सर्वकिल्बिषैः ।
भुञ्जते ते त्वघं पापा ये पचन्त्यात्मकारणात् ॥१३॥

yajña-śiṣṭāśinaḥ santo mucyante sarva-kilbiṣaiḥ/
bhuñjate te tv aghaṁ pāpā ye pacanty ātma-kāraṇāt//

yajña-śiṣṭa—of food taken after performance of *yajña; aśinaḥ*—eaters; *santaḥ*—the saintly; *mucyante*—are released; *sarva*—all; *kilbiṣaiḥ*—from evil; *bhuñjate*—enjoy; *te*—they; *tu*—but; *agham*—impurity; *pāpāḥ*—wicked; *ye*—who; *pacanti*—prepare food; *ātma-kāraṇāt*—for themselves.

The saintly, who even while eating perform sacrifice by offering food and then eating the remnants, are released from all evil. The wicked, who cook only for themselves, eat only impurities.

Here Kṛṣṇa cites the common act of eating as an example of how far-reaching the principle of sacrifice is for human society. The very act of eating should be one of sacrifice. Enjoyment is truly only that which is the fruit of sacrifice.

The act of "saying grace" before one's meals is the heart of Kṛṣṇa's instruction in this verse. In the strict Vedic sense this verse refers to the means by which the householder is freed from evil acts performed inadvertently. Five types of sacrifice are enjoined for the householder that absolve him from evils committed through five everyday household accessories essential to the householder: the pestle, grinder, oven, water pot, and broom. It is said that on account of these five items the householder does not attain heaven, for their use in household life causes harm to other living beings (insects, etc.). Thus by performing the five sacrifices one counteracts the sins inadvertently committed through these five items. Central to these sacrifices is the offering of food to the gods in the *vaiśvadeva-yajña.*

Taking this verse beyond the scope of the Vedic law to the heart of the principle of sacrifice, Bhaktivedanta Swami Prabhupāda comments that the devotees, who are truly saintly people, are freed from all sins merely by the act of offering all of their food to Kṛṣṇa and partaking of the remnants.

Kṛṣṇa next further explains the system that calls for sacrifice on the part of humanity, thereby connecting humanity with divinity.

Text 14

अन्नाद्भवन्ति भूतानि पर्जन्यादन्नसम्भवः ।
यज्ञाद्भवति पर्जन्यो यज्ञः कर्मसमुद्भवः ॥१४॥

annād bhavanti bhūtāni parjanyād anna-sambhavaḥ/
yajñād bhavati parjanyo yajñaḥ karma-samudbhavaḥ//

annāt—from food; *bhavanti*—subsist; *bhūtāni*—beings; *parjanyāt*—from the rain cloud; *anna*—food; *sambhavaḥ*—product; *yajñāt*—from sacrifice; *bhavati*—becomes possible; *parjanyaḥ*—rain cloud; *yajñaḥ*—sacrifice; *karma*—prescribed duties; *samudbhavaḥ*—born of.

Humanity subsists on food, and food is a product of rain. Rain in turn is a product of sacrifice, and sacrifice is born of prescribed duties and ritual.

Text 15

कर्म ब्रह्मोद्भवं विद्धि ब्रह्माक्षरसमुद्भवम् ।
तस्मात्सर्वगतं ब्रह्म नित्यं यज्ञे प्रतिष्ठितम् ॥१५॥

karma brahmodbhavaṁ viddhi brahmākṣara-samudbhavam/
tasmāt sarva-gataṁ brahma nityaṁ yajñe pratiṣṭhitam//

karma—prescribed duties; *brahma*—the *Vedas; udbhavam*—originating; *viddhi*—know; *brahma*—the *Vedas; akṣara*—imperishable; *samudbhavam*—originating; *tasmāt*—therefore; *sarva-gatam*—all-pervading; *brahma*—the Absolute; *nityam*—eternally; *yajñe*—in sacrifice; *pratiṣṭhitam*—situated.

Ritual and prescribed duties originate from the sacred literature (Vedas), and the sacred literature arises from the imperishable Absolute. Therefore, the all-pervading Absolute is eternally situated in acts of sacrifice.

In verses 15 and 16 Kṛṣṇa says that it is sacrifice that makes the world go 'round. While we often hear that love keeps the world turning on its axis, we do not stop to think that love arises out of sacrifice. Without such introspection one often mistakes selfishness for love, the result of which is that one goes around in confusion as to what the world is really all about.

When food is eaten and transformed into blood and blood into semen, the reproduction of the different species becomes possible. Food is dependent on rain. All of this is understandable to modern society. The idea that rain is produced through sacrifice is not apparent. According to Madhusūdana Saraswatī this science is detailed in the *aṣṭādhyāyī-kāṇḍa* of the *Śatapatha-Brāhmaṇa,* in the section containing six questions in the form of a dialogue between Janaka and Yajñavalkya. Otherwise, it is common knowledge that through sacrifice one gains. It should be clear that sacrifice is enjoined in scripture. Scripture (the *Veda*) is an expression of the Absolute and is that by which the Absolute can be known. It has no human origin, and it is eternally situated in acts of sacrifice.

Text 16

एवं प्रवर्तितं चक्रं नानुवर्तयतीह यः ।
अघायुरिन्द्रियारामो मोघं पार्थ स जीवति ॥१६॥

evaṁ pravartitaṁ cakraṁ nānuvartayatīha yaḥ/
aghāyur indriyārāmo moghaṁ pārtha sa jīvati//

evam—thus; *pravartitam*—set in motion; *cakram*—cycle; *na*—not; *anuvartayati*—causes to turn; *iha*—in this life; *yaḥ*—one who; *agha-āyuḥ*—whose life is full of sins; *indriya-ārāmaḥ*—satisfied in sense pleasure; *mogham*—in vain; *pārtha*—O Pārtha; *saḥ*—he; *jīvati*—lives.

My dear Pārtha, one who in human life does not acknowledge this cycle lives irresponsibly for sense pleasure and thus in vain.

This section beginning with verse 10 and ending with this verse is not merely a mandate for ritualistic offerings to the gods, a magical technique of bargaining with supernatural powers for one's maintenance. Those who think that this is all that Kṛṣṇa is saying miss the deeper implication of his words. In this section Kṛṣṇa advocates sacrifice not as a means, but as the end itself, for he has said that life both begins with sacrifice and is thenceforth meant for further sacrifice. The bounty of life is not a product of chance. It is a result of detached action. Getting is a result of giving; and moreover, giving is getting. Life really consists of effectively and actively surrendering one's own power and resources to a supernatural, personal source.

He who does not follow the system described here as a cycle or wheel *(cakra)* of life would be better off dead, for he would then have the opportunity to do so in the next life. Although he enjoys through the senses and is thus obliged to participate in religious sacrificial rites, he does not do so. His life is most certainly spent in vain.

Kṛṣṇa next contrasts those who are obliged to observe religious injunctions for purification with those who are already purified. In doing so, he elaborates in two verses on the position of the self-satisfied soul, who has no need to engage in purificatory sacrificial rituals.

Text 17

यस्त्वात्मरतिरेव स्यादात्मतृप्तश्च मानवः ।
आत्मन्येव च सन्तुष्टस्तस्य कार्यं न विद्यते ॥१७॥

yas tv ātma-ratir eva syād ātma-tṛptaś ca mānavaḥ/
ātmany eva ca santuṣṭas tasya kāryaṁ na vidyate//

yaḥ—one who; *tu*—but; *ātma-ratiḥ*—taking pleasure in the self; *eva*— certainly; *syāt*—remains; *ātma-tṛptaḥ*—self-satisfied; *ca*—and; *mānavaḥ*—a man; *ātmani*—in the self; *eva*—only; *ca*—and; *santuṣṭaḥ*—content; *tasya*—his; *kāryam*—duty; *na*—not; *vidyate*—exists.

One who takes pleasure in the self, whose satisfaction is derived from the self, and who is content in the self alone has no need to perform duties.

Text 18

नैव तस्य कृतेनार्थो नाकृतेनेह कश्चन ।
न चास्य सर्वभूतेषु कश्चिदर्थव्यपाश्रयः ॥१८॥

naiva tasya kṛtenārtho nākṛteneha kaścana/
na cāsya sarva-bhūteṣu kaścid artha-vyapāśrayaḥ//

na—never; *eva*—certainly; *tasya*—his; *kṛtena*—by acting; *arthaḥ*—gain; *na*—nor; *akṛtena*—by not acting; *iha*—in this world; *kaścana*—anything; *na*—never; *ca*—and; *asya*—of him; *sarva-bhūteṣu*—among all living beings; *kaścit*—any; *artha*—purpose; *vyapāśrayaḥ*—dependent.

He has nothing to gain by acting and nothing to lose by not acting. He needs no one for any purpose.

One who is *ātma-ratiḥ* derives pleasure from the self alone. He has no obligatory work to perform, nor is he dependent on others, either humans or gods. Such a person is in perfect harmony with the aforementioned cosmic order. Having sacrificed his material ego altogether he eventually transcends it.

Arjuna's position is such that he is neither overly attached to material acquisition and thereby in need of petitioning the gods, nor qualified to take up a life of contemplation. His eligibility for spiritual progress lies in between these two paths. Therefore, after having described the course for both the attached person and the one in knowledge, Kṛṣṇa next concludes that Arjuna should perform selfless *karma-yoga*, continuing to drive this point home to his disciple. He advises Arjuna on how he can attain the state of God consciousness he has just described in verses 17 and 18 by engaging in *niṣkāma-karma-yoga*.

Text 19

तस्मादसक्तः सततं कार्यं कर्म समाचर ।
असक्तो ह्याचरन् कर्म परमाप्नोति पूरुषः ॥१९॥

tasmād asaktaḥ satataṁ kāryaṁ karma samācara/
asakto hy ācaran karma param āpnoti pūruṣaḥ//

tasmāt—therefore; *asaktaḥ*—without attachment; *satatam*—constantly; *kāryam*—as duty; *karma*—action; *samācara*—perform; *asaktaḥ*—unattached; *hi*—certainly; *ācaran*—performing; *karma*—action; *param*—the Supreme; *āpnoti*—achieves; *pūruṣaḥ*—a man.

Therefore, without attachment to the fruits of your work, constantly engage in your duty as a warrior, for by acting without attachment one attains God consciousness.

Arjuna wonders if there are any examples of persons who attained God consciousness by *karma-yoga*. Thus Kṛṣṇa next cites the example of other warriors who attained success through action.

Text 20

कर्मणैव हि संसिद्धिमास्थिता जनकादयः ।
लोकसंग्रहमेवापि सम्पश्यन् कर्तुमर्हसि ॥२०॥

karmaṇaiva hi saṁsiddhim āsthitā janakādayaḥ/
loka-saṅgraham evāpi sampaśyan kartum arhasi//

karmaṇā—by action; *eva*—even; *hi*—certainly; *saṁsiddhim*—perfection; *āsthitāḥ*—attained; *janaka-ādayaḥ*—Janaka and other kings; *loka-saṅgraham*—the people in general; *eva api*—also; *sampaśyan*—considering; *kartum*—to act; *arhasi*—you should.

Janaka and other kings attained perfection by proper action alone. Thus, in consideration of the people in general, you should take to proper action.

Here Kṛṣṇa offers still another reason in support of detached action over contemplative life: setting an example for others. A great person like Arjuna certainly does have some obligation to the masses with regard to his personal example. Kṛṣṇa cites the example of Janaka and others, who were warriors like Arjuna. They were successful by means of detached action rather than renunciation of action altogether. Whether one is a seeker of knowledge or situated in knowledge, Kṛṣṇa advises that one should set a proper example.

Text 21

यद्यदाचरति श्रेष्ठस्तत्तदेवेतरो जनः ।
स यत् प्रमाणं कुरुते लोकस्तदनुवर्तते ॥२१॥

yad yad ācarati śreṣṭhas tat tad evetaro janaḥ/
sa yat pramāṇaṁ kurute lokas tad anuvartate//

yat yat—whatever; *ācarati*—does; *śreṣṭhaḥ*—best; *tat*—that; *tat*—that; *eva*—certainly; *itaraḥ*—the other; *janaḥ*—person; *saḥ*—he; *yat*—whichever; *pramāṇam*—standard; *kurute*—perform; *lokaḥ*—all the world; *tat*—that; *anuvartate*—follows in the footsteps.

Whatever a great man does, the world follows. Whatever standards he sets, the world pursues.

Kṛṣṇadāsa Kavirāja Goswāmī cites this verse in *Caitanya-caritāmṛta.*[1] Gauḍīya Vaiṣṇavas consider Śrī Caitanya to be Kṛṣṇa himself, who in desiring others to love him in the intimacy of Vraja *bhakti* realized that only he could bestow this love, and that to explain it to others, he had to personally practice it. Thus he reasoned, "Unless a person practices devotional service himself, he cannot teach it to others. This conclusion is indeed confirmed throughout the *Gītā* and the *Bhāgavatam.*" (Cc. Ādi 3.21) While Kṛṣṇa's expansions and incarnations can certainly establish religious principles, only he can bestow Vraja *bhakti*. Desiring to do so, he descends as Śrī Caitanya, assuming the form of a devotee of himself.

1. See Cc. Ādi 3.25 and Madhya 17.178. Bg. 3.24 and 4.7–8 are also cited in support of the same point.

The word *yat* (whatever) in this verse implies that common people follow a great person's example, be it scripturally ordained or otherwise. Common people cannot discriminate between that which is scripturally sanctioned and that which is not. Therefore, they are not able to dismiss what a great person might do that is not sanctioned by scripture and accept scripturally enjoined actions as the proper course of action. Thus they are in need of a proper example, and great souls, although above scripture themselves, should set this example.

As Kṛṣṇa further implores Arjuna to set an example for others, in the next three verses he cites his own standard in this regard.

Text 22

न मे पार्थास्ति कर्तव्यं त्रिषु लोकेषु किञ्चन ।
नानवाप्तमवाप्तव्यं वर्त एव च कर्मणि ॥२२॥

na me pārthāsti kartavyaṁ triṣu lokeṣu kiñcana/
nānavāptam avāptavyaṁ varta eva ca karmaṇi//

na—not; *me*—my; *pārtha*—O Pārtha; *asti*—there is; *kartavyam*—to be done; *triṣu*—in three; *lokeṣu*—in the worlds; *kiñcana*—any; *na*—not; *anavāptam*—unattained; *avāptavyam*—to be attained; *varte*—I am engaged; *eva*—certainly; *ca*—also; *karmaṇi*—in prescribed duty.

O son of Pṛthā, there is no work that I need to perform in all the three worlds, nor is there anything to be attained by me. In spite of this, I nevertheless perform prescribed duties.

Kṛṣṇa addresses Arjuna as Pārtha, and thus in terms of their common family heritage. Kṛṣṇa and Arjuna are cousins. Kṛṣṇa speaks in a very endearing voice to his cousin brother as if to say, "You were born in a pure warrior family as I was, and thus we are very similar. Therefore you should behave as I do."

In this and the following two verses, Kṛṣṇa explains the nature of his conduct.

Text 23

यदि ह्यहं न वर्तेयं जातु कर्मण्यतन्द्रितः ।
मम वर्त्मानुवर्तन्ते मनुष्याः पार्थ सर्वशः ॥२३॥

yadi hy ahaṁ na varteyaṁ jātu karmaṇy atandritaḥ/
mama vartmānuvartante manuṣyāḥ pārtha sarvaśaḥ//

yadi—if; *hi*—certainly; *aham*—I; *na*—not; *varteyam*—should engage; *jātu*—ever; *karmaṇi*—in proper action; *atandritaḥ*—with great care; *mama*—my; *vartma*—path; *anuvartante*—follow; *manuṣyāḥ*—men; *pārtha*—O Pārtha; *sarvaśaḥ*—in every way.

For if I should fail to engage in proper action, O Pārtha, people would follow my footsteps in every way.

Text 24

उत्सीदेयुरिमे लोका न कुर्यां कर्म चेदहम् ।
सङ्करस्य च कर्ता स्यामुपहन्यामिमाः प्रजाः ॥२४॥

utsīdeyur ime lokā na kuryāṁ karma ced aham/
saṅkarasya ca kartā syām upahanyām imāḥ prajāḥ//

utsīdeyuḥ—would perish; *ime*—these; *lokāḥ*—worlds; *na*—not; *kuryām*—I should perform; *karma*—prescribed duties; *cet*—if; *aham*—I; *saṅkarasya*—of confusion; *ca*—and; *kartā*—creator; *syām*—would be; *upahanyām*—would destroy; *imāḥ*—these; *prajāḥ*—population.

If I did not act properly, the world would perish and I would be the cause of social chaos, thereby ruining the population.

This is not Vraja Kṛṣṇa speaking here! Although he can do no wrong, Kṛṣṇa certainly *appears* to set a poor example in his affairs with the *gopīs*. Thus after hearing of Vraja Kṛṣṇa's *rāsa* dance with others' wives, Mahārāja Parīkṣit asked Śukadeva how the very support of *dharma*, Kṛṣṇa himself, could act out of character,[2] apparently contradicting what he says in this verse. Śukadeva answered by explaining that great persons *(īśvaraḥ)* can do what others cannot. They act without selfish motive and are thus not implicated in karmic reaction by their seemingly material activities. Furthermore, from an ontological point of view, Kṛṣṇa was the husband/maintainer of the husbands of the *gopīs*, for he resides in the hearts of all.[3] Everyone

2. ŚB. 10.33.26–28
3. ŚB. 10.33.35

belongs to Kṛṣṇa, but not everyone acknowledges this. The *gopīs* of Kṛṣṇa *līlā* exemplify for us the acknowledgment of this principle to the extreme. We are to learn from them the ideal life of devotion to God that *Bhagavad-gītā* points to in its concluding words. The *gopīs* were Kṛṣṇa's most surrendered devotees, and his union with them, while appearing inappropriate on the surface, was in fact most appropriate.

Kṛṣṇa is easier to understand as the prince and statesman of the *Bhagavad-gītā* than he is in his *līlā* of divine love with the *gopīs*. However, readers should understand that Kṛṣṇa's noble and majestic character *(aiśvarya)* brought out in this verse is not absent in his Vraja *līlā*. It lies beneath the surface of that *līlā* and is foundational to it, for were Vraja Kṛṣṇa not God himself, the very support of *dharma*, his *līlā* with the *gopīs* would hold little charm for us. It is only because he *is* God that his most humanlike *līlā* is so sweet *(mādhurya)*. This point is central to Gauḍīya Vedānta.

For the pleasure of his devotees like the *gopīs*, Kṛṣṇa may violate the scripture, otherwise not. To please Kṛṣṇa's devotees is the essence of scriptural adherence. Scripture tells us that the criterion for evaluating the perfection of action is the extent to which it pleases God, *saṁsiddhir hari-toṣaṇam* (ŚB. 1.2.13), and there is nothing that pleases Kṛṣṇa more than the pleasure of his devotees. However, under scrutiny Kṛṣṇa does not violate scripture, nor would this be pleasing to his devotees.

Arjuna's concern for keeping the social order intact, which was voiced in chapter 1, is addressed here by Kṛṣṇa. He says that he acts with this in mind. Previous commentators have given this verse a narrow interpretation: Kṛṣṇa's concern for the social order means the conservation of caste within the traditional *varṇāśrama* socioreligious system.[4]

Ironically, concern for an improved social order today involves a breaking down of what are considered artificial boundaries, such as race, sex, religion, and so on. An improved world order is thought to be one in which people relate to one another based on what they have in common as human beings, a vision that transcends material differences. This is the spirit of the essential message of the *Gītā* as well, wherein the common tie between all humanity—even all species—is their common spiritual essence. It is in pursuit of realizing this common ground that the *Gītā* stresses adherence to its social order, but since the likelihood of reestablishing this socioreligious system in the modern world is slight, it may be best to stress the essential message

4. See Bg. 4.13.

of the *Gītā*, which is to elevate the understanding of humanity's common bond from one that is species-centered to one that is based in spirituality. In doing so, the spirit behind the *Gītā*'s concern for preserving the social order can also be stressed by emphasizing the importance of social morality in general and avoiding the watering down of values, understanding these concerns as the religious and moral underpinnings of a spiritual reality.

Most of the world's religions contain a kind of socially oriented teaching that validates social activism. These teachings are rarely seen as the means to enlightenment itself, but are certainly not seen as being opposed to it. Devotees who, like Arjuna, are not ready to take up a life of renunciation can perhaps find in these teachings models of a contemporary social framework in support of enlightened life. Vaiṣṇavas share many of the values inherent in the environmental movement, vegetarian and animal protection movements, certain aspects of liberal social thought, and various other related types of activism, and there is no reason why *karma-yoga* to promote these values would militate against a Vaiṣṇava's gradual advancement. Indeed, since Kṛṣṇa himself speaks in favor of these values, working to promote them could be considered pleasing to God in the most general sense, as is adherence to the prescribed duties of *varṇāśrama dharma*. Selflessness, renunciation of the fruits of one's work, knowledge of an underlying spiritual purpose of all things, and the desire to please God are the basic principles that, when combined with a culture of devotion to God, lead one gradually to the supreme destination.

Text 25

सक्ताः कर्मण्यविद्वांसो यथा कुर्वन्ति भारत ।
कुर्याद्विद्वांस्तथासक्तश्चिकीर्षुर्लोकसंग्रहम् ॥२५॥

saktāḥ karmaṇy avidvāṁso yathā kurvanti bhārata/
kuryād vidvāṁs tathāsaktaś cikīrṣur loka-saṅgraham//

saktāḥ—attached; *karmaṇi*—in prescribed duties; *avidvāṁsaḥ*—the unwise; *yathā*—as; *kurvanti*—they do; *bhārata*—O descendant of Bharata; *kuryāt*—he must do; *vidvān*—the wise; *tathā*—so; *asaktaḥ*—without attachment; *cikīrṣuḥ*—desiring to do; *loka-saṅgraham*—uplifting the world.

O scion of Bharata, as those who are unwise act out of attachment for the results of their action, so the wise should act without attachment for the sake of uplifting the world.

The name Bhārata indicates one devoted *(rata)* to knowledge *(bhā)*. Arjuna is thus characterized as one so devoted, who should not act out of attachment but for the sake of uplifting others by his example.

Text 26

न बुद्धिभेदं जनयेदज्ञानां कर्मसङ्गिनाम् ।
जोषयेत् सर्वकर्माणि विद्वान्युक्तः समाचरन् ॥२६॥

na buddhi-bhedaṁ janayed ajñānāṁ karma-saṅginām/
joṣayet sarva-karmāṇi vidvān yuktaḥ samācaran//

na—not; *buddhi-bhedam*—disruption of intelligence; *janayet*—he should cause; *ajñānām*—of the ignorant; *karma-saṅginām*—who are attached to fruitive work; *joṣayet*—he should cause to delight; *sarva*—all; *karmāṇi*—duties; *vidvān*—the wise; *yuktaḥ*—engaged; *samācaran*—practicing.

The wise should not unsettle the minds of the ignorant who are attached to fruitive work. They should make them delight in all prescribed duties while acting themselves with discipline.

Truth must be revealed in installments relative to the eligibility of the student. This is a general principle observed in all spheres of learning. Thus restrictions on who is privileged to study the *Upaniṣads* is not a social bias but observance of a universal principle. Although loving God is everyone's right, persons are eligible to do so in consideration of the extent of their material conditioning.

The stricture in this verse applies primarily to the *jñānī*. He should not encourage the ignorant to give up work. Although devotees are also bound to observe the principle described in this verse, this does not mean that they are forbidden to encourage the ignorant to engage in Kṛṣṇa's service. Such service will not disturb the minds of the ignorant inasmuch as it can be dovetailed with one's karmic propensity. *Bhakti* does not require that a person first purify his heart by another means before engaging in it. However, devotees must teach the ignorant about devotion and engage people in *bhakti* in consideration of the level of their eligibility. Beginners on the path of *bhakti* should engage in congregational hearing and chanting about Kṛṣṇa, whereas advanced devotees can sit in solitude meditating on Kṛṣṇa's *līlās* with undisturbed minds. However, such advanced devotees should also set an example for beginners to emulate.

Here Kṛṣṇa says that those in knowledge should not encourage the ignorant to give up prescribed duties in the name of self-realization when they are unqualified to do so. This will only disturb their minds. Instead such persons should be encouraged to engage in scripturally enjoined work. Indeed, the self-realized soul should encourage this to the extent of setting an example himself.

Kṛṣṇa next describes in two verses what the action of the unenlightened and enlightened person consists of.

Text 27

प्रकृतेः क्रियमाणानि गुणैः कर्माणि सर्वशः ।
अहंकारविमूढात्मा कर्ताहमिति मन्यते ॥२७॥

prakṛteḥ kriyamāṇāni guṇaiḥ karmāṇi sarvaśaḥ/
ahaṅkāra-vimūḍhātmā kartāham iti manyate//

prakṛteḥ—of material nature; *kriyamāṇāni*—being performed; *guṇaiḥ*—by the modes; *karmāṇi*—actions; *sarvaśaḥ*—entirely; *ahaṅkāra-vimūḍha*—bewildered by egotism; *ātmā*—self; *kartā*—doer; *aham*—I; *iti*—thus; *manyate*—he thinks.

All actions are performed by the guṇas. One who misidentifies with the body in false ego imagines "I am the doer."

In this verse Kṛṣṇa describes the bewilderment of the ignorant, who identify themselves with the body and mind. In ignorance, people think themselves to be independent in their action, seeing themselves as the agents of action. If they are enlightened, they can understand the nature of action: whence it arises and how it can be harnessed to bring about emancipation. The functions of the body are the movements of material nature, whereas the soul is the nondoer. Without this understanding, ignorant people do not realize that they are embodied souls and that their physical actions and thoughts are not really their own—not the movement of their self, but movement under the influence of material nature, overseen by God.

While this verse stresses the difference between spirit and matter, the former being a witness to the action of the latter, the *Gītā*'s message is not entirely dualistic, and thus this verse understood in the context of the entire *Gītā* cannot be equated with Sāṅkhya philosophy, which maintains complete dualism of matter and spirit. Baladeva Vidyābhūṣaṇa points out that the individual soul is a factor in action, although only one among others. He cites *Bhagavad-gīta* 18.14 where Kṛṣṇa says as much himself. Material nature acts only as a result of contact with spirit, both God and the individual soul. Thus the soul is not without its influence over actions of the body. The limited sense in which the soul also acts is brought out in the following verse wherein we learn that rather than becoming attached to the senses and sense objects, one can do otherwise.

Text 28

तत्त्ववित्तु महाबाहो गुणकर्मविभागयोः ।
गुणा गुणेषु वर्तन्त इति मत्वा न सज्जते ॥२८॥

tattva-vit tu mahā-bāho guṇa-karma-vibhāgayoḥ/
guṇā guṇeṣu vartanta iti matvā na sajjate//

tattva-vit—the knower of the truth; *tu*—however; *mahā-bāho*—O mighty-armed one; *guṇa-karma-vibhāgayoḥ*—in the two spheres of *guṇa* and action; *guṇāḥ*—the *guṇas; guṇeṣu*—in the *guṇas; vartante*—they engage; *iti*—thus; *matvā*—thinking; *na*—never; *sajjate*—becomes attached.

However, O mighty-armed one, one who knows the truth concerning the two spheres, action and the guṇas, and thus thinks that only the guṇas interact with one another, remains unattached.

In this verse Kṛṣṇa distinguishes the enlightened from the unenlightened. The enlightened understand the influence of material nature's *guṇas* and the actions they cause the body to perform *(karma)*. The word *vibhāga* in this verse can also be understood to indicate the soul. It is that which is categorically different from *guṇa* and *karma* by virtue of its being the revealer of all that is insentient within the realm of *guṇa* and *karma*.[5] The enlightened know not only *guṇa* and *karma*, they also know the soul. Here the soul is described as a nondoer. It is, however, a doer in terms of being the only initiator of action through its desire. The soul as doer/nondoer will be further explained in chapter 5.

One who is in full knowledge of the influence of the three *guṇas* and material nature in relation to the gods, senses, sense objects, and so on, knows that in all action only the senses interact with the sense objects,

5. Madhusūdana Saraswatī explains *guṇa-karma-vibhāgayoḥ* as a *samāhāra-dvandva* in the collective singular.

while the soul remains aloof. The bewildered soul suffers and enjoys vicariously through his identification with material nature.

In the next verse Kṛṣṇa explains the logical conclusion of the previous two verses. It is also the conclusion of the theme that began with verse 26.

Text 29

प्रकृतेर्गुणसम्मूढाः सज्जन्ते गुणकर्मसु ।
तानकृत्स्नविदो मन्दान् कृत्स्नविन्न विचालयेत् ॥२९॥

prakṛter guṇa-sammūḍhāḥ sajjante guṇa-karmasu/
tān akṛtsna-vido mandān kṛtsna-vin na vicālayet//

prakṛteḥ—of material nature; *guṇa-sammūḍhāḥ*—deluded by the *guṇas*; *sajjante*—they are attached; *guṇa-karmasu*—in material activities; *tān*—those; *akṛtsna-vidaḥ*—not knowing entirely; *mandān*—fools; *kṛtsna-vit*—the knower; *na*—not; *vicālayet*—should disturb.

Those deluded by the influence of material nature are attached to the senses and sense objects. The wise should not disturb these foolish people, whose knowledge is incomplete.

Although the futility of attached work is a reality, merely advising the ignorant of this without engaging them in detached action will not be useful.

Text 30

मयि सर्वाणि कर्माणि सन्न्यस्याध्यात्मचेतसा ।
निराशीर्निर्ममो भूत्वा युध्यस्व विगतज्वरः ॥३०॥

mayi sarvāṇi karmāṇi sannyasyādhyātma-cetasā/
nirāśīr nirmamo bhūtvā yudhyasva vigata-jvaraḥ//

mayi—unto me; *sarvāṇi*—all; *karmāṇi*—actions; *sannyasya*—giving up; *adhyātma-cetasā*—in knowledge of the Supersoul; *nirāśīḥ*—without desire; *nirmamaḥ*—without selfishness; *bhūtvā*—being; *yudhyasva*—fight; *vigata-jvaraḥ*—without grief.

Offering all of one's actions unto me in knowledge of the indwelling Supersoul, free from desire, selfishness, and grief, fight!

This is the remedy for the material fever of the soul. *Jvaraḥ* means fever, and the fever for sense enjoyment brings only grief to the soul. Under its influence the soul is delirious. In addition to selfless action Kṛṣṇa adds dedication to God to the remedial measures required to treat this fever. Kṛṣṇa implores Arjuna to fight not only in knowledge of the fact that he is not the enjoyer and that action is carried out by material nature, but also in devotion to the indwelling guide (Paramātmā), who is a partial manifestation of himself. B. R. Śrīdhara Deva Goswāmī glosses *adhyātma-cetasā* as "with the understanding, 'All my actions are under the control of the indwelling Lord.' "

However, Kṛṣṇa is not telling Arjuna to act out of love for him, and thus at this point he implores him to engage in *niṣkāma-karma-yoga* more so than *bhakti*. Arjuna should fight because he is a warrior. He should do so without attachment to the results for the sake of purifying his heart and thereby gaining knowledge of the self. The results of his actions should be offered unto Kṛṣṇa, laying a foundation for devotion. The immediate result of this course of action is liberation.

Text 31

ये मे मतमिदं नित्यमनुतिष्ठन्ति मानवाः ।
श्रद्धावन्तोऽनसूयन्तो मुच्यन्ते तेऽपि कर्मभिः ॥३१॥

ye me matam idaṁ nityam anutiṣṭhanti mānavāḥ/
śraddhāvanto 'nasūyanto mucyante te 'pi karmabhiḥ//

ye—who; *me*—my; *matam*—doctrine; *idam*—this; *nityam*—constantly; *anutiṣṭhanti*—practice; *mānavāḥ*—human beings; *śraddhā-vantaḥ*—with faith; *anasūyantaḥ*—without envy; *mucyante*—are released; *te*—they; *api*—even; *karmabhiḥ*—from karmic reactions.

Persons who constantly practice this, my own doctrine, with full faith and without envy are also released from karmic reactions.

The positive result of *niṣkāma-karma-yoga* is liberation. The paths of selfless action and knowledge beget liberation when mixed with devotion. The word *nityam* has a twofold meaning—constant and eternal. Thus Kṛṣṇa is saying that his path should be constantly practiced and it is itself eternal, being enjoined in the scripture. Its use also indicates that a person will be liberated if he is fixed in his spiritual objective, free from envy, and faithful. The word *śraddhā* implies faith in scripture and thus a descending path involving revelation. This path is for a person free from envy of the preceptor. Those who decry this path are discussed next.

Text 32

ये त्वेतदभ्यसूयन्तो नानुतिष्ठन्ति मे मतम् ।
सर्वज्ञानविमूढांस्तान्विद्धि नष्टानचेतसः ॥३२॥

ye tv etad abhyasūyanto nānutiṣṭhanti me matam/
sarva-jñāna-vimūḍhāṁs tān viddhi naṣṭān acetasaḥ//

ye—those; *tu*—however; *etat*—this; *abhyasūyantaḥ*—out of envy; *na*—not; *anutiṣṭhanti*—practice; *me*—my; *matam*—doctrine; *sarva-jñāna-vimūḍhān*—confusing all knowledge; *tān*—they; *viddhi*—know; *naṣṭān*—deprived of the goal of life; *acetasaḥ*—mindless.

However, those who out of envy of my doctrine do not practice it are deluded and bereft of knowledge. Know that such people have lost their minds and are deprived of the goal of life.

Finding fault in something that is good for you can be an expression of envy. The result of harboring this envy is that one becomes bereft of knowledge and thus deluded. Why do people act in this way? It is difficult to overcome one's acquired nature.

Text 33

सदृशं चेष्टते स्वस्याः प्रकृतेर्ज्ञानवानपि ।
प्रकृतिं यान्ति भूतानि निग्रहः किं करिष्यति ॥३३॥

sadṛśaṁ ceṣṭate svasyāḥ prakṛter jñānavān api/
prakṛtiṁ yānti bhūtāni nigrahaḥ kiṁ kariṣyati//

sadṛśam—accordingly; *ceṣṭate*—tries; *svasyāḥ*—by his own; *prakṛteḥ*—from material nature; *jñāna-vān*—wise; *api*—even; *prakṛtim*—nature; *yānti*—follow; *bhūtāni*—beings; *nigrahaḥ*—repression; *kim*—what; *kariṣyati*—will accomplish.

Even wise people act according to the nature they have acquired in this world. People follow their acquired nature. What will repression accomplish?

Here Kṛṣṇa further stresses the path of selfless action by stating that even the wise, *jñānīs*, act in accordance with their natures. If this is so for the wise, how much more is this true for those in ignorance? Thus repressing one's nature is very difficult and often counterproductive. This being so, the question arises as to the value of scriptural injunctions. If everyone is induced to follow his own nature as if by force, what is the value of scriptural proscriptions and prohibitions? This is answered in the following verse.

Text 34

इन्द्रियस्येन्द्रियस्यार्थे रागद्वेषौ व्यवस्थितौ ।
तयोर्न वशमागच्छेत्तौ ह्यस्य परिपन्थिनौ ॥३४॥

indriyasyendriyasyārthe rāga-dveṣau vyavasthitau/
tayor na vaśam āgacchet tau hy asya paripanthinau//

indriyasya—of each of the senses; *indriyasya arthe*—in relation to their objects; *rāga-dveṣau*—attachment and aversion; *vyavasthitau*—seated; *tayoḥ*—of them; *na*—never; *vaśam*—control; *āgacchet*—one should come; *tau*—those; *hi*—certainly; *asya*—his; *paripanthinau*—two enemies.

Attachment and aversion in relation to the sense objects are deeply rooted in the senses. One should not come under the control of these two, for they are one's enemies.

Overcoming one's karmically acquired nature is possible with the help of scripture. The sacred literature takes our nature into consideration by recommending appropriate action. Contemplation of sense objects produces attachment and aversion. The unhappy result of this is that one comes under their sway. However, scripture reveals the fact that the so-called desirable and undesirable sense objects are not really so. The ignorance that underlies the sense of an object's being desirable or otherwise is exposed through theoretical knowledge acquired from scripture. It is removed by scripturally guided action. Thus Arjuna is next advised to follow scripture and work in accordance with his own socioreligious duties as a warrior.

Text 35

श्रेयान् स्वधर्मो विगुणः परधर्मात् स्वनुष्ठितात् ।
स्वधर्मे निधनं श्रेयः परधर्मो भयावहः ॥३५॥

śreyān sva-dharmo viguṇaḥ para-dharmāt sv-anuṣṭhitāt/
sva-dharme nidhanaṁ śreyaḥ para-dharmo bhayāvahaḥ//

śreyān—better; *sva-dharmaḥ*—duties according to one's own nature; *viguṇaḥ*—faulty; *para-dharmāt*—than another's duties; *su-anuṣṭhitāt*—perfectly executed; *sva-dharme*—in one's prescribed duties; *nidhanam*—destruction; *śreyaḥ*—better; *para-dharmaḥ*—duties prescribed for others; *bhaya-āvahaḥ*—inviting peril.

One should act in accordance with one's own nature, even though in doing so one may appear faulty. This course of action is better than engaging in any other duties, however well you might attend to them. It is better to die engaged in accordance with one's own nature, for others' duties invite peril.

Verses 30 through 35 are a covert advocacy of *bhakti*, which, as B. R. Śrīdhara Deva Goswāmī says, "is the eternal superexcellent natural function of the soul." In the words of Śrī Caitanya, the *jīva* soul is the eternal servant of Kṛṣṇa, *jīvera 'svarūpa' haya—kṛṣṇera 'nitya-dāsa'* (Cc. Mad. 20.108). This is ultimately what Kṛṣṇa has in mind for Arjuna, and *niṣkāma-karma-yoga*, in which the fruit of one's work is offered to Kṛṣṇa, is similar to *bhakti*. In verse 30, Kṛṣṇa introduces himself into the equation of selfless work as the one to whom one's actions should be dedicated *(mayi sarvāṇi karmāṇi)*. His commanding Arjuna to fight only overtly appears to be a directive in consideration of Arjuna's warrior nature. Covertly, Kṛṣṇa commands Arjuna to act in accordance with his soul's interest in terms of an eternal loving relationship with him. In verse 31, Kṛṣṇa describes the path he wants Arjuna to tread as his own *(me matam)*, a path that is eternal and arises out of faith *(śraddhā)*, devoid of envy *(anasūya)* of himself. Again in verse 32 Kṛṣṇa identifies this path as his own *(me matam)*. In verse 33, Kṛṣṇa subtly plays down the path of *jñāna (jñānavān api)*.

In the present verse, Kṛṣṇa says that pure devotion is the natural function of the soul. Even if acting in the soul's interest appears inappropriate from the vantage point of socioreligious considerations, it is far superior to mere moral conformity. In the pursuit of the soul's eternal interest, even death is auspicious. In contrast, pursuance of any interest other than one's spiritual interest is perilous, however perfectly it is pursued.[6]

6. In this connection, B. R. Śrīdhara Deva Goswāmī cites ŚB. 11.2.37.

Looking at these verses in light of *bhakti*, one can find parallels between this verse and the *Gītā*'s conclusion (Bg. 18.66). The *Gītā* concludes by telling us that abandoning socioreligious concerns and surrendering to Kṛṣṇa himself is the essence of all *dharma*—*prema-dharma*. Here he covertly says the same thing: "You should act in accordance with your own nature (as a devotee), even though in doing so you may appear faulty (for neglecting worldly concerns). This course of action is better than engaging in any other duties, however well you might attend to them. It would be better to die acting in accordance with your own (eternal) nature, for other duties invite peril (of continued birth and death)."

The customary interpretation of this verse renders it a socioreligious instruction of relative value, in apparent contradiction with the *Gītā*'s conclusion. However, there need not be any contradiction for truth is administered in installments. Understanding this verse in terms of *niṣkāma-karma-yoga* sheds further light on the importance of scripture. Kṛṣṇa told Arjuna not to think that he could perform another's duty to avoid fighting. Scripture is to be followed. Baladeva Vidyābhūṣaṇa says that just as one sees with eyes and not other senses, we learn about religion from scripture. Doing another's duty or acting against one's own nature will disturb the socioreligious order.

With this Kṛṣṇa stops as if he is getting ahead of himself in his instructions to Arjuna. As Kṛṣṇa pauses collecting himself to continue his emphasis on *karma-yoga*, Arjuna asks a pertinent question. He wants to know what it is that causes one to act contrary to scripture even after gaining knowledge of it.

Text 36

अर्जुन उवाच
अथ केन प्रयुक्तोऽयं पापं चरति पूरुषः ।
अनिच्छन्नपि वार्ष्णेय बलादिव नियोजितः ॥३६॥

arjuna uvāca
atha kena prayukto 'yaṁ pāpaṁ carati pūruṣaḥ/
anicchann api vārṣṇeya balād iva niyojitaḥ//

arjunaḥ uvāca—Arjuna said; *atha*—then; *kena*—by what; *prayuktaḥ*—forced; *ayam*—one; *pāpam*—evil; *carati*—does; *pūruṣaḥ*—a man; *anicchan*—without desiring; *api*—although; *vārṣṇeya*—O descendant of Vṛṣṇi; *balāt*—by force; *iva*—as if; *niyojitaḥ*—engaged.

Arjuna said: By what influence then, O descendant of Vṛṣṇi, does one act improperly, as if forced to do so against his own will?

Previously Kṛṣṇa explained that delusion is caused by contemplating sense objects. He also attributed delusion to the influence of the *guṇas*. Is there any other cause of delusion, eradicating which all others are done away with at the same time? These questions are at the heart of Arjuna's present inquiry.

Text 37

श्रीभगवानुवाच
काम एष क्रोध एष रजोगुणसमुद्भवः ।
महाशनो महापाप्मा विद्ध्येनमिह वैरिणम् ॥३७॥

śrī-bhagavān uvāca
kāma eṣa krodha eṣa rajo-guṇa-samudbhavaḥ/
mahāśano mahā-pāpmā viddhy enam iha vairiṇam//

śri-bhagavān uvāca—the Lord of Śrī said; *kāmaḥ*—lust; *eṣaḥ*—this; *krodhaḥ*—anger; *eṣaḥ*—this; *rajaḥ-guṇa*—the mode of passion; *samudbhavaḥ*—born of; *mahā-aśanaḥ*—insatiable; *mahā-pāpmā*—very injurious; *viddhi*—know; *enam*—this; *iha*—in the material world; *vairiṇam*—enemy.

The Lord of Śrī said: This force is lust, born of rajo-guṇa. It eventually transforms into anger. It is insatiable like a great fire and very injurious. Know this to be the enemy.

Kṛṣṇa says that the force that impels one to act contrary to scripturally guided intelligence is desire *(kāma)*, the lust for material enjoyment. This lust resides within the heart like a cancer, and it is very subtle and difficult to uproot. It is born of the material *guṇa* of passion *(rajas)*. When desire is obstructed, it turns to anger, a manifestation of the material *guṇa* of ignorance *(tamas)*.

It is said in *Śrīmad-Bhāgavatam* (9.19.13) that all the paddy, barley, gold, cattle, and women in the world are not enough to satisfy one man (suffering from *kāma*). Therefore one should resort to desirelessness. Because *kāma* is so powerful *(mahāśanaḥ)* and very injurious *(mahāpāpmā)*, it cannot be subjugated by anything less than the most comprehensive treatment.

In dealing with enemies it is said that one should first seek conciliation, then try bribery. If this is unsuccessful, one should attempt to sow dissension in the ranks of the enemy. If this fails, one must resort to punishment. Punishment of *kāma* is best accomplished by invoking the help of the transcendental Kāmadeva,[7] Kṛṣṇa, who proceeds to instruct Arjuna how to conquer *kāma* from the next verse to the end of the chapter.

Text 38

धूमेनाव्रियते वह्निर्यथादर्शो मलेन च ।
यथोल्बेनावृतो गर्भस्तथा तेनेदमावृतम् ॥३८॥

dhūmenāvriyate vahnir yathādarśo malena ca/
yatholbenāvṛto garbhas tathā tenedam āvṛtam//

dhūmena—by smoke; *āvriyate*—is covered; *vahniḥ*—fire; *yathā*—as; *ādarśaḥ*—mirror; *malena*—by dust; *ca*—also; *yathā*—as; *ulbena*—by the womb; *āvṛtaḥ*—covered; *garbhaḥ*—embryo; *tathā*—so; *tena*—by that lust; *idam*—this; *āvṛtam*—covered.

As a fire is covered by smoke, a mirror by dust, and an embryo by the womb, so one's proper understanding is covered by inordinate desire.

In this verse Kṛṣṇa gives an example to illustrate the different degrees to which intelligence is covered by *kāma*. Smoke represents one who in spite of *kāma*'s influence can continue to engage in spiritual practice, as fire is not extinguished by smoke. Dust covering the mirror represents one who can understand the necessity to engage in spiritual practice, but nonetheless cannot act practically in this regard, as a dusty mirror does not give a reflection. The womb covering the embryo represents one who cannot even theoretically understand the problem of *kāma*, as the embryo within the womb cannot see the light of day. These three examples—fire covered by smoke, the mirror covered by dust, and the embryo covered by membrane—represent the influence of the three modes of material nature, *sattva*, *rajas*, and *tamas*.

Text 39

आवृतं ज्ञानमेतेन ज्ञानिनो नित्यवैरिणा ।
कामरूपेण कौन्तेय दुष्पूरेणानलेन च ॥३९॥

7. Kāmadeva is the god *(deva)* of *kāma*. This god is Cupid, but Kṛṣṇa is also known as Kāmadeva, the transcendental Cupid. His *rāsa-līlā* is thus referred to by Śrīdhara Swāmī as *kāma-vijaya*, the conquest of Cupid.

āvṛtaṁ jñānam etena jñānino nitya-vairiṇā/
kāma-rūpeṇa kaunteya duṣpūreṇānalena ca//

āvṛtam—covered; *jñānam*—knowledge; *etena*—by this; *jñāninaḥ*—of the knower; *nitya-vairiṇā*—by the perpetual enemy; *kāma-rūpeṇa*—in the form of lust; *kaunteya*—O son of Kuntī; *duṣpūreṇa*—by the insatiable; *analena*—by the fire; *ca*—also.

O son of Kuntī, even the understanding of the wise contemplative is obscured by this perpetual enemy in the form of lust, which has an appetite like fire.

For the wise, the desire that inevitably leads to sorrow is recognized as an enemy even while the object of desire is being experienced. Thus the wise know that *kāma* is a constant enemy (*nitya-vairiṇā*). Those who are not wise enjoy desire when it brings fruit and regret its sorrowful consequences only afterward. Thus the ignorant do not understand that *kāma* is a constant enemy. The wise who understand *kāma* to be a constant and powerful enemy resort to whatever means necessary to destroy it. So also should the unwise, for this *kāma* burns like fire and is never satiated by feeding it with the fuel of sense enjoyment. This example is given here to help the unwise understand the nature of the enemy known as *kāma*. Kṛṣṇa cites another example in the following verse.

Text 40

इन्द्रियाणि मनो बुद्धिरस्याधिष्ठानमुच्यते ।
एतैर्विमोहयत्येष ज्ञानमावृत्य देहिनम् ॥४०॥

indriyāṇi mano buddhir asyādhiṣṭhānam ucyate/
etair vimohayaty eṣa jñānam āvṛtya dehinam//

indriyāṇi—the senses; *manaḥ*—the mind; *buddhiḥ*—the intelligence; *asya*—of it; *adhiṣṭhānam*—sitting place; *ucyate*—is called; *etaiḥ*—by these; *vimohayati*—bewilders; *eṣaḥ*—this; *jñānam*—knowledge; *āvṛtya*—covering; *dehinam*—the embodied.

It is seated in the senses, mind, and intelligence. From there it influences the embodied soul, bewildering him and covering his knowledge.

In this verse Kṛṣṇa identifies *kāma*'s haunts: the body consisting of sense organs, both perceiving and acting, the mental realm, and the faculty of judgment, intellect. From these strategic points, *kāma* acts to cover one's discriminating wisdom. First it must be routed out of the senses.

Text 41

तस्मात्त्वमिन्द्रियाण्यादौ नियम्य भरतर्षभ ।
पाप्मानं प्रजहि ह्येनं ज्ञानविज्ञाननाशनम् ॥४१॥

tasmāt tvam indriyāṇy ādau niyamya bharatarṣabha/
pāpmānaṁ prajahi hy enaṁ jñāna-vijñāna-nāśanam//

tasmāt—therefore; *tvam*—you; *indriyāṇi*—senses; *ādau*—at the outset; *niyamya*—by regulating; *bharata-ṛṣabha*—O best of the Bhāratas; *pāpmānam*—devil; *prajahi*—kill; *hi*—certainly; *enam*—this; *jñāna*—knowledge; *vijñāna*—self-realization; *nāśanam*—the destroyer.

Therefore, O best of the Bhāratas, at the very outset regulate your senses and kill this devil that destroys knowledge and self-realization.

By curbing the sensual outlets for *kāma*, one also effectively routs it out of the mind and intellect, because both the mind and intellect must be involved in the effort to control the senses. When the sensual outlets are effectively curbed, *kāma* is left with no means to express itself. Thus it gradually leaves the mind and intellect altogether. By engaging these senses in the service of Godhead one acquires a higher taste,[8] and thus inner hankering is also destroyed. Although senses, mind, and intellect were mentioned separately in text 40, all three of them are implied in this verse by mention of the senses.

Kṛṣṇa next describes the material hierarchy leading to the soul to further implore Arjuna to follow his instructions.

Text 42

इन्द्रियाणि पराण्याहुरिन्द्रियेभ्यः परं मनः ।
मनसस्तु परा बुद्धिर्यो बुद्धेः परतस्तु सः ॥४२॥

8. See Bg. 2.59.

indriyāṇi parāṇy āhur indriyebhyaḥ paraṁ manaḥ/
manasas tu parā buddhir yo buddheḥ paratas tu saḥ//

indriyāṇi—senses; *parāṇi*—superior; *āhuḥ*—are said; *indriyebhyaḥ*—than the senses; *param*—superior; *manaḥ*—the mind; *manasaḥ*—than the mind; *tu*—however; *parā*—superior; *buddhiḥ*—intelligence; *yaḥ*—who; *buddheḥ*—than the intelligence; *parataḥ*—superior; *tu*—but; *saḥ*—he.

It is said that senses are superior to the sense objects, the mind is superior to the senses, and moreover, the intellect is superior to the mind. Superior even to the intellect is the self.

In this verse Kṛṣṇa outlines the material hierarchy and then touches the soul. The authorities he refers to are either the wise or the *śruti*. They say that the senses are superior to the sense objects. This also means that the senses are superior to the body, as the actual senses are situated in the subtle body with their external representation appearing in the gross body. Superior to the senses is the mind, which is subordinate to the intellect. This is the material hierarchy.

The word *saḥ* in this verse means "this" or "he." It refers to either *kāma* itself, the individual soul, or God. If we understand the word *saḥ* as a reference to *kāma*, the principal subject of this section, such a rendering serves to stress the power of desire. It can corrupt all; it is the all-powerful enemy of the soul. Without underestimating the power of *kāma*, however, a more plausible rendering of *saḥ* here is the individual soul. Above the intellect is the soul, a unit of consciousness. By knowing oneself as a unit of consciousness one can conquer over *kāma*. This is confirmed in the next verse.

Text 43

एवं बुद्धेः परं बुद्ध्वा संस्तभ्यात्मानमात्मना ।
जहि शत्रुं महाबाहो कामरूपं दुरासदम् ॥४३॥

evaṁ buddheḥ paraṁ buddhvā saṁstabhyātmānam ātmanā/
jahi śatruṁ mahā-bāho kāma-rūpaṁ durāsadam//

evam—thus; *buddheḥ*—to intelligence; *param*—superior; *buddhvā*—knowing; *saṁstabhya*—by controlling; *ātmānam*—the mind; *ātmanā*—by the intellect; *jahi*—kill; *śatrum*—the enemy; *mahā-bāho*—O mighty-armed one; *kāma-rūpam*—in the form of lust; *durāsadam*—difficult to conquer.

Thus, knowing oneself to be superior to the intellect, control the mind with intellect. In this way, O mighty-armed one, destroy the unconquerable enemy in the form of desire.

Here Kṛṣṇa emphasizes the strength of the soul, one's self. The self is superior to all three of the seats of lust—senses, mind, and intellect. Being theoretically aware of one's own position as a pure soul, one can begin to differentiate oneself from the sensual, mental, and intellectual planes of experience and thus rise above lust. The awakened soul is in a position to direct his intellect. Later in chapter 10 (Bg. 10.10) Kṛṣṇa reveals himself to be the source of divine intelligence in the awakened soul. However, at this point in the *Gītā* he is restraining himself from saying too much too soon, as he gradually builds his case for *bhakti*.

Chapter Four

ज्ञानयोगः

Jñāna-yoga

YOGA OF KNOWLEDGE

Text 1

श्रीभगवानुवाच
इमं विवस्वते योगं प्रोक्तवानहमव्ययम् ।
विवस्वान् मनवे प्राह मनुरिक्ष्वाकवेऽब्रवीत् ॥१॥

śrī-bhagavān uvāca
imaṁ vivasvate yogaṁ proktavān aham avyayam/
vivasvān manave prāha manur ikṣvākave 'bravīt//

śrī-bhagavān uvāca—the Lord of Śrī said; *imam*—this; *vivasvate*—to Vivasvān; *yogam*—yoga; *proktavān*—explained; *aham*—I; *avyayam*—imperishable; *vivasvān*—Vivasvān; *manave*—to Manu; *prāha*—spoke; *manuḥ*—Manu; *ikṣvākave*—to Ikṣvāku; *abravīt*—imparted.

The Lord of Śrī said: I explained this imperishable science of yoga to Vivasvān. Vivasvān spoke it to Manu, and Manu in turn imparted it to Ikṣvāku.

In this chapter Kṛṣṇa explains how through *karma-yoga* one attains *jñāna* and eligibility for *jñāna-yoga*. Here the word *jñāna* conveys much more than merely the theoretical knowledge that informs the action of the *karma-yogī*, causing him to act with the spirit of detachment—*jñāna* is insight or wisdom into the nature of nondual consciousness. It gradually awakens in the heart that is free from selfish desire. While the previous chapter stressed *karma-yoga* and this chapter stresses *jñāna-yoga*, it will become clear in chapter 5 that Kṛṣṇa's teaching to Arjuna advocates an integration of the two, and in his conclusion to chapter 6 he makes it clear that this integration culminates in the spiritually emotional life of *bhakti*.

To further convince Arjuna about the value of this science of *yoga*, here Kṛṣṇa speaks of the doctrine's historical legacy: how it came to the world and through whom it has been disseminated. In doing so, he mentions his own involvement in its dissemination, extending into the far distant past.

In the course of explaining the history of the science of *yoga*, Kṛṣṇa will introduce the principle of divine descent, the *avatāra*. In so doing, he will explain to Arjuna things about himself that are foundational to *bhakti-yoga*.

Śaṅkara comments that it is the goal and not the path of *yoga* that is imperishable *(avyayam)*. However, Baladeva Vidyābhūṣaṇa says that the path of *yoga* itself is imperishable because it is the essential meaning of the *Vedas* and it unfailingly delivers the supreme goal. As *karma-yoga* it consistently delivers its fruit of inner wisdom. When the fruit of *karma-yoga* in the form of self-knowledge ripens and one acts in devotion to God, this liberated yogic action is *bhakti*.

Text 2

एवं परम्पराप्राप्तमिमं राजर्षयो विदुः ।
स कालेनेह महता योगो नष्टः परन्तप ॥२॥

evaṁ paramparā-prāptam imaṁ rājarṣayo viduḥ/
sa kāleneha mahatā yogo naṣṭaḥ parantapa//

evam—thus; *paramparā*—through disciplic succession; *prāptam*—obtained; *imam*—this; *rāja-ṛṣayaḥ*—saintly kings; *viduḥ*—they knew; *saḥ*—it; *kālena*—under the influence of time; *iha*—here, on earth; *mahatā*—extended; *yogaḥ*—*yoga*; *naṣṭaḥ*—lost; *parantapa*—O Arjuna, conqueror of the enemy.

O conqueror of the enemy, visionary kings thus obtained this knowledge through disciplic succession. At present, under the influence of extended time here on earth, this teaching of yoga has been obscured.

As Kṛṣṇa prepares to explain the principle of the *avatāra*, or divine descent, he introduces another important principle, that of *guru-paramparā*, or disciplic succession. The two are intertwined. Kṛṣṇa says that he inaugurates the divine lineage through which knowledge of himself is then revealed by his devotees appearing in that lineage. He also says that under the influence of time this lineage can become broken, thus requiring that it be resurrected. Kṛṣṇa himself becomes involved in revitalizing the lineage during his descent, as described in text three. Later in the *Gītā*, Kṛṣṇa identifies time, described here as the influence under which the essential message of the lineage is obscured, with himself. Thus the hand of God is as much involved in obscuring the lineage as it is in establishing it.

As circumstances and social considerations change over time, the need arises to re-explain the spirit of the lineage relevant to time and circumstances. That which is essential in the message must be separated from that which is relative. In delivering the principle the details must be altered. This is the task of great souls.

The mystery of *guru-paramparā* is that while it suggests conformity to a lineage dating into antiquity, at the same time its spirit is that of nonconformity. Becoming a member, one conforms with the Absolute, the supreme nonconformist, who is absolutely independent. To be in the *guru-paramparā*, one must sometimes leave what appears to be the lineage. One must distinguish between the form and substance of the tradition. Thus we find the most prominent members of the lineage are involved in renovation of the tradition, revealing its truth in a way relevant to time and circumstance, such that often those who are members in form only cannot appreciate them. To recognize reformers of the mission, practitioners themselves must also become essence seekers on a deeper level and thus remain vital in their practice. Failure to do so involves a break from the tradition despite superficial adherence to its external symbols.

In pursuit of the spirit of the lineage, the practitioner must take note of this verse, both with regard to recognizing the work of great souls when it outwardly appears to be different in detail from previous teachers and with regard to their own practicing life. The spirit of the teaching is not as much obscured for the practitioner at a particular time as it is continuously. We glimpse the true meaning of the teaching only to lose sight of it again, being distracted by material conditioning under the influence of the mind and senses due to our external, sensual orientation in life. We tend to gravitate toward the outer body of the message rather than to its heartbeat. The message is more than the cultural trappings in which it is presented. It answers to a sense of urgency in the soul striving for self-perfection. The spirit with which one initially embraces the lineage may over time become suppressed, as the practitioner settles for pat answers to the problems of life, rather than taking up the challenge of applying those answers in progressive spiritual life. Thus there is an ongoing need to resurrect the spirit of the teaching, not only in terms of revitalizing its message generation after generation, but also in our everyday life of spiritual practice.

When one representative passes the torch to another, this is the formal institution of *guru-paramparā* ("from one to another"). However, its essence is that in bearing the torch the current link sheds new light. At the same time, renovators of the tradition must be distinguished from renegades of the tradition. The scriptural canon can help us to some extent in this task. Renovators justify their innovations with scriptural references, yet they also dynamically revise the scripture itself.[1]

Renovators of the tradition cite those scriptures that they feel are essential, and in this way they support their innovations. However, not everyone will necessarily agree with their particular interpretations. Thus more important than their ability to cite scripture (which even the devil can do) is their ability to make their vision credible by dint of their obvious spiritual power.

The illustrious members of the *guru-paramparā* are kings of the world in the sense that they have conquered their own minds and senses, and these two—the mind and senses—rule everyday life on earth. In this verse Kṛṣṇa uses the word *rājarṣi* to describe the prominent members of the *guru-paramparā*. Although he is literally referring to the kings mentioned in the previous verse,[2] anyone representing the *guru-paramparā* is both a king and a seer *(rājarṣi)*.

Text 3

स एवायं मया तेऽद्य योगः प्रोक्तः पुरातनः ।
भक्तोऽसि मे सखा चेति रहस्यं ह्येतदुत्तमम् ॥३॥

sa evāyaṁ mayā te 'dya yogaḥ proktaḥ purātanaḥ/
bhakto 'si me sakhā ceti rahasyaṁ hy etad uttamam//

saḥ—it; *eva*—certainly; *ayam*—this; *mayā*—by me; *te*—to you; *adya*—today; *yogaḥ*—the teaching of *yoga*; *proktaḥ*—imparted; *purātanaḥ*—ancient; *bhaktaḥ*—devotee; *asi*—you are; *me*—my; *sakhā*—friend; *ca*—and; *iti*—therefore; *rahasyam*—secret; *hi*—indeed; *etat*—this; *uttamam*—supreme.

1. See Śrī Jīva Goswāmī's argument in his *Tattva-sandarbha* for dismissing various texts in search of the flawless *pramāṇa* (*Śrīmad-Bhāgavatam*). In the *Gītā* itself, we find that Arjuna has quoted scripture while Kṛṣṇa rejects his citations, calling his attention to higher principles. The conclusion of scripture brings one to a point beyond "what has been heard and what is to be heard."

2. Vivasvān (the sun god), Manu (the father of humanity), and Ikṣvāku (Manu's son, a powerful earthly king).

It is this very same ancient teaching of yoga that I am teaching you today. It is the ultimate secret, but I tell it to you because you are my trusted devotee and friend.

Kṛṣṇa privileges Arjuna with this secret knowledge because of their mutual friendship and Arjuna's devotion to him. In the humility natural to a devotee of Kṛṣṇa, Arjuna did not consider himself to have the stature of great kings and gods, much less a spiritual visionary. However, in actuality true devotees of Kṛṣṇa, what to speak of his friends, are much greater than either kings or gods, and they set the standard for saintliness.

Kṛṣṇa begins to introduce the qualifications of Arjuna in verse 2 by addressing him as Parantapa, destroyer of enemies. Here it indicates his sense control, as in the case of his well-known indifference towards the heavenly damsel Urvaśī.[3] Kṛṣṇa then reveals that the transmission of spiritual knowledge from guru to disciple requires that the disciple understand the heart of the guru, as in talks between friends in the language of love. By using the words *rahasyam* and *uttamam*, Kṛṣṇa indicates that *karma-yoga*, as he is teaching it, culminates in *bhakti*, the supreme secret.[4] In this verse the word *bhakti (bhakto)* appears for the first time in the *Gītā*. Arjuna's devotion is his principal qualification for understanding the mystery of the *Gītā*.

As much as Kṛṣṇa's introductory statements regarding the history and dissemination of his teaching are intended to solidify Arjuna's conviction, the first verse of this chapter also causes further confusion in Arjuna's mind. In questioning it, Arjuna enables Kṛṣṇa to explain the nature of his descent.

Text 4

अर्जुन उवाच
अपरं भवतो जन्म परं जन्म विवस्वतः ।
कथमेतद्विजानीयां त्वमादौ प्रोक्तवानिति ॥४॥

arjuna uvāca
aparaṁ bhavato janma paraṁ janma vivasvataḥ/
katham etad vijānīyāṁ tvam ādau proktavān iti//

3. Urvaśī was very eager to have an affair with Arjuna, whom she considered the strongest human being. She met him and expressed her desires, but Arjuna sustained his impeccable character by closing his eyes before her and addressing her as mother of the Kuru dynasty.

4. See Bg. 9.2, *rāja-guhyam*.

arjunaḥ uvāca—Arjuna said; *aparam*—later; *bhavataḥ*—your; *janma*—birth; *param*—previous; *janma*—birth; *vivasvataḥ*—of Vivasvān; *katham*—how; *etat*—this; *vijānīyām*—I should understand; *tvam*—you; *ādau*—in the beginning; *proktavān*—instructed; *iti*—thus.

Arjuna said: You took birth long after Vivasvān was born. How then am I to understand that you instructed him previously?

Although the historical legacy of the doctrine of *yoga* is itself impressive, Kṛṣṇa's alleged involvement in it is bewildering to Arjuna. Arjuna, in confusion as to how Kṛṣṇa, who was standing before him, could have taught this art of work to the ancient sun god, conjectures thus: "If Kṛṣṇa taught this to the sun god, it certainly testifies to his own divinity, for it is improper for humans to instruct gods, and unusual for them to remember their previous lives."

By asking about Kṛṣṇa's apparent recent human birth in contrast with the ancient celestial birth of the sun god at the dawn of creation, Arjuna has paved the way for Kṛṣṇa to enlighten him about the divine nature of his appearance in this world. In this way, he is inching a discussion centered on self-realization in the direction of God-realization. Although this discussion of the *avatāra* is tangential to the topic at hand, it is foundational to devotion, the central theme of Kṛṣṇa's discourse.

What Kṛṣṇa has said about his instructing the sun god previously is humanly impossible. If Kṛṣṇa taught the sun god in another body, he could not remember it in his present human body. Neither could Kṛṣṇa have taught the sun god in his present body at the dawn of creation due to its apparent human and temporal nature. Thus the teaching of the *Gītā* as to the omniscient and eternal nature of Kṛṣṇa's humanlike form is introduced by Arjuna's question. Although Arjuna knows that Kṛṣṇa is God, his friendship with him sometimes covers that knowledge. Furthermore, according to Baladeva Vidyābhūṣaṇa, only Kṛṣṇa knows his own nature. Thus Kṛṣṇa explains his omniscience in verse 5 and his eternality in verse 6.

Text 5

श्रीभगवानुवाच
बहूनि मे व्यतीतानि जन्मानि तव चार्जुन ।
तान्यहं वेद सर्वाणि न त्वं वेत्थ परन्तप ॥५॥

śrī-bhagavān uvāca
bahūni me vyatītāni janmāni tava cārjuna/
tāny ahaṁ veda sarvāṇi na tvaṁ vettha parantapa//

śrī-bhagavān uvāca—the Lord of Śrī said; *bahūni*—many; *me*—of me; *vyatītāni*—passed; *janmāni*—births; *tava*—yours; *ca*—and; *arjuna*—O Arjuna; *tāni*—those; *aham*—I; *veda*—know; *sarvāṇi*—all; *na*—not; *tvam*—you; *vettha*—know; *parantapa*—O subduer of the enemy.

The Lord of Śrī said: Arjuna, both of us have passed through many births. I know all of them, whereas you, subduer of enemies, do not.

Kṛṣṇa addresses his disciple in this verse as "Arjuna" because he considers that Arjuna's question betrays the ignorance of a tree. Kṛṣṇa considers him to be covered with ignorance like the well-known arjuna tree,[5] albeit by Kṛṣṇa's own divine arrangement. Here Arjuna represents all illusioned *jīva* souls, who are ignorant of the nature and background of their own birth, and more so that of others.

By addressing Arjuna as Parantapa (slayer of enemies) Kṛṣṇa indicates that Arjuna has become further deluded. He is seeing in terms of illusory differences and thus thinking he has enemies to destroy and friends to protect. Madhusūdana Saraswatī comments that through these two addresses, Arjuna and Parantapa, the twofold nature of *māyā-śakti* is explained: *āvaraṇātmikā* (initial covering) and *prakṣepātmikā* (distorting influence). The thoughts and actions of one covered by ignorance are distorted. The address "Arjuna" indicates that *māyā* covers the soul with ignorance, and the name "Parantapa" indicates that the soul's subsequent thoughts and actions make for a distorted reality.

Baladeva Vidyābhūṣaṇa says that verses 5 through 14 contain the seeds of chapters 7 through 12, wherein Kṛṣṇa speaks directly about himself, his opulences, and devotion to himself. A gentleman does not initiate discussion about his own glory without being asked, and thus Arjuna has asked an appropriate question in order that Kṛṣṇa can begin to do so and the world can benefit from hearing him speak about himself. Parantapa also means one who gives to others. Thus we learn of Kṛṣṇa's omniscience in

5. See ŚB. 10.10 for a description of the ignorance of the arjuna tree in Kṛṣṇa *līlā*. It is a deciduous tree found throughout India. Its bark has been used in Ayurvedic medicine for over three centuries, primarily as a cardiac tonic.

this verse and next his eternality, and for this we are eternally indebted to Arjuna who has given Kṛṣṇa the opportunity to enlighten us in this regard.

Text 6

अजोऽपि सन्नव्ययात्मा भूतानामीश्वरोऽपि सन् ।
प्रकृतिं स्वामधिष्ठाय सम्भवाम्यात्ममायया ॥६॥

ajo 'pi sann avyayātmā bhūtānām īśvaro 'pi san/
prakṛtiṁ svām adhiṣṭhāya sambhavāmy ātma-māyayā//

ajaḥ—birthless; *api*—although; *san*—being; *avyaya*—imperishable; *ātmā*—myself; *bhūtānām*—of beings; *īśvaraḥ*—controller; *api*—although; *san*—being; *prakṛtim*—nature; *svām*—own; *adhiṣṭhāya*—being in control; *sambhavāmi*—I manifest; *ātma-māyayā*—by my own inner power.

Although I myself am birthless and by nature imperishable, and although I am the controller of all beings, nevertheless, remaining in control of my material energy, I manifest by my own inner power.

The latter part of this verse can also read "nevertheless, being situated *(adhiṣṭhāya)* in my own form *(prakṛtiṁ svām)*." In this rendering, *prakṛti* refers not to Kṛṣṇa's material energy, but rather to his own identity or nature. Śrīdhara Swāmī says, "Resorting to my own *prakṛti* which is made of *śuddha-sattva* (transcendence)," implying the divine nature of Kṛṣṇa's form. Rāmānuja concurs, as does Jīva Goswāmī in his *Kṛṣṇa-sandarbha* (105). In either case the purport is the same: Kṛṣṇa's form and descent are not tinged with material qualities, for he descends in a spiritual form under the influence of his primary *śakti*.

Madhusūdana Saraswatī offers a different purport to the above translation in conformance with Adwaita-vāda. At the same time, he acknowledges that "others, however, do not admit that there is a relationship of a body and possessor of the body in the case of the Supreme Lord, but that he is Vāsudeva, eternal, omnipresent, existence-knowledge-bliss through and through, full, unconditioned, and the Supreme Self. He is himself that body, and it is not anything material or made of *māyā*." Showing regard for this Vaiṣṇava interpretation, he makes no effort to refute it.

In accordance with Vaiṣṇava theology this verse as rendered above clearly distinguishes Kṛṣṇa's secondary *śakti* (*prakṛti*, material nature), which he controls, from his own inner nature, or primary *śakti* (*ātma-māyayā*), which he allows himself to come under the influence of. Kṛṣṇa's primary *śakti*, by which the affairs of the *avatāra* are carried out, is introduced for the first time in this verse.

Kṛṣṇa's primary *śakti* is mentioned again in chapter 9 with regard to his unalloyed devotees coming under its influence (Bg. 9.13). This *śakti* enables God in his appearance in the material world to be in the world but not of it. As the influence of Kṛṣṇa's secondary *śakti* is deluding, the influence of his primary *śakti* is enlightening. However, this primary *śakti* also deludes in a positive sense in the course of bringing a soul to the zenith of enlightened life. It does so by suppressing the knowledge of Kṛṣṇa's Godhood in the interest of intimate loving dealings between Kṛṣṇa and the liberated *jīva* soul. It makes Kṛṣṇa appear humanlike in spite of his Godhood. In order that the finite soul might intimately associate with the infinite, the infinite appears finite even while remaining infinite. This takes place under the influence of Kṛṣṇa's primary *śakti*. Although Kṛṣṇa says that he has passed through many births, here he qualifies this statement by explaining that he is at the same time birthless, for birth takes place under the jurisdiction of the material energy whereas his appearance is not under her jurisdiction.

The birth of Kṛṣṇa is a complex subject. He is born, but he is not born. Kṛṣṇa has already taught that all souls are unborn (Bg. 2.20), while they appear to undergo birth when identified with material bodies. In order to distinguish himself from the *jīva* souls, Kṛṣṇa says further that his form and nature are imperishable *(avyayātmā)*. Even though he is birthless, and even though his nature and form are imperishable, he appears to take birth. Yet his appearance is not a product of piety or impiety, the force of *karma* carrying one into a future life. This is so because even though he takes birth as if he were one of the living beings, he remains the controller of the destiny *(karma)* of all living beings *(bhūtānām īśvaraḥ)*. Kṛṣṇa appears in the world of our experience just as the sun appears to take birth at sunrise. He appears by his own influence, as an act of mercy *(ātma-māyayā)*. Another meaning of the word *māyā* is mercy.

Before Arjuna could ask, "If you are birthless and imperishable, when and why would you choose to appear in this world of birth and death?" Kṛṣṇa answers in the following two verses.

Text 7

यदा यदा हि धर्मस्य ग्लानिर्भवति भारत ।
अभ्युत्थानमधर्मस्य तदात्मानं सृजाम्यहम् ॥७॥

yadā yadā hi dharmasya glānir bhavati bhārata/
abhyutthānam adharmasya tadātmānaṁ sṛjāmy aham//

yadā yadā—whenever; *hi*—certainly; *dharmasya*—of *dharma*; *glāniḥ*—decrease; *bhavati*—become manifested; *bhārata*—O descendant of Bharata; *abhyutthānam*—rise; *adharmasya*—of unrighteousness; *tadā*—at that time; *ātmānam*—myself; *sṛjāmi*—manifest; *aham*—I.

Whenever, O descendant of Bharata, dharma is diminished and unrighteousness is on the rise, at that time I myself manifest.

To say that unrighteousness precedes Kṛṣṇa's appearance does not imply that his appearance is caused by it. Kṛṣṇa continues his explanation in the following verse to clarify that the time of his appearance is a time of unrighteousness, yet he himself comes to destroy it.

Text 8

परित्राणाय साधूनां विनाशाय च दुष्कृताम् ।
धर्मसंस्थापनार्थाय सम्भवामि युगे युगे ॥८॥

paritrāṇāya sādhūnāṁ vināśāya ca duṣkṛtām/
dharma-saṁsthāpanārthāya sambhavāmi yuge yuge//

paritrāṇāya—for the protection; *sādhūnām*—of the saintly; *vināśāya*—for the destruction; *ca*—and; *duṣkṛtām*—of the evil doers; *dharma*—*dharma*; *saṁsthāpana-arthāya*—to reestablish; *sambhavāmi*—I manifest; *yuge yuge*—age after age.

For the protection of the saintly and the destruction of evil doers, as well as for the purpose of establishing dharma, I manifest in every age.

Because Kṛṣṇa's saintly devotees are beyond the joy and suffering of this world, the only suffering they undergo is the pain of separation from him that they feel in his absence—the dark night of the soul. Thus Kṛṣṇa appears to mitigate their spiritual anguish. Establishing *dharma* and subduing the unrighteous come as by-products of this principal reason for Kṛṣṇa's descent. The punishment of the wicked has the goal of correcting their behavior and removing them from the world. Bhaktivedanta Swami Prabhupāda comments that Kṛṣṇa has many agents who are capable of dealing with the unrighteous, and thus his primary reason for descending involves his dealings with his devotees. Viśvanātha Cakravartī points out that Kṛṣṇa's apparent punishment of the unrighteous is in fact an act of mercy because the final result of this punishment is liberation. However, it is worth mentioning that the specific type of liberation *(sāyujya-mukti)* attained by the unrighteous through Kṛṣṇa's chastisement is undesirable for the devotees.

The unrighteous who are killed by Kṛṣṇa experience not only the death of their gross material body, but the demise of their subtle body as well. The subtle body carries the soul from one gross body to another. The subtle body consisting of a state of mind is the basis of the gross body one acquires in the next life. When the subtle body of the unrighteous person is destroyed, that person's attitude toward Kṛṣṇa immediately changes, for his opposition to Kṛṣṇa was a product of his subtle body—his unrighteous disposition. On the demise of the subtle body, his hostility toward Kṛṣṇa is transformed into love for Kṛṣṇa. Thus at the moment of death he sees Kṛṣṇa as the greatest object of affection. His liberation is not directly a result of being killed by Kṛṣṇa, but rather a result of his newfound love for him. This is the opinion of Baladeva Vidyābhūṣaṇa voiced in his *Govinda Bhāṣya* commentary on *Vedānta-sūtra.*

Having explained the nature of his descent, Kṛṣṇa next explains the result of understanding it.

Text 9

जन्म कर्म च मे दिव्यमेवं यो वेत्ति तत्त्वतः ।
त्यक्त्वा देहं पुनर्जन्म नैति मामेति सोऽर्जुन ॥९॥

janma karma ca me divyam evaṁ yo vetti tattvataḥ/
tyaktvā dehaṁ punar janma naiti mām eti so 'rjuna//

janma—birth; *karma*—activities; *ca*—and; *me*—my; *divyam*—divine; *evam*—thus; *yaḥ*—one who; *vetti*—knows; *tattvataḥ*—truly; *tyaktvā*—on giving up; *deham*—body; *punaḥ*—again; *janma*—birth; *na*—not; *eti*—goes; *mām*—me; *eti*—comes (to); *saḥ*—he; *arjuna*—O Arjuna.

One who truly understands the divine nature of my birth and activities is not reborn upon giving up his body but comes to me, O Arjuna.

Liberation is not easily attained, yet it is possible to attain it simply by understanding and accepting with faith what Kṛṣṇa has said about his appearance and activities. They are *divyam*, divine and transcendental.

Rāmānuja and the Gauḍīya commentators are of one mind in saying that here *divyam* means transcendental, not merely celestial. Śrīdhara Swāmī says *divyam* indicates that Kṛṣṇa's activities are supernatural and impossible for anyone other than God.

Jīva Goswāmī has cited this verse in his *Bhagavat-sandarbha* (48), wherein a lengthy discussion of *Śrīmad-Bhāgavatam* 8.3.8 takes place. In this section of *Bhāgavatam*, Gajendra prays for the one who is formless, nameless, and without qualities or attributes—the Absolute—to descend. In response to his prayers, Viṣṇu appears replete with form, name, qualities, and attributes. Jīva Goswāmī thus concludes that Viṣṇu is formless in the sense that his form is not material. He is birthless in the sense that his appearance in the world is not a material birth. Similarly, his qualities and activities are all transcendental. Jīva Goswāmī has presented overwhelming evidence from various scriptures to support this point of view. As stated in the *Vedas* (*Puruṣa-bodhinī Upaniṣad*), *eko devo nitya-līlānurakto bhakta-vyāpī hṛdy antarātmā:* "The one Godhead eternally sports in many diverse transcendental forms in relation to his devotees." Many other quotes are also given in the *Laghu-bhāgavatāmṛta* by Rūpa Goswāmī, establishing the eternal nature of Kṛṣṇa's birth and activities.

In this verse the word *tattvataḥ* implies faith in what Kṛṣṇa has said in verses seven, eight, and nine. Faith in Kṛṣṇa's words amounts to knowing Kṛṣṇa. Such faith does not require any logical argument as proof. The word *tattvataḥ* also means in truth, and truth is of the nature of Brahman. Indeed, later in the *Gītā* (Bg. 17.23) the sacred syllable *tat* is considered to indicate Brahman. Thus Kṛṣṇa says that one who knows him to be Brahman attains Brahman. Such a person attains *para-brahman*, Śrī Kṛṣṇa himself. Here Kṛṣṇa explains that not taking birth again (*punar janma na*), which is tantamount to liberation, means attaining him. Attaining Kṛṣṇa is true liberation. Baladeva Vidyābhūṣaṇa cites the *Śvetāśvatara Upaniṣad* (6.15): "Only by knowing him can one cross over death. There is no other path than this for liberation."

Bhakti is mentioned in this chapter in verses 3 and 11. Kṛṣṇa's own divinity is also introduced in this section, and the integration of the individual soul and God is mentioned later in verse 35. However, these themes, *bhakti* and the *Gītā's* theology, are not fully explained until we reach the second set of six chapters (Bg. 7–12). Because this chapter deals with inner wisdom (*jñāna*), knowledge is still emphasized over *bhakti*.

Text 10

वीतरागभयक्रोधा मन्मया मामुपाश्रिताः ।
बहवो ज्ञानतपसा पूता मद्भावमागताः ॥१०॥

vīta-rāga-bhaya-krodhā man-mayā mām upāśritāḥ/
bahavo jñāna-tapasā pūtā mad-bhāvam āgatāḥ//

vīta—gone away; *rāga*—attachment; *bhaya*—fear; *krodhāḥ*—anger; *mat-mayā*—thinking of me; *mām*—in me; *upāśritāḥ*—taking refuge; *bahavaḥ*—many; *jñāna*—of knowledge; *tapasā*—by the fire; *pūtāḥ*—purified; *mat-bhāvam*—my state of being; *āgatāḥ*—attained.

Free from attachment, fear, and anger, with mind absorbed in thinking of me and taking refuge in me, many persons in the past were purified by the fire of knowledge and attained me.

Here *tapasā* (austerity) also means knowledge. From austerity, knowledge develops. One deals with the pain of voluntary austerity through philosophy. It is also an austerity to try to understand the inconceivable nature of Kṛṣṇa's appearance. Those who have done so have attained the knowledge by which Kṛṣṇa is attained. Viśvanātha Cakravartī Ṭhākura also gives a novel interpretation of the words *jñāna-tapasā:* the suffering that a devotee undergoes on hearing misleading information regarding Kṛṣṇa's appearance and activities, which burns his heart like the venom of a snake. By remaining faithful to the conception Kṛṣṇa presents here, the devotee becomes purified and attains Kṛṣṇa. In keeping with this interpretation, Viśvanātha Cakravartī also takes *vīta-rāga-bhaya-krodhā* to mean that the devotee does not show affection, fear, or anger to people who express such erroneous understandings of God's nature and pastimes. This is possible because he takes shelter of Kṛṣṇa and constantly engages in glorifying him.

Cultivating the proper understanding of Kṛṣṇa is a powerful spiritual practice. In spite of all that he has taught thus far concerning *karma-yoga,* Kṛṣṇa says here that simply hearing about him, his appearance and activities *(līlā)*, is sufficient to bring about one's liberation, and more, love of God. Viśvanātha Cakravartī understands *mad-bhāvam āgatāḥ* (attained my state of being) in this verse to mean that purified persons have "attained love for me." Here Kṛṣṇa says that many persons in the past have experienced this. This is the path taken by his devotees. Knowledge of the nature of Kṛṣṇa's transcendental *līlā* is much higher than mere knowledge of the difference between the self and matter. As confirmed in this verse, those who understand Kṛṣṇa's birth and activities in truth are free from attachment, fear, and anger. Their minds are absorbed in thinking of him. They take refuge in Kṛṣṇa and are purified by the fire of knowledge. All of this is involved in attaining him, and it constitutes the foundation of understanding Kṛṣṇa.

Madhusūdana Saraswatī says that after attaining the status of *jīvanmukta*, persons can develop an affectionate attitude toward Kṛṣṇa called *rati* (love). However, although he says this, he teaches that this *rati*, through which the *jīvanmukta* relishes Kṛṣṇa *līlā*, does not extend into *videha-mukti* (final release). This is in sharp contrast to Vaiṣṇavism, where the *jivanmukta* experiences *rati* for Kṛṣṇa and continues to do so in Kṛṣṇa *līlā* after final release.

As the devotional path surfaces in Kṛṣṇa's mind, he reflects on his different types of devotees in whose hearts spiritual emotion for him arises, dictating their particular loving approach. He thinks of his servants, friends, elders, and lovers who participate in the drama of divine love. As those in whose hearts deep spiritual emotion *(bhāva/rati)* for Kṛṣṇa has awakened take refuge completely in him, they enter his *līlā* accordingly. Reflecting in the following verse primarily on these devotees, Kṛṣṇa also reflects secondarily on all beings and their relationship with him, even in the state of bondage. He does so as Arjuna mentally questions, "Your devotees know your birth and activities to be eternally true, but others, such as the *jñānīs*, think of them in a different way. So what happens to them? In response to this, Kṛṣṇa speaks the following verse.

Text 11

ये यथा मां प्रपद्यन्ते तांस्तथैव भजाम्यहम् ।
मम वर्त्मानुवर्तन्ते मनुष्याः पार्थ सर्वशः ॥११॥

ye yathā māṁ prapadyante tāṁs tathaiva bhajāmy aham/
mama vartmānuvartante manuṣyāḥ pārtha sarvaśaḥ//

ye—those who; *yathā*—in whatever way; *mām*—me; *prapadyante*—take refuge in; *tān*—them; *tathā*—that way; *eva*—certainly; *bhajāmi*—reciprocate; *aham*—I; *mama*—my; *vartma*—path; *anuvartante*—follow; *manuṣyāḥ*—men; *pārtha*—O son of Pṛthā; *sarvaśaḥ*—all.

In whatever way people take refuge in me, I reciprocate with them accordingly. Everyone in all circumstances, O son of Pṛthā, follows my path.

Kṛṣṇa is speaking primarily about his devotees here, but at the same time he addresses others who directly or indirectly approach him for something other than entering his *līlā*—such as those interested in self-realization, both *karma* and *jñāna-yogīs*. He has also addressed those who unknowingly approach him as well, by stating that all persons follow his path whether they realize it or not. Those who worship the gods for material gain also worship Kṛṣṇa indirectly because the gods are partial manifestations of Kṛṣṇa. Such worshippers are unaware that the gods are dependent on Kṛṣṇa to fulfill anyone's desires.

Although Kṛṣṇa reciprocates with all who approach him, they do not all get the same result. Yet he is not partial. While the paths of *karma-yoga, jñāna-yoga,* and *bhakti-yoga* all lead to him in varying degrees, those approaching through *karma* and *jñāna* have desires. The *karma-yogī*'s desires are purified and he attains knowledge of the self. In self-knowledge such *jñāna-yogīs* desire and attain liberation. This attainment is Kṛṣṇa's reciprocation relative to their approach. Those on the path of *bhakti* attain love of Kṛṣṇa *(mad-bhāvam āgatāḥ)* in accordance with their particular *bhāva*. They do not desire anything material, nor do they aspire for liberation, which is a by-product of entering Kṛṣṇa's divine *līlā*.

Among Kṛṣṇa's devotees the Vraja *gopīs*' approach to him is most notable. Although Kṛṣṇa promises in this verse to reciprocate the measure of his devotees' love, he found it difficult to fulfill this promise after experiencing the *gopīs*' love. Therefore he told them that they must be satisfied with their love itself, for he himself surrenders to this love, *na pāraye 'haṁ niravadya-saṁyujām* (ŚB. 10.32.22). Because their love is more powerful than his, in accordance with his statement in this verse, he worships them. He is purchased by their love. Kṛṣṇa surrendering to the mystery of the *gopīs*' love is the deepest significance of the appearance and precepts of Śrī Caitanya, who taught that there is no superior means of approaching Kṛṣṇa than that which was conceived by the Vraja *gopīs*. The Vraja *gopīs*' love is thus the deepest import of this verse. The object of love that corresponds with the *gopīs*' standard of love is *svayaṁ bhagavān* Kṛṣṇa.

Overall, Kṛṣṇa is the architect of the cosmic order, but not its author. Desire writes the story. The desire or ideal of people determines their conception of God.

Text 12

काङ्क्षन्तः कर्मणां सिद्धिं यजन्त इह देवताः ।
क्षिप्रं हि मानुषे लोके सिद्धिर्भवति कर्मजा ॥१२॥

kāṅkṣantaḥ karmaṇāṁ siddhiṁ yajanta iha devatāḥ/
kṣipraṁ hi mānuṣe loke siddhir bhavati karma-jā//

kāṅkṣantaḥ—desiring; *karmaṇām*—of activities; *siddhim*—success; *yajante*—they perform sacrifices; *iha*—in this world; *devatāḥ*—to the gods; *kṣipram*—quickly; *hi*—surely; *mānuṣe*—in human society; *loke*—in the world; *siddhiḥ*—success; *bhavati*—comes; *karma-jā*—born of ritualistic acts.

Worldly people who desire material success perform sacrifice in worship of the gods. Surely in this world they quickly get results from such ritualistic acts.

The vast majority of people are interested in material enjoyment. Thus they do not worship Kṛṣṇa. In times gone by such people worshipped his agents, the gods. They attained their desired result quickly in comparison to how long it took for those interested in spiritual matters to attain a result.

Material goals are much more common than spiritual ones, and in our times people seem to attain them without any type of worship at all. However, the principle of worship is not limited to the realm of religion. Gurus and gods abound in all spheres of social and political life. Kowtowing to the growing corporate globalization wins elections, yet it imprisons the victors themselves. We may resist such worship in pursuit of human dignity, but our highest prospect lies in realizing the dignity of the soul.

We must answer to no one other than our own soul and God, and to do so we must withdraw our patronage of the material ego itself, championing neither the rich nor the poor. This is the nondual ground on which the devotee kneels in prayer; it is the drum he beats; it is the key in which he sings in praise of Kṛṣṇa. Such devotees find freedom and dignity in the act of being both an instrument and ingredient of worship, not merely participating in the act of worship while keeping themselves apart. The dignity of the soul is won at the cost of one's very self, a price many are not prepared to pay.

Pure devotion is rarely attained, and thus people in general are less interested in this, even though the results of such devotion far exceed that of any other course of action. Those interested in spiritual life are rare and devotees rarer still. Even so, Kṛṣṇa has not neglected the masses. He suggests a God-centered socioreligious system that will help them gradually become free from material desire. This is a system in which people can strive to perform their God-given duty in life responsibly without concern for the immediate result, knowing that the proper execution of one's ordained duty is itself a greater reward that will develop and eventually mature into spiritual realization. Kṛṣṇa mentions this system next in the overall context of explaining the secret of impartiality and detachment in action, citing himself as an example.

Text 13

चातुर्वर्ण्यं मया सृष्टं गुणकर्मविभागशः ।
तस्य कर्तारमपि मां विद्ध्यकर्तारमव्ययम् ॥१३॥

cātur-varṇyaṁ mayā sṛṣṭaṁ guṇa-karma-vibhāgaśaḥ/
tasya kartāram api māṁ viddhy akartāram avyayam//

cātuḥ-varṇyam—socioreligious order with its fourfold division; *mayā*— by me; *sṛṣṭam*—created; *guṇa*—quality; *karma*—propensity to act; *vibhāgaśaḥ*—according to; *tasya*—of that; *kartāram*—the author; *api*—although; *mām*—me; *viddhi*—you should know; *akartāram*—as the nondoer; *avyayam*—imperishable.

In consideration of the influence of the guṇas and one's karma, I created the fourfold division of socioreligious order (caste). Although I created this system, you should know that I am imperishable and not responsible for the results derived from it.

Kṛṣṇa creates the socioreligious system of the four orders. In this system, prescribed duties correspond with one's acquired karmic propensity, which is determined by the threefold influence *(guṇas)* of material nature. Thus persons predominantly influenced by *sattva* (goodness) are prescribed the religious work suitable for intellectuals, whereas warriors like Arjuna who are predominantly influenced by *rajas* (passion) are enjoined to administer, organize, and lead people in religious life. Those whose psyche is predominantly influenced by an admixture of *rajas* and *tamas* (ignorance) are enjoined to mercantile and agricultural activity, while those predominantly under the influence of *tamas* are enjoined to labor. Kṛṣṇa will speak more about the influence of these modes of nature *(guṇas)* and thereby indirectly about this socioreligious system later, in chapters 14, 17, and 18. Otherwise, the system itself is well known to Arjuna, as it was in place at the time.

Varṇāśrama-dharma is rooted in ultimate reality in that it superficially governs interaction in Kṛṣṇa *līlā* and is mentioned here as having been created by God himself. Thus its essence must have universal application. It is essentially a systematic attempt to organize society so that in the course of realizing material values, spiritual values are also pursued. It is a system in which the spiritual is given the highest priority. However, many of its particulars relevant to Vedic times, such as its monarchical form of government, would be counterproductive to attempt to implement in today's society. Indeed, any attempt to resurrect *varṇāśrama-dharma* in all respects will be fraught with obstacles, while its essence, its spirit of dutiful work, and the ultimate ideal it seeks to gently push one in the direction of should meet with wide acceptance.

Here Kṛṣṇa seeks not to explain this system, but merely to point out his own position in relationship to it: although he is its creator, he stands aloof from it. The system itself gives results in accordance with how individuals apply themselves.

Kṛṣṇa is beyond the socioreligious system he sets in motion, and thus the method of attaining love for him and entering his *līlā* cannot come from merely following this system alone. Other than making this important point in the context of his ultimate advocacy of devotion, Kṛṣṇa points here to himself as an example of one who acts without accruing karmic reactions. One could hardly imagine doing something more than establishing a socioreligious system, yet although he has done so, Kṛṣṇa says that he is not bound by it. This is what Kṛṣṇa wants Arjuna to do at present: act such that he is not bound by karmic reactions. Kṛṣṇa also wants Arjuna to understand his supreme status. Thus while explaining his unique position, knowledge of which is essential for devotion, Kṛṣṇa also points to his own example in the next verse to further inspire Arjuna to act in *karma-yoga*.

Text 14

न मां कर्माणि लिम्पन्ति न मे कर्मफले स्पृहा ।
इति मां योऽभिजानाति कर्मभिर्न स बध्यते ॥१४॥

na māṁ karmāṇi limpanti na me karma-phale spṛhā/
iti māṁ yo 'bhijānāti karmabhir na sa badhyate//

na—not; *mām*—me; *karmāṇi*—works; *limpanti*—implicate; *na*—not; *me*—my; *karma-phale*—in the fruits of action; *spṛhā*—desire; *iti*—thus; *mām*—me; *yaḥ*—one who; *abhijānāti*—understands; *karmabhiḥ*—by karmic reactions; *na*—not; *saḥ*—he; *badhyate*—becomes bound.

There is no work that implicates me. I have no desire for the fruits of action. One who understands me thus is not bound by reactions to work.

Baladeva Vidyābhūṣaṇa comments that Kṛṣṇa's position is like that of rain. Rain causes the creation of vegetation, yet it derives nothing from the vegetation it creates. Kṛṣṇa is free from partiality because he is self-satisfied. He acts only for the welfare of others. Thus detachment from the results of one's work causes freedom from bondage. It is not action that binds one, but the desire to enjoy the fruit of one's actions.

Text 15

एवं ज्ञात्वा कृतं कर्म पूर्वैरपि मुमुक्षुभिः ।
कुरु कर्मैव तस्मात्त्वं पूर्वैः पूर्वतरं कृतम् ॥१५॥

evaṁ jñātvā kṛtaṁ karma pūrvair api mumukṣubhiḥ/
kuru karmaiva tasmāt tvaṁ pūrvaiḥ pūrvataraṁ kṛtam//

evam—thus; *jñātvā*—knowing; *kṛtam*—performed; *karma*—action; *pūrvaiḥ*—by the ancients; *api*—also; *mumukṣubhiḥ*—by those who seek liberation; *kuru*—perform; *karma*—action; *eva*—certainly; *tasmāt*—therefore; *tvam*—you; *pūrvaiḥ*—by the ancients; *pūrva-taram*—in the past; *kṛtam*—as performed.

Having known this, ancient seekers of transcendence also performed action. Therefore, now you should also act as the ancients did.

The ancient seekers referred to in this verse are Vivasvān, Manu, and Ikṣvāku. They are all mentioned in the first verse of this chapter. Kṛṣṇa implores Arjuna to follow their example. Here Kṛṣṇa says, "Knowing means acting." If one's heart is not pure, one should perform detached action, and if one's heart is pure, one should act to set an example for others. Next Kṛṣṇa begins to explain the intricacies of action.

Text 16

किं कर्म किमकर्मेति कवयोऽप्यत्र मोहिताः ।
तत्ते कर्म प्रवक्ष्यामि यज्ज्ञात्वा मोक्ष्यसेऽशुभात् ॥१६॥

kiṁ karma kim akarmeti kavayo 'py atra mohitāḥ/
tat te karma pravakṣyāmi yaj jñātvā mokṣyase 'śubhāt//

kim—what; *karma*—action; *kim*—what; *akarma*—inaction; *iti*—thus; *kavayaḥ*—learned persons; *api*—also; *atra*—in this matter; *mohitāḥ*—are confused; *tat*—that; *te*—to you; *karma*—action; *pravakṣyāmi*—I will explain; *yat*—which; *jñātvā*—knowing; *mokṣyase*—you will be freed; *aśubhāt*—from evil.

Even learned people are confused as to what constitutes action and what constitutes inaction. I will now explain action, understanding which you shall be freed from evil.

One may question what is so difficult about understanding action or inaction. One either acts or does not. However, the truth of the intricacies of action and inaction are unknown even to discriminating persons. Thus Kṛṣṇa next explains the intricacies of action prescribed in the sacred literature, the action prohibited therein, and selfless action performed without egotism that constitutes true inaction.

Text 17

कर्मणो ह्यपि बोद्धव्यं बोद्धव्यं च विकर्मणः ।
अकर्मणश्च बोद्धव्यं गहना कमणो गतिः ॥१७॥

karmaṇo hy api boddhavyaṁ boddhavyaṁ ca vikarmaṇaḥ/
akarmaṇaś ca boddhavyaṁ gahanā karmaṇo gatiḥ//

karmaṇaḥ—of prescribed action; *hi*—certainly; *api*—also; *boddhavyam*—to be understood; *boddhavyam*—to be understood; *ca*—also; *vikarmaṇaḥ*—of prohibited action; *akarmaṇaḥ*—of inaction; *ca*—also; *boddhavyam*—to be understood; *gahanā*—mysterious; *karmaṇaḥ*—of action; *gatiḥ*—path.

One must know the nature of prescribed action, the nature of prohibited action, and also the nature of inaction. The path of action is mysterious.

Text 18

कर्मण्यकर्म यः पश्येदकर्मणि च कर्म यः ।
स बुद्धिमान् मनुष्येषु स युक्तः कृत्स्नकर्मकृत् ॥१८॥

karmaṇy akarma yaḥ paśyed akarmaṇi ca karma yaḥ/
sa buddhimān manuṣyeṣu sa yuktaḥ kṛtsna-karma-kṛt//

karmaṇi—in action; *akarma*—inaction; *yaḥ*—one who; *paśyet*—perceives; *akarmaṇi*—in inaction; *ca*—and; *karma*—action; *yaḥ*—one who; *saḥ*—he;

buddhi-mān—wise; *manuṣyeṣu*—in human society; *saḥ*—he; *yuktaḥ*—spiritually situated; *kṛtsna-karma-kṛt*—while engaged in all activities.

One who perceives inaction in action and action in inaction is wise in human society. Such a person is spiritually situated while engaged in all types of work.

The emphasis here is on egoless action. In egoless action one accrues no karmic reaction and remains thereby inactive. This should be adopted, and one should avoid artificial attempts at inaction, in which one acts nonetheless and accrues karmic reactions. As Kṛṣṇa has said earlier, "No one can be free from action even for a moment." Kṛṣṇa wants to make it abundantly clear to Arjuna that the type of selfless action he advocates is itself knowledge. Perfectly executed, *karma-yoga* is perfect knowledge. Kṛṣṇa elaborates on this point in the following five verses, and in doing so he describes the life of the true practitioner of *karma-yoga*, as well as the life of one who has attained perfection.

Text 19

यस्य सर्वे समारम्भाः कामसङ्कल्पवर्जिताः ।
ज्ञानाग्निदग्धकर्माणं तमाहुः पण्डितं बुधाः ॥१९॥

yasya sarve samārambhāḥ kāma-saṅkalpa-varjitāḥ/
jñānāgni-dagdha-karmāṇaṁ tam āhuḥ paṇḍitaṁ budhāḥ//

yasya—of whom; *sarve*—all; *samārambhaḥ*—undertakings; *kāma*—desire for sense gratification; *saṅkalpa*—motivation; *varjitāḥ*—devoid; *jñāna*—knowledge; *agni*—fire; *dagdha*—consumed; *karmāṇam*—karmic reactions; *tam*—him; *āhuḥ*—call; *paṇḍitam*—sage; *budhāḥ*—the wise.

A person who has removed desire and motivation from his undertakings, and consumed his karmic reactions in the fire of knowledge is called a sage by the wise.

According to Madhusūdana Saraswatī, here desire *(kāma)* means hankering for results, and motivation *(saṅkalpa)* indicates the sense of agentship, thinking oneself the doer. The word *sarve* in this verse indicates that all actions, those prescribed in the *Vedas* or otherwise, including even prohibited actions, have no capacity to bind one whose actions are *kāma-saṅkalpa-varjitāḥ*.

Baladeva Vidyābhūṣaṇa glosses *kāma-saṅkalpa-varjitāḥ* as "activities directed to the self or personal objectives" *(karmabhiḥ ātmoddeśinaḥ bhavanti)*. Both he and Viśvanātha Cakravartī Ṭhākura agree with Śrīdhara Swāmī's comments, who glosses *kāma* as "fruits" and *saṅkalpa* as "the desire for fruits."

Text 20

त्यक्त्वा कर्मफलासङ्गं नित्यतृप्तो निराश्रयः ।
कर्मण्यभिप्रवृत्तोऽपि नैव किञ्चित् करोति सः ॥२०॥

tyaktvā karma-phalāsaṅgaṁ nitya-tṛpto nirāśrayaḥ/
karmaṇy abhipravṛtto 'pi naiva kiñcit karoti saḥ//

tyaktvā—abandoning; *karma-phala-āsaṅgam*—attachment to the fruits of action; *nitya*—always; *tṛptaḥ*—satisfied; *nirāśrayaḥ*—independent; *karmaṇi*—in action; *abhipravṛttaḥ*—engaged; *api*—even; *na*—not; *eva*—at all; *kiñcit*—anything; *karoti*—does; *saḥ*—he.

Abandoning attachment to the fruits of action, always satisfied and independent, even while acting, such a person does nothing at all.

One who acts without desire to attain something mundane is always satisfied *(nitya-tṛpto)* and independent *(nirāśrayaḥ)* from the body.

Text 21

निराशीर्यतचित्तात्मा त्यक्तसर्वपरिग्रहः ।
शारीरं केवलं कर्म कुर्वन्नाप्नोति किल्बिषम् ॥२१॥

nirāśīr yata-cittātmā tyakta-sarva-parigrahaḥ/
śārīraṁ kevalaṁ karma kurvan nāpnoti kilbiṣam//

nirāśīḥ—without desire; *yata*—disciplined; *citta-ātmā*—mind and intelligence; *tyakta*—given up; *sarva*—all; *parigrahaḥ*—sense of proprietorship; *śārīram*—body; *kevalam*—only; *karma*—action; *kurvan*—doing; *na*—not; *āpnoti*—incurs; *kilbiṣam*—evil.

Having given up all sense of proprietorship, such a person of disciplined spiritual intelligence, who performs only bodily actions, incurs no evil.

Emerging from *samādhi (vyutthāna* from *samādhi)* for the maintenance of the body and engaging in begging alms does not implicate the sage in karmic reactions. Here Kṛṣṇa reasons that if one whose actions are devoid of desire and resolve is not implicated even when engaged in elaborate Vedic rites for material acquisition, how much more is this so for one who merely acts for the maintenance of the body.

Text 22

यदृच्छालाभसन्तुष्टो द्वन्द्वातीतो विमत्सरः ।
समः सिद्धावसिद्धौ च कृत्वापि न निबध्यते ॥२२॥

yadṛcchā-lābha-santuṣṭo dvandvātīto vimatsaraḥ/
samaḥ siddhāv asiddhau ca kṛtvāpi na nibadhyate//

yadṛcchā—of its own accord; *lābha*—gain; *santuṣṭaḥ*—content; *dvandva*—duality; *atītaḥ*—transcended; *vimatsaraḥ*—free from envy; *samaḥ*—steady; *siddhau*—in success; *asiddhau*—in failure; *ca*—also; *kṛtvā*—doing; *api*—even though; *na*—not; *nibadhyate*—becomes bound.

Content with that which comes of its own accord, transcending dualities, free from envy, and steady in the face of success or failure, even though acting, such a person is not bound by karmic reactions.

Scripture enjoins that monks can collect alms and minimally clothe themselves. Such acquisition on their part is called *yadṛcchā-lābha*. The word *yadṛcchā* means "without being asked for." This verse speaks of one who is satisfied with this, *yadṛcchā-lābha-santuṣṭaḥ*. By stating this in the present verse, Kṛṣṇa clarifies "possessionless" *(tyakta-sarva-parigrahaḥ)* in the previous verse.

In the state of *samādhi* one has no perception of dualities such as heat and cold. However upon emerging from *samādhi* one becomes aware of them. In this state of emergence, the sage, although afflicted by dualities, is not perturbed by them. Thus he lives his life transcendent to material dualities, and because of this he is not envious of anyone. *Vimatsaraḥ* means freedom from *mātsarya*, the inability to tolerate the excellence of another. Such a person is equipoised *(samaḥ)* amidst material success and failure.

Text 23

गतसङ्गस्य मुक्तस्य ज्ञानावस्थितचेतसः ।
यज्ञायाचरतः कर्म समग्रं प्रविलीयते ॥२३॥

gata-saṅgasya muktasya jñānāvasthita-cetasaḥ/
yajñāyācarataḥ karma samagraṁ pravilīyate//

gata-saṅgasya—of one unattached; *muktasya*—of the liberated; *jñāna-avasthita*—established in knowledge; *cetasaḥ*—thought; *yajñāya*—for the sake of sacrifice; *ācarataḥ*—acting; *karma*—*karma*; *samagram*—wholly; *pravilīyate*—dissolved.

A liberated soul established in knowledge, who is free from attachment and acts only in sacrifice, dissipates all his karma.

Madhusūdana Saraswatī comments that *yajñāyācarataḥ* means acts performed for the satisfaction of Viṣṇu. Such actions do not bind the performer. Thus not only the monk who performs action for the maintenance of his body is free from material consequences, but he who engages in any action for the satisfaction of Viṣṇu. This part of the verse is a reiteration of verse 19. It also leads into the following verse, which explains the spiritual quality of sacrifice.

Text 24

ब्रह्मार्पणं ब्रह्म हविर्ब्रह्माग्नौ ब्रह्मणा हुतम् ।
ब्रह्मैव तेन गन्तव्यं ब्रह्मकर्मसमाधिना ॥२४॥

brahmārpaṇaṁ brahma havir brahmāgnau brahmaṇā hutam/
brahmaiva tena gantavyaṁ brahma-karma-samādhinā//

brahma—Brahman; *arpaṇam*—offering; *brahma*—Brahman; *haviḥ*—oblation; *brahma*—Brahman; *agnau*—in the fire; *brahmaṇā*—by Brahman; *hutam*—offered; *brahma*—Brahman; *eva*—certainly; *tena*—by him; *gantavyam*—to be reached; *brahma*—Brahman; *karma*—action; *samādhinā*—by absorption.

In acts of sacrifice, that by which the offering is made is Brahman, as is the offering itself. Sacrifice is offered by one who is himself Brahman into the fire of Brahman. One who is absorbed thus in thoughts of Brahman in relation to sacrificial action attains Brahman.

Having described the union of action and knowledge resulting from self-knowledge, Kṛṣṇa explains in this section from verse 24 to 30 how persons acting sacrificially understand that Brahman permeates all sacrificial action by pervading and sustaining everything related to it. The action performed by one concerned with liberation is permeated by the consciousness that everything involved with sacrificial action is an embodiment of the Absolute. Such action is itself an expression of that consciousness. Thus action in the spirit of sacrifice is a form of knowledge directly leading to self-realization without the necessity of a separate endeavor in contemplative life. When Brahman is realized, the cause of reactionary work—ignorance—ceases to exist even in the midst of action.

In this verse Kṛṣṇa describes the goal of sacrificial performance. Then, in order to praise this attainment, he describes different types of sacrifices that serve as a means of attaining realization of the all-pervasive nature of Brahman.

Text 25

दैवमेवापरे यज्ञं योगिनः पर्युपासते ।
ब्रह्माग्नावपरे यज्ञं यज्ञेनैवोपजुह्वति ॥२५॥

daivam evāpare yajñaṁ yoginaḥ paryupāsate/
brahmāgnāv apare yajñaṁ yajñenaivopajuhvati//

daivam—to a god; *eva*—indeed; *apare*—others; *yajñam*—sacrifice; *yoginaḥ*—yogīs; *paryupāsate*—practice; *brahma*—Brahman; *agnau*—in the fire; *apare*—others; *yajñam*—sacrifice; *yajñena*—by sacrifice; *eva*—thus; *upajuhvati*—offer.

Others offer sacrifices to the gods. Still others offer themselves into the fire of Brahman.

The first two lines of this verse refer to *karma-yogīs* who worship the gods through Vedic sacrifice. They worship the Godhead indirectly. Those already in knowledge of the self by *karma-yoga* are referred to in the second half of the verse. Metaphorically speaking, they offer themselves directly to the Absolute, as if they themselves were the sacrificial clarified butter used in the worship of the gods. The fire of Brahman mentioned in this verse is the same as that mentioned in verses 19 and 37, the fire of transcendental wisdom.

Baladeva Vidyābhūṣaṇa understands this verse and all of the verses in the following section to refer to *karma-yoga*. Because they have the search for spiritual realization at their heart, they are to be considered forms of knowledge.

Text 26

श्रोत्रादीनीन्द्रियाण्यन्ये संयमाग्निषु जुह्वति ।
शब्दादीन्विषयानन्य इन्द्रियाग्निषु जुह्वति ॥२६॥

śrotrādīnīndriyāṇy anye saṁyamāgniṣu juhvati/
śabdādīn viṣayān anya indriyāgniṣu juhvati//

śrotra-ādīni—such as the sense of hearing; *indriyāṇi*—senses; *anye*—others; *saṁyama*—controlled; *agniṣu*—in the fires; *juhvati*—offer; *śabda-ādīn*—sound, etc.; *viṣayān*—sense objects; *anye*—others; *indriya*—sense organ; *agniṣu*—in the fires; *juhvati*—offer.

Others offer the senses such as the sense of hearing into the fire of the controlled mind, while others offer sound and the other sense objects themselves into the fire of the senses.

In this verse Kṛṣṇa first describes life-long celibates, and then those involved in household life, who more readily interact with sense objects. The life-long celibates renounce ordinary action and engage in hearing continuously about the Absolute. In this way they sacrifice their senses' activities into the sacrificial fire of the controlled mind. The householder engages his senses in ordinary actions such that they become an offering unto the Absolute. In this way the objects of his senses are sacrificed into the figurative fire of controlled senses.

Text 27

सर्वाणीन्द्रियकर्माणि प्राणकर्माणि चापरे ।
आत्मसंयमयोगाग्नौ जुह्वति ज्ञानदीपिते ॥२७॥

sarvāṇīndriya-karmāṇi prāṇa-karmāṇi cāpare/
ātma-saṁyama-yogāgnau juhvati jñāna-dīpite//

sarvāṇi—all; *indriya*—senses; *karmāṇi*—functions; *prāṇa-karmāṇi*—functions of the life airs; *ca*—also; *apare*—others; *ātma-saṁyama*—self-restraint; *yoga*—yoga; *agnau*—in the fire; *juhvati*—offer; *jñāna-dīpite*—ignite by knowledge.

Others offer the functions of all the organs and the functions of the life airs in the fire of self-restrained yoga, which is ignited by knowledge.

Here Kṛṣṇa refers to those who follow the *Yoga-sūtras*. They offer the knowledge-acquiring faculties of seeing, hearing, and so on, and the working senses, such as hands and legs, as well as the life airs into the symbolic fire of self-restraint in *yoga-sādhana*. This figurative fire is ignited by knowledge of the object of meditation—Brahman—which retires the ordinary functions of the knowledge-acquiring and working senses.

Text 28

द्रव्ययज्ञास्तपोयज्ञा योगयज्ञास्तथापरे ।
स्वाध्यायज्ञानयज्ञाश्च यतयः संशितव्रताः ॥२८॥

dravya-yajñās tapo-yajñā yoga-yajñās tathāpare/
svādhyāya-jñāna-yajñāś ca yatayaḥ saṁśita-vratāḥ//

dravya-yajñāḥ—sacrifices of one's possessions; *tapaḥ-yajñāḥ*—sacrifices through austerities; *yoga-yajñāḥ*—sacrifices through *yoga*; *tathā*—and; *apare*—others; *svādhyāya*—reciting the scriptures to oneself; *jñāna-yajñāḥ*—sacrifices through knowledge; *ca*—also; *yatayaḥ*—ascetics; *saṁśita-vratāḥ*—of severe vows.

Some sacrifice through acts of charity, others sacrifice through austerities, and others through yoga practice, while ascetics of severe vows do so through scriptural study and knowledge.

Text 29

अपाने जुह्वति प्राणं प्राणेऽपानं तथापरे ।
प्राणापानगती रुद्ध्वा प्राणायामपरायणाः ।
अपरे नियताहाराः प्राणान् प्राणेषु जुह्वति ॥२९॥

apāne juhvati prāṇaṁ prāṇe 'pānaṁ tathāpare/
prāṇāpāna-gatī ruddhvā prāṇāyāma-parāyaṇāḥ/
apare niyatāhārāḥ prāṇān prāṇeṣu juhvati//

apāne—in exhalation; *juhvati*—offer; *prāṇam*—inhalation; *prāṇe*—in inhalation; *apānam*—exhalation; *tathā*—also; *apare*—others; *prāṇa-apāna-gatī*—the movement of inhalation and exhalation; *ruddhvā*—restraining; *prāṇa-āyāma*—breath control; *parāyaṇāḥ*—intent on; *apare*—others; *niyata*—having controlled; *āhārāḥ*—eating; *prāṇān*—vital airs; *prāṇeṣu*—in the airs; *juhvati*—offer.

Others practice breath control. They offer inhalation into exhalation and exhalation into inhalation thereby restraining both. Still others restrict their intake of food and restrain their breath, sacrificing their vital force.

Breath control is known a *prāṇāyāma*. In this practice the *yogī* closes the right nostril and inhales through the left nostril and in this way offers his inhalation into his exhalation. Reversing this process he offers his exhalation into his inhalation and thereby restrains both his ingoing and outgoing breath.

Another type of *yogī* restricts his intake of food by filling his stomach with only two parts food and one part water, leaving one part empty for air to circulate. He restrains his breath such that he causes his life airs to merge into a singular vital force concentrated in the mouth.

Verses 26 through 29 refer to eightfold mystic *yoga*. In verse 28, *yama*, *niyama*, and *āsana* are implied in the word *yoga-yajñāḥ*. In this verse, *prāṇāyāma* is referred to. Verse 26 refers to *pratyāhāra* in the words, "others offer the senses." The three stages known as *dhāraṇa*, *dhyāna*, and *samādhi* are referred to in verse 27 through the word *saṁyama*.

Texts 30–31

सर्वेऽप्येते यज्ञविदो यज्ञक्षपितकल्मषाः ।
यज्ञशिष्टामृतभुजो यान्ति ब्रह्म सनातनम् ॥३०॥
नायं लोकोऽस्त्ययज्ञस्य कुतोऽन्यः कुरुसत्तम ॥३१॥

sarve 'py ete yajña-vido yajña-kṣapita-kalmaṣāḥ/
yajña-śiṣṭāmṛta-bhujo yānti brahma sanātanam//
nāyaṁ loko 'sty ayajñasya kuto 'nyaḥ kuru-sattama//

sarve—all; *api*—also; *ete*—these; *yajña-vidaḥ*—those with knowledge of sacrifice; *yajña-kṣapita*—purified through sacrifice; *kalmaṣāḥ*—evils; *yajña-śiṣṭa*—sacrificial remnants; *amṛta-bhujaḥ*—those who have tasted nectar; *yānti*—attain; *brahma*—Brahman; *sanātanam*—eternal; *na*—not; *ayam*—this; *lokaḥ*—world; *asti*—there is; *ayajñasya*—of one who performs no sacrifice; *kutaḥ*—how; *anyaḥ*—other; *kuru-sat-tama*—O best of the Kurus.

All these persons know well the purpose of sacrifice and are purified from evil through its performance. They enjoy the nectar of sacrificial remnants and attain eternal Brahman. O best of the Kuru dynasty, without sacrifice no one can live happily even in this world; what then of the other?

Sacrifice yields results in this world in the form of knowledge, mystic power, and material opulence. After leaving this world such sacrificers attain Brahman/Paramātmā. All of the various sacrificers mentioned in the preceding verses attain their respective goals in this world and ultimately attain the fruit of self-realization.

Text 32

एवं बहुविधा यज्ञा वितता ब्रह्मणो मुखे ।
कर्मजान्विद्धि तान् सर्वानेवं ज्ञात्वा विमोक्ष्यसे ॥३२॥

evaṁ bahu-vidhā yajñā vitatā brahmaṇo mukhe/
karma-jān viddhi tān sarvān evaṁ jñātvā vimokṣyase//

evam—thus; *bahu-vidhāḥ*—various kinds; *yajñāḥ*—sacrifices; *vitatāḥ*—spread; *brahmaṇaḥ*—of the sacred literature; *mukhe*—through the mouth; *karma-jān*—born from action; *viddhi*—you should know; *tān*—them; *sarvān*—all; *evam*—thus; *jñātvā*—knowing; *vimokṣyase*—you shall be liberated.

In this way, there are many sacrifices that have emanated from the mouth of the sacred literature. You should know that they are born from action. Thus knowing, you shall be liberated.

In verse 31 Kṛṣṇa says that without sacrifice one has no standing in this world, what to speak of the next world. In this verse he implies that this opinion is supported by the *Vedas*, *vitatā brahmaṇo mukhe*. Śaṅkara takes "Brahman" in this verse to mean the *Vedas*. Both Baladeva Vidyābhūṣaṇa and Viśvanātha Cakravartī concur with Śaṅkara. Sacrifice is mandated in the *Vedas* as a basis for life in this world, and such sacrifice assures one's standing in the next. Life is about sacrifice, giving. Short of this, we do not get and do not live.

Another possible rendering of the phrase *vitatā brahmaṇo mukhe* is "offered in the presence of Brahman." Sacrificial acts are born of Brahman and are themselves Brahman, thus acting as a link between time and eternity. They are not, as Śaṅkara would have it, entirely foreign to the self. Śrīpāda Rāmānuja says that they are a means by which one gains possession of one's own self. They emanate from Brahman and lead to the wisdom of Brahman.

Text 33

श्रेयान् द्रव्यमयाद्यज्ञाज्ज्ञानयज्ञः परन्तप ।
सर्वं कर्माखिलं पार्थ ज्ञाने परिसमाप्यते ॥३३॥

śreyān dravya-mayād yajñāj jñāna-yajñaḥ parantapa/
sarvaṁ karmākhilaṁ pārtha jñāne parisamāpyate//

śreyān—superior; *dravya-mayāt*—than material possessions; *yajñāt*—than the sacrifice; *jñāna-yajñaḥ*—sacrifice of knowledge; *parantapa*—O subduer of the enemy; *sarvam*—all; *karma*—action; *akhilam*—completely; *pārtha*—O son of Pṛthā; *jñāne*—in knowledge; *parisamāpyate*—is accomplished.

O subduer of the enemy, of the various sacrifices, that of wisdom is far superior to the sacrifice of material possessions, for whatever may be accomplished by action is realized in wisdom.

Here Kṛṣṇa tells Arjuna that the inner element of wisdom that serves as the proper orientation to sacrificial action is more important than the actual work of sacrifice itself. Work is ultimately about wisdom. That sacrifice that is directly involved with the culture of inner wisdom *(jñāna-yajñaḥ)* is better than sacrifice in which material ingredients are offered *(dravya-mayād yajñāt)*, because the latter at best leads to the former.

In the most general sense this verse tells us that psychological sacrifice of one's inner attachments is more valuable than merely giving up one's external possessions. The pain involved in conscious, unmotivated giving to another, even if it involves very little in the way of tangible goods, brings greater reward than the sacrifice of great material wealth offered with a motive of personal gain. In chapter 3 Kṛṣṇa spoke of performing one's prescribed duty with the spirit of detachment. In this chapter, and in this section in particular, he takes Arjuna deeper. From the surface of dutifully conforming to the socioreligious norms in a spirit of detachment, we dive into activities that are directly involved with wisdom: sacrificial acts, *yoga*, and meditation.

The importance of inner wisdom being what it is, Kṛṣṇa next speaks of the direct method of acquiring that wisdom and the means to sustain it. The implication is that there are many types of sacrifices or purificatory rites, and one needs to find a wise person in order to understand which specific acts one should engage in and what the goal of such practice will be. What *sādhana* should one perform, and what is the *sādhya* one will attain thereby? The answer to this question lies with the *sādhu*, *śrī guru*.

Text 34

तद्विद्धि प्रणिपातेन परिप्रश्नेन सेवया ।
उपदेक्ष्यन्ति ते ज्ञानं ज्ञानिनस्तत्त्वदर्शिनः ॥३४॥

tad viddhi praṇipātena paripraśnena sevayā/
upadekṣyanti te jñānaṁ jñāninas tattva-darśinaḥ//

tat—that; *viddhi*—know; *praṇipātena*—through submission; *paripraśn-ena*—through inquiry; *sevayā*—through service; *upadekṣyanti*—they will teach; *te*—you; *jñānam*—knowledge; *jñāninaḥ*—the wise; *tattva*—truth; *darśinaḥ*—seers.

Acquire that wisdom through humble resignation, relevant inquiry, and rendering service to the wise who have realized the truth. They in turn will impart wisdom unto you.

By resigning oneself to the preceptor, knowledge is revealed. Proper action, Kṛṣṇa teaches, bears the fruit of knowledge. The disciple should learn to make spiritual practice his life's duty and stick to it. Identification with a particular guru is the recognition of a specific direction valid for oneself in spiritual life. This identification involves glimpsing one's own spiritual potential. The practitioner's own heart free from the clutter of material desire appears before him in the form of *śrī guru.*

We are accustomed to making material knowledge part of our agenda, but spiritual knowledge has an agenda of its own. This knowledge reveals its agenda and the fact that we are part of it when we approach this knowledge on its terms. These terms are laid out in this verse: humble submission *(praṇipātena)*, relevant inquiry *(paripraśnena)*, and the rendering of service *(sevayā)* to realized souls who represent divine knowledge in this world. When we do this, spiritual wisdom chooses to reveal itself to us, not otherwise.

Praṇipāta means humble submission to the guru out of respect for the wisdom he represents. This submission is natural, and it creates an inner state of receptivity. *Paripraśna* means asking questions, such as "Who am I?" and "Why am I suffering?" Relevant inquiries are not those questions asked merely out of desire for intellectual stimulation, but rather from a sense of urgency for spiritual growth. Such inquires are relevant to one's immediate advancement in spiritual life. Here the word *sevā* indicates affectionate service.

Although the scripture mandates that one must learn from the guru, this scriptural law has love at its heart. The sincere disciple genuinely feels that his highest prospect lies in hearing and serving the knowledge imparted by the guru: "I *must* surrender here, for my life's highest prospect will be realized in this." This feeling arises within when we hear from one who has been commissioned to collect our soul for divine service. It is love that forms the bond between guru and disciple, not law.

In this verse Kṛṣṇa speaks of a plurality of gurus *(jñāninaḥ)* and at the same time of the singularity of *guru tattva.* The word *jñāninaḥ* is plural. However, in Sanskrit the plural is often used to indicate respect for one person, rather than to indicate more than one person. The spiritual preceptor is worthy of the highest regard, and this is indicated by the use of the plural in the word *jñāninaḥ*. In principle the guru is one. He represents the singular Godhead. In the *Śrīmad-Bhāgavatam* (11.17.27) Kṛṣṇa says that he himself is the guru, *ācāryaṁ māṁ vijānīyāt*. This does not mean that the guru is God. It means that God chooses one or more of his devotees to represent him, and such a devotee should be honored as though he were Kṛṣṇa himself. Thus, even behind the multiplicity of instruction, the disciple detects the direction of the one Godhead.

The singular Godhead has many representatives. Thus within the oneness of *śrī guru* there is simultaneously a plurality. In the Gauḍīya tradition there are both initiating *(dīkṣā)* and instructing *(śikṣā)* gurus. They are to be honored equally, yet their functions differ. The initiating guru is usually the one who prescribes the practice for the disciple, while the instructing gurus help to fine-tune this practice. The initiating guru must be singular, whereas one can embrace a plurality of instructing gurus. If one enrolls in spiritual culture under the guidance of a guru, one will simultaneously experience a plurality of gurus, for in discipleship one is linked through one guru to a succession of gurus *(guru-paramparā)*, all of whom benevolently lend support to the disciple's progress. Such a sincere disciple may also get support from other saints or instructing gurus to pass through the door of opportunity opened by one's initiating guru. However, one who in the name of accepting many gurus does not submit to one guru experiences neither the singularity nor plurality of gurus.

The force of Kṛṣṇa's emphasis on hearing from and serving a realized soul in this verse is noteworthy. All of the methods of sacrifice previously mentioned require that we learn how to practice them from a teacher, the guru. Here Kṛṣṇa implores us to approach such a guru, his representative. The power inherent in approaching a realized soul is such that it can make one immediately eligible for the direct culture of spiritual life without one's having to qualify oneself gradually through other means. While the study of Vedānta *(brahma-jijñāsā)* generally requires that one first inquire into and pass through religious practice *(dharma-jijñāsā)*, this prerequisite can be waived if one is fortunate to associate with a realized soul. This is the opinion of both Śaṅkara and Baladeva Vidyābhūṣaṇa.[6]

Over the next four verses Kṛṣṇa describes the nature of the knowledge one receives from *śrī guru.*

Text 35

यज्ज्ञात्वा न पुनर्मोहमेवं यास्यसि पाण्डव ।
येन भूतान्यशेषाणि द्रक्ष्यस्यात्मन्यथो मयि ॥३५॥

yaj jñātvā na punar moham evaṁ yāsyasi pāṇḍava/
yena bhūtāny aśeṣāṇi drakṣyasy ātmany atho mayi//

yat—which; *jñātvā*—knowing; *na*—not; *punaḥ*—again; *moham*—illusion; *evam*—indeed; *yāsyasi*—you shall go; *pāṇḍava*—O son of Pāṇḍu; *yena*—by which; *bhūtāni*—living beings; *aśeṣāṇi*—all; *drakṣyasi*—you will see; *ātmani*—in the self; *athau*—then; *mayi*—in me.

Having acquired this knowledge, you shall not be deluded again, O son of Pāṇḍu, for by that knowledge you shall see all living beings in terms of their common spiritual essence as one with you and abiding in me.

In this verse and the following three verses, Kṛṣṇa details the glory of spiritual wisdom and the result of acquiring it. Here Kṛṣṇa tells Arjuna that having acquired wisdom he will see all living beings such as his friends and relatives assembled on the battlefield as one in terms of their common spiritual essence, and not in terms of differences arising from bodily identification. Baladeva Vidyābhūṣaṇa says that Arjuna will be freed from the illusion *(moha)* that he must kill friends and relatives. Viśvanātha Cakravartī Ṭhākura comments that Kṛṣṇa's use of the word *mayi* in this verse means that Arjuna will see all beings as effects of Kṛṣṇa, the supreme cause.

The fruits of acquiring transcendental knowledge are listed herein as (1) knowing the common spiritual essence shared by all beings regardless of their bodily appearance, (2) never falling into illusion, (3) understanding that all souls abide in Kṛṣṇa's all-pervading Paramātmā feature (Viṣṇu). Here the eternal plurality of all souls is posited, while for the first time

6. See their commentaries on Vs. 1.1.1.

in the *Gītā* the individual soul and God are brought into juxtaposition as Kṛṣṇa further develops the text's theology.

Text 36

अपि चेदसि पापेभ्यः सर्वेभ्यः पापकृत्तमः ।
सर्वं ज्ञानप्लवेनैव वृजिनं सन्तरिष्यसि ॥३६॥

api ced asi pāpebhyaḥ sarvebhyaḥ pāpa-kṛt-tamaḥ/
sarvaṁ jñāna-plavenaiva vṛjinaṁ santariṣyasi//

api—even; *cet*—if; *asi*—you are; *pāpebhyaḥ*—of sinners; *sarvebhyaḥ*—of all; *pāpa-kṛt-tamaḥ*—the worst sinner; *sarvam*—all; *jñāna-plavena*—by the boat of transcendental knowledge; *eva*—certainly; *vṛjinam*—sin; *santariṣyasi*—you will cross over.

Even if you are the worst of sinful persons, you can cross over all sin by the boat of transcendental knowledge.

How can one who is most evil directly acquire self-knowledge without undergoing acts of purification? Madhusūdana Saraswatī answers this apparent contradiction. He says this verse is a glorification of knowledge, "theoretically accepting the impossible as possible."

Here Kṛṣṇa says that knowledge is like a boat carrying one across the ocean of evil. In the next verse Kṛṣṇa gives an example to further illustrate the efficacy of the power of knowledge.

Text 37

यथैधांसि समिद्धोऽग्निर्भस्मसात्कुरुतेऽर्जुन ।
ज्ञानाग्निः सर्वकर्माणि भस्मसात्कुरुते तथा ॥३७॥

yathaidhāṁsi samiddho 'gnir bhasma-sāt kurute 'rjuna/
jñānāgniḥ sarva-karmāṇi bhasma-sāt kurute tathā//

yathā—as; *edhāṁsi*—firewood; *samiddhaḥ*—blazing; *agniḥ*—fire; *bhasma-sāt kurute*—burns to ashes; *arjuna*—O Arjuna; *jñāna-agniḥ*—the fire of knowledge; *sarva-karmāṇi*—all karmic reactions; *bhasma-sāt kurute*—it burns to ashes; *tathā*—so.

As a blazing fire burns wood to ashes, Arjuna, so does the fire of transcendental knowledge reduce all karmic reactions to ashes.

Here Kṛṣṇa continues to stress the purifying effects of knowledge. He gives an example in which he seems to say that even the manifest *(prārabdha) karma* of one can be destroyed by knowledge. However, only *bhakti* has this power. The opinion that the knowledge under discussion has such power due to its fruition in *bhakti* is supported by Bhaktivedanta Swami Prabhupāda's commentary on this and the following verse: "Perfect knowledge of self and Superself and of their relationship is compared herein to fire. This fire not only burns up all reactions to impious activities, but also all reactions to pious activities, turning them to ashes. There are many stages of reaction: reaction in the making, reaction fructifying, reaction already achieved, and reaction *a priori*. But knowledge of the constitutional position of the living entity burns everything to ashes. When one is in complete knowledge, all reactions, both *a priori* and *a posteriori*, are consumed. In the *Vedas* (*Bṛhad-āraṅyaka Upaniṣad* 4.4.22) it is stated, *ubhe uhaivaiṣa ete taraty amṛtaḥ sādhv-asādhūnī*: 'One overcomes both the pious and impious reactions of work.' When we speak of transcendental knowledge, we do so in terms of spiritual understanding. As such, there is nothing so sublime and pure as transcendental knowledge. Ignorance is the cause of our bondage, and knowledge is the cause of our liberation. This knowledge is the mature fruit of devotional service, and when one is situated in transcendental knowledge, he need not search for peace elsewhere, for he enjoys peace within himself. In other words, this knowledge and peace culminate in Kṛṣṇa consciousness. That is the last word in the *Bhagavad-gītā*."

In the previous verse Kṛṣṇa spoke of crossing the karmic ocean. When one crosses the ocean on the boat of knowledge, the water remains. This water is the *prārabdha-karma* that remains in the life of the *jīvanmukta*. However, when wood is burnt to ashes, the wood no longer remains. Similarly *bhakti*, the furthest reach of knowledge, has the power to remove even one's *prārabdha-karma*, as Kṛṣṇa takes over the body of his devotee using him as his instrument.

With regard to the aforementioned practices of sacrifice, in the next verse Kṛṣṇa again asserts the superiority of transcendental knowledge, the very fruit of such practices.

Text 38

न हि ज्ञानेन सदृशं पवित्रमिह विद्यते ।
तत्स्वयं योगसंसिद्धः कालेनात्मनि विन्दति ॥३८॥

na hi jñānena sadṛśaṁ pavitram iha vidyate/
tat svayaṁ yoga-saṁsiddhaḥ kālenātmani vindati//

na—not; *hi*—certainly; *jñānena*—with knowledge; *sadṛśam*—similar; *pavitram*—purifier; *iha*—here; *vidyate*—exists; *tat*—that; *svayam*—himself; *yoga*—*yoga*; *saṁsiddhaḥ*—perfect; *kālena*—in the course of time; *ātmani*—in himself; *vindati*—finds.

There is nothing here that is as purifying as transcendental knowledge. One who is perfect in yoga realizes this wisdom within himself in due course.

The word *iha* (here) refers to this world. Inner wisdom is the purest thing in this world. *Iha* can also refer to the sacrificial practices mentioned previously. Among all varieties of sacrificial acts, it is the wisdom that arises from them that justifies their performance. Thus Kṛṣṇa stresses that realized knowledge awakens naturally within one who has learned how to acquire that knowledge from a seer by engaging himself under that seer's direction. Realized knowledge will awaken within the practitioner of its own accord as his heart becomes purified.

Kṛṣṇa speaks next of the relationship between faith and knowledge.

Text 39

श्रद्धावाँल्लभते ज्ञानं तत्परः संयतेन्द्रियः ।
ज्ञानं लब्ध्वा परां शान्तिमचिरेणाधिगच्छति ॥३९॥

śraddhāvāl labhate jñānaṁ tat-paraḥ saṁyatendriyaḥ/
jñānaṁ labdhvā parāṁ śāntim acireṇādhigacchati//

śraddhā-vān—one who has faith; *labhate*—attains; *jñānam*—knowledge; *tat-paraḥ*—devoted to it; *saṁyata*—controlled; *indriyaḥ*—sense; *jñānam*—knowledge; *labdhvā*—having attained; *parām*—supreme; *śāntim*—peace; *acireṇa*—quickly; *adhigacchati*—attains.

One who has faith and devotes himself with controlled senses to attaining this wisdom is successful in his effort. Having wisdom and knowledge, he quickly attains the supreme peace.

The faithful stand on firm ground, for divine faith is a most tangible reality and not merely a product of the mind and intellect. Faith is the prerogative of the soul, while belief belongs to the intellect. Faith picks up where reason leaves off. It is not unreasonable, but rather a transrational vehicle to the land beyond intellect, the home of the soul.

A person who trusts in that which he has learned from the guru and thus acts with controlled senses, detached from the fruits of his work in devotion, attains transcendental knowledge. He who has confidence that through *niṣkāma-karma-yoga* his heart will be purified, and not merely by renunciation of work, attains peace.

To emphasize his point through contrast, Kṛṣṇa next describes the fate of those devoid of the requisite faith in the scripture and the guru—the ignorant. Such suspicious persons are suspended, unable to be successful in any sphere.

Text 40

अज्ञश्चाश्रद्दधानश्च संशयात्मा विनश्यति ।
नायं लोकोऽस्ति न परो न सुखं संशयात्मनः ॥४०॥

ajñaś cāśraddadhānaś ca saṁśayātmā vinaśyati/
nāyaṁ loko 'sti na paro na sukhaṁ saṁśayātmanaḥ//

ajñaḥ—the ignorant; *ca*—and; *aśraddadhānaḥ*—without faith; *ca*—also; *saṁśayātmā*—those who doubt; *vinaśyati*—is lost; *na*—not; *ayam*—this; *lokaḥ*—world; *asti*—there is; *na*—not; *paraḥ*—next; *na*—not; *sukham*—happiness; *saṁśaya-ātmanaḥ*—of the doubtful.

Those who are ignorant, faithless, or doubting are lost. There is neither happiness nor success in this world or the next for the doubting soul.

The disciple should have faith in the scripture and the guru's explanation of it. Those who question whether knowledge will ever fructify in themselves and are thus doubtful will never be successful. They lack faith in the inconceivable power of God and remain preoccupied with their own shortcomings.

Other than the doubtful, Kṛṣṇa mentions the ignorant *(ajñaḥ)* and faithless *(aśraddadhānaḥ)*. These two persons are in one sense better off than the doubtful, for at least they enjoy the bliss of their ignorance and happiness in this world. Those without faith in the next world find some happiness in the here and now. Those who doubt that they will be successful on the spiritual path, yet believe in it, cannot find happiness in this world nor will they attain the next. They cannot find happiness in this world because they know from scripture that there is no enduring happiness here, and they lack the self-confidence necessary for happiness and success in general. Viśvanātha Cakravartī argues that the three persons mentioned in this verse are in a hierarchical order beginning with the lowest ignorant *(ajñaḥ)* to the faithless *(aśraddadhānaḥ)* to the doubtful *(saṁśayātmā)*.

In the last two verses of this chapter, Kṛṣṇa introduces chapter 5 by imploring Arjuna to realize the fruit of *karma-yoga* through diligent execution and thereby qualify himself for renunciation.

Text 41

योगसन्न्यस्तकर्माणं ज्ञानसञ्छिन्नसंशयम् ।
आत्मवन्तं न कर्माणि निबध्नन्ति धनञ्जय ॥४१॥

yoga-sannyasta-karmāṇaṁ jñāna-sañchinna-saṁśayam/
ātmavantaṁ na karmāṇi nibadhnanti dhanañjaya//

yoga—*yoga*; *sannyasta*—renounced; *karmāṇam*—action; *jñāna*—knowledge; *sañchinna*—cut; *saṁśayam*—doubt; *ātma-vantam*—composed in the self; *na*—not; *karmāṇi*—actions; *nibadhnanti*—bind; *dhanañjaya*—O conqueror of riches.

One who has renounced action through yoga and whose doubt is cut asunder by knowledge and is thus composed in his self, O Dhanañjaya, is not bound by karma.

Here Kṛṣṇa speaks of *karma-yoga* in the words *yoga-sannyasta-karmāṇam*. The *karma-yogī* is one who has disciplined his actions in consideration of the principle of sacrifice outlined in this chapter. Madhusūdana Saraswatī says, "He has dedicated his actions to God through *yoga* consisting of the attitude of equanimity characterized by adoration of God, as mentioned in chapter 2 (Bg. 2.48)." This *karma-yogī* is not bound by his actions, and continues to practice *karma-yoga*, cultivating the inner spirit of renunciation leading to meditation and devotion proper. This cultivation is what Kṛṣṇa instructs Arjuna to do in the next chapter, while also describing the dynamics of renouncing action in the direct culture of inner wisdom—the contemplative life.

Kṛṣṇa also speaks of the results of *karma-yoga:* the removal of doubt through knowledge *(jñāna-sañchinna-saṁśayam)*, the firm resolve of self-composure required for a contemplative life of renunciation (*ātma-vantam*), and freedom from the obligation to act further in terms of *karma-yoga* (*na karmāṇi nibadhnanti*).

Viśvanātha Cakravartī understands the word *ātmavantam* as *pratyag-ātmani*, "knowledge of the self as an individual soul." In this rendering self-knowledge serves as a precursor to the doctrine of devotion that is only beginning to unfold at this point. Kṛṣṇa has not yet begun his discourse on devotion itself. He is building up to it by setting a firm foundation for spiritual life. *Bhakti* assimilates both *karma* and *jñāna*, as it involves the acts of the senses and working organs as well as the subtler mental powers and consciousness. However, in both these domains, *bhakti* involves the culture of spiritual emotion for God. *Karma-yoga* involves dutiful, detached action and *jñāna* is emotionless. *Bhakti*, while including the objectivity and absence of material emotion involved in *karma* and *jñāna*, is based in positive spiritual emotion for God, either that shared with the neophyte by an advanced devotee or that arising from the soul proper in advanced stages of devotional culture.

Text 42

तस्मादज्ञानसम्भूतं हृत्स्थं ज्ञानासिनात्मनः ।
छित्त्वैनं संशयं योगमातिष्ठोत्तिष्ठ भारत ॥४२॥

tasmād ajñāna-sambhūtaṁ hṛt-sthaṁ jñānāsinātmanaḥ/
chittvainaṁ saṁśayaṁ yogam ātiṣṭhottiṣṭha bhārata//

tasmāt—therefore; *ajñāna-sambhūtam*—arising from ignorance; *hṛt-stham*—situated in the heart; *jñāna*—knowledge; *asinā*—with the sword; *ātmanaḥ*—own; *chittvā*—having cut; *enam*—this; *saṁśayam*—doubt; *yogam*—*yoga*; *ātiṣṭha*—take refuge; *uttiṣṭha*—stand up; *bhārata*—O descendant of Bharata.

Therefore, having cut away with the sword of knowledge your doubt arising from ignorance that lurks in your heart, take refuge in yoga and stand for battle, O descendant of Bharata!

Verses 41 and 42 conclude this chapter with emphasis on knowledge as the fruit of detached action. Baladeva Vidyābhūṣaṇa comments that knowledge and action are like the two aspects of rice paddy, the husk and the rice grain itself. *Karma* is compared to the husk and *jñāna* to the rice. *Jñāna* develops out of the protective husk of detached action, yet the rice of *jñāna* itself is superior to such action, being the fruit of the harvest. This, he says, is the lesson of chapter 4.

These two concluding verses also introduce chapter 5. Verse 41 speaks of the result of *karma-yoga* that qualifies one for the renunciation of contemplative life. In verse 42 Kṛṣṇa implores Arjuna to take shelter of *karma-yoga* having gained theoretical knowledge from him and thus conviction about the self. This is what he instructs Arjuna to do in chapter 5—continue to practice *karma-yoga* with a view to attain the qualification for renunciation and meditation. However, this concluding verse can also be construed to be a covert directive for the culture of *bhakti*, for knowledge by which doubts are destroyed is more than theoretical knowledge. It is the ground of inner wisdom that is the fruit of *karma-yoga* upon which the emotional life of *bhakti* stands. Viewing it in this light, here Kṛṣṇa instructs Arjuna to fight, not out of duty with a sense of detachment but rather because this battle is Kṛṣṇa's work.

CHAPTER FIVE

कर्मसन्न्यासयोगः
Karma-Sannyāsa-yoga
YOGA OF RENUNCIATION OF ACTION

Text 1

अर्जुन उवाच
सन्न्यासं कर्मणां कृष्ण पुनर्योगं च शंससि ।
यच्छ्रेय एतयोरेकं तन् मे ब्रूहि सुनिश्चितम् ॥१॥

arjuna uvāca
sannyāsaṁ karmaṇāṁ kṛṣṇa punar yogaṁ ca śaṁsasi/
yac chreya etayor ekaṁ tan me brūhi su-niścitam//

arjunaḥ uvāca—Arjuna said; *sannyāsam*—renunciation; *karmaṇām*—of actions; *kṛṣṇa*—O Kṛṣṇa; *punaḥ*—again; *yogam*—yoga; *ca*—also; *śaṁsasi*—you praise; *yat*—which; *śreyaḥ*—better; *etayoḥ*—of the two; *ekam*—one; *tat*—that; *me*—to me; *brūhi*—tell; *su-niścitam*—with certainty.

Arjuna said: O Kṛṣṇa, on the one hand you advocate renunciation of action and on the other you advocate yoga. Tell me with certainty, which of the two is better?

In chapter 3 Kṛṣṇa stressed selfless action. In chapter 4 Kṛṣṇa glorified knowledge over selfless action, inasmuch as knowledge is the fruit of selfless action. In this chapter, Kṛṣṇa stresses the renunciation of action that deepens knowledge. While selfless action is indirectly helpful in awakening knowledge, renunciation of action involves the direct culture of knowledge. Selfless action prepares the heart for knowledge to manifest by awakening dispassion and the firm resolve to attain wisdom. Subsequently, action that interferes with meditation should be renounced as dispassion arises. This renunciation of action makes one eligible for the contemplative life and meditation that directly awaken wisdom. The contemplative's renunciation and meditation are the subjects discussed in chapters 5 and 6 from which they receive their names, *Karma-sannyāsa-yoga* and *Dhyāna-yoga*, respectively. Both chapters are an elaboration on the concluding section of chapter 2 (Bg. 2.55–72), in which the *samādhi* of the enlightened soul is described.

This chapter further clarifies the apparent difference between action and renunciation by pointing out that the two are really inseparable because renunciation is the very state of mind the *karma-yogī* must possess. At the same time, the life of the *karma-yogī* and that of the contemplative are outwardly different. *Karma-yoga* is better because it is safer and easier for the beginner. Furthermore, while engaging in it, renunciation develops naturally and can be strengthened through its continued practice.

The integrated person that Kṛṣṇa further elaborates on in this chapter is ultimately his devotee. Thus this chapter ends with a verse in which Kṛṣṇa, in speaking of the attainment of Brahman and the cessation of material suffering *(brahma-nirvāṇam)*, thrusts himself, the object of devotion, into his description of the perfect static peace *(śānti)* of liberation, declaring that knowing him, the Lord of all, one attains true peace and does so quickly.

Arjuna's question in this opening verse picks up from the last two stanzas of the previous chapter. When Kṛṣṇa urged Arjuna to attain the status of renunciation and self-composure through *karma-yoga* (Bg. 4.41), the words "renounce action" *(sannyāsta-karmāṇaṁ)* stood out in Arjuna's mind. Thus when Kṛṣṇa at the same time implored him to "stand for battle" (Bg. 4.42), Arjuna asks for clarification, as renouncing action and fighting appear to be opposites. However, when Kṛṣṇa told Arjuna to renounce action, he told him to do so through the practice of *karma-yoga (yoga-sannyāsta-karmāṇam)*. Thus he spoke of the action of *karma-yoga* as the means to attain the self-composure necessary for renunciation and contemplative life. He was also instructing Arjuna that selfless action itself is not materially binding on the self and thus constitutes a dynamic expression of inaction. Kṛṣṇa was not instructing Arjuna to then and there overtly renounce action. When Kṛṣṇa told Arjuna to fight in the following verse (Bg. 4.42), he did not contradict himself. When he implored Arjuna to act in battle, he meant that he should act in *karma-yoga* inspired by theoretical knowledge and the conviction to attain self-realization, which he compared to a sword of knowledge *(jñānāsin)* that destroys ignorance. Thus while this chapter advocates the renunciation of action that is no longer necessary for one entering contemplative life, it also emphasizes once again the idea that selfless action itself is not binding. This is another way of understanding the term *karma sannyāsa*, renunciation of action through renunciation of attachment to the result of action. Seen in this light, chapter 5 reemphasizes the essence of chapter 3, given that the notion of inaction in action is difficult to grasp. In chapter 4 Kṛṣṇa also spoke covertly about engaging in battle as a result of having actually attained inner wisdom—liberated action. As we shall see at the end of chapter 6, this mature *yoga* Kṛṣṇa alludes to is *bhakti*.

Text 2

श्रीभगवानुवाच
सन्न्यासः कर्मयोगश्च निःश्रेयसकरावुभौ ।
तयोस्तु कर्मसन्न्यासात् कर्मयोगो विशिष्यते ॥२॥

śrī-bhagavān uvāca
sannyāsaḥ karma-yogaś ca niḥśreyasa-karāv ubhau/
tayos tu karma-sannyāsāt karma-yogo viśiṣyate//

śrī-bhagavān uvāca—the Lord of Śrī said; *sannyāsaḥ*—renunciation; *karma-yogaḥ*—*yoga* of action; *ca*—also; *niḥśreyasa-karau*—leading to the ultimate happiness; *ubhau*—both; *tayoḥ*—of the two; *tu*—but; *karma-sannyāsāt*—than renunciation of action; *karma-yogaḥ*—*karma-yoga*; *viśiṣyate*—is better.

The Lord of Śrī said: Both renunciation of action and selfless action lead to ultimate happiness. However, of the two, selfless action is better than the renunciation of action.

Selfless action is better for one who is ineligible for the path of renunciation of action. The path of selfless action is easier than a contemplative life of introspection (*sannyāsa*) in the sense that once a monk formally renounces prescribed actions and adopts the renounced order of life, should any impurity surface in his heart, he cannot return to the world of prescribed action to remove it without being condemned as fallen. According to Baladeva Vidyābhūṣaṇa, statements advising renunciation apply to those who have attained attachment to the spiritual platform (*ātmā-rati*). However, on the whole a person who has attained inner wisdom can still engage in *karma-yoga* without incurring fault, and furthermore it strengthens one's realization in that it has wisdom at its heart. Baladeva Vidyābhūṣaṇa comments further that knowledge is within *karma-yoga* as a child is within the womb or as fire is within wood. As Kṛṣṇa elaborates in the following verse, that which is accomplished by the renunciation of action is accomplished as well by one engaged in selfless action.

Text 3

ज्ञेयः स नित्यसन्न्यासी यो न द्वेष्टि न काङ्क्षति ।
निर्द्वन्द्वो हि महाबाहो सुखं बन्धात् प्रमुच्यते ॥३॥

jñeyaḥ sa nitya-sannyāsī yo na dveṣṭi na kāṅkṣati/
nirdvandvo hi mahā-bāho sukhaṁ bandhāt pramucyate//

jñeyaḥ—to be known; *saḥ*—he; *nitya*—always; *sannyāsī*—renouncer; *yaḥ*—who; *na*—not; *dveṣṭi*—hates; *na*—not; *kāṅkṣati*—desires; *nirdvandvaḥ*—indifferent to dualities; *hi*—certainly; *mahā-bāho*—O mighty-armed; *sukham*—easily; *bandhāt*—from bondage; *pramucyate*—is liberated.

A person who is free from both hatred and desire is always renounced. Being indifferent to dualities, O mighty-armed, he is easily freed from bondage and attains liberation.

One who is free from prejudices is renounced even while acting. Here Kṛṣṇa explains how the *karma-yogī* himself is already a renouncer of action and thus a candidate for liberation even while apparently acting. Such a person is not formally a monk, but more importantly he is one in spirit.

Having spoken of the relative superiority of *karma-yoga*, Kṛṣṇa next speaks of that which the paths of *karma-yoga* and *jñāna-yoga* have in common.

Text 4

सांख्ययोगौ पृथग् बालाः प्रवदन्ति न पण्डिताः ।
एकमप्यास्थितः सम्यगुभयोर्विन्दते फलम् ॥४॥

sāṅkhya-yogau pṛthag bālāḥ pravadanti na paṇḍitāḥ/
ekam apy āsthitaḥ samyag ubhayor vindate phalam//

sāṅkhya—contemplative life; *yogau*—selfless action; *pṛthak*—different; *bālāḥ*—the childish; *pravadanti*—declare; *na*—not; *paṇḍitāḥ*—the learned; *ekam*—one; *api*—even; *āsthitaḥ*—followed; *samyak*—correctly; *ubhayoḥ*—of both; *vindate*—finds; *phalam*—the result.

Childish persons, not the learned, declare that contemplative life and selfless action are separate. One who practices either of these correctly achieves the same result.

In this verse the terms *sāṅkhya* and *yoga* (*sāṅkhya-yogau*) take on different meanings than they did in chapter 2 (Bg. 2.39). There *sāṅkhya* meant "theory" and *yoga* meant "practice." According to Śaṅkara, while using the same terms here, Kṛṣṇa uses them in a different way. Here the meaning of *yoga* is practice associated with action, and the meaning of *sāṅkhya* has developed from theory in chapter 2 (Bg. 2.39) to contemplation in chapter 3 (Bg. 3.3) to contemplation associated with renunciation here in chapter 5.

Text 5

यत्सांख्यैः प्राप्यते स्थानं तद्योगैरपि गम्यते ।
एकं सांख्यं च योगं च यः पश्यति स पश्यति ॥५॥

yat sāṅkhyaiḥ prāpyate sthānaṁ tad yogair api gamyate/
ekaṁ sāṅkhyaṁ ca yogaṁ ca yaḥ paśyati sa paśyati//

yat—which; *sāṅkhyaiḥ*—by contemplative life; *prāpyate*—attained; *sthānam*—position; *tat*—that; *yogaiḥ*—by *yoga*; *api*—also; *gamyate*—is attained; *ekam*—one; *sāṅkhyam*—contemplative life; *ca*—and; *yogam*—*yoga*; *ca*—and; *yaḥ*—one who; *paśyati*—sees; *saḥ*—he; *paśyati*—sees.

That destination attained by the contemplatives is also attained by the yogīs. Contemplative life and karma-yoga are one. One who perceives this sees things as they are.

Here Kṛṣṇa explains in what sense the two paths are equal. The two paths are one because they deliver the same result. The relative superiority of *karma-yoga* is in terms of its being easier and more expedient, of which Kṛṣṇa speaks in the following verse. In doing so he stresses that renunciation that does not arise out of *karma-yoga* should not be embraced.

Text 6

सन्न्यासस्तु महाबाहो दुःखमाप्तुमयोगतः ।
योगयुक्तो मुनिर्ब्रह्म न चिरेणाधिगच्छति ॥६॥

sannyāsas tu mahā-bāho duḥkham āptum ayogataḥ/
yoga-yukto munir brahma na cireṇādhigacchati//

sannyāsaḥ—renunciation; *tu*—however; *mahā-bāho*—O mighty-armed; *duḥkham*—difficult; *āptum*—to obtain; *ayogataḥ*—without *yoga*; *yoga-yuktaḥ*—practiced in *yoga*; *muniḥ*—sage; *brahma*—Brahman; *na cireṇa*—without delay; *adhigacchati*—attains.

However, renunciation of action without yoga, O Arjuna, is difficult. The sage who is practiced in yoga, however, quickly attains the Absolute.

Renunciation and a contemplative life must be prefaced by detached action that purifies the heart. Without a pure heart, no one can meditate effectively. Here Kṛṣṇa indicates that the *karma-yogī* also practices meditation in due course, *yoga-yukto munir brahma*.

How does the *karma-yogī* embrace the spirit of renunciation? Kṛṣṇa explains this next.

Text 7

योगयुक्तो विशुद्धात्मा विजितात्मा जितेन्द्रियः ।
सर्वभूतात्मभूतात्मा कुर्वन्नपि न लिप्यते ॥७॥

yoga-yukto viśuddhātmā vijitātmā jitendriyaḥ/
sarva-bhūtātma-bhūtātmā kurvann api na lipyate//

yoga-yuktaḥ—engaged in *yoga*; *viśuddha-ātmā*—one whose intelligence is purified; *vijita-ātmā*—whose mind is controlled; *jita-indriyaḥ*—whose senses are conquered; *sarva-bhūta-ātma-bhūta-ātmā*—who has identified with the self of all beings; *kurvan api*—even when acting; *na*—not; *lipyate*—is implicated.

Engaged in yoga, one whose intelligence is purified, whose mind is controlled, and whose senses are conquered, and who has thus identified with the self of all beings, is not implicated even when acting.

Here Kṛṣṇa stresses the dynamic sense of oneness that the *karma-yogī* attains with other living beings, one in which the sorrow and joy of others is identified with as if it were one's own. In this compassionate state, he works for the welfare of others without karmic reaction. Because he makes God his very being, he becomes like the soul of all beings and is thus dear to them. This is the Vaiṣṇava reading of *sarva-bhūtātma-bhūtātmā*. The Adwaita rendering of this compound word is that the *ātmān* and Brahman are one in all respects.

Madhusūdana Saraswatī sees this verse as referring to one who is controlled in mind, body, and speech. He quotes *Manu-saṁhitā:* "Speech is a *daṇḍa*, mind is a *daṇḍa*, so also the body is a *daṇḍa*. One who has these three *daṇḍas* under control is called a *tridaṇḍi*." (*Manu-saṁhitā* 12.10) The *daṇḍa* symbolizes the rod of chastisement one invokes to curb the intelligence, mind, and senses from straying away from a God-centered life. It is carried by those in the renounced order *(sannyāsa)*. Vaiṣṇava *sannyāsīs* in particular carry the *tridaṇḍa* (triple *daṇḍa*) and are thus often referred to as *tridaṇḍi-sannyāsīs*. They actively engage their body, mind, and speech in the service of God. Monists of Śaṅkara's lineage, on the other hand, carry the *ekadaṇḍa* (single *daṇḍa*) that symbolizes their monistic worldview.

According to Viśvanātha Cakravartī Ṭhākura, this verse describes three types of *karma-yogīs:* those whose intelligence is purified, those whose minds are controlled, and those who have conquered their senses.

In the next verse Kṛṣṇa explains the psychology of the sense-controlled entry-level *karma-yogī*.

Texts 8–9

नैव किञ्चित् करोमीति युक्तो मन्येत तत्त्ववित् ।
पश्यञ् शृण्वन् स्पृशञ् जिघ्रन्नश्नन् गच्छन् स्वपन् श्वसन् ॥८॥
प्रलपन् विसृजन् गृह्णन्नुन्मिषन् निमिषन्नपि ।
इन्द्रियाणीन्द्रियार्थेषु वर्तन्त इति धारयन् ॥९॥

naiva kiñcit karomīti yukto manyeta tattva-vit/
paśyañ śṛṇvan spṛśañ jighrann aśnan gacchan svapan śvasan//
pralapan visṛjan gṛhṇann unmiṣan nimiṣann api/
indriyāṇīndriyārtheṣu vartanta iti dhārayan//

na—not; *eva*—certainly; *kiñcit*—anything; *karomi*—I do; *iti*—thus; *yuktaḥ*—steadfast in *yoga*; *manyeta*—thinks; *tattva-vit*—one who knows the truth; *paśyan*—seeing; *śṛṇvan*—hearing; *spṛśan*—touching; *jighran*—smelling; *aśnan*—eating; *gacchan*—walking; *svapan*—sleeping; *śvasan*—breathing; *pralapan*—talking; *visṛjan*—evacuating; *gṛhṇan*—accepting; *unmiṣan*—opening the eyes; *nimiṣan*—closing the eyes; *api*—even; *indriyāṇi*—senses; *indriya-artheṣu*—in the sense objects; *vartante*—they are working; *iti*—thus; *dhārayan*—convinced.

A person who is steadfast in yoga and knows things as they are should think, "I am not doing anything, even while I am seeing, hearing,

touching, smelling, eating, walking, sleeping, breathing, talking, evacuating, accepting things, and blinking my eyes. Rather, it is the senses alone that are acting in relation to the sense objects."

Here Kṛṣṇa begins to describe the state of inner renunciation in which the self is experienced as being inactive in relation to the movements of the body. In these two verses, the five senses of perception and the five working senses are indicated. Breathing indicates the five internal airs and blinking indicates the five vital forces identified in the *Yoga-sūtra (kūrma, nāga, kṛkala, devadatta,* and *dhanañjaya)*. Sleeping indicates the fourfold function of the internal organ (mind, intellect, *citta*, and ego), for during sleep, when the physical body retires, this organ continues to function. All of these functions are distinct from the self. Thus this verse is an elaboration on verse 28 of chapter 3.

Next Kṛṣṇa gives an example of how the sense-controlled *karma-yogī* is in the world but not of it. Thus he continues to stress the beginning stage of *karma-yoga*, in which the senses alone are controlled, and by which the mind and intelligence are also eventually mastered.

Text 10

ब्रह्मण्याधाय कर्माणि सङ्गं त्यक्त्वा करोति यः ।
लिप्यते न स पापेन पद्मपत्रमिवाम्भसा ॥१०॥

brahmaṇy ādhāya karmāṇi saṅgaṁ tyaktvā karoti yaḥ/
lipyate na sa pāpena padma-patram ivāmbhasā//

brahmaṇi—in Brahman; *ādhāya*—placing; *karmāṇi*—in action; *saṅgam*—attachment; *tyaktvā*—giving up; *karoti*—performs; *yaḥ*—who; *lipyate*—is affected; *na*—not; *saḥ*—he; *pāpena*—by evil; *padma-patram*—a lotus leaf; *iva*—like; *ambhasā*—by the water.

One who works without attachment ascribing his actions to Brahman is not tainted by evil, just as a lotus leaf is untouched by water.

The lotus stem lies within the water but its flower never gets wet. Following this example, the perfect *karma-yogī* is in the world but not of it. He has renounced attachment *(saṅgaṁ tyaktvā)* in the midst of his action.

The word *brahmaṇi* in this verse has been explained by both Śrīdhara Swāmī and Viśvanātha Cakravartī to indicate God *(parameśvara)*. Śaṅkara also understands *brahmaṇi* to be *īśvara*, considering the person described in this verse to be "like a servant who renounces all works and attachment to the fruits of his action, even liberation, for the sake of his master." Rāmānuja differs, identifying *brahmaṇi* with the original state of nature in which the *guṇas* are in equilibrium. In support of this he cites the third verse of chapter 14. His explanation follows the idea that this section is elaborating on verse 28 of chapter 3, and Baladeva Vidyābhūṣaṇa agrees with this understanding, arguing strongly that no other interpretation is appropriate. However, in either interpretation the action of one who works without attachment is not his own. It is either God working through him, the *yogī* being God's (Brahman's) instrument, or material nature's (Brahman's) movements that the self is not involved with.

Text 11

कायेन मनसा बुद्ध्या केवलैरिन्द्रियैरपि ।
योगिनः कर्म कुर्वन्ति सङ्गं त्यक्त्वात्मशुद्धये ॥११॥

kāyena manasā buddhyā kevalair indriyair api/
yoginaḥ karma kurvanti saṅgaṁ tyaktvātma-śuddhaye//

kāyena—with the body; *manasā*—with the mind; *buddhyā*—with the intellect; *kevalaiḥ*—solely; *indriyaiḥ*—with the senses; *api*—even; *yoginaḥ*—*yogīs*; *karma*—actions; *kurvanti*—act; *saṅgam*—attachment; *tyaktvā*—abandoning; *ātma*—self; *śuddhaye*—for the purpose of purification.

Karma-yogīs act with the body, mind, intellect, and even senses, solely for the purpose of purification, having renounced attachment.

The word *kevala* here also implies that one who works in *karma-yoga* with only his senses gradually becomes purified, even though his mind wanders elsewhere. In the next verse, Kṛṣṇa summarizes his description of the *karma-yogī*, contrasting him with someone who does not follow the yogic path.

Text 12

युक्तः कर्मफलं त्यक्त्वा शान्तिमाप्नोति नैष्ठिकीम् ।
अयुक्तः कामकारेण फले सक्तो निबध्यते॥१२॥

yuktaḥ karma-phalaṁ tyaktvā śāntim āpnoti naiṣṭhikīm/
ayuktaḥ kāma-kāreṇa phale sakto nibadhyate//

yuktaḥ—one who is disciplined; *karma-phalam*—the fruit of action; *tyaktvā*—having renounced; *śāntim*—peace; *āpnoti*—attains; *naiṣṭhikīm*—lasting; *ayuktaḥ*—one who is not practiced in *yoga*; *kāma-kāreṇa*—by the action coming from desire; *phale*—in the fruit; *saktaḥ*—attached; *nibadhyate*—is entangled.

A person disciplined in karma-yoga, having renounced the fruit of action, attains lasting peace. A person who does not practice karma-yoga remains attached to the fruit of work and is entangled by his actions.

The *karma-yogī* knows that he himself is not really acting at all. He is free from the ego of considering himself the doer even while acting, and he is free from considering himself the initiator of the body's action while engaging the body.

Text 13

सर्वकर्माणि मनसा सन्न्यस्यास्ते सुखं वशी ।
नवद्वारे पुरे देही नैव कुर्वन्न कारयन् ॥१३॥

sarva-karmāṇi manasā sannyasyāste sukhaṁ vaśī/
nava-dvāre pure dehī naiva kurvan na kārayan//

sarva—all; *karmāṇi*—actions; *manasā*—with the mind; *sannyasya*—renouncing; *āste*—resides; *sukham*—happily; *vaśī*—one who is controlled; *nava-dvāre*—with nine gates; *pure*—in the city; *dehī*—the embodied; *na*—not; *eva*—certainly; *kurvan*—acting; *na*—not; *kārayan*—causing to act.

Mentally renouncing all actions, the embodied one happily resides with self-control in the city of nine gates, neither acting nor causing action to be performed.

The city of nine gates is the body with its two eyes, two ears, two nostrils, mouth, anus, and genital through which a person becomes implicated in the world of sense objects. Residing happily in this city means to reside there without attachment. He is self-controlled and indifferent to the actions of the body without any sense of identity with it. Such a person neither acts nor causes others or his own body to act other than in the service of God.

At this point, Arjuna, attentively listening to Kṛṣṇa's extended answer, mentally questions him thus: "Who acts and who is responsible for the results of action? If it is not the one enlightened in *karma-yoga*, perhaps it is material nature or God, who is in control of material nature. Or is it the living being in ignorance?" Knowing the mind of his disciple, Kṛṣṇa replies in the following verse.

Text 14

न कर्तृत्वं न कर्माणि लोकस्य सृजति प्रभुः ।
न कर्मफलसंयोगं स्वभावस्तु प्रवर्तते ॥१४॥

na kartṛtvaṁ na karmāṇi lokasya sṛjati prabhuḥ/
na karma-phala-saṁyogaṁ svabhāvas tu pravartate//

na—not; *kartṛtvam*—agency of action; *na*—not; *karmāṇi*—action; *lokasya*—of the people; *sṛjati*—creates; *prabhuḥ*—lord; *na*—not; *karma-phala*—the results of action; *saṁyogam*—connection; *svabhāvaḥ*—conditioned nature; *tu*—but; *pravartate*—proceeds.

The Lord creates neither a person's agency of action nor his actions nor the result. All this is done by a person's conditioned nature.

In this verse Kṛṣṇa reiterates his instruction found in verse 27 of chapter 3, which is the seed verse for his instruction found in this section. The means by which action is accomplished—its agency—is the ignorance of false proprietorship brought about by identification with material nature and desire. All actions are performed by the *guṇas*. The word *na* (not) is used three times here for emphasizing that God is not directly responsible for the agency of action, our actions, or their results. Thus the individual soul has been described in its true state as being situated in an inner state of renunciation removed from the action of the body. Here God is also described as being in a state of renunciation, removed from the action of those in material life.

The word *prabhuḥ* in this verse can also be interpreted to mean the individual self. Although this word is usually used to indicate God, not the individual soul, nonetheless, many commentators understand it in this way, including some of the Vaiṣṇava commentators. Following this interpretation, it is not the self-controlled person residing in the city of the body who creates either the agency or the actions of the body. This is done by material nature, which the self-controlled person is a witness to. The self-controlled *yogī* is God's instrument, and thus, as the actions of material nature characterized by ignorance are not ascribed to God, neither are they to be ascribed to his servant who does his bidding in the world. The individual soul, whether realized or not, is always distinct from matter, yet it becomes identified with matter through beginningless ignorance. This ignorance is called *anādi-avidyā*. Bhaktivedanta Swami Prabhupāda comments that "it is ignorance acquired from time immemorial that is the cause of bodily suffering and distress. As soon as the living entity becomes aloof from the activities of the body, he becomes free from the reactions as well."

Text 15

नादत्ते कस्यचित् पापं न चैव सुकृतं विभुः ।
अज्ञानेनावृतं ज्ञानं तेन मुह्यन्ति जन्तवः ॥१५॥

nādatte kasyacit pāpaṁ na caiva sukṛtaṁ vibhuḥ/
ajñānenāvṛtaṁ jñānaṁ tena muhyanti jantavaḥ//

na—not; *ādatte*—accepts; *kasyacit*—of anyone; *pāpam*—evil deed; *na*—not; *ca*—and; *eva*—certainly; *su-kṛtam*—pious deeds; *vibhuḥ*—the Omnipresent; *ajñānena*—by ignorance; *āvṛtam*—covered; *jñānam*—knowledge; *tena*—by that; *muhyanti*—are deluded; *jantavaḥ*—the living beings.

The omniscient Godhead does not accept responsibility for anyone's good or evil deeds. Beings are deluded because their knowledge is covered by ignorance.

With the exception of Rāmānuja, all of the commentators who identified *prabhuḥ* in the previous verse with the individual soul have identified *vibhuḥ* in this verse with God.

Jīva Goswāmī thoughtfully concludes that in the second half of this verse Kṛṣṇa explains that the individual souls are eternally individual, their knowledge being covered by the influence of ignorance, *ajñānenāvṛtaṁ jñānam* (Ts. 32 and Ps. 22). It is not that they themselves are a product of ignorance, disappearing with the removal of ignorance. When their ignorance is removed, they continue to exist in enlightened life, one in purpose with the Absolute.

Central to God's noninvolvement is the principle of free will inherent in the finite soul, as is the principle of beginningless *karma*. The notion of beginningless *karma* is explained in *Vedānta-sūtra* (2.1.34–35). It refers to the condition of the bound souls. Their conditioning under the influence of material nature, while having no beginning, can come to an end through the exercise of their inherent free will in relation to the hand of God's grace, which is perpetually extended to them.

God does not create an individual soul's agency for action. It is the soul's lower nature arising out of ignorance and timeless karmic implication that is the true agent of action. The living beings are disposed to material action through the influence of desire arising from timeless ignorance. God engages them in such action, but he does not make them act. Because God is self-satisfied, he does not direct the living beings for the fulfillment of his selfish desire. He directs in accordance with the living beings' previous actions. He does this through the power of his illusory energy *(māyā)*. In doing so, he acquires no sin or virtue, as do the living beings.

As for God's apparent partiality toward his devotees, this is a spiritual partiality. Rather than a fault, it is God's most beautiful ornament. He is perceived as being materially partial by those whose knowledge is covered by ignorance. They do not understand that his chastisement is also a form of grace. Kṛṣṇa's apparent partiality is the special grace he extends to his devotees. It is not arbitrary. Were he not the lover of those who love him, all of his other qualities would not be sufficient to evoke devotion and love. Moreover, it is the impartiality of the individual soul to the dualities of this world that serves as the passport for leaving it, but his spiritual partiality or individual preference that serves as his visa to the spiritual world of Kṛṣṇa's play.[1]

Text 16

ज्ञानेन तु तदज्ञानं येषां नाशितमात्मनः ।
तेषामादित्यवज्ज्ञानं प्रकाशयति तत् परम् ॥१६॥

jñānena tu tad ajñānaṁ yeṣāṁ nāśitam ātmanaḥ/
teṣāṁ āditya-vaj jñānaṁ prakāśayati tat param//

jñānena—by knowledge; *tu*—but; *tat*—that; *ajñānam*—ignorance; *yeṣām*—whose; *nāśitam*—is destroyed; *ātmanaḥ*—of the self; *teṣām*—their; *āditya-vat*—like the sun; *jñānam*—knowledge; *prakāśayati*—illumines; *tat*—that; *param*—God/relationship with God.

1. See Vs. 2.1.36.

For those whose ignorance of the self has been destroyed by knowledge, that same knowledge reveals like the shining sun the nature of their relationship with God.

Kṛṣṇa has been speaking about God himself, the Lord, referred to as *prabhuḥ* and *vibhuḥ* in verses 14 and 15, respectively. In consideration of this, *param* in this verse and the *tad* in verse 17 can be understood to refer to him as well, rather than the individual soul. While Viśvanātha Cakravartī Ṭhākura understands *param* to refer to the awakening of the inherent nature of the soul in relation to God, Baladeva Vidyābhūṣaṇa comments that the word refers to both the individual soul as well as to the Supreme Soul. He states further that although knowledge itself (referring to *sattva-guṇa*) does not reveal God, the knowledge given by the guru who acts on behalf of God does reveal both God and the true self. Thus in the opinion of Baladeva Vidyābhūṣaṇa, *param* here indicates both the individual soul and God. He says that "just as the sun when it rises obliterates the darkness and shows everything in its true form, so too does the knowledge of the self received from the pure spiritual master show the soul in its true form." The true self is the eternal servant of God.

Here Kṛṣṇa speaks of the undeluded and the nature and effect of transcendental knowledge. This knowledge involves proper understanding of the relationship between God, material nature, and the deluded as well as the enlightened soul. Such knowledge removes the ignorance that causes one to attribute mundane partiality to God.

In this verse Kṛṣṇa continues to affirm that souls are many in their essential nature, rather than only appearing so in the illusioned condition. Their plurality after the destruction of ignorance is essential for a life of enlightened devotion, and knowledge is an inalienable attribute of their self. The soul's knowledge is subject to expansion and contraction in relation to the Absolute and material nature, respectively. This is the opinion of Rāmānuja. Similarly, Baladeva Vidyābhūṣaṇa comments, "Here by mentioning the plurality of the living beings whose ignorance has been destroyed, Kṛṣṇa confirms what he said at the very beginning of the *Gītā* in verse 2.12: 'The individual nature of the soul is not conditional and does not disappear with liberation.' "

Text 17

तद्बुद्धयस्तदात्मानस्तन्निष्ठास्तत्परायणाः ।
गच्छन्त्यपुनरावृत्तिं ज्ञाननिर्धूतकल्मषाः ॥१७॥

tad-buddhayas tad-ātmānas tan-niṣṭhās tat-parāyaṇāḥ/
gacchanty apunar-āvṛttiṁ jñāna-nirdhūta-kalmaṣāḥ//

tat-buddhayaḥ—those whose intelligence is in that; *tat-ātmānaḥ*—those whose selves are in that; *tat-niṣṭhāḥ*—those whose faith is in that; *tat-parāyaṇāḥ*—those who are devoted to that; *gacchanti*—go; *apunaḥ-āvṛttim*—to the end of rebirth; *jñāna*—knowledge; *nirdhūta*—cast off; *kalmaṣāḥ*—impious acts.

Those whose intelligence is absorbed in God, whose minds are fixed on God, whose faith is in God, who are devoted to God, and whose impiety has been thus cast off through knowledge, go to that place where one does not again take birth.

Here the word *tat* repeated throughout this verse refers to God, who has been referred to in the previous verses in this section as *prabhuḥ*, *vibhuḥ*, and *param*. Viśvanātha Cakravartī Ṭhākura comments that knowledge or learning can reveal knowledge of the individual soul, but it cannot give realization of God. Therefore *jñānīs* must engage in *bhakti* if they wish to advance from self-realization to God-realization. Kṛṣṇa emphasizes this here, clarifying his statement in the previous verse as to the nature of the knowledge under discussion. It is the knowledge concomitant to *bhakti* that reveals the self as different from matter and God. It also reveals one's relationship with God.

Those whose intelligence is absorbed in God are always reflecting on him. Their minds are always absorbed in meditation on him. Faithful to him, they have surrendered even their self-knowledge to him in his service. Devoted, they are always engaged in hearing and chanting about him. The words *jñāna-nirdhūta-kalmaṣāḥ* refer to the destruction of ignorance through the influence of spiritual knowledge, as stated in the previous verse.

Baladeva Vidyābhūṣaṇa says that those who recognize God's freedom from partiality and meditate on him develop the fixed intelligence mentioned in this verse. They too become impartial, experiencing an inner state of renunciation.

Text 18

विद्याविनयसम्पन्ने ब्राह्मणे गवि हस्तिनि ।
शुनि चैव श्वपाके च पण्डिताः समदर्शिनः ॥१८॥

vidyā-vinaya-sampanne brāhmaṇe gavi hastini/
śuni caiva śva-pāke ca paṇḍitāḥ sama-darśinaḥ//

vidyā—learning; *vinaya*—culture; *sampanne*—endowed; *brāhmaṇe*—in the *brāhmaṇa; gavi*—in the cow; *hastini*—in the elephant; *śuni*—in the dog; *ca*—and; *eva*—certainly; *śva-pāke*—in the dog-eater; *ca*—and; *sama-darśinaḥ*—seeing equally; *paṇḍitāḥ*—the wise.

The wise see equally a brāhmaṇa endowed with learning and culture, a cow, an elephant, and even a dog or a dog-eater.

The enlightened soul, like God, is free from mundane partiality as a result of contemplating the impartiality of the Absolute. He regards all equally regardless of the species in which they appear or their conduct, be they *brāhmaṇas* or outcastes. Here the cow, elephant, and dog are mentioned to show that distinctions of species are not made by the sage of equal vision. That he makes no distinctions on the basis of conduct or caste is shown by the mention of the *brāhmaṇa* and the dog-eater. According to Viśvanātha Cakravartī, the cow and *brāhmaṇa* are representative of the mode of goodness and are therefore superior in material estimation; the elephant is in the mode of passion and therefore a creature of moderate value by the same standard. The dog-eater and the dog are representative of ignorance and therefore they are inferior. However, since the learned sage of equal vision acknowledges the soul, he does not make such judgments. He is free from prejudice and relates to everyone in light of their spiritual reality, beyond the three constituents of the material nature.

This verse speaks of *jīvanmukti*, whereas final liberation after the death of the body *(videha-mukti)* is described in the previous verse.

Text 19

इहैव तैर्जितः सर्गो येषां साम्ये स्थितं मनः ।
निर्दोषं हि समं ब्रह्म तस्माद् ब्रह्मणि ते स्थिताः ॥१९॥

ihaiva tair jitaḥ sargo yeṣāṁ sāmye sthitaṁ manaḥ/
nirdoṣaṁ hi samaṁ brahma tasmād brahmaṇi te sthitāḥ//

iha—here, in this world; *eva*—certainly; *taiḥ*—by them; *jitaḥ*—conquered; *sargaḥ*—rebirth; *yeṣām*—whose; *sāmye*—in equanimity; *sthitam*—situated; *manaḥ*—mind; *nirdoṣam*—faultless; *hi*—certainly; *samam*—impartial;

brahma—Brahman; *tasmāt*—therefore; *brahmaṇi*—in Brahman; *te*—they; *sthitāḥ*—established.

Even here in this world those whose minds are established in impartiality conquer rebirth. As the Absolute is faultless and impartial, they too become established in the Absolute.

Here Kṛṣṇa speaks of those in this world who meditate on the Absolute and thus realize impartiality. Jīva Goswāmī says that the idea that the liberated are established in Brahman (*tasmād brahmaṇi te sthitāḥ*) means that the *jīvas* are of this nature (Ps. 32). In their pure state they are of the nature of Brahman, which is faultless (*nirdoṣam*) and impartial (*samam*). Their nature is not adulterated by the influence of the material energy.

Text 20

न प्रहृष्येत् प्रियं प्राप्य नोद्विजेत् प्राप्य चाप्रियम् ।
स्थिरबुद्धिरसम्मूढो ब्रह्मविद् ब्रह्मणि स्थितः ॥२०॥

na prahṛṣyet priyaṁ prāpya nodvijet prāpya cāpriyam/
sthira-buddhir asammūḍho brahma-vid brahmaṇi sthitaḥ//

na—not; *prahṛṣyet*—should rejoice; *priyam*—pleasant; *prāpya*—attaining; *na*—not; *udvijet*—become repulsed; *prāpya*—attaining; *ca*—and; *apriyam*—unpleasant; *sthira-buddhiḥ*—whose intelligence is fixed; *asammūḍhaḥ*—unbewildered; *brahma-vit*—one who knows the Absolute; *brahmaṇi*—in the Absolute; *sthitaḥ*—established.

One who knows the Absolute, who is established in the Absolute, and who is fixed in intelligence does not rejoice on attaining something pleasant or become repulsed on attaining something unpleasant.

The characteristics of the *jīvanmukta* are further described in this verse, which reiterates the explanation found in verse 56 of the second chapter. Here Kṛṣṇa implies that those aspiring for self-realization should strive for the natural qualities of the liberated soul described in this verse.

Text 21

बाह्यस्पर्शेष्वसक्तात्मा विन्दत्यात्मनि यत् सुखम् ।
स ब्रह्मयोगयुक्तात्मा सुखमक्षयमश्नुते ॥२१॥

bāhya-sparśeṣv asaktātmā vindaty ātmani yat sukham/
sa brahma-yoga-yuktātmā sukham akṣayam aśnute//

bāhya-sparśeṣu—in external sensations; *asakta-ātmā*—one whose mind is not attached; *vindati*—finds; *ātmani*—in the self; *yat*—which; *sukham*—joy; *saḥ*—he; *brahma-yoga-yukta-ātmā*—whose self is united with the Absolute in *yoga*; *sukham*—happiness; *akṣayam*—unlimited; *aśnute*—attains.

One whose mind is not attracted to sense pleasure, who finds joy in the self, and whose self is united with God in yoga attains unlimited happiness.

The practitioner must be fixed in his intelligence as to the unhappy reality of sense pleasure. Following this intelligence he finds joy in the self, attains *yoga (sa brahma-yoga-yuktātmā)*, and comes to know unlimited happiness *(sukham akṣayam aśnute)*. One who finds joy in the self *(tvam)*, upon attaining *yoga* comes to know that *(tat)* which is God—*tat tvam asi*. God-realization follows self-realization.

Next Kṛṣṇa contrasts the unlimited happiness of God-realization with the so-called happiness of sense indulgence.

Text 22

ये हि संस्पर्शजा भोगा दुःखयोनय एव ते ।
आद्यन्तवन्तः कौन्तेय न तेषु रमते बुधः ॥२२॥

ye hi saṁsparśa-jā bhogā duḥkha-yonaya eva te/
ādy-antavantaḥ kaunteya na teṣu ramate budhaḥ//

ye—which; *hi*—certainly; *saṁsparśa-jāḥ*—born of contact; *bhogāḥ*—pleasures; *duḥkha*—misery; *yonayaḥ*—wombs; *eva*—certainly; *te*—they are; *ādi*—beginning; *anta*—end; *vantaḥ*—having; *kaunteya*—O son of Kuntī; *na*—not; *teṣu*—in them; *ramate*—rejoice; *budhaḥ*—the wise.

Certainly pleasures born of sensual contact are nothing but wombs of misery. Since they have a beginning and end, O son of Kuntī, the wise do not rejoice in them.

Here Kṛṣṇa poetically elaborates on the nature of pleasure born of sense indulgence. Such pleasures born out of contact with sense objects are wombs of misery that give birth to suffering. The wise who seek eternal life take no pleasure in contact between the senses and their objects, knowing the pleasure born of this contact to be nonenduring in the least.

That which does not exist at some point in time, yet appears to come into being, only to cease from existing afterwards, does not really exist in the present any more than in a dreamlike condition. Such is the ephemeral nature of sense pleasure. In Kṛṣṇa's critique of sense pleasure, he appeals to wise persons. They alone will concur with him as to the unhappy nature of all variety of sense indulgence. According to Patañjali's *Yoga-sūtra* (2.15) the wise understand that sense pleasure begets suffering either as a direct consequence *(pariṇāma)* in the form of anticipation *(tāpa)* of its inevitable loss or in the form of new craving *(saṁskāra)* for sense pleasure that arises from impressions of it imbedded in the mind. Thus sense pleasure is mixed with suffering in all three phases of time.

The cause of sensual happiness is one with its effect. The cause is attachment, for it is not possible to derive pleasure from an object one has no attachment for. Initial attachment for an object is transformed into the effect of so-called happiness on obtaining that object, an object that will inevitably be lost. When the material object is lost, attachment remains either for that same object or another, all of which are transformations of the same basic material ingredients. As the result of acquiring happiness from sense objects is suffering, so too is its cause—attachment. Furthermore, while experiencing sensual happiness one simultaneously experiences displeasure in relation to that which opposes this so-called happiness. Dealing with this opposition brings suffering to others.

Reaching the above conclusion involves applying one's entire intellectual faculty in spiritual pursuit. Only such a wise person can know the unending joy of spiritual life, for spiritual bliss follows the fullest measure of intelligent life. To reach this conclusion and act accordingly is not easy. Therefore Kṛṣṇa speaks next of the effort involved.

Text 23

शक्नोतीहैव यः सोढुं प्राक् शरीरविमोक्षणात् ।
कामक्रोधोद्भवं वेगं स युक्तः स सुखी नरः ॥२३॥

śaknotīhaiva yaḥ soḍhuṁ prāk śarīra-vimokṣaṇāt/
kāma-krodhodbhavaṁ vegaṁ sa yuktaḥ sa sukhī naraḥ//

śaknoti—is able; *iha eva*—here in this world; *yaḥ*—one who; *soḍhum*—to tolerate; *prāk*—before; *śarīra*—body; *vimokṣaṇāt*—from liberation; *kāma*—

desire; *krodha*—frustration; *udbhavam*—origination; *vegam*—agitation; *saḥ*—he; *yuktaḥ*—fixed in *yoga*; *saḥ*—he; *sukhī*—happy; *naraḥ*—human being.

A person in this world who can tolerate the agitation that arises from desire and frustration until he is liberated from the body is fixed in yoga. He is happy; he is a human being.

The word *vega* is used in this verse to denote the similarity between one's being on the verge of acting in relation to sense pleasure, even though one has repeatedly contemplated its true nature, and the rushing of a river during the rainy season. A person who can withstand the forceful internal current arising from desire for sense objects and the frustration of not acquiring the sense objects is poised to realize his human potential. Such a person differentiates himself from the animal species through practical exhibition of his capacity to reason meaningfully and thus solve the problems of life, opening the door to actual happiness.

The body does not feel pleasure or pain after the soul has departed. The practitioner who can live in the body with this understanding, knowing that pain and pleasure are merely perceptions born of bodily identification, lives a life that begets liberation. Such a person rejoices within. He finds intrinsic happiness in his own nature, as opposed to deriving happiness from external objects.

Text 24

योऽन्तःसुखोऽन्तरारामस्तथान्तर्ज्योतिरेव यः ।
स योगी ब्रह्मनिर्वाणं ब्रह्मभूतोऽधिगच्छति ॥२४॥

yo 'ntaḥ-sukho 'ntar-ārāmas tathāntar-jyotir eva yaḥ/
sa yogī brahma-nirvāṇaṁ brahma-bhūto 'dhigacchati//

yaḥ—one who; *antaḥ-sukhaḥ*—happiness within; *antaḥ-ārāmaḥ*—delight within; *tathā*—and; *antaḥ-jyotiḥ*—illumined within; *eva*—certainly; *yaḥ*—anyone; *saḥ*—this; *yogī*—*yogī*; *brahma-nirvāṇam*—liberation in Brahman; *brahma-bhūtaḥ*—self-realized; *adhigacchati*—attains.

One who finds happiness within, who delights within, who is illumined within, such a yogī established in self-realization, attains the cessation of material existence in Brahman.

Here the word *brahma-nirvāṇam* refers to cessation of material existence arising from identifying oneself with Brahman, as opposed to the Buddhist conception of *nirvāṇa*, which does not acknowledge the eternal existence of consciousness *(ātman)*. In contrast, the Buddhist conception of *nirvāṇa* could be termed *prakṛti-nirvāṇa*, which involves identification with matter through all of its transformations, as opposed to identifying with one particular stage of transformation.

The term *brahma-nirvāṇam* first appeared at the end of chapter 2 (Bg. 2.72). Kṛṣṇa elaborates on this liberated condition in this and the following two verses. At the end of this chapter he implies that this liberated status is included within realization of himself, and in chapter 6 (Bg. 6.15) he states that *brahma-nirvāṇam* is subsumed within himself. The term *brahma-bhūtaḥ* in this verse is also found in chapter 18 (Bg. 18.54), where it describes the liberated status from which one enters into *bhakti* proper.

A person who is happy within no longer takes pleasure in sense objects. His happiness is independent of them and derived from the intrinsic nature of the self. He takes pleasure in the self *(ātmārāma)*.

Text 25

लभन्ते ब्रह्मनिर्वाणमृषयः क्षीणकल्मषाः ।
छिन्नद्वैधा यतात्मानः सर्वभूतहिते रताः ॥२५॥

labhante brahma-nirvāṇam ṛṣayaḥ kṣīṇa-kalmaṣāḥ/
chinna-dvaidhā yatātmānaḥ sarva-bhūta-hite ratāḥ//

labhante—attain; *brahma-nirvāṇam*—liberation in the Absolute; *ṛṣayaḥ*—the seers; *kṣīṇa-kalmaṣāḥ*—whose impiety is destroyed; *chinna*—slashed; *dvaidhāḥ*—doubts; *yata-ātmānaḥ*—the self-controlled; *sarva-bhūta*—for all beings; *hite*—in welfare; *ratāḥ*—engaged.

The seers, whose impiety has been vanquished, whose doubts have been slashed, who are self-controlled and live for the welfare of all beings, attain the cessation of material existence in Brahman.

Text 26

कामक्रोधविमुक्तानां यतीनां यतचेतसाम् ।
अभितो ब्रह्मनिर्वाणं वर्तते विदितात्मनाम् ॥२६॥

kāma-krodha-vimuktānāṁ yatīnāṁ yata-cetasām/
abhito brahma-nirvāṇaṁ vartate viditātmanām//

kāma—desire; *krodha*—anger; *vimuktānām*—of those who are free; *yatīnām*—of the renunciate; *yata-cetasām*—who have control over the mind; *abhitaḥ*—near; *brahma-nirvāṇam*—liberation in the Absolute; *vartate*—is there; *vidita-ātmanām*—of those who know the self.

Those renunciates who are free from desire and anger, who have control of their minds and know the self, attain the cessation of material existence in Brahman, both here and in the hereafter.

After speaking at length regarding attaining the Absolute, the means of doing so, and the experience of those who have, Kṛṣṇa here emphasizes as he did in the beginning of this chapter that *karma-yogīs* are also renouncers of action in a dynamic sense by referring to them as renunciates or *sannyāsīs* (*yatīnām*). Viśvanātha Cakravartī says this verse states that the *yogī* under discussion attains *brahma-nirvāṇam* quickly.

Kṛṣṇa next introduces the techniques of meditation (*dhyāna*) that are common to all types of *yoga* and are sometimes employed in the advanced practice of *karma-yoga* and *jñāna-yoga* in particular.[2] First, in the next two verses, Kṛṣṇa mentions yogic techniques and their results in brief, and then in the third verse, he elaborates on the results of practicing these techniques. By speaking of meditation (*dhyāna*) and its techniques along with its result in the following three verses, Kṛṣṇa also introduces the next chapter, *dhyāna-yoga*.

Texts 27–28

स्पर्शान् कृत्वा बहिर्बाह्यांश्चक्षुश्चैवान्तरे भ्रुवोः ।
प्राणापानौ समौ कृत्वा नासाभ्यन्तरचारिणौ ॥२७॥
यतेन्द्रियमनोबुद्धिर्मुनिर्मोक्षपरायणः ।
विगतेच्छाभयक्रोधो यः सदा मुक्त एव सः ॥२८॥

sparśān kṛtvā bahir bāhyāṁś cakṣuś caivāntare bhruvoḥ/
prāṇāpānau samau kṛtvā nāsābhyantara-cāriṇau//
yatendriya-mano-buddhir munir mokṣa-parāyaṇaḥ/
vigatecchā-bhaya-krodho yaḥ sadā mukta eva saḥ//

2. Elsewhere Viśvanātha Cakravartī Ṭhākura has proclaimed *prāṇāyāma* to be *pratikūla*, or unfavorable, for *bhakti*; however, it is mentioned in *Hari-bhakti-vilāsa* in reference to *mantra-dhyāna* of the Gauḍīyas.

sparśān—contacts; *kṛtvā*—making; *bahiḥ*—outside; *bāhyān*—external; *cakṣuḥ*—eye; *ca*—and; *eva*—certainly; *antare*—between; *bhruvoḥ*—of the eyebrows; *prāṇa-apānau*—incoming and outgoing breath; *samau*—equal; *kṛtvā*—making; *nāsa-abhyantara*—within the nostrils; *cāriṇau*—moving; *yata*—restrained; *indriya*—sense; *manaḥ*—mind; *buddhiḥ*—intelligence; *muniḥ*—the transcendentalist; *mokṣa*—liberation; *parāyaṇaḥ*—dedicated; *vigata*—departed; *icchā*—desire; *bhaya*—fear; *krodhaḥ*—anger; *yaḥ*—one who; *sadā*—always; *muktaḥ*—liberated; *eva*—certainly; *saḥ*—he.

Shutting out external sense objects and fixing the eyesight between the two eyebrows, equalizing the incoming and outgoing breaths that move through the nostrils, restraining the senses, mind, and intelligence, and dedicating oneself to liberation, he from whom desire, fear, and anger have departed is forever liberated.

Those situated in inner renunciation, either in contemplative life or in the ongoing culture of *karma-yoga*, practice meditation. Without evolving to the stage of inner renunciation, meditative attempts will not be very successful.

The *yogī* must learn to expel from the mind thoughts of contact with sense objects in the name of pleasure. Fixing the eyesight between the eyebrows on the "third eye" helps him to inhibit random thought, as eye movement often accompanies thought. Expelling external contacts (*sparśān kṛtvā bahir bāhyān*) refers to sense indulgence in general. The word *sparśān* (contact/touch) is understood to represent the functions of all the senses, as the sense of touch is connected with all of the working senses through skin, which pervades the entire body.

Having introduced the meditation that is the subject of chapter 6 in this verse, Kṛṣṇa declares himself to be the object of the *yogī*'s meditation in the last verse of this chapter. He also places all that enlightenment involves for the *jñānī*, *yogī*, and devotee within himself, and declares that the enlightened state he has been discussing is quickly attained by acknowledging his supreme position. Thus *bhakti* is alluded to yet again, this time as we enter chapter 6 wherein Kṛṣṇa openly states his preference for devotion and implores Arjuna to be his devotee—the perfectly integrated being.

Text 29

भोक्तारं यज्ञतपसां सर्वलोकमहेश्वरम् ।
सुहृदं सर्वभूतानां ज्ञात्वा मां शान्तिमृच्छति ॥२९॥

bhoktāraṁ yajña-tapasāṁ sarva-loka-maheśvaram/
suhṛdaṁ sarva-bhūtānāṁ jñātvā māṁ śāntim ṛcchati//

bhoktāram—enjoyer; *yajña*—sacrifice; *tapasām*—of austerities; *sarva-loka*—all worlds; *mahā-īśvaram*—great controller; *su-hṛdam*—friend; *sarva*—all; *bhūtānām*—of the creatures; *jñātvā*—knowing; *mām*—me; *śāntim*—peace; *ṛcchati*—attains.

Knowing me to be the enjoyer of the results of sacrifice and austerities, the great controller of the entire world, and the friend of all creatures, one quickly attains peace.

Kṛṣṇa is the enjoyer of the results of sacrifices performed by ritualists *(yajña)*. He is also the enjoyer of the results of austerities performed by *jñānīs (tapasām)*. He is the Paramātmā *(sarva-loka-maheśvaram)* of the world in the eyes of the *yogīs* and reverential devotees. His devotees, who know his Brahman and Paramātmā features, also know him as Bhagavān, the loving friend of all creatures *(suhṛdaṁ sarva-bhūtānām)*. Thus after describing the practice of meditation and mystic *yoga* in brief, here Kṛṣṇa further identifies the indwelling Supersoul and overseer of the material world (Paramātmā), who is the object of the *yogī*'s meditation, with himself. Previously, he identified himself with Brahman, the object of the *jñānī*'s attainment. Here for the first time in the *Gītā* he also indicates that he is Bhagavān, the loving friend of his devotees, and that the *karma-yogī* whose appropriately God-centered *yoga* turns to loving devotion *(bhakti)* will attain him.

To know him as one's dear friend is to be in a better position than to approach him for material gain, liberation, or even dutiful devotion, for the results of all of these and more are easily attained by one who becomes the intimate friend of the one who owns and controls all, the rightful enjoyer of all sacrifice and austerity—God himself. We are not the rightful enjoyers of anything, nor the controllers of anything, much less the entire world. However, we can be on intimate terms with the one who is. What then could be lacking for us?

CHAPTER SIX

ध्यानयोगः
Dhyāna-yoga

YOGA OF MEDITATION

Text 1

श्रीभगवानुवाच
अनाश्रितः कर्मफलं कार्यं कर्म करोति यः ।
स सन्न्यासी च योगी च न निरग्निर्न चाक्रियः ॥१॥

śrī-bhagavān uvāca
anāśritaḥ karma-phalaṁ kāryaṁ karma karoti yaḥ/
sa sannyāsī ca yogī ca na niragnir na cākriyaḥ//

śrī-bhagavān uvāca—the Lord of Śrī said; *anāśritaḥ*—without depending; *karma-phalam*—the fruit of work; *kāryam*—prescribed; *karma*—work; *karoti*—does; *yaḥ*—one who; *saḥ*—he; *sannyāsī*—renunciate; *ca*—and; *yogī*—yogī; *ca*—and; *na*—not; *niragniḥ*—one who forgoes the sacrificial fire; *na*—not; *ca*—also; *akriyaḥ*—without rite.

The Lord of Śrī said: A person who performs his duties renouncing the fruit of his action is both a renunciate and a yogī. One does not become a sannyāsi merely by forgoing work and the sacrificial fire.

At the beginning of this chapter Kṛṣṇa continues to stress *karma-yoga* centered on himself, leading to knowledge, meditation, and ultimately *bhakti*. This chapter discusses meditation in greater detail, both in its physical and psychic aspects. *Karma-yoga* refers to all activities executed with the body. Thus the discussion of physical *(haṭha) yoga* and psychic *(aṣṭāṅga) yoga* in this chapter are essential aspects of the practice of *karma-yoga* required to facilitate the training of the mind in meditation. While the discussion of *haṭha-yoga* and *aṣṭāṅga-yoga* takes up much of the chapter, Kṛṣṇa brings his discussion of *yoga* to its zenith by emphasizing *bhakti*. He does so by stressing his own position as that in which liberation subsists (Bg. 6.15) by describing the highest yogic experience of his devotees (Bg. 6.29–32) and by stating at the end of the chapter that *bhakti-yoga* is the *yoga* most dear to him (Bg. 6.47). It should be noted that this chapter stresses practice *(sādhana)*. Regardless of which *yoga* path or rung of the ladder of *yoga* one identifies with, one cannot avoid the spiritual practice involved in controlling the mind and senses.

In this verse Kṛṣṇa tells Arjuna that the *karma-yogī* is both a renunciate, and thus as good as a *jñānī*, as well as a *yogī* in spirit, for self-sacrifice is at the heart of *yoga*. One who lights no fire *(niragniḥ)* is one in whose life there is no self-sacrifice. Because the *karma-yogī* is a true *yogī*, he is eligible to engage in yogic techniques that are helpful in meditation as his heart becomes purified.

One in advanced stages of *karma-yoga* employs meditative techniques as *jñāna* awakens. Even the *bhakti-yogī*, the devotee, engages in *dhyāna*, and thus some of the techniques of this type of *yoga* are also relevant to his practice.[1]

Text 2

यं सन्न्यासमिति प्राहुर्योगं तं विद्धि पाण्डव ।
न ह्यसन्न्यस्तसङ्कल्पो योगी भवति कश्चन ॥२॥

yaṁ sannyāsam iti prāhur yogaṁ taṁ viddhi pāṇḍava/
na hy asannyasta-saṅkalpo yogī bhavati kaścana//

yam—what; *sannyāsam*—renunciation; *iti*—thus; *prāhuḥ*—they say; *yogam*—*yoga*; *tam*—that; *viddhi*—know; *pāṇḍava*—O son of Pāṇḍu; *na*—not; *hi*—certainly; *asannyasta*—without renouncing; *saṅkalpaḥ*—(selfish) motivation; *yogī*—*yogī*; *bhavati*—becomes; *kaścana*—anyone.

O son of Pāṇḍu, know that which is sannyāsa to be yoga, for without renouncing selfish motivation, no one becomes a yogī.

Here Kṛṣṇa tells Arjuna he should understand that one who is actually a renouncer, the *karma-yogī* he has been describing, is also a mystic *yogī*. *Yoga* implies selflessness. It involves restraint of the mental modifications that

1. In the *bhakti* school of the Gauḍīyas, *dhyāna* is one of the fivefold aspects of *smaraṇam* (remembrance).

occur in the form of desires for sense objects. Thus renunciation, which involves realizing the nature of material desire, and *yoga*, which involves the cessation of material desires, are one.

In underscoring the heart of *yoga* by declaring here that it is first and foremost selflessness that makes one a *yogī*, Kṛṣṇa lays the foundation for establishing his ultimate premise: *bhakti-yoga* is the most complete *yoga*, including within itself union with God through action (as in *karma-yoga*), introspection (as in *jñāna-yoga*), and meditation (as in *dhyāna-yoga*), for the body, intelligence, and mind all follow the heart. The devotee not only forgoes selfish concerns, abnegating material desire to attain peace, but embraces the desire of God, becoming his instrument in divine slavery.

Having stressed the heart of *yoga* in the form of renunciation of selfish desire, Kṛṣṇa next begins to describe the path of mystic *yoga* itself in detail. To begin this path, one must pass through selfless action and purification of the heart. Only then can one sit peacefully culturing meditation without being distracted by the call of the world, religious or otherwise.

Text 3

आरुरुक्षोर्मुनेर्योगं कर्म कारणमुच्यते ।
योगारूढस्य तस्यैव शमः कारणमुच्यते ॥३॥

ārurukṣor muner yogaṁ karma kāraṇam ucyate/
yogārūḍhasya tasyaiva śamaḥ kāraṇam ucyate//

ārurukṣoḥ—of the beginner; *muneḥ*—of the sage; *yogam*—*yoga*; *karma*—work; *kāraṇam*—the means; *ucyate*—is said; *yoga*—*yoga*; *ārūḍhasya*—of one who has attained; *tasya*—his; *eva*—certainly; *śamaḥ*—cessation of activities; *kāraṇam*—the means; *ucyate*—is said to be.

For the beginner desiring perfection in yoga, action is the means, whereas for one who has attained yoga, cessation of activity is the means.

One who desires perfection in mystic *yoga* must first engage in selfless action. On the other hand, one who has attained perfection in mystic *yoga* is able to remain in continuous trance through cessation of activity that would otherwise be disturbing to the mind.

Kṛṣṇa next describes the symptoms of yogic attainment followed by its techniques.

Text 4

यदा हि नेन्द्रियार्थेषु न कर्मस्वनुषज्जते ।
सर्वसङ्कल्पसन्न्यासी योगारूढस्तदोच्यते ॥४॥

yadā hi nendriyārtheṣu na karmasv anuṣajjate/
sarva-saṅkalpa-sannyāsī yogārūḍhas tadocyate//

yadā—when; *hi*—certainly; *na*—not; *indriya-artheṣu*—in sense objects; *na*—not; *karmasu*—in actions; *anuṣajjate*—is attached; *sarva-saṅkalpa*—all (material) motivation; *sannyāsī*—renouncer; *yoga-ārūḍhaḥ*—elevated in *yoga*; *tadā*—at that time; *ucyate*—is said to be.

When one is attached to neither sense objects nor to action itself and has renounced all material motivation, one is said to have attained yoga.

The mature *yogī* has no purpose to fulfill. He is not attached to sense objects, nor any type of work, nor does his attainment in *yoga* depend any longer on a particular spiritual practice. He does not entertain the idea that he is the doer or that the results of action are for his enjoyment. Kṛṣṇa says again that he is *sarva-saṅkalpa-sannyāsī*. Baladeva Vidyābhūṣaṇa comments that Kṛṣṇa has not said *sarva-karma-sannyāsī*. The mature *yogī* gives up all desire *(sarva-saṅkalpa)* for the results of his work and not all work *(sarva-karma)*. Such a *yogī* is established in *yoga (yogārūḍhaḥ)*.

In the context of discussing yogic attainment, because meditation deals with mastering the mind, Kṛṣṇa next speaks both of the mind's power to degrade and elevate one relative to the extent that it has been mastered by the self.

Text 5

उद्धरेदात्मनात्मानं नात्मानमवसादयेत् ।
आत्मैव ह्यात्मनो बन्धुरात्मैव रिपुरात्मनः ॥५॥

uddhared ātmanātmānaṁ nātmānam avasādayet/
ātmaiva hy ātmano bandhurātmaiva ripur ātmanaḥ//

uddharet—one should deliver; *ātmanā*—by the mind; *ātmānam*—oneself; *na*—not; *ātmānam*—oneself; *avasādayet*—one should degrade; *ātmā*—mind; *eva*—certainly; *hi*—indeed; *ātmanaḥ*—of the self; *bandhuḥ*—friend; *ātmā*—mind; *eva*—certainly; *ripuḥ*—enemy; *ātmanaḥ*—of the self.

One should elevate oneself by the mind, not degrade oneself. Indeed, the mind can be the self's friend or its enemy.

In consideration of the context in which it appears, *ātmā* can mean mind, intelligence, body, or soul, as the "self" we speak of is often a bodily, mental, or intellectual self, rather than the self proper, the soul. In verses 5 through 7, *ātmā* refers primarily to the mind. Here Kṛṣṇa says that the mind influenced by spiritual discrimination has the power to uplift the self from worldliness. However, when the mind is not fortified in this way, it causes degradation.

A friend is one who can help us in times of need. The trained mind is such a friend. The uncontrolled mind, on the other hand, is the greatest enemy of the soul. Kṛṣṇa next elaborates on just how the mind can be either one's friend or enemy, followed by a description of the symptoms of one who has controlled the mind—the *sthita-prajñā*, discussed earlier in chapter 2 (Bg. 2.55–72).

Text 6

बन्धुरात्मात्मनस्तस्य येनात्मैवात्मना जितः ।
अनात्मनस्तु शत्रुत्वे वर्तेतात्मैव शत्रुवत् ॥६॥

bandhur ātmātmanas tasya yenātmaivātmanā jitaḥ/
anātmanas tu śatrutve vartetātmaiva śatru-vat//

bandhuḥ—friend; *ātmā*—the mind; *ātmanaḥ*—of the self; *tasya*—of him; *yena*—by whom; *ātmā*—the mind; *eva*—certainly; *ātmanā*—by the self; *jitaḥ*—conquered; *anātmanaḥ*—of one who has not conquered the mind; *tu*—but; *śatrutve*—in enmity; *varteta*—it might be; *ātmā eva*—the very mind; *śatru-vat*—as an enemy.

For one who has conquered the mind, the mind is the best of friends, but for one who has not conquered the mind, it acts like one's enemy.

The uncontrolled mind acts as one's enemy. This is true even with regard to material pursuit, not to speak of spiritual pursuit. However, as the mind is trained through spiritual discipline, it acts as one's friend by thinking naturally of God and all things in relation to him. There is an illuminating story in this connection from the Gauḍīya tradition. Two devotees were walking side by side when a vulture flew overhead. Noticing the vulture, one devotee cried out "*hari bol*" (chant the name of God). Hearing this from his comrade, the other devotee exclaimed, "Why are you so overjoyed on seeing a vulture, whose preoccupation is death? Seeing this bird does not ordinarily give rise to chanting the names of God." To this the first devotee replied, "When I see the vulture, my mind goes to the cremation grounds where cows who have died naturally are skinned. This skin is then tanned and the hide is used to make the traditional drum used in Hari *kīrtana* (chanting of God's name)." Seeing the vulture, his trained mind, acting as his friend, drew him naturally to his spiritual practice.

Text 7

जितात्मनः प्रशान्तस्य परमात्मा समाहितः ।
शीतोष्णसुखदुःखेषु तथा मानापमानयोः ॥७॥

jitātmanaḥ praśāntasya paramātmā samāhitaḥ/
śītoṣṇa-sukha-duḥkheṣu tathā mānāpamānayoḥ//

jita-ātmanaḥ—of one who has conquered the mind; *praśāntasya*—of the peaceful; *parama-ātmā*—the Supreme Soul; *samāhitaḥ*—poised; *śīta-uṣṇa*—in cold and heat; *sukha-duḥkheṣu*—in pleasure and pain; *tathā*—and; *māna-apamānayoḥ*—in honor and dishonor.

A person who has conquered the mind and is thus peaceful is poised in realization of the Supreme Soul. Heat and cold, pleasure and pain, honor and dishonor are all the same to him.

In this verse the word Paramātmā is used for the first time in the *Gītā*. The concept of the Paramātmā, however, was introduced at the end of chapter 5 with the words *sarva-loka-maheśvaram*. The Paramātmā is the object of the *aṣṭāṅga-yogī*'s meditation.

Bhaktivedanta Swami Prabhupāda comments, "The effect of controlling the mind is that one automatically follows the dictation of the Paramātmā, or Supersoul.... the devotee of the Lord is unaffected by the dualities of material existence, namely distress and happiness, cold and heat, etc. This state is practical *samādhi*, or absorption in the Supreme."

Here Kṛṣṇa uses the word *samādhi (samāhitaḥ)* for the first time in this chapter. He has referred to it earlier using the word *yoga* in its stead in verse 3 and 4. There he speaks of attaining *yoga (samādhi)*. *Samādhi* was first mentioned in the *Gītā* in chapter 2 (Bg. 2.44). Therein Kṛṣṇa told Arjuna that those who are too attached to sense objects cannot experience *samādhi*. Later in the same chapter (Bg. 2.54) Arjuna asked Kṛṣṇa about the characteristics of one who has attained *samādhi*. In chapter 4 (Bg. 4.24–29) Kṛṣṇa also spoke of *samādhi* when he described being absorbed in various types of sacrifices to attain Brahman: *brahmaiva tena gantavyaṁ brahma-karma-samādhinā*. Here in chapter 6 Kṛṣṇa elaborates further on his initial response to Arjuna's question in chapter 2 concerning the characteristics of one who has attained *samādhi*. He also speaks of different kinds of *samādhi* and their results.

Text 8

ज्ञानविज्ञानतृप्तात्मा कूटस्थो विजितेन्द्रियः ।
युक्त इत्युच्यते योगी समलोष्ट्राश्मकाञ्चनः ॥८॥

jñāna-vijñāna-tṛptātmā kūṭa-stho vijitendriyaḥ/
yukta ity ucyate yogī sama-loṣṭrāśma-kāñcanaḥ//

jñāna—knowledge; *vijñāna*—realization; *tṛpta*—satisfied; *ātmā*—self; *kūṭa-sthaḥ*—steady; *vijita-indriyaḥ*—whose senses are conquered; *yuktaḥ*—fixed; *iti*—thus; *ucyate*—is said; *yogī*—*yogī*; *sama*—equally; *loṣṭra*—earth; *aśma*—stone; *kāñcanaḥ*—gold.

One who is self-satisfied by dint of scriptural knowledge and realization and is steadfast and sense controlled sees a piece of earth, a stone, and gold equally. One so fixed is said to be a yogī.

Seeing a piece of earth, a jewel, or gold equally means seeing them as the same substance in different states of transformation. In this verse Kṛṣṇa speaks of equal vision in relation to inanimate objects. In the next verse he speaks of a higher stage in which one sees the animate world with the same equal vision.

Text 9

सुहृन्मित्रार्युदासीनमध्यस्थद्वेष्यबन्धुषु ।
साधुष्वपि च पापेषु समबुद्धिर्विशिष्यते ॥९॥

suhṛn-mitrāry-udāsīna-madhyastha-dveṣya-bandhuṣu/
sādhuṣv api ca pāpeṣu sama-buddhir viśiṣyate//

su-hṛt—friend; *mitra*—associate; *ari*—enemy; *udāsīna*—equal-minded; *madhya-stha*—neutral amidst; *dveṣya-bandhuṣu*—enemies and friends;

sādhuṣu—among saints; *api*—even; *ca*—and; *pāpeṣu*—among sinners; *sama-buddhiḥ*—having equal intelligence; *viśiṣyate*—is superlative.

The superlative yogī is one who looks equally on a close friend, an associate, and an enemy, and who is thus equal in his dealings with everyone be they saints or sinners.

This verse is comparable to Kṛṣṇa's description of the impartial vision of the wise in chapter 5 (Bg. 5.18), with the difference that here the people the *yogī* is to see equally are those with whom one is personally involved—like the people with whom Arjuna has to fight.

Having explained the nature of yogic attainment in brief, Kṛṣṇa next explains the practices involved in achieving *yoga-samādhi*. These practices include the culture of *samprajñāta-samādhi*, mental absorption wherein one's thoughts are concentrated on one object *(ekāgra)*. *Samprajñāta-samādhi* leads to the perfection of *asamprajñāta-samādhi*, the mental stage in which all thought is restrained *(nirodha)*.

Text 10

योगी युञ्जीत सततमात्मानं रहसि स्थितः ।
एकाकी यतचित्तात्मा निराशीरपरिग्रहः ॥१०॥

yogī yuñjīta satatam ātmānaṁ rahasi sthitaḥ/
ekākī yata-cittātmā nirāśīr aparigrahaḥ//

yogī—the *yogī*; *yuñjīta*—should concentrate; *satatam*—always; *ātmānam*—on the self; *rahasi*—in a secluded place; *sthitaḥ*—remaining; *ekākī*—alone; *yata-citta-ātmā*—mind and body controlled; *nirāśīḥ*—free from desire; *aparigrahaḥ*—devoid of possessions.

The yogī should always concentrate his mind on the self, remaining alone in a secluded place with mind and body controlled, free from desire and devoid of possessions.

In verses 10 through 13 Kṛṣṇa explains how the *yogī* should sit for meditation. He should do so in a secluded *(rahasi)* place. Other than the fact that meditation itself involves entering the private hollow of the heart in utmost earnestness, the sense of this verse is that one should find a peaceful place free from disruptive influences and conducive to spiritual practice. The *yogī* should be alone to tend to his mind with controlled senses. The mind must be free from distraction if one is to be successful in *yoga*.

There are five mental planes or stages, only two of which are really conducive to *yoga*. *Kṣipta* refers to the mental plane in which under the influence of likes and dislikes the mind becomes engrossed in material objects; *mūḍha* refers to mental drowsiness; *vikṣipta* refers to the restless condition of the mind; *ekāgra* refers to one-pointed concentration of the mind; *nirodha* involves the restraint of thought altogether.

The planes of *kṣipta* and *mūḍha* are governed by *tamo-guṇa*. They are not at all conducive to the culture of *yoga-samādhi*. *Vikṣipta* is the influence of *rajo-guṇa*. This restless condition of the mind allows one to experience occasional *samādhi*. In this mental plane, the restless mind that is preoccupied with sense objects can sometimes concentrate in meditation. However, this *dhyāna* is short lived. It is in the stage of *ekāgra*, when the *guṇa* of *sattva* predominates, that the *yoga* practitioner can experience continued *samādhi*. This is known as *samprajñāta-samādhi*, which Kṛṣṇa is recommending the cultivation of here. In the mental stage of *nirodha*, all thought is restrained and one experiences *asamprajñāta-samādhi*. This will be discussed later in this same chapter. One should practice meditation and *bhajana* with knowledge of these mental planes and judge one's success accordingly.

Text 11

शुचौ देशे प्रतिष्ठाप्य स्थिरमासनमात्मनः ।
नात्युच्छ्रितं नातिनीचं चैलाजिनकुशोत्तरम् ॥११॥

śucau deśe pratiṣṭhāpya sthiram āsanam ātmanaḥ/
nāty-ucchritaṁ nāti-nīcaṁ cailājina-kuśottaram//

śucau—in a clean; *deśe*—in a place; *pratiṣṭhāpya*—establishing; *sthiram*—firm; *āsanam*—seat; *ātmanaḥ*—own; *na*—not; *ati*—too; *ucchritam*—high; *na*—nor; *ati*—too; *nīcam*—low; *caila-ajina*—soft cloth and deerskin; *kuśa*—kuśa grass; *uttaram*—covering.

He should establish a firm seat for himself in a clean place. It should be neither too high nor too low and should be covered with kuśa grass, a deer skin, and a cloth.

The meditator's seat should be slightly elevated and firm so that it will give sufficient support and not be subject to movement. If his *āsana* is too high or too low it will be a cause of disturbance. If it is too high he could fall from it during trance, and if too low forest creatures could disturb him and thus his *samādhi*. In ancient times it consisted of *kuśa* grass on top of which a tiger or deer skin was placed and then covered by a layer of cloth (*cailājina-kuśottaram*). Patañjali reveals the spirit of the *āsana* to be a seat that is firm and pleasant (Ys. 2.46). This seat should be one's own (*āsanam ātmanaḥ*) and used exclusively for the purpose of meditation. If the seat belongs to another, one may be disturbed due to uncertainty whether its owner wants to use it.

Text 12

तत्रैकाग्रं मनः कृत्वा यतचित्तेन्द्रियक्रियः ।
उपविश्यासने युञ्ज्याद्योगमात्मविशुद्धये ॥१२॥

tatraikāgraṁ manaḥ kṛtvā yata-cittendriya-kriyaḥ/
upaviśyāsane yuñjyād yogam ātma-viśuddhaye//

tatra—in that place; *eka-agram*—one-pointed; *manaḥ*—mind; *kṛtvā*—making; *yata-citta*—controlling the mind; *indriya-kriyaḥ*—sense activities; *upaviśya*—seated; *āsane*—on the seat; *yuñjyāt*—should practice; *yogam*—yoga; *ātma*—heart; *viśuddhaye*—for purifying.

Making his mind one-pointed and controlling all the activities of his senses, he should sit on that seat and engage in yoga for the sake of self-purification.

Here Kṛṣṇa says that one should practice *ekāgra—samprajñāta-samādhi*. Stress on sitting implies that meditation should not be attempted lying down or standing. Such an injunction is also found in *Vedānta-sūtra* (4.1.7–10), *dhyānāc ca*, "And because meditation is possible only in a sitting posture." However, one-pointedness, or concentration of the mind, is at the heart of meditation. The conditions set forth for meditating are subordinate to actually doing so. These conditions are favorable for accomplishing mental concentration; nevertheless, wherever, whenever, or however one can concentrate the mind on God one should do so. The above scriptural injunctions with regard to detail are not violated should they not be in place. Hence the best place for meditation is that which is conducive to concentrating the mind, *yatra ekāgratā tatrāviśeṣāt* (Vs. 4.1.11).

Text 13

समं कायशिरोग्रीवं धारयन्नचलं स्थिरः ।
सम्प्रेक्ष्य नासिकाग्रं स्वं दिशश्चानवलोकयन् ॥१३॥

samaṁ kāya-śiro-grīvaṁ dhārayann acalaṁ sthiraḥ/
samprekṣya nāsikāgraṁ svaṁ diśaś cānavalokayan//

samam—erect; *kāya*—body; *śiraḥ*—head; *grīvam*—neck; *dhārayan*—holding; *acalam*—motionless; *sthiraḥ*—steady; *samprekṣya*—concentrating the eyes on; *nāsikā*—nose; *agram*—tip; *svam*—own; *diśaḥ*—directions; *ca*—also; *anavalokayan*—not looking.

Holding his body, head, and neck erect, he should remain motionless and steady, concentrating his vision on the tip of his nose without letting it stray here and there.

After completing his description of how one should sit for meditation with the first half of this verse, Kṛṣṇa continues to discuss how one should meditate in the culture of *samprajñāta-samādhi* in the second half of this verse. He continues this description in the following verse.

Text 14

प्रशान्तात्मा विगतभीर्ब्रह्मचारिव्रते स्थितः ।
मनः संयम्य मच्चित्तो युक्त आसीत मत्परः ॥१४॥

praśāntātmā vigata-bhīr brahmacāri-vrate sthitaḥ/
manaḥ saṁyamya mac-citto yukta āsīta mat-paraḥ//

praśānta—quieted; *ātmā*—mind; *vigata-bhīḥ*—fearless; *brahmacāri-vrate*—in the vow of chastity; *sthitaḥ*—situated; *manaḥ*—mind; *saṁyamya*—controlling; *mat*—on me; *cittaḥ*—thought; *yuktaḥ*—the *yogī*; *āsīta*—should sit; *mat*—me; *paraḥ*—holding as the highest object.

With his mind quieted, fearless, observing a vow of chastity, controlling his mind by fixing his thoughts on me, he should sit concentrated in devotion, holding me as the highest object.

Central to all that has been described thus far is Kṛṣṇa's instruction in this verse, "Holding me as the highest object." Indeed, if a person somehow or other is able to fix his mind on Kṛṣṇa, he becomes situated in *yoga*. In describing himself as the central focus of *dhyāna-yoga*, Kṛṣṇa has identified himself with the Paramātmā seated in the heart of all living beings. Here Kṛṣṇa indirectly disparages the acquisition of yogic powers *(siddhis)*, which can be acquired by one-pointed concentration on material objects.

Text 15

युञ्जन्नेवं सदात्मानं योगी नियतमानसः ।
शान्तिं निर्वाणपरमां मत्संस्थामधिगच्छति ॥१५॥

yuñjann evaṁ sadātmānaṁ yogī niyata-mānasaḥ/
śāntiṁ nirvāṇa-paramāṁ mat-saṁsthām adhigacchati//

yuñjan—disciplining; *evam*—thus; *sadā*—always; *ātmānam*—the self; *yogī*—the *yogī*; *niyata-mānasaḥ*—with a controlled mind; *śāntim*—peace; *nirvāṇa-paramām*—cessation of material existence; *mat-saṁsthām*—standing with me; *adhigacchati*—attains.

Thus always disciplining the self, the yogī whose mind is controlled attains the supreme peace situated in me, beyond the cessation of material existence.

Here Kṛṣṇa defines that which lies beyond the mere cessation of material existence *(nirvāṇa-paramām)* to be the ultimate goal of *yoga*—union in love with Kṛṣṇa *(mat-saṁsthām)*. This is attained after prolonged practice. Baladeva Vidyābhūṣaṇa calls it "the highest limit of liberation." Here the conception of *nirvāṇa* first mentioned in chapter 2 (Bg. 2.72) has been subsumed in Kṛṣṇa. The highest peace that lies beyond the cessation of material existence is incorporated within the experience of Kṛṣṇa himself. What then must the direct experience of Kṛṣṇa be for his devotee? This is *asamprajñāta-samādhi*, in which thought is restrained *(niyata-mānasaḥ)*, stolen by the charm and beauty of Kṛṣṇa. It is attained through the constant practice *(yuñjan)* of fixing one's mind on Kṛṣṇa in *samprajñāta-samādhi*.

Kṛṣṇa speaks next of the moderation that is central to the path of *yoga*, making clear that *yoga* is not concerned with the material world, either in terms of chasing after it or running away from it.

Text 16

नात्यश्नतस्तु योगोऽस्ति न चैकान्तमनश्नतः ।
न चातिस्वप्नशीलस्य जाग्रतो नैव चार्जुन ॥१६॥

nāty-aśnatas tu yogo 'sti na caikāntam anaśnataḥ/
na cāti-svapna-śīlasya jāgrato naiva cārjuna//

na—not; *ati*—too much; *aśnataḥ*—of eating; *tu*—but; *yogaḥ*—*yoga*; *asti*—there is; *ca*—and; *ekāntam*—exclusively; *anaśnataḥ*—abstaining from eating; *na*—not; *ca*—and; *ati*—too much; *svapna-śīlasya*—of one who has the habit of sleeping; *jāgrataḥ*—or keeping awake; *na*—not; *eva*—even; *ca*—and; *arjuna*—O Arjuna.

O Arjuna, yoga is not attained by eating too much or eating too little. Nor is it for those habituated to sleeping too much or sleeping too little.

Overeating will cause disease. If one eats too little, the body will not be properly sustained. Not too much and not too little eating can also refer to the yogic prescription of filling one half of the stomach with food and one quarter with water, leaving the remaining quarter empty for the circulation of air. Regarding sleep, the *yogī* remains awake at the beginning and end of the night, sleeping only in the middle period.

Having spoken of what a *yogī* should not do, Kṛṣṇa next explains what he should do.

Text 17

युक्ताहारविहारस्य युक्तचेष्टस्य कर्मसु ।
युक्तस्वप्नावबोधस्य योगो भवति दुःखहा ॥१७॥

yuktāhāra-vihārasya yukta-ceṣṭasya karmasu/
yukta-svapnāvabodhasya yogo bhavati duḥkha-hā//

yukta—moderate; *āhāra*—eating; *vihārasya*—relaxation; *yukta*—regulated; *ceṣṭasya*—of action; *karmasu*—in actions; *yukta*—regulated; *svapna-avabodhasya*—of sleeping and being awake; *yogaḥ*—*yoga*; *bhavati*—becomes; *duḥkha-hā*—misery destroying.

The practice of yoga destroys the miseries of a person who is disciplined in his eating and relaxation, who performs his duties diligently, and who is balanced in his sleeping and waking.

The need for the discipline of moderation in eating, sleeping, relaxation, and so on applies not only to spiritual pursuit but also to material well-being.

Extreme fasting and sleep deprivation are not recommended here. The word *yukta* implies that which is acquired without excessive difficulty. One must be sensible in the practice of *yoga*.

Text 18

यदा विनियतं चित्तमात्मन्येवावतिष्ठते ।
निस्पृहः सर्वकामेभ्यो युक्त इत्युच्यते तदा ॥१८॥

yadā viniyataṁ cittam ātmany evāvatiṣṭhate/
nispṛhaḥ sarva-kāmebhyo yukta ity ucyate tadā//

yadā—when; *viniyatam*—controlled; *cittam*—mind; *ātmani*—in the self; *eva*—certainly; *avatiṣṭhate*—abides; *nispṛhaḥ*—free from longing; *sarva*—all; *kāmebhyaḥ*—from desires; *yuktaḥ*—situated in *yoga*; *iti*—thus; *ucyate*—is said; *tadā*—at that time.

When a yogī abides in the self alone with mind controlled and free from longing in relation to all material desires, at that time he is said to have attained yoga.

Text 19

यथा दीपो निवातस्थो नेङ्गते सोपमा स्मृता ।
योगिनो यतचित्तस्य युञ्जतो योगमात्मनः ॥१९॥

yathā dīpo nivāta-stho neṅgate sopamā smṛtā/
yogīno yata-cittasya yuñjato yogam ātmanaḥ//

yathā—as; *dīpaḥ*—a lamp; *nivāta-sthaḥ*—in a windless place; *na*—not; *iṅgate*—flickers; *sā*—this; *upamā*—comparison; *smṛtā*—is considered; *yogīnaḥ*—of the *yogī*; *yata-cittasya*—whose mind is controlled; *yuñjataḥ*—of the concentrated; *yogam*—*yoga*; *ātmanaḥ*—of the self.

A yogī whose mind is controlled and situated in yoga is like an unflickering lamp in a windless place.

Texts 20–25

यत्रोपरमते चित्तं निरुद्धं योगसेवया ।
यत्र चैवात्मनात्मानं पश्यन्नात्मनि तुष्यति ॥२०॥
सुखमात्यन्तिकं यत्तद्बुद्धिग्राह्यमतीन्द्रियम् ।
वेत्ति यत्र न चैवायं स्थितश्चलति तत्त्वतः ॥२१॥

यं लब्ध्वा चापरं लाभं मन्यते नाधिकं ततः ।
यस्मिन् स्थितो न दुःखेन गुरुणापि विचाल्यते ॥२२॥
तं विद्याद्दुःखसंयोगवियोगं योगसंज्ञितं ।
स निश्चयेन योक्तव्यो योगोऽनिर्विण्णचेतसा ॥२३॥
सङ्कल्पप्रभवान् कामांस्त्यक्त्वा सर्वानशेषतः ।
मनसैवेन्द्रियग्रामं विनियम्य समन्ततः ॥२४॥
शनैः शनैरुपरमेद् बुद्ध्या धृतिगृहीतया ।
आत्मसंस्थं मनः कृत्वा न किञ्चिदपि चिन्तयेत् ॥२५॥

yatroparamate cittaṁ niruddhaṁ yoga-sevayā/
yatra caivātmanātmānaṁ paśyann ātmani tuṣyati//
sukham ātyantikaṁ yat tad buddhi-grāhyam atīndriyam/
vetti yatra na caivāyaṁ sthitaś calati tattvataḥ//
yaṁ labdhvā cāparaṁ lābhaṁ manyate nādhikaṁ tataḥ/
yasmin sthito na duḥkhena guruṇāpi vicālyate//
taṁ vidyād duḥkha-saṁyoga-viyogaṁ yoga-saṁjñitam/
sa niścayena yoktavyo yogo 'nirviṇṇa-cetasā//
saṅkalpa-prabhavān kāmāṁs tyaktvā sarvān aśeṣataḥ/
manasaivendriya-grāmaṁ viniyamya samantataḥ//
śanaiḥ śanair uparamed buddhyā dhṛti-gṛhītayā/
ātma-saṁsthaṁ manaḥ kṛtvā na kiñcid api cintayet//

saḥ—that; *niścayena*—with determination; *yoktavyaḥ*—to be practiced; *yogaḥ*—*yoga*; *anirviṇṇa-cetasā*—with undismayed mind; *saṅkalpa*—cravings; *prabhavān*—born; *kāmān*—material desires; *tyaktvā*—abandoning; *sarvān*—all; *aśeṣataḥ*—without exception; *manasā*—by the mind; *eva*—certainly; *indriya-grāmam*—the full set of senses; *viniyamya*—controlling; *samantataḥ*—on all sides; *yatra*—where; *uparamate*—stops; *cittam*—mind; *niruddham*—restrained; *yoga-sevayā*—by *yoga* practice; *yatra*—where; *ca*—and; *eva*—certainly; *ātmanā*—by the self; *ātmānam*—the self; *paśyan*—beholds; *ātmani*—in the self; *tuṣyati*—becomes satisfied; *sukham*—joy; *ātyantikam*—boundless; *yat*—which; *tat*—that; *buddhi-grāhyam*—grasped by intelligence; *atīndriyam*—transcending the senses; *vetti*—knows; *yatra*—where; *na*—not; *ca*—and; *eva*—certainly; *ayam*—he; *sthitaḥ*—established; *calati*—wavers; *tattvataḥ*—from the truth; *yam*—that which; *labdhvā*—upon gaining; *ca*—also; *aparam*—other; *lābham*—gain; *manyate*—thinks; *na*—not; *adhikam*—greater; *tataḥ*—than that; *yasmin*—in which; *sthitaḥ*—situated; *na*—not; *duḥkhena*—by distress; *guruṇā*—by difficult; *api*—even; *vicālyate*—is perturbed; *tam*—that; *vidyāt*—let it be known; *duḥkha-saṁyoga*—sorrow arising from material contact; *viyogam*—dissolution; *yoga-saṁjñitam*—known as *yoga*; *śanaiḥ śanaiḥ*—step-by-step; *uparamet*—one should become still; *buddhyā*—by intelligence; *dhṛti-gṛhītayā*—carried by conviction; *ātma-saṁstham*—established in self-realization; *manaḥ*—mind; *kṛtvā*—making; *na*—not; *kiñcit*—anything else; *api*—even; *cintayet*—should think.

Yoga is the name given to the state of dissolution of all sorrow arising from material contact, in which the adept's mind comes to a halt, being restrained by his disciplined practice, in which he beholds the self by the self and is thus self-satisfied, in which he comes to know the boundless joy that is beyond the senses but is apprehended by the pure intelligence of the soul, in which once established he never wavers from the truth, upon gaining which he thinks there is nothing greater to be attained, and situated in which he is not perturbed even in the face of great difficulty. To attain this a person should engage himself in yoga practice with determination, his mind always confident of success. Without exception he should abandon all cravings born of desires and control the senses on all sides by the mind. Gradually, step-by-step he should become still. With intelligence carried by conviction, his mind established in self-realization, he should cease all mental activity.

From verse 20 through 23, Kṛṣṇa speaks about *asamprajñāta-samādhi*. In verses 24 and 25, Kṛṣṇa speaks of the practices at the beginning and end of the *yoga* process: Giving up cravings is the symptom of the beginning of the process of *yoga*, while ceasing all mental activity is the sign of having completed it. Ceasing all mental activity is accomplished when the mind is taken over by the Absolute. Viśvanātha Cakravartī Ṭhākura comments that all these verses (Bg. 6. 20–25) are to be read together as descriptions of the condition called *yoga* (*samādhi*).

Text 26

यतो यतो निश्चलति मनश्चञ्चलमस्थिरम् ।
ततस्ततो नियम्यैतदात्मन्येव वशं नयेत् ॥२६॥

yato yato niścalati manaś cañcalam asthiram/
tatas tato niyamyaitad ātmany eva vaśaṁ nayet//

yataḥ yataḥ—wherever; *niścalati*—wanders; *manaḥ*—mind; *cañcalam*—fickle; *asthiram*—unsteady; *tataḥ tataḥ*—from there; *niyamya*—controlling; *etat*—

this; *ātmani*—in the self; *eva*—certainly; *vaśam*—control; *nayet*—should bring.

From wherever the unsteady, fickle mind wanders, the yogī should draw it back under the control of the self.

Text 27

प्रशान्तमनसं ह्येनं योगिनं सुखमुत्तमम् ।
उपैति शान्तरजसं ब्रह्मभूतमकल्मषम् ॥२७॥

praśānta-manasaṁ hy enaṁ yoginaṁ sukham uttamam/
upaiti śānta-rajasaṁ brahma-bhūtam akalmaṣam//

praśānta—peaceful; *manasam*—mind; *hi*—certainly; *enam*—this; *yoginam*—yogī; *sukham*—happiness; *uttamam*—the highest; *upaiti*—attains; *śānta-rajasam*—his passion subdued; *brahma-bhūtam*—self-realization; *akalmaṣam*—free from evil.

The yogī whose mind is truly composed, who has subdued his passion and is free from evil, attains ultimate happiness in self-realization.

Text 28

युञ्जन्नेवं सदात्मानं योगी विगतकल्मशः ।
सुखेन ब्रह्मसंस्पर्शमत्यन्तं सुखमश्नुते ॥२८॥

yuñjann evaṁ sadātmānaṁ yogī vigata-kalmaṣaḥ/
sukhena brahma-saṁsparśam atyantaṁ sukham aśnute//

yuñjan—practicing *yoga*; *evam*—thus; *sadā*—constantly; *ātmānam*—himself; *yogī*—yogī; *vigata*—gone away; *kalmaṣaḥ*—evil; *sukhena*—in happiness; *brahma-saṁsparśam*—contact with Brahman; *atyantam*—boundless; *sukham*—happiness; *aśnute*—attains.

In this way through constant practice, the yogī, free from any trace of evil, easily reaches Brahman, attaining boundless happiness.

Text 29

सर्वभूतस्थमात्मानं सर्वभूतानि चात्मनि ।
ईक्षते योगयुक्तात्मा सर्वत्र समदर्शनः ॥२९॥

sarva-bhūta-stham ātmānaṁ sarva-bhūtāni cātmani/
īkṣate yoga-yuktātmā sarvatra sama-darśanaḥ//

sarva-bhūta-stham—situated in all beings; *ātmānam*—the Self; *sarva*—all; *bhūtāni*—beings; *ca*—also; *ātmani*—in the Self; *īkṣate*—sees; *yoga-yukta-ātmā*—one who is disciplined in *yoga*; *sarvatra*—everywhere; *sama-darśa-naḥ*—seeing equally.

He who is disciplined in yoga sees the Supreme Self existing in all beings and all beings existing in the Supreme Self. He sees equally at all times.

Here Kṛṣṇa describes the vision of the *jīvanmukta*. He sees equally, and he sees God in everything and everything in God. Although he sees only God, this involves seeing all things in relation to him. The famous Upaniṣadic dictum *sarvaṁ khalv idaṁ brahma*, "Everything is Brahman," hardly does away with "all things." They exist as the energy of God. Thus the perfect *yogī* sees only God and his energy.

Most of the Vaiṣṇava commentators render *ātmān* in this verse as God (Paramātmā). Here Kṛṣṇa speaks of a further development in yogic perfection from that mentioned in the previous verse. From Brahman realization, the *yogī* advances to realization of the Paramātmā feature of God.

Bhaktivedanta Swami Prabhupāda renders *ātman* as "me," referring to Kṛṣṇa himself. This rendering senses the emotion of Kṛṣṇa as he speaks of the perfection of *yoga* that culminates in devotion to himself. Indeed, the following verse seems to confirm this. As a person in love sees only his lover wherever he looks, so the highest devotee sees Kṛṣṇa all the more so, for in reality all things are but his energy. Such a devotee lives in Kṛṣṇa, beyond the necessity of the rules of *yoga* mentioned previously. Whatever he does is done out of love for Kṛṣṇa, and because he is so motivated no one can predict what he will do.

Text 30

यो मां पश्यति सर्वत्र सर्वं च मयि पश्यति ।
तस्याहं न प्रणश्यामि स च मे न प्रणश्यति ॥३०॥

yo māṁ paśyati sarvatra sarvaṁ ca mayi paśyati/
tasyāhaṁ na praṇaśyāmi sa ca me na praṇaśyati//

yaḥ—whoever; *mām*—me; *paśyati*—sees; *sarvatra*—everywhere; *sarvam*—everything; *ca*—and; *mayi*—in me; *paśyati*—sees; *tasya*—of him; *aham*—I;

na—not; *praṇaśyāmi*—am lost; *saḥ*—he; *ca*—also; *me*—to me; *na*—not; *praṇaśyati*—is lost.

I am never lost to one who sees me everywhere and sees all things in me, nor is such a person ever lost to me.

Speaking of himself, Bhagavān Śrī Kṛṣṇa describes the vision of his highest devotees: *mahātmās, mahābhāgavatas*. As we shall see at the end of this chapter, they are the best *yogīs*. Their vision is further described in the *Śrīmad-Bhāgavatam* thus:

sarva-bhūteṣu yaḥ paśyed bhagavad-bhāvam ātmanaḥ bhūtāni bhagavaty
ātmany eṣa bhāgavatottamaḥ

"One who sees the soul of all souls within everything and thus everything in relation to God, realizing that existence itself is situated within God, such a person is a superlative devotee." (ŚB. 11.2.45) The best example of this is found in the Vraja *gopīs*, and it appears that Kurukṣetra Kṛṣṇa is remembering them here.

After Vraja Kṛṣṇa disappeared from the *rāsa* dance on the night designated to consummate his relationship with the *gopīs*, their love for him in separation caused him to reappear. How did they express their love in separation? They spoke to the trees, the earth, the deer, and other forest inhabitants, inquiring from them about Kṛṣṇa's whereabouts. They addressed them as if they were better devotees than themselves. They projected their own love onto others, even inanimate objects, bringing them and the world to life in divine love. Devoid of the tendency to criticize others, they found fault only in themselves. Whatever they saw reminded them of Kṛṣṇa. They saw him in everything, and he was captured by their love.[2]

Text 31

सर्वभूतस्थितं यो मां भजत्येकत्वमास्थितः ।
सर्वथा वर्तमानोऽपि स योगी मयि वर्तते ॥३१॥

sarva-bhūta-sthitaṁ yo māṁ bhajaty ekatvam āsthitaḥ/
sarvathā vartamāno 'pi sa yogī mayi vartate//

sarva-bhūta-sthitam—situated in all beings; *yaḥ*—he who; *mām*—me; *bhajati*—worships; *ekatvam*—in oneness; *āsthitaḥ*—situated; *sarvathā*—in

2. See ŚB. 10.29–33.

whatever way; *vartamānaḥ*—existing; *api*—in spite of; *sa*—he; *yogī*—*yogī*; *mayi*—in me; *vartate*—lives.

That yogī who worships me in the oneness of understanding that it is I who am situated in all beings lives in me regardless of how he acts.

Kṛṣṇa's words *sarvathā vartamāno 'pi* (regardless of how he acts), keep his instruction in this section focused on the highest devotion. Those who appeared to cross over *dharma* by stealing away in the night to meet with Kṛṣṇa, the Vraja *gopīs*, are the kind of *yogīs* Kṛṣṇa is speaking of here. They had little concern for sitting postures and breathing exercises, for they had embraced the heart of *yoga*, which caused them to get up to sing and dance. While the average *yogī* tries to think of Kṛṣṇa, they tried to forget him in the madness of divine love but could not! The techniques of mystic *yoga* Kṛṣṇa has spoken of apply to Kṛṣṇa's devotees in terms of their meditation on their *mantra* and their *japa*. Singing in *kīrtana* about Kṛṣṇa, however, is not subject to these regulations. Such chanting and subsequent dancing can be performed anywhere at any time, in all circumstances. Furthermore, such practice, while potent for the practitioner and an outpouring of love for the perfected devotee, simultaneously benedicts others.

Arjuna thought, "If such a devotional *yogī* sees Kṛṣṇa in everything, how does he relate to 'others'?" To his query Kṛṣṇa responds, speaking of his devotee's compassion, the overflowing of the vessel of his love.

Text 32

आत्मौपम्येन सर्वत्र समं पश्यति योऽर्जुन ।
सुखं वा यदि वा दुःखं स योगी परमो मतः ॥३२॥

ātmaupamyena sarvatra samaṁ paśyati yo 'rjuna/
sukhaṁ vā yadi vā duḥkhaṁ sa yogī paramo mataḥ//

ātma—self; *aupamyena*—by comparison; *sarvatra*—everywhere; *samam*—equally; *paśyati*—sees; *yaḥ*—he who; *arjuna*—O Arjuna; *sukham*—pleasure; *vā*—or; *yadi*—if; *vā*—or; *duḥkham*—pain; *saḥ*—that; *yogī*—*yogī*; *paramaḥ*—best; *mataḥ*—considered.

The yogī who measures the pain and pleasure of others as if it were his own, O Arjuna, is considered to be the best of all.

Kṛṣṇa's devotees possess such compassionate hearts that they broadcast his holy name and virtuous deeds wherever they go. In the words of the *gopīs*, they are the most munificent welfare workers.[3] They identify with the joys and sorrows of others as if they were their own, and thus they tirelessly canvass to lift others beyond the duality of joy and sorrow by showering them with the immortal nectar of *hari-kathā*. To see another's sorrow as one's own is to see through the eyes of God, for all souls are eternally related with God, as parts are to the whole. Mature *yoga* is recognizable by the outward symptoms indicated in this verse.

Here we find the practical application of *yoga* in the world, what *yoga* practice will do to improve the world. Although this and the previous verses in this section refer to advanced *yogīs*, it is they whom practitioners should try to emulate. Practitioners should strive to follow this golden rule of *yoga*. Only when practitioners do so will their practice of meditation be effective. How we deal with others and the world in everyday life will have considerable impact on our attempts at meditation. In *Śrīmad-Bhāgavatam* it is mentioned that without cultivating this outlook, one's devotional practices are performed in vain. Therein Kṛṣṇa's incarnation Kapiladeva instructs his mother thus: "I am present in every living entity as the Supersoul. If someone neglects or disregards that Supersoul everywhere and engages himself in the worship of the Deity in the temple, that is simply imitation. One who worships the Deity of Godhead in the temple but does not know that God, as Paramātmā, is situated in every living entity's heart, must be in ignorance and is compared to one who offers oblations unto ashes." Kṛṣṇa himself instructed Arjuna along these lines earlier in the *Gītā* (Bg. 5.25): "Those who are self-controlled and live for the welfare of all beings *(sarva-bhūta-hite ratāḥ)* attain *brahma-nirvāṇa*."

Verses 29 through 33 foreshadow Kṛṣṇa's concluding statement on *yoga* in verse 47. Finally, as we near the end of the first six chapters that constitute the *yoga* psychology of the *Gītā*, we arrive at the highest ideal. After describing the entire process of self-realization, discussing all its different levels of self-control and experience, *sthita-prajña*, *brahma-bhūta*, *brahma-nirvāṇa*, and so on, we come to *bhakti* and Kṛṣṇa himself. Kṛṣṇa has been revealing himself little by little throughout these six chapters almost at regular intervals (Bg. 2.61, 3.30, 4.35, 5.29, 6.14–15). Now it is definite—he is the one we have to see everywhere and in everything. As

3. See ŚB. 10.31.9.

he emphatically concludes at the end of this chapter, the means to do so is *bhakti*.

As Kṛṣṇa's mind floods with thoughts of his devotees, Arjuna asks him about the practicality of that which he had proposed earlier. Inasmuch as controlling the mind is central to the system of *yoga* that Kṛṣṇa has explained, Arjuna expressed his reservation, knowing well from his own experience the restless nature of the mind. After all, his mind had been reeling at the thought of doing battle with his own kinsmen.

Text 33

अर्जुन उवाच
योऽयं योगस्त्वया प्रोक्तः साम्येन मधुसूदन ।
एतस्याहं न पश्यामि चञ्चलत्वात् स्थितिं स्थिराम् ॥३३॥

arjuna uvāca
yo 'yaṁ yogas tvayā proktaḥ sāmyena madhusūdana/
etasyāhaṁ na paśyāmi cañcalatvāt sthitiṁ sthirām//

arjunaḥ uvāca—Arjuna said; *yaḥ ayam*—this which; *yogaḥ*—*yoga*; *tvayā*—by you; *proktaḥ*—described; *sāmyena*—with evenness of mind; *madhusūdana*—O killer of Madhu; *etasya*—of this; *aham*—I; *na*—not; *paśyāmi*—see; *cañcalatvāt*—from unsteadiness; *sthitim*—situation; *sthirām*—permanent.

Arjuna said: O Madhusūdana, the system of yoga you have described that calls for evenness of mind does not appear realistic, because of the mind's unsteady nature.

Arjuna's reservation is partly related to his lack of inclination for the techniques of *yoga*, such as breath control *(prāṇāyāma)* and other such devices that Kṛṣṇa has described. Being at heart a devotee, he is not overly inclined to the techniques of mystic *yoga* and its goal of union with the Paramātmā. He is, however, disposed to the central theme of *yoga*: thinking of Kṛṣṇa and loving him as Bhagavān. However, actually loving Kṛṣṇa involves passing through the stages of yogic attainment discussed thus far. This is an enormous undertaking, and Arjuna is understandably overwhelmed by the task before him.

Arjuna next attempts to justify his doubts and gives an example to further illustrate them.

Text 34

चञ्चलं हि मनः कृष्ण प्रमाथि बलवद्दृढम् ।
तस्याहं निग्रहं मन्ये वायोरिव सुदुष्करम् ॥३४॥

cañcalaṁ hi manaḥ kṛṣṇa pramāthi balavad dṛḍham/
tasyāhaṁ nigrahaṁ manye vāyor iva su-duṣkaram//

cañcalam—fickle; *hi*—certainly; *manaḥ*—mind; *kṛṣṇa*—O Kṛṣṇa; *pramāthi*—disturbing; *bala-vat*—powerful; *dṛḍham*—obstinate; *tasya*—its; *aham*—I; *nigraham*—subjugation; *manye*—think; *vāyoḥ*—of the wind; *iva*—like; *su-duṣkaram*—difficult to do.

For the mind is so fickle, disturbing, powerful, and obstinate, O Kṛṣṇa, that I think that subduing it is as difficult as trying to control the wind.

Use of the word *hi* (certainly) in this verse indicates that Arjuna's depiction of the mind is something that is universally experienced. Arjuna's reservations are thus well founded. *Yoga* is not for the squeamish. It is no easy task for Arjuna to look upon his own brothers and Duryodhana, the leader of the opposition, with impartiality. He will have to die an ego death to live in this reality, and this is much more difficult than dying in battle. One's mind is his most formidable enemy.

The mind is not only fickle *(cañcalam)*, it also disturbs *(pramāthi)* the other senses. Furthermore, it is powerful *(balavat)* and obstinate *(dṛḍham)*. Śaṅkara has compared it to an octopus. Viśvanātha Cakravartī comments that the mind is so powerful that it does not care for the counsel of intelligence.

While Arjuna speaks here of the predicament, he also indicates the solution by invoking Kṛṣṇa's holy name. Kṛṣṇa means he who removes *(karṣati)* even the greatest faults in his devotees—reactions to evil deeds for which there is no other remedial measure. There is no more effective means recommended anywhere in the sacred literature for conquering the mind than invoking the name of Kṛṣṇa. Here Arjuna has done so without thinking due to his natural position in devotion. In doing so, he indicates his natural love for the heart of *yoga*, the very principle of spiritual life, in relation to which the various techniques mentioned are details subject to modification in accordance with time and circumstance.

Text 35

श्रीभगवानुवाच
असंशयं महाबाहो मनो दुर्निग्रहं चलम् ।
अभ्यासेन तु कौन्तेय वैराग्येण च गृह्यते ॥३५॥

śrī-bhagavān uvāca
asaṁśayaṁ mahā-bāho mano durnigrahaṁ calam/
abhyāsena tu kaunteya vairāgyeṇa ca gṛhyate//

śrī-bhagavān uvāca—the Lord of Śrī said; *asaṁśayam*—undoubtedly; *mahā-bāho*—O mighty-armed one; *manaḥ*—the mind; *durnigraham*—difficult to control; *calam*—fickle; *abhyāsena*—by practice; *tu*—but; *kaunteya*—O son of Kuntī; *vairāgyeṇa*—by detachment; *ca*—also; *gṛhyate*—is controlled.

The Lord of Śrī said: No doubt, O mighty-armed one, the fickle mind is difficult to control. However, O son of Kuntī, it can be controlled by practice and detachment.

Kṛṣṇa sympathizes with Arjuna in this verse, and he appreciates Arjuna's natural devotion. Thus he addresses Arjuna encouragingly as *mahā-bāho*, "mighty-armed." Through this address Kṛṣṇa implies that by his grace Arjuna will be successful in his battle with the obstinate mind. He underscores this with the word *asaṁśayam* (without doubt). Both God's grace and great effort on our part are required for successful *yoga* practice. Kṛṣṇa's grace is further implied here when he identifies Arjuna as his dear relative, *kaunteya*. Surely for such a dear one Kṛṣṇa will be merciful. Thus one should try to endear oneself to Kṛṣṇa. This is real *yoga*.

The relationship between practice and grace is not always clear. Through grace one is empowered to practice, and by practice one secures God's grace. In Viśvanātha Cakravartī's comments on verse 41 of chapter 2 we find that the grace of the guru that is so essential for success is equated with wholeheartedly embracing the practices he outlines.

Here Kṛṣṇa further recommends that practice *(abhyāsa)* and detachment *(vairāgya)* are essential if one is to conquer the mind. By detaching the mind from thoughts of sense indulgence, one dams the river of its perpetual flow. By *yoga* practice the *sādhaka* diverts the mind's current in the direction of God. This practice involves not only spiritual practices relative to one's chosen path, such as hearing and chanting about Kṛṣṇa, associating with saintly persons, hearing the scripture, venerating the Deity, living in a sacred place, and other such forms of *sādhana*, but practicing to steady the mind itself in *samādhi*. One must practice restraining the mind. Spiritual practice, *sādhana*, is the emphasis of this entire chapter. There is no replacement for spiritual practice. Detachment involves a lifestyle in which one abstains from those things that tend to disturb the mind. Without such detachment, one's practice will be like pouring water in a leaking bucket. Whatever gains are made are simultaneously lost rather than accumulated.

Text 36

असंयतात्मना योगो दुष्प्राप इति मे मतिः ।
वश्यात्मना तु यतता शक्योऽवाप्तुमुपायतः ॥३६॥

asaṁyatātmanā yogo duṣprāpa iti me matiḥ/
vaśyātmanā tu yatatā śakyo 'vāptum upāyataḥ//

asaṁyata—uncontrolled; *ātmanā*—by the mind; *yogaḥ*—*yoga*; *duṣprāpaḥ*—difficult to attain; *iti*—thus; *me*—my; *matiḥ*—opinion; *vaśya*—controlled; *ātmanā*—by the mind; *tu*—but; *yatatā*—by striving; *śakyaḥ*—possible; *avāptum*—to attain; *upāyataḥ*—by the proper method.

I agree that yoga is difficult to attain for one whose mind is out of control, but for one whose mind is under control and who strives by the proper method, it is possible.

Kṛṣṇa agrees with Arjuna that *yoga* is difficult to achieve for one with an uncontrolled mind. By this he means to say that one cannot attain *yoga* if one has not cultivated detachment and engaged regularly in spiritual practice as prescribed in the previous verse. The proper method *(upāyataḥ)* mentioned in this verse refers to repeated efforts *(sādhan-bhāyastvam)*.

Hearing Kṛṣṇa stress practice and detachment, Arjuna wonders about the fate of one who fails in his practice.

Text 37

अर्जुन उवाच
अयतिः श्रद्धयोपेतो योगाच्चलितमानसः ।
अप्राप्य योगसंसिद्धिं कां गतिं कृष्ण गच्छति ॥३७॥

arjuna uvāca
ayatiḥ śraddhayopeto yogāc calita-mānasaḥ/
aprāpya yoga-saṁsiddhiṁ kāṁ gatiṁ kṛṣṇa gacchati//

arjunaḥ uvāca—Arjuna said; *ayatiḥ*—the uncontrolled; *śraddhayā*—with faith; *upetaḥ*—arrived at; *yogāt*—from *yoga*; *calita*—deviated; *mānasaḥ*—mind; *aprāpya*—failing to attain; *yoga-saṁsiddhim*—yogic perfection; *kām*—which; *gatim*—destination; *kṛṣṇa*—O Kṛṣṇa; *gacchati*—attains.

Arjuna said: O Kṛṣṇa, what destination befalls one who, although possessed of faith, is nevertheless uncontrolled? What happens to one whose mind has fallen away from yoga practice without having achieved perfection?

Text 38

कच्चिन्नोभयविभ्रष्टश्छिन्नाभ्रमिव नश्यति ।
अप्रतिष्ठो महाबाहो विमूढो ब्रह्मणः पथि ॥३८॥

kaccin nobhaya-vibhraṣṭaś chinnābhram iva naśyati/
apratiṣṭho mahā-bāho vimūḍho brahmaṇaḥ pathi//

kaccit—whether; *na*—not; *ubhaya*—both; *vibhraṣṭaḥ*—deviated; *chinna*—cut off; *abhram*—cloud; *iva*—like; *naśyati*—is lost; *apratiṣṭhaḥ*—without footing; *mahā-bāho*—O mighty-armed; *vimūḍhaḥ*—bewildered; *brahmaṇaḥ*—of transcendence; *pathi*—on the path.

O mighty-armed, is he not lost in his pursuit of transcendence like a riven cloud with no solid footing in either world?

Text 39

एतन्मे संशयं कृष्ण छेत्तुमर्हस्यशेषतः ।
त्वदन्यः संशयस्यास्य छेत्ता न ह्युपपद्यते ॥३९॥

etan me saṁśayaṁ kṛṣṇa chettum arhasy aśeṣataḥ/
tvad-anyaḥ saṁśayasyāsya chettā na hy upapadyate//

etat—this; *me*—my; *saṁśayam*—doubt; *kṛṣṇa*—O Kṛṣṇa; *chettum*—cut through; *arhasi*—you can; *aśeṣataḥ*—completely; *tvat*—than you; *anyaḥ*—other; *saṁśayasya*—of the doubt; *asya*—of this; *chettā*—remover; *na*—not; *hi*—certainly; *upapadyate*—exists.

These are my doubts, O Kṛṣṇa! Please cut through them, for other than you, no one is capable of destroying them completely.

Arjuna's question is thoughtful. Should a person leave the *karma-mārga*, he will not attain heaven or material success in the next life. That is fine if in doing so he embraces *yoga* in pursuit of liberation. However, should he be unsuccessful in *yoga* practice, what will his position be then? It would seem that he attains neither heaven nor liberation, neither material nor spiritual perfection.

Arjuna has implicit faith in Kṛṣṇa, and Kṛṣṇa responds to his sincere inquiry with great affection.

Text 40

श्रीभगवानुवाच
पार्थ नैवेह नामुत्र विनाशस्तस्य विद्यते ।
न हि कल्याणकृत् कश्चिद्दुर्गतिं तात गच्छति ॥४०॥

śrī-bhagavān uvāca
pārtha naiveha nāmutra vināśas tasya vidyate/
na hi kalyāṇa-kṛt kaścid durgatiṁ tāta gacchati//

śrī-bhagavān uvāca—the Lord of Śrī said; *pārtha*—O son of Pṛthā; *na*—not; *eva*—certainly; *iha*—in this world; *na*—not; *amutra*—there in heaven; *vināśaḥ*—destruction; *tasya*—his; *vidyate*—exists; *na*—not; *hi*—certainly; *kalyāṇa-kṛt*—virtuous; *kaścit*—anyone; *durgatim*—to misfortune; *tāta*—my dear friend; *gacchati*—goes.

The Lord of Śrī said: O son of Pṛthā, neither here in this world nor in the next is he vanquished. Anyone who is sincere, my dear friend, walks not the road of misfortune.

Here the all-compassionate Kṛṣṇa replies, his heart going out to Arjuna and all of his devotees. His assurance is that "sincerity is invincible," *na hi kalyāṇa-kṛt kaścid durgatiṁ tāta gacchati*. Anyone who does good is never overcome by evil. With this assurance one should practice *yoga*, difficult though it may be. The use of the word *tāta* indicates great affection on the part of Kṛṣṇa, who speaks here as fatherly guru to his son-like disciple. Although Kṛṣṇa's words are relevant for *yoga* practitioners in general, this verse is intended for his devotees in particular.

Text 41–42

प्राप्य पुण्यकृतां लोकान् उषित्वा शाश्वतीः समाः ।
शुचीनां श्रीमतां गेहे योगभ्रष्टोऽभिजायते ॥४१॥

अथवा योगिनामेव कुले भवति धीमताम्।
एतद्धि दुर्लभतरं लोके जन्म यदीदृशम् ॥४२॥

prāpya puṇya-kṛtāṁ lokān uṣitvā śāśvatīḥ samāḥ/
śucīnāṁ śrīmatāṁ gehe yoga-bhraṣṭo 'bhijāyate//
athavā yogīnām eva kule bhavati dhīmatām/
etad dhi durlabhataraṁ loke janma yad īdṛśam//

prāpya—after achieving; *puṇya-kṛtām*—of those who performed pious activities; *lokān*—planets; *uṣitvā*—after dwelling; *śāśvatīḥ*—many; *samāḥ*—years; *śucīnām*—of the pious; *śrī-matām*—of the aristocratic; *gehe*—in the house; *yoga-bhraṣṭaḥ*—one who has fallen from the path of *yoga*; *abhijāyate*—is born; *atha vā*—or; *yogīnām*—of *yogīs*; *eva*—certainly; *kule*—in the family; *bhavati*—is born; *dhī-matām*—of the learned; *etat*—this; *hi*—certainly; *durlabha-taram*—very rare; *loke*—in this world; *janma*—birth; *yat*—that which; *īdṛśam*—such.

He who has fallen from the path of yoga attains heaven and dwells there for what seems an eternity. Then he is born again in a pious or aristocratic family. Or he may be born directly into a family of wise transcendentalists. Rare is such a birth in this world.

Contrary to Arjuna's thinking, Kṛṣṇa reveals that the unsuccessful *yogī* attains both material happiness and eventually liberation. Here we are reminded of Kṛṣṇa's first instruction on the nature of *yoga-dharma* found in chapter 2 (Bg. 2.40), wherein he taught that efforts on the path of *yoga* never go in vain. The immature *yogī* or devotee attains material heaven where he is free to enjoy without karmic repercussion that sense pleasure that distracted him from his practice. This, however, does not include distractions that lead the practitioner off the path—deviations from pious, scripturally regulated life. It refers to distractions such as the desire to visit heaven itself. When the neophyte *yogī* has exhausted this propensity, he again takes birth on earth in a family that provides him the economic freedom or pious situation from which to pick up where he left off in his spiritual practice.

The advanced *yogī* referred to in verse 42 who falls from his practice need not go to heaven to exhaust his enjoying propensity. He takes birth directly in a family that is involved in *yoga* practice, receiving instruction in *yoga* from his very birth. Both the mature and immature *yogīs* are assisted by efforts spent on the spiritual path, as the yogic tendency again asserts itself in their life. Kṛṣṇa affirms this in the following verses.

Text 43

तत्र तं बुद्धिसंयोगं लभते पौर्वदेहिकम् ।
यतते च ततो भूयः संसिद्धौ कुरुनन्दन ॥४३॥

tatra taṁ buddhi-saṁyogaṁ labhate paurva-dehikam/
yatate ca tato bhūyaḥ saṁsiddhau kuru-nandana//

tatra—thereupon; *tam*—that; *buddhi-saṁyogam*—yogic intelligence; *labhate*—gains; *paurva-dehikam*—from the previous body; *yatate*—he strives; *ca*—also; *tataḥ*—thereafter; *bhūyaḥ*—again; *saṁsiddhau*—for perfection; *kuru-nandana*—O son of Kuru.

Thereupon he regains the yogic intelligence cultivated in his previous life and once again strives for perfection, O son of Kuru.

Text 44

पूर्वाभ्यासेन तेनैव ह्रियते ह्यवशोऽपि सः ।
जिज्ञासुरपि योगस्य शब्दब्रह्मातिवर्तते ॥४४॥

pūrvābhyāsena tenaiva hriyate hy avaśo 'pi saḥ/
jijñāsur api yogasya śabda-brahmātivartate//

pūrva—previous; *abhyāsena*—by practice; *tena*—by that; *eva*—certainly; *hriyate*—is attracted; *hi*—surely; *avaśaḥ*—spontaneously; *api*—also; *saḥ*—he; *jijñāsuḥ*—inquisitive; *api*—even; *yogasya*—about *yoga*; *śabda-brahma*—ritualistic recitation of scriptures; *ativartate*—transcends.

Due to his prior practice, he is carried along spontaneously. Even one who merely inquires about yoga transcends the ritualistic recitation of the Vedas.

Text 45

प्रयत्नाद्यतमानस्तु योगी संशुद्धकिल्बिषः ।
अनेकजन्मसंसिद्धस्ततो याति परां गतिम् ॥४५॥

prayatnād yatamānas tu yogī saṁśuddha-kilbiṣaḥ/
aneka-janma-saṁsiddhas tato yāti parāṁ gatim//

prayatnāt—from persevering; *yatamānaḥ*—restrained; *tu*—but; *yogī*—the yogī; *saṁśuddha*—completely cleansed; *kilbiṣaḥ*—evil; *aneka*—many; *janma*—birth; *saṁsiddhaḥ*—perfected; *tataḥ*—thereafter; *yāti*—attains; *parām*—supreme; *gatim*—goal.

In this way, by persevering and restraining his mind, the yogī, completely cleansed of all evil tendencies and perfected through many births, finally attains the supreme goal.

Text 46

तपस्विभ्योऽधिको योगी ज्ञानिभ्योऽपि मतोऽधिकः ।
कर्मिभ्यश्चाधिको योगी तस्माद्योगी भवार्जुन ॥४६॥

tapasvibhyo 'dhiko yogī jñānibhyo 'pi mato 'dhikaḥ/
karmibhyaś cādhiko yogī tasmād yogī bhavārjuna//

tapasvibhyaḥ—than the ascetics; *adhikaḥ*—superior; *yogī*—the yogī; *jñānibhyaḥ*—than the *jñānis; api*—also; *mataḥ*—considered; *adhikaḥ*—superior; *karmibhyaḥ*—than the ritualists; *ca*—also; *adhikaḥ*—superior; *yogī*—*yogī*; *tasmāt*—therefore; *yogī*—*yogī*; *bhava*—be; *arjuna*—O Arjuna.

The yogī is superior to the ascetic, superior to the jñāni, and superior to the ritualist as well. Therefore, Arjuna, be a yogī!

Here Kṛṣṇa summarizes his teaching thus far: "Become a *yogī*, Arjuna." He addresses his disciple as Arjuna, indicating his purity. In the concluding verse of this chapter, Kṛṣṇa tells Arjuna that of all types of *yogīs*, his devotee is the best.

Text 47

योगिनामपि सर्वेषां मद्गतेनान्तरात्मना ।
श्रद्धावान् भजते यो मां स मे युक्ततमो मतः ॥४७॥

yogīnām api sarveṣāṁ mad-gatenāntar-ātmanā/
śraddhāvān bhajate yo māṁ sa me yuktatamo mataḥ//

yogīnām—of yogīs; *api*—also; *sarveṣām*—of all; *mat-gatena*—abiding in me; *antaḥ-ātmanā*—within himself; *śraddhā-vān*—with full faith; *bhajate*—worships; *yaḥ*—he who; *mām*—to me; *saḥ*—he; *me*—to me; *yukta-tamaḥ*—the best *yogī*; *mataḥ*—is considered.

Of all yogīs, he who abides in me with full faith, worshipping me in devotion, is most intimately united with me and considered the best of all.

After the considerable discussion of *yoga* that began in the second chapter (Bg. 2.39), Kṛṣṇa concludes his *yoga* discourse with this verse. Here he places his devotees on the highest rung of the ladder of *yoga*. Devotion to Kṛṣṇa is the last word on *yoga*. He has indicated this throughout the first six chapters and at the end of chapters 2 through 6 he has indicated that it is *bhakti* that Arjuna is to attain if he is to be the person Kṛṣṇa wants him to be. The perfectly integrated person that Kṛṣṇa has been teaching Arjuna about is his devotee. He is dutiful and responsible in all his actions. His actions are informed by higher knowledge, and he has realized the fruit of this detached action in the form of inner wisdom. His action is integrated with knowledge, and thus he is renounced even while acting. He is absorbed in meditation on God, and his heart swells with love for God and love for all beings. He has realized the cessation of material suffering, and he knows God as Brahman, Paramātmā, and Bhagavān. Arjuna is spellbound at what it means to be Kṛṣṇa's devotee!

As the first six chapters describing the psychology of the ideal person come to a close, Kṛṣṇa turns next to theology and a discussion of different types of devotees.

CHAPTER SEVEN

ज्ञानविज्ञानयोगाः

Jñāna-Vijñāna-yoga

YOGA OF KNOWLEDGE AND REALIZATION

Text 1

श्रीभगवानुवाच
मय्यासक्तमनाः पार्थ योगं युञ्जन्मदाश्रयः ।
असंशयं समग्रं मां यथा ज्ञास्यसि तच्छृणु ॥१॥

śrī-bhagavān uvāca
mayy āsakta-manāḥ pārtha yogaṁ yuñjan mad-āśrayaḥ/
asaṁśayaṁ samagraṁ māṁ yathā jñāsyasi tac chṛṇu//

śrī-bhagavān uvāca—the Lord of Śrī said; *mayi*—to me; *āsakta-manāḥ*—mind attached; *pārtha*—O son of Pṛthā; *yogam*—*yoga*; *yuñjan*—practicing; *mat-āśrayaḥ*—taking refuge in me; *asaṁśayam*—without doubt; *samagram*—completely; *mām*—me; *yathā*—how; *jñāsyasi*—you will know; *tat*—that; *śṛṇu*—listen.

The Lord of Śrī said: Listen, O Pārtha, how with mind attached to me, practicing yoga and taking refuge in me, you can know me completely without doubt.

Having concluded the sixth chapter by emphasizing devotion to himself, Kṛṣṇa continues speaking about devotion as the seventh chapter opens. While knowledge of the self (*tvam*, you) is revealed in the first six chapters, knowledge of that with which the self is to be united in love (*tat*, his) is revealed in chapters 7 through 12. Thus the famous Upaniṣadic dictum *tat tvam asi*, "you are his," is explained.[1]

1. This phrase, usually rendered "you are that," can also be translated "you are his." In this rendering it indicates a union between self and God in love, wherein both self and God continue to exist individually, yet united in purpose.

When Kṛṣṇa told Arjuna to fix his mind on him, Arjuna naturally wondered how one does so. Sensing his mental question, Kṛṣṇa speaks without waiting for Arjuna to ask, enthused to be speaking directly about devotion, by which he can be known completely. In the previous six chapters, knowledge of the individual spiritual self's likeness to Brahman and the nature of the Brahman and Paramātmā feature of the Absolute have been described. Now in this chapter, Kṛṣṇa will discuss the Bhagavān feature of Godhead.

Bhagavān is the personal, lovable aspect of Godhead, replete with eternal form, abode, associates, and pastimes. Reality exists, is cognizant of itself, and has a purpose. As Brahman, Godhead exists. As Paramātmā, cognizance comes into play, and as Bhagavān, a cognizant existence plays. This play, the inner life of the Absolute, is the *līlā* of Bhagavān, which overflows into the world of our experience from time to time when Bhagavān enters this plane. Knowing this feature of Godhead amounts to knowing him completely *(samagram)*.

Knowledge of Bhagavān, which includes all of his *śaktis*, is required if one is to practice the devotional *yoga* Kṛṣṇa characterized as the best of all at the end of the previous chapter. His primary *śakti* was introduced in the fourth chapter (Bg. 4.6). His intermediate and secondary *śaktis* are introduced in this chapter.

Complete *(samagram)* knowing is the knowledge that is inherent in love. When one loves, one knows what to do. When one loves God, one knows everything one needs to know. This knowing is characterized further as freeing one from doubt *(asaṁśayam)*. Doubt is a function of the mind. When it is overridden, we are able to move freely. Intellect driven movement suggests surety, yet following its lead amounts to proceeding with caution. It is not the movement of the heart. Here Kṛṣṇa speaks of the homeland of the heart, and a life in which mind and intellect are subordinate to one's heart. In this land, one does not doubt the virtue of serving God, but questions how one can serve him best in any given circumstance.

How does one reach this plane? One begins by hearing, indicated here by the words *tat śṛṇu*. Kṛṣṇa says further, *yogaṁ yuñjan*, one attains comprehensive knowing in love through *yoga* practice. Devotional *yoga* has three developmental stages: devotion in practice *(sādhana-bhakti)*, devotion in ecstasy *(bhāva-bhakti)*, and devotion in love *(prema-bhakti)*.[2] Here Kṛṣṇa speaks of devotion in practice. He is speaking, however, of the final stage

2. See Brs. 1.2.1.

of *sādhana-bhakti*, invoking as he has the word *āsakti*, spiritual attachment. *Āsakti* is the stage of practice in which the practitioner's mind is attached to Kṛṣṇa, the object of devotion *(mayy āsakta-manāḥ)*. At this stage, due to intense attachment, one's spiritual identity is glimpsed as one enters devotion in ecstasy, taking refuge in Kṛṣṇa alone.

Kṛṣṇa next eulogizes the topics discussed in this chapter in order to stress their importance to Arjuna.

Text 2

ज्ञानं तेऽहं सविज्ञानमिदं वक्ष्याम्यशेषतः ।
यज्ज्ञात्वा नेह भूयोऽन्यज्ज्ञातव्यमवशिष्यते ॥२॥

jñānaṁ te 'haṁ sa-vijñānam idaṁ vakṣyāmy aśeṣataḥ/
yaj jñātvā neha bhūyo 'nyaj jñātavyam avaśiṣyate//

jñānam—knowledge; *te*—to you; *aham*—I; *sa*—with; *vijñānam*—realization; *idam*—this; *vakṣyāmi*—shall expound; *aśeṣataḥ*—in full; *yat*—which; *jñātvā*—understanding; *na*—not; *iha*—in this world; *bhūyaḥ*—further; *anyat*—anything; *jñātavyam*—to be known; *avaśiṣyate*—remains.

Without holding anything back, I shall expound on this knowledge and its realization, understanding which there remains nothing further to be known in this world.

Here *jñāna* refers to theoretical knowledge derived from scripture. *Vijñānam* is the practical wisdom that constitutes realization of the theory. Generally, the latter follows the former. Theoretical knowledge is required, and by applying this knowledge practically, one gains wisdom.

Regarding the sacred literature, it is said that nothing exists outside the mind of Vyāsa, its compiler. However, possessing theoretical knowledge alone does not make one's knowledge complete. It is the realization of this knowledge that leaves nothing further to be known.

The knowledge that Kṛṣṇa will explain is knowledge of himself, Bhagavān, and not knowledge of lesser manifestations of the Absolute. This is implied in his willingness to speak without reservation *(aśeṣataḥ)*. Knowledge relating to the nature of the self is more confidential than knowledge of how to prosper materially through religious adherence. More confidential still is knowledge relating to the personality of the Absolute. This knowledge also has two divisions, that of Bhagavān's opulence and that of his sweetness. Viśvanātha Cakravartī Ṭhākura comments that both of these are discussed in this chapter, and thus the words *jñāna* and *vijñānam* in this verse can also be understood to refer to these two aspects of Bhagavān.

Next Kṛṣṇa further glorifies this knowledge by addressing the rarity of its attainment.

Text 3

मनुष्याणां सहस्रेषु कश्चिद्यतति सिद्धये ।
यततामपि सिद्धानां कश्चिन्मां वेत्ति तत्त्वतः ॥३॥

manuṣyāṇāṁ sahasreṣu kaścid yatati siddhaye/
yatatām api siddhānāṁ kaścin māṁ vetti tattvataḥ//

manuṣyāṇām—of men; *sahasreṣu*—of thousands; *kaścit*—someone; *yatati*—strives; *siddhaye*—for perfection; *yatatām*—of those endeavoring; *api*—indeed; *siddhānām*—of those who have attained perfection; *kaścit*—someone; *mām*—me; *vetti*—knows; *tattvataḥ*—in truth.

Among many thousands of men, one may strive for perfection, and among those who attain perfection, only a very rare soul knows me in truth.

Although in one sense everyone pursues perfection on some level, very few people are interested in striving for spiritual perfection systematically in accordance with the sacred literature and advice of saints. One reason for lackluster enthusiasm among those who are aware of the path is the rarity of success.

In this verse, Kṛṣṇa makes a startling point: even among liberated souls *(siddhānām)* very few know him in truth. According to Śrīdhara Swāmī, the spirit of this verse is that "even among thousands of those who are perfect through knowledge of the self, only one perchance, through my grace, knows me in truth as the Supreme Self." Kṛṣṇa, Mukunda, the giver of liberation, stands above liberation, and if he should grace the liberated, their perfection knows perfection.

Knowing Kṛṣṇa as *paraṁ brahma* is a post-liberated realization. The example of Śukadeva Goswāmī from *Śrīmad-Bhāgavatam* serves to illustrate this important point. Although he was a liberated *siddha* who had realized Brahman, Śukadeva became attracted to Kṛṣṇa's form, qualities, and *līlā*. What then is the nature of Kṛṣṇa? This question was touched on in the fourth chapter during the tangential discussion of the *avatāra*. It will be more fully addressed in this chapter.

Having aroused Arjuna's interest, Kṛṣṇa next speaks about himself in the following verses in terms of his *śaktis* that make up the material world. First he speaks of his secondary power *(māyā-śakti)* and then his intermediate power *(jīva-śakti)*. He does so not with a view to explain these *śaktis* in any detail, but to define their ontological status. Further discussion of them will be taken up in chapter 13.

Text 4

भूमिरापोऽनलो वायुः खं मनो बुद्धिरेव च ।
अहङ्कार इतीयं मे भिन्ना प्रकृतिरष्टधा ॥४॥

bhūmir āpo 'nalo vāyuḥ khaṁ mano buddhir eva ca/
ahaṅkāra itīyaṁ me bhinnā prakṛtir aṣṭadhā//

bhūmiḥ—earth; *āpaḥ*—water; *analaḥ*—fire; *vāyuḥ*—air; *kham*—ether; *manaḥ*—mind; *buddhiḥ*—intellect; *eva*—certainly; *ca*—and; *ahaṅkāraḥ*—egoism; *iti*—thus; *iyam*—this; *me*—my; *bhinnā*—separated; *prakṛtiḥ*—nature; *aṣṭadhā*—eightfold.

Earth, water, fire, air, ether, mind, intellect, and egoism—this material nature of mine is so divided eightfold.

Here Kṛṣṇa describes in brief the makeup of matter. Matter constitutes one of his *śaktis*. In the next verse he will refer back to this *śakti*, describing it as his inferior nature or secondary power. Inside each of the elements mentioned are their subtle origins.

Earth, water, fire, air, and ether are the five gross elements known as *mahā-bhūtas*. Included within these five are sixteen transformations: the five knowledge-acquiring senses (nose, tongue, eyes, tactile sense, and ears), the five working senses (hands, legs, genitals, the organ of speech, and the organ of evacuation), the eleventh internal sense (the mind), and the five sense objects (manifestations of smell, taste, sight, touch, and sound).

Mind, intelligence, and egoism are the three subtle elements mentioned in this verse. If we count the mind among the senses, both working senses because the mind directs them and the senses of perception because they inform the mind, the word *manaḥ* (mind) in this verse appears unnecessary. The mind itself is included within the uncompounded elements *(mahā-bhūtas)* as the eleventh sense. However, here *manaḥ* can be understood to refer to *pradhāna*, the unmanifest stage of the three modes of material nature, on account of its being correlated with the word *prakṛti* in this verse. From *pradhāna*, the *mahat-tattva*, or great intellect, manifests. *Mahat-tattva* in turn gives rise to *ahaṅkāra*, or ego, the principle of material identification, which in turn is the subtle cause of the sense objects and mind/senses. After the sense objects manifest, the necessity for the senses to manifest arises.

Thus in the form of a *sūtra* Kṛṣṇa has described his secondary power that makes up material nature and its divisions. He has also indicated that the material nature itself is separated from himself *(bhinnā prakṛtiḥ)*. This is the explanation of Bhaktivedanta Swami Prabhupāda. Separated means that it acts as if independent of God once God sets it in motion, much like a tape recording acts independently of the person whose words it has recorded, while being wholly dependent on him at the same time.

The world as we experience it, however, is not merely matter. Thus Kṛṣṇa next describes his *jīva-śakti*, which is of the nature of consciousness.

Text 5

अपरेयमितस्त्वान्यां प्रकृतिं विद्धि मे पराम्।
जीवभूतां महाबाहो ययेदं धार्यते जगत् ॥५॥

apareyam itas tv anyāṁ prakṛtiṁ viddhi me parām/
jīva-bhūtāṁ mahā-bāho yayedaṁ dhāryate jagat//

aparā—inferior; *iyam*—this; *itaḥ*—here; *tu*—but; *anyām*—another; *prakṛtim*—energy; *viddhi*—know; *me*—my; *parām*—superior; *jīva-bhūtām*—consisting of souls; *mahā-bāho*—O mighty-armed one; *yayā*—by which; *idam*—this; *dhāryate*—is sustained; *jagat*—the material world.

However, other than this, O mighty-armed one, you should know that I have another, superior nature consisting of souls, by which this universe is sustained.

Material nature is inferior to consciousness. It is that which is experienced, as opposed to that which experiences. Matter is insentient, while consciousness is life itself.

The *jīva-śakti* consisting of individual souls is God's intermediate power. It is similar in nature to God and dissimilar to matter. It is at the same time dissimilar to God in that it is prone to being deluded by the influence of material nature. How can the *jīva-śakti* be deluded by material nature if it is superior to matter? Such is the power of illusion. Even while souls, units of consciousness, sustain the material world by their presence, due to their association with matter they think their existence is dependent on material conditions.

Kṛṣṇa has described his intermediate power here as *jīva-bhūta*. In using the singular, he refers to the entire class of individual souls. The source of both the individual souls and matter is Kṛṣṇa himself, as he affirms in the next verse.

Text 6

एतद्योनीनि भूतानि सर्वाणीत्युपधारय ।
अहं कृत्स्नस्य जगतः प्रभवः प्रलयस्तथा ॥६॥

etad-yonīni bhūtāni sarvāṇīty upadhāraya/
ahaṁ kṛtsnasya jagataḥ prabhavaḥ pralayas tathā//

etat—this; *yonīni*—sources; *bhūtāni*—beings; *sarvāṇi*—all; *iti*—thus; *upadhāraya*—understand; *aham*—I; *kṛtsnasya*—of the entire; *jagataḥ*—of the universe; *prabhavaḥ*—the origin; *pralayaḥ*—dissolution; *tathā*—also.

You should understand that all beings are born of these two powers and that I am the origin and destroyer of the entire universe.

All beings as we know them in this world are a product of Kṛṣṇa's two *śaktis*, secondary and intermediate. They are a combination of consciousness and matter, be they men, women, animals, or plants. Souls in touch with matter animate material nature and identify themselves with the particular gross shape and subtle mental condition that matter surrounds them with. Although unborn and eternal, souls take birth in terms of material life when in connection with matter.

Kṛṣṇa will describe his intermediate and secondary *śaktis* in greater detail in chapter 13. In this verse Kṛṣṇa mentions these *śaktis* in the course of stressing his point thus far: they are the world as we know it, they belong to him, and they are thus subordinate to him.

Text 7

मत्तः परतरं नान्यत् किञ्चिदस्ति धनञ्जय ।
मयि सर्वमिदं प्रोतं सूत्रे मणिगणा इव ॥७॥

mattaḥ parataraṁ nānyat kiñcid asti dhanañjaya/
mayi sarvam idaṁ protaṁ sūtre maṇi-gaṇā iva//

mattaḥ—than me; *para-taram*—superior; *na*—not; *anyat kiñcit*—anything else; *asti*—there is; *dhanañjaya*—O winner of wealth; *mayi*—in me; *sarvam*—all; *idam*—this; *protam*—strung; *sūtre*—on a thread; *maṇi-gaṇāḥ*—pearls; *iva*—like.

Nothing whatsoever is superior to me, O winner of wealth. Everything rests on me like pearls strung on a thread.

This is one of a number of statements in the *Gītā* in which Kṛṣṇa asserts his supreme position. According to Śaṅkara, Kṛṣṇa is a manifestation of what he terms *saguṇa* Brahman, Brahman with material qualities. He considers the so-called *saguṇa* manifestation of Brahman as Kṛṣṇa to be an inferior manifestation of the Absolute, which in its highest expression is formless and without qualities (*nirguṇa* Brahman). In his Vedānta commentary, Baladeva Vidyābhūṣaṇa asks sarcastically, "When Kṛṣṇa says, 'O Dhanañjaya! No one is higher than myself,' was Śrī Kṛṣṇa *saguṇa* or *nirguṇa*?"[3] If he was *saguṇa*, Kṛṣṇa must have been mistaken when he said that there is nothing superior to himself. If he was *nirguṇa*, we must understand *nirguṇa* to indicate that God, Kṛṣṇa, has no material qualities. His form is spiritual, and thus nothing like material forms which are ephemeral.

Kṛṣṇa has explained that he is the world and he is the cause of the world. He is the world inasmuch as the effect is present in the cause. Moreover, he has entered into this effect and is now standing before his friend Arjuna in order to explain this metaphysical reality. Thus Kṛṣṇa's example: he is the invisible thread that has entered the world and is its ultimate support, as a thread strings pearls together and supports them. He is invisible in that it is not apparent that he, as Arjuna's charioteer, is the support of all existence. Thus knowing this is required if we are to understand the worshippable nature of humanlike Kṛṣṇa. Who would have thought him to be so?

After a forced effort to explain this verse in support of Adwaita Vedānta, Madhusūdana Saraswatī admits the possibility of other interpretations. Without mentioning names, he appears to refer to Vaiṣṇava Vedānta. He comments that Kṛṣṇa's example of pearls on a thread refers to the fact that

3. See Baladeva's *Govinda Bhāṣya* 1.1.10. Baladeva renders *gatiḥ sāmānyāt*, "*Saguṇa* Brahman is not taught anywhere in the *Vedas*, which uniformly describe only *nirguṇa* Brahman."

the world rests on Kṛṣṇa, whereas it does not explain how he is also its material cause. He then suggests that a better example would have been "like gold earrings in relation to gold," as gold both supports and is the cause of gold earrings. However, this example illustrates the Advaita position of *vivarta-vāda*, in which the Absolute is the material cause by way of the Absolute's appearing to be transformed into the material world, just as a piece of gold becomes a gold earring. This is opposed to the Vaiṣṇava position of *pariṇāma-vāda*, in which the world is considered to be a transformation of God's *śakti*, rather than an apparent transformation of the Absolute itself. Although Madhusūdana Saraswatī's criticism of the limitation of Kṛṣṇa's example is valid, Kṛṣṇa has already described himself as the independent cause of the material world in the previous verse. He is not transformed in the course of its manifestation, which is the interaction of his intermediate and secondary *śaktis*.

In the next five verses, Kṛṣṇa gives examples of how he may be thought of as the essence of all things, their very support. This follows the reasoning of this verse, in which Kṛṣṇa has said that he, along with being the one who creates the world and destroys it, is its support as well.

Text 8

रसोऽहमप्सु कौन्तेय प्रभास्मि शशिसूर्ययोः ।
प्रणवः सर्ववेदेषु शब्दः खे पौरुषं नृषु ॥८॥

raso 'ham apsu kaunteya prabhāsmi śaśi-sūryayoḥ/
praṇavaḥ sarva-vedeṣu śabdaḥ khe pauruṣaṁ nṛṣu//

rasaḥ—taste; *aham*—I; *apsu*—in water; *kaunteya*—O son of Kuntī; *prabhā*—the shine; *asmi*—I am; *śaśi-sūryayoḥ*—of the moon and the sun; *praṇavaḥ*—the syllable *oṁ; sarva*—all; *vedeṣu*—in the *Vedas; śabdaḥ*—sound; *khe*—in the ether; *pauruṣam*—manhood; *nṛṣu*—in men.

O son of Kuntī, I am the taste in water, the shine in the moon and the sun, the sacred syllable (oṁ) in all the Vedas, the sound in ether, and humanity's drive to achieve.

As the *tanmātras* (sense objects) of taste and sound, Kṛṣṇa is present everywhere in water and ether. The radiance of the sun and moon are inseparable from them. Similarly, the sacred syllable *oṁ* pervades the *Vedas*, as all Vedic *mantras* are prefaced by *oṁ*. In this five-verse section Kṛṣṇa speaks of being one with all things while simultaneously being different from them as well. We can talk about humanity and we can talk about its drive to achieve, yet the two are at the same time inseparable. Viśvanātha Cakravartī comments, *pauruṣaṁ saphala udyama-viśeṣa eva manuṣya-sāra:* "*Pauruṣaṁ* is the drive to achieve that is the distinguishing feature of humanity." Baladeva Vidyābhūṣaṇa comments that this *pauruṣam* is that by which humanity has its existence, and this is why it represents Kṛṣṇa.

Text 9

पुण्यो गन्धः पृथिव्यां च तेजश्चास्मि विभावसौ ।
जीवनं सर्वभूतेषु तपश्चास्मि तपस्विषु ॥९॥

puṇyo gandhaḥ pṛthivyāṁ ca tejaś cāsmi vibhāvasau/
jīvanaṁ sarva-bhūteṣu tapaś cāsmi tapasviṣu//

puṇyaḥ—original; *gandhaḥ*—fragrance; *pṛthivyām*—in the earth; *ca*—also; *tejaḥ*—light; *ca*—also; *asmi*—I am; *vibhāvasau*—in the fire; *jīvanam*—life; *sarva*—all; *bhūteṣu*—in the living being; *tapaḥ*—austerity; *ca*—also; *asmi*—I am; *tapasviṣu*—in the ascetics.

I am the original fragrance in earth, the light in fire, the life in all living beings, and the austerity of ascetics.

Kṛṣṇa describes fragrance as *puṇyaḥ* (original, pure). By this, he refers to the fragrance of the earth in its pristine state, before it is polluted by the misdeeds of humans. Viśvanātha Cakravartī comments that here *ca* (and) following *pṛthivyām* refers to the *tanmātras* mentioned in the previous verse.

Kṛṣṇa is the light in fire. The use of *ca* (also) following this description indicates heat as well as light, as warmth is associated with light. *Ca* can also be construed to imply the cooling effect of air that comforts those afflicted by excessive heat.

Kṛṣṇa is the life of all living beings, whose life is service to something, be it a manifestation of Kṛṣṇa's lower nature for the materialist or himself for the enlightened. That which sustains the ascetic, his austerity, is Kṛṣṇa as well.

Text 10

बीजं मां सर्वभूतानां विद्धि पार्थ सनातनम् ।
बुद्धिर्बुद्धिमतामस्मि तेजस्तेजस्विनामहम् ॥१०॥

bījaṁ māṁ sarva-bhūtānāṁ viddhi pārtha sanātanam/
buddhir buddhimatām asmi tejas tejasvinām aham//

bījam—the seed; *mām*—me; *sarva-bhūtānām*—of all beings; *viddhi*—know; *pārtha*—O son of Pṛthā; *sanātanam*—primeval; *buddhiḥ*—intelligence; *buddhi-matām*—of the intelligent; *asmi*—I am; *tejaḥ*—prowess; *tejasvinām*—of the powerful; *aham*—I am.

O Pārtha, know me to be the primeval seed of all beings, the wisdom of the wise, and the splendor of the splendid.

Text 11

बलं बलवतां चाहं कामरागविवर्जितम् ।
धर्माविरुद्धो भूतेषु कामोऽस्मि भरतर्षभ ॥११॥

balaṁ balavatāṁ cāhaṁ kāma-rāga-vivarjitam/
dharmāviruddho bhūteṣu kāmo 'smi bharatarṣabha//

balam—strength; *bala-vatām*—of the strong; *ca*—and; *aham*—I am; *kāma*—desire; *rāga*—attachment; *vivarjitam*—devoid; *dharma-aviruddhaḥ*—not against religious principles; *bhūteṣu*—in beings; *kāmaḥ*—love; *asmi*—I am; *bharata-ṛṣabha*—O best of the Bhāratas.

Of the strong I am strength devoid of desire and attachment, and I am love that is righteous, O best of the Bhāratas.

The strength mentioned here is of the nature of purity *(sattva)*. *Kāma* (desire) represents the material influence of passion *(rajas)*, and *rāga* (attachment) indicates the material influence of ignorance *(tamas)*. Passion is active, whereas attachment is passive, being synonymous with the thirst for more of an object already attained.

In the least, Kṛṣṇa refers here to the strength necessary to maintain one's body and mind for the sake of performing one's religious duty. It is strength devoid of desire and attachment born of the lower influence of material nature, in which there is no scope for spiritual advancement. In the optimum, Kṛṣṇa speaks of the strength of those who have turned their back on the illusion of material life.

Kṛṣṇa also identifies himself with love that is in accordance with scriptural law. While love by nature is lawless, Kṛṣṇa advocates the taming of material love. The effect of this is the awakening of the soul and its prospect for love on the spiritual plane, real love arising out of self-sacrifice. Although love is lawless, in material life its unbridled pursuit amounts to ignoring obvious laws of nature, which in the least render such love unenduring. Scripture points this out and advocates that material love be redirected in order that it be fulfilled. When love is fully spiritualized, it transcends scripture.

Concluding this brief elaboration on his presence in all things as their essence, Kṛṣṇa next tells Arjuna that this description is endless. Rather than go into further detail, he states in summary that the entire material existence is a product of the threefold influence of material nature *(triguṇa)*, which emanates from him. He is the primal cause and the essence of the effect. The world as an effect is in him, but he is aloof from it.

Text 12

ये चैव सात्त्विका भावा राजसास्तामसाश्च ये ।
मत्त एवेति तान् विद्धि न त्वहं तेषु ते मयि ॥१२॥

ye caiva sāttvikā bhāvā rājasās tāmasāś ca ye/
matta eveti tān viddhi na tv ahaṁ teṣu te mayi//

ye—which; *ca*—and; *eva*—certainly; *sāttvikāḥ*—derived from the *sattva-guṇa*; *bhāvāḥ*—states of being; *rājasāḥ*—in the mode of passion; *tāmasāḥ*—in the mode of ignorance; *ca*—also; *ye*—which; *mattaḥ*—from me; *eva*—certainly; *iti*—thus; *tān*—those; *viddhi*—know; *na*—not; *tu*—but; *aham*—I; *teṣu*—in them; *te*—they; *mayi*—in me.

And, indeed, know that all things constituted of the guṇas of purity, passion, and ignorance issue from me alone. At the same time, I am not in them—they are in me!

If what Kṛṣṇa has said about his being the cause of the entire world and its very essence is true, Arjuna wonders, "Why don't people know about it? Why don't they serve you?" Kṛṣṇa responds to this doubt in the next verse.

Text 13

त्रिभिर्गुणमयैर्भावैरेभिः सर्वमिदं जगत् ।
मोहितं नाभिजानाति मामेभ्यः परमव्ययम् ॥१३॥

tribhir guṇa-mayair bhāvair ebhiḥ sarvam idaṁ jagat/
mohitaṁ nābhijānāti mām ebhyaḥ param avyayam//

tribhiḥ—by the three; *guṇa-mayaiḥ bhāvaiḥ*—by the states of being consisting of the *guṇas*; *ebhiḥ*—by these; *sarvam*—whole; *idam*—this; *jagat*—universe; *mohitam*—deluded; *na abhijānāti*—does not recognize; *mām*—me; *ebhyaḥ*—than these; *param*—transcendental; *avyayam*—inexhaustible.

Being deluded by the three guṇas, the entire universe does not recognize me, who am transcendental to the guṇas and inexhaustible.

In answering Arjuna's doubt, Kṛṣṇa explains that under the influence of the three *guṇas (tribhir guṇa-mayaiḥ)*, beings mistake the transformations of material nature to be enduring and worthy of pursuit. Thus they cannot recognize him, who is enduring *(avyayam)* and not a product of these transformations. Simply put, Kṛṣṇa says souls are bewildered *(mohitam)* and the cause is the *guṇas* of his *māyā*.

At this point, Arjuna wonders how this bewilderment can be overcome. Souls lost to their own higher nature look for this nature in a place where it will never be found. Viśvanātha Cakravartī Ṭhākura comments that in response, Kṛṣṇa points to his chest and emphatically declares that surrender to himself in his form of Śyāmasundara (Vraja Kṛṣṇa) is the solution, and there is no other remedy.

Text 14

दैवी ह्येषा गुणमयी मम माया दुरत्यया ।
मामेव ये प्रपद्यन्ते मायामेतां तरन्ति ते ॥१४॥

daivī hy eṣā guṇa-mayī mama māyā duratyayā/
mām eva ye prapadyante māyām etāṁ taranti te//

daivī—divine; *hi*—certainly; *eṣā*—this; *guṇa-mayī*—consisting of the *guṇas*; *mama*—my; *māyā*—energy; *duratyayā*—very difficult to overcome; *mām*—unto me; *eva*—certainly; *ye*—those who; *prapadyante*—surrender; *māyām etām*—this energy; *taranti*—transcend; *te*—they.

This divine energy of mine consisting of the guṇas is certainly difficult to go beyond. Those who take refuge in me alone transcend this illusion.

Kṛṣṇa here describes the illusion cast by his material nature as divine *(daivī)* because he is its master *(mama māyā)*. The illusion consisting of the three *guṇas*, or ropes *(guṇa-mayī)*, is impenetrable. As one bound not by one rope but by three ropes intertwined is indeed bound tightly, so are the souls of this world bound by Kṛṣṇa's divine illusion. While the world itself is real, its effect on the *jīvas* is such that they misread reality.

Struggling with material nature is futile. Surrender to Kṛṣṇa, its master, on the other hand, allows one to easily cross over *māyā*. Through the words *mām eva*, Kṛṣṇa stresses himself, as opposed to other manifestations of God, be they governing agents of the material manifestation or expansions or incarnations of himself. The word *eva* also implies the certainty and expediency of deliverance by surrender to Kṛṣṇa, as opposed to surrender to any of Kṛṣṇa's *avatāras*. Although *avatāras* of Kṛṣṇa can deliver one from illusion, surrender to Kṛṣṇa in particular makes this deliverance comparatively easy. Taken in this sense, Kṛṣṇa refers here to the path of Vraja *bhakti*, in which hearing and chanting about his charming *līlās* is the primary means of surrender. As the propensity to love is inherent in all souls, and Kṛṣṇa means the all-attractive, irresistible manifestation of the Absolute, surrender to him is easy and natural.

Madhusūdana Saraswatī admits that *prapadyante* implies, "those who by taking shelter of me alone pass their days thinking constantly of only me, who am the essence of infinite beauty in its entirety, who am possessed of the luster of two lotus-like feet that surpass the beauty of a newly born, blooming lotus, who am ever engaged in playing on a flute, whose mind is absorbed in Vṛndāvana (Vraja) sport, who playfully holds aloft the hill called Govardhana, who am a cowherd, destroyer of evil ones such as Śiśupāla, Kāṁsa, and others, whose feet defeat the beauty of rain clouds, who possesses a form made of supreme bliss through and through, who transcends the phenomenal creation of Brahmā—they on account of having their minds immersed in love for me, which is a great ocean of joy, are not overwhelmed by the *guṇas* of *māyā*."

Madhusūdana Saraswatī goes on to say that *māyā* herself, as though out of fear that she could be entirely uprooted by such devotion to Kṛṣṇa, her ultimate source, withdraws from those who surrender to Kṛṣṇa, in the same way that a prostitute withdraws from those in the renounced order who are prone to outbursts of anger and thus sometimes cast curses on ladies of ill repute.

Understandably, Arjuna continues to wonder why some people don't surrender to Kṛṣṇa. In the next verse, Kṛṣṇa informs him that those who are impious *(duṣkṛtīs)* do not surrender to him.

Text 15

न मां दुष्कृतिनो मूढाः प्रपद्यन्ते नराधमाः ।
माययापहृतज्ञाना आसुरं भावमाश्रिताः ॥१५॥

na māṁ duṣkṛtino mūḍhāḥ prapadyante narādhamāḥ/
māyayāpahṛta-jñānā āsuraṁ bhāvam āśritāḥ//

na—not; *mām*—to me; *duṣkṛtinaḥ*—the impious; *mūḍhāḥ*—foolish; *prapadyante*—surrender; *nara-adhamāḥ*—lowest of men; *māyayā*—by illusion; *apahṛta*—stolen; *jñānāḥ*—those whose knowledge; *āsuram*—demoniac; *bhāvam*—existence; *āśritāḥ*—surrendered.

Those who are grossly foolish, the lowest of men, the so-called learned who are bereft of wisdom owing to the influence of illusion, and those whose very existence is demoniac do not surrender to me.

In this verse, Kṛṣṇa describes four types of persons whose *karma* is such that they do not rise to the point of surrendering to him. The first and best of this unfortunate lot suffers from a failure of understanding. They cannot grasp the basic difference between that which is spiritual and that which is material even in terms of theoretical knowledge. They are the best of the four types mentioned in this verse because their lack of surrender is based on ignorance.

The second type suffers from a failure of spiritual inclination. While they have a general understanding of the nature of reality, they are not inclined to take the steps to perfect their understanding. They are labeled *narādhama* (low-life) for their lack of interest in that which is not only entirely in their interest but available to them as well. Persons of good birth and spiritual background who do not take advantage of spiritual opportunity when it knocks are examples of the *narādhama*.

The third group suffers from a failure of reason. Their understanding of God is undermined by innumerable theories both spiritual and mundane, which together render the Absolute relative in the mind of this unfortunate group. Their wisdom is stolen by the illusion of the power and potential of logic to arrive at conclusive truth *(māyayāpahṛta-jñānā)*. While the second group lacks the intellectual prowess to understand, this third group suffers from its excess.

The fourth and worst of these *duṣkṛtīs* suffer from a failure of heart. They are those in whose hearts hatred for God *(āsuraṁ bhāvam)* is generated despite being established in theoretical understanding of the nature of God-centered reality. Jīva Goswāmī says in *Bhakti-sandarbha* (115) that this verse describes that which is to be avoided in the culture of the mystery of *bhakti*. Such avoidance constitutes the indirect *(vyatireka)* culture of devotion (ŚB. 2.9.36). Madhusūdana Saraswatī sees this verse as describing the impious in general and not four types of impious persons. Vaiṣṇava *ācāryas* all understand the verse to be referring to four types, while differing slightly in their description of them.[4]

Kṛṣṇa next describes four types of pious souls who do turn to him.

Text 16

चतुर्विधा भजन्ते मां जनाः सुकृतिनोऽर्जुन ।
आर्तो जिज्ञासुरर्थार्थी ज्ञानी च भरतर्षभ ॥१६॥

catur-vidhā bhajante māṁ janāḥ sukṛtino 'rjuna/
ārto jijñāsur arthārthī jñānī ca bharatarṣabha//

catuḥ-vidhāḥ—four kinds; *bhajante*—worship; *mām*—me; *janāḥ*—persons; *sukṛtinaḥ*—the pious; *arjuna*—O Arjuna; *ārtaḥ*—the distressed; *jijñāsuḥ*—the inquisitive; *artha-arthī*—one who desires wealth; *jñānī*—the knowledgeable; *ca*—also; *bharata-ṛṣabha*—O best of the Bhāratas.

Among the pious, Arjuna, four kinds of men worship me: the distressed, the seekers of wealth, the inquisitive, and the knowledgeable, O best of the Bhāratas.

In this and the next three verses, Kṛṣṇa speaks about *miśra-bhakti*, or devotion mixed with either material desire *(karma-miśra)* or desire for knowledge/liberation *(jñāna-miśra)*. Three persons mentioned in this verse, the distressed *(ārta)*, those desiring wealth *(arthārthī)*, and the inquisitive *(jiñāsu)*, are examples of *karma-miśra-bhakti*. The person in knowledge who

4. My explanation follows the lead of Rāmānuja, whose commentary on this verse lends itself well to a contemporary explanation.

takes to *bhakti* is an example of *jñāna-miśra-bhakti*. This is the opinion of Baladeva Vidyābhūṣaṇa, while Kṛṣṇadāsa Kavirāja Goswāmī differs slightly, dividing the four types into two categories. He considers the distressed and those desiring wealth to be involved in *karma-miśra-bhakti* and the inquisitive and those in knowledge to be involved in *jñāna-miśra-bhakti*.[5] Both of these *ācāryas* concur that such persons gradually give up material desires and become unalloyed devotees engaged in *śuddha-bhakti*—pure, unmixed devotion—after having received the grace of Kṛṣṇa or his devotees.

The word *sukṛti* in this verse is significant. There are three types of piety, or *sukṛti:* piety in relation to *karma*, piety in relation to *jñāna*, and piety in relation to pure devotion *(bhakty-unmukhī-sukṛti)*. Those whose *sukṛti* has developed in connection with *bhakti* will develop faith *(śraddhā)* in *bhakti* and take directly to devotional life. However, in this verse Kṛṣṇa is describing pious souls in general who follow the socioreligious life ordained in the scriptural canon *(varṇāśrama-dharma)*. They surrender to Kṛṣṇa in their hour of necessity.[6] In association with devotees they eventually become purified and take directly to *bhakti*.

The lowest of the four pious souls mentioned here are those who approach Kṛṣṇa for wealth *(arthārthī)*. Indeed, this seems almost diametrically opposed to the thrust of the *Gītā*. Some commentators, including Rāmānuja, have dismissed this rendering of *arthārthī* because of this, offering as an alternative, "One who desires the highest necessity *(artha)*." However, the *Śrīmad-Bhāgavatam* (2.3.10) agrees with the notion that one desirous of wealth should approach Kṛṣṇa on the *bhakti-mārga*. The example of Dhruva Mahārāja is found in the *Bhāgavatam*,[7] and Gauḍīya Vaiṣṇava commentators, as well as Madhusūdana Saraswatī, have cited Dhruva as an example of one who, desirous of material gain, approached Kṛṣṇa (Viṣṇu).[8] One has to begin somewhere.

In his commentary on this verse, Viśvanātha Cakravartī Ṭhākura explains that those on a path in which *bhakti* does not predominate attain their respective goals of knowledge and liberation as outlined in the first six chapters of the *Gītā*. Those on a path in which *bhakti* comes to predominate are discussed in this verse. They will ultimately attain pure devotion.

5. See Cc. Madhya 24.95.

6. See Brs. 1.2.14–21.

7. For a description of Dhruva see ŚB. 4.8–12.

8. Examples of the other three are Gajendra (the distressed), Śaunaka Ṛṣi (the inquisitive seeker/philosopher), and the four Kumāras (those in knowledge).

According to Baladeva Vidyābhūṣaṇa, those desiring wealth and those in distress *(arthārthī, ārtaḥ)* will eventually become inquisitive *(jijñāsuḥ)*, and the inquisitive will eventually become knowledgeable *(jñānī)*. This is the natural progression, in which devotion waxes and desire wanes as knowledge develops. Thus the best of this group is the person in knowledge of the soul, as Kṛṣṇa affirms in the following verse.

Text 17

तेषां ज्ञानी नित्ययुक्त एकभक्तिर्विशिष्यते ।
प्रियो हि ज्ञानिनोऽत्यर्थमहं स च मम प्रियः ॥१७॥

teṣāṁ jñānī nitya-yukta eka-bhaktir viśiṣyate/
priyo hi jñānino 'tyartham ahaṁ sa ca mama priyaḥ//

teṣām—of them; *jñānī*—the man in knowledge; *nitya-yuktaḥ*—always united; *eka*—one; *bhaktiḥ*—devotion; *viśiṣyate*—is distinguished; *priyaḥ*—fond; *hi*—certainly; *jñāninaḥ*—to the person in knowledge; *atyartham*—very; *aham*—I; *saḥ*—he; *ca*—also; *mama*—to me; *priyaḥ*—dear.

Of these, the man in knowledge, who is ever united and one with me in devotion, is best. Indeed, I am very affectionate to a person in knowledge, and he is fond of me.

The word *eka-bhakti* implies a dynamic oneness with Kṛṣṇa in devotion. In conjunction with *nitya-yukta*, it is a reference to devotion that is eternal in nature. Those who are in knowledge and are devoted to Kṛṣṇa, but whose devotion is a means to a nondevotional monistic end, are not the subject of this verse. This is obvious from the fact that the self-realized soul is described as one with Kṛṣṇa in devotion and not engaged in devotion as a means to self-realization. The wise person in this verse has already attained self-realization, which distinguishes him from the seeker. He is a *jīvanmukta*, one who is liberated while in this world.

Jīvanmuktas are of two types, those in the *jñāna-mārga* and those in the *bhakti-mārga*. Those on the path of knowledge attain the *jīvanmukta* status and await the expiration of their manifest *karma* to enter ultimate reality in unembodied liberation *(videha-mukti)*. *Jīvanmuktas* on the path of devotion, on the other hand, are free from all manifest *karma*, their bodies having been taken over by Kṛṣṇa's primary *śakti* in order that they may do his bidding in this world. He in this verse who is very dear to Kṛṣṇa is a *jīvanmukta* from the path of knowledge who takes to *bhakti*. This person reminds us of the progression described in the first six chapters, where through *karma-yoga* the inner wisdom of *jñāna* develops and one is thus eligible to enter *bhakti* proper.

In the next verse Kṛṣṇa explains further just how dear to him the *jñānī-bhakta* is, while assuring Arjuna that the other three types of souls who worship him are also dear. All are dear because all eventually become unalloyed devotees.

Text 18

उदाराः सर्व एवैते ज्ञानी त्वात्मैव मे मतम् ।
आस्थितः स हि युक्तात्मा मामेवानुत्तमां गतिम् ॥१८॥

udārāḥ sarva evaite jñānī tv ātmaiva me matam/
āsthitaḥ sa hi yuktātmā mām evānuttamāṁ gatim//

udārāḥ—exalted; *sarve*—all; *eva*—certainly; *ete*—these; *jñānī*—the *jñānī*; *tu*—however; *ātmā eva*—just like myself; *me*—my; *matam*—opinion; *āsthitaḥ*—situated; *saḥ*—he; *hi*—certainly; *yukta-ātmā*—with fixed mind; *mām*—in me; *eva*—certainly; *anuttamām*—the highest; *gatim*—goal.

All of these are no doubt exalted. However, the self-realized soul I regard as my very self. Indeed, his mind fixed on me, he abides in me, the ultimate goal.

Rāmānuja says that the word *udārāḥ* indicates generosity. Kṛṣṇa says that the exalted character of those who worship him for any of the above reasons is such that they become recipients of his grace, and thus these seekers are themselves benefactors, for the spiritual need of the Absolute is to affectionately bestow grace. This need is so great that opportunities provided by the devoted for God to express his grace are hailed as generosity.

If Kṛṣṇa is so moved by the slightest devotion even when it is tinged with desire for something other than devotion itself, it is understandable how much more moved he would be by those whose devotion is free from any material concern. Here Kṛṣṇa glorifies such devotees by saying that they are one with him. There are also devotees who Kṛṣṇa considers greater than himself, such as the *gopīs*, whose motivation for serving him is a love so strong that it suppresses knowledge of his opulence.[9]

9. See ŚB. 10.29.42.

When the self-realized *jñānī* becomes a *bhakta*, Kṛṣṇa accepts him as his own self. Although metaphysically speaking Kṛṣṇa is the soul of all souls, here Kṛṣṇa speaks the truth of love, in which his devotee is seen as his soul. The spirit of the identity that Kṛṣṇa expresses here is that of one who says about someone dear, "He and I are one." Nārāyaṇa said these very words to the Kumāras when they knocked on the door of Vaikuṇṭha (ŚB. 3.16.4). At that time, when the gatekeepers refused to allow the Kumāras entrance to his abode, Nārāyaṇa took responsibility for the gatekeepers' actions as if they were his own. Understanding the implication of Nārāyaṇa's speech, in which he indicated that his devotees are one with him, the Kumāras themselves became devotees, concluding that self-realization is merely a stepping stone to God-realization.

Echoing the third verse of this chapter, Kṛṣṇa next describes how rare it is for a soul to attain self-knowledge and from there to become his devotee. He also explains the vision attained by such a devotee.

Text 19

बहूनां जन्मनामन्ते ज्ञानवान् मां प्रपद्यते ।
वासुदेवः सर्वमिति स महात्मा सुदुर्लभः ॥१९॥

bahūnāṁ janmanām ante jñānavān māṁ prapadyate/
vāsudevaḥ sarvam iti sa mahātmā su-durlabhaḥ//

bahūnām—of many; *janmanām*—of births; *ante*—at the end; *jñāna-vān*—one who is in knowledge; *mām*—to me; *prapadyate*—surrenders; *vāsudevaḥ*—Vāsudeva, Kṛṣṇa; *sarvam*—everything; *iti*—thus; *saḥ*—that; *mahā-ātmā*—great soul; *su-durlabhaḥ*—very rare.

After many births, the person possessing self-knowledge surrenders to me upon realizing that Vāsudeva is everything. Such a great soul is very rare.

Kṛṣṇa uses the word *mahātmā* for the first time in this verse. He will use it once again in the eighth chapter and again in the ninth.[10] Although he describes many types of transcendentalists and religious persons in the *Gītā*, he reserves this term for his unalloyed devotees. The spirit of this verse is that it takes many lives to arrive at self-realization, which is a prerequisite for realizing that everything is Kṛṣṇa and his energy, including oneself.

10. See Bg. 8.15 and 9.13.

As Kṛṣṇa concludes this section, Arjuna wonders what becomes of those who lack knowledge and thus have material desires, but petition other gods instead of taking refuge in Kṛṣṇa like those mentioned in verse 16. Kṛṣṇa answers Arjuna's thoughts in four verses. By providing contrast, he further defines *bhakti*.

Text 20

कामैस्तैस्तैर्हृतज्ञानाः प्रपद्यन्तेऽन्य देवताः ।
तं तं नियममास्थाय प्रकृत्या नियताः स्वया ॥२०॥

kāmais tais tair hṛta-jñānāḥ prapadyante 'nya-devatāḥ/
taṁ taṁ niyamam āsthāya prakṛtyā niyatāḥ svayā//

kāmaiḥ—by desires; *taiḥ taiḥ*—by various; *hṛta*—stolen; *jñānāḥ*—those whose knowledge; *prapadyante*—surrender; *anya*—other; *devatāḥ*—gods; *tam tam*—this or that; *niyamam*—rituals; *āsthāya*—following; *prakṛtyā*—by nature; *niyatāḥ*—controlled; *svayā*—by their own.

Those whose intelligence has been stolen by various desires take refuge in other gods. Impelled by their own natures, they engage in various religious rituals.

Those who have no background of piety in relation to *bhakti* worship various deities to attain their material goals. At best, they can attain these goals, but they will not awaken knowledge and devotion.

In this section, Kṛṣṇa dismisses the notion that worship of any god or goddess results in liberation. The word *anya-devatāḥ* means "other gods." Gods other than himself are those invested with his power for the express purpose of conducting affairs in the material world. These gods of limited jurisdiction are innumerable.

Lest one fault Kṛṣṇa for sectarian propaganda in our pluralistic times, it is important to point out just what "Kṛṣṇa" means. This is precisely what Kṛṣṇa is doing in this chapter. He is telling Arjuna that he, Kṛṣṇa, is the all-attractive person by virtue of his being everything and beyond everything at the same time. Kṛṣṇa is not a sectarian God. He is the heart of divinity itself. The affairs of the other gods are all within the world consisting of his two energies. Their power to function as gods is relative to their empowerment by Kṛṣṇa.

Text 21

यो यो यां यां तनुं भक्तः श्रद्धयार्चितुमिच्छति ।
तस्य तस्याचलां श्रद्धां तामेव विदधाम्यहम् ॥२१॥

yo yo yāṁ yāṁ tanuṁ bhaktaḥ śraddhayārcitum icchati/
tasya tasyācalāṁ śraddhāṁ tām eva vidadhāmy aham//

yaḥ yaḥ—whoever; *yām yām*—whichever; *tanum*—form; *bhaktaḥ*—devotee; *śraddhayā*—with faith; *arcitum*—to worship; *icchati*—desires; *tasya tasya*—of him; *acalām*—steady; *śraddhām*—faith; *tām*—that; *eva*—surely; *vidadhāmi*—give; *aham*—I.

Whoever desires to faithfully worship a particular form, whichever one it is, I grant him the necessary conviction to do so.

Text 22

स तया श्रद्धया युक्तस्तस्याराधनमीहते ।
लभते च ततः कामान् मयैव विहितान् हि तान् ॥२२॥

sa tayā śraddhayā yuktas tasyārādhanam īhate/
labhate ca tataḥ kāmān mayaiva vihitān hi tān//

saḥ—he; *tayā*—by that; *śraddhayā*—by faith; *yuktaḥ*—endowed; *tasya*—of him; *ārādhanam*—worship; *īhate*—he desires; *labhate*—attains; *ca*—and; *tataḥ*—from that; *kāmān*—desires; *mayā*—by me; *eva*—alone; *vihitān*—decreed; *hi*—certainly; *tān*—those.

A person endowed with this faith desires to worship that form, and surely he attains the fulfillment of his desires only because of me.

Although those who worship other gods are indirectly worshipping Kṛṣṇa, those mentioned here are unaware of this fact. Were they aware of what Kṛṣṇa is saying here, they could worship these gods without receiving the undesirable results mentioned in the next verse or the sharp criticism of Kṛṣṇa.

Text 23

अन्तवत्तु फलं तेषां तद्भवत्यल्पमेधसाम् ।
देवान् देवयजो यान्ति मद्भक्ता यान्ति मामपि ॥२३॥

antavat tu phalaṁ teṣāṁ tad bhavaty alpa-medhasām/
devān deva-yajo yānti mad-bhaktā yānti mām api//

anta-vat—perishable; *tu*—however; *phalam*—fruit; *teṣām*—of them; *tat*—that; *bhavati*—becomes; *alpa-medhasām*—of those of meager intellect; *devān*—to the gods; *deva-yajaḥ*—the worshippers of the gods; *yānti*—go; *mat*—my; *bhaktāḥ*—devotees; *yānti*—go; *mām*—to me; *api*—indeed.

However, the results of these persons of meager intellect are perishable. Those who worship the gods attain the gods, but my devotees attain me.

Although the *Gītā* establishes Kṛṣṇa's supremacy and extols the worship of Kṛṣṇa over all other types of worship, it remains a work of religious tolerance, acknowledging other gods and their worship as other forms of religious expression.

If anyone worships Kṛṣṇa in pursuit of material goals, he not only attains them but eventually develops the knowledge and devotion that lead to eternal life. On the other hand, by worshipping other gods, one attains only one's material objectives. Thus the difference between worshipping Kṛṣṇa directly and worshipping other gods without understanding that the gods themselves are dependent on Kṛṣṇa is one of attainment. While both groups of worshippers attain their immediate desired objectives, after doing so, their ultimate destination is relative to the object of their worship. Those who worship Kṛṣṇa attain eternal life, whereas those who worship other gods attain only perishable results. One obvious reason for this is that the gods themselves are perishable.

Although the preceding paragraph represents the instruction of the *Gītā*, we are left to wonder how it is that devotees of Kṛṣṇa often do not seem to attain their material objectives. History reveals that superstition has been replaced with religion, and religion with science in pursuit of actually attaining material objectives. In response the *Gītā*'s adherents will say that in such cases the material objectives sought after are either not obtained until one's next life or they are withheld by Kṛṣṇa in order to awaken detachment in his devotees and thus bring them nearer to him.

While Kṛṣṇa considers those who worship other gods to be less intelligent, he next speaks of the unintelligent.

Text 24

अव्यक्तं व्यक्तिमापन्नं मन्यन्ते मामबुद्धयः ।
परं भावमजानन्तो ममाव्ययमनुत्तमम् ॥२४॥

avyaktaṁ vyaktim āpannaṁ manyante mām abuddhayaḥ/
paraṁ bhāvam ajānanto mamāvyayam anuttamam//

avyaktam—unmanifest; *vyaktim*—manifestation; *āpannam*—achieved; *manyante*—think; *mām*—me; *abuddhayaḥ*—the unintelligent; *param*—supreme; *bhāvam*—existence; *ajānantaḥ*—unaware; *mama*—my; *avyayam*—eternal; *anuttamam*—unsurpassable.

The unintelligent, being unaware of my supreme nature, which is eternal and unsurpassable, think me to be the unmanifest that has become embodied!

With a tone of indignation, Kṛṣṇa decries those who think him to be different from his form and his form thereby to be material. Even if they think that his form is constituted of the material quality of purity *(sattva)*, which has an elevating effect on the soul, they are not free from his wrath.

To Vaiṣṇava commentators this verse speaks of Monists, who consider Brahman to be the undifferentiated Absolute that enters the world in a material form with the purpose of serving as a focal point of meditation for *sādhakas*. According to Monists, Kṛṣṇa's form, however special and extraordinary a manifestation it is considered, is nonetheless not transcendental or eternal—it is Brahman with material adjuncts. This theory is untenable for Vaiṣṇavas, and it does not get much support from this verse.

Kṛṣṇa's form and humanlike activities lead the uninformed, who are equally lacking *bhakti*, to believe that either Kṛṣṇa is not worshippable at all or that such worship is a means to an end in which the form of Kṛṣṇa is transcended. To the ignorant latter, who think themselves too intelligent to believe that the form of Kṛṣṇa could be anything but a limitation on the Absolute, worship of Kṛṣṇa is considered ultimately unnecessary. The foolish former group, misunderstanding his humanlike activities, turn to other gods for their needs or do not worship at all.

Kṛṣṇa is known only to those he chooses to reveal himself to. Those lacking in devotion are not privileged to know him in full. This is the thrust of the chapter. Accordingly, Kṛṣṇa next speaks of how the ignorant mentioned in this verse and the foolish in the preceding verses are kept from understanding him.

Text 25

नाहं प्रकाशः सर्वस्य योगमायासमावृतः ।
मूढोऽयं नाभिजानाति लोको मामजमव्ययम् ॥२५॥

nāhaṁ prakāśaḥ sarvasya yoga-māyā-samāvṛtaḥ/
mūḍho 'yaṁ nābhijānāti loko mām ajam avyayam//

na—not; *aham*—I; *prakāśaḥ*—manifest; *sarvasya*—of everyone; *yoga-māyā-samāvṛtaḥ*—hidden in yogic illusion; *mūḍhaḥ*—confused; *ayam*—this; *na*—not; *abhijānāti*—recognize; *lokaḥ*—world; *mām*—me; *ajam*—birthless; *avyayam*—eternal.

I am not revealed to everyone, being hidden by the power of māyā, and thus the world does not recognize me, the birthless and infallible one.

The juxtaposition of the words *yoga* and *māyā* is curious. *Yoga* overlaps with *māyā* in several meanings—magic, trick, power—and in general strengthens the meaning of the word *māyā*. In the devotional literature *yoga-māyā* often refers to Kṛṣṇa's internal primary *śakti*. However, we cannot really talk about Kṛṣṇa's internal potency here without first discussing his external potency. In this verse *yoga-māyā* refers to the magical power of Kṛṣṇa's *māyā-śakti* that deludes those who are not his devotees.

When we speak of *yoga-māyā* with regard to Kṛṣṇa's primary *śakti*, this influence creates an enlightened illusion within divinity. Such is the nature of the illusion by which Kṛṣṇa's devotees are enabled to relate with him not as God, but as friend, lover, and so on. It is under the influence of this mystic illusion that Kṛṣṇa allows himself to be intimately related with his devotees, bordering on forgetfulness of his own divinity at times. Although absolutely divine, his divinity cannot be understood by those without devotion.

Kṛṣṇa appears in his human form and all types of people see him but nevertheless do not understand who he is. This is the exercise of *yoga-māyā* as internal *śakti* rather than *yoga-māyā* as *māyā-śakti*, which is broader in scope and involves creation as a whole. Since *yoga-māyā* thus involves perception of Kṛṣṇa's person, it is equally applicable to the devotees and those who are averse to him. He hides from those adverse to him in his human-like relationships with his devotees under his own self-imposed *yoga-māyā*.

Jīva Goswāmī comments in *Kṛṣṇa-sandarbha* (29) that in this verse Kṛṣṇa explains why some people, even in some instances those devoted to him, think he is an incarnation, rather than the source of Viṣṇu. According to this verse, even when the complete manifestation of God (Kṛṣṇa) appears to the common person, such a person may take Kṛṣṇa to be an incarnation of Viṣṇu because Kṛṣṇa only reveals himself partially, relative to that person's belief.

While hiding from others, Kṛṣṇa is aware of their position. Although they cannot see him, he is not blind to their affairs.

Text 26

वेदाहं समतीतानि वर्तमानानि चार्जुन ।
भविष्याणि च भूतानि मां तु वेद न कश्चन ॥२६॥

vedāhaṁ samatītāni vartamānāni cārjuna/
bhaviṣyāṇi ca bhūtāni māṁ tu veda na kaścana//

veda—knows; *aham*—I; *samatītāni*—the past ones; *vartamānāni*—the present ones; *ca*—and; *arjuna*—O Arjuna; *bhaviṣyāṇi*—the ones to be; *ca*—also; *bhūtāni*—beings; *mām*—me; *tu*—but; *veda*—know; *na*—not; *kaścana*—anyone.

O Arjuna, I know the past, present, future, and all beings, but no one knows me.

Here Kṛṣṇa contrasts his position with that of others. He is omniscient and undeluded by *māyā*, appearing under the influence of his own internal *yoga-māyā*. The *jīvas* are deluded by his *mahā-māyā* (secondary potency) and certainly cannot understand the enlightening influence of his *yoga-māyā*, under whose influence he performs humanlike activities in subordination to his devotees' love, while remaining omniscient.[11] Understanding and thereby transcending the influence of *māyā*, one realizes self-perfection. When one understands Kṛṣṇa's *yoga-māyā*, one is the very rare soul Kṛṣṇa refers to in verse 3 and again in verse 19. He knows Kṛṣṇa as much as one can know him through love, while Kṛṣṇa himself remains unknowable.

Kṛṣṇa next describes further the influence of his *māyā*.

Text 27

इच्छाद्वेषसमुत्थेन द्वन्द्वमोहेन भारत ।
सर्वभूतानि संमोहं सर्गे यान्ति परन्तप ॥२७॥

icchā-dveṣa-samutthena dvandva-mohena bhārata/
sarva-bhūtāni saṁmohaṁ sarge yānti parantapa//

11. See KK. 83 and ŚB. 3.4.17.

icchā—desire; *dveṣa*—hate; *samutthena*—by the rising; *dvandva*—duality; *mohena*—by the illusion; *bhārata*—O descendant of Bharata; *sarva*—all; *bhūtāni*—beings; *sammoham*—delusion; *sarge*—at birth; *yānti*—go; *paran-tapa*—O destroyer of foes.

O descendant of Bharata, destroyer of foes, all beings are born deluded, bewildered by the dualities arising from desire and hate.

Kṛṣṇa addresses Arjuna here as Bhārata and Parantapa as if to say, "Because you are of noble heritage and well-known for your ability to destroy your enemies, you should not succumb to the influences of desire and hate." These two sides of the coin of material existence deprive the soul of knowledge of the true nature of the material world. So deluded, one suffers from a wrong sense of values and is hardly fit to understand the truth of the self, much less the truth about Kṛṣṇa.

Kṛṣṇa next qualifies his statement regarding the bewilderment of all beings in this world. There are those who, although physically in the world, are not of it.

Text 28

येषां त्वन्तगतं पापं जनानां पुण्यकर्मणाम् ।
ते द्वन्द्वमोहनिर्मुक्ता भजन्ते मां दृढव्रताः ॥२८॥

yeṣāṁ tv anta-gataṁ pāpaṁ janānāṁ puṇya-karmaṇām/
te dvandva-moha-nirmuktā bhajante māṁ dṛḍha-vratāḥ//

yeṣām—whose; *tu*—however; *anta-gatam*—finished; *pāpam*—sin; *janānām*—of the persons; *puṇya-karmaṇām*—of those who act piously; *te*—they; *dvandva*—duality; *moha*—delusion; *nirmuktāḥ*—free; *bhajante*—adore; *mām*—me; *dṛḍha-vratāḥ*—with firm vows.

However, those persons who act piously, in whom evil is finished, being liberated from the delusion of dualities, adore me with firm vows.

As mentioned earlier, piety that gives rise to devotion is piety in relation to *bhakti*. Opportunities for this kind of piety are created by those who are already devotees of Kṛṣṇa. Baladeva Vidyābhūṣaṇa says in his commentary on this verse that merely by the merciful glance of great devotees this devotional piety is created.

Bhakty-unmukhī-sukṛti takes two forms: *sukṛti* gained without the recipient's knowledge *(ajñāta-sukṛti)* and in a more developed stage, *sukṛti* earned by acting with some knowledge of the value of devotional life *(jñāta-sukṛti)*. *Jñāta-sukṛti* matures into *śraddhā*, which grants one eligibility for the direct culture of *bhakti*. Under discussion in this verse is a further developmental stage known as *niṣṭhā*. In this stage, the practitioner has been freed from vice and his faith is thus firm.

This verse reiterates the progression already given earlier in this chapter in verses 16 through 19. Devotionally pious persons approach Kṛṣṇa. Their desires are fulfilled and they gradually lose interest in them by coming to the platform of knowledge of the self, at which time their devotion becomes unwavering.

Kṛṣṇa concludes this chapter by way of introducing the next.

Text 29

जरामरणमोक्षाय मामाश्रित्य यतन्ति ये ।
ते ब्रह्म तद् विदुः कृत्स्नमध्यात्मं कर्म चाखिलम् ॥२९॥

jarā-maraṇa-mokṣāya mām āśritya yatanti ye/
te brahma tad viduḥ kṛtsnam adhyātmaṁ karma cākhilam//

jarā—old age; *maraṇa*—death; *mokṣāya*—for freedom; *mām*—me; *āśritya*—resorting; *yatanti*—endeavor; *ye*—those who; *te*—they; *brahma*—Brahman; *tat*—actually that; *viduḥ*—know; *kṛtsnam*—everything; *adhyātmam*—the individual self; *karma*—activities; *ca*—also; *akhilam*—entirely.

Those who strive for freedom from old age and death by resorting to me know Brahman, the individual self, and the principle of karma.

Here Kṛṣṇa says that if anyone wants freedom from death, taking shelter of him *(mām āśritya)* will bring success. They will realize Brahman and the individual self. Were the individual self and Brahman one and the same in all respects, the two would not have been mentioned separately. Such devotees who realize Brahman and the individual self also understand the principle of *karma*, having transcended it.

Viśvanātha Cakravartī Ṭhākura comments that in this verse Kṛṣṇa describes a devotee who desires liberation.

Text 30

साधिभूताधिदैवं मां साधियज्ञं च ये विदुः ।
प्रयाणकालेऽपि च मां ते विदुर्युक्तचेतसः ॥३०॥

sādhibhūtādhidaivaṁ māṁ sādhiyajñaṁ ca ye viduḥ/
prayāṇa-kāle 'pi ca māṁ te vidur yukta-cetasaḥ//

sa-adhibhūta—along with the *adhibhūta*; *adhidaivam*—along with the *adhidaiva*; *mām*—me; *sa-adhiyajñam*—along with the *adhiyajña*; *ca*—and; *ye*—those who; *viduḥ*—know; *prayāṇa*—death; *kāle*—at the time; *api*—even; *ca*—and; *mām*—me; *te*—they; *viduḥ*—know; *yukta-cetasaḥ*—their minds fixed.

Those who know me along with the adhibhūta, the adhidaiva, and the adhiyajña, their minds fixed on me, can know me even at the time of death.

Kṛṣṇa has introduced three topics in the previous verse that require further elaboration: Brahman, *adhyātmā*, and *karma*. In this verse he introduces three more: *adhibhūta*, *adhidaiva*, and *adhiyajña*, as well as the idea that by understanding these principles through devotion to Kṛṣṇa one can attain him at the time of death.

Jīva Goswāmī explains in his *Kṛṣṇa-sandarbha* that this verse reveals the superiority of Kṛṣṇa over the Paramātmā situated in the heart of all living beings.[12] According to Pāṇini (2.3.19), a word that is accompanied by the word "with" *(sa)* is secondary to the subject of the verb in a sentence. In the example, "The father came with his son," "father" is the primary noun in the sentence, and "son" is secondary. Thus, by using the compound noun *sādhiyajña*, which simply means "with the Supersoul," Kṛṣṇa indicates that the *adhiyajña*, or indwelling Supersoul, is secondary to himself, and that he is superior to it.

In the next chapter, Arjuna will ask further about the seven topics introduced in the last two verses of this chapter and Kṛṣṇa will elaborate on them.

12. See Ks. 82, *Sarvasaṁvādinī* commentary.

CHAPTER EIGHT

तारकब्रह्मयोगः
Tāraka-Brahma-yoga

YOGA OF ATTAINING THE ABSOLUTE

Text 1–2

अर्जुन उवाच
किं तद् ब्रह्म किमाध्यात्मं किं कर्म पुरुषोत्तम ।
अधिभूतं च किं प्रोक्तमधिदैवं किमुच्यते ॥१॥
अधियज्ञः कथं कोऽत्र देहेऽस्मिन्मधुसूदन ।
प्रयाणकाले च कथं ज्ञेयोऽसि नियतात्मभिः ॥२॥

arjuna uvāca
kiṁ tad brahma kim adhyātmaṁ kiṁ karma puruṣottama/
adhibhūtaṁ ca kiṁ proktam adhidaivaṁ kim ucyate//
adhiyajñaḥ kathaṁ ko 'tra dehe 'smin madhusūdana/
prayāṇa-kāle ca kathaṁ jñeyo 'si niyatātmabhiḥ//

arjunaḥ uvāca—Arjuna said; *kim*—what; *tat*—that; *brahma*—Brahman; *kim*—what; *adhyātmam*—*adhyātmā; kim*—what; *karma*—*karma; puruṣa-uttama*—O Supreme Person; *adhibhūtam*—*adhibhūta; ca*—and; *kim*—what; *proktam*—called; *adhidaivam*—*adhidaiva; kim*—what; *ucyate*—is said; *adhiyajñaḥ*—*adhiyajña; katham*—how; *kaḥ*—who; *atra*—here; *dehe*—in the body; *asmin*—this; *madhusūdana*—O Madhusūdana; *prayāṇa-kāle*—at the time of death; *ca*—and; *katham*—how; *jñeyaḥ asi*—you are to be known; *niyata-ātmabhiḥ*—by the self-controlled.

Arjuna said: O Supreme Person, what is meant by Brahman, what is adhyātma, what is karma, what is adhibhūta, and what is adhidaiva? Who is the adhiyajña and how is he situated within the body, O Madhusūdana, and how are you to be known at the time of death by those who are self-controlled?

Arjuna begins this chapter by asking Kṛṣṇa to elaborate on the seven topics mentioned at the end of the previous chapter: Brahman, *adhyātmā*, *karma*, *adhibhūta*, *adhidaiva*, *adhiyajña*, and how by understanding them in relation to Kṛṣṇa one can attain the Absolute at the time of death. Kṛṣṇa has rather mysteriously ended the seventh chapter by introducing these terms, some of which we have seen before, such as Brahman and *karma*, and others that are familiar in the *Upaniṣads* but have not yet been discussed in the *Gītā*: *adhyātma*, *adhibhūta*, *adhidaiva*, and *adhiyajña*. When Arjuna inquires into their meaning, Kṛṣṇa is brief in his replies. The result is that the *Gītā*'s many commentators have interpreted Kṛṣṇa's replies in a wide variety of ways.

Here in the first verse of this chapter, Arjuna addresses Kṛṣṇa as Puruṣottama, Supreme Person. By this he indicates that Kṛṣṇa's opinion is conclusive. This epithet further underscores the nature of the knowledge Kṛṣṇa explains in the middle six chapters of the *Gītā*: knowledge of God and the means to attain him. This chapter deals specifically with how to attain God at the time of death. It is to be understood that comprehending the first six topics about which Arjuna is asking is a prerequisite for attaining that state of consciousness by which one can remember Kṛṣṇa at the time of death and thus attain him.

The terms Arjuna asks about require explanation. Arjuna wonders if Kṛṣṇa means *paraṁ-brahma* when he mentions Brahman. Does he mean the Paramātmā when he mentions *adhyātmā*, or does he mean the individual soul? By *karma* does he mean scriptural rites or social duties? Does he mean the material body when he says *adhibhūta*? Who is the *adhidaiva*? Does this refer to the gods or God himself? Who is the *adhiyajña*—Indra or Viṣṇu—and in what form does he exist? How is one to conceive of *adhiyajña* during spiritual practice in terms of his being situated within the body?

The answers to Arjuna's questions must be understood in the context of the two verses that end the seventh chapter. Kṛṣṇa's answer in verse 3 is related to verse 29 of the previous chapter, and his answer in verse 4 is connected with verse 30 of chapter 7.

Text 3

श्रीभगवानुवाच
अक्षरं ब्रह्म परमं स्वभावोऽध्यात्ममुच्यते ।
भूतभावोद्भवकरो विसर्गः कर्मसंज्ञितः ॥३॥

śrī-bhagavān uvāca
akṣaraṁ brahma paramaṁ svabhāvo 'dhyātmam ucyate/
bhūta-bhāvodbhava-karo visargaḥ karma-saṁjñitaḥ//

śrī-bhagavān uvāca—the Lord of Śrī said; *akṣaram*—imperishable; *brahma*—Brahman; *paramam*—supreme; *svabhāvaḥ*—own nature; *adhyātmam*—the self; *ucyate*—is called; *bhūta-bhāva-udbhava-karaḥ*—producing the birth and growth of things; *visargaḥ*—creation; *karma*—*karma*; *saṁjñitaḥ*—called.

The Lord of Śrī said: Brahman is the supreme imperishable; adhyātmā is said to be the nature of the individual self. That action which brings about the birth and growth of things is called karma.

When Kṛṣṇa explains Brahman, he describes it as both infallible *(akṣara)* and supreme *(paramam)*. The word *akṣara* is used throughout the *Upaniṣads* to describe Brahman. Thus Brahman is both differentiated from all things material, the fallible *(kṣara)*, and identified with Kṛṣṇa himself *(paramam)*.[1]

Adhyātmā refers to the *jīva*, who, although embodied, is of the nature of Brahman in that it is consciousness. This *jīva* has been mentioned earlier in the previous chapter (Bg. 7.5) and will be discussed in detail in chapter 13. According to Gauḍīya Vaiṣṇava theology, the Supreme Brahman as *jīva* is called *vibhinnāṁśa*. The individual self is a particle of one of Brahman's *śaktis*. It is not unqualified Brahman temporarily embodied. It is not supreme *(paramam)*, nor infallible *(akṣara)*, and it does not realize supremacy on transcending bodily identification, although it does realize infallibility in connection with the Supreme Brahman. Later in the fifteenth chapter (Bg. 15.16), Kṛṣṇa describes two types of souls, fallible *(kṣara)* and infallible *(akṣara)*, both of whom are subordinate to the Supreme Person.

The *jīva* soul is *adhyātmā*, he who presides over the body and thus lives in the context *(adhi)* of the body *(ātmā)*. Here *ātmā* means the material body. Such a rendering owes itself to the soul's tendency to misidentify itself with the body.

Baladeva Vidyābhūṣaṇa says that the inherent nature of the self *(svabhāva)* is the *jīvātmā* and its desire. Its *svabhāva* is that aspect of itself that

1. Jīva Goswāmī understands *akṣara* as a reference to the Brahman feature of Godhead, and he understands the *adhidaiva* and *adhiyajña* to refer to the Paramātmā feature of Godhead (Bs. 176).

is characterized by subtle desires from the past that tie it to the material body. He says that Kṛṣṇa calls this *svabhāva adhyātma* because one's material desire has the power to bind the soul to the body *(ātmā)*.

Viśvanātha Cakravartī Ṭhākura understands *svabhāvo 'dhyātmam* in this verse to indicate either the nature of the self conditioned by material influence or the inherent serving nature of the self, its predisposition to the culture of devotion to the all-blissful Godhead, *svaṁ bhāvayati param-ātmānaṁ prāpayatīti svabhāvaḥ śuddha-jīvaḥ*. In the case of the former, *ātmā* means the material body. In the latter, *ātmā* indicates the Paramātmā. In his latter explanation, Viśvanātha Cakravartī Ṭhākura seems to be following the lead of Śrī Jīva Goswāmī in *Bhakti-sandarbha* (Bs. 216). Śrī Jīva cites this verse in support of the Vaiṣṇava conception of *sārūpya-mukti* (attaining a liberated form like God's). He says, "*Svabhāva* refers to the thoughts or meditation *(bhāvanā)* of the pure soul *(sva)*." Because such thought is situated in the self, it is called *adhyātmā*."

Karma is that influence by which the world revolves. It thus gives birth to the world. *Visargaḥ* denotes creative power. That action on the part of the *jīva* that is possessed of creative power, or the power to regenerate, is what Kṛṣṇa refers to here as *karma*. More specifically, by the word *karma* Kṛṣṇa refers to religious sacrifice governed by the *Vedas*. Jīva Goswāmī says *visargaḥ* means "making offerings to the gods" (Bs. 225). This action is to some extent of the nature of self-abnegation, in which one parts with something of his own in honor of a particular god, the overt result of which is heavenly attainment and subsequent rebirth in human society. Thus by extension, *karma* refers to religious activity. However, Jīva Goswāmī says that the special characteristic *(dharma)* of religious activity *(karma)* is that it leads to some association with *bhakti*. In support of this, he cites *Śrīmad-Bhāgavatam* (11.19.27), *dharmo mad-bhakti-kṛt proktaḥ:* "Religious activity is that which leads to my devotion." Commenting on this verse from *Śrīmad-Bhāgavatam*, Viśvanātha Cakravartī Ṭhākura says, "An entity's intrinsic characteristic, its *dharma*, is that which gives rise to Kṛṣṇa *bhakti*." In the words of Śrī Caitanya, the nature of the *jīva* is service to Kṛṣṇa, *jīvera svarūpa haya kṛṣṇera nitya-dāsa* (Cc. Madhya 20.108). Thus knowledge of the intrinsic nature *(dharma)* of an object leads to *bhakti*, and it is *bhakti* that brings the animate and inanimate world to life in the fullest sense.

Text 4

अधिभूतं क्षरो भावः पुरुषश्चाधिदैवतम् ।
अधियज्ञोऽहमेवात्र देहे देहभृतां वर ॥४॥

adhibhūtaṁ kṣaro bhāvaḥ puruṣaś cādhidaivatam/
adhiyajño 'ham evātra dehe deha-bhṛtāṁ vara//

adhibhūtam—the *adhibhūta*; *kṣaraḥ*—perishable; *bhāvaḥ*—existence; *puruṣaḥ*—person; *ca*—and; *adhidaivatam*—the *adhidaiva*; *adhiyajñaḥ*—the *adhiyajña*; *aham*—I; *eva*—certainly; *atra*—in this; *dehe*—body; *deha-bhṛtāṁ vara*—O best of the embodied.

The adhibhūta is fallible existence, and the adhidaiva, the agency of universal governance, is the divine person. I alone am the adhiyajña, the Lord of sacrifice, situated within the body, O best of embodied beings.

Adhibhūta refers to material existence and the soul's embodiment. *Adhidaiva* refers to the divine controlling agency, the gods and goddesses, all of whom move under the direction of the Supreme God. It is thus God represented as the gods and goddesses. The *adhiyajña*, however, is God himself, the Lord of sacrifice, Viṣṇu, who is nondifferent from Kṛṣṇa, being his expansion, as the *śruti* loudly proclaims *(yajño vai viṣṇuḥ)*.[2] Indeed, sacrifice *(yajña)* is one of his names. For the sake of conceptualization during meditation he is to be thought of as sitting within the heart, the size of one's thumb. Distinct from the individual souls and all human faculties including intellect, he is present in those humans who perform sacrifice. Although he is everywhere, his presence as the Lord of sacrifice is known only to those humans who engage in sacrifice. Indirectly, Kṛṣṇa has stressed sacrifice here as imperative for all souls.

In this verse, Kṛṣṇa's affection for Arjuna surfaces amidst this technical explanation through his address *deha-bhṛtāṁ vara*, best of the embodied. Kṛṣṇa is situated within the body as one's friend, and Arjuna, who has been made aware of this and is thus listening to him, is the best of those so embodied. By reminding Arjuna that he is the best of all beings due to being his devotee and friend, Kṛṣṇa is hinting at the qualifications which are needed to remember him at the time of death, the subject of the next verse.

Text 5

अन्तकाले च मामेव स्मरन्मुक्त्वा कलेवरम् ।
यः प्रयाति स मद्भावं याति नास्त्यत्र संशयः ॥५॥

2. Jīva Goswāmī explains that when Kṛṣṇa says he is the Supersoul, this does not mean that he is personally present in this form, rather the Supersoul is Kṛṣṇa's expansion by which he is partially present (*Sarvasaṁvādinī* commentary on Ks. 82).

anta-kāle ca mām eva smaran muktvā kalevaram/
yaḥ prayāti sa mad-bhāvaṁ yāti nāsty atra saṁśayaḥ//

anta-kāle—at the end (of life); *ca*—also; *mām*—me; *eva*—certainly; *smaran*—remembering; *muktvā*—relinquishing; *kalevaram*—body; *yaḥ*—he who; *prayāti*—goes; *saḥ*—he; *mat-bhāvam*—my nature; *yāti*—achieves; *na*—not; *asti*—there is; *atra*—here; *saṁśayaḥ*—doubt.

At the time of death, a person who relinquishes his body, remembering me alone, attains my nature. Of this there is no doubt.

In this verse, Kṛṣṇa begins to answer Arjuna's last question as to how he can be known at the time of death. The essence of his answer, extending through verse 7, is that he can be known by meditation on or remembrance (*smaran*) of himself.

The words *mām eva* indicate exclusive devotion to Kṛṣṇa. *Mad-bhāvam* is explained by Baladeva Vidyābhūṣaṇa as *mat-svabhāvam* (my own nature). Attaining the nature of Kṛṣṇa means to come under the influence of his *svarūpa-śakti* and thereby participate in his eternal *līlā*.

The time of death is significant. The implication is that at the time of death the mind is disturbed and difficult to control, but if one remembers Kṛṣṇa even imperfectly at that time one will attain Kṛṣṇa nonetheless. Such remembrance will not result without spiritual practice. Viśvanātha Cakravartī says that here *smaran* means knowledge.

Kṛṣṇa continues to assure Arjuna of the efficacy of remembering him at the time of death by saying that one's consciousness at the time of death determines one's next life.

Text 6

यं यं वापि स्मरन् भावं त्यजत्यन्ते कलेवरम् ।
तं तमेवैति कौन्तेय सदा तद्भावभावितः ॥६॥

yaṁ yaṁ vāpi smaran bhāvaṁ tyajaty ante kalevaram/
taṁ tam evaiti kaunteya sadā tad-bhāva-bhāvitaḥ//

yam yam vā api—whatever, anything at all; *smaran*—remembering; *bhāvam*—state of being; *tyajati*—relinquishes; *ante*—at the end; *kalevaram*—body; *tam tam*—respectively that; *eva*—certainly; *eti*—attains; *kaunteya*—O son of Kuntī; *sadā*—always; *tat*—that; *bhāva*—state of being; *bhāvitaḥ*—absorbed.

O son of Kuntī, whatever state of being a person remembers at the time of relinquishing the body, that state he will attain, being absorbed in its thought.

Our present life is a product of our net consciousness at the end of our previous life. The medium of reincarnation, or transmigration, is the subtle mental body. When the physical body expires, one acquires another one through the vehicle of the mind—the mind is expressed in the form of the new physical body to facilitate one's thoughts and desires.

This verse explains the possibility of transmigration. King/sage Bharata of the *Bhāgavata*, after whom India became known as Bhārata, is the classic example of transmigration cited by most commentators. Unbecoming his stature, he fell prey to attachment for a motherless fawn in the forest and died in thought of the fawn. In his next life he was born as a deer, but due to his spiritual practices he could remember his previous life.

In this verse, Kṛṣṇa continues to assure Arjuna through his manner of address: O son of Kuntī. Kṛṣṇa is overflowing with affection for Arjuna, the son of his father's sister, and he does not hide his partiality toward him. He wants to say to his friend that in this there is no deception—even though Kṛṣṇa is known to deceive, there is no chance of it here.[3] Although Kṛṣṇa has already made it clear that one who remembers him at the time of death attains him, in this verse he further assures Arjuna of this. He does so by stating the general rule that whatever one remembers at the time of death determines one's next life. Next Kṛṣṇa explains that which determines one's thoughts at the time of death and thereby one's future.

Text 7

तस्मात्सर्वेषु कालेषु मामनुस्मर युध्य च ।
मय्यर्पितमनोबुद्धिर्मामेवैष्यस्यसंशयः ॥७॥

tasmāt sarveṣu kāleṣu mām anusmara yudhya ca/
mayy arpita-mano-buddhir mām evaiṣyasy asaṁśayaḥ//

tasmāt—therefore; *sarveṣu*—in all; *kāleṣu*—in times; *mām*—me; *anusmara*—remember; *yudhya*—fight; *ca*—also; *mayi*—in me; *arpita*—placed;

3. Kṛṣṇa was known to lie and steal in his childhood *līlā*. He will also break his word for the sake of his devotee, should he deem it necessary. How can one trust such a person? Become his devotee.

manaḥ—mind; *buddhiḥ*—intellect; *mām*—me; *eva*—surely; *eṣyasi*—you will come; *asaṁśayaḥ*—beyond a doubt.

Therefore, remember me at all times and fight. With your mind and intellect fixed on me, you shall come to me without doubt.

At the time of death, thinking of anything in particular is difficult. However, tendency resulting from past habit causes remembrance. At the time of death, a person will remember that which he has contemplated throughout his life, especially what he has remembered during difficult times. Fighting implies difficulty. Here Kṛṣṇa advises Arjuna to remember him always, and in particular while fighting.

Fighting also refers to Arjuna's prescribed duty, which happens to run parallel with Kṛṣṇa's will, not only in a general religious sense, but relative to the particular circumstances in Kṛṣṇa's *līlā* (establishing *dharma*) as well. He does not want Arjuna to forgo fighting in the name of remembering him. Rather, fighting in this instance constitutes a form of remembrance of Kṛṣṇa, for it is Kṛṣṇa who has advised Arjuna to fight. Fighting, as the prescribed duty of a warrior, will cleanse Arjuna's heart, enabling him to remember and meditate on Kṛṣṇa.

One will constantly remember that which one loves. Mind and intellect follow the heart. Kṛṣṇa thus implores Arjuna to love him, thereby further exposing his own love and the *raison d'être* of *bhakti*: emotion is more powerful than intellect.

For the balance of the chapter Kṛṣṇa explains how to meditate on him. He does so through comparative analysis and discussion of mixed and pure devotion.

Text 8

अभ्यासयोगयुक्तेन चेतसा नान्यगामिना ।
परमं पुरुषं दिव्यं याति पार्थानुचिन्तयन् ॥८॥

abhyāsa-yoga-yuktena cetasā nānya-gāminā/
paramaṁ puruṣaṁ divyaṁ yāti pārthānucintayan//

abhyāsa-yoga—*yoga* practice; *yuktena*—being engaged; *cetasā*—by the mind; *na anya-gāminā*—without deviation; *paramam puruṣam*—Supreme Person; *divyam*—divine; *yāti*—attains; *pārtha*—O son of Pṛthā; *anucintayan*—meditating.

O Pārtha, a person who fixes his mind in yoga practice without deviation, meditating on the divine Supreme Person, attains him.

In this and the following five verses, Kṛṣṇa speaks of *yoga* mixed with devotion *(yoga-miśra-bhakti)*. He does so to emphasize that success in *yoga* requires *bhakti*. He also speaks of *yoga-miśra-bhakti* and its requirements and techniques to compare it with the path of exclusive devotion.

Here the words *abhyāsa-yoga-yuktena* indicate a constant flow of thought resulting from practice. When this stream of thought is undeviated by any other thought *(nānya-gāminā)* and the stream of thought is all in relation to the Supreme Person, one attains that Supreme Being. In the word *anucintayan*, the prefix *anu* implies that such meditation should be in accordance with scriptural descriptions of the Supreme Person and it should follow the direction of the succession of spiritual preceptors *(sampradāya/paramparā)*.

The tone of Kṛṣṇa's voice in this verse continues to be reassuring to Arjuna, if not emphatic that attainment results from devotion. In the next two verses, Kṛṣṇa gives further details as to the nature of devotional meditation and *yoga*.

Text 9–10

कविं पुराणमनुशासितार-
मणोरणीयांसमनुस्मरेद् यः ।
सर्वस्य धातारमचिन्त्यरूप-
मादित्यवर्णं तमसः परस्तात् ॥९॥
प्रयाणकाले मनसाचलेन
भक्त्या युक्तो योगबलेन चैव ।
भ्रुवोर्मध्ये प्राणमावेश्य सम्यक्
स तं परं पुरुषमुपैति दिव्यम् ॥१०॥

kaviṁ purāṇam anuśāsitāram
aṇor aṇīyāṁsam anusmared yaḥ/
sarvasya dhātāram acintya-rūpam
āditya-varṇaṁ tamasaḥ parastāt//
prayāṇa-kāle manasācalena
bhaktyā yukto yoga-balena caiva/
bhruvor madhye prāṇam āveśya samyak
sa taṁ paraṁ puruṣam upaiti divyam//

kavim—all-knowing seer; *purāṇam*—ancient; *anuśāsitāram*—ruler; *aṇoḥ*—than the atom; *aṇīyāṁsam*—smaller; *anusmaret*—one should meditate; *yaḥ*—one who; *sarvasya*—of everything; *dhātāram*—the maintainer; *acintya*—inconceivable; *rūpam*—form; *āditya-varṇam*—effulgent like the sun; *tamasaḥ*—than darkness; *parastāt*—beyond; *prayāṇa-kāle*—at the time of death; *manasā*—by the mind; *acalena*—without deviating; *bhaktyā*—with devotion; *yuktaḥ*—united; *yoga-balena*—by yogic power; *ca*—also; *eva*—certainly; *bhruvoḥ*—of the two eyebrows; *madhye*—between; *prāṇam*—life air; *āveśya*—having caused to enter; *samyak*—completely; *saḥ*—he; *tam*—that; *param puruṣam*—Supreme Person; *upaiti*—achieves; *divyam*—divine.

He who, imbued with devotion and the power of yoga at the time of death, perfectly places the life airs between the eyebrows while constantly meditating on God as the all-knowing seer, the ancient one, the ruler who is smaller than the atom and yet the support of all, of inconceivable form and effulgent like the sun beyond the darkness, attains the divine Supreme Person.

Vedānta-sūtra (4.2.17) discusses the *yoga* technique of raising the vital force, or life air, from the heart after having controlled it along the *suṣumṇā* nerve and fixing it on the point between the eyebrows, or the *ājñā-cakra*. *Yoga* practitioners will be familiar with this terminology. However, it is important to note that yogic power *(yoga-balena)* must be accompanied by the integrating force of love and devotion *(bhaktyā yukto)* for it to produce the desired result.

All of the above *yoga* terminology and that which follows in the next three verses has been prefaced by a description of the Supreme Person, the object of meditation. He is the all-knowing seer and poet, who speaks the language of love. Although ancient, he does not age. *Śrutis* such as *Gopāla-tāpanī* describe him as eternally adolescent. He is the ruler of all. To be so, his ruling power must ultimately be the force of affection, for only love can conquer all. This characterizes the ruling power of Kṛṣṇa, who conquers even Cupid by his irresistible power of attraction and charm. He is smaller than the smallest and bigger than the biggest, and thereby both infinite and infinitesimal, and thus immeasurable. In his Paramātmā feature, he both manifests the world and enters the heart of every soul. Yet he appears as Kṛṣṇa *(svayaṁ bhagavān)* in medium size, apparently measurable. Thus his form is inconceivable *(acintya-rūpam)*. He is effulgent like the sun and therefore one cannot look at him or see him with material eyes, even while it is he who is the light by which we see and who dispels all darkness.

As Arjuna wonders if there is anything more to this practice of *yoga* other than fixing the life air between the eyebrows, Kṛṣṇa continues with other technical details of the practice.

Text 11

यदक्षरं वेदविदो वदन्ति
  विशन्ति यद् यतयो वीतरागाः ।
यदिच्छन्तो ब्रह्मचर्यं चरन्ति
  तत्ते पदं संग्रहेण प्रवक्ष्ये ॥११॥

yad akṣaraṁ veda-vido vadanti
  viśanti yad yatayo vīta-rāgāḥ/
yad icchanto brahmacaryaṁ caranti
  tat te padaṁ saṅgraheṇa pravakṣye//

yat—which; *akṣaram*—imperishable; *veda-vidaḥ*—the knowers of the Vedas; *vadanti*—describe; *viśanti*—enter; *yat*—which; *yatayaḥ*—ascetics; *vīta-rāgāḥ*—free from attachment; *yat*—which; *icchantaḥ*—desiring; *brahmacaryam*—celibacy; *caranti*—practice; *tat*—that; *te*—to you; *padam*—situation; *saṅgraheṇa*—briefly; *pravakṣye*—I shall speak.

I shall speak briefly to you of that infallible goal which knowers of the Vedas describe, into which ascetics free from attachment enter, and desiring which they practice celibacy.

Text 12–13

सर्वद्वाराणि संयम्य मनो हृदि निरुध्य च ।
  मूर्ध्न्याधायात्मनः प्राणमास्थितो योगधारणाम् ॥१२॥
ॐ इत्येकाक्षरं ब्रह्म व्याहरन्मामनुस्मरन् ।
  यः प्रयाति त्यजन् देहं स याति परमां गतिम् ॥१३॥

sarva-dvārāṇi saṁyamya mano hṛdi nirudhya ca/
  mūrdhny ādhāyātmanaḥ prāṇam āsthito yoga-dhāraṇām//
oṁ ity ekākṣaraṁ brahma vyāharan mām anusmaran/
  yaḥ prayāti tyajan dehaṁ sa yāti paramāṁ gatim//

sarva-dvārāṇi—all the gates; *saṁyamya*—controlling; *manaḥ*—the mind; *hṛdi*—in the heart; *nirudhya*—confining; *ca*—also; *mūrdhni*—in the head;

ādhāya—fixing; *ātmanaḥ*—own; *prāṇam*—vital force; *āsthitaḥ*—established; *yoga-dhāraṇām*—yogic concentration; *oṁ*—*oṁ*; *iti*—thus; *eka-akṣaram*—the monosyllable; *brahma*—Brahman; *vyāharan*—uttering; *mām*—me; *anu-smaran*—remembering; *yaḥ*—one who; *prayāti*—departs; *tyajan*—quitting; *deham*—body; *saḥ*—he; *yāti*—attains; *paramām*—supreme; *gatim*—goal.

A person who is situated in yogic concentration by controlling all the gates of the body, confining the mind within the heart, and fixing the vital force at the top of the head, and then utters oṁ, the single-syllable form of Brahman, and remembers me as he quits the body, attains the supreme goal.

In verse 11 the word *akṣaram*, infallible, is synonymous with *oṁ*. Thus its utterance is indicated, as it is directly mentioned in verse 13. Kṛṣṇa describes *oṁ* as monosyllabic to stress the ease of its utterance. It is nondifferent from himself. Otherwise, everything else in this yogic equation is difficult. Celibacy is a prerequisite. Life-long celibacy is implied. The gates of the body refer to the senses of perception: eyes, ears, nose, and mouth (tongue). Controlling these gates or closing them implies not perceiving external objects. Confining the mind in the heart means not contemplating external objects.

Here Kṛṣṇa ends his discussion of *yoga-miśra-bhakti* with a brief description of the techniques and prerequisites involved. If anything makes success on this path easy or realistic, it is the element of devotion, not any of the techniques or prerequisites described. This practice does not appeal to Arjuna, nor is he practiced in it, whereas its essence, devotion, does appeal to him and is natural for him. Thus Kṛṣṇa next speaks about the path of pure devotion in two verses, contrasting its simplicity with the difficulties involved in *yoga-miśra-bhakti*.

Text 14

अनन्यचेताः सततं यो मां स्मरति नित्यशः ।
तस्याहं सुलभः पार्थ नित्ययुक्तस्य योगिनः ॥१४॥

ananya-cetāḥ satataṁ yo māṁ smarati nityaśaḥ/
tasyāhaṁ sulabhaḥ pārtha nitya-yuktasya yoginaḥ//

ananya-cetāḥ—whose consciousness is devoid of any consideration; *satatam*—always; *yaḥ*—one who; *mām*—me; *smarati*—remembers; *nityaśaḥ*—

regularly; *tasya*—of him; *aham*—I am; *su-labhaḥ*—easy to attain; *pārtha*—O son of Pṛthā; *nitya*—constantly; *yuktasya*—of the united; *yoginaḥ*—of the *yogī*.

But Pārtha, how easily am I won by one who remembers me constantly with undivided attention, for he is a [true] yogī who is ever united with me.

In this verse Kṛṣṇa's voice is full of love, and he again addresses Arjuna affectionately as Pārtha. Kṛṣṇa speaks to Arjuna about Arjuna's own status in *yoga*. The words *ananya-cetāḥ* imply consciousness devoid of desire for any goal other than devotion itself or interest in any path other than *bhakti*.

By use of the word *satatam*, Kṛṣṇa differentiates between unalloyed *bhakti* and the *yoga-miśra-bhakti* he has been explaining. The path of pure devotion is not concerned with time, place, and other details to the same extent that they are important in the paths of *karma*, *jñāna*, and *yoga*. Love has the power to attract the heart of the Absolute, causing him to overlook what might otherwise be a discrepancy. Kṛṣṇa's use of the word *satatam* indicates devotion's application in all circumstances. Chanting Kṛṣṇa's name in particular is so powerful an expression of love that no rules are attached to it. It can be done at any time, in any place, by anyone. It promotes constant remembrance of Kṛṣṇa like no other practice.

Madhusūdana Saraswatī acknowledges the distinction between the *yoga* practice Kṛṣṇa has been describing, with all its requirements and difficult practices, and that which he speaks of in this verse. He explains that the phrase *ananya-cetāḥ* indicates great veneration and love. He further points out that it is remembrance of God that is the essential ingredient for success, while the aforementioned techniques and prerequisites are nonessential.

No meditation is more powerful than that of a devotee who aspires for an intimate relationship with Kṛṣṇa. Such spiritual relationships capture Kṛṣṇa's heart. This advanced stage of meditation or remembrance (*smarati*) is what Kṛṣṇa is alluding to in this verse. He says, *tasya yoginaḥ*, "For such a *yogī* (devotee) in intimate spiritual rapport with me (*nitya-yuktasya*), I am easily attained (*tasyāhaṁ sulabhaḥ*)."

The words *nitya-yuktasya* here indicate the devotee who aspires to be eternally united in loving relationship with Kṛṣṇa. Kṛṣṇa assures Arjuna, who has already expressed his lack of confidence in yogic techniques in the sixth chapter, that devotees who constantly remember him easily attain him. This ease is such that they attain Kṛṣṇa regardless of when they leave the body or whether they have perfected yogic techniques, such as focusing the vital force between the eyebrows. Kṛṣṇa further describes these souls in the next verse in terms of their greatness and level of attainment.

Text 15

मामुपेत्य पुनर्जन्म दुःखालयमशाश्वतम् ।
नाप्नुवन्ति महात्मानः संसिद्धिं परमां गताः ॥१५॥

mām upetya punar janma duḥkhālayam aśāśvatam/
nāpnuvanti mahātmānaḥ saṁsiddhiṁ paramāṁ gatāḥ//

mām—me; *upetya*—coming near; *punaḥ*—again; *janma*—birth; *duḥkha-ālayam*—abode of misery; *aśāśvatam*—temporary; *na*—never; *āpnuvanti*—reach; *mahā-ātmānaḥ*—great souls; *saṁsiddhim*—perfection; *paramām*—ultimate; *gatāḥ*—having attained.

Reaching me, these great souls never again experience birth in this temporal abode of misery, for they have attained the ultimate perfection.

In this verse, Kṛṣṇa invokes the term *mahātmā* (great soul) for the second time.[4] He will do so once again in the next chapter (Bg. 9.13). In each instance he refers to his unalloyed devotees. He does not describe any other type of transcendentalist so flatteringly. Such perfect beings are those rare souls referred to in the third verse of the seventh chapter, the most perfect among the perfect. They come near to Kṛṣṇa in loving relationships of sacred rapture.

Here Kṛṣṇa has summed up material existence in two words, *duḥkhālayam* and *aśāśvatam*. It is miserable and temporary. If a person disagrees with Kṛṣṇa's description of material existence being an abode of misery and insists that he likes this world, Kṛṣṇa replies that it is then all the more miserable, for one cannot remain here.

It is well known that Kṛṣṇa's devotees *do* take birth along with him when he appears in this world. His eternal associates accompany him, and perfected *sādhakas* take advantage of their association through birth in his *līlā*. However, in either case they do not experience any misery, nor is the *līlā* temporary even while appearing in the material world. This is why Kṛṣṇa states that such *mahātmās* do not take birth in a temporal abode of misery instead of saying that they do not take birth at all.

4. The first time was in 7.19.

While Kṛṣṇa's devotees do not undergo the misery of rebirth, those who in their next life attain any of the various material planes are not assured the same status. In the next four verses Kṛṣṇa discusses these planes to contrast their attainment with that of his devotees, both unalloyed and *yoga-miśra bhaktas*.

Text 16

आब्रह्मभुवनाल्लोकाः पुनरावर्तिनोऽर्जुन ।
मामुपेत्य तु कौन्तेय पुनर्जन्म न विद्यते ॥१६॥

ā-brahma-bhuvanāl lokāḥ punar āvartino 'rjuna/
mām upetya tu kaunteya punar janma na vidyate//

ā-brahma-bhuvanāt—all the way up to Brahmā's realm; *lokāḥ*—realms of existence; *punaḥ*—again; *āvartinaḥ*—rebirths; *arjuna*—O Arjuna; *mām*—me; *upetya*—attaining; *tu*—but; *kaunteya*—O son of Kuntī; *punaḥ janma*—rebirth; *na*—not; *vidyate*—takes place.

O Arjuna, all realms of existence up to and including the abode of Brahmā are places from which one must again return. Only one who reaches me is never reborn.

The sacred literature describes many planes of experience, worlds (*lokas*), corresponding with the development of one's spiritual consciousness and piety. Brahmā's realm is considered to be the highest attainment in the material world. Brahmaloka is a realm of pure intellect. For the most part, those dwelling there have attained that plane through the culture of spiritual knowledge, which involves controlling the mental and physical urges. Other sense-controlled persons attain material realms that correspond with their level of spiritual attainment. Just below Brahmaloka, planes such as Mahārloka, Tapaloka, and Siddhaloka are primarily populated by spiritual seekers who in their previous life renounced the procreative urge. These seekers generally evolve to take birth in Brahmaloka, from which they, along with Brahmā at the end of his life, attain liberation, the cessation of birth and death. However, because the possibility exists that one can attain residence in Brahmaloka through immense piety rather than spiritual culture, Kṛṣṇa states that even the highest material realm is subject to rebirth.

Here Kṛṣṇa stresses the futility of material attainment, however great, in comparison with spiritual attainment. While the former, with all of its frills, ultimately grants only rebirth, the latter begets eternity. Thus there is really no comparison between the two. Kṛṣṇa wants to say that a life of spiritual culture is infinitely better than a life motivated by materialistic values. Those familiar with Hindu cosmography and the importance of Brahmā, the god of creation, will be astounded by this statement in which the pious position of the god of creation is belittled. As Kṛṣṇa next explains, the reason that all material realms are subject to rebirth is that they are within the influence of time.

Text 17

सहस्रयुगपर्यन्तमहर्यद् ब्रह्मणो विदुः ।
रात्रिं युगसहस्रान्तां तेऽहोरात्रविदो जनाः ॥१७॥

sahasra-yuga-paryantam ahar yad brahmaṇo viduḥ/
rātriṁ yuga-sahasrāntāṁ te 'ho-rātra-vido janāḥ//

sahasra-yuga—one thousand *yugas; paryantam*—extent; *ahaḥ*—day; *yat*—which; *brahmaṇaḥ*—of Brahmā; *viduḥ*—they know; *rātrim*—night; *yuga-sahasra-antām*—ending after one thousand *yugas*; *te*—they; *ahaḥ-rātra*—day and night; *vidaḥ*—knowers; *janāḥ*—people.

Those who know that the day of Brahmā lasts for a thousand yugas and that his night lasts for a thousand yugas know what day and night are.

The length of Brahmā's day is *sahasra-yuga*, one thousand *yuga* cycles. Hindus recognize four ages *(yugas)*, which revolve in cycles from Satya-yuga to Tretā-yuga to Dwāpara-yuga to Kali-yuga over and over again. One thousand of these cycles makes up the duration of Brahmā's day, and another one thousand cycles his night. One of these cycles alone consists of 4,320,000 years. Here the *Gītā* asks us to expand our frame of reference. It is worth remembering what Kṛṣṇa has said earlier: "Even those who think they know what day and night are, do not really know what they are." (Bg. 2.69)

We have no experience of people living lives the length of Brahmā's, although we do have experience of species of insects whose entire life consists of only the twenty-four hours that make up our day and night. Brahmā's life span is as inconceivable to us as ours would be to an insect. If we were to come in contact with one exemplifying the measure of piety or spiritual culture required for attaining birth in Brahmā's realm, it would make the corresponding birth for such a pious life and its descriptions in sacred literature more plausible, for it would be apparent that such a person does not belong here in this world among us.

Speaking microcosmically, a life ruled by discriminating intellect is one that passes at a slower pace. The discriminating person takes time to make a thorough analysis before acting. He investigates with interest even minute aspects of the creation in relation to a bigger, spiritually-based picture. The true intellectual is not preoccupied with all the imaginable material possibilities, for his fascination with the underlying essence of material creation extends his power of discrimination beyond matter. In the material hierarchy mentioned in chapter 3 (Bg. 3.42), intellect takes its seat above the mind, senses, and sense objects, just beneath the soul.

It may be better for the culture of one's spiritual life not to rationalize away concepts such as the long life of Brahmā. It will no doubt be helpful for spiritual advancement to accept the limitations of our experience based as it is on the faulty and inconclusive mediums of sense perception and reason.

We may think our days to be long at times, but material life is all too short in comparison to eternity. According to this verse, the duration of Brahmā's days and nights are incredibly long from the human standpoint. Yet all of them put together are not enough to save him from death. Those who know the truth about the days and nights of Brahmā truly know the nature of day and night. They know them to be, however long, unable to deliver enduring experience. Regardless of just how long Brahmā lives, Kṛṣṇa's main point here is that however long a person lives on any material plane, his life is temporary. Thus Kṛṣṇa reminds us of the all-pervading influence of time.

As Brahmā is subject to death and even the possibility of rebirth, it is understood that those realms below his mentioned in verse 16 are subject to the same. These inferior planes are not only those populated primarily by spiritual seekers, but also the mental and physical realms populated primarily by those in pursuit of sense enjoyment. In verse 18, Kṛṣṇa discusses the particulars of time's influence on Brahmā's abode. In verse 19, he speaks more specifically about the inferior realms. For the sake of emphasis, Kṛṣṇa points out the temporal nature of these domains.

Text 18

अव्यक्ताद्‍ व्यक्तयः सर्वाः प्रभवन्त्यहरागमे ।
रात्र्यागमे प्रलीयन्ते तत्रैवाव्यक्तसंज्ञके ॥१८॥

avyaktād vyaktayaḥ sarvāḥ prabhavanty ahar-āgame/
rātry-āgame pralīyante tatraivāvyakta-saṁjñake//

avyaktāt—from the unmanifest; *vyaktayaḥ*—manifestations; *sarvāḥ*—all; *prabhavanti*—come forth; *ahaḥ-āgame*—with the arrival of the day; *rātri-āgame*—with the arrival of night; *pralīyante*—are reabsorbed; *tatra*—there; *eva*—certainly; *avyakta*—the unmanifest; *saṁjñake*—known as.

With the arrival of the day of Brahmā all things come forth from the unmanifest state; with the arrival of Brahmā's night, they are reabsorbed into that known as the unmanifest state.

Here the word *avyakta*, the unmanifest, refers to Brahmā in his sleeping state. The worlds of material enjoyment populated by sense enjoyers are manifest during the partial creation of Brahmā's day. Mental and physical realms are controlled by intellect. During his night they become unmanifest, only to again manifest at the dawn of his next day. They come into being replete with living beings under the influence of *karma*. Kṛṣṇa explains this next to make clear that the material merit of beings under the influence of *karma* is not lost during Brahmā's night. It is the very force by which they again become manifest.

Text 19

भूतग्रामः स एवायं भूत्वा भूत्वा प्रलीयते ।
राज्यागमेऽवशः पार्थ प्रभवत्यहरागमे ॥१९॥

bhūta-grāmaḥ sa evāyaṁ bhūtvā bhūtvā pralīyate/
rātry-āgame 'vaśaḥ pārtha prabhavaty ahar-āgame//

bhūta-grāmaḥ—the multitude of creatures; *saḥ*—that; *eva*—certainly; *ayam*—this; *bhūtvā bhūtvā*—repeatedly coming into being; *pralīyate*—is reabsorbed; *rātri-āgame*—with the arrival of night; *avaśaḥ*—helplessly; *pārtha*—O son of Pṛthā; *prabhavati*—comes into being; *ahaḥ āgame*—with the arrival of day.

Having come into being, O Pārtha, the multitude of creatures is helplessly reabsorbed with the arrival of Brahmā's night, and they again come into being with the arrival of his day.

The implication of this verse is that there is no such thing as creation in the sense of something being created out of nothing. That which exists will always exist and that which is nonexistent will never exist. The *śruti* states that the creator (Brahmā) recreated the sun and moon just as they were before (Ṛg. 10.190.3). Thus there is a perpetuity even to the temporal. The desires and karmic tendencies *(saṁskāras)* of the living beings remain with them during the unmanifest state and assure that beings under the influence of *karma* will again manifest to play out their desires. Accordingly, the material manifestation itself manifests along with them to facilitate their desires.

The word *avaśaḥ* in this verse, rendered "helplessly," describes the condition of one under the influence of ignorance and material desire, which characterizes materially conditioned souls. Kṛṣṇa uses this word in concluding his depiction of the material realms and their inhabitants to indirectly stress his own position. Like those lost in the waves of the ocean, souls drift helplessly in a sea of material desire based on misplaced values arising from ignorance. They are helpless without the intervention of God.

Having described in brief yet compelling verses the futility of material attainment, Kṛṣṇa returns to a description of his own abode, the destination of the devoted. Consistent with his previous assurances, his voice is forceful and emphatic.

Text 20

परस्तस्मात्तु भावोऽन्योऽव्यक्तोऽव्यक्तात्सनातनः ।
यः स सर्वेषु भूतेषु नश्यत्सु न विनश्यति ॥२०॥

paras tasmāt tu bhāvo 'nyo 'vyakto 'vyaktāt sanātanaḥ/
yaḥ sa sarveṣu bhūteṣu naśyatsu na vinaśyati//

paraḥ—higher; *tasmāt*—than that; *tu*—however; *bhāvaḥ*—state of being; *anyaḥ*—other; *avyaktaḥ*—unmanifest; *avyaktāt*—than the unmanifest; *sanātanaḥ*—eternal; *yaḥ*—which; *saḥ*—that; *sarveṣu*—in all; *bhūteṣu*—in beings; *naśyatsu*—in the losses; *na*—not; *vinaśyati*—perishes.

However, higher than this unmanifest is another eternal unmanifest, which does not perish when created things perish.

The other unmanifest *(avyaktaḥ)* mentioned in this verse is categorically different from Brahmā during his sleep, who has also been called *avyakta* in verse 18. Because *avyakta* refers to the person of Brahmā in verse 18, there should be little doubt that the same term used here to indicate the source of Brahmā also describes a person. This person is *avyakta* in the sense that he is not manifest to the material eye. It is he into whom the entire material manifestation is reabsorbed, as effect becomes unmanifest while in its causal state. When Brahmā sleeps, his creation is dissolved into himself, becoming unmanifest. Similarly, when Viṣṇu sleeps, the entire material manifestation including Brahmā is dissolved into himself.

The word *tu* (however) indicates the categorical difference between the two types of *avyakta*. This *avyakta* is *anya* (of different characteristics). The imperceptible unmanifest has its own distinguishing characteristics. Thus *avyakta* here refers to Viṣṇu, who is ever-existing *(sanātanaḥ)* as is his realm, which is nondifferent from himself.

Text 21

अव्यक्तोऽक्षर इत्युक्तस्तमाहुः परमां गतिम् ।
यं प्राप्य न निवर्तन्ते तद्धाम परमं मम ॥२१॥

avyakto 'kṣara ity uktas tam āhuḥ paramāṁ gatim/
yaṁ prāpya na nivartante tad dhāma paramaṁ mama//

avyaktaḥ—unmanifest; *akṣaraḥ*—infallible; *iti*—thus; *uktaḥ*—said; *tam*—that; *āhuḥ*—they call; *paramām*—supreme; *gatim*—goal; *yam*—which; *prāpya*—attaining; *na*—not; *nivartante*—return; *tat*—that; *dhāma*—abode; *paramam*—supreme; *mama*—my.

That other unmanifest realm is said to be infallible. They call it the supreme goal, on attaining which one does not return. It is my supreme abode.

Here "they" who say this *avyakta* is infallible and call it the supreme destination are the *Upaniṣads*. They do so in verses such as, "There is nothing higher than the Supreme Person *(puruṣa)*. He is the culmination. He is the highest goal." (Ka. Up. 1.3.11)

According to Madhusūdana Saraswatī, Kṛṣṇa's use of *mama dhāma* (my abode) in the sixth case implies nondifference between his abode and himself.[5] Such is the nature of his abode, although replete with form, qualities, and *līlā*, it is distinct from the material manifestation and eternal in nature, a veritable world of pure consciousness and bliss. This is an elaborate subject of Vaiṣṇava theology.

5. As in the case of "Rāhu's head," when indeed Rāhu is nothing but a head.

Kṛṣṇa concludes this section by echoing verse 14 and reiterating the means of attaining him and his abode.

Text 22

पुरुषः स परः पार्थ भक्त्या लभ्यस्त्वनन्यया ।
यस्यान्तःस्थानि भूतानि येन सर्वमिदं ततम् ॥२२॥

puruṣaḥ sa paraḥ pārtha bhaktyā labhyas tv ananyayā/
yasyāntaḥ-sthāni bhūtāni yena sarvam idaṁ tatam//

puruṣaḥ—person; *saḥ*—he; *paraḥ*—supreme; *pārtha*—O son of Pṛthā; *bhaktyā*—by devotion; *labhyaḥ*—to be attained; *tu*—but; *ananyayā*—unalloyed; *yasya*—of whom; *antaḥ-sthāni*—standing within; *bhūtāni*—created things; *yena*—by whom; *sarvam*—all; *idam*—this; *tatam*—pervaded.

O Pārtha, the Supreme Person, in whom all things stand and by whom all things are pervaded, is attainable by unalloyed devotion.

The word *puruṣa* has a number of meanings, but in this case it refers to God's expansions, the *puruṣāvatāras*, known most commonly as Nārāyaṇa or Viṣṇu. Nārāyaṇa means "the resting place of all people," as Kṛṣṇa says here, "in whom all beings stand." Viṣṇu means "all-pervading," and it is because God pervades everything that all things rest in him. Kṛṣṇa is the source of Viṣṇu/Nārāyaṇa,[6] but in this verse he is speaking directly of the *puruṣa*, Viṣṇu, and only indirectly about himself.

However, Kṛṣṇa has also demonstrated that he is all-pervading and the resting place of all things in his pastimes described in *Śrīmad-Bhāgavatam*. The all-pervading nature of Kṛṣṇa's form is illustrated in the *Śrīmad-Bhāgavatam*'s description of his childhood *līlā*, in which his mother looked into his mouth to see if he had eaten dirt, only to see the entire universe within Kṛṣṇa, including herself looking into his mouth (ŚB. 10.8). In the *dāmodara-līlā* (ŚB. 10.9), in which Yaśodā tried to bind Kṛṣṇa with rope, Kṛṣṇa also demonstrated that all the rope in the world could not fit around his waist. He did this while remaining the same size, thus demonstrating his simultaneous all-pervasive and humanlike nature.

Kṛṣṇa hinted at the subject of *yoga-miśra-bhakti* in the two concluding verses of chapter 7. He then elaborated on this form of mixed devotion in

6. See ŚB. 1.3.28.

verses 8 through 13 of this chapter. Therein, he stressed devotion to God and meditation on the Supreme Person as the essential elements of this practice. In verse 14 Kṛṣṇa turned from his description of *yoga-miśra-bhakti* to unalloyed *bhakti*, in which even *yoga* techniques and prerequisites can be dispensed with and by which Kṛṣṇa himself is easily attained. After comparing this with material attainment, Kṛṣṇa spoke further of the nature of the ultimate goal, concluding with this verse. Here he says that attaining him and his own personal abode is possible only by devotion, not by any other means. He says, *bhaktyā labhyaḥ* (by devotion) *tv ananyayā* (indeed, not by anything else). Viṣṇu or any of his *avatāras'* abodes can be attained only if devotion is the primary factor in one's particular practice, but Kṛṣṇa is attained only by unalloyed devotion, devoid of even the desire for liberation or one's own spiritual benefit. Devotion for love's sake is the emphasis in this verse, as it was in text 14.

Here Kṛṣṇa is once again assuring Arjuna of his success, should he take recourse to unalloyed devotion even while remaining a householder and warrior. Such is the mystical nature of *bhakti*. It is the power of pure love by which the Absolute, the source of all realms material and spiritual, is conquered and rendered humanlike. This humanity is epitomized by his falling in love with his devotee. Afflicted by this love here, Kṛṣṇa addresses Arjuna as Pārtha.

Kṛṣṇa next describes details of the paths to liberation and rebirth. He does so to emphasize the virtue and logic of spiritual practice, and more, the unique position of his unalloyed devotees in relation to the two routes of passage.

Text 23

यत्र काले त्वनावृत्तिमावृत्तिं चैव योगिनः ।
प्रयाता यान्ति तं कालं वक्ष्यामि भरतर्षभ ॥२३॥

yatra kāle tv anāvṛttim āvṛttiṁ caiva yoginaḥ/
prayātā yānti taṁ kālaṁ vakṣyāmi bharatarṣabha//

yatra—at which; *kāle*—in time; *tu*—indeed; *anāvṛttim*—nonreturn; *āvṛttim*—return; *ca*—also; *va*—certainly; *yoginaḥ*—*yogīs*; *prayātāḥ*—departing; *yānti*—attain; *tam*—that; *kālam*—time; *vakṣyāmi*—I shall speak; *bharata-ṛṣabha*—O best of the Bharata dynasty.

O best of the Bharata dynasty, I shall now explain to you those times when yogīs departing at death either return or do not return.

Text 24

अग्निर्ज्योतिरहः शुक्लः षण्मासा उत्तरायणम् ।
तत्र प्रयाता गच्छन्ति ब्रह्म ब्रह्मविदो जनाः ॥२४॥

agnir jyotir ahaḥ śuklaḥ ṣaṇ-māsā uttarāyaṇam/
tatra prayātā gacchanti brahma brahma-vido janāḥ//

agniḥ—fire; *jyotiḥ*—light; *ahaḥ*—day; *śuklaḥ*—the bright fortnight; *ṣaṭ-māsāḥ*—six months; *uttara-ayanam*—northern phase of the sun; *tatra*—there; *prayātāḥ*—departing; *gacchanti*—go; *brahma*—(to) Brahman; *brahma-vidaḥ*—knowers of Brahman; *janāḥ*—persons.

Those who know Brahman and depart during fire, light, day, the bright lunar fortnight, and the six months of the sun's northern solstice go to Brahman.

Text 25

धूमो रात्रिस्तथा कृष्णः षण्मासा दक्षिणायनम् ।
तत्र चान्द्रमसं ज्योतिर्योगी प्राप्य निवर्तते ॥२५॥

dhūmo rātris tathā kṛṣṇaḥ ṣaṇ-māsā dakṣiṇāyanam/
tatra cāndramasaṁ jyotir yogī prāpya nivartate//

dhūmaḥ—smoke; *rātriḥ*—night; *tathā*—also; *kṛṣṇaḥ*—the dark fortnight; *ṣaṭ-māsāḥ*—six months; *dakṣiṇa-ayanam*—southern phase of the sun; *tatra*—there; *cāndra-masam*—moon; *jyotiḥ*—light; *yogī*—*yogī; prāpya*—attaining; *nivartate*—returns.

The yogī who departs during smoke, night, the dark lunar fortnight, and the sun's six month southern solstice attains the lunar light and returns.

Text 26

शुक्लकृष्णे गती ह्येते जगतः शाश्वते मते ।
एकया यात्यनावृत्तिमन्ययावर्तते पुनः ॥२६॥

śukla-kṛṣṇe gatī hy ete jagataḥ śāśvate mate/
ekayā yāty anāvṛttim anyayāvartate punaḥ//

śukla—light; *kṛṣṇe*—dark; *gatī*—paths; *hi*—certainly; *ete*—these two; *jagataḥ*—of the world; *śāśvate*—primeval; *mate*—opinion; *ekayā*—by one;

yāti—goes; *anāvṛttim*—nonreturn; *anyayā*—by the other; *āvartate*—returns; *punaḥ*—again.

These two well-known paths of this world, that of light and that of darkness, are considered primeval. By one, one does not return, by the other, one returns.

In verse 24 Kṛṣṇa describes *jñāna-yogīs*, who know Brahman. They take the path of light and attain Brahman. In verse 25 Kṛṣṇa describes *karma-yogīs*, who still have material desire. They take the dark path and return, remaining in *saṁsāra*. Having discussed these two paths and their respective travellers, Kṛṣṇa turns his attention to his unalloyed devotees, *bhakti-yogīs*. They are aware of both the dark and light paths, but take another alternative.

Text 27

नैते सृती पार्थ जानन् योगी मुह्यति कश्चन ।
तस्मात्सर्वेषु कालेषु योगयुक्तो भवार्जुन ॥२७॥

naite sṛtī pārtha jānan yogī muhyati kaścana/
tasmāt sarveṣu kāleṣu yoga-yukto bhavārjuna//

na—not; *ete*—these two; *sṛtī*—paths; *pārtha*—O son of Pṛthā; *jānan*—knowing; *yogī*—*yogī*; *muhyati*—is confused; *kaścana*—any; *tasmāt*—therefore; *sarveṣu kāleṣu*—at all times; *yoga-yuktaḥ*—steadfast in *yoga*; *bhava*—be; *arjuna*—O Arjuna.

Knowing these two paths, the yogī is not confused at all. Therefore, at all times be steadfast in yoga, Arjuna.

After having spoken about pure devotion (*ananya-cetāḥ satataṁ yo māṁ smarati nityaśaḥ*) and how his devotees easily (*sulabhaḥ*) attain his abode, Kṛṣṇa tells Arjuna of two paths taken by departed souls: one in light, the other in darkness.

This section of *Śrī Gītā* is taken metaphorically by Baladeva Vidyābhūṣaṇa. He also understands it as referring to the paths of devotion mixed with both material desire (the dark path) and desire for liberation (the path of light). Furthermore, this section indirectly underscores by way of contrast the sublime nature of the path of pure devotion. After describing the path of light and that of darkness, Kṛṣṇa remarks that pure devotees need not be concerned with either of them.

Metaphorically, the two paths speak of time *(kāla)*. Śrī Kṛṣṇa says, *yatra kāle tv anāvṛttim āvṛttiṁ caiva yoginaḥ prayātā:* "I shall now speak of that time at which departing *yogīs* return and do not return." Kṛṣṇa appears to be speaking about a particular time, yet in describing the path of light, he mentions not only time, but objects: fire, light, day, the fortnight of the bright moon, *uttarāyaṇa (agnir jyotir ahaḥ śuklaḥ ṣaṇ-māsā uttarāyaṇam)*. The path of darkness is also described in terms of times and objects: *dakṣiṇāyana*, smoke, night, the dark fortnight *(dhūmo rātris tathā kṛṣṇaḥ ṣaṇ-māsā dakṣiṇāyanam)*. Had Kṛṣṇa not been speaking of time metaphorically, the objects such as fire, light, and smoke would not be included, as they have nothing to do with time.

What then is Kṛṣṇa describing? By mentioning particular times and objects, he is referring to the deities that preside over them, deities that are designated to assist the soul in its passage *(ātivāhika-devas)*, as mentioned in the *Upaniṣads*.[7] As a grove that has a majority of mangos is called a mango grove, even when other trees are also present there, similarly, since the series of deities that the passing soul meets is predominated by deities of time—the day, fortnight, six months—the word *time* is used to refer to the entire series of deities.

Stressing two paths, one of return, the other of no return, Kṛṣṇa tells us that in the least we should take the path of no return by way of culturing spiritual knowledge. We should be concerned with this—passing beyond time—not any particular time of passage. More than the details of the paths, Kṛṣṇa stresses that there are two of them: one of return, the other of no return. Those who know these two, he concludes, are not bewildered. He implies in his conclusion that they are not bewildered because they take the path of no return, which is obviously better. Thus the wise follow the path of light, as do most devotees.

However, not all devotees follow the path of light Kṛṣṇa refers to. Here we come to the greater value of understanding this abstract section of the *Gītā*. It highlights the complexity involved in passage for those on paths other than that of pure devotion. The sublime nature of *śuddha-bhakti* is that it has the power to attract Kṛṣṇa *(kṛṣṇākarṣiṇī)*.[8] For those unalloyed *(ananya)* devotees who have spent their lives pining for Kṛṣṇa *(nitya-yuktasya)*, as their time of passage approaches, Kṛṣṇa himself loses patience

7. See *Govinda Bhāṣya* on Vs. 4.3. See also Vs. 4.2.20.
8. Brs. 1.1.17

and cannot wait for them to gradually come to him through the presiding deities on the path of light.

Gopāla-tāpanī (1.23) informs us that Kṛṣṇa directly reveals himself to those who worship him (the cowherd) by the *gopāla-mantra*. This is confirmed later in the *Gītā* (12.6–7) when Kṛṣṇa tells Arjuna that *mat-parāḥ* (those who are attached to me as the highest goal) *teṣām ahaṁ samuddhartā* (I personally deliver them) *na cirāt* (very quickly). In chapter 9 of the *Gītā*, Kṛṣṇa assures Arjuna that he personally carries his unalloyed devotees *(vahāmy aham)* as a husband carries his bride across the threshold into the house of *prema-bhakti*. In chapter 12, verses 6 and 7, Kṛṣṇa also affirms his personal involvement in the deliverance of his unalloyed devotees.

Bādarāyaṇa says in his *sūtras* (4.3.16), *viśeṣam ca darṣayati*, implying that the scripture declares a difference between the passing from the world of *ananya* devotees and that of others. Nārada Muni's life and liberation related in his own words in the *Bhāgavata* (1.6.27–28) also serve to illustrate this difference, as do the words of the *Varāha Purāṇa*, "By my sweet will I place him on Garuḍa's[9] shoulders and bring him unhindered to the supreme abode without any need for the path of *arcirādi*."[10]

Arcirādi refers to the path of light under discussion, in which the first deity is Arci, the *deva* of light, the last being four-faced Prajāpati Brahmā. After reaching Brahmā, *jñānīs* and *yogīs* attain liberation along with him at the end of his very long life. Altogether there are thirteen deities on the path of light, all of which are not directly mentioned in the *Gītā*. As the desireless *jñānī* or *yogī* leaves his body through the 101st coronary artery, he moves along the path of light from one deity to the next, never to return to birth and death. This path is also tread by some devotees, for only the unalloyed devotees are directly delivered by their Lord.

Thus the import of *Śrī Gītā* in describing the paths of light and darkness is twofold. Kṛṣṇa tells us that in general we should take the path of light through the culture of spiritual knowledge, lest we for all of our efforts gain but a return ticket to the world of birth and death. Furthermore, he tells us that those who are *mahātmās*, great souls, while in knowledge of these paths, need not be concerned with either of them, complicated as they are.[11] Their path is simple and expedient, *tasyāhaṁ sulabhaḥ pārtha*.

9. Kṛṣṇa/Viṣṇu's bird carrier.
10. Cited in *Govinda Bhāṣya* 4.3.16.
11. See Bg. 8.15.

Furthermore, as Kṛṣṇa concludes in the next verse, the path of devotion is surpassed by no other practice.

Text 28

वेदेषु यज्ञेषु तपःसु चैव
दानेषु यत्पुण्यफलं प्रदिष्टम् ।
अत्येति तत्सर्वमिदं विदित्वा
योगी परं स्थानमुपैति चाद्यम् ॥२८॥

vedeṣu yajñeṣu tapaḥsu caiva
dāneṣu yat puṇya-phalaṁ pradiṣṭam/
atyeti tat sarvam idaṁ viditvā
yogī paraṁ sthānam upaiti cādyam//

vedeṣu—in the *Vedas; yajñeṣu*—in the *yajñas; tapaḥsu*—in austerities; *ca*—also; *eva*—certainly; *dāneṣu*—in charities; *yat*—which; *puṇya-phalam*—fruit of piety; *pradiṣṭam*—prescribed; *atyeti*—transcends; *tat sarvam*—all this; *idam*—this; *viditvā*—knowing; *yogī*—the *yogī; param*—supreme; *sthānam*—abode; *upaiti*—attains; *ca*—also; *ādyam*—primal.

Knowing all of this, the yogī transcends whatever results are attained by study of the Vedas, sacrifice, austerity, charity, as well as the fruit of piety. He attains the supreme primal abode.

Such is the virtue of knowing that which Kṛṣṇa teaches Arjuna in this chapter. All of this (*sarvam idam*)—studying the *Vedas*, sacrifice, austerity, charity, as well as piety and its fruit—is surpassed by one who understands what Kṛṣṇa teaches in this chapter. That which is surpassed is not limited to the specific practices mentioned. Further implied is that even when performing these acts optimally (under the direction of the guru, at the appropriate time, and so on) the subsequent results are not comparable to understanding this chapter.

This chapter's glory, however, rests not merely on the fact that its knowledge surpasses all of the above, but that one who understands it attains Kṛṣṇa's primal and supreme abode, *yogī paraṁ sthānam upaiti cādyam*. The abode of Kṛṣṇa is described throughout the sacred literature: a mystic, poetic land of love, where all things are possible, as all desire is in concert with the Absolute. Where talking is song and walking is dance, one can only imagine what the song and dance of that place must be, a realm known by only a very few transcendentalists as Goloka.[12]

The *yogī* referred to herein is the true spiritual practitioner in general and the unalloyed devotee in particular. Kṛṣṇa himself and his abode are attained only by unalloyed devotion. This is the attainment Kṛṣṇa speaks of here. Thus Kṛṣṇa compellingly concludes this chapter with emphasis on devotion and carries this emphasis into the next, wherein pure devotion reaches its climax, only to overflow into chapter 10.

12. Br. Sm. 5.56. The fifth chapter of Br. Sm. describes the abode of Kṛṣṇa, known as Goloka.

CHAPTER NINE

राजगुह्ययोगः
Rāja-Guhya-yoga

YOGA OF HIDDEN TREASURE

Text 1

श्रीभगवानुवाच
इदं तु ते गुह्यतमं प्रवक्ष्याम्यनसूयवे ।
ज्ञानं विज्ञानसहितं यज्ज्ञात्वा मोक्ष्यसेऽशुभात् ॥१॥

śrī-bhagavān uvāca
idaṁ tu te guhyatamaṁ pravakṣyāmy anasūyave/
jñānaṁ vijñāna-sahitaṁ yaj jñātvā mokṣyase 'śubhāt//

śrī-bhagavān uvāca—the Lord of Śrī said; *idam*—this; *tu*—but; *te*—to you; *guhya-tamam*—the most secret; *pravakṣyāmi*—I shall explain; *anasūyave*—to the nonenvious; *jñānam*—theoretical knowledge; *vijñāna*—realized knowledge; *sahitam*—with; *yat*—which; *jñātvā*—knowing; *mokṣyase*—you shall be free; *aśubhāt*—from inauspiciousness.

The Lord of Śrī said: O Arjuna, you are nonenvious, and therefore I shall impart this supreme secret to you, in terms of both theory and experience, knowing which you shall be free from inauspiciousness.

Kṛṣṇa begins this chapter with three verses eulogizing the knowledge he will reveal. Here he wants to get Arjuna's undivided attention, as the knowledge to be revealed is very important. Furthermore, Kṛṣṇa himself is filled with emotion as he begins to speak about that by which he is conquered—pure devotion. Śrīdhara Swāmī says that Kṛṣṇa, having first taught in the previous two chapters that he is attained through devotion alone and by no other means, introduces this chapter to expound his own incomprehensible glory and the extraordinary power of devotion.

Here the word *tu* (but) indicates that this knowledge is more confidential than that which he has already described. After concluding the previous chapter with glorification of that which was revealed therein, here Kṛṣṇa says, "But now I shall impart higher understanding." Arjuna's *adhikāra* (eligibility) is also stated: he is nonenvious. Arjuna never tires of hearing the glory of Kṛṣṇa. That is, even after hearing Kṛṣṇa praise himself repeatedly, Arjuna finds no fault in him, nor does he lose interest. Arjuna is thus characterized as both sincere and self-controlled.

The wisdom Kṛṣṇa imparts in this chapter is explained theoretically in scripture. It is the knowledge of his Godhood, knowing which his devotee, through its application, gradually experiences Kṛṣṇa's sweetness in love. Being the knowledge of pure devotion, it is most confidential *(guhyatamam)*, more so than the wisdom of the difference between matter and spirit, the realization of Brahman and Paramātmā stressed in the first six chapters, and the culture of devotion mixed with *karma*, *jñāna*, and *yoga* mentioned in the previous two chapters. It is the esoteric mystery of divine love that has surfaced here and there throughout the text and particularly in the previous two chapters. This is the essence of the *Gītā*, and here it will be brought out in detail, both its philosophical underpinning and practical application.

The insight revealed in this chapter is the same divine knowledge that Kṛṣṇa revealed to Brahmā in the original four verses of *Śrīmad-Bhāgavatam*. There Kṛṣṇa says, *jñānaṁ parama-guhyaṁ me yad vijñāna-samanvitam sarahasyam:* "Knowledge about me as described in the scriptures is very confidential, and it has to be realized in conjunction with confidential devotional service." (ŚB. 2.9.31) Gauḍīya Vaiṣṇava *ācāryas* have consistently rendered *sarahasyam* as "with devotional service." Both Jīva Goswāmī and Viśvanātha Cakravartī Ṭhākura have labeled this devotional service *prema-bhakti*. The idea that knowledge culminates in devotion and love was also discussed in the *Gītā*'s seventh chapter (Bg. 7.19).

Text 2

राजविद्या राजगुह्यं पवित्रमिदमुत्तमम् ।
प्रत्यक्षावगमं धर्म्यं सुसुखं कर्तुमव्ययम् ॥२॥

rāja-vidyā rāja-guhyaṁ pavitram idam uttamam/
pratyakṣāvagamaṁ dharmyaṁ su-sukhaṁ kartum avyayam//

rāja-vidyā—the king of knowledge; *rāja-guhyam*—the king of secrets; *pavitram*—the purifier; *idam*—this; *uttamam*—ultimate; *pratyakṣa*—directly;

avagamam—perceivable; *dharmyam*—religious; *su-sukham*—easy; *kartum*—to practice; *avyayam*—imperishable.

This is the king of knowledge, the king of secrets, the ultimate purifier. It is directly perceivable, religious, easy to practice, and imperishable.

The knowledge of pure devotion is both the king of knowledge *(rāja-vidyā)* and the knowledge of kings *(rājānāṁ vidyā)*.[1] The kings of this world are the senses, and one who conquers them is a true king. This knowledge is for such persons, and it will also make such persons kings. What is the knowledge of kings? It is their wisdom—the knowledge by which they are kings in reality. It is that which they keep hidden. Thus it is secret knowledge as well. It is the king of secrets *(rāja-guhya)* because it is hidden away in the scripture, and thus it is concealed here in the middle of the *Gītā*'s eighteen chapters.

Jīva Goswāmī comments both in his *Kṛṣṇa-sandarbha* (186) and his commentary on *Gopāla-tāpanī Upaniṣad* (1.5) that the word *vidyā* refers to the highest *bhakti*. He cites this verse in explaining *Gopāla-tāpanī Upaniṣad*'s statement, *gopījanāvidyā-kalā-prerakaḥ:* "[Kṛṣṇa] is the master *(preraka)* of the *gopīs*, who are potencies *(kalā)* of the knowledge *(vidyā)* that is love characterized by compassion." Śrī Jīva further states in his *Gopāla-tāpanī* commentary: "Those who are the forms or parts *(kalāḥ)* of the perfect knowledge *(ā-vidyā)* that is loving devotion in a specific mood are the *gopī-jana*. He who inspires them—who engages them in his personal pastimes—is their lover." Thus the word *vidyā* in this verse also indicates the highest devotion.

The word *vidyā* is often rendered "practical knowledge," differentiating it from abstract and theoretical knowledge. This common understanding of *vidyā* finds the word often used in reference to magical spells, which have a practical effect. *Bhakti* is also practical knowledge that results in the magical effect of loving Kṛṣṇa. It is the magic that transforms all things by way of unveiling their connection with their spiritual origin.

It has been said that Vedānta deals with secret knowledge, not the common knowledge in which the dualities of good, bad, happy, and sad are apparent. It deals with the knowledge of the underlying unity of all

1. Ordinarily, the words *rāja-vidyā* and *rāja-guhyam* mean "knowledge of kings" and "the secret of kings"; however, according to *Pāṇini Sūtras* secondary words *(upasarjana)* can be placed first. Thus *rāja-vidyā* and *rāja-guhyam* mean "the king of knowledge" and "the king of secrets."

things—knowledge of oneness, as opposed to the knowledge of duality. However, Baladeva Vidyābhūṣaṇa in his Vedānta commentary, *Govinda Bhāṣya*,[2] alludes to the idea that uncommon, or secret, knowledge is not the mere opposite of common knowledge. Secret knowledge is not concerned merely with the underlying unity of all things, but with the fact that within the unity of Brahman there is simultaneously a variegatedness that does not compromise its unity. Indeed, such knowledge makes the knowledge of the underlying unity of Brahman common knowledge in comparison.

This secret knowledge is directly perceivable *(pratyakṣāvagamam)*. It is *rasānanda*, the taste and feeling of devotional life. That it is declared religious *(dharmyam)* indicates that this knowledge is transcendental devotion. Generally, spiritual knowledge retires religious practice. As one's heart is purified through religious practice, knowledge of the self manifests, and this knowledge frees one from religious duties. This has been taught in the first six chapters of the *Gītā*. Thus with the word *dharmyam*, Kṛṣṇa speaks of *bhakti* as religious life in transcendence replete with knowledge that delivers one from material duality. This *dharma* is an eternal suprareligious expression—the *prema-dharma* of devotional life.

Jīva Goswāmī has coined the term *acintya-bhedābheda* (inconceivable simultaneous identity and difference) to describe the Vedānta of Gauḍīya Vaiṣṇavism. The *abheda* (identity) is the philosophical reality of the nondifference between God and all things, while the *bheda* (difference) is Gauḍīya Vedānta's religious expression in transcendence that makes for an undivided yet variegated Absolute. This doctrine is an apt description of the knowledge of this chapter, love *(prema)* that is by nature a oneness expressing itself variously.

The knowledge that is *bhakti* is supremely purifying. Purification involves the clearing of *karma*. Our *karma* exists not only in terms of that which we are presently experiencing; it is also stored in seed in the form of desire and acquired tendencies. Whereas knowledge of the self has the power to destroy *karma* before it bears fruit, it cannot change one's manifest *karma*, or *prārabdha-karma*. Pure devotion, on the other hand, can clear even one's *prārabdha-karma*, that which is already bearing fruit in this life.[3]

Kṛṣṇa says that *bhakti* is easily or happily performed. At the same time, it is imperishable. While most things easily performed do not produce lasting

2. See commentary on Vs. 1.1.2.

3. See ŚB. 3.33.6 and Brs. 1.1.23, citing *Padma Purāṇa*.

results, this is not the case with *śuddha-bhakti*. It is easily performed, yet the result is permanent.

Having eulogized its virtues directly, Kṛṣṇa further glorifies *bhakti* by way of stating the adverse effects that result from not accepting it. He does so in the next verse anticipating Arjuna's question: "If this path is both the best and easiest, why are there so many souls still in *saṁsāra*? Why don't they take to *bhakti*?"

Text 3

अश्रद्दधानाः पुरुषा धर्मस्यास्य परन्तप ।
अप्राप्य मां निवर्तन्ते मृत्युसंसारवर्त्मनि ॥३॥

aśraddadhānāḥ puruṣā dharmasyāsya parantapa/
aprāpya māṁ nivartante mṛtyu-saṁsāra-vartmani//

aśraddadhānāḥ—faithless; *puruṣāḥ*—people; *dharmasya*—of *dharma*; *asya*—of it; *parantapa*—O destroyer of enemies; *aprāpya*—without attaining; *mām*—me; *nivartante*—come back; *mṛtyu*—death; *saṁsāra*—transmigration; *vartmani*—on the path.

People who do not have faith in this (prema) dharma, O destroyer of enemies, do not attain me. They are reborn on the path of death and transmigration.

Śraddhā (faith) that simply by serving Kṛṣṇa one's life will be perfect indicates one's eligibility for *bhakti*. Rūpa Goswāmī says, *ādau śraddhā: bhakti* begins with *śraddhā* (Brs. 1.4.15). Those lacking *śraddhā (aśraddadhānāḥ)* remain in *saṁsāra*. They do not take to *bhakti* because they do not believe what Kṛṣṇa says about it. It is, after all, hard to imagine that the highest thing is so easily attainable. The combination of these two things—exalted status and accessibility—makes for true magnanimity: giving the highest thing to the least qualified. Such magnanimity is nowhere better exemplified than in Śrī Caitanya, who distributed *prema-bhakti* to anyone and everyone without consideration of their social or religious status.

Here Kṛṣṇa indicates that liberation by any means requires that the element of *bhakti* be present in one's practice, and when *bhakti* itself is unalloyed, one attains the highest form of liberation, *prema-dharma*.

In the next three texts, Kṛṣṇa begins to discuss the most confidential knowledge by first explaining its metaphysical basis in two verses and then giving an example to help Arjuna understand the philosophical underpinning of this knowledge.

Text 4

मया ततमिदं सर्वं जगदव्यक्तमूर्तिना ।
मत्स्थानि सर्वभूतानि न चाहं तेष्ववस्थितः ॥४॥

mayā tatam idaṁ sarvaṁ jagad avyakta-mūrtinā/
mat-sthāni sarva-bhūtāni na cāhaṁ teṣv avasthitaḥ//

mayā—by me; *tatam*—pervaded; *idam*—this; *sarvam*—entire; *jagat*—creation; *avyakta-mūrtinā*—by the unmanifested form; *mat-sthāni*—in me; *sarva-bhūtāni*—all created beings; *na*—not; *ca*—also; *aham*—I; *teṣu*—in them; *avasthitaḥ*—situated.

This entire creation is pervaded by me in my unmanifest form. All created beings are situated in me, but I am not situated in them.

In this chapter Kṛṣṇa will reveal something about the nature of "sweet" devotion, Vraja *bhakti*. This devotion involves the ultimate manifestation of divinity (Vraja Kṛṣṇa) relating intimately with his devotees, such that his Godhood is concealed. Were it not concealed, such intimacy could not take place, nor would it be sweet if it did not manifest in relation to the ultimate feature of divinity. When the Supreme Godhead relates with his devotee as if he were not God, and as if his devotee were the highest object of love, this is sweet devotion. Thus sweet devotion has as its background the Godhood of the Absolute. In this verse through the tenth, Kṛṣṇa speaks of his majesty *(aiśvarya)*, knowledge of which is necessary for entering the realm of sweet devotion, wherein it is ultimately suppressed by the power of devotion itself. The theological basis for this loving devotion is Kṛṣṇa's majesty—his Godhood. First philosophy and theology (theory/*tattva*), then love (realization/*bhāva*).

Kṛṣṇa says here that although his form is unmanifest, it is all-pervasive. The words *avyakta-mūrtinā* are significant. Kṛṣṇa is not ultimately formless and thereby all-pervasive. His form is all-pervasive, although unmanifest to mundane eyes. All beings exist in Kṛṣṇa, but he is not in them, in that he is not attached to the mundane world as are the living beings. Otherwise, the *śruti* says, "Having projected it (the world), he entered into it." (Tai. Up. 2.6) He is in the world, but not of it.

Kṛṣṇa is the cause, the world is the effect. The effect is present in the cause, and the cause invisibly pervades the effect.

Text 5

न च मत्स्थानि भूतानि पश्य मे योगमैश्वरम् ।
भूतभृन्न च भूतस्थो ममात्मा भूतभावनः ॥५॥

na ca mat-sthāni bhūtāni paśya me yogam aiśvaram/
bhūta-bhṛn na ca bhūta-stho mamātmā bhūta-bhāvanaḥ//

na—not; *ca*—also; *mat-sthāni*—abiding in me; *bhūtāni*—beings; *paśya*—behold; *me*—my; *yogam aiśvaram*—Godly power; *bhūta-bhṛt*—the sustainer of beings; *na*—never; *ca*—also; *bhūta-sthaḥ*—in the created beings; *mama*—my; *ātmā*—self; *bhūta-bhāvanaḥ*—the cause of beings.

And yet beings do not abide in me. Behold my Godly power! While I am the sustainer and cause of beings, my Self is not contained in created beings.

Here Kṛṣṇa appears to contradict himself. In the previous verse he said that all beings are within him, yet here he says the opposite: "beings do not abide in me." Created beings of this world do and do not abide in him at the same time. How does Kṛṣṇa accomplish this impossible task? He says, *paśya me yogam aiśvaram:* "Behold my Godly power, by which I do the impossible!"[4]

In the metaphysic of the Gauḍīya Vaiṣṇavas, Jīva Goswāmī has included the word *acintya* (inconceivable). Kṛṣṇa's inconceivable *śakti* reconciles all apparent contradictions *(acintya-bhedābheda)*. He is one with the world while simultaneously different from it. He maintains all living beings without being within them!

While created beings are within their bodies and sustain them due to being attached to them, Kṛṣṇa enters and sustains all without attachment. It is not out of a sense of self-preservation that Kṛṣṇa sustains the world.

Kṛṣṇa next gives an example to help Arjuna understand. However, in doing so, he appears to contradict himself again by saying that all beings do abide in him!

4. Here the word *yoga* must be understood as power and not spiritual discipline. Baladeva Vidyābhūṣaṇa explains *yoga* thus: "The etymological root of the word *yoga* is 'that which is used in difficult tasks.' In other words, *yoga* is Kṛṣṇa's capacity *(dharma)* characterized by the determination to fulfill his promises through a body of inconceivable energies."

Text 6

यथाकाशस्थितो नित्यं वायुः सर्वत्रगो महान् ।
तथा सर्वाणि भूतानि मत्स्थानीत्युपधारय ॥६॥

yathākāśa-sthito nityaṁ vāyuḥ sarvatra-go mahān/
tathā sarvāṇi bhūtāni mat-sthānīty upadhāraya//

yathā—as; *ākāśa-sthitaḥ*—situated in the sky; *nityam*—always; *vāyuḥ*—the wind; *sarvatra-gaḥ*—blowing everywhere; *mahān*—mighty; *tathā*—similarly; *sarvāṇi bhūtāni*—all created beings; *mat-sthāni*—situated in me; *iti*—thus; *upadhāraya*—know.

Just as the air blows everywhere, being always situated within the sky, so are all beings situated in me.

While Kṛṣṇa says here that all beings are situated in him, as opposed to having said they are not in the previous verse, he qualifies his statement to explain himself to Arjuna. All beings *are* in him inasmuch as the wind is contained in space. Although wind is contained in space, space is not attached to or dependent on wind. Although the two, space and wind, have a relationship as sustainer and sustained, they are not in contact with one another. Just as the wind, although everywhere, is always in space, for without space nothing can exist, at the same time wind has no connection with space because space has no parts to be connected with, being all-pervading.

Viśvanātha Cakravartī Ṭhākura explains that this example does not entirely explain the nature of Kṛṣṇa's relationship with the world, which Kṛṣṇa himself has said he maintains by his mystic opulence, or inconceivable power. The example falls short inasmuch as while both the sky and wind are unconscious, Kṛṣṇa and the living beings are conscious. Consciousness is the basis of attachment, yet Kṛṣṇa remains unattached to that which he sustains. This is the inconceivable mystic reality of Kṛṣṇa's identity with and difference from the world and the living beings, to which Viśvanātha Cakravartī Ṭhākura says we must simply fold our hands and offer respect, acknowledging Kṛṣṇa's greatness.

Having explained his greatness in relation to the sustenance of the world, Kṛṣṇa next explains his position in relation to its creation and destruction. He does so in accordance with Arjuna's mental question concerning the state of affairs at the time of the cosmic dissolution. What happens to all the living beings who abide in Kṛṣṇa at that time?

Text 7

सर्वभूतानि कौन्तेय प्रकृतिं यान्ति मामिकाम् ।
कल्पक्षये पुनस्तानि कल्पादौ विसृजाम्यहम् ॥७॥

sarva-bhūtāni kaunteya prakṛtiṁ yānti māmikām/
kalpa-kṣaye punas tāni kalpādau visṛjāmy aham//

sarva-bhūtāni—all beings; *kaunteya*—O son of Kuntī; *prakṛtim*—material nature; *yānti*—enter; *māmikām*—my; *kalpa-kṣaye*—at the end of the *kalpa*; *punaḥ*—again; *tāni*—those; *kalpa-ādau*—at the beginning of the *kalpa*; *visṛjāmi*—send forth; *aham*—I.

At the end of a cycle of kalpas, O son of Kuntī, all beings enter my material nature; at the beginning of the next cycle, I again send them forth.

Kṛṣṇa speaks to Arjuna, the son of Kuntī, with compassion for the living beings trapped in the endless cycle of material nature, as he explains his position in relation to their plight. He sends them forth through his manifestation as primary creator (Mahā-Viṣṇu). As explained in chapter 4, he then enters the world to liberate them. He does this in his original form as Kṛṣṇa or as one of his *avatāras*.

Here *kalpa-kṣaye* and *kalpādau* indicate, respectively, the end of the cycle of *kalpas* that make up Brahmā's life and the beginning of a new life of Brahmā. The living beings' merger into Kṛṣṇa's material nature involves their being suspended in subtle form as the modes of material nature *(guṇas)* become unmanifest. This merging of the living beings into the unmanifest state is different than that described in chapter 8 (Bg. 8.18). In chapter 8 Kṛṣṇa spoke of the partial dissolution of the world at the end of each of Brahmā's days. Here he is speaking about the complete dissolution of the manifest world at the end of Brahmā's life.

Kṛṣṇa next explains how he sends the living beings forth at the beginning of the next cycle of creation, remaining unattached and changeless himself.

Text 8

प्रकृतिं स्वामवष्टभ्य विसृजामि पुनः पुनः ।
भूतग्राममिमं कृत्स्नमवशं प्रकृतेर्वशात् ॥८॥

prakṛtiṁ svām avaṣṭabhya visṛjāmi punaḥ punaḥ/
bhūta-grāmam imaṁ kṛtsnam avaśaṁ prakṛter vaśāt//

prakṛtim—material nature; *svām*—my own; *avaṣṭabhya*—presiding over; *visṛjāmi*—I send forth; *punaḥ punaḥ*—again and again; *bhūta-grāmam*—the aggregate of beings; *imam*—this; *kṛtsnam*—entire; *avaśam*—helpless; *prakṛteḥ vaśāt*—in accordance with their natures.

Presiding over my material nature, I again and again send forth this entire aggregate of helpless beings in accordance with their natures.

In this verse, Kṛṣṇa uses the same words he used in chapter 4 (Bg. 4.6), *prakṛtiṁ svām avaṣṭabhya*. The words *adhiṣṭhāya* and *avaṣṭabhya* are synonymous. In chapter 4 Kṛṣṇa was speaking about his own descent as the *avatāra*. As the *avatāra*, God enters the world for *līlā* and remains unaffected by the world's influence, just as a governor enters a prison but does not become a prisoner. Here Kṛṣṇa is speaking about how as God (Viṣṇu) he rules over material nature in the act of creation.

As he who presides over his own material nature, God sends forth the living beings at the time of creation in accordance with their *karma*, or acquired natures. Nature itself is the agency through which creation takes place, and though presiding over the creation, God is personally neither transformed nor attached. Deferring to the principle of *karma*, which he himself has put in place, he allows the living beings to become manifest again in accordance with the desires and qualities they had acquired at the time of dissolution. As such, God remains uninvolved, although he is behind the entire cosmic manifestation.

Text 9

न च मां तानि कर्माणि निबध्नन्ति धनञ्जय ।
उदासीनवदासीनमसक्तं तेषु कर्मसु ॥९॥

na ca māṁ tāni karmāṇi nibadhnanti dhanañjaya/
udāsīna-vad āsīnam asaktaṁ teṣu karmasu//

na—not; *ca*—also; *mām*—me; *tāni*—these; *karmāṇi*—actions; *nibadhnanti*—bind; *dhanañjaya*—O conqueror of wealth; *udāsīna-vat*—like one who is indifferent; *āsīnam*—remaining; *asaktam*—unattached; *teṣu*—to those; *karmasu*—activities.

O Dhanañjaya, these actions do not bind me, as I remain unattached to them like one indifferent.

The *Bhagavad-gītā* is based on the *Upaniṣads*. Thus it preserves the impartiality of the Absolute while introducing the concept of a personal, merciful, loving God. Here Kṛṣṇa describes himself as impartial, yet as we shall see later on in this chapter, he is also merciful and loving at heart. As the great God of justice he is impartial like a high court judge, but in his private life with his intimate friends he is motivated by the spiritual partiality of love. This contrast is brought out in verse 29 of this chapter.

The birth of living beings is a result of beginningless *karma*, not God's desire. Kṛṣṇa describes himself as *udāsīnavad āsīnam*, seated as if neutral. As God he is not affected by partiality. Observing the principle of beginningless *karma*, God is just. Were he not so, there would be no question of mercy, which involves occasionally overriding justice. Were justice overruled in all cases, there would be no meaning to mercy, and justice would have no say. Thus mercy requires observance of the principle of justice, as it does overruling it. God does just that. Because he remains neutral, he is impartial, yet he is at the same time the doer. *Udāsīnavat* means "as if neutral." In reality, he is neutral, active, just, and impartial. In the form of his incarnations he is merciful, and as Kṛṣṇa he is particularly so. Mercifully here, he continues to explain these points to Arjuna in the next verse.

Text 10

मयाध्यक्षेण प्रकृतिः सूयते सचराचरम् ।
हेतुनानेन कौन्तेय जगद् विपरिवर्तते ॥१०॥

mayādhyakṣeṇa prakṛtiḥ sūyate sa-carācaram/
hetunānena kaunteya jagad viparivartate//

mayā—by me; *adhyakṣeṇa*—as overseer; *prakṛtiḥ*—material nature; *sūyate*—brings forth; *sa-cara-acaram*—both the animate and the inanimate things; *hetunā*—for the reason; *anena*—this; *kaunteya*—O son of Kuntī; *jagat*—the world; *viparivartate*—revolves.

Under my supervision, material nature brings forth the world of animate and inanimate things; on account of this, O son of Kuntī, the world revolves.

Here Kṛṣṇa reiterates: he is neutral, yet the doer inasmuch as material nature is dependent on him and by his will she carries out the work of creation. God sanctions and material nature acts, yet because material nature belongs to and is thus presided over *(mayādhyakṣena prakṛtiḥ)* by God, he is both the efficient *(nimitta)* and ingredient *(upādāna)* cause of the world.

This verse concludes this section in which Kṛṣṇa explains the theoretical knowledge of his extraordinary opulence. The theoretical basis of the reality of Kṛṣṇa's inconceivable simultaneous identity and difference with the world has been explained in verses 4 and 5, and Kṛṣṇa has stated his position clearly, identifying the cosmic life of Viṣṇu as an aspect of himself in verses 7 and 8. All of this knowledge of *tattva* is called *sambandha-jñāna* in the devotional school of Gauḍīya Vedānta. Such knowledge is essential for entering a life of pure devotion to Kṛṣṇa, the subject of this chapter.

Hearing Kṛṣṇa speak about himself in this way, Arjuna accepts everything Kṛṣṇa has said and is overwhelmed. He wonders why people don't revere Kṛṣṇa. Sensing Arjuna's question, Kṛṣṇa answers.

Text 11

अवजानन्ति मां मूढा मानुषीं तनुमाश्रितम् ।
परं भावमजानन्तो मम भूतमहेश्वरम् ॥११॥

avajānanti māṁ mūḍhā mānuṣīṁ tanum āśritam/
paraṁ bhāvam ajānanto mama bhūta-maheśvaram//

avajānanti—deride; *mām*—me; *mūḍhāḥ*—fools; *mānuṣīm*—in a human form; *tanum*—a body; *āśritam*—assuming; *param*—transcendental; *bhāvam*—existence; *ajānantaḥ*—not knowing; *mama*—my; *bhūta*—of all beings; *mahā-īśvaram*—the great Lord.

Fools deride me, who have assumed human form, not understanding my transcendental existence as the great Lord of all beings.

The transcendental nature of Kṛṣṇa's humanlike form is raised in this verse. Although he has explained himself to be the source of the world, it is hard to imagine that he could be so, owing to his human appearance and the limitation that accompanies the human form. How can he be the Lord of all beings?

Kṛṣṇa's acceptance of human form, *mānuṣīṁ tanum āśritam*, corresponds with his devotees' love for him. According to *Śrīmad-Bhāgavatam* (3.9.11), God appears in the heart of a mature *(paribhāvita)* devotee in a particular form relative to the devotee's pure love, *yad-yad-dhiyā ta urugāya vibhāvayanti tat-tad-vapuḥ praṇayase sad-anugrahāya*.

God's appearance in the heart of his devotee is not an event in time, as the form of God is eternally existing, and the *bhāva*, or love, of the devotee is as well. This *bhāva* is not a product of spiritual practice, *sādhya kabhu naya* (Cc. Madhya 22.107). It awakens in the purified heart of the devotee by virtue of God's grace. Those devoid of this love think that Kṛṣṇa acquired his form at some point in time as a result of previous pious deeds and austerities. Here Kṛṣṇa says that such people are fools.

Love of God has power over God, who fully gives himself to his devotee in his appearance as Kṛṣṇa. As such, Kṛṣṇa's assuming a humanlike form is spiritual and eternal, although appearing here as though within the jurisdiction of time. Humanlike in appearance, Kṛṣṇa remains the Supreme Godhead.

People often assume that the humanlike appearance of Kṛṣṇa precludes his being the ultimate expression of divinity, the Lord of all beings, *avatāras* included. People more readily accept a powerful image of the divine rather than a playful one when conceiving of the God of gods. However, play requires power. The more power one has, the more one can play. As mentioned earlier, Viśvanātha Cakravartī Ṭhākura reminds us that playing with his mother in his earthly *līlā*, Kṛṣṇa once showed her the entire universe within his mouth. In this *līlā* he demonstrated that Bhagavān is also Brahman (unlimited). He is *paraṁ-brahma*. Playful Kṛṣṇa in humanlike appearance is most powerful. At the very least, he is the Lord of all beings, more, the heart of transcendence.

Arjuna naturally wondered what happens to fools who deride Kṛṣṇa's humanlike appearance, not acknowledging its spirituality.

Text 12

मोघाशा मोघकर्माणो मोघज्ञाना विचेतसः ।
राक्षसीमासुरीं चैव प्रकृतिं मोहिनीं श्रिताः ॥१२॥

moghāśā mogha-karmāṇo mogha-jñānā vicetasaḥ/
rākṣasīm āsurīṁ caiva prakṛtiṁ mohinīṁ śritāḥ//

mogha-āśāḥ—their hopes are in vain; *mogha-karmāṇaḥ*—their actions are in vain; *mogha-jñānāḥ*—their knowledge is in vain; *vicetasaḥ*—senseless; *rākṣasīm*—the hateful and envious; *āsurīm*—ungodly sense enjoyers; *ca*—and; *eva*—certainly; *prakṛtim*—nature; *mohinīm*—bewildering; *śritāḥ*—taking shelter in.

Their hopes are in vain, their actions are in vain, their knowledge is in vain. They are senseless, taking shelter of the deluding dispositions of fiends and demons.

Baladeva Vidyābhūṣaṇa says that *rākṣasas* are those who are strongly influenced by ignorance *(tamo-guṇa)* and thus dominated by a spirit of envy, hatred, and violence. Present-day society's perpetrators of hate crimes fall into this category. The term *āsura* indicates one who takes pleasure in the senses, indicating the gross materialist influenced by passion and ignorance *(rajo-guṇa* and *tamo-guṇa)* and dominated by pride and desire. The āsuric disposition will be discussed in greater detail in chapter 16.

Viśvanātha Cakravartī explains the words *moghāśāḥ*, *mogha-karmāṇaḥ*, and *mogha-jnānāḥ* in relation to devotees, fruitive workers, and *jñānīs*, respectively. He says that those (mixed) devotees who do not consider God's form eternal have no hope *(mogha-āśāḥ)* of attaining liberation. Those desiring material gain and heavenly attainment are also frustrated in their efforts *(mogha-karmāṇaḥ)*. *Jñānīs* desiring liberation cannot attain it *(mogha-jnānāḥ)*.

Implied here is that by offending God, who descends to the world for the upliftment of humanity, people become possessed of the above dispositions in their next life or are so in this life as a result of previous offenses. Those who hope *(āśā)* that they can derive their desired result from actions irrespective of God's will fail in their attempts *(karma)*. Both their hopes and actions are in vain, as is their knowledge that appears to support their view. In short, no good can come from deriding the form of God, whereas respecting God is praiseworthy and brings about ultimate good.

Text 13

महात्मानस्तु मां पार्थ दैवीं प्रकृतिमाश्रिताः ।
भजन्त्यनन्यमनसो ज्ञात्वा भूतादिमव्ययम् ॥१३॥

mahātmānas tu māṁ pārtha daivīṁ prakṛtim āśritāḥ/
bhajanty ananya-manaso jñātvā bhūtādim avyayam//

mahā-ātmānaḥ—the great souls; *tu*—however; *mām*—me; *pārtha*—O Pārtha; *daivīm*—divine; *prakṛtim*—nature; *āśritāḥ*—having taken shelter of; *bhajanti*—worship; *ananya-manasaḥ*—with undeviated mind; *jñātvā*—knowing; *bhūta*—of beings; *ādim*—the origin; *avyayam*—imperishable.

On the other hand, O Pārtha, those great souls who take refuge in the divine nature worship me with undeviated minds, knowing me to be the origin of all beings and imperishable.

In this verse Kṛṣṇa uses the word *mahātmā* for the third and last time in the *Gītā*. Once again he uses it in reference to his unalloyed devotees. Here he describes them as having taken shelter of divine nature *(daivīṁ prakṛtim)*. This is God's internal, or primary, potency referred to in the fourth chapter (Bg. 4.6) with regard to the nature of Kṛṣṇa's descent. As Kṛṣṇa appears under the influence of his internal *śakti*, so also do his devotees move in this world under its influence.

Bhakti proper is constituted of the ingress of Kṛṣṇa's divine *śakti (svarūpa-śakti)* in the heart of the individual soul. Rūpa Goswāmī has explained this with the words *śuddha-sattva-viśeṣātmā prema-sūryāṁśu-sāmya-bhāk* (Brs. 1.3.1). *Bhāva* (ecstatic/cognitive spiritual emotion) dawns like rays of the sun of love of God in the hearts of the mature devotees with the ingress of God's primary *śakti*. When this occurs, the practitioner's mind becomes undeviated from thoughts of Kṛṣṇa, knowing him to be the origin of all *(bhūtādim)* and imperishable *(avyayam)*. Viśvanātha Cakravartī says that *avyayam* refers to the eternal, cognitive, blissful form of God *(saccidānanda-vigraham)*, which those mentioned in verses 11 and 12 deride.

In the second half of this verse, internal characteristics of *mahātmās* are mentioned *(bhajanty ananya-manaso)*. In the first three lines of the next verse, Kṛṣṇa speaks of external characteristics of his unalloyed devotees, followed by a further explanation of the nature of their internal worship. He thus explains that great souls worship him, as well as how they do so.

Text 14

सततं कीर्तयन्तो मां यतन्तश्च दृढव्रताः ।
नमस्यन्तश्च मां भक्त्या नित्ययुक्ता उपासते ॥१४॥

satataṁ kīrtayanto māṁ yatantaś ca dṛḍha-vratāḥ/
namasyantaś ca māṁ bhaktyā nitya-yuktā upāsate//

satatam—always; *kīrtayantaḥ*—chanting; *mām*—me; *yatantaḥ*—striving; *ca*—also; *dṛḍha-vratāḥ*—firmly in their vows; *namasyantaḥ*—offering obeisances; *ca*—and; *mām*—me; *bhaktyā*—with devotion; *nitya-yuktāḥ*—continuous longing for union; *upāsate*—worship.

Always chanting about me, striving firmly in their vows, and offering obeisances unto me with devotion, they worship (me) with continuous longing for union.

The words *nitya-yuktā upāsate* indicate the aspired-for spiritual relationship with Kṛṣṇa that devotees cultivate inwardly while engaged outwardly in devotional practices. They worship *(upāsate)* in quest of an eternal *(nitya)* union in *yoga (yuktā)*. Perpetual union in devotional *yoga* is a dynamic union in love. It is a union with the Absolute in purpose, in which there is a perpetual loving exchange between God and individual soul. Monistic union is not referred to in this verse. It is discussed separately in the next verse with regard to those who worship Kṛṣṇa by means other than pure devotion. Viśvanātha Cakravartī Ṭhākura further explains that the words *nitya-yuktā* indicate that *mahātmās* aspire for devotional union with Kṛṣṇa and that they will attain it in due course. It appears that Kṛṣṇa refers here not only to those who have attained *prema*. His love for his devotees causes him to address intermediate *bhāva-bhaktas* as *mahātmās* as well.[5]

The principal expression of devotion mentioned here is chanting about Kṛṣṇa *(kīrtayanto mām)*, as it is spoken of first. *Kīrti* also indicates fame. Engaging in *kīrtana* spreads the fame of God. As a by-product of this act, a person becomes famous himself by doing welfare work for others. *Kīrtana* is *para upakāra*, the highest welfare work, as the *gopīs* declare in their own *gītā* within *Śrīmad-Bhāgavatam*.[6]

The word *satatam* qualifies the practice of *kīrtana*. As in chapter 8 (Bg. 8.14), *satatam* here indicates that chanting about Kṛṣṇa is not subject to time and place. It can be performed by everyone at any time. Chanting the sacred name of Kṛṣṇa takes one to the highest spiritual attainment and reaches down to even those who are the least eligible for such attainment. In all the Hindu sacred literature, there is no more efficacious or universal practice mentioned than that of chanting the name of God and Kṛṣṇa in particular. Indeed, this is so much the case that one can find persons of all disciplines and ideals incorporating the chanting of Kṛṣṇa's name into their particular practice in order to better assure and expedite attaining their desired goal. Here, however, Kṛṣṇa speaks of those who chant for no

5. Brs. details three stages of devotion: devotion in practice *(sādhana-bhakti)*, devotion in ecstasy *(bhāva-bhakti)*, and devotion in love of God *(prema-bhakti)*.

6. ŚB. 10.31. This chapter is also known as *Gopī-gītā*.

other reason than that they love him. They chant for the sake of chanting. The *mahātmās* do this both in the stage of practice as well as in the stage of perfection—always, *satatam*.

Although there are no hard and fast rules for chanting Kṛṣṇa's name, if there are any favorable conditions or practices that assist one in chanting, *mahātmās* seek them out and incorporate them into their practice. They observe vows that are favorable to their practice with great determination (*dṛḍha-vratāḥ*). Devotees of Kṛṣṇa embrace various observances that are said to enhance devotion to Kṛṣṇa, such as fasting on Ekādaśī and honoring holy days.[7] Conversely, they avoid offending the name of Kṛṣṇa.[8]

Kṛṣṇa says that *mahātmās* bow to him with devotion. Viśvanātha Cakravartī Ṭhākura comments that Kṛṣṇa says *namasyantaś ca*, indicating the practice of paying homage as well as all other expressions of devotion (*ca*). When we offer obeisances, we say *namaḥ*: "not (*na*) me (*ma*)." *Padma Purāṇa* explains the word *namaḥ* thus: *ahaṅkṛtir ma-kāraḥ syān na-kāra tan niṣedhakaḥ*, "The Sanskrit syllable *ma* means 'material ego'; the Sanskrit syllable *na* means 'that which forbids'." Thus obeisances are to be directed to God, by which a person acknowledges that he is forbidden from acting independently from God's will. Here Kṛṣṇa says, *namasyantaś ca mām*. *Mām* (me) would be redundant were Kṛṣṇa not invoking it for emphasis: "Offering homage unto *me*, performing *kīrtana* about *me*."

To make abundantly clear who he considers a *mahātmā*, Kṛṣṇa next speaks of others who, although they worship him, are not *mahātmās*.

Text 15

ज्ञानयज्ञेन चाप्यन्ये यजन्तो मामुपासते ।
एकत्वेन पृथक्त्वेन बहुधा विश्वतोमुखम् ॥१५॥

jñāna-yajñena cāpy anye yajanto mām upāsate/
ekatvena pṛthaktvena bahudhā viśvato-mukham//

jñāna-yajñena—through knowledge; *ca*—also; *api*—certainly; *anye*—others; *yajantaḥ*—sacrifice; *mām*—me; *upāsate*—worship; *ekatvena*—in oneness; *pṛthaktvena*—as the manifold; *bahudhā*—diversity; *viśvataḥ-mukham*—pantheistic.

7. See Brs. 1.2, entire chapter.

8. *Padma Purāṇa* cites ten offenses one can commit while chanting Kṛṣṇa's name that are to be avoided, ultimately through nothing other than repeated chanting.

Others also worship me as one with themselves through the sacrifice of knowledge. Other people worship me as the manifold diversity through sacrifice, while another group worships me by viewing the universe as God.

Three types of worshippers are mentioned in this verse, none of whom are eligible for the practices mentioned in the previous verse. Unlike those culturing unalloyed devotion, they are engaged in the sacrifice of knowledge (*jñāna-yajñena*). Some are engaged in the culture of knowledge of the self's oneness (*ekatvena*) with the Absolute. Others worship various gods (*pṛthaktvena*), viewing them as symbols representing the one undifferentiated Absolute (Brahman). Others worship manifestations of nature, viewing the universe itself as God (*viśvato-mukham*).

The sacrifice of knowledge involves the culture of transcendence, which can culminate in either love of God or merely liberation, depending on one's approach. The first group mentioned in this verse directly cultures the self's likeness to Brahman. Such persons hardly worship, for worship implies a difference between worshipper and worshipped. Although such persons are in one sense the highest of the three mentioned in this verse due to their being involved in the direct culture of self-knowledge, evaluating from a devotional perspective, Bhaktivedanta Swami Prabhupāda comments that they are the lowest of the three. They have little interest in the devotion that is so dear to Kṛṣṇa, even as a means to a monistic end. If they worship at all, they worship themselves, following such scriptural mandates as "one should think, 'I am Gopāla.'" (Gt. Up. 2.38) in terms of a monistic understanding.[9] Viśvanātha Cakravartī Ṭhākura, considering from a neutral standpoint, comments that they are the highest of the three under discussion, having risen above duality.

The second class of worshippers are those who differentiate between God and themselves enough to worship various gods, understanding them to be symbolic representations of Brahman. Although their aim is also monistic, as is that of the first group, their method of approach involves worship other than that of themselves, and their practice thus acknowledges at least a provisional differentiation between themselves and God. They can be considered either lower or higher than the first group, for they are less aware of their oneness with God, yet more involved in worship,

9. According to Jīva Goswāmī, Gauḍīya Vaiṣṇavas understand this section of Gt. Up., in which one is instructed to think, "I am Gopāla," as follows: "My existence is to his as the rays of the sun are to the sun itself."

which from the devotional perspective is intrinsic to the very nature of the soul.

The third group consists of those who worship nature as God. While they are less aware of the nature of the self as consciousness, and thus its likeness to God, they are worshipful at every turn. Detailing a gradual course to devotional enlightenment in love of Kṛṣṇa, *Śrīmad-Bhāgavatam* discusses this type of conceptual orientation to devotional life, considering it to be the first step in God-realization. The *Bhāgavatam* thus recommends a provisional form of pantheism to promote the sense of worship in general. When viewed from this standpoint, this group is the best of the three. Otherwise, owing to their lack of direct experience of the self as consciousness, they can be considered the lowest of the three.

Kṛṣṇa next elaborates on how he is universally represented *(bahudhā viśvato-mukham)*. This is the second instance in which Kṛṣṇa speaks of himself in this way. He did so earlier in chapter 7 (Bg. 7.8–12). He will do so with greater elaboration in the tenth chapter and actually demonstrate his universal form in chapter 11.

Text 16

अहं क्रतुरहं यज्ञः स्वधाहमहमौषधम् ।
मन्त्रोऽहमहमेवाज्यमहमग्निरहं हुतम् ॥१६॥

ahaṁ kratur ahaṁ yajñaḥ svadhāham aham auṣadham/
mantro 'ham aham evājyam aham agnir ahaṁ hutam//

aham—I; *kratuḥ*—ritual; *aham*—I; *yajñaḥ*—sacrifice; *svadhā*—offering; *aham*—I; *aham*—I; *auṣadham*—medicinal herb; *mantraḥ*—*mantra; aham*—I; *aham*—I; *eva*—certainly; *ājyam*—ghee; *aham*—I; *agniḥ*—fire; *aham*—I; *hutam*—act of offering.

It is I who am the ritual, the sacrifice, and the offering. I am the medicinal herb, the mantra, and also the ghee. I am the fire, and I am the act of offering.

In this and the next three verses Kṛṣṇa gives some idea of how he can be thought of in the most general way. Here he identifies himself with the ritual, sacrifice, and offering that he previously identified with Brahman (Bg. 4.24). *Kratu* and *yajña* are different types of sacrifices, such as Agniṣṭoma and Vaiśvadeva, respectively. *Svadhā* refers to offerings on behalf of the deceased, such as the *śrāddha* ceremony. *Auṣadha* is the medicine derived from plants that give their life when harvested. Ghee is clarified butter, which is essential for performing Vedic rituals. *Mantra*, sacrificial fire, and the act of offering require no explanation. Here Kṛṣṇa implies that there is nothing in the aggregate of action, agent, and result that is different from him.

Text 17

पिताहमस्य जगतो माता धाता पितामहः ।
वेद्यं पवित्रम् ॐकार ऋक् साम यजुरेव च ॥१७॥

pitāham asya jagato mātā dhātā pitāmahaḥ/
vedyaṁ pavitram oṁkāra ṛk sāma yajur eva ca//

pitā—father; *aham*—I; *asya*—of this; *jagataḥ*—world; *mātā*—mother; *dhātā*—nurse; *pitāmahaḥ*—grandfather; *vedyam*—what is to be known; *pavitram*—purifier; *oṁ-kāra*—the syllable *oṁ*; *ṛk*—the *Ṛg Veda; sāma*—the *Sāma Veda; yajuḥ*—the *Yajur Veda; eva*—certainly; *ca*—and.

I am the father of the world, its mother, its nurse, and its grandfather; I am that which is to be known, the purifier, the sacred syllable oṁ, the Ṛg, Sāma, Yajur, and Atharva Vedas.

Kṛṣṇa is the father of the universe in that the glance of God is said to inject the seed of consciousness into the womb of material nature. As material nature is a product of God's secondary *śakti*, he too is this womb and thereby the mother of all. *Dhātā* is the nurse, the one who feeds.

In another sense, Brahmā, the secondary creator, is the father of the universe, whose days and nights generate and dissolve worlds. In consideration of this, Kṛṣṇa, as the source of Brahmā, is the grandfather of all.

Kṛṣṇa again identifies himself with *oṁ*, as he did in the seventh chapter (Bg. 7.8). *Gopāla-tāpanī Upaniṣad* explains the syllable *oṁ* in terms of its being identical with the *bīja-mantra* "*klīṁ*," as well as how it represents Kṛṣṇa. Jīva Goswāmī has also explained *oṁ* in terms of its signifying Kṛṣṇa, Rādhā, and the *jīva* souls.

By use of the word *ca*, the *Atharva Veda* is included with the other three: *Ṛg*, *Sāma*, and *Yajur*.

Text 18

गतिर्भर्ता प्रभुः साक्षी निवासः शरणं सुहृत् ।
प्रभवः प्रलयः स्थानं निधानं बीजमव्ययम् ॥१८॥

gatir bhartā prabhuḥ sākṣī nivāsaḥ śaraṇaṁ suhṛt/
prabhavaḥ pralayaḥ sthānaṁ nidhānaṁ bījam avyayam//

gatiḥ—goal; *bhartā*—supporter; *prabhuḥ*—master; *sākṣī*—witness; *nivāsaḥ*—abode; *śaraṇam*—refuge; *su-hṛt*—friend; *prabhavaḥ*—origin; *pralayaḥ*—dissolution; *sthānam*—maintenance; *nidhānam*—storehouse; *bījam*—seed; *avyayam*—imperishable.

I am the goal, support, master, witness, abode, refuge, friend, origin, dissolution, maintenance, storehouse, and imperishable seed.

Origin, dissolution, and maintenance affect all material manifestations. Although Kṛṣṇa is the seed, unlike other seeds which disappear with the appearance of the plant, he is imperishable.

Text 19

तपाम्यहमहं वर्षं निगृह्णाम्युत्सृजामि च ।
अमृतं चैव मृत्युश्च सदसच्चाहमर्जुन ॥१९॥

tapāmy aham ahaṁ varṣaṁ nigṛhṇāmy utsṛjāmi ca/
amṛtaṁ caiva mṛtyuś ca sad asac cāham arjuna//

tapāmi—radiate heat; *aham*—I; *aham*—I; *varṣam*—rain; *nigṛhṇāmi*—withhold; *utsṛjāmi*—send forth; *ca*—and; *amṛtam*—immortality; *ca*—and; *eva*—certainly; *mṛtyuḥ*—death; *ca*—and; *sat*—existence; *asat*—nonexistence; *ca*—and; *aham*—I; *arjuna*—O Arjuna.

O Arjuna, I radiate heat; I withhold and send forth rain. I am immortality and I am death, and I am both that which exists and that which does not exist.

With the words *sad asac cāham*, Kṛṣṇa concludes this section, declaring himself to be everything, as he has earlier in chapter 7 with the words *vāsudevaḥ sarvam iti* (Bg. 7.19). All that he has mentioned in verses 16 through 19 is an explanation of the words *bahudhā viśvato-mukham*, the concluding words of verse 15.

In verse 16 Kṛṣṇa begins by identifying himself, as he has in chapter 4 (Bg. 4.24), with sacrifice, and thus Brahman. Next in verses 17 and 18 he speaks of all the aspects of creation as well as the *Vedas* identifying them with himself. In the present verse, each one of the words is related to the functions of one of the universal gods, which as Kṛṣṇa points out here are ultimately dependent on him. Thus *tapāmy aham ahaṁ varṣam*, he is the sun (Sūrya), the rain (Indra), and so on. He is everything that exists and everything that does not ultimately endure—both spiritual and material manifestations *(sad asat)*. "Since I am all these things," Kṛṣṇa says, "one should worship me as *viśvato-mukham* (the universe)." This is a good beginning, the end result of which is actually realizing Kṛṣṇa himself to be everything *(vāsudevaḥ sarvam iti)*. One attains this realization by worshipping him exclusively, he who is immortality for those who remember him and death for those who forget his proprietorship.

Having contrasted the worship of those engaged in unalloyed devotion with those who practice the sacrifice of knowledge, Kṛṣṇa next speaks about another class of worshippers: those desirous of material gain. Their approach is not through selfless devotion, nor are they involved in the sacrifice of knowledge for the sake of liberation. While the devotees and *jñānīs* attain love of God and liberation, respectively, those mentioned next do not transcend material existence but remain in the cycle of birth and death. They worship minor gods such as those mentioned above, while unaware of the fact that it is Kṛṣṇa who empowers the gods to bestow benedictions.

Text 20

त्रैविद्या मां सोमपाः पूतपापा
 यज्ञैरिष्ट्वा स्वर्गतिं प्रार्थयन्ते ।
ते पुण्यमासाद्य सुरेन्द्रलोक-
 मश्नन्ति दिव्यान् दिवि देवभोगान् ॥२०॥

trai-vidyā māṁ soma-pāḥ pūta-pāpā
 yajñair iṣṭvā svar-gatiṁ prārthayante/
te puṇyam āsādya surendra-lokam
 aśnanti divyān divi deva-bhogān//

trai-vidyāḥ—the knowers of the three *Vedas; mām*—me; *soma-pāḥ*—drinkers of soma; *pūta*—purified; *pāpāḥ*—sins; *yajñaiḥ*—through sacrifices; *iṣṭvā*—worshipping; *svaḥ-gatim*—heavenly attainment; *prārthayante*—seek; *te*—they; *puṇyam*—pious; *āsādya*—attaining; *sura-indra*—of Indra; *lokam*—the abode; *aśnanti*—enjoy; *divyān*—godly; *divi*—in heaven; *deva-bhogān*—delights.

Those well versed in the three Vedas seek heavenly attainment after worshipping (me) through sacrifices, drinking soma, and thus becoming

purified of sin. Having acquired the results of their piety, they attain the abode of Indra, where they enjoy godly delights in heaven.

Knowers of the three *Vedas*—*Ṛg*, *Sāma*, and *Yajur*—are called Trivedī (*traividyāḥ*). They are acquainted with the technical rites performed by the Hotā, Adhvaryu, and Udgātā priests. As mentioned in the second chapter (Bg. 2.45), the *Vedas* mostly deal with the three modes of material nature and not transcendental subject matter. Only the latter portion of the *Vedas* concerns transcendental knowledge. The Trivedīs' scope of attainment lies within the three material modes. They seek heaven, the abode of Indra.

Indra, as his name indicates, is the "chief" of the gods. Etymologically related to his name is *indriya*, "senses." Indra is depicted as the chief of the sense enjoyers whose heavenly delights are the fruits of material piety. Extensive descriptions are found throughout the sacred literature of subtle, heavenly material abodes, where mind rather than the physical body predominates with all of its imaginable delights. Such descriptions, replete with details of rituals designed for attaining heavenly abodes, offer compelling impetus for a pious life. Their value pales, however, when viewed in juxtaposition to eternal life and love of Godhead.

Here Kṛṣṇa says that Trivedīs also worship him. They do so through their offerings to various gods who represent the cosmic order. As such, their worship of Kṛṣṇa is very indirect. It is devoid of knowledge of who Kṛṣṇa is or the fact that they are indirectly worshipping him. Those outside of the Vedic worldview who worship God for material advancement fall in a general sense within the category of the worshippers mentioned herein. The result of their worship is further detailed in the next verse.

Text 21

ते तं भुक्त्वा स्वर्गलोकं विशालं
क्षीणे पुण्ये मर्त्यलोकं विशन्ति ।
एवं त्रयीधर्ममनुप्रपन्ना
गतागतं कामकामा लभन्ते ॥२१॥

te taṁ bhuktvā svarga-lokaṁ viśālaṁ
kṣīṇe puṇye martya-lokaṁ viśanti/
evaṁ trayī-dharmam anuprapannā
gatāgataṁ kāma-kāmā labhante//

te—they; *tam*—that; *bhuktvā*—having enjoyed; *svarga-lokam*—heavenly realm; *viśālam*—vast; *kṣīṇe*—being exhausted; *puṇye*—merit; *martya-lokam*—the world of mortals; *viśanti*—enter; *evam*—thus; *trayī*—of the three *Vedas*; *dharmam*—religion; *anuprapannāḥ*—following; *gata-āgatam*—going and coming; *kāma-kāmāḥ*—desiring material pleasure; *labhante*—obtain.

After having enjoyed the vast heavenly realm, when their merit is exhausted, they enter the world of mortals once again. Thus those following the religion of the three Vedas, desiring material pleasure, obtain a reward that comes and goes.

Under scrutiny this path is not desirable. Although the heavenly realm is sometimes billed as immortal, such scriptural propaganda constitutes exaggeration with a view to inspire pious acts. The scripture takes a license in this regard. A life in which six of our months equal twelve heavenly hours is indeed long, but, again, when compared with eternity and love of God, it falls short, its participants doomed to earthly return.

At this point, Arjuna wonders who takes care of Kṛṣṇa's devotees' material needs. If they make no arrangement to secure material necessities, as those mentioned in this and the previous verse do in excess, how will their basic needs be met? In answer to this, Kṛṣṇa returns to speaking directly about his unalloyed devotees, having compared them with *jñānīs* and those on the *karma-mārga*.

Text 22

अनन्याश्चिन्तयन्तो मां ये जनाः पर्युपासते ।
तेषां नित्याभियुक्तानां योगक्षेमं वहाम्यहम् ॥२२॥

ananyāś cintayanto māṁ ye janāḥ paryupāsate/
teṣāṁ nityābhiyuktānāṁ yoga-kṣemaṁ vahāmy aham//

ananyāḥ—without deviation; *cintayantaḥ*—concentrating; *mām*—on me; *ye*—those who; *janāḥ*—persons; *paryupāsate*—worship; *teṣām*—of them; *nitya*—always; *abhiyuktānām*—united; *yoga-kṣemam*—acquisition; *vahāmi*—carry; *aham*—I.

For those persons who worship me, directing their thoughts to me without deviation, who are always united with me in (bhakti) yoga, I carry what they lack and preserve what they have.

Here the word *nityābhiyuktānām* indicates unalloyed devotion. Those who are ever united with Kṛṣṇa in *yoga* are the *mahātmās* mentioned earlier. As it did in verse 13, here *ananyāḥ* also indicates interest in nothing other than devotion.

Kṛṣṇa has not stopped speaking either directly or indirectly about his unalloyed devotees since his first mention of them in verse 13. Here, as in verses 13 and 14, he speaks directly about them, describing how dear they are to him. As such, Kṛṣṇa's heart is in his throat as he speaks lovingly, revealing his most prominent quality—he is *bhakta-vatsala*, partial to his devotees, ruled by their love.

How do those devotees who are so concerned with Kṛṣṇa's service that they neglect their bodily necessities survive? Kṛṣṇa says that he himself serves them by carrying what they lack and preserving what they have. Kṛṣṇa sees their bodies as extensions of his own. Although he is indirectly the maintainer of everyone, he personally cares for his devotees. Kṛṣṇa uses the word *vahāmi* (I carry) in this verse rather than *karomi* (I do) to dispel the idea that he accomplishes the task of maintaining his devotees through an agent rather than doing it personally. Viśvanātha Cakravartī Ṭhākura says that he does so "just like a householder 'carries' the burden (*bhāram* means 'weight') of maintaining his wife and children." In carrying the burden of his devotees' maintenance, Kṛṣṇa is not burdened by this labor of love. Neither do his devotees ask him to provide for them. They simply love and serve him, and as they enter into a union of love with him, they are maintained as though they were his own bodily parts. Baladeva Vidyābhūṣaṇa cites this verse in his commentary to *Vedānta-sūtra* (3.4.44) where a similar discussion takes place.

To further stress unalloyed devotion to himself, Kṛṣṇa continues his discussion of various modes of worship. In doing so, he answers the possible doubt of Arjuna: "But as there is really no other God than you, worshippers of Indra and other gods are your devotees as well. Why then should they rise to heaven only to return again, whereas other devotees attain you?"

Text 23

येऽप्यन्यदेवताभक्ता यजन्ते श्रद्धयान्विताः ।
तेऽपि मामेव कौन्तेय यजन्त्यविधिपूर्वकम् ॥२३॥

ye 'py anya-devatā-bhaktā yajante śraddhayānvitāḥ/
te 'pi mām eva kaunteya yajanty avidhi-pūrvakam//

ye—those who; *api*—even; *anya*—of other; *devatā*—gods; *bhaktāḥ*—devotees; *yajante*—worship; *śraddhayā anvitāḥ*—with faith; *te*—they; *api*—although; *mām*—me; *eva*—only; *kaunteya*—O son of Kuntī; *yajanti*—they worship; *avidhi-pūrvakam*—improperly.

Even those who worship other gods with faith also worship only me, O son of Kuntī, although they do so improperly.

The word *avidhi-pūrvakam* means "not according to rule." Here Kṛṣṇa speaks of improper worship in terms of the worshipper being unaware that it is he whom one worships when one worships other gods, who are manifestations of Kṛṣṇa for particular material purposes. "Other gods" here does not refer to Kṛṣṇa's *avatāras*.

The result of improper worship is discussed next, followed by a general yet important statement regarding the results of different types of worship.

Text 24

अहं हि सर्वयज्ञानां भोक्ता च प्रभुरेव च ।
न तु मामभिजानन्ति तत्त्वेनातश्च्यवन्ति ते ॥२४॥

ahaṁ hi sarva-yajñānāṁ bhoktā ca prabhur eva ca/
na tu mām abhijānanti tattvenātaś cyavanti te//

aham—I; *hi*—surely; *sarva*—of all; *yajñānām*—sacrifices; *bhoktā*—enjoyer; *ca*—and; *prabhuḥ*—master; *eva*—also; *ca*—and; *na*—not; *tu*—but; *mām*—me; *abhijānanti*—they know; *tattvena*—in truth; *ataḥ*—therefore; *cyavanti*—fall down; *te*—they.

For I am the enjoyer and master of all sacrifices, but not knowing me in truth, they fall down.

Kṛṣṇa enjoys the fruit of all sacrifices through the agency of the gods, and as the master of all sacrifice, he awards results through them as well. Not knowing this, such ignorant worshippers, after attaining heaven through the aforementioned dark path, fall down, as detailed earlier in chapter 8 (Bg. 8.25). It is implied in this verse that those who worship the gods while understanding them to be representatives of Kṛṣṇa do eventually attain liberation through the path of light.

Text 25

यान्ति देवव्रता देवान् पितॄन् यान्ति पितृव्रताः ।
भूतानि यान्ति भूतेज्या यान्ति मद्याजिनोऽपि माम् ॥२५॥

yānti deva-vratā devān pitṛn yānti pitṛ-vratāḥ/
bhūtāni yānti bhūtejyā yānti mad-yājino 'pi mām//

yānti—go; *deva-vratāḥ*—devoted to the gods; *devān*—to the gods; *pitṛn*—to the ancestors; *yānti*—go; *pitṛ-vratāḥ*—devoted to the ancestors; *bhūtāni*—to the ghosts; *yānti*—go; *bhūta-ijyāḥ*—devoted to ghosts; *yānti*—go; *mat-yājinaḥ*—devoted to me; *api*—certainly; *mām*—unto me.

Those devoted to the gods go to the gods; those devoted to the ancestors go to the ancestors; those devoted to the ghosts go to the ghosts; those who worship me surely attain me.

All forms of worship are not equal. Worshippers of the gods worship in the material mode of goodness *(sattva-guṇa)*. Those who worship the ancestors worship in the mode of passion *(rajo-guṇa)*. Worshippers of ghosts and spirits worship in the mode of ignorance *(tamo-guṇa)*.

Kṛṣṇa's emphasis on the certainty *(api)* of attaining him through worship of himself indicates an attainment from which one does not return to another birth. Such worship is not material in quality *(nirguṇa)*.

Here Kṛṣṇa indirectly says that although in general the effort of worship is similar, the object to which it is directed determines the result. If anything, the effort and requisite paraphernalia for worship of other gods is considerable in comparison to that required for worshipping Kṛṣṇa. He thus goes on to detail the simplicity of his worship.

Text 26

पत्रं पुष्पं फलं तोयं यो मे भक्त्या प्रयच्छति ।
तदहं भक्त्युपहृतमश्नामि प्रयतात्मनः ॥२६॥

patraṁ puṣpaṁ phalaṁ toyaṁ yo me bhaktyā prayacchati/
tad ahaṁ bhakty-upahṛtam aśnāmi prayatātmanaḥ//

patram—leaf; *puṣpam*—flower; *phalam*—fruit; *toyam*—water; *yaḥ*—anyone; *me*—unto me; *bhaktyā*—with devotion; *prayacchati*—offers; *tat*—that; *aham*—I; *bhakti-upahṛtam*—offering of devotion; *aśnāmi*—accept; *prayata-ātmanaḥ*—from one in pure consciousness.

If anyone offers me with devotion and purity a leaf, a flower, a fruit, or water, I accept that offering of devotion.

Here we are reminded of the eulogy of the king of knowledge at the beginning of this chapter. There Kṛṣṇa described the knowledge of pure devotion as easy to perform yet bearing imperishable fruit, *susukhaṁ kartum avyayam.*

The mention of items in the singular emphasizes just how little in terms of external offerings is necessary to satisfy Kṛṣṇa: one leaf, one flower, one fruit, or water, all of which are available to everyone, is sufficient. All four items are not necessary, nor more than any one of them. Kṛṣṇa's statement is not limited to these four items. They merely represent that which is easily available to anyone. By saying "anyone" *(yaḥ)*, Kṛṣṇa means that he will accept the offering of a person from any background if they take to devotional life.

Here it is implied that while the offering itself in terms of its material ingredients is somehow important to the gods, this is not the case in the worship of Kṛṣṇa. By offering the gods valuable material ingredients that one is attached to, one at least enters the arena of sacrifice. The ultimate sacrifice, however, is called for in unalloyed devotion to Kṛṣṇa. One must offer one's heart.

Kṛṣṇa is self-satisfied, the one who has everything. What then can we give him? We can give him our hearts, for his own heart has been stolen by the love of his devotees. It is the devotion with which one offers that he accepts, and thus devotion is mentioned twice in this verse, which as in verses 13, 14, and 22 speaks of the pure devotion that is the heart of this chapter.

While devotion is the essential ingredient, *prayatātmanaḥ* indicates that the offering should be done with a pure heart, or in accordance with standards of purity such as cleanliness. In the optimum, Kṛṣṇa refers here to offerings that are an act of devotion from start to finish; in which, for example, the devotee plants, grows, picks, prepares, and offers the fruit to him. Such preoccupation with Kṛṣṇa's service assures purity of heart and gives Kṛṣṇa an appetite.

At this point, Kṛṣṇa is barely able to contain himself as he glorifies and explains how dear pure devotion and his devotees are to him—*paraṁ-brahma.*

Text 27

यत्करोषि यदश्नासि यज्जुहोषि ददासि यत् ।
यत्तपस्यसि कौन्तेय तत्कुरुष्व मदर्पणम् ॥२७॥

yat karoṣi yad aśnāsi yaj juhoṣi dadāsi yat/
yat tapasyasi kaunteya tat kuruṣva mad-arpaṇam//

yat—whatever; *karoṣi*—you do; *yat*—whatever; *aśnāsi*—you eat; *yat*—whatever; *juhoṣi*—you offer; *dadāsi*—you give away; *yat*—whatever; *yat*—whatever; *tapasyasi*—austerities you perform; *kaunteya*—O son of Kuntī; *tat*—that; *kuruṣva*—do; *mat*—unto me; *arpaṇam*—as an offering.

Whatever you do, whatever you eat, whatever you offer or give away, whatever austerities you perform, O son of Kuntī, do that as an offering unto me.

Having said "whoever offers me" in the previous verse, Kṛṣṇa understands that not everyone is capable of offering themselves to him in unalloyed devotion. Thus in this verse, without straying from his emphasis on devotion, he proposes how others who are not pure in heart can nonetheless make offerings unto him. He says that although such offerings may not be offered with purity of heart or be perfect in terms of standards and ingredients, they should be offered anyway. However, he does not say that he will necessarily accept these offerings; nonetheless, whatever devotion is present will gradually purify the offerer, bringing him eventually to the standard of pure devotion. The resultant sanctity of such persons and their destination are described next.

Text 28

शुभाशुभफलैरेवं मोक्ष्यसे कर्मबन्धनैः ।
सन्न्यासयोगयुक्तात्मा विमुक्तो मामुपैष्यसि ॥२८॥

śubhāśubha-phalair evaṁ mokṣyase karma-bandhanaiḥ/
sannyāsa-yoga-yuktātmā vimukto mām upaiṣyasi//

śubha—good; *aśubha*—bad; *phalaiḥ*—from the fruits; *evam*—thus; *mokṣyase*—you shall be liberated; *karma*—*karma*; *bandhanaiḥ*—from the bondage; *sannyāsa*—renunciation; *yoga*—*yoga*; *yukta-ātmā*—self united; *vimuktaḥ*—liberated status; *mām*—to me; *upaiṣyasi*—you will attain.

In this way, you shall surely be liberated from the bondage of karma, both its good and bad fruits. Being renounced from the fruit of your actions, your self united with me in yoga, you shall come to me, attaining a special liberated status.

Here Kṛṣṇa explains that a person who offers whatever he does to him, whether his actions are scripturally enjoined or not, will gradually become liberated from the bondage of *karma*. Reaching thereby the stage of knowledge and concomitant detachment (*sannyāsa*), he attains devotional union with Kṛṣṇa and liberation. Śaṅkara says, "*Sannyāsa-yoga* means actions done as offerings to Kṛṣṇa, *sannyāsa* implying the offering, *yoga* the action itself that is being offered."

Here *vimukti* indicates more than the general idea of liberation (*mukti*), in which one is freed from karmic bondage alone. *Vimukti* refers as well to positive attainment, devotional liberation in love of God.[10]

In the first six chapters, Kṛṣṇa detailed gradual progress from *niṣkāma-karma-yoga* to *jñāna* to *bhakti* in order to stress that *bhakti* is liberated *yoga* and thus its highest expression. Here he highlights another feature of *bhakti*'s superexcellence. Speaking from his heart, he says that *bhakti* is so efficacious that nonliberated persons can engage in some form of it and by this alone pass through karmic bondage and attain knowledge and *bhakti* proper. In the previous verse Kṛṣṇa suggests that one offer him the fruits not only of one's prescribed duties as enjoined in scripture, but of *any* activities. This is a mixed form of devotion in which one offers the fruits of one's activities and not first oneself, as in the case of the pure devotion detailed in verse 26. In that verse the offering pales in comparison to the devotion and the devotee has no life of his own. He belongs to Kṛṣṇa, and more, Kṛṣṇa belongs to him. In this section, on the other hand, there is scope for one's own separate life, given one offers the fruits of one's work to Kṛṣṇa. One has to start somewhere, and Kṛṣṇa recommends that one do so with some form of devotion.

With all this talk of devotion, Kṛṣṇa has begun to appear partial, a quality that seems unbecoming for God. In the next verse, Kṛṣṇa refutes this notion only to enlighten Arjuna concerning the nature of spiritual partiality.

Text 29

समोऽहं सर्वभूतेषु न मे द्वेष्योऽस्ति न प्रियः ।
ये भजन्ति तु मां भक्त्या मयि ते तेषु चाप्यहम् ॥२९॥

samo 'haṁ sarva-bhūteṣu na me dveṣyo 'sti na priyaḥ/
ye bhajanti tu māṁ bhaktyā mayi te teṣu cāpy aham//

10. See ŚB. 10.9.20.

samaḥ—impartial; *aham*—I; *sarva-bhūteṣu*—to all beings; *na*—no one; *me*—to me; *dveṣyaḥ*—hateful; *asti*—is; *na*—nor; *priyaḥ*—dear; *ye*—those who; *bhajanti*—worship; *tu*—however; *mām*—me; *bhaktyā*—with devotion; *mayi*—are in me; *te*—they; *teṣu*—in them; *ca*—also; *api*—certainly; *aham*—I.

I am impartial to all beings. I hate no one and I favor no one. However, those who worship me with devotion are in me, and I am also in them.

In the first two lines of this verse, Kṛṣṇa speaks as the Paramātmā, the Supreme Soul situated within the heart of all beings. In the last two, Kṛṣṇa himself, Bhagavān, is speaking. As Paramātmā, God is the impartial witness; as Bhagavān, he is partial to his devotees. While partiality on the part of Paramātmā would be a blemish, partiality toward his devotees is the greatest ornament of Bhagavān.

God is free from ordinary attachment and aversion. To rise above these two misperceptions, which blind one to the equality of all souls, is the beginning of actual spiritual life. Attachment and aversion are two sides of the same coin of false currency—ignorance *(avidyā)*. Thus Kṛṣṇa first declares his impartiality as the just Lord of all beings who dispenses equally the bitter and sweet fruits from the karmic tree of life.

The apparent contradiction in this verse can be resolved in two ways. As stated above, Kṛṣṇa is speaking from different aspects of himself, Paramātmā and Bhagavān. Moreover, Bhagavān encourages everyone to become his devotee.

Although philosophically Kṛṣṇa is impartial, when viewed with devotional eyes he is partial, and this partiality is what makes him Bhagavān. It is partiality that fuels the land of divine love. One devotee is partial to Rāma, another Kṛṣṇa, and Kṛṣṇa is partial to all those who are partial to him. He is in them and they are in him, as one holds a dear one within one's heart. The question as to whether living beings are one with God or different from him is transcended, because *bhakti* introduces another option. Love is complete self-giving and total interpenetration, and thus Kṛṣṇa abides in his loving devotees and they in him. In this equation the Adwaita notion of the so-called fixed, motionless state of Brahman finds no scope. In *bhakti* there is a complete union in love that preserves the individuality of both the soul and God. This is experienced only by the soul who has already achieved liberation.

Kṛṣṇa's love for his devotees also takes the form of his not liking one who is envious of them. This, after all, is the nature of love. While divine love is often considered to transcend such partiality, Kṛṣṇa's love for his devotees transcends the general conception of divine love. When Bhagavān's attention is drawn toward one who envies his devotee, such attention, even when wrathful, is more beneficial for the envious than no attention at all. Everyone has the impartial attention of Paramātmā, but the Lord with *līlā*—Bhagavān, and more, Kṛṣṇa himself *(svayaṁ bhagavān)*—only interacts with his devotees, and as a by-product of that interaction, with those inimical to them.

Having briefly defended himself against the charge of partiality, only to openly admit his preference for his devotees, announcing it to the public, Kṛṣṇa continues unabated to the end of this chapter, extolling the virtues of devotion to himself. Beginning with verse 26 and culminating in the thirty-fourth and final verse, we come to the high point of the *Gītā*, which is again reiterated in its closing words, nine chapters later.

Text 30–31

अपि चेत्सुदुराचारो भजते मामनन्यभाक् ।
साधुरेव स मन्तव्यः सम्यग् व्यवसितो हि सः ॥३०॥
क्षिप्रं भवति धर्मात्मा शश्वच्छान्तिं निगच्छति ।
कौन्तेय प्रतिजानीहि न मे भक्तः प्रणश्यति ॥३१॥

api cet su-durācāro bhajate mām ananya-bhāk/
sādhur eva sa mantavyaḥ samyag vyavasito hi saḥ//
kṣipraṁ bhavati dharmātmā śaśvac-chāntiṁ nigacchati/
kaunteya pratijānīhi na me bhaktaḥ praṇaśyati//

api—even; *cet*—if; *su-durācāraḥ*—a person of very bad behavior; *bhajate*—worships; *mām*—me; *ananya-bhāk*—with undivided devotion; *sādhuḥ*—saint; *eva*—certainly; *saḥ*—he; *mantavyaḥ*—is to be thought; *samyak*—properly; *vyavasitaḥ*—resolved; *hi*—certainly; *saḥ*—he; *kṣipram*—quickly; *bhavati*—becomes; *dharma-ātmā*—righteous; *śaśvat-śāntim*—lasting peace; *nigacchati*—attains; *kaunteya*—O son of Kuntī; *pratijānīhi*—declare; *na*—never; *me*—my; *bhaktaḥ*—devotee; *praṇaśyati*—is lost.

Even if a person of very bad behavior worships me with undivided devotion, he is to be thought of as saintly, for he has the proper resolution.

He quickly becomes righteous and attains lasting peace. O son of Kuntī, declare it boldly that no devotee of mine is ever lost.

In these two verses the extent of *bhakti*'s power to award salvation are feelingly expressed by the connoisseur of love, Śrī Kṛṣṇa. Kṛṣṇa says here that the sinner *(sudurācāraḥ)*, worshipping him exclusively *(ananya-bhāk)*, is definitely a saint *(sādhur eva)* despite his bad character, owing to his resignation *(vyavasitaḥ)* to the service/worship of Kṛṣṇa. For emphasis, the word *mantavyaḥ*, "he is to be thought of (as saintly)," is spoken as if it were a law with undesirable consequences that arrests those who disregard it. One may get the impression from this statement that *bhakti*, even in its immature stage of practice, is in some sense antinomian. Kṛṣṇa appears to be saying that his devotees are not bound by moral obligation. Understandably, these verses have been explained in numerous ways to qualify what Kṛṣṇa is saying so that one cannot cite them to support bad character in the name of *bhakti*. However, in evoking these explanations, one must be careful not to undermine the power of *bhakti*, which is the spirit of the text.

Characteristically, Viśvanātha Cakravartī Ṭhākura emphasizes the power of *bhakti*, siding largely with the reasoning that the devotee, owing to his devotion, is to be considered above the law. In such a generous rendering, what is stressed is the ideal of the devotee—that which he will become—as opposed to judging him by his present condition, much less his past. His devotional ideal, which represents his *svarūpa-lakṣaṇa*, or principal characteristic, overrides his marginal characteristic of bad character.

Śrīdhara Swāmī's rendering of *ananya-bhāk* is such that it does away with an apparent contradiction. If a devotee is *ananya-bhāk*, meaning undeviating in pure devotional life, this contradicts *sudurācāra* (very badly misbehaved). How can one be undeviating in the sense of *bhajate mām ananya bhāk* and *ananyāś cintayanto mām*, found, respectively, in verses 30 and 22, and at the same time misbehave? To avoid this difficulty, Śrīdhara Swāmī explains *ananya-bhāk* as devotion to Kṛṣṇa alone and not to any other god or goddess. Viśvanātha Cakravartī Ṭhākura adds to this "unencumbered by any practice other than devotion, such as *jñāna* or *karma*, and without desire for anything other than Kṛṣṇa, such as worldly power or riches." This could easily apply to an intermediate devotee.

Following Śrīdhara Swāmī's lead, an *ananya bhakta* could also be a neophyte devotee, for such devotees are devoted to Kṛṣṇa alone. Beginners have some love for Kṛṣṇa, but their sense of the reality of Kṛṣṇa has not yet developed to the point of seeing the world in relation to him. True morality beyond convention is the result of seeing God in the world. The neophyte may lack strong moral fiber due to his underdeveloped realization of the all-encompassing nature of his object of love. Still he is properly situated to realize this in due course and become righteous thereby in all respects.

Due to being in the present tense, the words *kṣipraṁ bhavati dharmātmā* in verse 31 are understood by Viśvanātha Cakravartī to indicate the immediate or continued attainment of righteous status. Thus, the person who chooses to serve no one other than Kṛṣṇa, even if he is very badly behaved, must be considered saintly. As for the blemish resulting from his misbehavior, he is immediately rectified owing to his repentance and continued resolve. One who thinks otherwise is himself condemned, having ignored Kṛṣṇa's order, which is a scriptural mandate.

Viśvanātha Cakravartī Ṭhākura says that, should one agree with the above understanding on the condition that the devotee in question actually does become righteous *(bhavati dharmātmā)*, giving up his bad character, this conditional acceptance of his words invokes Kṛṣṇa's wrath. The thought that someone will take such a position makes Kṛṣṇa say, *kaunteya pratijānīhi na me bhaktaḥ praṇaśyati*: "O son of Kuntī, declare it boldly that no devotee of mine is ever lost." Thus even if the devotee is not seen to rectify himself, still he is to be considered saintly. Kṛṣṇa orders Arjuna to declare this fact publicly because his devotee's promise will never be broken, as Kṛṣṇa sees to this even more than upholding his own promises. Following Śrīdhara Swāmī, Viśvanātha Cakravartī says the spirit of Kṛṣṇa's words is "publicly declare it boldly with cymbals and drums like a town crier." The result will be that the public will worship one who does so.

Although Viśvanātha Cakravartī Ṭhākura's comments are the liberal side of the pendulum, it should be noted that the wayward devotee he sees in these verses is always remorseful for his misbehavior. Even if he cannot give up his wrongdoing, he continues to condemn himself for it. Thus even Cakravartī Ṭhākura does not give a license for flouting the moral law in the name of devotion.

Conservative explanations of these verses are in no shortage. In his *Bhakti-sandarbha*, Jīva Goswāmī says that the verses are intended to instill initial faith in unalloyed *bhakti*, on attaining which one evolves to deeper faith, faith in scriptural descriptions regarding the proper practice of *bhakti*.

There is no dearth of scriptural statements condemning wrongdoing of all kinds. Jīva Goswāmī says that the understanding that devotees are absolved from transgressions is the opinion of those persons who are scripturally uneducated. For Śrī Jīva, the words *api cet* in verse 30 mean "even though," indicating that real misbehavior on the part of the devoted is indeed a blemish and an aberration.

Api cet can also mean "even if." Even if a devotee does something improper in the name of devotion, such as deceiving another to involve them in Kṛṣṇa's service, he should be considered saintly. Or if a devotee comes from a background steeped in vice, his lack of moral culture may carry over into his new devotional life. For this he should not be condemned, because his heart is in the right place. In this way, it is possible to make less of the nature of the transgression Kṛṣṇa describes, as it is possible to make more of *bhakti*'s dearness to Kṛṣṇa and its resultant efficacy.

Another understanding is that "even if" implies that verse 30 speaks of only a hypothetical case in which a devotee does that which for an *ananya-bhakta* is not possible. Undeviating *(ananya)* devotees *(bhaktas)* simply do not engage in moral transgressions. If such a devotee exhibits the impossible, then his misbehavior may be an arrangement of Kṛṣṇa for his own purpose. Kṛṣṇa may cause a near-perfect devotee to fall, after which the devotee rises up with the humility necessary to attain the perfectional stage of devotion.

A third solution to this quandary can be drawn from Jīva Goswāmī's discussion of *rāgānugā-bhakti* (sacred passionate love) in his *Bhakti-sandarbha*. Śrī Jīva cites verse 30 to support the idea that devotees on the path of *rāgānugā-bhakti* are absolved from following the religious codes detailed in the *dharma-śāstra*. Ordinarily, violation of these codes is considered irreligious. However, because the devotee has come under the jurisdiction of *bhakti*, the supreme expression of *dharma (prema-dharma)*, he need not be concerned with lesser religious mandates. Indeed, this is the conclusion of the *Gītā*, wherein Kṛṣṇa implores Arjuna to forgo all *dharma* and surrender unto him to attain *prema* (Bg. 18.66). Kedarnātha Bhaktivinoda Ṭhākura has used this logic to offer a unique and charming resolution to the apparent contradiction arising from Kṛṣṇa's use of the words *ananya-bhāk* and *sudurācāra* to describe the same devotee.

Bhaktivinoda Ṭhākura renders *ananya-bhāk* in terms of its meaning found in verse 13, indicating not only one who worships Kṛṣṇa and no other God, but one who worships Kṛṣṇa with the highest standard of devotion—an unalloyed devotee. How can an unalloyed devotee be immoral? He also finds an apparent contradiction in the idea that an unalloyed devotee, after somehow acting inappropriately, would then become righteous *(dharmātmā)*. This implies that after falling from the plane of unalloyed devotion, he is reestablished in the plane of religion, which lies in between moral transgression and unalloyed devotion.

Ṭhākura Bhaktivinoda harmonizes all of the above points by applying these verses to Kṛṣṇa's *gopīs*, who are *ananya-bhaktas*, yet immoral in terms of violating socioreligious codes. They went to Kṛṣṇa following their hearts, ravaged by the sound of Kṛṣṇa's flute. In doing so, they violated religious mandates with regard to marital fidelity. Although they were *ananya-bhāk* to the extreme, they were morally corrupt to the mundane religious mind, which does not understand the significance of Kṛṣṇa.

How then did the *gopīs* become religiously reformed? As there is no instance of this, nor would it ever be an appropriate theological conclusion, Bhaktivinoda Ṭhākura says that it is not the *gopīs* who become righteous. He who proclaims the purity of the *gopīs*' apparent misbehavior—the forgoing of *dharma-śāstra* in pursuit of sacred passionate love—immediately becomes righteous by speaking about their so-called violation. And by glorifying their apparent transgression everywhere, he attains salvation *(śaśvac-chāntiṁ nigacchati)*. In other words, "One (who declares it boldly that my unalloyed devotee is never fallen) quickly becomes righteous and attains lasting peace."

Having glorified even those on the path of devotion who appear to have fallen from the path itself, Kṛṣṇa next makes it clear that the path of devotion can deliver those who are born in less opportune circumstances for spiritual practice owing to their previous life's actions.

Text 32

मां हि पार्थ व्यपाश्रित्य येऽपि स्युः पापयोनयः ।
स्त्रियो वैश्यास्तथा शूद्रास्तेऽपि यान्ति परां गतिम् ॥३२॥

māṁ hi pārtha vyapāśritya ye 'pi syuḥ pāpa-yonayaḥ/
striyo vaiśyās tathā śūdrās te 'pi yānti parāṁ gatim//

mām—me; *hi*—certainly; *pārtha*—O Pārtha; *vyapāśritya*—taking refuge; *ye*—those who; *api*—also; *syuḥ*—are; *pāpa-yonayaḥ*—lowborn; *striyaḥ*—women; *vaiśyāḥ*—merchants; *tathā*—also; *śūdrāḥ*—working-class men; *te api*—even they; *yānti*—go; *parām*—highest; *gatim*—goal.

It is certain, O Pārtha, that those who take refuge in me, even the lowborn, women, merchants, as well as the working class, attain the highest goal.

In this verse Kṛṣṇa says that even the lowborn, who due to impiety in their previous life have taken such births, regardless of what they harvest from the seeds they have sown in the present or past, can overcome their impiety if they take shelter of him in devotion. The sacred literature cites numerous examples of animal killers and animals themselves being so delivered by the direct and indirect influence of *bhakti*.

Women are mentioned in this verse because of the social impediment to their study of the *Vedas* in times gone by, as well as the fact that a woman's birth can subject one to the kind of discrimination they have suffered from over the centuries.

Merchants are notorious for stretching the truth, and the laborers for their lack of interest in and qualification for scriptural study. Regardless of the background of all of the above, Kṛṣṇa does not withhold himself from them should they try to love him. Indeed, they will surpass others of greater material qualification who take paths other than *bhakti*.

Text 33

किं पुनर्ब्राह्मणाः पुण्या भक्ता राजर्षयस्तथा ।
अनित्यमसुखं लोकमिमं प्राप्य भजस्व माम् ॥३३॥

kiṁ punar brāhmaṇāḥ puṇyā bhaktā rājarṣayas tathā/
anityam asukhaṁ lokam imaṁ prāpya bhajasva mām//

kim—how much; *punaḥ*—more; *brāhmaṇāḥ*—priestly; *puṇyāḥ*—pure; *bhaktāḥ*—devotees; *rāja-ṛṣayaḥ*—saintly kings; *tathā*—also; *anityam*—ephemeral; *asukham*—unhappy; *lokam*—world; *imam*—this; *prāpya*—having attained; *bhajasva*—devote yourself; *mām*—to me.

How much more is this the case for the pure priests and saintly kings! You have been born in this ephemeral and unhappy world, now devote yourself to me.

The words *lokam imaṁ prāpya* here imply that attaining human birth in this world is itself difficult. *Imaṁ lokam* means both "this world" and "this body." Kṛṣṇa refers to human birth in this world, which is attained after many, many births. The human body is fit for attaining higher goals that are not attainable in other births. Yet it is itself ephemeral *(anityam)*.[11] So

11. Here Kṛṣṇa describes the world as *anityam* (noneternal), not *mithyā* (false), as does Śaṅkara.

too is the world. Because of this and because one can only be aware of this fact in human birth, Kṛṣṇa says, "How much one should strive through devotion to me for that which is human life's perfection! One should do so now, while the gift of human life lasts, and one should not be distracted from this undertaking by that which surrounds one in the name of happiness, for in reality the world is unhappy (*asukham*)—both the world (sense objects) and the body made of senses bent on enjoying sense objects."

Just how one—anyone—can devote himself to Kṛṣṇa is described next, as Kṛṣṇa concludes this chapter with great spiritual emotion.

Text 34

मन्मना भव मद्भक्तो मद्याजी मां नमस्कुरु ।
मामेवैष्यसि युक्त्वैवमात्मानं मत्परायणः ॥३४॥

man-manā bhava mad-bhakto mad-yājī māṁ namaskuru/
mām evaiṣyasi yuktvaivam ātmānaṁ mat-parāyaṇaḥ//

mat-manāḥ—thinking of me; *bhava*—become; *mat*—my; *bhaktaḥ*—devotee; *mat*—my; *yājī*—one who sacrifices; *mām*—to me; *namaskuru*—offer obeisance; *mām*—to me; *eva*—alone; *eṣyasi*—you will come; *yuktvā*—being absorbed; *evam*—thus; *ātmānam*—your soul; *mat-parāyaṇaḥ*—devoted to me.

Fix your mind on me. Be my devotee! Sacrifice for me. Offer obeisance unto me. Absorbed thus in me alone, you shall come to me.

One whose mind is fixed on Kṛṣṇa is one who is Kṛṣṇa's devotee. Thus devotion proper requires more than the physical act of service. We are where our minds are regardless of where we appear to be physically. Both Baladeva Vidyābhūṣaṇa and Madhusūdana Saraswatī give the example of a king's servant, who although serving the king physically has his mind on his own family. Thus Kṛṣṇa says one should both devote oneself to him and think of him. The word *bhava* is an imperative in this regard, as if Kṛṣṇa is commanding and empowering one to be his devotee by the force of his heartfelt words.

Kṛṣṇa says that such a devotee should sacrifice for him. This is the heart of worship and the basis of love. Love arises out of sacrifice, labor's beautiful child. As in text 14, here again Kṛṣṇa says *māṁ namaskuru*: "Offer obeisance unto me," symbolizing the offering of nothing less than one's entire self, mind, body, and speech, as all of these are involved in the act of obeisance.

This verse is the essence and conclusion of the *Bhagavad-gītā* and it is repeated almost verbatim in the sixty-fifth verse of the eighteenth chapter. Preceding it there in verse 64, Kṛṣṇa describes this knowledge and path of *bhakti* as *sarva-guhyatamam*, the most confidential knowledge. Although many paths have been discussed and recommended at different times thus far, here they are all superseded as Kṛṣṇa fully opens his heart to Arjuna.

At the end of chapter 6 Kṛṣṇa revealed that his idea of the perfectly integrated being was his devotee. Thus he implored Arjuna to be a devotee. In chapters 7 through 9 different kinds of devotees are discussed: *karma-miśra*, *jñāna-miśra*, *yoga-miśra*, and unalloyed *bhaktas*. As Kṛṣṇa concludes this chapter, he makes it clear that his ideal person is not merely his devotee, but an unalloyed devotee.

When all is said and done, spiritual life is as simple as this verse makes it out to be. Devotion, love, the heart's domain, rules over all. It is *the* path, the ocean into which all rivers must flow and are worthy of rafting only if they reach her shore.

Chapter Ten

विभूतियोगः
Vibhūti-yoga

YOGA OF DIVINE MANIFESTATION

Text 1

श्रीभगवानुवाच
भूय एव महाबाहो शृणु मे परमं वचः ।
यत्तेऽहं प्रीयमाणाय वक्ष्यामि हितकाम्यया ॥१॥

śrī-bhagavān uvāca
bhūya eva mahā-bāho śṛṇu me paramaṁ vacaḥ/
yat te 'haṁ prīyamāṇāya vakṣyāmi hita-kāmyayā//

śrī-bhagavān uvāca—the Lord of Śrī said; *bhūyaḥ*—again; *eva*—certainly; *mahā-bāho*—O mighty-armed one; *śṛṇu*—listen; *me*—my; *paramam*—supreme; *vacaḥ*—advice; *yat*—which; *te*—to you; *aham*—I; *prīyamāṇāya*—to the beloved one; *vakṣyāmi*—I shall speak; *hita-kāmyayā*—desiring your welfare.

The Lord of Śrī said: O mighty-armed one, listen again to my supreme advice, which I shall speak to you, beloved one, desiring your welfare.

In this chapter, Kṛṣṇa continues to speak confidentially to Arjuna. He has not given Arjuna a chance to ask any questions due to his own enthusiasm to reveal to Arjuna that which will ground him in devotion—confidential knowledge of his opulence and knowledge of the nature of devotion itself. Kṛṣṇa says "listen again" *(bhūyaḥ)*, indicating that he has more to say about himself than he has revealed so far. Kṛṣṇa has spoken of his opulence in previous chapters, and in this chapter he will say more about it. Knowing Kṛṣṇa to be the Supreme Being inspires one to worship him and to properly regard his *līlās*, which are otherwise difficult to understand. The confidential knowledge of this chapter is an extension of that revealed in the previous chapter, and it reaches its apex in verses 8 through 11. Viśvanātha Cakravartī Ṭhākura comments that the knowledge of this chapter is superior to what has been given thus far. This is the meaning of the words *paramaṁ vacaḥ*. Kṛṣṇa says that he reveals this knowledge "to you who love me" *(prīyamāṇāya)*, referring to Arjuna.

Here Kṛṣṇa speaks to Arjuna in terms of their friendly relationship *(sakhya-rasa)*. The word *hita-kāmyayā* means "desiring welfare." As his dear friend, Kṛṣṇa desires Arjuna's welfare. He is not speaking for his own benefit, nor has he anything to gain from his speaking. He speaks out of love for Arjuna and all of his devotees, who like Arjuna take pleasure in hearing his advice.

As this chapter begins, Kṛṣṇa addresses Arjuna as mighty-armed, implying that although he is competent in military science, more than this is required for understanding what he will reveal about himself in this chapter. Although Arjuna is competent, and Kṛṣṇa has already spoken about his own opulence, Arjuna must pay special attention to Kṛṣṇa's supreme advice. It is so confidential that it is unknown even to the gods and sages.

Text 2

न मे विदुः सुरगणाः प्रभवं न महर्षयः ।
अहमादिर्हि देवानां महर्षीणां च सर्वशः ॥२॥

na me viduḥ sura-gaṇāḥ prabhavaṁ na maharṣayaḥ/
aham ādir hi devānāṁ maharṣīṇāṁ ca sarvaśaḥ//

na—not; *me*—my; *viduḥ*—they know; *sura-gaṇāḥ*—the gods; *prabhavam*—origin; *na*—not; *mahā-ṛṣayaḥ*—the great sages; *aham*—I; *ādiḥ*—source; *hi*—indeed; *devānām*—of the gods; *mahā-ṛṣiṇām*—of the great sages; *ca*—also; *sarvaśaḥ*—in all respects.

Neither the gods nor the great sages know my origin. Indeed, I am in all respects the source of the gods and great sages.

As it is difficult to know the source of one's birth unless informed about it, similarly, although the gods and sages know of him and even worship him, they do not know what he will reveal about himself in this chapter. Kṛṣṇa, Arjuna's chariot driver, is the source of everything including the gods and great sages, and he answers to the devotional necessity of his devotees.

The gods are bewildered about Kṛṣṇa, as confirmed in the opening stanza of *Śrīmad-Bhāgavatam, muhyanti yat sūrayaḥ* (ŚB. 1.1.1). This is illustrated later in the same *Purāṇa* by Brahmā's and Indra's confusion about Kṛṣṇa.[1] The great sages referred to here are Bhṛgu and others who are referred to again in verse 6. They are said to be omniscient, yet what Kṛṣṇa tells Arjuna in this chapter is still unknown to them. Unlike the gods, the sages have no material attachment and are thus wise. However, their intellect is controlled by their source, and thus without Kṛṣṇa's grace they cannot know him in all respects. They are confused about his origin, for although Kṛṣṇa appears to take birth as the son of Devakī, he is at the same time birthless.

Kṛṣṇa next tells Arjuna the partial result of knowing him in truth, and he will reveal the entire fruit in verse 7.

Text 3

यो मामजमनादिं च वेत्ति लोकमहेश्वरम् ।
असम्मूढः स मर्त्येषु सर्वपापैः प्रमुच्यते ॥३॥

yo mām ajam anādiṁ ca vetti loka-maheśvaram/
asaṁmūḍhaḥ sa martyeṣu sarva-pāpaiḥ pramucyate//

yaḥ—one who; *mām*—me; *ajam*—birthless; *anādim*—beginningless; *ca*—and; *vetti*—knows; *loka*—world; *mahā-īśvaram*—the great Lord; *asaṁmūḍhaḥ*—undeluded; *saḥ*—he; *martyeṣu*—of mortals; *sarva-pāpaiḥ*—from all evils; *pramucyate*—is released.

He who undeluded among mortals knows me as birthless and beginningless, the great Lord of the world, is released from all evils.

Kṛṣṇa tells Arjuna that he is birthless *(ajam)*, even while appearing to have taken birth. The mystery of his apparent birth and the result of understanding its spiritual nature was discussed in chapter 4 (Bg. 4.9). While Kṛṣṇa previously mentioned his birth and the fact that one who understands it in truth attains liberation, in this chapter Kṛṣṇa emphasizes that one who understands such opulence as his birthlessness becomes his devotee, thereby becoming liberated. The means to liberation is devotion, initially fueled by understanding Kṛṣṇa's opulence. While knowledge of Kṛṣṇa's opulence

1. ŚB. 10.12–14 and 10.24–27.

leads to devotion, hearing of it is itself devotion as well. Thus devotion is both the means and end of spiritual life.

To distinguish himself from Brahmā, who is commonly known as *aja*, Kṛṣṇa adds that he is also beginningless *(anādim)*, a quality not found in Brahmā. Also implied is the fact that, unlike Brahmā, Kṛṣṇa's existence does not come to an end. By stating that he is the Lord of the world *(loka-maheśvaram)*, Kṛṣṇa distinguishes himself from eternally liberated souls *(nitya-muktas)*. They are birthless and beginningless, and their lives never come to an end. However, they are not lords of the world.

While the result of knowing these things about Kṛṣṇa is devotion, it first takes the form of liberating one from all inauspicious karmic reactions *(sarva-pāpaiḥ)*. This is the natural result of destroying the cause of improper action—ignorance of Kṛṣṇa's proprietorship *(loka-maheśvaram)*—for improper action amounts to acting as though one were the proprietor. Thus one with this knowledge is undeluded *(asaṁmūḍhaḥ)* in this world and acts accordingly in devotion. To entirely uproot ignorance of his proprietorship, Kṛṣṇa elaborates on this feature of himself as the Lord of the world *(loka-maheśvaram)* in the next three verses.

Text 4–5

बुद्धिर्ज्ञानमसंमोहः क्षमा सत्यं दमः शमः ।
सुखं दुःखं भवोऽभावो भयं चाभयमेव च ॥४॥
अहिंसा समता तुष्टिस्तपो दानं यशोऽयशः ।
भवन्ति भावा भूतानां मत्त एव पृथग्विधाः ॥५॥

buddhir jñānam asaṁmohaḥ kṣamā satyaṁ damaḥ śamaḥ/
sukhaṁ duḥkhaṁ bhavo 'bhāvo bhayaṁ cābhayam eva ca//
ahiṁsā samatā tuṣṭis tapo dānaṁ yaśo 'yaśaḥ/
bhavanti bhāvā bhūtānāṁ matta eva pṛthag-vidhāḥ//

buddhiḥ—intelligence; *jñānam*—knowledge; *asaṁmohaḥ*—freedom from delusion; *kṣamā*—forgiveness; *satyam*—truthfulness; *damaḥ*—self-control; *śamaḥ*—tranquillity; *sukham*—happiness; *duḥkham*—misery; *bhavaḥ*—existence; *abhāvaḥ*—nonexistence; *bhayam*—fear; *ca*—and; *abhayam*—fearlessness; *eva*—indeed; *ca*—and; *ahiṁsā*—nonviolence; *samatā*—impartiality; *tuṣṭiḥ*—satisfaction; *tapaḥ*—austerity; *dānam*—charity; *yaśaḥ*—fame; *ayaśaḥ*—infamy; *bhavanti*—arise; *bhāvāḥ*—dispositions; *bhūtānām*—of living entities; *mattaḥ*—from me; *eva*—certainly; *pṛthak-vidhāḥ*—various.

Intelligence, knowledge, freedom from delusion, forgiveness, truthfulness, self-control, tranquillity, happiness, misery, existence, nonexistence, fear, fearlessness, nonviolence, impartiality, satisfaction, austerity, charity, fame, infamy—indeed, all of these various dispositions found in living beings arise from me.

Jīva Goswāmī cites these two verses in his *Bhagavat-sandarbha* (102) as evidence that the Absolute, although beyond words according to the *śruti*,[2] can nonetheless be described to an extent. It is not that we cannot say anything about God, but that not enough can be said to fully describe him. Such descriptions make up the greater balance of the scripture. The dispositions mentioned in this verse arise from him and are found in him in their purest expression. Thus God has all of the above qualities.

Here Kṛṣṇa explains first that even the qualities of the sages—proper discrimination *(buddhiḥ)*, scriptural knowledge of the difference between matter and spirit *(jñānam)*, and freedom from delusion *(asaṁmohaḥ)*—arise from him. As such, they cannot in and of themselves reveal him in full. They are needed for spiritual progress, but are insufficient in terms of attaining ultimate beatitude, which requires God's grace.

Forgiveness *(kṣamā)* involves remaining unperturbed in mind when abused by others and possessing the power to punish abusers yet refraining from doing so. It is the foremost quality of the *brāhmaṇas*. Truthfulness refers to speaking of something as it is understood through valid evidence *(pramāṇa)*, principally that of sacred literature. Truthfulness also requires that one's mind and actions be in concert with one's speech. Self-control *(damaḥ)* refers to restraining the external senses by withdrawing them from sense objects, and tranquillity *(śamaḥ)* refers to controlling the internal organ, the mind. All of these dispositions are products of the material influence of goodness *(sattva-guṇa)* and have no expression in the other modes of nature.

Happiness *(sukham)* is of different kinds relative to the influence of material nature. Happiness arising from *sattva-guṇa* is the feeling derived from the performance of virtuous acts. Misery *(duḥkham)* is the pain arising from nonvirtuous acts, which ultimately appears when the superficial happiness derived from such acts dissipates. Existence *(bhavaḥ)* and nonexistence *(abhāvaḥ)* refer to birth and death.

2. See Ka. Up. 2.15.

Fear *(bhayam)* is the all-pervading experience of material existence, in which we appear threatened with the possibility of nonexistence at every moment. Fearlessness *(abhayam)* appears in all modes of nature. In *sattva-guṇa* it arises from knowledge. In *rajo-guṇa* it appears as the foolishness of risking one's life for fame, and in *tamo-guṇa* it appears when one should be afraid.

Nonviolence *(ahiṁsā)* refers ultimately to not hindering the spiritual progress of any living being—not merely refraining from physical violence, which, although rarely, has its positive application even in spiritual practice in the instance of protecting saints and the sacred in general. Impartiality *(samatā)* is sattvic and refers to equal vision and a state of mind that is free from attraction and repulsion. Satisfaction *(tuṣṭiḥ)* arises in both passion and goodness, with and without cause, respectively. It causes one to feel "this is enough" with regard to material enjoyment. Austerity *(tapaḥ)* appears in all modes of nature. Only that sanctioned by the scripture is recommended. Charity *(dāna)* appears in both goodness and passion. In goodness it is offered in consideration of one's capacity and among deserving people with due respect and in consideration of appropriate times and places. Fame *(yaśaḥ)* in goodness arises from praise that is a result of virtue, and infamy *(ayaśaḥ)* is to be known for one's vices.

Kṛṣṇa says here that all of the above dispositions certainly *(eva)* arise *(bhavanti)* from me *(mattaḥ)*, and thus he continues to explain how he is the Lord of the world *(loka-maheśvaram)*.

Text 6

महर्षयः सप्त पूर्वे चत्वारो मनवस्तथा ।
मद्भावा मानसा जाता येषां लोक इमाः प्रजाः ॥६॥

maharṣayaḥ sapta pūrve catvāro manavas tathā/
mad-bhāvā mānasā jātā yeṣāṁ loka imāḥ prajāḥ//

mahā-ṛṣayaḥ—the great sages; *sapta*—seven; *pūrve*—previously; *catvāraḥ*—four; *manavaḥ*—Manus; *tathā*—as well; *mat-bhāvāḥ*—originated in me; *mānasāḥ*—from the mind; *jātāḥ*—born; *yeṣām*—of whom; *loke*—in the world; *imāḥ*—these; *prajāḥ*—creatures.

The seven great sages of old, as well as the four (Kumāras) and the Manus from whom the world's creatures have come, originated in me, born of my mind.

With this verse, in which he refers to the seven sages of Vedic lore—Bhṛgu, Marīci, Atri, Aṅgirā, Pulastya, Pulaha, and Kratu—Kṛṣṇa concludes his brief explanation of how he is the Lord of the world. These great sages, as well as "the four," referring to the four Kumāras, are considered the mental sons of Prajāpati Brahmā, who represents Kṛṣṇa in the act of creation. They are pure in terms of their birth. The Manus mentioned here are progenitors who are fourteen in number. Those acquainted with these persons and their prominence in Vedic literature with regard to universal affairs, both procreation and the dissemination of knowledge, will appreciate the significance of the one who is their source.

In the next verse Kṛṣṇa explains the ripened fruit of knowing his position as the origin of all of the above, as well as the *yoga* of devotion, under discussion since the previous chapter.

Text 7

एतां विभूतिं योगं च मम यो वेत्ति तत्त्वतः ।
सोऽविकल्पेन योगेन युज्यते नात्र संशयः ॥७॥

etāṁ vibhūtiṁ yogaṁ ca mama yo vetti tattvataḥ/
so 'vikampena yogena yujyate nātra saṁśayaḥ//

etām—this; *vibhūtim*—opulence; *yogam*—*yoga*; *ca*—and; *mama*—my; *yaḥ*—one who; *vetti*—knows; *tattvataḥ*—in truth; *saḥ*—he; *avikampena*—by unwavering; *yogena*—by *yoga*; *yujyate*—is united; *na*—not; *atra*—here; *saṁśayaḥ*—doubt.

One who knows my opulence and power in truth is united with me in unwavering yoga; of this there is no doubt.

The fruit of understanding both Kṛṣṇa's opulence (*vibhūtim*) and his power (*yogaṁ ca mama*) is that one becomes fixed (*avikampena*) in the culture of devotional *yoga* (*yogena yujyate*). Here Kṛṣṇa assures Arjuna of this (*nātra saṁśayaḥ*).

Bhakti in practice is either *aniṣṭhā* (wavering) or *niṣṭhā* (unwavering). One reaches the stage of *niṣṭhā* through acquiring knowledge in relation to Kṛṣṇa along with engaging in devotional practices. This knowledge is both *tat-padārtha-jñāna* and *tvam-padārtha-jñāna*, knowledge of God and knowledge of the individual soul (*tat tvam asi*). Beginning with chapter 7, Kṛṣṇa has revealed *tat-padārtha-jñāna*; *tvam-padārtha-jñāna* was revealed in the first six chapters. The practice of *bhakti* arising out of a proper conceptual orientation as to the position of Kṛṣṇa, his relation to the world and the individual souls and their relationship with one another, eventually unites one with Kṛṣṇa in love.

Having spoken about his opulence and his personal *yoga* of devotion, Kṛṣṇa, brimming with spiritual emotion, next elaborates in four essential verses on his position as the source of everything as well as on the nature of *bhakti* proper.

Text 8

अहं सर्वस्य प्रभवो मत्तः सर्वं प्रवर्तते ।
इति मत्वा भजन्ते मां बुधा भावसमन्विताः ॥८॥

ahaṁ sarvasya prabhavo mattaḥ sarvaṁ pravartate/
iti matvā bhajante māṁ budhā bhāva-samanvitāḥ//

aham—I; *sarvasya*—of everything; *prabhavaḥ*—the source; *mattaḥ*—from me; *sarvam*—everything; *pravartate*—proceeds; *iti*—thus; *matvā*—considering; *bhajante*—adore; *mām*—me; *budhāḥ*—the wise; *bhāva-samanvitāḥ*—imbued with love.

I am the source of everything; all proceeds from me. Realizing this, the wise imbued with love adore me.

Viśvanātha Cakravartī Ṭhākura has called verses 8 through 11 the *catuḥ-ślokī* of the *Bhagavad-gītā*, playing off the well-known four *(catur)* essential verses *(śloka)* of the *Śrīmad-Bhāgavatam* (ŚB. 2.9.33–36), originally spoken by Kṛṣṇa to Brahmā. All four verses have a general meaning for practicing devotees *(sādhakas)*, as well as an esoteric meaning relative to Kṛṣṇa's devotees of Vraja and the *gopīs* and their followers in particular. They deal with the nature of devotion that follows the realization of the first two lines of this verse, in which Kṛṣṇa, as he does in the *Śrīmad-Bhāgavatam*,[3] proclaims himself to be the original Supreme Person *(svayaṁ bhagavān)*.

Kṛṣṇa first says, "I *(aham)* am the source *(prabhavo)* of everything *(sarvasya)*, and everything *(sarvam)* proceeds *(pravartate)* from me *(mattaḥ)*." Here Kṛṣṇa declares himself to be both the efficient and ingredient cause of

3. ŚB. 1.3.28. See also ŚB. 1.1.1. In this verse Kṛṣṇa is described as the source of everything *(janmādyasya yataḥ)*, who is to be meditated on in devotion *(satyaṁ paraṁ dhīmahi)*.

the world. In pottery, the potter and the clay are the efficient and ingredient causes, respectively. However, in the case of the world, all systems of Vedānta recognize Brahman to be both causes, efficient and ingredient.

Not only is Kṛṣṇa the source of both the material and spiritual worlds, he oversees their maintenance as well. The spiritual domain is maintained by his incarnations and expansions. The material world is presided over by his expansion as Paramātmā. Brahmā and Śiva, his partial incarnations *(guṇāvatāras)*, create and destroy the material world, respectively. Furthermore, order in the civilized world, by the direction of the sacred *Vedas*, emanates from him as well. Kṛṣṇa is the Godhead himself *(svayaṁ bhagavān)*. Those who understand this are wise, the expression of which is their devotion to him. This is the general import.

The deeper meaning reveals that he who is *svayaṁ bhagavān*, the original Godhead from whom all other expressions of divinity emanate is *dhīra-lalita* Kṛṣṇa of Vraja, the playful Casanova subjugated by Rādhā's love. *Dhīra-praśānta* Kṛṣṇa of Dwārakā (Dwārakeśa Kṛṣṇa), the sober statesman who gives Upaniṣadic council to Arjuna on the battlefield, is a partial manifestation of Kṛṣṇa of Vraja. Although Kṛṣṇa of the *Gītā* preaches a sermon of love, the full face of love *(mukhya-rasa)* is expressed in Vraja alone. The fullest expression of love is the source of all other expressions of love. Thus in this verse, Kṛṣṇa of Vraja is speaking, as Dwārakeśa Kṛṣṇa's mind shifts from the battlefield to Vraja due to the influence of sacred Kurukṣetra.

Earlier in Kurukṣetra, Dwārakeśa Kṛṣṇa met with Rādhā and others from Vraja after killing the evil king Kaṁsa. They came to Kurukṣetra, as he did, to observe the solar eclipse. Amidst royal paraphernalia, entourage, and elephants, Dwārakeśa Kṛṣṇa, the ever-youthful prince, met with the beloved devotees of Vraja. Reminded of their love, he admitted that he was entirely purchased by them. At that time, his mother, Devakī, seeing the love of his so-called foster mother of Vraja by whom he had been raised, acknowledged that Kṛṣṇa was in fact Yaśodā's son in consideration of the intensity of her love. To Nanda and Yaśodā of Vraja, prince Kṛṣṇa was just their young boy, his princely paraphernalia merely an ornament.

Śrī Rādhā and the *gopīs* drew the *dhīra-lalita nāyaka* of Vraja from Kṛṣṇa's heart, reminding Kṛṣṇa of their youthful days of love in carefree Vraja: frolicking in its beautiful forests, Mount Govardhana, and the sandy banks of the Yamunā. They were not attracted to Kṛṣṇa's regal attire, for he remained to them their adolescent love. They were not city girls, and the formalities of high society held no attraction for them. Their Kṛṣṇa was not a prince to bow before, rather he who bowed to their love, attesting to its supremacy.[4] For the *gopīs*, Kṛṣṇa was, although the best of them, a mere village boy of Vraja, and by the force of their love, Kṛṣṇa admitted to the *gopīs* that even in the midst of princely life his heart was always with them, subjugated by their love.[5] It is thus through the lens of love, sacred aesthetic rapture, that Śrī Caitanya's disciples have envisioned Vraja's *dhīra-lalita* Kṛṣṇa at sacred Kurukṣetra in this verse, a vision of love *(bhāva- samanvitāḥ)* philosophically grounded *(budhā)*.

Spiritual love that knows no reason cares little for the Godhood of Godhead, yet it is this kind of love that brings one in touch with the fullest expression of the Absolute, the source of everything and its feeling, the Supreme God. At the same time, according to this verse, initially it is knowledge of Kṛṣṇa's supremacy and thus his supreme capacity to love that inspires one to approach him in absolute love—to give fully of oneself.

In the language of Rūpa Goswāmī, the fullest expression of the Absolute is Kṛṣṇa, who is *akhila-rasāmṛta-murtiḥ*, the reservoir of loving reciprocation in sacred aesthetic rapture (Brs. 1.1.1). Thus *svayaṁ bhagavān* Kṛṣṇa, after explaining his position as the source of all, speaks in the second half of this verse about the type of devotion he relishes—and by which he is realized.

Through the sacred literature Kṛṣṇa explains his own devotional *yoga*. B. R. Śrīdhara Deva Goswāmī comments that the words *mattaḥ sarvaṁ pravartate* in this verse indicate, "Every attempt and movement begins with me, including the methods by which everyone worships and serves me in devotion." Kṛṣṇa reveals himself through the methods of devotion he himself has given in the scripture. Study of the scripture in and of itself does not reveal him, but therein Kṛṣṇa reveals the means by which he can be known, his grace, and the means of attracting this grace, acts of devotion under the guidance of *śrī guru*.

B. R. Śrīdhara Deva Goswāmī cites the famous *Bhāgavata* verse in which Kṛṣṇa identifies the guru with himself, *ācāryaṁ māṁ vijānīyāt:* "I am the guru *(ācārya)*." (ŚB. 11.17.27) Thus it is Kṛṣṇa himself who teaches his devotional *yoga* to one who understands *(budhā)* him as *svayaṁ bhagavān*, the origin of all. He does so through his potency, Śrī Rādhā, who for the Gauḍīyas is represented by *śrī guru*, for she knows Kṛṣṇa like no one else. She knows everything about him: the original person, *svayaṁ bhagavān*.

4. See ŚB. 10.32.22.
5. See ŚB. 10.82.44.

Under her influence, the influence of Vraja *bhakti*, devotees worship Kṛṣṇa imbued with spontaneous love *(bhāva-samanvitāḥ)*.

Bhāva-samanvitāḥ indicates the sacred path of passionate love *(rāgānuga-bhakti)*. This is the path demarcated by Śrī Caitanya. B. R. Śrīdhara Deva Goswāmī remarks that the insight into the ultimacy of Vraja Kṛṣṇa is mentioned in the *Bhāgavata* (11.5.32) in relation to the worship of Śrī Caitanya himself, *yajanti hi sumedhasaḥ*. Endowed with divine wisdom begetting subtle theistic intelligence, devotees worship Śrī Caitanya as the combined form of Rādhā and Kṛṣṇa by means of *saṅkīrtana* (chanting God's name in unison). Such wisdom is described in this verse as *budhā*, and the subsequent worship as *bhāva-samanvitāḥ*.

The words *budhā* and *bhāva-samanvitāḥ* indicate the essence of *bhakti*. It is a wise existence, wise love, in which one is cognizant of one's relationship with Kṛṣṇa and joyfully functions in that loving relationship. This takes place on firm existential ground. Rūpa Goswāmī describes that one possessed of *bhāva* is under the influence of the cognitive *(saṁvit)* and joy *(hlādinī)* features of Kṛṣṇa's primary *śakti*, which is also composed of an existential feature *(sandhinī)*.[6] This is *budhā bhāva-samanvitāḥ*.

A feeling existence is not always a wise one. Misplaced feeling amounts to the experience of material existence, an existence rooted in ignorance. When our feeling *(bhāva)* is wise *(budhā)*, due to its being reposed in the perfect object of love that Kṛṣṇa describes himself to be in this verse, we dwell in a corresponding eternal existence. *Bhāva* means feeling, love, as well as existence. Our love is our existence. Kṛṣṇa next describes how his loving devotees exist and express their love for him.

Text 9

मच्चित्ता मद्गतप्राणा बोधयन्तः परस्परम् ।
कथयन्तश्च मां नित्यं तुष्यन्ति च रमन्ति च ॥९॥

mac-cittā mad-gata-prāṇā bodhayantaḥ parasparam/
kathayantaś ca māṁ nityaṁ tuṣyanti ca ramanti ca//

mat-cittāḥ—those whose minds are fixed on me; *mat-gata-prāṇāḥ*—those whose lives are absorbed in me; *bodhayantaḥ*—enlightening; *parasparam*—one another; *kathayantaḥ*—speaking; *ca*—and; *mām*—me; *nityam*—always; *tuṣyanti*—they derive satisfaction; *ca*—and; *ramanti*—they rejoice; *ca*—also.

6. Brs. 1.3.1

Those whose minds are fixed on me and whose lives are absorbed in me derive satisfaction and delight from enlightening one another and always speaking of me.

Even in Kṛṣṇa's absence from Vraja, his devotees continued to exist only for him. Their minds were fixed on him *(mac-cittā)*, and their lives absorbed in him, their very life breath *(mad-gata-prāṇā)*. They eternally discussed only Kṛṣṇa and his Vraja *līlās (kathayantaś ca māṁ nityam)*. From this they derived great satisfaction *(tuṣyanti)* even in his absence, and the *gopīs*' hearts grew fonder for him in conjugal love *(ramanti)*.

Here Kṛṣṇa continues to think of his devotees in Vraja and those aspiring for their standard of devotion. Although they derive satisfaction even in his separation by constantly speaking about him in their own assembly and ministering to the public about him as well, this is so because it increases their anticipation of meeting with him, in which they feel his presence.

Madhusūdana Saraswatī, following Śaṅkara himself, acknowledges that the word *ramanti* in this verse implies the delight of love that a young girl feels for a young boy, as the *gopīs* felt for Kṛṣṇa. Śaṅkara says, "They [devotees] find their contentment and delight as though they have met with their beloved." *Ramanti* speaks of the *gopīs* and those in this world who tread the path of *rāgānuga-bhakti* in search of Kṛṣṇa following in the wake of the *gopīs*' love. It speaks of union with Kṛṣṇa through longing in separation, the dark night of the soul. As Kṛṣṇa continues to explain, such devotees constantly worship him, and he assists them in their efforts for union with him.

Text 10

तेषां सततयुक्तानां भजतां प्रीतिपूर्वकम् ।
ददामि बुद्धियोगं तं येन मामुपयान्ति ते ॥१०॥

teṣāṁ satata-yuktānāṁ bhajatāṁ prīti-pūrvakam/
dadāmi buddhi-yogaṁ taṁ yena mām upayānti te//

teṣām—to them; *satata-yuktānām*—constantly devoted; *bhajatām*—to those who worship; *prīti-pūrvakam*—with love; *dadāmi*—I give; *buddhi-yogam*—power of discrimination; *tam*—it; *yena*—by which; *mām*—(to) me; *upayānti*—they come; *te*—they.

To those who are constantly devoted, who worship me with love, I give the power of discrimination by which they come to me.

Madhusūdana Saraswatī acknowledges that the words *satata-yuktānām* indicate those who are ever devoted to Kṛṣṇa, as well as that *prīti-pūrvakam* indicates selfless love. Regarding the previous verse, he says that the contentment *(tuṣyanti)* of the devotees under discussion is such that they feel, "We have attained everything through this much [devotion] alone. There is no need for anything else to be achieved." However, in contradiction to this he writes in his commentary on the present verse that Kṛṣṇa gives *(dadāmi)* the power of discrimination, the *yoga* of wisdom *(buddhi-yoga* or *jñāna-yoga)* to such selfless devotees. This implies that *bhakti* is merely the means to *jñāna* and thereby salvation. According to Adwaita Vedānta, upon attaining salvation, devotion retires. This implies that in and of itself *bhakti* does not bear the fruit of absolute contentment, yet Kṛṣṇa himself has already instructed Arjuna at the close of the ninth chapter that his devotees come to him by devotion alone (Bg. 9.34). Knowledge and detachment are concomitant factors of devotion.[7] Thus in a general sense, the power of discrimination that Kṛṣṇa gives his devotees is the cognitive aspect of *bhakti* proper. He gives them knowledge of their eternal relationship with him, and cultivating this relationship, his devotees come to him. From his use of the term *buddhi-yogam* in this verse, it is apparent that Kṛṣṇa's use of the same term earlier in the second chapter (Bg. 2.39), while overtly referring to *niṣkāma-karma-yoga*, implies *bhakti-yoga*. The full sense of *buddhi-yoga* is *bhakti*.

Kṛṣṇadāsa Kavirāja Goswāmī cites this verse three times in *Caitanya-caritāmṛta*.[8] In his initial citing he connects it with the *Śrīmad-Bhāgavatam*'s *catuḥ-ślokī* in the context of explaining the nature of the instructing guru *(śikṣā-guru)*, who enlightens one with transcendental knowledge. In his commentary on Kavirāja Goswāmī's citation, Bhaktivedanta Swami Prabhupāda writes, "The Lord declares that by enlightenment in theistic knowledge he awards attachment for him to those who constantly engage in his transcendental loving service. This awakening of divine consciousness enthralls a devotee, who thus relishes his eternal transcendental mellow *(rasa)*."

Relative to Kṛṣṇa's emotional state from which this verse issues, there is a deeper meaning to consider. For one who is constantly *(satatam)* devoted *(yuktānām)* to Kṛṣṇa, worshipping him *(bhajatām)* with love *(prīti-pūrvakam)*, what need does such a devotee have for power of discrimination

7. See ŚB. 1.2.7.
8. Cc. Ādi 1.49, Madhya 24.173,192.

(buddhi-yogam) or even attachment for Kṛṣṇa in terms of sacred aesthetic rapture, when this attachment is the very basis of their perpetual loving worship? Such devotees are not practitioners, they are Kṛṣṇa's devotees of Vraja, who embody the ideals of natural, inborn spontaneous love *(rāgātmika)*.[9] Here Kṛṣṇa is speaking of the *gopīs* in particular, as he flows into this verse from the previous one on the nectar ocean of the word *ramanti* (conjugal love) and its implications. The *gopīs* have already discriminated between matter and spirit, and exercised powerful discrimination within that which is spiritual as well, choosing, for example, Kṛṣṇa over Nārāyaṇa. What further need do they have for the power of discrimination? Having already attained Kṛṣṇa, the words *yena mām upayanti te* (they come to me) in this verse also appear redundant. Furthermore, the term *buddhi-yoga* in the *Gītā*'s second chapter, verse 39, is often understood to indicate *niṣkāma-karma-yoga*, detached action within the context of scripturally prescribed duties.[10] What need do elevated devotees such as the *gopīs* have for practicing detachment or prescribed duties?

If we take *buddhi-yoga* to mean *niṣkāma-karma-yoga*, we will have to think that Kṛṣṇa inspires the *gopīs* in selfless action, for they attend to household affairs and their socioreligious duties responsibly lest their family members become suspicious. They do so with no attachment whatsoever to the results, their minds absorbed in the hope of meeting secretly with Kṛṣṇa. Because they do meet him in the dead of night when all of the other devotees of Vraja's *līlā* sleep and dream of Kṛṣṇa but have no active service, the *gopīs*' loving service is sometimes referred to as "twenty-four hour" service in Kṛṣṇa's *nitya-līlā (satata-yuktānām)*.

Those who hear *dhīra-lalita* Kṛṣṇa of Vraja, *pūrṇatama svayaṁ bhagavān*, speaking in this verse understand *buddhi-yogam* in light of Kṛṣṇa's Vraja *līlā*. Kṛṣṇa is the paramour of the *gopīs*. They cannot meet with him openly. How do they meet with him? Kṛṣṇa gives them the power of discrimination through his sidelong glances as to how to steal away in the night and meet him *(mām upayanti)* on the banks of the Yamunā.

Text 11

तेषामेवानुकम्पार्थमहमज्ञानजं तमः ।
नाशयाम्यात्मभावस्थो ज्ञानदीपेन भास्वता ॥११॥

9. See Brs. 1.2.271–289.

10. In this edition *buddhi-yoga* in Bg. 2.39 has been explained to indicate *bhakti* in accordance with the commentary of Viśvanātha Cakravartī Ṭhākura.

teṣām evānukampārtham aham ajñāna-jaṁ tamaḥ/
nāśayāmy ātma-bhāva-stho jñāna-dīpena bhāsvatā//

teṣām—for them; *eva*—indeed; *anukampā-artham*—out of compassion; *aham*—I; *ajñāna-jam*—born of ignorance; *tamaḥ*—darkness; *nāśayāmi*—I destroy; *ātma-bhāva*—within their souls; *sthaḥ*—dwelling; *jñāna*—knowledge; *dīpena*—with the lamp; *bhāsvatā*—effulgent.

Out of compassion for them, I, dwelling within their soul, destroy the darkness born of ignorance with the effulgent lamp of knowledge.

Kṛṣṇa shows compassion to practitioners on the path of devotion by illuminating their hearts with the highest knowledge of himself and their relationship with him. This knowledge is not of the nature of *sattva-guṇa*. It is transcendental. Kṛṣṇa reveals it from within the devotee who keeps him on the altar of his heart.

While other means of removing ignorance are available to those on paths other than unalloyed *bhakti*, Kṛṣṇa's devotees rely solely on him for destroying their ignorance. Thus he is personally involved in removing the ignorance of only his devotees, and only in their hearts does he personally dwell, witnessing their trials and tribulations life after life. As his devotees search for him everywhere, begging from door to door on his behalf, suffering ridicule, and shedding tears for him, he is aware of all these things. He knows the trouble they take to come to him, and it is difficult for him to bear. Thus he illumines their path, holding a lamp to their dark night of separation, revealing himself within their hearts and enabling them to realize all that they have heard about him from scripture. As *jñāna* also refers to scriptural knowledge, the lamp of knowledge *(jñāna-dīpena)* also refers to Kṛṣṇa's illuminating from within his devotee's heart the esoteric meaning of the sacred literature, its deepest import regarding the practice of *rāgānuga-bhakti*.

Relative to Vraja *bhakti* and the feeling of this verse, Kṛṣṇa continues to speak of the Vraja *gopīs* and how their love affects him. In consideration of this, the present verse appears to suffer from the same inconsistency found in the previous verse. What need do the Vraja *gopīs* have for the lamplight of knowledge *(jñāna-dīpa)*? This is the query of B. R. Śrīdhara Deva Goswāmī, who bases his esoteric rendering on Viśvanātha Cakravartī's claim that the *jñāna* mentioned in this verse is not the knowledge of this world *(sattva-guṇa)* leading to purity and transcendental realization, but rather *vilakṣaṇa-jñāna*, "extraordinary knowledge." B. R. Śrīdhara Deva Goswāmī goes on to offer an alternative translation based on the words *teṣām evānukampārtham*, which have been rendered above as "out of compassion for them." He informs us that it can also be rendered, "I want *their* favor, I aspire for the favor of those devotees of the highest order. Being conquered by the love of those devotees, when I cannot tolerate their pain of separation, I at once come running to satisfy them, and reveal to them with special light, special consciousness, 'I have returned to you—see me now.' With powerful brilliance *(jñāna-dīpena)* I show them my presence when they are very much in need of me, and I relieve their pain of separation." Perhaps the best example in all of the sacred literature of Kṛṣṇa's brightening the dark night of the soul's separation from him is Kṛṣṇa's return to the *gopīs* after his disappearance during the *rāsa-līlā* (ŚB. 10.32.2).

Silenced by Kṛṣṇa's speech and concerned by his sudden pause as he drifted emotionally from the battlefield, Arjuna considered how to bring Kṛṣṇa back to the present reality. He does so in seven verses of his own by praising and accepting what Kṛṣṇa had said about his Godliness and asking Kṛṣṇa to continue in this vein.

Texts 12–13

अर्जुन उवाच
परं ब्रह्म परं धाम पवित्रं परमं भवान् ।
पुरुषं शाश्वतं दिव्यमादिदेवमजं विभुम् ॥१२॥
आहुस्त्वामृषयः सर्वे देवर्षिर्नारदस्तथा ।
असितो देवलो व्यासः स्वयं चैव ब्रवीषि मे ॥१३॥

arjuna uvāca
paraṁ brahma paraṁ dhāma pavitraṁ paramaṁ bhavān/
puruṣaṁ śāśvataṁ divyam ādi-devam ajaṁ vibhum//
āhus tvām ṛṣayaḥ sarve devarṣir nāradas tathā/
asito devalo vyāsaḥ svayaṁ caiva bravīṣi me//

arjunaḥ uvāca—Arjuna said; *param*—supreme; *brahma*—Brahman; *param*—supreme; *dhāma*—abode; *pavitram*—purifier; *paramam*—supreme; *bhavān*—you; *puruṣam*—person; *śāśvatam*—eternal; *divyam*—divine; *ādi-devam*—the primal God; *ajam*—unborn; *vibhum*—omnipresent; *āhuḥ*—they say; *tvām*—you; *ṛṣayaḥ*—the sages; *sarve*—all; *deva-ṛṣiḥ*—the sage among the gods; *nāradaḥ*—Nārada; *tathā*—also; *asitaḥ*—Asita; *devalaḥ*—Devala; *vyāsaḥ*—Vyāsa; *svayam*—yourself; *ca*—also; *eva*—certainly; *bravīṣi*—you say; *me*—(to) me.

Arjuna said: You are the Supreme Brahman, the supreme abode, the supreme purifier, the eternal divine person, the primal God, unborn and omnipresent, for all the sages (including) Nārada, Asita, Devala, and Vyāsa (Kṛṣṇa-dvaipāyana) say so, as have you yourself (just now).

Arjuna speaks here for the first time since the second verse of the eighth chapter. He does so after Kṛṣṇa's speech has reached a crescendo, rendering him speechless, his mind no longer on the battlefield. Arjuna brings Kṛṣṇa back by speaking of his opulence, confirming aloud that he has understood what Kṛṣṇa has said about himself. Thus the topic reverts from devotion back to its initial impetus: knowledge of Kṛṣṇa's opulence. This topic will continue almost to the end of the eleventh chapter. At the end of the eleventh chapter and throughout the twelfth, the discussion will revert back to devotion.

For one interested in a life of devotion, the importance of knowing Kṛṣṇa's opulence cannot be underestimated. Thus there is considerable emphasis on this in the *Gītā*'s middle six chapters dealing with devotion. At the same time, the knowledge of Kṛṣṇa's opulence, while initially important, ultimately takes a subordinate position to devotion itself. This is the import of the balance of chapters 10 and 11.

Before asking Kṛṣṇa to continue to speak about his opulence, Arjuna praises him in terms of that which he has said about his majesty earlier. Praising Kṛṣṇa as the Supreme Brahman *(paraṁ brahma)* and the supreme abode *(paraṁ dhāma)* is in striking contrast to Kṛṣṇa's characterization of himself as one dependent on his devotees *(teṣām evānukampārtham)*. Arjuna's speech effectively brings Kṛṣṇa down from the lofty love of Vraja to continue his discourse. At the conclusion of the *Gītā*, Kṛṣṇa will again drift to Vraja, thus bringing the *Song of God* to a close.

The sages referred to in this verse are many. Their praises of Kṛṣṇa are found throughout the sacred literature. Those mentioned by name are particularly prominent, and among them Nārada is preeminent.[11]

Text 14

सर्वमेतदृतं मन्ये यन्मां वदसि केशव ।
न हि ते भगवन् व्यक्तिं विदुर्देवा न दानवाः ॥१४॥

11. Nārada is the famous *devarṣi*, sage among the gods, described throughout the *Purāṇas*. He is said to have authored the *Nārada-bhakti-sūtra*, an important treatise on devotion. Kṛṣṇa is his Deity.

sarvam etad ṛtaṁ manye yan māṁ vadasi keśava/
na hi te bhagavan vyaktiṁ vidur devā na dānavāḥ//

sarvam—all; *etat*—this; *ṛtam*—truth; *manye*—I believe; *yat*—which; *mām*—me; *vadasi*—you tell; *keśava*—O Keśava; *na*—not; *hi*—certainly; *te*—your; *bhagavan*—O Blessed One; *vyaktim*—manifestation; *viduḥ*—they know; *devāḥ*—the gods; *na*—not; *dānavāḥ*—the demons.

O Keśava, I accept all that you have said as true, for, O Blessed One, neither the gods nor the demons know your glorious manifestation!

Addressing Kṛṣṇa as Keśava and Bhagavān, Arjuna acknowledges Kṛṣṇa's omniscience. Thus he says, "I accept all that you have said, and I know that you are aware of my acceptance, being omniscient." Gauḍīya commentators, as well as Madhusūdana Saraswatī, understand the name Keśava to indicate supremacy over Brahmā *(ka)* and Śiva *(īśa)*. Madhusūdana Saraswatī glorifies Keśava as "He who looks upon Brahmā and Śiva with compassion, even though they rule over all." This person is the Blessed Lord (Bhagavān).

In this verse, Arjuna confirms that which Kṛṣṇa said in the second verse of this chapter regarding the gods being unaware of Kṛṣṇa's position. Mention of the demons' ignorance is for the purpose of including everyone in between. Implied also is the ignorance of the sages in this regard—even though they know Kṛṣṇa as the Supreme Brahman—for they do not know how he can be the son of Devakī.

Text 15

स्वयमेवात्मनात्मानं वेत्थ त्वं पुरुषोत्तम ।
भूतभावन भूतेष देवदेव जगत्पते ॥१५॥

svayam evātmanātmānaṁ vettha tvaṁ puruṣottama/
bhūta-bhāvana bhūteśa deva-deva jagat-pate//

svayam—yourself; *eva*—alone; *ātmanā*—by yourself; *ātmānam*—yourself; *vettha*—you know; *tvam*—you; *puruṣa-uttama*—O best of persons; *bhūta-bhāvana*—O cause of the welfare of beings; *bhūta-īśa*—O Lord of beings; *deva-deva*—O God of gods; *jagat-pate*—O Lord of the universe.

You alone know yourself through your own power, O best of persons, cause of the welfare of beings, Lord of beings, God of gods, Lord of the universe.

Arjuna attests to Kṛṣṇa's supremacy by saying first that, unlike others who know themselves by the help of the gods or sages, Kṛṣṇa, being above them, knows himself in full by his own power alone. He knows himself by dint of his primary *śakti*.

Arjuna's pronouncement is in response to any possible playful rebuttal of Kṛṣṇa such as, "How can I know that which no one else knows?" Following this challenge, Arjuna addresses Kṛṣṇa as Puruṣottama, "best of persons." Madhusūdana Saraswatī says, "O Puruṣottama, in comparison with you all persons without exception are inferior. Therefore what is impossible for them is surely possible for you."

After declaring Kṛṣṇa to be the Supreme Person, Arjuna substantiates his claim by explaining the position of the Puruṣottama. He is the one who brings other beings into existence *(bhūta-bhāvana)* and causes their welfare, the benevolent father of all. He is the Lord of the created *(bhūteśa)* as well. He is the God of gods *(deva-deva)*, the one who is worshipped by all the *devas*, and the Lord of the universe *(jagat-pate)*, by virtue of manifesting the *Vedas* which govern its inhabitants.

Text 16

वक्तुमर्हस्यशेषेण दिव्या ह्यात्मविभूतयः ।
याभिर्विभूतिभिर्लोकानिमांस्त्वं व्याप्य तिष्ठसि ॥१६॥

vaktum arhasy aśeṣeṇa divyā hy ātma-vibhūtayaḥ/
yābhir vibhūtibhir lokān imāṁs tvaṁ vyāpya tiṣṭhasi//

vaktum arhasi—please speak; *aśeṣeṇa*—completely; *divyāḥ*—divine; *hi*—certainly; *ātma*—your own; *vibhūtayaḥ*—manifestations; *yābhiḥ*—by which; *vibhūtibhiḥ*—by the manifestations; *lokān*—all the worlds; *imān*—these; *tvam*—you; *vyāpya*—pervading; *tiṣṭhasi*—you abide.

Please speak without reservation about the divine manifestations by which you pervade all the worlds and abide in them.

Arjuna asks Kṛṣṇa to speak further about his divine manifestations *(ātma-vibhūtayaḥ)* so that he can better follow Kṛṣṇa's advice to always think of him. He should do so, Arjuna says, without reservation *(aśeṣeṇa)*, as friend to friend even though Kṛṣṇa is God and Arjuna his devotee. As will be clear from Kṛṣṇa's reply, which takes one through the majority of chapter 11, such descriptions are for beginners to help them understand the glory of Kṛṣṇa, he who pervades everything and is represented as the best and essence of all things. Thinking of these representations of Kṛṣṇa in material nature as such, one naturally begins to think of Kṛṣṇa himself.

Text 17

कथं विद्यामहं योगिंस्त्वां सदा परिचिन्तयन् ।
केषु केषु च भावेषु चिन्त्योऽसि भगवन्मया ॥१७॥

kathaṁ vidyām ahaṁ yogiṁs tvāṁ sadā paricintayan/
keṣu keṣu ca bhāveṣu cintyo 'si bhagavan mayā//

katham—how; *vidyām*—shall I know; *aham*—I; *yogin*—O mystic; *tvām*—you; *sadā*—constantly; *paricintayan*—meditating on; *keṣu keṣu*—in what various; *ca*—and; *bhāveṣu*—aspects of being; *cintyaḥ asi*—you are to be thought of; *bhagavan*—O Blessed One; *mayā*—by me.

O mystic, how can I know you in constant meditation, and in what various aspects of being am I to think of you, O Blessed One?

By contemplating Kṛṣṇa though his various manifestations mentioned in this chapter and in chapters 7 and 9 that parallel these descriptions, one comes to appreciate the personal form of Kṛṣṇa as the source of all being, the supreme mystic who possesses the *śakti* known as *yoga-māyā*. At that time, one can meditate on his personal name, form, and *līlās* without distraction, one's heart sufficiently purified. This is the verdict of *Śrīmad-Bhāgavatam* (2.2.14), and particularly the commentary of Viśvanātha Cakravartī Ṭhākura. As an introduction to the theology of the *Bhāgavata*, *Śrī Gītā* suggests the same course.

The *Bhāgavata* cautions that those without love for the personality of Godhead should not meditate on his personal form. Such persons are advised to meditate first on the universal form of God (*viśva-rūpa*), in which his form is imagined in terms of the mountains, seas, sun, moon, and so on. Viśvanātha Cakravartī goes further in commenting that those whose intelligence is still impure should not even meditate on the four-armed form of Viṣṇu. Thus out of his own humility and under the influence of Kṛṣṇa's divine bewilderment for the sake of teaching others through him, Arjuna asks Kṛṣṇa how he can meditate on his divine universal manifestations. Arjuna considers himself dull and unfit to understand the opulence of Kṛṣṇa, when even gods and sages have difficulty. Thus he asks the following question, which leads to the description of Kṛṣṇa's universal form.

Text 18

विस्तरेणात्मनो योगं विभूतिं च जनार्दन ।
भूयः कथय तृप्तिर्हि शृण्वतो नास्ति मेऽमृतम् ॥१८॥

vistareṇātmano yogaṁ vibhūtiṁ ca janārdana/
bhūyaḥ kathaya tṛptir hi śṛṇvato nāsti me 'mṛtam//

vistareṇa—in detail; *ātmanaḥ*—your; *yogam*—mystic power; *vibhūtim*—opulence; *ca*—and; *janārdana*—O Janārdana; *bhūyaḥ*—again; *kathaya*—tell; *tṛptiḥ*—satisfaction; *hi*—certainly; *śṛṇvataḥ*—of hearing; *na asti*—there is not; *me*—my; *amṛtam*—nectar.

O Janārdana, tell me again in detail of your mystic power and opulence, for I am never satiated hearing your nectar.

Although Kṛṣṇa has already stated that he is the source of everything, Arjuna asks to hear about this metaphysical truth in greater detail. Arjuna's question is practical, and it is further justified by his addressing Kṛṣṇa as Janārdana. Madhusūdana Saraswatī explains "Janārdana" as one who is prayed to *(ardana)* by all people *(jana)*. Madhusūdana Saraswatī further notes the use of three figures of speech in this verse,[12] the combined effect of which indicates great eagerness on the part of Arjuna resulting from his experience of overwhelming sweetness in his exchange with Kṛṣṇa thus far.

Viśvanātha Cakravartī says that by addressing Kṛṣṇa as Janārdana, Arjuna is saying, "By your nectarean instruction you make persons *(jana)* like myself hungry for more and thus make us beg you to continue." Here *ardayase* is taken as synonymous with *yācayasi*, "make us beg." This is a recondite use of the verb. An example of this usage is found in *Raghuvaṁśa* (5.17). Viśvanātha Cakravartī Ṭhākura says that Arjuna, more than praying, is begging Kṛṣṇa to satisfy his greed to hear more about him. His thirst remains unquenched even in the midst of the flow of immortal nectar he has been drinking through his ears. His addressing Kṛṣṇa as Janārdana thus

12. *Rūpaka*, *apahnuti*, and *atiśayokti*. The *rūpaka* (metaphor) is "nectar." The *apahnuti* (concealment) is in the fact that Kṛṣṇa's speech itself is not mentioned as the element being compared to nectar. The *atiśayokti* (hyperbole) is in identifying Kṛṣṇa's words with nectar.

reveals that he is qualified for more than meditation on Kṛṣṇa's universal form, for his greed to hear is a sign of his love for Kṛṣṇa.

Arjuna has endeared himself to Kṛṣṇa by making this request and thus Kṛṣṇa elaborates on his opulence.

Text 19

श्रीभगवानुवाच
हन्त ते कथयिष्यामि दिव्या ह्यात्मविभूतयः ।
प्राधान्यतः कुरुश्रेष्ठ नास्त्यन्तो विस्तरस्य मे ॥१९॥

śrī-bhagavān uvāca
hanta te kathayiṣyāmi divyā hy ātma-vibhūtayaḥ/
prādhānyataḥ kuru-śreṣṭha nāsty anto vistarasya me//

śrī-bhagavān uvāca—the Lord of Śrī said; *hanta*—listen; *te*—(to) you; *kathayiṣyāmi*—I shall explain; *divyāḥ*—divine; *hi*—certainly; *ātma-vibhūtayaḥ*—manifestations; *prādhānyataḥ*—prominent; *kuru-śreṣṭha*—O best of the Kurus; *na asti*—there is not; *antaḥ*—end; *vistarasya*—of the extent; *me*—my.

The Lord of Śrī said: Listen as I explain to you only those divine manifestations of my Self that are prominent, for there is no end to the extent of my opulence.

As Arjuna is charmed by Kṛṣṇa's words, so too is Kṛṣṇa charmed by Arjuna's request. Thus he consents to it using the word *hanta*, an affectionate affirmation. However, Kṛṣṇa qualifies his response in two ways. The word *prādhānyataḥ* means both those manifestations that are "most prominent" as well as "in the order of their prominence." Thus Kṛṣṇa begins in the next verse by mentioning his manifestation as the Supersoul.

Text 20

अहमात्मा गुडाकेश सर्वभूताशयस्थितः ।
अहमादिश्च मध्यं च भूतानामन्त एव च ॥२०॥

aham ātmā guḍākeśa sarva-bhūtāśaya-sthitaḥ/
aham ādiś ca madhyaṁ ca bhūtānām anta eva ca//

aham—I; *ātmā*—the Self; *guḍākeśa*—O Guḍākeśa; *sarva-bhūta*—of all beings; *āśaya-sthitaḥ*—abiding in the heart; *aham*—I; *ādiḥ*—the beginning; *ca*—and; *madhyam*—middle; *ca*—and; *bhūtānām*—of all beings; *antaḥ*—end; *eva*—certainly; *ca*—and.

I am the Self, O Guḍākeśa, abiding in the hearts of all beings. Of all beings I am the beginning, middle, and end.

Kṛṣṇa addresses Arjuna as Guḍākeśa, indicating his qualification for meditation. He is one who has conquered sleep and is thus qualified in the least to meditate on the four-armed form of Kṛṣṇa as Paramātmā. Kṛṣṇa says, "I, *svayaṁ bhagavān*, am the Supersoul in all souls' hearts." In this way he makes it clear that the Paramātmā *(ātmā)* is a manifestation of himself. It is through his Paramātmā feature that Kṛṣṇa is the cause *(ādiḥ)* of the world and the living beings. Through this feature he further oversees the maintenance of material existence in its middle phase *(madhyam)* and sees to its annihilation in the end *(antaḥ)*.

Having spoken first of the qualification for internal meditation on the form of God, Kṛṣṇa next speaks at length of how less qualified persons can begin to contemplate him.

Text 21

आदित्यानामहं विष्णुर्ज्योतिषां रविरंशुमान् ।
मरीचिर्मरुतामस्मि नक्षत्राणामहं शशी ॥२१॥

ādityānām ahaṁ viṣṇur jyotiṣāṁ ravir aṁśumān/
marīcir marutām asmi nakṣatrāṇām ahaṁ śaśī//

ādityānām—of the Ādityas; *aham*—I; *viṣṇuḥ*—Viṣṇu; *jyotiṣām*—of lights; *raviḥ*—the sun; *aṁśu-mān*—radiant; *marīciḥ*—Marīci; *marutām*—of the Maruts; *asmi*—I am; *nakṣatrāṇām*—of the stars; *aham*—I; *śaśī*—the moon.

Of the Ādityas I am Viṣṇu; of lights, the radiant sun; of the Maruts I am Marīci; of heavenly bodies I am the moon.

The Viṣṇu among the twelve *ādityas* is the incarnation known as Vāmana. Later Kṛṣṇa will also mention Rāma and Vāsudeva within the list of his opulences *(vibhūtis)*. However, incarnations of Kṛṣṇa such as Vāmana and Rāma and expansions such as Vāsudeva are not Kṛṣṇa's *vibhūtis* but God himself. They are included in this section because of their appearing in the material world as if part of it.

Text 22

वेदानां सामवेदोऽस्मि देवानामस्मि वासवः ।
इन्द्रियाणां मनश्चास्मि भूतानामस्मि चेतना ॥२२॥

vedānāṁ sāma-vedo 'smi devānām asmi vāsavaḥ/
indriyāṇāṁ manaś cāsmi bhūtānām asmi cetanā//

vedānām—of the *Vedas; sāma-vedaḥ*—the *Sāma Veda; asmi*—I am; *devānām*—of the gods; *asmi*—I am; *vāsavaḥ*—Indra; *indriyāṇām*—of the senses; *manaḥ*—the mind; *ca*—also; *asmi*—I am; *bhūtānām*—of the living beings; *asmi*—I am; *cetanā*—consciousness.

Of the Vedas I am the Sāma Veda; of the gods I am Indra. Of the senses I am the mind, and of the living beings I am consciousness.

The *Sāma Veda* is originally derived from the *Ṛg Veda*. It consists of hymns of praise and is very beautiful. Indra is the chief *(indra)* of the gods. The mind is the sixth sense, the most powerful and subtle of all. That which is the essence of living beings is consciousness.

Text 23

रुद्राणां शंकरश्चास्मि वित्तेशो यक्षरक्षसाम् ।
वसूनां पावकश्चास्मि मेरुः शिखरिणामहम् ॥२३॥

rudrāṇāṁ śaṅkaraś cāsmi vitteśo yakṣa-rakṣasām/
vasūnāṁ pāvakaś cāsmi meruḥ śikhariṇām aham//

rudrāṇām—of the Rudras; *śaṅkaraḥ*—Śaṅkara; *ca*—also; *asmi*—I am; *vitta-īśaḥ*—Kuvera; *yakṣa-rakṣasām*—of the Yakṣas and Rākṣasas; *vasūnām*—of the Vasus; *pāvakaḥ*—fire; *ca*—also; *asmi*—I am; *meruḥ*—Meru; *śikhariṇām*—of mountains; *aham*—I.

Of the Rudras I am Śaṅkara; of the Yakṣas I am Kuvera. Of the Vasus I am fire (Agni), and of mountains I am Meru.

The eleven Rudras are manifestations of Śiva. Śaṅkara is Śiva himself. Kuvera is the treasurer of the gods and a ghostly associate of Śiva. Agni is the god of fire, and Meru the mythic mountain of the Himālayas involved in such things as creation.

Text 24

पुरोधसां च मुख्यं मां विद्धि पार्थ बृहस्पतिम् ।
सेनानीनामहं स्कन्दः सरसामस्मि सागरः ॥२४॥

purodhasāṁ ca mukhyaṁ māṁ viddhi pārtha bṛhaspatim/
senānīnām ahaṁ skandaḥ sarasām asmi sāgaraḥ//

purodhasām—of priests; *ca*—also; *mukhyam*—the chief; *mām*—me; *viddhi*—know; *pārtha*—O Pārtha; *bṛhaspatim*—Bṛhaspati; *senānīnām*—of military commanders; *aham*—I; *skandaḥ*—Skanda; *sarasām*—of bodies of water; *asmi*—I; *sāgaraḥ*—the ocean.

Of priests, O Pārtha, know me to be the chief, Bṛhaspati. Of military commanders I am Skanda; of bodies of water I am the ocean.

Indra is the king of the gods and Bṛhaspati is his priest. The sense of the unlimited experienced when gazing at the ocean reminds one of God.

Text 25

महर्षीणां भृगुरहं गिरामस्म्येकमक्षरम् ।
यज्ञानां जपयज्ञोऽस्मि स्थावराणां हिमालयः ॥२५॥

maharṣīṇāṁ bhṛgur ahaṁ girām asmy ekam akṣaram/
yajñānāṁ japa-yajño 'smi sthāvarāṇāṁ himālayaḥ//

mahā-ṛṣīṇām—of the great sages; *bhṛguḥ*—Bhṛgu; *aham*—I; *girām*—of utterances; *asmi*—I am; *ekam akṣaram*—the single syllable; *yajñānām*—of sacrifices; *japa-yajñaḥ*—*japa*; *asmi*—I am; *sthāvarāṇām*—of immovable things; *himālayaḥ*—the Himālayas.

Of the great sages I am Bhṛgu; of utterances, the single syllable (oṁ); of sacrifices I am japa; of that which is immovable I am the Himālayas.

Japa refers to the sacrifice of inaudibly reciting one's *mantra*, an important aspect of spiritual practice.

Text 26

अश्वत्थः सर्ववृक्षाणां देवर्षीणां च नारदः ।
गन्धर्वाणां चित्ररथः सिद्धानां कपिलो मुनिः ॥२६॥

aśvatthaḥ sarva-vṛkṣāṇāṁ devarṣīṇāṁ ca nāradaḥ/
gandharvāṇāṁ citrarathaḥ siddhānāṁ kapilo muniḥ//

aśvatthaḥ—Pippala tree; *sarva-vṛkṣāṇām*—of all trees; *deva-ṛṣīṇām*—of the godly seers; *ca*—and; *nāradaḥ*—Nārada; *gandharvāṇām*—of Gandharvas;

citrarathaḥ—Citraratha; *siddhānām*—of the *siddhas*; *kapilaḥ muniḥ*—Kapila Muni.

Of trees I am the Aśvattha (Pippala tree); of the godly seers I am Nārada; of Gandharvas (heavenly musicians) I am Citraratha; of the siddhas I am Kapila.

Text 27

उच्चैःश्रवसमश्वानां विद्धि माममृतोद्भवम् ।
ऐरावतं गजेन्द्राणां नराणां च नराधिपम् ॥२७॥

uccaiḥśravasam aśvānāṁ viddhi mām amṛtodbhavam/
airāvataṁ gajendrāṇāṁ narāṇāṁ ca narādhipam//

uccaiḥśravasam—Uccaiḥśravā; *aśvānām*—of horses; *viddhi*—know; *mām*—me; *amṛta-udbhavam*—born of nectar; *airāvatam*—Airāvata; *gaja-indrāṇām*—of lordly elephants; *narāṇām*—of human beings; *ca*—and; *nara-adhipam*—the king.

Of horses know me as Uccaiḥśravā, born of the nectar of immortality. Of lordly elephants, Airāvata, and of men, the king.

Uccaiḥśravā and Airāvata are said to have been churned from the milk ocean at the dawn of creation. That kings are to be taken as representatives of God speaks of the *Gītā*'s standard of world leadership.

Text 28

आयुधानामहं वज्रं धेनूनामस्मि कामधुक् ।
प्रजनश्चास्मि कन्दर्पः सर्पाणामस्मि वासुकिः ॥२८॥

āyudhānām ahaṁ vajraṁ dhenūnām asmi kāmadhuk/
prajanaś cāsmi kandarpaḥ sarpāṇām asmi vāsukiḥ//

āyudhānām—of weapons; *aham*—I; *vajram*—the thunderbolt; *dhenūnām*—of cows; *asmi*—I am; *kāma-dhuk*—the *kāma-dhenu*; *prajanaḥ*—procreating; *ca*—and; *asmi*—I am; *kandarpaḥ*—Cupid; *sarpāṇām*—of serpents; *asmi*—I am; *vāsukiḥ*—Vāsuki.

Of weapons I am the thunderbolt; of cows, the wish-fulfilling kāmadhenu. Of progenitors I am Cupid, and of serpents I am Vāsuki.

The thunderbolt is considered to be the weapon of Indra, king of the gods. The magical *kāmadhenu* is well known in Purāṇic lore, as is the serpent Vāsuki.

Text 29

अनन्तश्चास्मि नागानां वरुणो यादसामहम् ।
पितॄणामर्यमा चास्मि यमः संयमतामहम् ॥२९॥

anantaś cāsmi nāgānāṁ varuṇo yādasām aham/
pitṝṇām aryamā cāsmi yamaḥ saṁyamatām aham//

anantaḥ—Ananta; *ca*—and; *asmi*—I am; *nāgānām*—of *nāgas*; *varuṇaḥ*—Varuṇa; *yādasām*—of aquatics; *aham*—I; *pitṝṇām*—of the ancestors; *aryamā*—Aryamā; *ca*—and; *asmi*—I am; *yamaḥ*—Yama; *saṁyamatām*—of all regulators; *aham*—I.

Of nāgas I am Ananta; of aquatics, Varuṇa. Of the ancestors I am Aryamā, and of those who punish and reward I am Yama.

Varuṇa and Aryamā are the leaders of their constituents: aquatics and ancestors, respectively. Yama is the god to whom the soul must account at death.

Text 30

प्रह्लादश्चास्मि दैत्यानां कालः कलयतामहम् ।
मृगाणां च मृगेन्द्रोऽहं वैनतेयश्च पक्षिणाम् ॥३०॥

prahlādaś cāsmi daityānāṁ kālaḥ kalayatām aham/
mṛgāṇāṁ ca mṛgendro 'haṁ vainateyaś ca pakṣiṇām//

prahlādaḥ—Prahlāda; *ca*—and; *asmi*—I am; *daityānām*—of demons; *kālaḥ*—time; *kalayatām*—of calculators; *aham*—I; *mṛgāṇām*—of animals; *ca*—and; *mṛga-indraḥ*—the lion; *aham*—I; *vainateyaḥ*—Garuḍa; *ca*—and; *pakṣiṇām*—of birds.

Of demons I am Prahlāda; of calculators I am time. Of animals I am the lion, and of birds, Garuḍa.

Prahlāda, a great devotee, was born in a family of demons. His name indicates one who delights all. Garuḍa is the carrier of Viṣṇu.

Text 31

पवनः पवतामस्मि रामः शस्त्रभृतामहम् ।
झषाणां मकरश्चास्मि स्रोतसामस्मि जाह्नवी ॥३१॥

pavanaḥ pavatām asmi rāmaḥ śastra-bhṛtām aham/
jhaṣāṇāṁ makaraś cāsmi srotasām asmi jāhnavī//

pavanaḥ—the wind; *pavatām*—of purifiers; *asmi*—I am; *rāmaḥ*—Rāma; *śastra-bhṛtām*—of the carriers of weapons; *aham*—I; *jhaṣāṇām*—of the fish; *makaraḥ*—the shark; *ca*—and; *asmi*—I am; *srotasām*—of rivers; *asmi*—I am; *jāhnavī*—the Ganges.

Of purifiers I am the wind; of warriors I am Rāma; of fish I am the shark; of rivers I am the Ganges.

Text 32

सर्गाणामादिरन्तश्च मध्यं चैवाहमर्जुन ।
अध्यात्मविद्या विद्यानां वादः प्रवदतामहम् ॥३२॥

sargāṇām ādir antaś ca madhyaṁ caivāham arjuna/
adhyātma-vidyā vidyānāṁ vādaḥ pravadatām aham//

sargāṇām—of creations; *ādiḥ*—the beginning; *antaḥ*—the end; *ca*—and; *madhyam*—the middle; *ca*—also; *eva*—certainly; *aham*—I; *arjuna*—O Arjuna; *adhyātma-vidyā*—knowledge of the Supreme Self; *vidyānām*—of knowledge; *vādaḥ*—discourse; *pravadatām*—of those who speak; *aham*—I.

O Arjuna, of creations I am the beginning, middle, and end; of knowledge I am knowledge of the Supreme Self; among speakers I am words that are unbiased and in pursuit of the truth.

Earlier Kṛṣṇa told Arjuna that he was the beginning, middle, and end of the created beings. Here he says he is the same for the insentient.

The word *vādaḥ* refers to debate in which both parties are concerned not with merely asserting their opinion, but rather with reaching the proper conclusion.

Text 33

अक्षराणामकारोऽस्मि द्वन्द्वः सामासिकस्य च ।
अहमेवाक्षयः कालो धाताहं विश्वतोमुखः ॥३३॥

akṣarāṇām a-kāro 'smi dvandvaḥ sāmāsikasya ca/
aham evākṣayaḥ kālo dhātāhaṁ viśvato-mukhaḥ//

akṣarāṇām—of letters; *a-kāraḥ*—the letter *a*; *asmi*—I am; *dvandvaḥ*—the dual; *sāmāsikasya*—of compound words; *ca*—and; *aham*—I; *eva*—certainly; *akṣayaḥ*—endless; *kālaḥ*—time; *dhātā*—the dispenser; *aham*—I; *viśvataḥ-mukhaḥ*—facing all directions (Brahmā).

Of letters I am the letter a, and of compound words I am the dual. I alone am endless time and the universal dispenser facing in all directions.

According to *śruti*, the sound *a* is said to pervade all speech (Ai. Ā. 2.3.7.13). It is the first letter in the Sanskrit alphabet, *a-kāra*, and inherent in every consonant of the Sanskrit alphabet. *Dvandva* is the compound in which the meaning of both words compounded are equally dominant. An example of the *dvandva* compound is "Rādhā-Kṛṣṇa." In all other Sanskrit compounds either the first word predominates *(avyayībhāva)*, the second *(tatpuruṣa)*, or some other word than those in the compound itself *(bahuvrīhi)*.

In this verse eternal time is referred to as opposed to the form of time mentioned in verse 30 that causes decay.

Text 34

मृत्युः सर्वहरश्चाहमुद्भवश्च भविष्यताम् ।
कीर्तिः श्रीर्वाक् च नारीणां स्मृतिर्मेधा धृतिः क्षमा ॥३४॥

mṛtyuḥ sarva-haraś cāham udbhavaś ca bhaviṣyatām/
kīrtiḥ śrīr vāk ca nārīṇāṁ smṛtir medhā dhṛtiḥ kṣamā//

mṛtyuḥ—death; *sarva-haraḥ*—destroyer of all; *ca*—and; *aham*—I; *udbhavaḥ*—source; *ca*—and; *bhaviṣyatām*—of future manifestations; *kīrtiḥ*—fame; *śrīḥ*—prosperity; *vāk*—speech; *ca*—and; *nārīṇām*—of women; *smṛtiḥ*—memory; *medhā*—intelligence; *dhṛtiḥ*—fortitude; *kṣamā*—forbearance.

I am death, destroyer of all; I am the source of all things yet to be. Of women I am fame, prosperity, speech, memory, intelligence, fortitude, and forbearance.

Fame, prosperity, speech, memory, intelligence, fortitude, and forbearance are considered the seven wives of *dharma*. As qualities they are very desirable and usually best expressed by women. Speech *(vāk)* is also identified with the Sanskrit language, which is said to be capable of expressing all ideas.

Text 35

बृहत्साम तथा साम्नां गायत्री छन्दसामहम् ।
मासानां मार्गशीर्षोऽहमृतूनां कुसुमाकरः ॥३५॥

bṛhat-sāma tathā sāmnāṁ gāyatrī chandasām aham/
māsānāṁ mārga-śīrṣo 'ham ṛtūnāṁ kusumākaraḥ//

bṛhat-sāma—the *Bṛhat-sāma;* *tathā*—also; *sāmnām*—of the *Sāma Veda* hymns; *gāyatrī*—the Gāyatrī; *chandasām*—of meters; *aham*—I; *māsānām*—of months; *mārga-śīrṣaḥ*—Mārga-śīrṣa; *aham*—I; *ṛtūnām*—of seasons; *kusuma-ākaraḥ*—flower-bearing (spring).

Of the Vedic hymns I am Bṛhat-sāma; of meters, Gāyatrī; of months, Mārga-śīrṣa; of seasons, flower-bearing spring.

The *Bṛhat-sāma* is that part of the *Sāma Veda* that originates in the *Ṛg Veda mantra* beginning with *tvāmiddhi havāmahe* (Ṛg 6.46.1).

Gāyatrī is the prototype of all Vedic *mantras*. Baladeva Vidyābhūṣaṇa says, "Of all the metrically bound Vedic *mantras*, I am the Gāyatrī, which is the best of all due to being the initiation into second birth of the *brāhmaṇas*." According to the *Upaniṣads*, *Gāyatrī* is identified with Brahman, and according to Gauḍīya Vedānta with the service of Rādhā.

Mārga-śīrṣa (November/December) is a harvest month for paddy. It follows Karttika, the month representing Rādhā.

Text 36

द्यूतं छलयतामस्मि तेजस्तेजस्विनामहम् ।
जयोऽस्मि व्यवसायोऽस्मि सत्त्वं सत्त्ववतामहम् ॥३६॥

dyūtaṁ chalayatām asmi tejas tejasvinām aham/
jayo 'smi vyavasāyo 'smi sattvaṁ sattvavatām aham//

dyūtam—gambling; *chalayatām*—of cheaters; *asmi*—I am; *tejaḥ*—influence; *tejasvinām*—of the influential; *aham*—I; *jayaḥ*—victory; *asmi*—I am; *vyavasāyaḥ*—effort; *asmi*—I; *sattvam*—goodness; *sattva-vatām*—of the good; *aham*—I.

Of cheaters I am gambling, and influence among the influential. I am victory, effort, and the goodness of the good.

Text 37

वृष्णीनां वासुदेवोऽस्मि पाण्डवानां धनञ्जयः ।
मुनीनामप्यहं व्यासः कवीनामुशना कविः ॥३७॥

vṛṣṇīnāṁ vāsudevo 'smi pāṇḍavānāṁ dhanañjayaḥ/
munīnām apy ahaṁ vyāsaḥ kavīnām uśanā kaviḥ//

vṛṣṇīnām—of Vṛṣṇis; *vāsudevaḥ*—Vāsudeva; *asmi*—I am; *pāṇḍavānām*—of the Pāṇḍavas; *dhanañjayaḥ*—Arjuna; *munīnām*—of the sages; *api*—also; *aham*—I; *vyāsaḥ*—Vyāsa; *kavīnām*—of poets; *uśanā*—Uśanā; *kaviḥ*—the poet.

Of Vṛṣṇis I am Vāsudeva; of the Pāṇḍavas, Dhanañjaya (Arjuna); of the wise I am Vyāsa; of poets, Uśanā.

Jīva Goswāmī considers Vāsudeva to refer to Kṛṣṇa's first expansion, Balarāma.

Text 38

दण्डो दमयतामस्मि नीतिरस्मि जिगीषताम् ।
मौनं चैवास्मि गुह्यानां ज्ञानं ज्ञानवतामहम् ॥३८॥

daṇḍo damayatām asmi nītir asmi jigīṣatām/
maunaṁ caivāsmi guhyānāṁ jñānaṁ jñānavatām aham//

daṇḍaḥ—rod; *damayatām*—of punishers; *asmi*—I am; *nītiḥ*—guidance; *asmi*—I am; *jigīṣatām*—of those who seek victory; *maunam*—silence; *ca*—and; *eva*—also; *asmi*—I am; *guhyānām*—of secret things; *jñānam*—wisdom; *jñāna-vatām*—of the wise; *aham*—I.

Of punishers I am the rod of chastisement; of victors I am the guidance they follow. Of secret things I am silence, and of the wise I am wisdom.

Text 39

यच्चापि सर्वभूतानां बीजं तदहमर्जुन ।
न तदस्ति विना यत्स्यान्मया भूतं चराचरम् ॥३९॥

yac cāpi sarva-bhūtānāṁ bījaṁ tad aham arjuna/
na tad asti vinā yat syān mayā bhūtaṁ carācaram//

yat—which; *ca*—and; *api*—even; *sarva-bhūtānām*—of all beings; *bījam*—seed; *tat*—that; *aham*—I; *arjuna*—O Arjuna; *na*—not; *tat*—that; *asti*—there is; *vinā*—without; *yat*—which; *syāt*—exists; *mayā*—by me; *bhūtam*—existing; *cara-acaram*—moving or unmoving.

Furthermore, O Arjuna, I am the seed of all existence. There is nothing moving or unmoving that can exist without me.

Text 40

नान्तोऽस्ति मम दिव्यानां विभूतीनां परन्तप ।
एष तूद्देशतः प्रोक्तो विभूतेर्विस्तरो मया ॥४०॥

nānto 'sti mama divyānāṁ vibhūtīnāṁ parantapa/
eṣa tūddeśataḥ prokto vibhūter vistaro mayā//

na—not; *antaḥ*—end; *asti*—there is; *mama*—of my; *divyānām*—of the divine; *vibhūtīnām*—of the manifestation; *parantapa*—O conqueror of enemies; *eṣaḥ*—this; *tu*—but; *uddeśataḥ*—for example; *proktaḥ*—told; *vibhūteḥ*—of opulence; *vistaraḥ*—the extent; *mayā*—by me.

O conqueror of enemies, there is no end to my divine manifestation. What I have told you is merely an indication of the extent of my opulence.

Text 41

यद्यद्विभूतिमत्सत्त्वं श्रीमदूर्जितमेव वा ।
तत्तदेवावगच्छ त्वं मम तेजोंऽशसम्भवम् ॥४१॥

yad yad vibhūtimat sattvaṁ śrīmad ūrjitam eva vā/
tat tad evāvagaccha tvaṁ mama tejo-'ṁśa-sambhavam//

yat yat—whatever; *vibhūti-mat*—powerful; *sattvam*—existence; *śrī-mat*—beautiful; *ūrjitam*—glorious; *eva*—certainly; *vā*—or; *tat tat*—all those; *eva*—certainly; *avagaccha*—know; *tvam*—you; *mama*—my; *tejaḥ*—of splendor; *aṁśa*—spark; *sambhavam*—origin.

Know that in all cases whatever in existence is powerful, glorious, and beautiful issues from but a spark of my splendor.

Text 42

अथ वा बहुनैतेन किं ज्ञातेन तवार्जुन ।
विष्टभ्याहमिदं कृत्स्नमेकांशेन स्थितो जगत् ॥४२॥

atha vā bahunaitena kiṁ jñātena tavārjuna/
viṣṭabhyāham idaṁ kṛtsnam ekāṁśena sthito jagat//

atha vā—or; *bahunā*—with extensive; *etena*—with this; *kim*—what; *jñātena*—with knowledge; *tava*—your; *arjuna*—O Arjuna; *viṣṭabhya*—sustaining; *aham*—I; *idam*—this; *kṛtsnam*—entire; *eka*—one; *aṁśena*—by a portion; *sthitaḥ*—constantly; *jagat*—universe.

But what need is there for all this extensive knowledge, Arjuna? I sustain this entire universe by a mere portion of myself!

Kṛṣṇa concludes this section by referring back to its beginning in verse 20. There Kṛṣṇa began describing his divine manifestations by mentioning the Paramātmā. Here in verses 41 and 42 he describes the Paramātmā as a fraction *(aṁśa)*, or plenary portion, of himself, by which the entire material manifestation is pervaded. Thus Kṛṣṇa has reiterated that he is the source of everything, including the Paramātmā, who is but a spark of his splendor. From this verse it should be clear that Kṛṣṇa is not an incarnation of the Paramātmā in the form of Mahā-Viṣṇu.

At the close of this chapter, Arjuna is overwhelmed at the thought of his friend's opulence—the fact that Kṛṣṇa is the source of Viṣṇu, who is his mere plenary portion. This awe inspires the next chapter.

CHAPTER ELEVEN

विश्वरूपदर्शनयोगः
Viśva-Rūpa-Darśana-yoga

YOGA OF THEOPHANY

Text 1

अर्जुन उवाच
मदनुग्रहाय परमं गुह्यमध्यात्मसंज्ञितम् ।
यत्त्वयोक्तं वचस्तेन मोहोऽयं विगतो मम ॥१॥

arjuna uvāca
mad-anugrahāya paramaṁ guhyam adhyātma-saṁjñitam/
yat tvayoktaṁ vacas tena moho 'yaṁ vigato mama//

arjunaḥ uvāca—Arjuna said; *mat-anugrahāya*—out of fondness for me; *paramam*—supreme; *guhyam*—secret; *adhyātma*—Supreme Self; *saṁjñitam*—known as; *yat*—what; *tvayā*—by you; *uktam*—spoken; *vacaḥ*—words; *tena*—by that; *mohaḥ*—illusion; *ayam*—this; *vigataḥ*—is gone; *mama*—my.

Arjuna said: Out of fondness for me you have spoken about your secret, supreme nature. Thus my delusion is gone.

As this chapter opens, Arjuna is overwhelmed: on the one hand his heart has been melted by Kṛṣṇa's affection *(anugrahāya)*; on the other he is awe-struck by the fact that Kṛṣṇa, his dear friend, is the source of the universal God (Paramātmā). Kṛṣṇa's fondness for Arjuna as a devotee and friend caused him to reveal confidential, spiritual knowledge about himself, and Arjuna's awareness of this honor causes him to tremble and this affects his speech. Arjuna's trembling is demonstrated by the metrical irregularity in the first line of this verse. The extra syllable that appears there would normally be considered a blemish, but because this irregularity serves to illustrate Arjuna's emotional state, it is in fact an ornament.

The nature of Arjuna's love for Kṛṣṇa is such that the opulence of Kṛṣṇa's Godhood can sometimes overshadow Arjuna's emotion of friendship. This begins to happen in this verse and fully manifests later in the chapter. The love of Vraja never suffers when a display of Kṛṣṇa's opulence appears. When Kṛṣṇa lifted Vraja's Mount Govardhana to protect his devotees from Indra's torrential rains, the young cowherds lifted their sticks to help him. In spite of Kṛṣṇa's extraordinary display of majesty, they never lost sight of him as their friend, and thus they tried to help him. The nature of the cowherds' love for Kṛṣṇa and that of the *gopīs* of Vraja is so intensely intimate that it can never be covered by knowledge of the fact that Kṛṣṇa is God. Arjuna's love on the other hand is mixed with a sense of Kṛṣṇa's Godhood. Thus as we shall see, when Kṛṣṇa manifests his opulence further, Arjuna questions the appropriateness of his intimate friendly behavior with Kṛṣṇa.[1]

When Arjuna says that his delusion is now gone *(moho 'yaṁ vigato mama)*, he refers to his delusion regarding both the nature of the self *(tvam)* and the nature of God *(tat)*. With regard to the self, he had been thinking earlier in terms of bodily egoic concerns. Now he understands that he is the soul within the body. Significantly, his understanding of this is voiced after Kṛṣṇa has revealed knowledge of his Godhood. The implication is that self-realization is most effectively accomplished in the context of pursuing God-realization and that upon realization of the individual soul, one continues to be interested in God himself. This is the path of devotion, as opposed to *niṣkāma-karma-yoga* or *jñāna-yoga* aimed merely at self-realization.

Regarding Arjuna's delusion about God, he had been thinking of Kṛṣṇa as his friend. While this kind of spiritual delusion is ultimately desirable, owing to Kṛṣṇa's speech about his opulence it has now receded to the back of Arjuna's mind. At this point in *Śrī Gītā*, no reader should be in confusion about the Godhood of Arjuna's chariot driver. As mentioned in the previous chapter, knowledge of Kṛṣṇa's Godhood is both initially necessary for inspiring a life of devotion to him and unnecessary, if not bothersome, to those exalted souls who develop intimate spiritual love for him. In chapter 11 Arjuna demonstrates this devotional psychology by first continuing to ask about Kṛṣṇa's extraordinary opulence, only to be bothered by it when it fully manifests later in the chapter.

Text 2

भवाप्ययौ हि भूतानां श्रुतौ विस्तरशो मया ।
त्वत्तः कमलपत्राक्ष माहात्म्यमपि चाव्ययम् ॥२॥

1. See Bg. 11.41.

bhavāpyayau hi bhūtānāṁ śrutau vistaraśo mayā/
tvattaḥ kamala-patrākṣa māhātmyam api cāvyayam//

bhava-apyayau—origin and dissolution; *hi*—indeed; *bhūtānām*—of beings; *śrutau*—have been heard; *vistaraśaḥ*—in detail; *mayā*—by me; *tvattaḥ*—from you; *kamala-patra-akṣa*—O you whose eyes resemble the petals of the lotus; *māhātmyam*—glory; *api*—also; *ca*—and; *avyayam*—imperishable.

I have heard in detail from you, whose eyes resemble the petals of the lotus, about the origin and dissolution of beings, as well as of your imperishable glory.

Arjuna says that he has heard in detail *(vistaraśaḥ)*, for Kṛṣṇa has repeatedly described himself as the origin and dissolution of all beings in chapters 7 through 10 and stated his eternal glories again and again. The name Kamala-patrākṣa (lotus-eyed one) reveals Arjuna's affection for Kṛṣṇa, who he lovingly describes as one whose eyes are elongated like the petals of the lotus and reddish at their ends, thus appearing very charming to the mind.

Text 3

एवमेतद्यथात्थ त्वमात्मानं परमेश्वर ।
द्रष्टुमिच्छामि ते रूपमैश्वरं पुरुषोत्तम ॥३॥

evam etad yathāttha tvam ātmānaṁ parameśvara/
draṣṭum icchāmi te rūpam aiśvaraṁ puruṣottama//

evam—thus; *etat*—this; *yathā*—as; *āttha*—you say; *tvam*—you; *ātmānam*—yourself; *parama-īśvara*—O Supreme Lord; *draṣṭum*—to see; *icchāmi*—I wish; *te*—your; *rūpam*—form; *aiśvaram*—opulent; *puruṣa-uttama*—O Supreme Person.

O Supreme Lord, as you speak of yourself so you are. O Supreme Person! I wish to see the form of your opulence.

Arjuna wants Kṛṣṇa to know that he himself has absolutely no doubt about Kṛṣṇa's position at this point. Thus he addresses him as Parameśvara, indicating Kṛṣṇa's omniscience as if to say, "As you who are omniscient surely know, I personally have no doubt about what you have said about yourself." Arjuna speaks in this way to preface his request in this verse.

Arjuna does not doubt Kṛṣṇa and therefore insist on seeing so that he might believe. He believes and reasons that he is thereby qualified to see. Indeed, by addressing Kṛṣṇa as Parameśvara, Arjuna further indicates that Kṛṣṇa himself residing within Arjuna's heart has awakened the desire to see Kṛṣṇa's godly form *(rūpam aiśvaram)*; otherwise, Arjuna was satisfied seeing Kṛṣṇa as *līlā-puruṣottama.*

That which Arjuna desires to see as prompted from within by Kṛṣṇa himself is a form that is rarely seen in this world. Thus even while Arjuna desires to see it, he doubts the possibility of doing so, not due to any inability on the part of Kṛṣṇa, but out of his own humility and assumed lack of qualification. Baladeva Vidyābhūṣaṇa says that Arjuna, having heard Kṛṣṇa say at the end of the previous chapter that by a mere portion of himself he holds up the universe, wishes to see that form.

Text 4

मन्यसे यदि तच्छक्यं मया द्रष्टुमिति प्रभो ।
योगेश्वर ततो मे त्वं दर्शयात्मानमव्ययम् ॥४॥

manyase yadi tac chakyaṁ mayā draṣṭum iti prabho/
yogeśvara tato me tvaṁ darśayātmānam avyayam//

manyase—you think; *yadi*—if; *tat*—that; *śakyam*—possible; *mayā*—by me; *draṣṭum*—to see; *iti*—thus; *prabho*—O Lord; *yoga-īśvara*—O master of mystics; *tataḥ*—then; *me*—to me; *tvam*—you; *darśaya*—show; *ātmānam*—your self; *avyayam*—imperishable.

O Lord, if you think it is possible for me to behold this, O master of mystics, then show me your imperishable Self.

Arjuna finishes his request in this verse, indicating that although what he has requested may be impossible, it will be possible because Kṛṣṇa is the supreme mystic. Indeed, Kṛṣṇa next blesses Arjuna with the capacity to see his universal form *(viśva-rūpa)*.

Text 5

श्रीभगवानुवाच
पश्य मे पार्थ रूपाणि शतशोऽथ सहस्रशः ।
नानाविधानि दिव्यानि नानावर्णाकृतीनि च ॥५॥

śrī-bhagavān uvāca
paśya me pārtha rūpāṇi śataśo 'tha sahasraśaḥ/
nānā-vidhāni divyāni nānā-varṇākṛtīni ca//

śrī-bhagavān uvāca—the Lord of Śrī said; *paśya*—behold; *me*—my; *pārtha*—O Pārtha; *rūpāṇi*—forms; *śataśaḥ*—a hundredfold; *atha*—also; *sahasraśaḥ*—a thousandfold; *nānā-vidhāni*—variegated; *divyāni*—divine; *nānā*—many; *varṇa*—color; *ākṛtīni*—shapes; *ca*—also.

The Lord of Śrī said: O Pārtha, behold my variegated, exceedingly wonderful, multicolored, and multishaped forms in their hundreds and thousands.

Kṛṣṇa tells Arjuna to behold *(paśya)* his godly form in this and the next three verses as if to bless him with the ability to see it. At the same time, *paśya*, being in the imperative mood, cautions Arjuna to be heedful of what Kṛṣṇa will reveal, for it is exceedingly wonderful *(divyāni)*. Although the form he will reveal is one, it is full of variety and thus spoken of in the plural. It is of different colors *(varṇa)* and shapes *(akṛtīni)* relative to the arrangement of limbs. Having mentioned the form that he will reveal, Kṛṣṇa next describes it in brief in two verses to help Arjuna understand what he will see.

Text 6

पश्यादित्यान् वसून् रुद्रानश्विनौ मरुतस्तथा ।
बहून्यदृष्टपूर्वाणि पश्याश्चर्याणि भारत ॥६॥

paśyādityān vasūn rudrān aśvinau marutas tathā/
bahūny adṛṣṭa-pūrvāṇi paśyāścaryāṇi bhārata//

paśya—behold; *ādityān*—the Ādityas; *vasūn*—the Vasus; *rudrān*—the Rudras; *aśvinau*—the two Aśvins; *marutaḥ*—the Maruts; *tathā*—also; *bahūni*—many; *adṛṣṭa*—not seen; *pūrvāṇi*—before; *paśya*—behold; *āścaryāṇi*—wonders; *bhārata*—O Bhārata.

Behold the Ādityas, Vasus, Rudras, the two Aśvins, as well as the Maruts, and others. Behold, O Bhārata, many wonderful things never before seen!

The Ādityas, Vasus, Rudras, Aśvins, and Maruts are various types of heavenly beings mentioned in the previous chapter, all of whom will be visible in the form Kṛṣṇa intends to reveal. The heavenly beings named here clarify what Kṛṣṇa meant when he spoke of hundreds of thousands of forms in the previous verse. By the word *adṛṣṭa-pūrvaṇi* (never seen before) Kṛṣṇa seeks to clarify "exceedingly wonderful" *(divyāni)* used in the previous verse. The form he will reveal has never been seen previously by any human being. The entire universe is contained within it.

Text 7

इहैकस्थं जगत्कृत्स्नं पश्याद्य सचराचरम् ।
मम देहे गुडाकेश यच्चान्यद्द्रष्टुमिच्छसि ॥७॥

ihaika-sthaṁ jagat kṛtsnaṁ paśyādya sa-carācaram/
mama dehe guḍākeśa yac cānyad draṣṭum icchasi//

iha—here; *eka-stham*—in one place; *jagat*—universe; *kṛtsnam*—entire; *paśya*—behold; *adya*—today; *sa*—with; *cara*—the moving; *acaram*—the nonmoving; *mama*—my; *dehe*—in this body; *guḍākeśa*—O Guḍākeśa; *yat*—whatever; *ca*—also; *anyat*—else; *draṣṭum*—to see; *icchasi*—you wish.

O Guḍākeśa, behold today the entire universe with the moving and nonmoving standing together here in my body along with whatever else you wish to see.

Text 8

न तु मां शक्यसे द्रष्टुमनेनैव स्वचक्षुषा ।
दिव्यं ददामि ते चक्षुः पश्य मे योगमैश्वरम् ॥८॥

na tu māṁ śakyase draṣṭum anenaiva sva-cakṣuṣā/
divyaṁ dadāmi te cakṣuḥ paśya me yogam aiśvaram//

na—not; *tu*—however; *mām*—me; *śakyase*—you are able; *draṣṭum*—to see; *anena*—with this; *eva*—certainly; *sva-cakṣuṣā*—your own eye; *divyam*—divine; *dadāmi*—I give; *te*—to you; *cakṣuḥ*—eye; *paśya*—see; *me*—my; *yogam aiśvaram*—mystic opulence.

However, you are not capable of seeing me in this form with your own eyes. I grant you a divine vision: behold my mystic opulence!

Arjuna was not capable of seeing Kṛṣṇa's *viśva-rūpa*, thus Kṛṣṇa granted him divine eyes. This is curious, for Arjuna was already seeing the divine personal form of Kṛṣṇa, a form that, as we shall see at the conclusion of this chapter, is more difficult to see than Kṛṣṇa's *viśva-rūpa*. Although the *viśva-rūpa* was never seen before in human society, it is possible for the gods to see it. Thus Kṛṣṇa granted Arjuna celestial, godly *(divyam)* vision. However, Arjuna's desire to see the *viśva-rūpa* did not change his mind's eye, which remained focused on the Lord of his heart, Pārthasārathī Kṛṣṇa.

Bracing himself as he related this event to Dhṛtarāṣṭra, Sañjaya next describes Kṛṣṇa's *viśva-rūpa* to the king, who was anxious to know what Arjuna saw. Previous to Kṛṣṇa's speaking the *Gīta*, Dhṛtarāṣṭra had seen a partial manifestation of this form himself, and even this partial manifestation of the *viśva-rūpa* had overwhelmed him.

Text 9

सञ्जय उवाच
एवमुक्त्वा ततो राजन्महायोगेश्वरो हरिः ।
दर्शयामास पार्थाय परमं रूपमैश्वरम् ॥९॥

sañjaya uvāca
evam uktvā tato rājan mahā-yogeśvaro hariḥ/
darśayām āsa pārthāya paramaṁ rūpam aiśvaram//

sañjayaḥ uvāca—Sañjaya said; *evam*—thus; *uktvā*—having spoken; *tataḥ*—then; *rājan*—O King; *mahā-yoga-īśvaraḥ*—the great master of mysticism; *hariḥ*—Hari; *darśayām āsa*—he showed; *pārthāya*—to the son of Pṛthā; *paramam*—supreme; *rūpam aiśvaram*—opulent form.

Sañjaya said: Having spoken in this way, O King, the master of mysticism, Hari, revealed his supremely opulent form to the son of Pṛthā.

Texts 10–11

अनेकवक्त्रनयनमनेकाद्भुतदर्शनम् ।
अनेकदिव्याभरणं दिव्यानेकोद्यतायुधम् ॥१०॥
दिव्यमाल्याम्बरधरं दिव्यगन्धानुलेपनम् ।
सर्वाश्चर्यमयं देवमनन्तं विश्वतोमुखम् ॥११॥

aneka-vaktra-nayanam anekādbhuta-darśanam/
aneka-divyābharaṇaṁ divyānekodyatāyudham//
divya-mālyāmbara-dharaṁ divya-gandhānulepanam/
sarvāścarya-mayaṁ devam anantaṁ viśvato-mukham//

aneka—many; *vaktra*—mouths; *nayanam*—eyes; *aneka*—many; *adbhuta*—wonderful; *darśanam*—visions; *aneka*—many; *divya*—divine; *ābharaṇam*—ornament; *divya*—divine; *aneka*—many; *udyata*—uplifted; *āyudham*—weapon; *divya*—divine; *mālya*—garland; *ambara*—apparel; *dharam*—wearing; *divya*—divine; *gandha*—scent; *anulepanam*—ointment; *sarva*—all; *āścarya-mayam*—wonderful; *devam*—resplendent; *anantam*—limitless; *viśvataḥ-mukham*—with faces in all directions.

In this form were many faces and eyes, many wonderful visions, divine ornaments, and uplifted divine weapons. It wore divine garlands and garments, was anointed with divine scents, abounded in many wonders; it was resplendent, limitless, and its faces were turned in every direction.

Text 12

दिवि सूर्यसहस्रस्य भवेद्युगपदुत्थिता ।
यदि भाः सदृशी सा स्याद् भासस्तस्य महात्मनः ॥१२॥

divi sūrya-sahasrasya bhaved yugapad utthitā/
yadi bhāḥ sadṛśī sā syād bhāsas tasya mahātmanaḥ//

divi—in the sky; *sūrya*—sun; *sahasrasya*—of a thousand; *bhavet*—there were; *yugapat*—at once; *utthitā*—risen; *yadi*—if; *bhāḥ*—light; *sadṛśī*—such; *sā*—that; *syāt*—it might be; *bhāsaḥ*—of splendor; *tasya*—of him; *mahā-ātmanaḥ*—of the exalted being.

If a thousand suns were to rise in the sky all at once, such splendor might resemble the splendor of that exalted being.

Text 13

तत्रैकस्थं जगत्कृत्स्नं प्रविभक्तमनेकधा ।
अपश्यद्देवदेवस्य शरीरे पाण्डवस्तदा ॥१३॥

tatraika-sthaṁ jagat kṛtsnaṁ pravibhaktam anekadhā/
apaśyad deva-devasya śarīre pāṇḍavas tadā//

tatra—there; *eka-stham*—in one place; *jagat*—universe; *kṛtsnam*—entire; *pravibhaktam*—divided; *anekadhā*—in many ways; *apaśyat*—he saw; *deva-devasya*—of the God of gods; *śarīre*—in the body; *pāṇḍavaḥ*—the son of Pāṇḍu; *tadā*—then.

Then and there the son of Pāṇḍu beheld the entire universal diversity in one place within the body of the God of gods.

Text 14

ततः स विस्मयाविष्टो हृष्टरोमा धनञ्जयः ।
प्रणम्य शिरसा देवं कृताञ्जलिरभाषत ॥१४॥

tataḥ sa vismayāviṣṭo hṛṣṭa-romā dhanañjayaḥ/
praṇamya śirasā devaṁ kṛtāñjalir abhāṣata//

tataḥ—then; *saḥ*—he; *vismaya-āviṣṭaḥ*—amazed; *hṛṣṭa-romā*—his hairs standing on end; *dhanañjayaḥ*—Dhanañjaya; *praṇamya*—offering obeisances; *śirasā*—with the head; *devam*—to the Lord; *kṛta-añjaliḥ*—with folded palms; *abhāṣata*—he said.

Then, filled with wonder, his hairs standing on end, bowing his head to the Lord with his palms folded, Dhanañjaya said:

Here Arjuna, who is known as Dhanañjaya because of his fire-like brilliance, is amazed *(vismayāviṣṭaḥ)*.[2] This amazement, which is both the basis of aesthetic rapture and the dominant emotion *(sthayī-bhāva)* in this verse, is nourished by the other ingredients of *rasa*.[3] The cause and object of the loving emotion *(viṣayālambana-vibhāva)* is Kṛṣṇa. The stimulus *(uddīpana)* is Kṛṣṇa manifesting his *viśva-rūpa*. The external expressions of *rasa (anubhāvas)* are Arjuna's bowed head and folded hands, while his horripilation is his ecstatic transformation *(sāttvika-bhāva)*. Arjuna's amazement is augmented by implied auxiliary emotions *(sañcārī-bhāvas)* of excitement, inertness, delight, and so on. Arjuna himself is the vessel of love *(aśrayālambana-vibhāva)*. Here his *sakhya-bhāva* has receded into the background.

Text 15

अर्जुन उवाच
पश्यामि देवांस्तव देव देहे
सर्वांस्तथा भूतविशेषसङ्घान् ।

2. Madhusūdana Saraswatī says that besides the common meaning of Dhanañjaya as winner of wealth, the word also means fire. He does not explain how this is so. However, according to Monier Williams it is used in this way in the *Kaṭha Upaniṣad*.

3. *Sāhitya-darpaṇa* (2.33) explains that all expressions of aesthetic rapture can be reduced to "amazement."

ब्रह्माणमीशं कमलासनस्थ-
मृषींश्च सर्वानुरगांश्च दिव्यान् ॥१५॥

arjuna uvāca
paśyāmi devāṁs tava deva dehe
sarvāṁs tathā bhūta-viśeṣa-saṅghān/
brahmāṇam īśaṁ kamalāsana-stham
ṛṣīṁś ca sarvān uragāṁś ca divyān//

arjunaḥ uvāca—Arjuna said; *paśyāmi*—I see; *devān*—the gods; *tava*—your; *deva*—O God; *dehe*—in the body; *sarvān*—all; *tathā*—also; *bhūta-viśeṣa-saṅghān*—varieties of beings assembled; *brahmāṇam*—Brahmā; *īśam*—lord; *kamala-āsana-stham*—on a lotus seat; *ṛṣīn*—great sages; *ca*—and; *sarvān*—all; *uragān*—serpents; *ca*—also; *divyān*—divine.

Arjuna said: O God, I see in your body the gods and all varieties of beings assembled—Brahmā on a lotus seat and all the sages and divine serpents.

Text 16

अनेकबाहूदरवक्त्रनेत्रं
पश्यामि त्वां सर्वतोऽनन्तरूपम् ।
नान्तं न मध्यं न पुनस्तवादिं
पश्यामि विश्वेश्वर विश्वरूप ॥१६॥

aneka-bāhūdara-vaktra-netraṁ
paśyāmi tvāṁ sarvato 'nanta-rūpam/
nāntaṁ na madhyaṁ na punas tavādiṁ
paśyāmi viśveśvara viśva-rūpa//

aneka—many; *bāhu*—arm; *udara*—belly; *vaktra*—mouth; *netram*—eye; *paśyāmi*—I see; *tvām*—you; *sarvataḥ*—everywhere; *ananta-rūpam*—infinite form; *na antam*—no end; *na madhyam*—no middle; *na punaḥ*—nor again; *tava*—your; *ādim*—beginning; *paśyāmi*—I see; *viśva-īśvara*—O Lord of the universe; *viśva-rūpa*—cosmic form.

I see your limitless form, with innumerable arms, bellies, mouths, and eyes in every direction. O Lord of the Universe, O universal form! I see no end and no middle to this form, nor can I find again its beginning.

Here the words *na punas tavādiṁ* indicate that Arjuna was able to see the beginning, but now, in the maelstrom of ever-multiplying forms, he can no longer find the beginning of this form, what to speak of the middle or end.

Text 17

किरीटिनं गदिनं चक्रिणं च
तेजोराशिं सर्वतो दीप्तिमन्तम् ।
पश्यामि त्वां दुर्निरीक्ष्यं समन्ताद्
दीप्तानलार्कद्युतिमप्रमेयम् ॥१७॥

kirīṭinaṁ gadiaṁ cakriṇaṁ ca
tejo-rāśiṁ sarvato dīptimantam/
paśyāmi tvāṁ durnirīkṣyaṁ samantād
dīptānalārka-dyutim aprameyam//

kirīṭinam—crowned; *gadinam*—with a club; *cakriṇam*—with a discus; *ca*—and; *tejaḥ-rāśim*—mass of brilliance; *sarvataḥ*—all around; *dīpti-mantam*—glowing; *paśyāmi*—I see; *tvām*—you; *durnirīkṣyam*—difficult to behold; *samantāt*—everywhere; *dīpta-anala*—blazing fire; *arka*—sun; *dyutim*—radiance; *aprameyam*—immeasurable.

Though you are impossible to see, I behold you crowned, armed with a club and bearing a discus, a mass of brilliance glowing all around you on all sides like the immeasurable radiance of blazing fire and the sun.

Text 18

त्वमक्षरं परमं वेदितव्यं
त्वमस्य विश्वस्य परं निधानम् ।
त्वमव्ययः शाश्वतधर्मगोप्ता
सनातनस्त्वं पुरुषो मतो मे ॥१८॥

tvam akṣaraṁ paramaṁ veditavyaṁ
tvam asya viśvasya paraṁ nidhānam/
tvam avyayaḥ śāśvata-dharma-goptā
sanātanas tvaṁ puruṣo mato me//

tvam—you; *akṣaram*—unchanging; *paramam*—supreme; *veditavyam*—to be known; *tvam*—you; *asya*—of this; *viśvasya*—of everything; *param*—supreme; *nidhānam*—resting place; *tvam*—you; *avyayaḥ*—imperishable;

śāśvata-dharma-goptā—defender of eternal *dharma; sanātanaḥ*—eternal; *tvam*—you; *puruṣaḥ*—person; *mataḥ me*—this is my opinion.

You are the unchanging, the supreme object of knowledge, the ultimate resting place of all, the imperishable defender of eternal dharma, known to me as the eternal person.

Text 19

अनादिमध्यान्तमनन्तवीर्य-
  मनन्तबाहुं शशिसूर्यनेत्रम् ।
पश्यामि त्वां दीप्तहुताशवक्त्रं
  स्वतेजसा विश्वमिदं तपन्तम् ॥१९॥

anādi-madhyāntam ananta-vīryam
  ananta-bāhuṁ śaśi-sūrya-netram/
paśyāmi tvāṁ dīpta-hutāśa-vaktraṁ
  sva-tejasā viśvam idaṁ tapantam//

anādi—without beginning; *madhya*—middle; *antam*—end; *ananta*—infinite; *vīryam*—power; *ananta*—innumerable; *bāhum*—arm; *śaśi*—moon; *sūrya*—sun; *netram*—eye; *paśyāmi*—I see; *tvām*—you; *dīpta*—blazing; *hutāśa-vaktram*—with fire in your mouth; *sva-tejasā*—with your brilliance; *viśvam*—universe; *idam*—this; *tapantam*—scorching.

I behold you without beginning, middle, or end, with infinite power, with innumerable arms, with the sun and moon as your eyes, with a mouth like blazing fire, scorching the universe with its brilliance.

Text 20

द्यावापृथिव्योरिदमन्तरं हि
  व्याप्तं त्वयैकेन दिशश्च सर्वाः ।
दृष्ट्वाद्भुतं रूपमुग्रं तवेदं
  लोकत्रयं प्रव्यथितं महात्मन् ॥२०॥

dyāv ā-pṛthivyor idam antaraṁ hi
  vyāptaṁ tvayaikena diśaś ca sarvāḥ/
dṛṣṭvādbhutaṁ rūpam ugraṁ tavedaṁ
  loka-trayaṁ pravyathitaṁ mahātman//

dyau ā-pṛthivyoḥ—of heaven and earth; *idam*—this; *antaram*—between; *hi*—certainly; *vyāptam*—pervaded; *tvayā*—by you; *ekena*—alone; *diśaḥ*—directions; *ca*—and; *sarvāḥ*—all; *dṛṣṭvā*—by seeing; *adbhutam*—wonderful; *rūpam*—form; *ugram*—formidable; *tava*—your; *idam*—this; *loka*—world; *trayam*—three; *pravyathitam*—trembling; *mahā-ātman*—O noble one.

You pervade the space between heaven and earth in every direction. O noble one, the three worlds tremble when they see your awesome and frightening form.

Here Arjuna hints that he has seen enough by addressing Kṛṣṇa as *mahātman* and speaking of the fear of others, including his own fear.

Text 21

अमी हि त्वां सुरसङ्घा विशन्ति
केचिद्भीताः प्राञ्जलयो गृणन्ति ।
स्वस्तीत्युक्त्वा महर्षिसिद्धसङ्घाः
स्तुवन्ति त्वां स्तुतिभिः पुष्कलाभिः ॥२१॥

amī hi tvāṁ sura-saṅghā viśanti
kecid bhītāḥ prāñjalayo gṛṇanti/
svastīty uktvā maharṣi-siddha-saṅghāḥ
stuvanti tvāṁ stutibhiḥ puṣkalābhiḥ//

amī—those; *hi*—certainly; *tvām*—you; *sura-saṅghāḥ*—hosts of gods; *viśanti*—they enter; *kecit*—some; *bhītāḥ*—fear stricken; *prāñjalayaḥ*—with folded palms; *gṛṇanti*—they praise; *svasti*—auspiciousness; *iti*—thus; *uktvā*—saying; *mahā-ṛṣi*—great sage; *siddha-saṅghāḥ*—hosts of perfect beings; *stuvanti*—they praise; *tvām*—you; *stutibhiḥ*—with hymns; *puṣkalābhiḥ*—abundant.

The host of gods enter into you. Fear stricken, some praise you with folded palms, while groups of perfected ṛṣis praise you with meaningful hymns saying, "May all auspiciousness prevail throughout the universe."

Text 22

रुद्रादित्या वसवो ये च साध्या
विश्वेऽश्विनौ मरुतश्चोष्मपाश्च ।
गन्धर्वयक्षासुरसिद्धसङ्घा
वीक्षन्ते त्वां विस्मिताश्चैव सर्वे ॥२२॥

rudrādityā vasavo ye ca sādhyā
viśve 'śvinau marutaś coṣmapāś ca/
gandharva-yakṣāsura-siddha-saṅghā
vīkṣante tvāṁ vismitāś caiva sarve//

rudra ādityāḥ—the Rudras and Ādityas; *vasavaḥ*—the Vasus; *ye*—who; *ca*—and; *sādhyāḥ*—the Sādhyas; *viśve*—the Viśvedevas; *aśvinau*—the Aśvins; *marutaḥ*—the Maruts; *ca*—and; *uṣma-pāḥ*—the ancestors; *ca*—and; *gandharva*—the Gandharvas; *yakṣa*—the Yakṣas; *asura*—the demons; *siddha*—the Siddhas; *saṅghāḥ*—assemblies; *vīkṣante*—they see; *tvām*—you; *vismitāḥ*—wonder struck; *ca*—also; *eva*—certainly; *sarve*—all.

The Rudras, Ādityas, Vasus, Sādhyas, Viśvedevas, Aśvins, Maruts, ancestors, Gandharvas, Yakṣas, demons, and Siddhas see you and are all struck with wonder.

Text 23

रूपं महत्ते बहुवक्त्रनेत्रं
महाबाहो बहुबाहूरुपादम् ।
बहूदरं बहुदंष्ट्राकरालं
दृष्ट्वा लोकाः प्रव्यथितास्तथाहम् ॥२३॥

rūpaṁ mahat te bahu-vaktra-netraṁ
mahā-bāho bahu-bāhūru-pādam/
bahūdaraṁ bahu-daṁṣṭrā-karālaṁ
dṛṣṭvā lokāḥ pravyathitās tathāham//

rūpam—form; *mahat*—great; *te*—of you; *bahu*—many; *vaktra*—mouth; *netram*—eye; *mahā-bāho*—O mighty-armed; *bahu*—many; *bāhu*—arm; *ūru*—thigh; *pādam*—foot; *bahu-udaram*—many bellies; *bahu-daṁṣṭrā*—many teeth; *karālam*—horrible; *dṛṣṭvā*—seeing; *lokāḥ*—the planets; *pravyathitāḥ*—trembling; *tathā*—similarly; *aham*—I.

Having seen your great form, which has many mouths, eyes, arms, thighs, feet, and bellies, and which bears many teeth, O mighty-armed, the world trembles, as do I.

Having tasted the sacred aesthetic rapture of astonishment, Arjuna begins to experience the divine *rasa* of fear *(bhayānaka)*.

Text 24

नभःस्पृशं दीप्तमनेकवर्णं
व्यात्ताननं दीप्तविशालनेत्रम् ।
दृष्ट्वा हि त्वां प्रव्यथितान्तरात्मा
धृतिं न विन्दामि शमं च विष्णो ॥२४॥

nabhaḥ-spṛśaṁ dīptam aneka-varṇaṁ
vyāttānanaṁ dīpta-viśāla-netram/
dṛṣṭvā hi tvāṁ pravyathitāntar-ātmā
dhṛtiṁ na vindāmi śamaṁ ca viṣṇo//

nabhaḥ-spṛśam—touching the sky; *dīptam*—blazing; *aneka*—many; *varṇam*—color; *vyātta*—gaping; *ānanam*—mouth; *dīpta*—glowing; *viśāla*—enormous; *netram*—eye; *dṛṣṭvā*—by seeing; *hi*—certainly; *tvām*—you; *pravyathita*—perturbed; *antaḥ*—within; *ātmā*—soul; *dhṛtim*—courage; *na*—not; *vindāmi*—I find; *śamam*—peace; *ca*—also; *viṣṇo*—O Viṣṇu.

O Viṣṇu! Merely by seeing you who are blazing and touching the sky, multicolored, mouth gaping, with enormous fiery eyes, I tremble at the core of my being. I find neither courage nor peace.

Text 25

दंष्ट्राकरालानि च ते मुखानि
दृष्ट्वैव कालानलसन्निभानि ।
दिशो न जाने न लभे च शर्म
प्रसीद देवेश जगन्निवास ॥२५॥

daṁṣṭrā-karālāni ca te mukhāni
dṛṣṭvaiva kālānala-sannibhāni/
diśo na jāne na labhe ca śarma
prasīda deveśa jagan-nivāsa//

daṁṣṭrā—teeth; *karālāni*—terrible; *ca*—also; *te*—your; *mukhāni*—faces; *dṛṣṭvā*—having seen; *eva*—thus; *kāla-anala*—the fire of destruction; *sannibhāni*—similar; *diśaḥ*—the directions; *na*—not; *jāne*—I know; *na*—not; *labhe*—I find; *ca*—and; *śarma*—comfort; *prasīda*—be merciful; *deva-īśa*—O God of gods; *jagat-nivāsa*—O abode of the universe.

Having seen your mouths made frightening by many teeth and glowing like the fire of universal destruction, I have lost my sense of

direction and find no comfort. Be merciful, O God of gods, abode of the universe.

Texts 26–27

अमी च त्वां धृतराष्ट्रस्य पुत्राः
सर्वे सहैवावनिपालसङ्घैः ।
भीष्मो द्रोणः सूतपुत्रस्तथासौ
सहास्मदीयैरपि योधमुख्यैः ॥२६॥
वक्त्राणि ते त्वरमाणा विशन्ति
दंष्ट्राकरालानि भयानकानि ।
केचिद् विलग्ना दशनान्तरेषु
सन्दृश्यन्ते चूर्णितैरुत्तमांगैः ॥२७॥

amī ca tvāṁ dhṛtarāṣṭrasya putrāḥ
sarve sahaivāvani-pāla-saṅghaiḥ/
bhīṣmo droṇaḥ sūta-putras tathāsau
sahāsmadīyair api yodha-mukhyaiḥ//
vaktrāṇi te tvaramāṇā viśanti
daṁṣṭrā-karālāni bhayānakāni/
kecid vilagnā daśanāntareṣu
sandṛśyante cūrṇitair uttamāṅgaiḥ//

amī—those; *ca*—also; *tvām*—you; *dhṛtarāṣṭrasya*—of Dhṛtarāṣṭra; *putrāḥ*—the sons; *sarve*—all; *saha*—with; *eva*—indeed; *avani-pāla*—earthly king; *saṅghaiḥ*—with the multitude; *bhīṣmaḥ*—Bhīṣma; *droṇaḥ*—Droṇa; *sūta-putraḥ*—Karṇa; *tathā*—also; *asau*—that; *saha*—with; *asmadīyaiḥ*—with our; *api*—also; *yodha-mukhyaiḥ*—with chief warriors; *vaktrāṇi*—mouths; *te*—your; *tvaramāṇāḥ*—rapidly; *viśanti*—they enter; *daṁṣṭrā-karālāni*—gaping with teeth; *bhayānakāni*—fearful; *kecit*—some; *vilagnāḥ*—clinging; *daśana-antareṣu*—between the teeth; *sandṛśyante*—they are seen; *cūrṇitaiḥ*—with crushed; *uttama-aṅgaiḥ*—with heads.

All the sons of Dhṛtarāṣṭra, along with the multitude of earthly kings such as Bhīṣma, Droṇa, and Karṇa, the son of a chariot driver, together with the principal warriors on our side, are rushing headlong into your fearfully gaping mouths with their many teeth. Some of them appear to have had their heads crushed and are now caught between those teeth.

At the beginning of this chapter (Bg. 11.7), Kṛṣṇa promised Arjuna that he would also show him anything else he wanted to see (*yac cānyad draṣṭum icchasi*). He now fulfills this promise by revealing to him what he desired to know—the outcome of the battle.

Text 28

यथा नदीनां बहवोऽम्बुवेगाः
समुद्रमेवाभिमुखा द्रवन्ति ।
तथा तवामी नरलोकवीरा
विशन्ति वक्त्राण्यभिविज्वलन्ति ॥२८॥

yathā nadīnāṁ bahavo 'mbu-vegāḥ
samudram evābhimukhā dravanti/
tathā tavāmī nara-loka-vīrā
viśanti vaktrāṇy abhivijvalanti//

yathā—as; *nadīnām*—of rivers; *bahavaḥ*—many; *ambu-vegāḥ*—currents; *samudram*—ocean; *eva*—certainly; *abhimukhāḥ*—toward; *dravanti*—they flow; *tathā*—similarly; *tava*—your; *amī*—these; *nara-loka-vīrāḥ*—worldly heroes; *viśanti*—they enter; *vaktrāṇi*—mouths; *abhivijvalanti*—flaming.

As rivers' currents rush toward the sea, so do these worldly heroes enter your flaming mouths.

Text 29

यथा प्रदीप्तं ज्वलनं पतङ्गा
विशन्ति नाशाय समृद्धवेगाः ।
तथैव नाशाय विशन्ति लोका-
स्तवापि वक्त्राणि समृद्धवेगाः ॥२९॥

yathā pradīptaṁ jvalanaṁ pataṅgā
viśanti nāśāya samṛddha-vegāḥ/
tathaiva nāśāya viśanti lokās
tavāpi vaktrāṇi samṛddha-vegāḥ//

yathā—as; *pradīptam*—blazing; *jvalanam*—fire; *pataṅgāḥ*—moths; *viśanti*—they enter; *nāśāya*—for destruction; *samṛddha-vegāḥ*—with increasing speed; *tathā eva*—similarly; *nāśāya*—for destruction; *viśanti*—they enter; *lokāḥ*—worlds; *tava*—your; *api*—also; *vaktrāṇi*—mouths; *samṛddha-vegāḥ*—swiftly.

All the worlds rush into your mouths, just like moths swiftly entering a blazing fire to be destroyed.

Baladeva Vidyābhūṣaṇa explains that as rivers flow into the sea without their own volition, being carried there by external forces, so too were great souls like Bhīṣma and Droṇa to meet with their destruction in the battle. They were never inimical to Kṛṣṇa or the Pāṇḍavas, but found themselves on the side of the opposition by force of circumstance. On the other hand, moths enter the fire consciously, so this comparison applies to Duryodhana, who in spite of knowing that the Pāṇḍavas were protected by Kṛṣṇa and even that he was the Supreme Person, still made deliberate efforts to destroy the Pāṇḍavas and thereby challenge Kṛṣṇa.

Text 30

लेलिह्यसे ग्रसमानः समन्ता-
　लोकान् समग्रान् वदनैर्ज्वलद्भिः ।
तेजोभिरापूर्य जगत्समग्रं
　भासस्तवोग्राः प्रतपन्ति विष्णो ॥३०॥

lelihyase grasamānaḥ samantāl
　lokān samagrān vadanair jvaladbhiḥ/
tejobhir āpūrya jagat samagraṁ
　bhāsas tavogrāḥ pratapanti viṣṇo//

lelihyase—you lick; *grasamānaḥ*—devouring; *samantāt*—from all sides; *lokān*—people; *samagrān*—all; *vadanaiḥ*—with mouths; *jvaladbhiḥ*—with flaming; *tejobhiḥ*—with splendor; *āpūrya*—filling; *jagat*—universe; *samagram*—all; *bhāsaḥ*—rays; *tava*—your; *ugrāḥ*—terrible; *pratapanti*—they scorch; *viṣṇo*—O Viṣṇu.

You lick your lips while devouring all creatures from all sides with your flaming mouths. O Viṣṇu, filling the entire universe with splendor, your terrible rays are scorching it.

Baladeva Vidyābhūṣaṇa says that "by saying 'Viṣṇu' Arjuna refers to the all-pervading nature of God, stressing that it is impossible for anyone to escape the Lord of time."

Text 31

आख्याहि मे को भवानुग्ररूपो
नमोऽस्तु ते देववर प्रसीद ।
विज्ञातुमिच्छामि भवन्तमाद्यं
न हि प्रजानामि तव प्रवृत्तिम् ॥३१॥

ākhyāhi me ko bhavān ugra-rūpo
namo 'stu te deva-vara prasīda/
vijñātum icchāmi bhavantam ādyaṁ
na hi prajānāmi tava pravṛttim//

ākhyāhi—explain; *me*—to me; *kaḥ*—who; *bhavān*—you; *ugra-rūpaḥ*—terrible form; *namaḥ astu*—let there be homage; *te*—to you; *deva-vara*—O best of the gods; *prasīda*—be merciful; *vijñātum*—to understand; *icchāmi*—I want; *bhavantam*—you; *ādyam*—primal; *na*—not; *hi*—certainly; *prajānāmi*—I know; *tava*—your; *pravṛttim*—purpose.

Tell me who you of such terrible form are. Homage to you, O best of gods, be merciful. I want to understand you, O primal one. Indeed, I cannot comprehend your actions.

In verse 20 Kṛṣṇa began to reveal his form of all-devouring time (*kāla-rūpa*, an aspect of his *viśvarūpa*), which brought fear to the heart of Arjuna. In response to Arjuna's inquiry, Kṛṣṇa will explain this form in the next three verses.

Baladeva Vidyābhūṣaṇa comments that Arjuna's use of the word *ugra* (terrible) indicates Arjuna's underlying request: he now wants Kṛṣṇa to withdraw this form.

Text 32

श्रीभगवानुवाच
कालोऽस्मि लोकक्षयकृत् प्रवृद्धो
लोकान् समाहर्तुमिह प्रवृत्तः ।
ऋतेऽपि त्वां न भविष्यन्ति सर्वे
येऽवस्थिताः प्रत्यनीकेषु योधाः ॥३२॥

śrī-bhagavān uvāca
kālo 'smi loka-kṣaya-kṛt pravṛddho

lokān samāhartum iha pravṛttaḥ/
ṛte 'pi tvāṁ na bhaviṣyanti sarve
ye 'vasthitāḥ pratyanīkeṣu yodhāḥ//

śrī-bhagavān uvāca—the Lord of Śrī said; *kālaḥ*—time; *asmi*—I am; *loka*—world; *kṣaya-kṛt*—destroyer; *pravṛddhaḥ*—powerful; *lokān*—people; *samāhartum*—to annihilate; *iha*—in this world; *pravṛttaḥ*—come forth; *ṛte*—without; *api*—even; *tvām*—you; *na*—not; *bhaviṣyanti*—they will be; *sarve*—all; *ye*—who; *avasthitāḥ*—arrayed; *prati-anīkeṣu*—in the opposite ranks; *yodhāḥ*—soldiers.

The Lord of Śrī said: I am time, powerful destroyer of the world, who has come forth to annihilate everyone. Even without your taking part, all those arrayed in the opposing ranks will be slain!

Text 33

तस्मात्त्वमुत्तिष्ठ यशो लभस्व
जित्वा शत्रून् भुङ्क्ष्व राज्यं समृद्धम् ।
मयैवैते निहताः पूर्वमेव
निमित्तमात्रं भव सव्यसाचिन् ॥३३॥

tasmāt tvam uttiṣṭha yaśo labhasva
jitvā śatrūn bhuṅkṣva rājyaṁ samṛddham/
mayaivaite nihatāḥ pūrvam eva
nimitta-mātraṁ bhava savya-sācin//

tasmāt—therefore; *tvam*—you; *uttiṣṭha*—rise up; *yaśaḥ*—fame; *labhasva*—gain; *jitvā*—conquering; *śatrūn*—enemies; *bhuṅkṣva*—enjoy; *rājyam*—kingdom; *samṛddham*—prosperous; *mayā*—by me; *eva*—certainly; *ete*—these; *nihatāḥ*—killed; *pūrvam eva*—previously; *nimitta-mātram*—instrument; *bhava*—be; *savya-sācin*—O Savyasācī.

Therefore rise up and become glorious. Defeat your enemies and enjoy a prosperous kingdom. These opposing warriors have already been killed by me and you will be but an instrument taking the credit, O Savyasācī.

Text 34

द्रोणं च भीष्मं च जयद्रथं च
कर्णं तथान्यानपि योधवीरान् ।

मया हतांस्त्वं जहि मा व्यथिष्ठा
युध्यस्व जेतासि रणे सपत्नान् ॥३४॥

droṇaṁ ca bhīṣmaṁ ca jayadrathaṁ ca
karṇaṁ tathānyān api yodha-vīrān/
mayā hatāṁs tvaṁ jahi mā vyathiṣṭhā
yudhyasva jetāsi raṇe sapatnān//

droṇam ca—also Droṇa; *bhīṣmam ca*—also Bhīṣma; *jayadratham ca*—also Jayadratha; *karṇam*—Karṇa; *tathā*—as well; *anyān*—others; *api*—certainly; *yodha-vīrān*—warriors; *mayā*—by me; *hatān*—killed; *tvam*—you; *jahi*—kill; *mā*—not; *vyathiṣṭhāḥ*—be afraid; *yudhyasva*—fight; *jetā asi*—you will conquer; *raṇe*—in battle; *sapatnān*—enemies.

Droṇa, Bhīṣma, Jayadratha, as well as Karṇa and other heroic warriors, have already been killed by me. Do not be afraid! Fight! You shall conquer the enemy in battle.

Kṛṣṇa, in the form of time personified, tells Arjuna that no one escapes his will. Time reveals its ultimate proprietorship by devouring all, and those who appear to destroy are merely the instruments by which he achieves his ends. Here Kṛṣṇa informs Arjuna that he need not fear, for the outcome of the battle will be that all of the opposing warriors will be slain. Kṛṣṇa thus confirms Duryodhana's words in chapter 1 (Bg. 1.9) when, unwittingly inspired by the goddess of learning, he predicted that all of his soldiers would lay down their lives for him.

The might of Droṇa, Bhīṣma, and Karṇa is indirectly underscored in this verse, as Kṛṣṇa answers the mental doubt of Arjuna regarding the possibility of their being slain, even in the face of time. Bhīṣma in particular had been blessed with the power of choosing the time at which he would die, and Jayadratha was once benedicted by Śiva with the power to diffuse the Pāṇḍavas. Thus Arjuna's doubt is dispelled by the force of Kṛṣṇa's proclamation imploring him to fight.

Although it is time, God's hand, that takes the life of all, people identify with the apparent cause of death, God's instrument. Thus Savyasācī Arjuna, the ambidextrous archer, will become famous in the eyes of common people for slaying great heroic warriors superior in prowess to himself. He will become famous among the learned and devoted for his willingness to be an instrument in God's hands.

Kṛṣṇa has justified Arjuna's fighting in many ways, but here for the first time he says that he should do so because he wants him to be his instrument. This implies that God has work to do in this world and that persons can be his instruments through which he executes it. If God has work to do in this world, then to that extent the world itself has value. However, we learned from chapter 4 (Bg. 4.7–8) that God's primary purpose for being in the world is mitigating his devotees' pangs of separation for him. Secondarily, in the course of tendering to the devoted, he vanquishes the ungodly. This is the work that Kṛṣṇa wants Arjuna to be instrumental in. He is not really concerned with Arjuna's fighting for *dharma*'s sake and all that *dharma* ordinarily implies. He clarifies this in chapter 18 (Bg. 18.66).

Text 35

सञ्जय उवाच
एतच्छ्रुत्वा वचनं केशवस्य
  कृताञ्जलिर्वेपमानः किरीटी ।
नमस्कृत्वा भूय एवाह कृष्णं
  सगद्गदं भीतभीतः प्रणम्य ॥३५॥

sañjaya uvāca
etac chrutvā vacanaṁ keśavasya
  kṛtāñjalir vepamānaḥ kirīṭī/
namaskṛtvā bhūya evāha kṛṣṇaṁ
  sa-gadgadaṁ bhīta-bhītaḥ praṇamya//

sañjayaḥ uvāca—Sañjaya said; *etat*—this; *śrutvā*—on hearing; *vacanam*—speech; *keśavasya*—of Keśava; *kṛta-añjaliḥ*—with folded palms; *vepamānaḥ*—trembling; *kirīṭī*—Arjuna; *namaskṛtvā*—offering homage; *bhūyaḥ*—again; *eva*—thus; *āha*—said; *kṛṣṇam*—(to) Kṛṣṇa; *sa-gadgadam*—in a faltering voice; *bhīta-bhītaḥ*—fearful; *praṇamya*—offering obeisances.

Sañjaya said: Upon hearing Keśava's speech, Kirīṭī (Arjuna), trembling with folded palms, offered homage in fear, prostrated himself, and spoke to Kṛṣṇa in a faltering voice.

Arjuna, the great archer whose head was decorated with the valuable helmet of gold and jewels (Kirīṭī) given to him by Indra, bowed again and again to Kṛṣṇa, as ecstatic symptoms *(sāttvika-bhāvas)* such as tears, choking of the voice, and trembling decorated his body. When a person's eyes become tearful owing to fear and delight, his throat chokes slightly causing his voice to falter. This is called *gadgada.*

Text 36

अर्जुन उवाच
स्थाने हृषीकेश तव प्रकीर्त्या
 जगत्प्रहृष्यत्यनुरज्यते च ।
रक्षांसि भीतानि दिशो द्रवन्ति
 सर्वे नमस्यन्ति च सिद्धसङ्घाः ॥३६॥

arjuna uvāca
sthāne hṛṣīkeśa tava prakīrtyā
 jagat prahṛṣyaty anurajyate ca/
rakṣāṁsi bhītāni diśo dravanti
 sarve namasyanti ca siddha-saṅghāḥ//

arjunaḥ uvāca—Arjuna said; *sthāne*—rightly; *hṛṣīka-īśa*—O Hṛṣīkeśa; *tava*—your; *prakīrtyā*—by the glories; *jagat*—the world; *prahṛṣyati*—becomes joyful; *anurajyate*—becomes attracted; *ca*—and; *rakṣāṁsi*—the demoniac; *bhītāni*—terrified; *diśaḥ*—directions; *dravanti*—they flee; *sarve*—all; *namasyanti*—they will bow down; *ca*—also; *siddha-saṅghāḥ*—the host of perfected beings.

Arjuna said: O Hṛṣīkeśa, it is appropriate that the entire universe should be joyful on hearing you praised and thus become attracted to you. At the same time, the demoniac, terrified, flee in all directions and the host of perfected beings reverently bows down before you.

In this verse, Arjuna begins to regain his sense of friendship with Kṛṣṇa and thus speaks to him about the joy he experiences on hearing Kṛṣṇa's glories. Here he remembers that the *viśva-rūpa* is a manifestation of Kṛṣṇa, who is his intimate friend sitting on his chariot. Arjuna reasons that, other than the demoniac, all people experience joy on hearing Kṛṣṇa's glories, and that it is appropriate that the demoniac flee in his presence, as it is for the perfected souls to perpetually bow before him. Arjuna's conclusion is derived from his direct experience, as he saw demons fleeing in the presence of Kṛṣṇa's *viśva-rūpa* and gods offering obeisances.

In the next two verses, Arjuna states why it is appropriate to offer homage to Kṛṣṇa and then he proceeds to do so in verses 39 through 46.

Text 37

कस्माच्च ते न नमेरन्महात्मन्
गरीयसे ब्रह्मणोऽप्यादिकर्त्रे ।
अनन्त देवेश जगन्निवास
त्वमक्षरं सदसत्तत्परं यत् ॥३७॥

kasmāc ca te na nameran mahātman
garīyase brahmaṇo 'py ādi-kartre/
ananta deveśa jagan-nivāsa
tvam akṣaraṁ sad-asat tat paraṁ yat//

kasmāt—why; *ca*—also; *te*—to you; *na*—not; *nameran*—they should bow down; *mahā-ātman*—O exalted one; *garīyase*—greater; *brahmaṇaḥ*—than Brahmā; *api*—even; *ādi-kartre*—to the original creator; *ananta*—O infinite; *deva-īśa*—O God of gods; *jagat-nivāsa*—O abode of the universe; *tvam*—you; *akṣaram*—imperishable; *sat-asat*—manifest and unmanifest; *tat param*—beyond that; *yat*—which.

And why should they not bow before you, O exalted one, who are even greater than Brahmā, being the original creator? O infinite one, God of gods, you are the abode of the universe, the imperishable, the manifest and the unmanifest, and that which lies beyond both.

Arjuna addresses Kṛṣṇa as *mahātmā* in this verse. *Mahātmā* literally means "great soul." Madhusūdana Saraswatī says that Arjuna uses this word to indicate the greatness *(mahān)* of Kṛṣṇa's heart *(ātmā)*. This is foremost in Arjuna's mind. Otherwise, the reason *(kasmāt)* that Kṛṣṇa is worthy of the praise of all *siddhas* is clear. He is even greater *(garīyase)* than Brahmā, who presides over the highest material planet inhabited by perfected souls. He is the original creator *(ādikartre)*. He is the source of the creative elements that Brahmā employs in his act of creation, having derived the power to create from Kṛṣṇa. Kṛṣṇa is the God of gods *(deva-īśa)* and the abode of the universe *(jagannivāsa)*. He is *akṣaram*, the infallible Brahman, and he is all that is manifest as well as all that is unmanifest, both existence and nonexistence *(sat-asat)* and that which lies beyond them.

Text 38

त्वमादिदेवः पुरुषः पुराण-
स्त्वमस्य विश्वस्य परं निधानम् ।

वेत्तासि वेद्यं च परं च धाम
त्वया ततं विश्वमनन्तरूप ॥३८॥

tvam ādi-devaḥ puruṣaḥ purāṇas
tvam asya viśvasya paraṁ nidhānam/
vettāsi vedyaṁ ca paraṁ ca dhāma
tvayā tataṁ viśvam ananta-rūpa//

tvam—you; *ādi-devaḥ*—the original God; *puruṣaḥ*—person; *purāṇaḥ*—old; *tvam*—you; *asya*—of this; *viśvasya*—of the universe; *param*—ultimate; *nidhānam*—refuge; *vettā*—knower; *asi*—you are; *vedyam*—the object of knowledge; *ca*—and; *param*—supreme; *ca*—and; *dhāma*—abode; *tvayā*—by you; *tatam*—pervaded; *viśvam*—universe; *ananta-rūpa*—O you of limitless form.

You are the original God, the oldest person, the ultimate resting place of the entire universe. You are the knower and you are that which is to be known, the supreme abode. You of limitless form pervade the entire universe!

Feeling love for Kṛṣṇa amidst the awe-inspiring display of the *viśva-rūpa*, Arjuna desires to offer something to Kṛṣṇa. However, realizing that Kṛṣṇa himself is everything, Arjuna offers only his obeisances again and again.

Text 39

वायुर्यमोऽग्निर्वरुणः शशाङ्कः
प्रजापतिस्त्वं प्रपितामहश्च ।
नमो नमस्तेऽस्तु सहस्रकृत्वः
पुनश्च भूयोऽपि नमो नमस्ते ॥३९॥

vāyur yamo 'gnir varuṇaḥ śaśāṅkaḥ
prajāpatis tvaṁ prapitāmahaś ca/
namo namas te 'stu sahasra-kṛtvaḥ
punaś ca bhūyo 'pi namo namas te//

vāyuḥ—Vāyu; *yamaḥ*—Yama; *agniḥ*—Agni; *varuṇaḥ*—Varuṇa; *śaśa-aṅkaḥ*—the moon; *prajāpatiḥ*—Lord of beings; *tvam*—you; *prapitāmahaḥ*—great-grandfather; *ca*—also; *namaḥ namaḥ*—salutations again and again; *te*—to you; *astu*—let there be; *sahasra-kṛtvaḥ*—a thousand times; *punaḥ ca*—and again; *bhūyaḥ*—again; *api*—also; *namaḥ namaḥ te*—repeated homage to you.

You are Vāyu, Yama, Agni, Varuṇa, the moon, the Lord of beings, and the great-grandfather. Salutations to you thousands of times; again and again, homage to you.

The various gods mentioned in this verse represent air (Vāyu), death (Yama), fire (Agni), and water (Varuṇa). The Lord of beings *(prajāpati)* is Brahmā. The moon *(śaśāṅkaḥ)* indicates the heavenly constellations. By his offering of repeated obeisances Arjuna demonstrates his humility. He feels unable to adequately glorify Kṛṣṇa, whose glory is unlimited.

Text 40

नमः पुरस्तादथ पृष्ठतस्ते
नमोऽस्तु ते सर्वत एव सर्व ।
अनन्तवीर्यामितविक्रमस्त्वं
सर्वं समाप्नोषि ततोऽसि सर्वः ॥४०॥

namaḥ purastād atha pṛṣṭhatas te
namo 'stu te sarvata eva sarva/
ananta-vīryāmita-vikramas tvaṁ
sarvaṁ samāpnoṣi tato 'si sarvaḥ//

namaḥ—obeisances; *purastāt*—from the front; *atha*—also; *pṛṣṭhataḥ*—from behind; *te*—to you; *namaḥ astu*—let there be obeisances; *te*—to you; *sarvataḥ*—from all sides; *eva*—indeed; *sarva*—all; *ananta-vīrya*—limitless valor; *amita-vikramaḥ*—infinite might; *tvam*—you; *sarvam*—all; *samāpnoṣi*—you pervade; *tataḥ*—therefore; *asi*—you are; *sarvaḥ*—everything.

Obeisances to you from the front and from behind. Obeisances to you on all sides as well, O all in all. You are infinite might and limitless valor. As you pervade all, you are everything.

While some warriors such as Bhīma are powerful by virtue of their strength, others like Droṇa are powerful by dint of their valor and skill in fighting. Here Arjuna says that Kṛṣṇa is superior in both ways. Kṛṣṇa has unlimited strength *(ananta-vīrya)* and immeasurable valor *(amita-vikrama)*.

Baladeva Vidyābhūṣaṇa cites this verse in his commentary on *Vedānta-sūtra* 1.1.30. This *sūtra* is part of a discussion regarding the sense in which the *śruti* proclaims identity between the individual soul *(jīvātmā)* and God. God is one with all souls and all things, yet this oneness is not an absolute oneness. In this verse Arjuna says, *sarvaṁ samāpnoṣi tato 'si sarvaḥ:* "As you pervade all, you are everything." Thus while realizing that Kṛṣṇa is everything, Arjuna qualifies this understanding by stating that Kṛṣṇa is so in as much as he pervades everything. All the parts of one's body are one's body, but the body and its parts are also different. My hand is my body, but it is also my hand.

Texts 41–42

सखेति मत्वा प्रसभं यदुक्तं
हे कृष्ण हे यादव हे सखेति ।
अजानता महिमानं तवेदं
मया प्रमादात्प्रणयेन वापि ॥४१॥
यच्चावहासार्थमसत्कृतोऽसि
विहारशय्यासनभोजनेषु ।
एकोऽथ वाप्यच्युत तत्समक्षं
तत्क्षामये त्वामहमप्रमेयम् ॥४२॥

sakheti matvā prasabhaṁ yad uktaṁ
he kṛṣṇa he yādava he sakheti/
ajānatā mahimānaṁ tavedaṁ
mayā pramādāt praṇayena vāpi//
yac cāvahāsārtham asat-kṛto 'si
vihāra-śayyāsana-bhojaneṣu/
eko 'tha vāpy acyuta tat-samakṣaṁ
tat kṣāmaye tvām aham aprameyam//

sakhā—friend; *iti*—thus; *matvā*—thinking; *prasabham*—rashly; *yat*—which; *uktam*—said; *he kṛṣṇa*—O Kṛṣṇa; *he yādava*—O Yādava; *he sakhe*—O comrade; *iti*—thus; *ajānatā*—in ignorance; *mahimānam*—majesty; *tava*—your; *idam*—this; *mayā*—by me; *pramādāt*—out of negligence; *praṇayena*—out of love; *vā api*—either; *yat*—whatever; *ca*—and; *avahāsa-artham*—for joking; *asat-kṛtaḥ*—disrespectfully treated; *asi*—you are; *vihāra-śayyā-āsana-bhojaneṣu*—in diversion, in bed, while seated, or while eating together; *ekaḥ*—alone; *atha vā*—or; *api*—also; *acyuta*—O Acyuta; *tat-samakṣam*—in front of others; *tat*—that; *kṣāmaye*—I ask forgiveness; *tvām*—you; *aham*—I; *aprameyam*—immeasurable.

Forgive me for things I may have rashly said in ignorance of your majesty. Out of negligence or even affection, I may have thought of you as an

ordinary friend and addressed you, "O Kṛṣṇa, O Yādava, O comrade!" O Acyuta, O immeasurable one, I ask forgiveness of you for having treated you disrespectfully by joking with you while playing, resting, sitting, or eating together, either privately or in front of other companions.

As Arjuna remembers his friendly relationship with Kṛṣṇa, he reflects on it in light of the obvious Godhood of his friend. It is apparent from this verse that although the opulence of Godhead is the background of the sweet relationship his devotees have with him, should it come to the foreground, sweet intimacy is impaired. If Kṛṣṇa were not God, his relationship with others would not be particularly charming. The fact that he is God, yet acts otherwise in love, is the charm of the Absolute. For this charm to manifest, the opulence of the Absolute must be suppressed. In the face of the opulence of the Absolute, Arjuna, although remembering his intimate relationship with Kṛṣṇa, questions the appropriateness of it.

Baladeva Vidyābhūṣaṇa says that Arjuna's address "O Kṛṣṇa" devoid of any honorific preface such as "Śrī" is irreverent. Ordinary people and the general class of devotees should take note of this. Addressing Kṛṣṇa "O Yādava!" as Arjuna often did also shows irreverence because on the one hand the Yādavas were minor kings, not emperors like the Kauravas or Pāṇḍavas, and furthermore, Kṛṣṇa was not even the king, but only a prince. Such an address implies superiority on the part of Arjuna, as does Arjuna's calling Kṛṣṇa "friend," as if Arjuna were in a position to benefit Kṛṣṇa. Viśvanātha Cakravartī Ṭhākura says that the name Kṛṣṇa describes the Lord in terms of his being the son of Vasudeva, who was a minister and not a warrior like Arjuna's father, either Pāṇḍu or Indra. Thus Arjuna laments that he has disrespected God *(acyuta)*, the infallible and immeasurable *(aprameyam)*. Arjuna's addressing Kṛṣṇa in this verse as Acyuta also implies that even though Arjuna was disrespectful in his dealing with Kṛṣṇa, Kṛṣṇa remained unruffled, a testimony to his greatness and the compassion that Arjuna seeks to draw on in this verse.

However, Arjuna's affectionate address in which Kṛṣṇa is referred to as a subordinate is hardly offensive. Indeed, his affectionate use of epithets and his intimate dealings, although not to be imitated, are more pleasing to Kṛṣṇa than Arjuna's deferential prayers. Here we glimpse the exalted devotional status of Arjuna, who continues to glorify Kṛṣṇa in terms of his opulence.

Text 43

पितासि लोकस्य चराचरस्य
त्वमस्य पूज्यश्च गुरुर्गरीयान् ।
न त्वत्समोऽस्त्यभ्यधिकः कुतोऽन्यो
लोकत्रयेऽप्यप्रतिमप्रभाव ॥४३॥

pitāsi lokasya carācarasya
tvam asya pūjyaś ca gurur garīyān/
na tvat-samo 'sty abhyadhikaḥ kuto 'nyo
loka-traye 'py apratima-prabhāva//

pitā—father; *asi*—you are; *lokasya*—of the world; *cara-acarasya*—of the moving and nonmoving; *tvam*—you; *asya*—of this; *pūjyaḥ*—worshippable; *ca*—also; *guruḥ*—guru; *garīyān*—more venerable; *na*—not; *tvat-samaḥ*—equal to you; *asti*—there is; *abhyadhikaḥ*—greater; *kutaḥ*—how; *anyaḥ*—other; *loka-traye*—in the three worlds; *api*—also; *apratima-prabhāva*—O you of unrivaled power.

You are the father of the world, of all things, moving and motionless. You are worshippable, the most venerable guru. There is no one like you in the three worlds. How could anyone be greater, O you of unrivaled power?

Text 44

तस्मात्प्रणम्य प्रणिधाय कायं
प्रसादये त्वामहमीशमीड्यम् ।
पितेव पुत्रस्य सखेव सख्युः
प्रियः प्रियायार्हसि देव सोढुम् ॥४४॥

tasmāt praṇamya praṇidhāya kāyaṁ
prasādaye tvām aham īśam īḍyam/
piteva putrasya sakheva sakhyuḥ
priyaḥ priyāyārhasi deva soḍhum//

tasmāt—therefore; *praṇamya*—bowing down; *praṇidhāya*—prostrating; *kāyam*—body; *prasādaye*—I ask forgiveness; *tvām*—you; *aham*—I; *īśam*—Lord; *īḍyam*—worshippable; *pitā iva*—like a father; *putrasya*—of a son; *sakhā iva*—like a friend; *sakhyuḥ*—of a friend; *priyaḥ*—a lover; *priyāyāḥ*—to the beloved; *arhasi*—you should; *deva*—O God; *soḍhum*—to be merciful.

I therefore prostrate myself on the ground before you in surrender, O Lord. O God, please be merciful to me and tolerate my offenses, just as a father tolerates his son, a friend his friend, and a lover his beloved.

Text 45–46

अदृष्टपूर्वं हृषितोऽस्मि दृष्ट्वा
भयेन च प्रव्यथितं मनो मे ।
तदेव मे दर्शय देव रूपं
प्रसीद देवेश जगन्निवास ॥४५॥
किरीटिनं गदिनं चक्रहस्तम्
इच्छामि त्वां द्रष्टुमहं तथैव ।
तेनैव रूपेन चतुर्भुजेन
सहस्रबाहो भव विश्वमूर्ते ॥४६॥

adṛṣṭa-pūrvaṁ hṛṣito 'smi dṛṣṭvā
bhayena ca pravyathitaṁ mano me/
tad eva me darśaya deva rūpaṁ
prasīda deveśa jagan-nivāsa//
kirīṭinaṁ gadinaṁ cakra-hastam
icchāmi tvāṁ draṣṭum ahaṁ tathaiva/
tenaiva rūpeṇa catur-bhujena
sahasra-bāho bhava viśva-mūrte//

adṛṣṭa-pūrvam—never seen before; *hṛṣitaḥ*—excited; *asmi*—I am; *dṛṣṭvā*—by seeing; *bhayena*—out of fear; *ca*—also; *pravyathitam*—trembling; *manaḥ*—mind; *me*—my; *tat*—that; *eva*—certainly; *me*—of me; *darśaya*—show; *deva*—O God; *rūpam*—form; *prasīda*—be merciful; *deva-īśa*—O God of gods; *jagat-nivāsa*—O shelter of the universe; *kirīṭinam*—with a crown; *gadinam*—with club; *cakra-hastam*—discus in hand; *icchāmi*—I want; *tvām*—you; *draṣṭum*—to see; *aham*—I; *tathā eva*—thus; *tena eva*—with that; *rūpeṇa*—with form; *catuḥ-bhujena*—with four arms; *sahasra-bāho*—O thousand-armed one; *bhava*—become; *viśva-mūrte*—O you of cosmic form.

I am thrilled to have seen this form, which has never been seen before. Now, O God of gods, shelter of the universe, be merciful and show me your familiar form. I want to see you in that form adorned with a crown, armed with club, discus in hand. O thousand-armed one, O you of cosmic form, show me that four-armed form.

Kṛṣṇa appeared to Vasudeva and Devakī in a four-armed form. This four-armed form is an expansion of *svayaṁ bhagavān* Kṛṣṇa of Vraja. In the language of *Śrīmad-Bhāgavatam* (10.3.11) it is described as *kṛṣṇāvatāra*, an *avatāra* of Kṛṣṇa. This is significant, as it explains that the four-armed form of Kṛṣṇa is an expansion of his two-armed humanlike form. This four-armed form is an opulent form of Kṛṣṇa. Arjuna saw it within the *viśva-rūpa*. Here he desires to see it again, a godly yet beautiful form, and be relieved of the vision of the *viśva-rūpa* before seeing Kṛṣṇa's beautiful two-armed form again. The theological implication of this sequence should be clear. From worship of the *viśva-rūpa*, it becomes possible to conceive of the four-armed Viṣṇu feature of Godhead in awe and reverence. Passing this stage, one can realize the two-armed Kṛṣṇa. Arjuna's desire to see Kṛṣṇa's four-armed form as he had heard of it from others and seen within the *viśva-rūpa* instructs us further about the opulence of Kṛṣṇa, the summum bonum of the Absolute.

Text 47

श्रीभगवानुवाच
मया प्रसन्नेन तवार्जुनेदं
    रूपं परं दर्शितमात्मयोगात्।
तेजोमयं विश्वमनन्तमाद्यं
    यन्मे त्वदन्येन न दृष्टपूर्वम् ॥४७॥

śrī-bhagavān uvāca
mayā prasannena tavārjunedaṁ
    rūpaṁ paraṁ darśitam ātma-yogāt/
tejo-mayaṁ viśvam anantam ādyaṁ
    yan me tvad anyena na dṛṣṭa-pūrvam//

śrī-bhagavān uvāca—the Lord of Śrī said; *mayā*—by me; *prasannena*—by being merciful; *tava*—of you; *arjuna*—O Arjuna; *idam*—this; *rūpam*—form; *param*—supreme; *darśitam*—shown; *ātma-yogāt*—by my spiritual power; *tejaḥ-mayam*—effulgent; *viśvam*—universal; *anantam*—unlimited; *ādyam*—primal; *yat*—which; *me*—my; *tvat anyena*—besides you; *na dṛṣṭa-pūrvam*—not seen before.

The Lord of Śrī said: Out of my mercy I have manifested this supreme form by the influence of my own spiritual power. This primal form of mine is effulgent, universal, and unlimited. It has never been seen before by anyone other than you.

Kṛṣṇa says that he manifested the *viśva-rūpa* by his own spiritual power *(ātmayogāt)*. Here he refers to his primary energy by which he reveals or hides himself. Earlier in the *Mahābhārata* Kṛṣṇa revealed a partial manifestation of his *viśva-rūpa* to Duryodhana that did not include his *kāla-rūpa*. Thus this particular form revealed to Arjuna had never been seen before by any human being. It was, however, visible to the gods because they are also devotees.

Text 48

न वेदयज्ञाध्ययनैर्न दानै-
 र्न च क्रियाभिर्न तपोभिरुग्रैः ।
एवंरूपः शक्य अहं नृलोके
 द्रष्टुं त्वदन्येन कुरुप्रवीर ॥४८॥

na veda-yajñādhyayanair na dānair
 na ca kriyābhir na tapobhir ugraiḥ/
evaṁ-rūpaḥ śakya ahaṁ nṛ-loke
 draṣṭuṁ tvad anyena kuru-pravīra//

na—not; *veda-yajña*—Vedic sacrifice; *adhyayanaiḥ*—by Vedic study; *na*—not; *dānaiḥ*—by charity; *na*—not; *ca*—also; *kriyābhiḥ*—by ritualistic acts; *na*—not; *tapobhiḥ*—by austerities; *ugraiḥ*—by severe; *evam-rūpaḥ*—in such form; *śakyaḥ*—I can; *aham*—I; *nṛ-loke*—in the world of men; *draṣṭum*—to see (to be seen); *tvat*—than you; *anyena*—by another; *kuru-pravīra*—O best among the Kuru heroes.

Other than you, no one in human society can see me in this form, not through performing Vedic sacrifice, nor through studying the Vedas, charity, ritualistic acts, or severe austerities.

Arjuna was able to see this form of Kṛṣṇa because of Kṛṣṇa's special grace. In fact, it is grace that makes it possible to see any of Kṛṣṇa's forms *(divyaṁ dadāmi te cakṣuḥ)*. Devotion is a separate goal from the achievement of mystical visions, but both mystical visions and devotion (or the restoration of one's "natural state") are both the result of grace. However, the experience of the *mysterium tremendum* is more of a disruption than a desired ideal to the devotee. The end of devotion is the deepening of devotion. The mystical experience of God's omnipresence is a gift that serves that end. By the same token, the feeling of separation also serves that end. Indeed, all of God's actions serve that end in one way or another.

Text 49

मा ते व्यथा मा च विमूढभावो
दृष्ट्वा रूपं घोरमीदृङ् ममेदम् ।
व्यपेतभीः प्रीतमनाः पुनस्त्वं
तदेव मे रूपमिदं प्रपश्य ॥४९॥

mā te vyathā mā ca vimūḍha-bhāvo
dṛṣṭvā rūpaṁ ghoram īdṛṅ mamedam/
vyapeta-bhīḥ prīta-manāḥ punas tvaṁ
tad eva me rūpam idaṁ prapaśya//

mā—never; *te*—of you; *vyathā*—you should trouble; *mā*—never; *ca*—also; *vimūḍha-bhāvaḥ*—bewilderment; *dṛṣṭvā*—by seeing; *rūpam*—form; *ghoram*—awesome; *īdṛk*—such; *mama*—my; *idam*—this; *vyapeta-bhīḥ*—free from fear; *prīta-manāḥ*—joyful heart; *punaḥ*—again; *tvam*—you; *tat*—that; *eva*—thus; *me*—my; *rūpam*—form; *idam*—this; *prapaśya*—behold.

Be free from fear and the bewilderment that came upon you as a result of seeing this awesome form of mine. With joyful heart once again behold my human form.

Text 50

सञ्जय उवाच
इत्यर्जुनं वासुदेवस्तथोक्त्वा
स्वकं रूपं दर्शयामास भूयः ।
आश्वासयामास च भीतमेनं
भूत्वा पुनः सौम्यवपुर्महात्मा ॥५०॥

sañjaya uvāca
ity arjunaṁ vāsudevas tathoktvā
svakaṁ rūpaṁ darśayām āsa bhūyaḥ/
āśvāsayām āsa ca bhītam enaṁ
bhūtvā punaḥ saumya-vapur mahātmā//

sañjayaḥ uvāca—Sañjaya said; *iti*—thus; *arjunam*—Arjuna; *vāsudevaḥ*—Kṛṣṇa; *tathā*—thus; *uktvā*—having spoken; *svakam*—own; *rūpam*—form; *darśayām āsa*—he showed; *bhūyaḥ*—again; *āśvāsayām āsa*—he pacified; *ca*—and; *bhītam*—frightened; *enam*—him; *bhūtvā*—becoming; *punaḥ*—again; *saumya-vapuḥ*—gentle form; *mahā-ātmā*—the great one.

Sañjaya said: Having spoken thus to Arjuna, Vāsudeva Kṛṣṇa gave Arjuna darśana of his own four-armed form again. Then once again he of compassionate heart resumed his gentle, wonderful, two-armed, humanlike form, pacifying the frightened Arjuna.

In the *Mahābhārata*, it is mentioned that some persons saw Kṛṣṇa appear in a four-armed form on the battlefield of Kurukṣetra. However, because of Arjuna's relationship with him as a friend *(sakhya-rasa)*, Kṛṣṇa always appeared to him in a two-armed form. Friendship is exchanged between equals. Had Arjuna been accustomed to associating with Kṛṣṇa in his four-armed form, he would never have sat with him on the same bed, he would never have joked with him and addressed him, "O Yādava, O Kṛṣṇa, O Sakhā." It was Kṛṣṇa in his two-armed form who showed Arjuna the *viśvā-rūpa* and this same two-armed Kṛṣṇa here showed Arjuna the four-armed form at his request. This verse states that after so doing, Kṛṣṇa resumed his *saumya-vapu*, a reference to his two-armed, humanlike form. Sañjaya does not say that Kṛṣṇa then manifested his two-armed form, because it is Kṛṣṇa in this form who has been revealing other aspects of himself in the *viśva-rūpa* and the *catur-bhuja*.

In the second line of this verse Sañjaya says that Kṛṣṇa again *(bhūyaḥ)* showed *(darśayām āsa)* Arjuna his own form *(svakam rūpam)*. This refers to his four-armed form. In the third and fourth lines, Sañjaya says that Kṛṣṇa again *(punaḥ)* assumed his two-armed form and thus pacified *(āśvāsayām āsa)* Arjuna. If Kṛṣṇa's pacifying Arjuna did not involve resuming this form, this verse would suffer from repetition. This understanding is further supported by the following verse. It will be made even more clear in the subsequent verse, where the two-armed humanlike form of Kṛṣṇa is glorified as the most rare and difficult to see, more so than either the *viśva-rūpa* or the four-armed form of Kṛṣṇa.

Text 51

अर्जुन उवाच
दृष्ट्वेदं मानुषं रूपं तव सौम्यं जनार्दन ।
इदानीमस्मि संवृत्तः सचेताः प्रकृतिं गतः ॥५१॥

arjuna uvāca
dṛṣṭvedaṁ mānuṣaṁ rūpaṁ tava saumyaṁ janārdana/
idānīm asmi saṁvṛttaḥ sa-cetāḥ prakṛtiṁ gataḥ//

arjunaḥ uvāca—Arjuna said; *dṛṣṭvā*—seeing; *idam*—this; *mānuṣam*—human; *rūpam*—form; *tava*—your; *saumyam*—gentle; *janārdana*—O Janārdana; *idānīm*—now; *asmi*—I am; *saṁvṛttaḥ*—composed; *sa-cetāḥ*—with my consciousness; *prakṛtim*—to natural; *gataḥ*—restored.

Arjuna said: Now that I see this gentle human form of yours, O Janārdana, I am composed and restored to my natural state.

Text 52

श्रीभगवानुवाच
सुदुर्दर्शमिदं रूपं दृष्टवानसि यन्मम ।
देवा अप्यस्य रूपस्य नित्यं दर्शनकांक्षिणः ॥५२॥

śrī-bhagavān uvāca
su-durdarśam idaṁ rūpaṁ dṛṣṭavān asi yan mama/
devā apy asya rūpasya nityaṁ darśana-kāṅkṣiṇaḥ//

śrī-bhagavān uvāca—the Lord of Śrī said; *su-durdarśam*—very difficult to see; *idam*—this; *rūpam*—form; *dṛṣṭavān asi*—you have seen; *yat*—which; *mama*—my; *devāḥ*—the gods; *api*—even; *asya*—of this; *rūpasya*—of the form; *nityam*—constantly; *darśana-kāṅkṣiṇaḥ*—longing to see.

The Lord of Śrī said: This form of mine you are beholding is very difficult to see. Even the gods constantly long to see it.

In this verse, the word *dṛṣṭavān* is a perfect participle that can be rendered either in reference to the present form that Arjuna is seeing or in reference to the *viśva-rūpa* that Arjuna has seen. In either case the significance is the same: Kṛṣṇa's two-armed form is higher than his *viśva-rūpa.*

If we take *dṛṣṭavān* to be speaking in the present in reference to the form that Arjuna is now seeing, this rendering is further supported grammatically by the word *idam* (this), which is used in reference to things that are nearby, as opposed to *tat*, which is used to refer to things at a distance. Kṛṣṇa is standing before Arjuna in his humanlike form, whereas his *viśva-rūpa* is now at a distance, an event gone by. Had Kṛṣṇa been referring to his *viśva-rūpa*, he would have used the word *tat* rather than *idam.*

Here Kṛṣṇa's two-armed form is either being extolled directly as very difficult to see *(su-durdarśam)* or indirectly as even more glorious than the *viśva-rūpa*, because Arjuna cares more for it, even after seeing the *viśva-rūpa* that is so difficult to see. If we take a more literal approach to the language of the verse and render *dṛṣṭavān* in reference to the *viśva-rūpa*, as some commentators have, we cannot ignore the feeling of this section. Arjuna lost interest in the *viśva-rūpa* and not the beatific vision of Kṛṣṇa's humanlike form.

Furthermore, Kṛṣṇa has also mentioned that the gods constantly desire to see the form under discussion. While there are no scriptural references supporting the idea that the gods always desire to see the *viśva-rūpa*, there are many prayers in the *Śrīmad-Bhāgavatam* in which the gods pray to see the form of Kṛṣṇa.[4]

Finally, text 53 also confirms that in this verse Kṛṣṇa is speaking of his humanlike form, inasmuch as it would be repetitive were it referring to the *viśva-rūpa*, for in text 48 Kṛṣṇa has already said that it is not possible to see the *viśva-rūpa* through study of the *Vedas*, etc.

Text 53

नाहं वेदैर्न तपसा न दानेन न चेज्यया ।
शक्य एवंविधो द्रष्टुं दृष्टवानसि मां यथा ॥५३॥

nāhaṁ vedair na tapasā na dānena na cejyayā/
śakya evaṁ-vidho draṣṭuṁ dṛṣṭavān asi māṁ yathā//

na—not; *aham*—I; *vedaiḥ*—by study of the *Vedas; na*—not; *tapasā*—by austerity; *na*—not; *dānena*—by charity; *na*—not; *ca*—and; *ijyayā*—by sacrifice; *śakyaḥ*—I can; *evam-vidhaḥ*—in this form; *draṣṭum*—to see; *dṛṣṭavān*—seeing; *asi*—you are; *mām*—me; *yathā*—as.

Not by study of the Vedas, not by austerity, not by giving in charity, not even by sacrifice can I be seen in this form as you have seen me.

In his introductory notes to chapter 12, Madhusūdana Saraswatī says that after the revelation of the cosmic form, the entity with form (two-armed Kṛṣṇa) has been referred to in this verse. Viśvanātha Cakravartī comments that if anyone wants to see Kṛṣṇa in his eternal two-armed humanlike form as Arjuna did, he cannot do so by any of the practices mentioned in this verse, even if they consider the vision of this form to be the perfection of human endeavor.

4. See ŚB. 10.2, entire chapter.

Text 54

भक्त्या त्वनन्यया शक्य अहमेवंविधोऽर्जुन ।
ज्ञातुं द्रष्टुं च तत्त्वेन प्रवेष्टुं च परन्तप ॥५४॥

bhaktyā tv ananyayā śakya aham evaṁ-vidho 'rjuna/
jñātuṁ draṣṭuṁ ca tattvena praveṣṭuṁ ca parantapa//

bhaktyā—by devotion; *tu*—but; *ananyayā*—by unalloyed; *śakyaḥ*—I can; *aham*—I; *evam-vidhaḥ*—in this form; *arjuna*—O Arjuna; *jñātum*—to know; *draṣṭum*—to see; *ca*—and; *tattvena*—in fact; *praveṣṭum*—to attain; *ca*—also; *parantapa*—O Parantapa.

Only by unalloyed devotion can one actually see and understand this form and attain me, O Parantapa.

If verses 52 through 54 are taken to be in reference to the *viśva-rūpa*, they are indirectly glorifying not only Kṛṣṇa's humanlike form, but devotion to Kṛṣṇa as well. The word *praveṣṭum* in this verse can also be rendered "entered into." Should one desire to enter into the *viśva-rūpa* and attain liberation without concern for attaining a transcendental relationship with Kṛṣṇa, here Kṛṣṇa emphatically declares that this can only be accomplished by devotion.

Text 55

मत्कर्मकृन्मत्परमो मद्भक्तः सङ्गवर्जितः ।
निर्वैरः सर्वभूतेषु यः स मामेति पाण्डव ॥५५॥

mat-karma-kṛn mat-paramo mad-bhaktaḥ saṅga-varjitaḥ/
nirvairaḥ sarva-bhūteṣu yaḥ sa mām eti pāṇḍava//

mat-karma-kṛt—doing work for me; *mat-paramaḥ*—considering me the highest; *mat-bhaktaḥ*—devoted to me; *saṅga-varjitaḥ*—abandoning attachment; *nirvairaḥ*—free from enmity; *sarva-bhūteṣu*—toward all living beings; *yaḥ*—who; *saḥ*—he; *mām*—(to) me; *eti*—comes; *pāṇḍava*—O son of Pāṇḍu.

A person who acts for me, considers me the highest object of attainment, devotes himself to me, abandons all attachment, and frees himself from enmity toward any living being comes to me, O son of Pāṇḍu.

As this chapter ends Kṛṣṇa glorifies unalloyed *bhakti*. He stressed this at the beginning of chapter 7 and again in chapter 8. In chapter 9 he personally became overwhelmed while speaking about his devotees and devotion. His emotional state overflowed into chapter 10. Following this, Arjuna brought him back to practical reality by asking him about his majesty—his Godhood. Kṛṣṇa theorized about this for the balance of chapter 10, and then, at Arjuna's request, he translated theory into experience—*jñāna* into *vijñāna*. Properly understood, the overwhelming revelation of his Godhood in this chapter has indirectly served to underscore the charm and beauty of unalloyed devotion. Thus we turn to the last of the six middle chapters dealing with the *Gītā*'s devotional theology.

CHAPTER TWELVE

भक्तियोगः
Bhakti-yoga

YOGA OF DEVOTION

Text 1

अर्जुन उवाच
एवं सततयुक्ता ये भक्तास्त्वां पर्युपासते ।
ये चाप्यक्षरमव्यक्तं तेषां के योगवित्तमाः ॥१॥

arjuna uvāca
evaṁ satata-yuktā ye bhaktās tvāṁ paryupāsate/
ye cāpy akṣaram avyaktaṁ teṣāṁ ke yoga-vittamāḥ//

arjunaḥ uvāca—Arjuna said; *evam*—thus; *satata*—always; *yuktāḥ*—united; *ye*—who; *bhaktāḥ*—devotees; *tvām*—you; *paryupāsate*—they worship; *ye*—who; *ca*—and; *api*—again; *akṣaram*—imperishable; *avyaktam*—unmanifest; *teṣām*—of them; *ke*—who; *yoga-vit-tamāḥ*—having the best knowledge of *yoga*.

Arjuna said: Who has the best understanding of yoga, those devotees who worship you and are thus always united with you in love or those who worship the imperishable unmanifest?

The middle six chapters of the *Gītā* are introduced with the final verse of the sixth chapter. Therein Kṛṣṇa tells Arjuna that devotion to himself is the highest form of *yoga* (Bg. 6.47). Thus in this verse, Arjuna seems to be asking a question that has already been answered. He does so for further clarification about worship and its object. Although Kṛṣṇa has already stated unequivocally that his devotee is the best *yogī*, here Arjuna gives him the opportunity to make a similar definitive statement regarding the highest object of worship as well.

Kṛṣṇa has just finished demonstrating that his personal form is a higher manifestation of divinity than his *virāṭa-rūpa*. This *virāṭa-rūpa* was discussed theoretically in chapter 9 when Kṛṣṇa spoke of pantheists (Bg. 9.15–19), and upon Arjuna's request he elaborated on this in chapter 10 leading up to the theophany of chapter 11. As chapter 12 commences with further glorification of Kṛṣṇa's personal form, any confusion remaining about this issue after reading chapter 11 is put to rest. Now Kṛṣṇa will explain that his personal form is also a higher manifestation of Godhead than his Brahman feature.

Here Arjuna clearly refers to the highest of devotees by his use of the words *satata-yuktāḥ*, which Kṛṣṇa used to describe them earlier in chapter 10 (Bg. 10.10). They are attached to Kṛṣṇa's beautiful form. They are the *mahātmās* of chapters 8 (Bg. 8.15) and 9 (Bg. 9.13–14). On the other hand, Arjuna refers here to *jñāna-yogīs*, whose object of meditation is the formless *akṣara*. Just before he mentioned pantheism, Kṛṣṇa spoke of those who worship him through the sacrifice of knowledge (*jñāna-yajñena*). These *jñāna-yogīs* are more spiritually developed than the other types of worshippers discussed in chapter 9. Are these *jñāna-yogīs* also better *yogīs* than Kṛṣṇa's devotees, the *mahātmās*? Arjuna wants to know which worshipper is the best *yogī* (*yoga-vittamāḥ*), and accordingly, whether the beautiful form of Śrī Kṛṣṇa that Arjuna loves so dearly—the *mahātmās*' object of worship—is a higher ideal than the Brahman feature of God, the *akṣara* adored by the *jñāna-yogīs*.

In his commentary on this verse, Rāmānuja makes the argument that the word *akṣara* does not refer to Brahman, for Brahman and Kṛṣṇa are synonymous in the *Gītā*. Nowhere in the *Gītā*, nor anywhere in the scripture, is Brahman described as superior to the person of Kṛṣṇa. Because Kṛṣṇa *is* Brahman, Rāmānuja opines that Arjuna cannot be asking if worship of Kṛṣṇa or worship of Brahman is superior. Thus he understands *akṣara* to refer to the individual soul.

Rāmānuja's argument is aimed at exposing the fault in Śaṅkara's explanation of this and the following verses concerning Arjuna's question. Śaṅkara reasons that Brahman is a superior expression of the Absolute. If there is any superiority to the form of Kṛṣṇa, Śaṅkara attributes it to the idea that this form facilitates liberation for those unable to meditate without conceptualization. Thus Śaṅkara restricts Kṛṣṇa's answer to address only what he considers the relative superiority of worship for those not qualified to meditate on the unmanifest, indeterminate Brahman.

Śaṅkara's argument is the lens through which he looks at all the scriptural references glorifying the form of God and devotion to it. It appears first in his highly interpretive explanation of *Vedānta-sūtra* 1.1.17. This *sūtra* appears in a section in which Brahman is described as having qualities. It begins with the statement *ānandamayo 'bhyāsāt*, "Brahman is joyful." (Vs. 1.1.12) *Sūtra* 1.1.13 states that Brahman is not made of joy (a creation), but rather possessed of an abundance of joy. Evidence for this is offered in 1.1.14, which states that since Brahman is designated elsewhere as the cause of joy (*Taittirīya Upaniṣad* 2.7) he must be full of joy. *Sūtra* 1.1.15 states that the scripture of joy *(Taittirīya Upaniṣad)* also celebrates Brahman as being joyful. Following this *sūtra* in 1.1.16, that which is Brahman and joyful is distinguished from the individual soul. The Brahman who is joyful is also described in the scripture as being the creator. Thus it is Brahman who is described as joyful and not the individual soul, for only Brahman is described as possessing the ability to create the world. *Sūtra* 1.1.17 then states that the individual soul and Brahman are declared to be different, *bheda-vyapadeśāc ca*. Even Śaṅkara himself admits that *sūtras* 1.1.16–17 concern the difference between Brahman and the individual soul. However, Śaṅkara adds his own comment, declaring that the difference only exists on a lower level of reality *(vyavahāric)*, whereas in ultimate reality *(paramārthic)* this illusion of difference ceases to exist. However, nowhere in *Vedānta-sūtra* is there any reference to Śaṅkara's two levels of reality and thus two levels of Brahman—a provisional manifestation of the Absolute (Kṛṣṇa/the *avatāra*/*īśvara*) and an ultimate reality (unmanifest, indeterminate Brahman).

Thus Śaṅkara appears to have attached his own doctrine to the *sūtras*. In this doctrine he calls his provisional manifestation of Brahman "*saguṇa* Brahman," Brahman with material adjuncts. The form of Kṛṣṇa as *saguṇa* Brahman is thus considered a manifestation of Brahman constituted of the material quality of *sattva* that serves the purpose of helping individual souls realize the illusion of their individuality, at which time the form and person of the *avatāra* is dispensed with as the enlightened realizes himself to be Brahman.

According to Śaṅkara, those not qualified to meditate on *akṣara* Brahman should worship his idea of *saguṇa* Brahman to gradually qualify themselves for meditation on the formless Brahman. This idea has no basis in the *sūtras*, nor does it find any support in the *Gītā*. Indeed, this section of the text in particular clearly establishes the supremacy of the form and person of Kṛṣṇa over the *akṣara* Brahman and reiterates the ultimacy of devotional *yoga*.

Thus, according to the *Gītā*, if there is any difference between Brahman and Kṛṣṇa, it is that Kṛṣṇa is superior to Brahman. Gauḍīya commentators, while agreeing wholeheartedly with Rāmānuja as to Kṛṣṇa's identity with

Brahman, lay stress on the fact that Kṛṣṇa asserts himself to be a superior manifestation of Brahman. Arjuna states this earlier (Bg. 10.12), and Kṛṣṇa will do so later in the text (Bg. 14.27, 15.18). He is the Supreme Person, whose aura is Brahman.

It seems unlikely that Kṛṣṇa would be referring to the individual soul here by his use of the word *akṣara*. This word has been used repeatedly in the *Gītā* in reference to the Brahman feature of Godhead, and Kṛṣṇa has consistently identified himself with Brahman. If we understand Brahman to be an aspect of Bhagavān that is subsumed within the person of Kṛṣṇa, as understood by the Gauḍīya Vaiṣṇavas, the contradiction that Rāmānuja perceives in rendering *akṣara* as Brahman is removed. Arjuna is asking about the Brahman feature of Kṛṣṇa and Kṛṣṇa himself.

The path of the *jñāna-yogīs* leads to realization of Kṛṣṇa's aura and the individual soul's oneness with the Absolute, whereas the superior path of devotion to Kṛṣṇa's personal form leads to realization of his person and the *jīva*'s simultaneous identity with and difference from God that makes possible a life of eternal love.

Thus it comes as no surprise that Kṛṣṇa replies to Arjuna stating his preference for the adoration of his devotees who worship his personal feature over meditation on his Brahman feature. Kṛṣṇa will explain that the path of devotion is more pleasing to him and easier as well. However, should one be unable to take directly to it, Kṛṣṇa recommends other alternatives leading gradually to unalloyed devotion. He then concludes this chapter with eight verses describing the qualities of his devotees.

Text 2

श्रीभगवानुवाच
मय्यावेश्य मनो ये मां नित्ययुक्ता उपासते ।
श्रद्धया परयोपेतास्ते मे युक्ततमा मताः ॥२॥

śrī-bhagavān uvāca
mayy āveśya mano ye māṁ nitya-yuktā upāsate/
śraddhayā parayopetās te me yuktatamā matāḥ//

śrī-bhagavān uvāca—the Lord of Śrī said; *mayi*—upon me; *āveśya*—fixing; *manaḥ*—mind; *ye*—who; *mām*—me; *nitya*—eternally; *yuktāḥ*—united; *upāsate*—they worship; *śraddhayā*—with faith; *parayā*—with supreme; *upetāḥ*—possessed; *te*—they; *me*—to me; *yukta-tamāḥ*—most devoted; *matāḥ*—are considered.

The Lord of Śrī said: Those who are eternally united with me in worship, their minds absorbed in me, possessed of supreme faith—I consider them to be the most devoted to me.

Viśvanātha Cakravartī Ṭhākura comments that here Kṛṣṇa is speaking of his form of Śyāmasundara. This is the most worshippable form of Kṛṣṇa. It generally refers to his Vraja *līlā*. Thus the Ṭhākura makes the connection between this verse and the famous *catuḥ-ślokī* of chapter 10 (Bg. 10.8–11), and verse 10 of that section in particular. Again, the words *satata-yuktāḥ*, in the previous verse are reminiscent of *satata-yuktānām* of Bg. 10.10.

The following verse, in which Kṛṣṇa also acknowledges the worship of his Brahman feature and his reciprocation with those who prefer this, reminds one of the gradation of transcendent experience referred to in chapter 4 (Bg. 4.11).

Texts 3–4

ये त्वक्षरमनिर्देश्यमव्यक्तं पर्युपासते ।
सर्वत्रगमचिन्त्यं च कूटस्थमचलं ध्रुवम् ॥३॥
सन्नियम्येन्द्रियग्रामं सर्वत्र समबुद्धयः ।
ते प्राप्नुवन्ति मामेव सर्वभूतहिते रताः ॥४॥

ye tv akṣaram anirdeśyam avyaktaṁ paryupāsate/
sarvatra-gam acintyaṁ ca kūṭa-stham acalaṁ dhruvam//
sanniyamyendriya-grāmaṁ sarvatra sama-buddhayaḥ/
te prāpnuvanti mām eva sarva-bhūta-hite ratāḥ//

ye—who; *tu*—however; *akṣaram*—imperishable; *anirdeśyam*—inexplicable; *avyaktam*—unmanifested; *paryupāsate*—they worship; *sarvatra-gam*—all-pervading; *acintyam*—incomprehensible; *ca*—and; *kūṭa- stham*—unchanging; *acalam*—immovable; *dhruvam*—fixed; *sanniyamya*—controlling; *indriya-grāmam*—all the senses; *sarvatra*—on all sides; *sama-buddhayaḥ*—even-minded; *te*—they; *prāpnuvanti*—they attain; *mām*—me; *eva*—certainly; *sarva-bhūta-hite*—in the welfare of all beings; *ratāḥ*—engaged.

However, those who worship the imperishable, the inexplicable, the unmanifest, which is all-pervading and incomprehensible, the unchanging, the immovable, the fixed, with all of the senses controlled, even-minded in all things, and engaged in the welfare of all beings, also attain me.

The attainment of those who worship the unmanifest Brahman feature of the Absolute is self-realization, in which one identifies with Brahman. Rāmānuja comments that the description of Brahman in this verse corresponds with the description of the individual soul found in chapter 2 (Bg. 2.19–30). In Brahman realization one realizes oneself to be of the nature of consciousness, that which pervades all. This reality escapes description. Brahman is undifferentiated and formless, the antithesis of material manifestations, the great reality that lies beneath the illusory appearance of material phenomenon.

Those who realize Brahman must have complete control of their senses and develop equanimity of mind. They are engaged in the welfare of all beings because the more one goes within oneself the more one helps others by way of abandoning the life of exploitation. One helps others by teaching fearlessness through one's example. The welfare of others also becomes identified with ones's own welfare, as one's sense of self emerges from duality.

Significantly, this verse in response to Arjuna's inquiry about devotion speaks of those who worship *(upāsate)* Brahman. Although the method of worshipping Brahman is meditation, the very spirit of this meditation is worship and devotion. Without devotion, no one can attain Brahman realization. Worshippers of Brahman attain Kṛṣṇa in the sense that they attain Brahman, which is nondifferent from him—his feature of all-pervading consciousness.

Ṭhākura Bhaktivinoda comments that those described in this verse, while engaged in philanthropic work *(sarva-bhūta-hite)* sometimes render service to great devotees. As a result of this, they too eventually become devotees and attain Kṛṣṇa personally. However, in whatever sense they attain Kṛṣṇa, they do so with great difficulty and thus their path is inferior.

Text 5

क्लेशोऽधिकतरस्तेषामव्यक्तासक्तचेतसाम् ।
अव्यक्ता हि गतिर्दुःखं देहवद्भिरवाप्यते ॥५॥

kleśo 'dhikataras teṣām avyaktāsakta-cetasām/
avyaktā hi gatir duḥkhaṁ dehavadbhir avāpyate//

kleśaḥ—tribulation; *adhika-taraḥ*—greater; *teṣām*—of them; *avyakta*—unmanifested; *āsakta*—attached; *cetasām*—of those whose minds; *avyaktā*—unmanifest; *hi*—certainly; *gatiḥ*—path, goal; *duḥkham*—with difficulty; *deha-vadbhiḥ*—by the embodied; *avāpyate*—is attained.

Those whose minds are attached to the unmanifest undergo excessive tribulation, for the path that leads to the unmanifest is only attained with great difficulty by embodied beings.

This verse reveals that the superiority of the path of devotion to a personal God over worship of the impersonal unmanifest feature of the Absolute includes its ease of practice. Worship of the Brahman feature of the Absolute is difficult, for it is not easy to conceptualize an undifferentiated ultimate reality, much less engage in its worship. Embodied beings *(dehavadbhiḥ)* are accustomed to contemplating and contacting sense objects. To refrain entirely from this and in its place fix the mind on a theoretical reality that is without form, qualities, and so on, is difficult, whereas meditation on Kṛṣṇa, the eternal adolescent transcendental Cupid, is comparatively easy.

While on one hand it is easy to think of Kṛṣṇa in comparison to conceptualizing his Brahman feature, on the other hand it is not easy to conceive of an Absolute who, although all-pervasive, has form and moves from place to place in *līlā*. The Vaiṣṇava conception of Kṛṣṇa as the *para-brahma* is not for the less intelligent. While thinking of Kṛṣṇa in a simplistic sense may be easy, understanding his ontology is not. Comparatively, the Adwaita philosophy is easy to understand, inasmuch as it posits an Absolute that is the mere antithesis of the illusory world of form and variety—a formless Absolute. When we speak of spiritual form that is all-pervasive, devoid of material qualities yet replete with spiritual attributes, we have taken a step up into ultimate reality (*nirguṇa* Brahman), not down to a so-called Brahman with material qualities (Śaṅkara's *saguṇa* Brahman).

The word *gatiḥ* in this verse means both "goal" and "path." It should not be misunderstood to indicate that the ultimate goal of spiritual culture is realization of the unmanifest Brahman feature of divinity. This misunderstanding contradicts the teaching of the *Gītā* as to the paramount position of the Puruṣottama, Kṛṣṇa himself. Kṛṣṇa is not saying that the ultimate goal of attaining the unmanifest, formless, *nirguṇa* Brahman is difficult for the embodied, who are thus advised to take an easier path, that of worshipping so-called *saguṇa* Brahman represented as Kṛṣṇa until they are no longer in need of such a conceptual aid. This Adwaitin understanding of Kṛṣṇa's answer requires one to import foreign ideas into the text of the *Gītā* for it to make any sense, notions brought to the text by the reader that are not found anywhere in the scripture. The foremost example of this is Śaṅkara's notion of *saguṇa* Brahman as a provisional manifestation of the Absolute that he inserts in his commentary on *Vedānta-sūtra* and unceremoniously identifies Kṛṣṇa with in his *Gītā Bhāṣya*.

Contrary to the Adwaitan position, *Vedānta-sūtra* (1.1.10) states, *gati-sāmānyāt:* "*Saguṇa* Brahman is not taught anywhere in the *Vedas*, which consistently describe only *nirguṇa* Brahman." If it is difficult to conceive of the unmanifest *nirguṇa* Brahman, it is that much more difficult to conceive of Kṛṣṇa in terms of his form and person being *nirguṇa*. However, this is the super-esoteric teaching of the *Bhagavad-gītā*, one that only the most intelligent devotees can understand. Nowhere does the scripture advocate meditation on the form of God only to later abandon this practice in favor of something higher. It should be abundantly clear from the text of the *Gītā* itself that Kṛṣṇa is more than a provisional manifestation of reality. He is the ultimate object of love and the highest attainment. In the next two verses he contrasts the difficulties involved in worshipping the unmanifest with the expediency of the path of devotion centered on his personality.

Texts 6–7

ये तु सर्वाणि कर्माणि मयि सन्न्यस्य मत्पराः ।
  अनन्ये नैव योगेन मां ध्यायन्त उपासते ॥६॥
तेषामहं समुद्धर्ता मृत्युसंसारसागरात् ।
  भवामि न चिरात्पार्थ मय्यावेशितचेतसाम् ॥७॥

ye tu sarvāṇi karmāṇi mayi sannyasya mat-parāḥ/
  ananyenaiva yogena māṁ dhyāyanta upāsate//
teṣām ahaṁ samuddhartā mṛtyu-saṁsāra-sāgarāt/
  bhavāmi na cirāt pārtha mayy āveśita-cetasām//

ye—who; *tu*—however; *sarvāṇi*—all; *karmāṇi*—actions; *mayi*—in me; *sannyasya*—renouncing; *mat-parāḥ*—regarding me as the Supreme; *ananyena*—without distraction; *eva*—certainly; *yogena*—by *yoga*; *mām*—me; *dhyāyantaḥ*—meditating on; *upāsate*—they worship; *teṣām*—of them; *aham*—I; *samuddhartā*—deliverer; *mṛtyu-saṁsāra*—the cycle of birth and death; *sāgarāt*—from the ocean; *bhavāmi*—I become; *na cirāt*—swiftly; *pārtha*—O son of Pṛthā; *mayi*—in me; *āveśita*—fixed; *cetasām*—of those whose minds.

But, O Pārtha, I swiftly deliver those whose consciousness is absorbed in me, who renounce all actions in service to me, who regard me as the

Supreme, and who worship and meditate on me in undistracted yoga. I lift them from the ocean of birth and death.

While worship of the unmanifest aspect of the Absolute is difficult, here Kṛṣṇa says that worship of him personally with the sense that he is the ultimate manifestation of divinity bears results expeditiously. The difficulty involved in conceptualizing Brahman involves the limitations of the mind, whereas the difficulty in conceptualizing the personal deity involves intellectual limitations. Realizing the personal Deity also involves greater emotional commitment *(upāsate)*. The *bhakti* school teaches that the emotional aspect of the living being is grounded in reality, and this in turn accounts for its ease of practice. *Bhakti* in practice is efficacious because it more closely resembles the true state of the living being in eternity.

Instead of renouncing all action, devotees of Kṛṣṇa act only for him. They worship him and meditate on his name, form, spiritual qualities, and *līlā*. In this way they become absorbed in Kṛṣṇa consciousness, and Kṛṣṇa swiftly delivers them from birth and death. While others aspire for liberation, Kṛṣṇa's devotees aspire only to serve him, and thus he personally delivers them from *saṁsāra*. As difficult as it is to acquire *brahma-jñāna*, Kṛṣṇa says in this verse that even if his devotees do not have it, he delivers them anyway.

Kṛṣṇa's endearing conclusion to his answer reminds us of the position of his devotees described in chapter 8 with regard to the paths of light and darkness. Kṛṣṇa's devotees transcend both of them, as Kṛṣṇa himself cannot bear their separation and is thus compelled to personally deliver them. He is the imperishable and more, and he is first and foremost a God of grace, assisting the individual soul in every stage of its development. Thus in the next three verses Kṛṣṇa enjoins Arjuna to pursue a life in love of God.

Text 8

मय्येव मन आधत्स्व मयि बुद्धिं निवेशय ।
निवसिष्यसि मय्येव अत ऊर्ध्वं न संशयः ॥८॥

mayy eva mana ādhatsva mayi buddhiṁ niveśaya/
nivasiṣyasi mayy eva ata ūrdhvaṁ na saṁśayaḥ//

mayi—on me; *eva*—certainly; *manaḥ*—mind; *ādhatsva*—keep; *mayi*—on me; *buddhim*—intelligence; *niveśaya*—cause to enter; *nivasiṣyasi*—you will reside; *mayi*—in me; *eva*—thus; *ataḥ ūrdhvam*—henceforth; *na*—not; *saṁśayaḥ*—doubt.

Fix your mind exclusively on me and place your intelligence in me. Thus without a doubt you will reside with me henceforth.

After answering Arjuna's question definitively, Kṛṣṇa speaks in this verse in the imperative *(ādhatsva, niveśaya)* as if issuing a mandate. Thus Kṛṣṇa underscores his answer by ordering Arjuna to fix his mind on his personal form and to place his intellect in him.

Viśvanātha Cakravartī Ṭhākura comments that the words *mayy eva* (exclusively on me) in this verse prohibit Arjuna from meditating on the unmanifest aspect of Kṛṣṇa *(akṣara)*. The word *eva* is used to emphasize that one should fix the mind exclusively on the beautiful threefold bending form of Kṛṣṇa *(mayi)*. Such constant remembrance of Kṛṣṇa *(mana ādhatsva)* should be supported by proper discrimination in conjunction with scripture that serves to give rise to actual meditation on Kṛṣṇa. This reflective discrimination is the import of the words *mayi buddhiṁ niveśaya.* Constant remembrance is often referred to as *nididhyāsana*, and reflective discrimination as *manana.*

Verse 8 is the first of four verses in which Kṛṣṇa begins to summarize the import of chapters 6 through 11, throughout which he has emphasized the *yoga* of devotion to himself. In the Gauḍīya tradition, the *yoga* of devotion is of two types: the path of ritual *(vaidhi-bhakti)* and the path of love *(rāgānugā-bhakti)*.

In this verse Kṛṣṇa stresses the highest form of devotion, in which one's intelligence is naturally absorbed in reflecting on Kṛṣṇa and all that is related to him, and following this, one's mind is absorbed in meditation through spontaneous remembrance of his divine *līlā*. Advanced devotees on the path of love are capable of controlling their minds in trance. They are the subject of this verse, whereas those who are not proficient in this method but are qualified to practice it are the subject of the following verse.

Text 9

अथ चित्तं समाधातुं न शक्नोषि मयि स्थिरम् ।
अभ्यासयोगेन ततो मामिच्छाप्तुं धनञ्जय ॥९॥

atha cittaṁ samādhātuṁ na śaknoṣi mayi sthiram/
abhyāsa-yogena tato mām icchāptuṁ dhanañjaya//

atha—if however; *cittam*—mind; *samādhātum*—to fix; *na*—not; *śaknoṣi*—you are able; *mayi*—on me; *sthiram*—steadily; *abhyāsa-yogena*—by *yoga* practice;

tataḥ—then; *mām*—me; *icchā*—desire; *āptum*—to attain; *dhanam-jaya*—O winner of wealth, Arjuna.

However, if you are unable to fix your mind on me, O Dhanañjaya, then try to attain me by discipline in practice.

The words *abhyāsa-yogena* speak of the practice (*abhyāsa*) of uniting (*yoga*) the mind with Kṛṣṇa, that which Kṛṣṇa recommends in the previous verse. Previously in chapter 6 Kṛṣṇa also recommended practice with regard to fixing the mind on himself, *abhyāsena tu kaunteya* (Bg. 6.35). As he did in chapter 6, here Kṛṣṇa speaks again of *samādhi* (*samādhātum*). Practice in remembering Kṛṣṇa means to again and again, from wherever the mind wanders, bring it back to the form of Kṛṣṇa. This struggle is the essence of *yoga* practice, by which one wins the wealth of spontaneous meditation described in the previous verse. Kṛṣṇa addresses Arjuna in this verse as Dhanañjaya, winner of wealth, that he might be further inspired to win the wealth of an inner life in love of Kṛṣṇa.

Should one find it difficult to live the inner life of sitting in *yoga-sādhana*, Kṛṣṇa next recommends external engagement in devotion by which one's heart becomes purified, qualifying one for the internal devotional culture recommended in this verse.

Text 10

अभ्यासेऽप्यसमर्थोऽसि मत्कर्मपरमो भव ।
मदर्थमपि कर्माणि कुर्वन् सिद्धिमवाप्स्यसि ॥१०॥

abhyāse 'py asamartho 'si mat-karma-paramo bhava/
mad-artham api karmāṇi kurvan siddhim avāpsyasi//

abhyāse—in practice; *api*—if even; *asamarthaḥ*—unable; *asi*—you are; *mat-karma*—my work; *paramaḥ*—supreme; *bhava*—become; *mat-artham*—for my sake; *api*—even; *karmāṇi*—work; *kurvan*—performing; *siddhim*—perfection; *avāpsyasi*—you will attain.

If you are unable to practice even this, hold my work as the supreme object. Merely by acting for my sake you will attain perfection.

If a devotee cannot sit regularly in devotional *yoga* practicing fixing his mind on Kṛṣṇa, he should keep his external senses busy in Kṛṣṇa's work. He should open temples for Kṛṣṇa, plant the sacred Tulasī so dear to Kṛṣṇa, serve his advanced devotees, and so on. He should absorb himself in Kṛṣṇa's work, putting aside all other considerations. This devotional work is so potent that even without conquering the mind a person engaged in it can attain perfection by Kṛṣṇa's grace. Otherwise, the mind of a person doing Kṛṣṇa's work will naturally come under control, and gradually he will be able to practice remembering Kṛṣṇa constantly, leading to spontaneous meditation. When he engages in Kṛṣṇa's work and the rituals related to this work with a view to tread the path of love, he will gradually advance to the point of being eligible for internal service on the path of love. Although the path of ritual has its own end wherein a devotee attains love of God steeped in a sense of his majesty, it can also be engaged in with a view to attain love of Kṛṣṇa in intimacy. When one engages in *vaidhi-bhakti* with a desire to progress to the direct culture of *rāgānugā-bhakti*, centering his devotional culture on chanting the name of Kṛṣṇa, his success is sure. In this regard, in his song *Kṛṣṇa-nāma dhare kata bala*, Bhaktivinoda Ṭhākura sings, *vidhi-mārga-rata-jane svādhīnatā-ratna-dāne rāga-mārge karān praveśa:* "That person who is fixed in following *vaidhi-bhakti* attains the jewel of independence (through the grace of Kṛṣṇa *nāma*), by which he is placed on the path of *rāgānugā- bhakti*." In the same song, Bhaktivinoda Ṭhākura clearly explains that experience of one's internal spiritual form *(svarūpa)* required for the culture of *rāgānugā-bhakti* proper is revealed by the grace of Kṛṣṇa *nāma:*

īsāt vikaśi punaḥ dekhāya nija rūpa guṇa citta hari laya kṛṣṇa pāśa pūrṇa
vikaśita haña vraje more jāya lañā dekhāya nija svarūpa vilāsa

"When the name is even slightly revealed it shows me my own spiritual form and characteristics. It steals my mind and takes it to Kṛṣṇa's side. When the name is fully revealed, it takes me directly to Vraja, where it shows me my personal role in the eternal pastimes."

Thus in verses 8 through 10, Kṛṣṇa speaks directly about engagement in *bhakti-yoga*, both internal and external. Those who are not yet qualified for this engagement are discussed next.

Text 11

अथैतदप्यशक्तोऽसि कर्तुं मद्योगमाश्रितः ।
सर्वकर्मफलत्यागं ततः कुरु यतात्मवान् ॥११॥

athaitad apy aśakto 'si kartuṁ mad-yogam āśritaḥ/
sarva-karma-phala-tyāgaṁ tataḥ kuru yatātmavān//

atha—but if; *etat*—this; *api*—even; *aśaktaḥ*—unable; *asi*—you are; *kartum*—to do; *mat yogam*—in my *yoga*; *āśritaḥ*—taking shelter; *sarva-karma*—all actions; *phala*—fruit; *tyāgam*—renunciation; *tataḥ*—then; *kuru*—do; *yata-ātma-vān*—with self-restraint.

But if even this is not possible for you, then, taking shelter of my yoga, act with self-restraint, renouncing all the fruits of action.

In this verse Kṛṣṇa recommends *niṣkāma-karma-yoga* in which the fruits of one's actions are offered to God. He calls this kind of *karma-yoga* "my *yoga*" (*mad-yogam*). Here Kṛṣṇa makes clear that his advocacy of *karma-yoga* throughout the first six chapters has been an advocacy of a form of *bhakti*. Viśvanātha Cakravartī Ṭhākura calls this expression of *bhakti-yoga* selfless action offered to God, *bhagavad-arpita-niṣkāma-karma-yoga*. This kind of *bhakti* will develop into the *bhakti* of doing Kṛṣṇa's work suggested in the previous verse. This external engagement in *bhakti* in turn qualifies one for internal practices in devotional *yoga*. Spiritual culture proper really begins with renunciation of the fruits of action. The more the fruits of one's work are directed to God, and the more realization of the nature of the self and Godhead develops with the ingress of knowledge and ultimately love, one's progress is determined.

With this verse Kṛṣṇa concludes his summary of the spiritual disciplines he personally recommends in the *Gītā*. Having concluded with stress on renunciation of the fruit of one's actions for the pleasure of God, he next glorifies further this foundational principle of spiritual life that leads to *bhakti*.

Text 12

श्रेयो हि ज्ञानमभ्यासाज्ज्ञानाद्ध्यानं विशिष्यते ।
ध्यानात्कर्मफलत्यागस्त्यागाच्छान्तिरनन्तरम् ।

śreyo hi jñānam abhyāsāj jñānād dhyānaṁ viśiṣyate/
dhyānāt karma-phala-tyāgas tyāgāc chāntir anantaram//

śreyaḥ—better; *hi*—certainly; *jñānam*—knowledge; *abhyāsāt*—than practice; *jñānāt*—than knowledge; *dhyānam*—meditation; *viśiṣyate*—is superior; *dhyānāt*—than meditation; *karma-phala-tyāgaḥ*—renunciation of the fruit of action; *tyāgāt*—from renunciation; *śāntiḥ*—peace; *anantaram*—immediately afterward.

Knowledge is better than practice, and meditation is superior to knowledge. From meditation comes renunciation of the fruit of action, from which peace quickly follows.

The general understanding of this verse is that knowledge of the self is better than mere practice that is devoid of this knowledge. This principle has been discussed in chapter 4. One who has sufficient knowledge of the self can actually meditate. This is brought out in chapter 6.

Better than self-knowledge is meditation *(dhyāna)* on the Paramātmā. This is a step from self-realization in the direction of God-realization. However, superior to this gradual process is renunciation of the fruit of one's work for the satisfaction of God, for this leads directly to liberation, *bhakti*, and God-realization. Śrīdhara Swāmī says, "From such renunciation of the fruit of action through the consequent nonattachment to work and its fruits, coupled with God's grace, liberation from material existence comes about immediately."

In this understanding, the meditation and practice under discussion here are different from that mentioned in verses 8 and 9, respectively. Indeed, this explanation seems to ignore the previous four verses and speak more of that which has been taught in the *Gītā* thus far. In contrast, both Baladeva Vidyābhūṣaṇa and Viśvanātha Cakravartī have offered novel interpretations of this verse that explain it in relation to verses 8 through 11 of this chapter.

Baladeva Vidyābhūṣaṇa understands the words *śreyaḥ* and *viśiṣyate* in this verse to mean "better" in the sense of being easier or more recommendable. Thus he says that this verse praises the *karma-yoga* mentioned in the previous verse *(sarva-karma-phala-tyāgaṁ)* as being easy for beginners and leading naturally to spiritual realization. For those incapable of meditation *(dhyāna)*, it is better to engage in *karma-yoga*. Meditation is recommended for those without self-knowledge, and the culture of self-knowledge is recommended for those who cannot practice the *abhyāsa-yoga* mentioned in verse 9. Thus *karma-yoga* leads to meditation and the knowledge of self-realization, which in turn leads to God-realization and the highest *bhakti*.

Viśvanātha Cakravartī interprets this verse differently. He says knowledge/reflection *(mananam)* that gives rise to meditation *(nididhyāsana)* on Kṛṣṇa is better than the *abhyāsa-yoga* that leads to reflection and meditation. This knowledge or reflection on Kṛṣṇa's significance is what he referred to in verse 8 with the words *mayi buddhiṁ niveśaya*. It is better than the practice that precedes it because when continued reflection manifests, success in meditation is more readily achieved. Better than reflection is actual meditation itself. Why is this so? Because meditation on Kṛṣṇa destroys all desire for material gain or even liberation, and thus the peace arising from indifference to material life becomes manifest automatically in Kṛṣṇa's devotee, whose mind and senses interact only with his name, form, qualities, and pastimes. Viśvanātha Cakravartī justifies his rendering by explaining that the words *śreyaḥ* and *viśiṣyate* "govern the ablatives (of comparison) in the first hemstitch, while the two ablatives in the second are governed by the indeclinable *anantaram* (after)." Thus he reads *dhyānāt anantaram* as "from *dhyāna* comes *tyāga*; from *tyāga* comes *śanti*," rather than the more standard rendering: "better than *dhyāna* is renunciation," which is followed by Baladeva Vidyābhūṣaṇa and others.

Kṛṣṇa next describes the glories of his devotees, enumerating thirty-five of their qualities from text 13 to the end of the chapter. Thus we learn from the following verses what a devotee becomes like after attaining the peace mentioned in this verse.

Texts 13–14

अद्वेष्टा सर्वभूतानां मैत्रः करुण एव च ।
निर्ममो निरहंकारः समदुःखसुखः क्षमी ॥१३॥
सन्तुष्टः सततं योगी यतात्मा दृढनिश्चयः ।
मय्यर्पितमनोबुद्धिर्यो मद्भक्तः स मे प्रियः ॥१४॥

adveṣṭā sarva-bhūtānāṁ maitraḥ karuṇa eva ca/
nirmamo nirahaṅkāraḥ sama-duḥkha-sukhaḥ kṣamī//
santuṣṭaḥ satataṁ yogī yatātmā dṛḍha-niścayaḥ/
mayy arpita-mano-buddhir yo mad-bhaktaḥ sa me priyaḥ//

adveṣṭā—nonenvious; *sarva-bhūtānām*—toward all living entities; *maitraḥ*—friendly; *karuṇaḥ*—compassionate; *eva*—certainly; *ca*—also; *nirmamaḥ*—free from possessiveness; *nirahaṅkāraḥ*—free from egotism; *sama*—equal; *duḥkha*—pain; *sukhaḥ*—pleasure; *kṣamī*—patient; *santuṣṭaḥ*—satisfied; *satatam*—always; *yogī*—*yogī*; *yata-ātmā*—self-controlled; *dṛḍha-niścayaḥ*—firm in his resolve; *mayi*—on me; *arpita*—fixed; *manaḥ*—mind; *buddhiḥ*—intelligence; *yaḥ*—who; *mat-bhaktaḥ*—my devotee; *saḥ*—he; *me*—to me; *priyaḥ*—dear.

He who hates no one, who is friendly and compassionate, free from possessiveness and egotism, equal in the face of pain and pleasure, patient,

who is a yogī who is always satisfied, self-controlled, and firm in his resolve, whose mind and intellect are fixed on me, and who is thus my devotee is dear to me.

In this section Kṛṣṇa describes the internal symptoms of his devotees, while stressing the very root of the advanced devotees' spiritual qualities, that which causes them to manifest—devotion to Kṛṣṇa. The spirit here is Kṛṣṇa's pleasure in describing his devotees. Kṛṣṇa drives home the point that devotion to himself in and of itself gives rise to all good qualities, ornamenting the soul of his devotee. Rather than attempt to acquire any of these qualities independently, one should do so in the context of loving Kṛṣṇa. The measure by which one can understand one's success in loving him is the extent to which the qualities mentioned in these and the following verses manifest in one. At the same time, developing these qualities is part of the attempt to love Kṛṣṇa.

The exalted qualities described in verses 13 through 20 are ultimately those of God-realized souls. The word *satatam* (always) in this verse should be connected with all of the qualities mentioned. Thus these are not qualities that manifest from time to time in one's mind. Many of these qualities are shared by self-realized souls, and thus it is apparent that Kṛṣṇa's devotees have passed through the self-realization or enlightenment experienced by *jñānīs* and the Buddhists. One should not misunderstand and think that their devotion is merely a means to attain the general conception of enlightenment. It is the eternal function of the soul—its intrinsic characteristic—that endears the soul to God. Again and again in this section Kṛṣṇa says that those who he is describing are his devotees and that such devotees are dear to him.

Although a semblance of some of the qualities mentioned in this section may appear in those who are not self-realized or God-realized, they are comparable to the honesty one sometimes finds in thieves as they divide their loot. Without devotion to Kṛṣṇa, in which one acknowledges God's absolute proprietorship, one lives contrary to reality.

Text 15

यस्मान्नोद्विजते लोको लोकान्नोद्विजते च यः ।
हर्षामर्षभयोद्वेगैर्मुक्तो यः स च मे प्रियः ॥१५॥

yasmān nodvijate loko lokān nodvijate ca yaḥ/
harṣāmarṣa-bhayodvegair mukto yaḥ sa ca me priyaḥ//

yasmāt—from whom; *na*—not; *udvijate*—it is disturbed; *lokaḥ*—world; *lokāt*—from the world; *na*—never; *udvijate*—it is disturbed; *ca*—and; *yaḥ*—who; *harṣa-amarṣa-bhaya-udvegaiḥ*—from happiness, impatience, fear, and agitation; *muktaḥ*—freed; *yaḥ*—who; *saḥ*—he; *ca*—also; *me*—to me; *priyaḥ*—dear.

He by whom no one is put into difficulty, and who is never disturbed by anyone, who is free from happiness, impatience, fear, and agitation, is dear to me.

Madhusūdana Saraswatī comments that the second use of the word *ca* in this verse refers back to the phrase "my devotee" in the previous verse. Thus Kṛṣṇa continues to speak only of his devotees. It is they who possess these qualities, and thus it is clear that they more than anyone else are the *sthita-prajñā* persons Kṛṣṇa described in the second chapter (Bg. 2.55–72)—even more than the liberated *jñānīs*.

Text 16

अनपेक्षः शुचिर्दक्ष उदासिनो गतव्यथः ।
सर्वारम्भपरित्यागी यो मद्भक्तः स मे प्रियः ॥१६॥

anapekṣaḥ śucir dakṣa udāsīno gata-vyathaḥ/
sarvārambha-parityāgī yo mad-bhaktaḥ sa me priyaḥ//

anapekṣaḥ—neutral; *śuciḥ*—pure; *dakṣaḥ*—expert; *udāsīnaḥ*—impartial; *gata-vyathaḥ*—free from anxiety; *sarva-ārambha*—all endeavors; *parityāgī*—renouncer; *yaḥ*—who; *mat-bhaktaḥ*—my devotee; *saḥ*—he; *me*—to me; *priyaḥ*—very dear.

My devotee who strives not for any result and is pure, expert, impartial, and free from desire and anxiety is very dear to me.

Text 17

यो न हृष्यति न द्वेष्टि न शोचति न काङ्क्षति ।
शुभाशुभपरित्यागी भक्तिमान्यः स मे प्रियः ॥१७॥

yo na hṛṣyati na dveṣṭi na śocati na kāṅkṣati/
śubhāśubha-parityāgī bhaktimān yaḥ sa me priyaḥ//

yaḥ—who; *na*—not; *hṛṣyati*—he rejoices; *na*—not; *dveṣṭi*—he frets; *na*—not; *śocati*—he laments; *na*—not; *kāṅkṣati*—he hankers; *śubha*—good; *aśubha*—evil; *parityāgī*—renouncer; *bhakti-mān*—filled with devotion; *yaḥ*—who; *saḥ*—he; *me*—to me; *priyaḥ*—dear.

One who neither rejoices nor frets, neither hankers nor laments, who has renounced both good and evil, and is filled with devotion to me is dear to me.

The words *na hṛṣyati na dveṣṭi* are an elaboration on the phrase "equal in the face of pain and pleasure" found in verse 13. Similarly the phrase *śubhāśubha-parityāgī* elaborates on the phrase "who strives not for any result" found in verse 16.

Texts 18–19

समः शत्रौ च मित्रे च तथा मानापमानयोः ।
शीतोष्णसुखदुःखेषु समः सङ्गविवर्जितः ॥१८॥
तुल्यनिन्दास्तुतिर्मौनी सन्तुष्टो येन केनचित् ।
अनिकेतः स्थिरमतिर्भक्तिमान्मे प्रियो नरः ॥१९॥

samaḥ śatrau ca mitre ca tathā mānāpamānayoḥ/
śītoṣṇa-sukha-duḥkheṣu samaḥ saṅga-vivarjitaḥ//
tulya-nindā-stutir maunī santuṣṭo yena kenacit/
aniketaḥ sthira-matir bhaktimān me priyo naraḥ//

samaḥ—equal; *śatrau*—to an enemy; *ca*—and; *mitre*—to a friend; *ca*—also; *tathā*—so; *māna-apamānayoḥ*—in honor and disgrace; *śīta-uṣṇa-sukha-duḥkheṣu*—in cold, heat, pleasure, and pain; *samaḥ*—equipoised; *saṅga-vivarjitaḥ*—free from attachment; *tulya*—equal; *nindā*—blame; *stutiḥ*—praise; *maunī*—silent; *santuṣṭaḥ*—satisfied; *yena kenacit*—with anything; *aniketaḥ*—having no residence; *sthira*—steady; *matiḥ*—mind; *bhakti-mān*—engaged in devotion; *me*—to me; *priyaḥ*—dear; *naraḥ*—man.

One who is equal to friends and enemies, equipoised in honor and disgrace, alike in heat and cold, pleasure and pain, free from attachment, indifferent to blame and praise, controlled in speech, satisfied in gain without endeavor, without any fixed residence, even-minded, fully engaged in acts of devotion, this person is dear to me.

Text 20

ये तु धर्मामृतमिदं यथोक्तं पर्युपासते ।
श्रद्दधाना मत्परमा भक्तास्तेऽतीव मे प्रियाः ॥२०॥

ye tu dharmāmṛtam idaṁ yathoktaṁ paryupāsate/
śraddadhānā mat-paramā bhaktās te 'tīva me priyāḥ//

ye—who; *tu*—indeed; *dharma*—religion; *amṛtam*—nectar; *idam*—this; *yathā*—as; *uktam*—said; *paryupāsate*—they worship; *śraddadhānāḥ*—with faith; *mat-paramāḥ*—taking me as the Supreme; *bhaktāḥ*—devotees; *te*—they; *atīva*—extremely; *me*—to me; *priyāḥ*—dear.

Indeed, I love those who, endowed with faith in my supremacy, are devoted to me.

The nectar-like spiritual culture *(dharmāmṛtam)* is *prema-dharma. Dharma* means "one's intrinsic characteristic." The wetness of water is its *dharma.* In this sense the *dharma* of the individual soul is service. In material life the soul renders service to material objects. When a fortunate soul reposes its inherent serving tendency in the perfect object of service and love—Kṛṣṇa—it experiences *dharma* as both perpetual and sweet. The word *amṛta* means both eternal and ambrosial. When the soul expresses its serving nature in relation to temporary material objects, such service is neither eternal nor sweet. Although this improperly directed service is perpetual in the sense that in material life one continues to serve one material object after another, it is not sweet. The fruit of this life is repeated birth and death, not the nectar of immortality and divine love.

Rāmānujācārya says that the seven verses under discussion in this section refer to Kṛṣṇa's devotees who come to *bhakti* through *karma-yoga.* He understands verses 13 through 19 to refer to the *karma-yogī*, whereas he sees verse 20 to be a reference to the *bhakti-yogī.* All of these verses follow the glorification of *karma-yoga* in verse 12. However, verse 20 is distinguished from the rest by the word *tu*, which can mean "but" or "however." It is also distinguished from the others in this section by the word *atīva* (extremely). There is no doubt that the devotee proper, as opposed to one whose devotion is mixed with worldly involvement *(karma)*, is dearest to Kṛṣṇa. Thus Rāmānuja sees a devotional gradation in this section that reaches its zenith in the final verse.

While Rāmānujācārya plays down Kṛṣṇa's repeated emphasis on his devotees in verses 13 through 19, Viśvanātha Cakravartī Ṭhākura sees all of the qualities mentioned in verses 13 through 19 to be present in the special devotee mentioned in verse 20. He understands each of the preceding verses to refer to a particular devotee who possesses only the qualities mentioned in that verse. Thus like Rāmānuja, Viśvanātha Cakravartī also sees a gradation of devotion within these verses, but his reading finds room only for *bhakti-yoga* in all of the verses under discussion. However, both Rāmānujācārya and Viśvanātha Cakravartī agree that the *karma-yoga* that Kṛṣṇa has spoken of in previous chapters and in verse 11 of this chapter leads naturally to *bhakti-yoga* and that *bhakti* is undoubtedly the supreme form of practice and attainment.

CHAPTER THIRTEEN

प्रकृतिपुरुषविवेकयोगः
Prakṛti-Puruṣa-Viveka-yoga:

YOGA OF DELIBERATION ON MATTER AND SPIRIT

Text 1

अर्जुन उवाच
प्रकृतिं पुरुषं चैव क्षेत्रं क्षेत्रज्ञमेव च ।
एतद् वेदितुमिच्छामि ज्ञानं ज्ञेयं च केशव ॥१॥

arjuna uvāca
prakṛtiṁ puruṣaṁ caiva kṣetraṁ kṣetra-jñam eva ca/
etad veditum icchāmi jñānaṁ jñeyaṁ ca keśava//

arjunaḥ uvāca—Arjuna said; *prakṛtim*—nature; *puruṣam*—person; *ca*—and; *eva*—certainly; *kṣetram*—field; *kṣetra-jñam*—the knower of the field; *eva*—certainly; *ca*—and; *etat*—this; *veditum*—to know; *icchāmi*—I wish; *jñānam*—knowledge; *jñeyam*—the object of knowledge; *ca*—and; *keśava*—O Keśava.

Arjuna said: O Keśava, I would like to know about prakṛti and puruṣa, the field of activity, the knower of that field, knowledge, and that which is to be known.

This chapter delineates the nature of the knowledge of Kṛṣṇa's dear devotees. It begins the final six chapters of the *Bhagavad-gītā*. In this final section of the *Gītā*, Kṛṣṇa instructs Arjuna in greater detail regarding the knowledge referred to in the previous chapters: the initial fruit of *niṣkāma-karma-yoga* and the mystic insight concomitant to *bhakti*. *Niṣkāma-karma-yoga* blossoms with the awakening of knowledge, and then, with the help of *bhakti*, it blooms into liberation and the flower and fruit of post-liberated *parā bhakti*. Thus as *karma-yoga* properly practiced leads ultimately to *bhakti*, so too does the culture of knowledge. This is brought out more fully in chapters 13 through 18.

In his introduction to this section, Viśvanātha Cakravartī Ṭhākura offers obeisances to *bhakti* by whose grace, he says, knowledge and action become fruitful. Baladeva Vidyābhūṣaṇa says that the knowledge found in this section—knowledge of material nature, the living entity, God, their relationship, and so on—is the gateway to the devotion that has been explained previously.

While the ignorant and materially attached person can through association with devotees take to the path of *bhakti*, *bhakti* proper stands on the ground of detachment and knowledge. As mentioned previously in chapters 2 and 9, the glory of *bhakti* is twofold.[1] *Bhakti devī* is generous in that she extends herself to the least qualified persons and at the same time she is the most exalted form of *yoga*, knowledge and detachment being concomitant to her mature expression. Now may those whose faith in *bhakti* has been aroused from the previous six chapters, those touched by her generosity, better understand the knowledge she is possessed of and her liberated status.

Arjuna's inquiry prepares the ground for Kṛṣṇa's philosophical discourse.[2] It enables Kṛṣṇa to summarize much of what has been discussed thus far, clarify this subject matter for the balance of the text, and reach a conclusion. Thus the entire scheme of the *Gītā* is indicated in the introduction to this chapter.

Text 2

श्रीभगवानुवाच
इदं शरीरं कौन्तेय क्षेत्रमित्यभिधीयते ।
एतद्यो वेत्ति तं प्राहुः क्षेत्रज्ञ इति तद्विदः ॥२॥

śrī-bhagavān uvāca
idaṁ śarīraṁ kaunteya kṣetram ity abhidhīyate/
etad yo vetti taṁ prāhuḥ kṣetra-jña iti tad-vidaḥ//

śrī-bhagavān uvāca—the Lord of Śrī said; *idam*—this; *śarīram*—body; *kaunteya*—O son of Kuntī; *kṣetram*—the field; *iti*—thus; *abhidhīyate*—it is called; *etat*—this; *yaḥ*—who; *vetti*—knows; *tam*—him; *prāhuḥ*—they call; *kṣetra-jñaḥ*—the knower of the field; *iti*—thus; *tat-vidaḥ*—those who know this.

1. See commentaries on Bg. 2.39 and 9.28.
2. Arjuna's inquiry in the first verse is not found in all editions.

The Lord of Śrī said: This body, O Arjuna, is considered to be the field of activity. One who knows this field is called the knower of the field by the self-realized.

The field and knower of the field were discussed earlier in the seventh chapter in terms of their representing the secondary *(aparā prakṛti)* and intermediate *(parā prakṛti)* potencies of God, respectively (Bg. 7.4–5). The difference between the soul constituted of consciousness and the body constituted of matter was also discussed in chapter 2 (Bg. 2.11–30) and was an important theme throughout the first six chapters.

With a view to explain further the nature of the body constituted of matter and the soul constituted of consciousness, Kṛṣṇa invokes in this chapter the metaphor of a field, which represents the material circumstance the soul finds itself in life after life—the material body. The fruits of action represent the crops that are repeatedly harvested. The true knower of this field is one who knows what the body actually is and is thus not involved with its illusory harvest of happiness and distress.

The material body is "*śarīram*," or that which is subject to deterioration. Kṛṣṇa says *idaṁ śarīram*, "this body," indicating that the body, though near to the soul, is different from it. One who knows that this body, which is very near to the soul (in terms of misidentification), is actually different from the soul and thus realizes that one is separate from this *(idam)* body, is the knower of the bodily field.

The body and all material manifestations are experienced, whereas the soul is the experiencer. The soul knows itself by first understanding its categorical difference from the body. The body and its extensions are the object of the soul's subjective experience. The soul is the subject who experiences the object of the body. Should its object of experience be another soul rather than a material manifestation, this brings to light the reality of a plurality of souls. Amidst the eternal plurality of souls, the Supreme Soul (Paramātmā) represents the supersubjective reality discussed in the next verse. He too in a deeper sense is the knower of the field, and he gives his opinion as to what constitutes knowledge.

Text 3

क्षेत्रज्ञं चापि मां विद्धि सर्व क्षेत्रेषु भारत ।
क्षेत्रक्षेत्रज्ञयोर्ज्ञानं यत्तज्ज्ञानं मतं मम ॥३॥

kṣetra-jñaṁ cāpi māṁ viddhi sarva-kṣetreṣu bhārata/
kṣetra-kṣetrajñayor jñānaṁ yat taj jñānaṁ mataṁ mama//

kṣetra-jñam—the knower of the field; *ca*—also; *api*—certainly; *mām*—me; *viddhi*—know; *sarva*—all; *kṣetreṣu*—in the fields; *bhārata*—O descendant of Bharata; *kṣetra-kṣetra-jñayoḥ*—of the field and the knower of the field; *jñānam*—knowledge; *yat*—which; *tat*—that; *jñānam*—knowledge; *matam*—opinion; *mama*—my.

O descendant of Bharata, know that I am also the knower in all fields. Knowledge of the field and its knower is actual knowledge. This is my opinion.

In this verse Kṛṣṇa establishes himself as the knower in all bodies, representing the immanence of the Absolute in his Paramātmā feature. He dwells within the heart of all individual souls. The straightforward reading of *kṣetrajñaṁ cāpi māṁ viddhi sarva-kṣetreṣu* is "know also that I am the knower of the field in all fields." In the previous verse Kṛṣṇa establishes that the individual soul is the knower of the field of his body. Here, in identifying himself as the knower of the bodily field as well, Kṛṣṇa makes an important distinction. He is the knower of all bodily fields. He knows all fields and all the individual knowers of those fields. He knows the individual knowers, the souls of each bodily field, who are the treasure hidden in the bodily field, the self hidden in the heart. The individual soul is the knower of his own body in the complete sense only when he is self-realized and thus has realized the hidden treasure of the bodily field—his own soul. The individual soul's success in this treasure hunt is dependent on the supreme knower of all bodily fields, who knows all fields and the treasure that lies within them. By his grace the individual soul can become a knower of the field in a complete sense. He can know that the purpose of his human body is to facilitate self-realization and God-realization, and he can attain these ends.

The understanding of Kṛṣṇa's words in this verse that reveals him to be the supreme knower of all bodily fields and thus different from the individual soul is supported by the Upaniṣadic background that this chapter draws from considerably. For example, in the *Śvetāśvatara Upaniṣad* (1.6–12) we find the following: "Forgiven by him with his grace he then becomes immortal.... But when the love of God comes down upon her, then she finds her own immortal life.... The two—the knower and the nonknower, God and non-God—are eternal; the one remains entangled in the objects, the enjoyer, the other, the infinite omnipresent one, remains passive.... There is the soul of man with wisdom and unwisdom, power and powerlessness; there is nature, *prakṛti*, which is creation for the sake of the soul; and there is God—infinite, omnipresent—who watches the work of creation. When a man knows the three he knows Brahman.... Matter in time passes away, but God is forever in eternity, and he rules both matter and soul.... When one sees God and the world and the soul, one sees the Three: one sees Brahman."

The Adwaita reading of this verse interprets Kṛṣṇa to be equating the Paramātmā with the *ātmā* by his use of the word *ca*—"Understand the knower in all fields also *(ca)* to be me." According to this understanding, the *kṣetrajña* (individual soul) mentioned in the previous verse is ultimately God. For Śaṅkara, the sense that there are many souls, or a *jīva* soul and God, is a product of illusion. However, Śrī Jīva Goswāmī in his *Paramātmā-sandarbha* challenges this rendering on the basis of Sanskrit grammar, logic, and the scriptural canon. Following his lead Viśvanātha Cakravartī Ṭhākura and Baladeva Vidyābhūṣaṇa also challenge it. Rāmānuja also replies to Śaṅkara's lengthy interpretive commentary with his own commentary, one longer than his commentary on any other verse of the *Bhagavad-gītā*.

Jīva Goswāmī says that the word *ca* should be understood thus: "By the words *kṣetrajñaṁ cāpi māṁ viddhi* in this verse, which in prose order become *māṁ ca kṣetrajñaṁ viddhi*, Kṛṣṇa says, 'Know me to also be the *kṣetrajña*, as the *kṣetrajña* in all fields *(sarva-kṣetreṣu)*.' " Evidence that the knower of all bodily fields is a personal God and not an undifferentiated spiritual substance is found later in this chapter where the object of knowledge *(jñeya)* is described as possessing characteristics. Jīva Goswāmī cites verses 13 and 14 in this regard. He also cites verse 10, in which knowledge *(jñāna)* is described as "constant unalloyed *yoga* in devotion to me." Baladeva Vidyābhūṣaṇa concurs with Jīva Goswāmī, and Viśvanātha Cakravartī points to chapter 15 (Bg. 15.17)—in which Kṛṣṇa describes two *puruṣas*—to counter the idea that there is only one knower of the bodily field.

In the previous verse Kṛṣṇa said that the wise/*jñānīs* *(tad-vidaḥ)* opine that the body and soul are different. In the present verse Kṛṣṇa offers his own opinion, which is a further development of this idea. It is the opinion of Kṛṣṇa *(mataṁ mama)* that knowledge constitutes knowing spirit and matter, and that spirit is twofold as *jīvātmā* and Paramātmā. *Jīvātmā* and matter are the intermediate and secondary potencies of the Godhead, respectively.

Knowing God involves knowing his potencies as well. Kṛṣṇa elaborates on these subjects for the balance of the chapter.

Text 4

तत्क्षेत्रं यच्च यादृक् च यद्विकारि यतश्च यत् ।
स च यो यत्प्रभावश्च तत्समासेन मे शृणु ॥४॥

tat-kṣetraṁ yac ca yādṛk ca yad-vikāri yataś ca yat/
sa ca yo yat-prabhāvaś ca tat-samāsena me śṛṇu//

tat—that; *kṣetram*—field; *yat*—which; *ca*—and; *yādṛk*—as it is; *ca*—and; *yat*—which; *vikāri*—modifications; *yataḥ*—from which; *ca*—and; *yat*—which; *saḥ*—he; *ca*—and; *yaḥ*—who; *yat*—which; *prabhāvaḥ*—potency; *ca*—and; *tat*—that; *samāsena*—in brief; *me*—from me; *śṛṇu*—listen.

Now hear from me in brief about the field, its nature, its transformations, its origins, as well as its knower and its influence.

In discussing the bodily field *(tat-kṣetram)* in greater depth, what it is in terms of its elemental constituents as a manifestation of the totality of the material nature must be analyzed, as well as its insentient nature and relationship to desire. What its transformations *(yad-vikāri)* in the form of the senses are must also be discussed. It must also be determined from what conjunction it arises *(yat)*. Who its knower is and what his potencies are *(sa ca yo yat-prabhāvaś ca)* must also be discussed. These are the topics that follow in the course of Kṛṣṇa's answering the balance of Arjuna's questions.

In this verse Kṛṣṇa tells Arjuna that the deliberation on matter and spirit that he will embark on further deals with a topic that is endless. Thus he will speak about these topics only briefly *(samāsena)*. In the next verse he refers Arjuna to *Vedānta-sūtra* and other source material should he be interested in any further discussion. In doing so he also implies that, should one speak on these topics, one should support one's position with reference to the *sūtras* and scriptural canon in general, as well as to others who are reputed for their knowledge.

Text 5

ऋषिभिर्बहुधा गीतं छन्दोभिर्विविधैः पृथक् ।
ब्रह्मसूत्रपदैश्चैव हेतुमद्भिर्विनिश्चितैः ॥५॥

ṛṣibhir bahudhā gītaṁ chandobhir vividhaiḥ pṛthak/
brahma-sūtra-padaiś caiva hetumadbhir viniścitaiḥ//

ṛṣibhiḥ—by the sages; *bahudhā*—in various ways; *gītam*—sung; *chando-bhiḥ*—by Vedic hymns; *vividhaiḥ*—by various; *pṛthak*—distinctly; *brahma-sūtra*—*Brahma-sūtra*; *padaiḥ*—by the aphorisms; *ca*—and; *eva*—certainly; *hetu-madbhiḥ*—with reasons; *viniścitaiḥ*—with conclusive.

It has been sung of in various ways by sages, in various sacred hymns of the Vedas, and particularly in the Brahma-sūtras replete with conclusive logic.

Sages such as Parāśara, Vasiṣṭha, Patañjali, and others have spoken from different angles about the questions raised in the previous verse. It is also understood as the import of the Vedic hymns that superficially appear to be concerned with only material enjoyment in religious life. The word *chandobhiḥ* may also refer to the *Chandogya Upaniṣad* and thus to the later portion of the *Vedas*. Lastly, it has been directly discussed in the aphorisms of the *Brahma-sūtras* in a convincing manner through a rigorous and unified presentation as if to debate the matter.

In the following two verses Kṛṣṇa begins to elaborate on the bodily field.

Texts 6–7

महाभूतान्यहंकारो बुद्धिरव्यक्तमेव च ।
इन्द्रियाणि दशैकं च पञ्च चेन्द्रियगोचराः ॥६॥
इच्छा द्वेषः सुखं दुःखं सङ्घातश्चेतना धृतिः ।
एतत्क्षेत्रं समासेन सविकारमुदाहृतम् ॥७॥

mahā-bhūtāny ahaṅkāro buddhir avyaktam eva ca/
indriyāṇi daśaikaṁ ca pañca cendriya-gocarāḥ//
icchā dveṣaḥ sukhaṁ duḥkhaṁ saṅghātaś cetanā dhṛtiḥ/
etat kṣetraṁ samāsena sa-vikāram udāhṛtam//

mahā-bhūtāni—the great elements; *ahaṅkāraḥ*—egoism; *buddhiḥ*—intelligence; *avyaktam*—unmanifest; *eva*—certainly; *ca*—and; *indriyāṇi*—senses; *daśa-ekam*—eleven; *ca*—and; *pañca*—five; *ca*—and; *indriya-go-carāḥ*—sense objects; *icchā*—desire; *dveṣaḥ*—repulsion; *sukham*—pleasure; *duḥkham*—pain; *saṅghātaḥ*—the organic whole; *cetanā*—consciousness; *dhṛtiḥ*—

conviction; *etat*—this; *kṣetram*—field; *samāsena*—in brief; *sa-vikāram*—with modifications; *udāhṛtam*—explained.

The great elements, egoism, intellect, the unmanifest, the ten senses and the mind, the five sense objects, desire, repulsion, pleasure, pain, the organic whole, consciousness, and conviction—in brief these are considered to be the field and its modifications.

The great elements *(mahā-bhūtas)* are five in number. They were first mentioned in the *Gītā* in chapter 7 (Bg. 7.4), where Kṛṣṇa defined the ontological status of his secondary potency, material nature. Everything spoken of in verses 6 and 7 was mentioned in *sūtra* form in chapter 7. Earth, water, fire, air, and ether (space) are the *mahā-bhūtas*. They manifest from egoism *(ahaṁkāra)*, whose characteristic is self-identification with objects. *Ahaṁkāra* originates from *buddhi*, collective intellect, or the *mahat*, the great. It has the characteristic of ascertainment and also involves the Absolute's visualization of the world that precedes its will to become many. The unmanifest *(avyaktam)* is also known as *pradhāna*, the unmanifest condition of the three modes of material nature. This *pradhāna* is the source of the *mahat*. It represents the *māyā-śakti* in its totality, the secondary potency of God.

The ten and one *(daśaikam)* mentioned in this verse are the senses, both motor and perceptual—hands, legs, anus, genital, mouth, ear, skin, eyes, tongue, and nose—and the mind. The five objects of the senses *(pañca cendriya-gocarāḥ)* are sound, touch, form, taste, and smell. These are sense objects in that they are made known by the perceptual senses and are modes of action for the motor senses.

Desire, repulsion, pleasure, pain, consciousness, and conviction mentioned in these verses refer to qualities of the self as they are reflected through the mind in the bodily field. Desire, repulsion, pleasure, and pain are mental modifications. Hankering to acquire pleasure is known as desire *(icchā)*, and repulsion *(dveśaḥ)* with regard to that which causes pain is its polar opposite. True happiness *(sukham)* has virtue as its cause, and actual suffering *(duḥkham)* originates in vice.

The organic whole *(saṁghātaḥ)* is the aggregate of the material constituents in the form of the body itself. Consciousness *(cetanā)* here refers to the mental modification that expresses the true nature of things arising from valid evidence, such as the scriptural canon. Conviction *(dhṛtiḥ)* is the mental modification that allows one to carry on in difficult circumstances.

Such is the field of activity together with its transformations *(sa-vikāram)* in the form of birth, growth, maintenance, generation, dwindling, and death. He who is the witness of these transformations cannot himself be part of them. This witness is the knower of the field and the knower of all fields as *jīvātmā* and Paramātmā, respectively. The two knowers are further discussed in the following five verses in terms of *sādhana*, or practices leading to the knowledge that enables one to understand them.

Texts 8–12

अमानित्वमदम्भित्वमहिंसा क्षान्तिरार्जवम् ।
आचार्यो पासनं शौचं स्थैर्यमात्मविनिग्रहः ॥८॥
इन्द्रियार्थेषु वैराग्यमनहंकार एव च ।
जन्ममृत्युजराव्याधिदुःखदोषानुदर्शनम् ॥९॥
असक्तिरनभिष्वङ्गः पुत्रदारगृहादिषु ।
नित्यं च समचित्तत्वमिष्टानिष्टोपपत्तिषु ॥१०॥
मयि चानन्ययोगेन भक्तिरव्यभिचारिणी ।
विविक्तदेशसेवित्वमरतिर्जनसंसदि ॥११॥
अध्यात्मज्ञाननित्यत्वं तत्त्वज्ञानार्थदर्शनम् ।
एतज्ज्ञानमिति प्रोक्तमज्ञानं यदतोऽन्यथा ॥१२॥

amānitvam adambhitvam ahiṁsā kṣāntir ārjavam/
ācāryopāsanaṁ śaucaṁ sthairyam ātma-vinigrahaḥ//
indriyārtheṣu vairāgyam anahaṅkāra eva ca/
janma-mṛtyu-jarā-vyādhi-duḥkha-doṣānudarśanam//
asaktir anabhiṣvaṅgaḥ putra-dāra-gṛhādiṣu/
nityaṁ ca sama-cittatvam iṣṭāniṣṭopapattiṣu//
mayi cānanya-yogena bhaktir avyabhicāriṇī/
vivikta-deśa-sevitvam aratir jana-saṁsadi//
adhyātma-jñāna-nityatvaṁ tattva-jñānārtha-darśanam/
etaj jñānam iti proktam ajñānaṁ yad ato 'nyathā//

amānitvam—humility; *adambhitvam*—unpretentiousness; *ahiṁsā*—nonviolence; *kṣāntiḥ*—tolerance; *ārjavam*—simplicity; *ācārya-upāsanam*—serving the guru; *śaucam*—cleanliness; *sthairyam*—persistence; *ātma-vinigrahaḥ*—self-restraint; *indriya-artheṣu*—toward the senses; *vairāgyam*—renunciation; *anahaṅkāraḥ*—absence of egotism; *eva*—certainly; *ca*—and; *janma*—birth; *mṛtyu*—death; *jarā*—old age; *vyādhi*—disease; *duḥkha*—pain; *doṣa*—shortcoming; *anudarśanam*—contemplation; *asaktiḥ*—detachment; *anabhiṣvaṅgaḥ*—freedom from entanglement; *putra*—son; *dāra*—wife;

gṛha-ādiṣu—home, etc.; *nityam*—constant; *ca*—and; *sama-cittatvam*—equanimity; *iṣṭa*—desirable; *aniṣṭa*—undesirable; *upapattiṣu*—with regard to; *mayi*—to me; *ca*—and; *ananya-yogena*—by exclusive; *bhaktiḥ*—devotion; *avyabhicāriṇī*—unswerving; *vivikta*—solitary; *deśa*—place; *sevitvam*—resorting to; *aratiḥ*—dislike; *jana-saṁsadi*—social gathering; *adhyātma-jñāna*—self-realization; *nityatvam*—steadiness; *tattva-jñāna*—philosophy; *artha*—purpose; *darśanam*—keeping in sight; *etat*—this; *jñānam*—knowledge; *iti*—thus; *proktam*—said; *ajñānam*—ignorance; *yat*—which; *ataḥ*—from this; *anyathā*—contrary.

Humility, unpretentiousness, nonviolence, patience, simplicity, service to the guru, cleanliness, persistence, self-restraint, renunciation of sense objects, absence of egotism, repeated contemplation of the painful shortcomings of birth, death, old age, and disease, detachment, freedom from the entanglement of family life, equanimity of mind with regard to that which is desirable and undesirable, unswerving exclusive yoga in devotion to me, resorting to secluded places, disinterest in social gatherings, steadiness in self-realization, keeping in sight the purpose of philosophy—this is said to be knowledge. Ignorance is that which is contrary to this.

Having completed his discussion on the unconscious bodily field, Kṛṣṇa speaks of the qualities that when cultivated bear the fruit of self-knowledge and God-realization before he speaks in greater detail about the two conscious entities (*kṣetrajña*) themselves. Thus he includes this culture in that which he defines as knowledge. Most important in this list of virtues is "unswerving exclusive *yoga* in devotion to me" (*mayi cānanya yogena bhaktir avyabhicāriṇī*). From this all other virtues follow like maidservants in service to the queen of *bhakti*.

Having discussed knowledge and the practices leading to it, next Kṛṣṇa speaks about the object of knowledge—the two knowers of the bodily field.

Text 13

ज्ञेयं यत्तत्प्रवक्ष्यामि यज्ज्ञात्वामृतमश्नुते ।
अनादि मत्परं ब्रह्म न सत्तन्नासदुच्यते ॥१३॥

jñeyaṁ yat tat pravakṣyāmi yaj jñātvāmṛtam aśnute/
anādi mat-paraṁ brahma na sat tan nāsad ucyate//

jñeyam—to be known; *yat*—which; *tat*—that; *pravakṣyāmi*—I shall explain; *yat*—which; *jñātvā*—knowing; *amṛtam*—nectar; *aśnute*—one attains; *anādi*—beginningless; *mat-param*—subordinate to me; *brahma*—spirit; *na*—neither; *sat*—cause; *tat*—that; *na*—nor; *asat*—effect; *ucyate*—it is said.

I shall clearly explain that which is to be known, knowing which one attains the nectar of immortality. It is beginningless Brahman, it is ruled by me, and it lies beyond cause and effect.

Verses 13 through 19 describe the object of knowledge. They sometimes speak of the *jīvātmā* and sometimes the Absolute in one or another of its threefold features: Bhagavān, Paramātmā, or Brahman.

The words *anādi mat-param* in this verse lend themselves to a number of different interpretations. Rāmānujācārya understands this verse to be speaking of the *jīvātmā*'s essential nature whose ultimate attainment and support is the Supreme Soul *(mat-param)*. Both Bhaktivedanta Swami Prabhupāda and B. R. Śrīdhara Deva Goswāmī read these words as Rāmānuja does, understanding them to indicate that beginningless Brahman, in the form of either the *jīvātmā* or the Brahman feature of the Godhead, is subordinate to Kṛṣṇa. Madhusūdana Saraswatī acknowledges the obvious validity of understanding these words in this way; however, he does not concede that it is valid to do so in this verse in consideration of the context, which in his estimation is a description of *nirviśeṣa-brahma*, the Adwaitin notion of ultimate reality. Thus he renders *anādi mat-param* as "the Supreme Brahman is without beginning." However, his sense of the context involves his own failure to acknowledge that Kṛṣṇa is speaking of two knowers of the bodily field in verses 2 and 3 of this chapter. Indeed, Jīva Goswāmī understands this verse to support his insights on verse 3. He also understands the following verse to be similarly supportive of the idea that there are two knowers of the bodily field.

Understanding this verse to say either "beginningless Brahman, ruled by me" or "the beginningless Supreme Brahman" works well in terms of the Vaiṣṇava understanding of the Absolute. The latter rendering, although consistent with the doctrine of Adwaita Vedānta, need not indicate unqualified Monism. In chapter 10 Arjuna addressed Kṛṣṇa as *paraṁ brahma*, the Supreme Brahman, who both the *jīvātmā* and the Brahman feature of the Absolute are subordinate to. The very word Brahman means "the greatest, the Supreme." Thus the words "Supreme Brahman" are somewhat redundant unless they refer to something greater than the greatest, its support. This is Bhagavān Śrī Kṛṣṇa, the full-fledged expression of that which is spirit, the ground of the spiritual ground of being, who clearly says as much in chapter 14 (Bg. 14.27). He is beginningless and exists beyond the karmic plane of cause and effect. Knowing him in any of his transcendental features, one attains the nectar of immortality. He is Bhagavān *(paraṁ brahma)* whose features of Paramātmā and Brahman represent his cognitive and existential aspects, respectively. This threefold collective of the nondual Absolute makes for an ultimate reality that exists (Brahman), is cognitive of its existence (Paramātmā), and whose only purpose is joy (Bhagavān).[3]

Text 14

सर्वतः पाणिपादं तत्सर्वतोऽक्षिशिरोमुखम् ।
सर्वतः श्रुतिमल्लोके सर्वमावृत्य तिष्ठति ॥१४॥

sarvataḥ pāṇi-pādaṁ tat sarvato 'kṣi-śiro-mukham/
sarvataḥ śrutimal loke sarvam āvṛtya tiṣṭhati//

sarvataḥ—everywhere; *pāṇi*—hand; *pādam*—leg; *tat*—that; *sarvataḥ*—everywhere; *akṣi*—eye; *śiraḥ*—head; *mukham*—face; *sarvataḥ*—everywhere; *śruti-mat*—having ears; *loke*—in the world; *sarvam*—everything; *āvṛtya*—pervading; *tiṣṭhati*—exists.

Everywhere are his hands, legs, eyes, heads, faces, and ears. In this way, he exists, pervading all.

Here Kṛṣṇa speaks once again in Upaniṣadic language, as he did earlier (Bg. 2.16, 8.9–10). Indeed, this same verse is found in the *Śvetāśvatara Upaniṣad* (3.16). Moreover, all of the verses in this seven-verse section of the *Gītā* resemble the third chapter of this famous *śruti*'s description of the Cosmic Person. Introducing its section describing the Cosmic Person, *Śvetāśvatara Upaniṣad* (3.11) says about that which it proceeds to describe, *sa bhagavān tasmāt sarva-gataḥ śivaḥ:* "He is Bhagavān, and therefore omnipresent and auspicious." In the *Śvetāśvatara Upaniṣad* verses echoed here in the *Gītā*, all three aspects of the Absolute are described, and thus they are also described in these verses of *Bhagavad-gītā*.

3. See ŚB. 1.2.11.

The present verse speaks of either the Bhagavān, Paramātmā, or Brahman feature of the Absolute, the object of knowledge. It may also be understood to refer to the *jīvātmā* through whom God experiences the world of the material senses. In accordance with Gauḍīya Vedānta, God is simultaneously one with and different from the *jīvātmā*.

Brahman is all-pervading. Here Kṛṣṇa speaks of the all-pervading feature of the Godhead. As Paramātmā resides in the hearts of all *jīvas* and in every atom, this verse also speaks of this feature of the Godhead. How does this verse speak of Bhagavān? It is he whose hands reach out anywhere and everywhere to accept the offerings of his devotees. With his feet he goes wherever his devotees make prostrations to him, standing before them. Wherever his devotees sing his praise or pray to him he hears them, and with his eyes he takes pleasure in watching his devotees serve him in diverse ways. His devotees also see him everywhere. Thus he is possessed of organs that are uncommon.

It is mentioned in *Caitanya Bhāgavata* (Madhya 10.115–133) that Adwaita Ācārya had difficulty coming up with an interpretation of this verse that was conducive to *bhakti*, but that Śrī Caitanya appeared to him in a dream and told him how it should be understood. The implication of his explanation is that the entire world when seen for what it is presents unlimited opportunity to satisfy the senses of God/Bhagavān.

Text 15

सर्वेन्द्रियगुणाभासं सर्वेन्द्रियविवर्जितम् ।
असक्तं सर्वभृच्चैव निर्गुणं गुणभोक्तृ च ॥१५॥

sarvendriya-guṇābhāsaṁ sarvendriya-vivarjitam/
asaktaṁ sarva-bhṛc caiva nirguṇaṁ guṇa-bhoktṛ ca//

sarva—all; *indriya*—sense; *guṇa*—function; *ābhāsam*—semblance; *sarva*—all; *indriya*—sense; *vivarjitam*—free; *asaktam*—detached; *sarva-bhṛt*—the maintainer of all; *ca*—and; *eva*—certainly; *nirguṇam*—without qualities; *guṇa-bhoktṛ*—enjoying qualities; *ca*—and.

He manifests the functions of the senses while free from all senses, detached yet maintaining all, without qualities yet enjoying qualities.

The first half of this verse is also found in *Śvetāśvatara Upaniṣad* (3.17). God manifests the senses of the living beings in this world, yet he himself is not controlled by them. Although detached, he nonetheless maintains all. Although he is devoid of material qualities and thus above the three modes of nature (*triguṇa*), he enjoys in *līlā* and exhibits transcendental qualities. When the *śruti* says that the Absolute has no qualities (*nirguṇa*), this means that God has no material qualities. God does have spiritual qualities, form, and *līlā*. If this were not so, numerous *śruti* statements about them would be nullified.

Text 16

बहिरन्तश्च भूतानामचरं चरमेव च ।
सूक्ष्मत्वात्तदविज्ञेयं दूरस्थं चान्तिके च तत् ॥१६॥

bahir antaś ca bhūtānām acaraṁ caram eva ca/
sūkṣmatvāt tad avijñeyaṁ dūra-sthaṁ cāntike ca tat//

bahiḥ—outside; *antaḥ*—inside; *ca*—and; *bhūtānām*—of all beings; *acaram*—not moving; *caram*—moving; *eva*—also; *ca*—and; *sūkṣmatvāt*—being subtle; *tat*—that; *avijñeyam*—incomprehensible; *dūra-stham*—far; *ca*—and; *antike*—near; *ca*—and; *tat*—that.

He is outside and inside all beings. He moves and yet remains still. Being subtle, he is incomprehensible; he is far, yet near as well.

Text 17

अविभक्तं च भूतेषु विभक्तमिव च स्थितम् ।
भूतभर्तृ च तज्ज्ञेयं ग्रसिष्णु प्रभविष्णु च ॥१७॥

avibhaktaṁ ca bhūteṣu vibhaktam iva ca sthitam/
bhūta-bhartṛ ca taj jñeyaṁ grasiṣṇu prabhaviṣṇu ca//

avibhaktam—undivided; *ca*—and; *bhūteṣu*—in living beings; *vibhaktam*—divided; *iva*—as if; *ca*—and; *sthitam*—situated; *bhūta-bhartṛ*—maintainer of beings; *ca*—and; *tat*—that; *jñeyam*—to be known; *grasiṣṇu*—devourer; *prabhaviṣṇu*—creator; *ca*—and.

He is undivided in living beings, and yet remains as if divided. He is to be known as the destroyer and the creator.

Text 18

ज्योतिषामपि तज्ज्योतिस्तमसः परमुच्यते ।
ज्ञानं ज्ञेयं ज्ञानगम्यं हृदि सर्वस्य विष्ठितम् ॥१८॥

jyotiṣām api taj jyotis tamasaḥ param ucyate/
jñānaṁ jñeyaṁ jñāna-gamyaṁ hṛdi sarvasya viṣṭhitam//

jyotiṣām—of lights; *api*—also; *tat*—that; *jyotiḥ*—light; *tamasaḥ*—darkness; *param*—beyond; *ucyate*—it is said; *jñānam*—knowledge; *jñeyam*—object of knowledge; *jñāna-gamyam*—goal of knowledge; *hṛdi*—in the heart; *sarvasya*—of everyone; *viṣṭhitam*—situated.

He is also said to be the light of lights that is beyond darkness. He is knowledge, the object of knowledge, and the goal of knowledge. In a special way he is situated in everyone's heart.

God is the light of lights—"Being illumined by whom the sun shines." (Tai. Br. 3.12.9.7) In chapter 15 Kṛṣṇa identifies himself as this light, "I am the light in the sun, moon, and fire." (Bg. 15.12) It is he who illumines even the light of the soul—consciousness—by which one perceives. This soul is the light of the world and it too is illumined by him. Wherever he shines, darkness cannot stand. From the darkness of our ignorance we must go to light, *tamasi mā jyotir gamaḥ*.

The word *jñāna-gamyam* implies direct, conscious experience of God. It also means "attained by knowledge." Viśvanātha Cakravartī Ṭhākura comments that this knowledge, by which God is attained, is concomitant to *bhakti*. In the language of Gauḍīya Vedānta it is *sambandha-jñāna*. The aforementioned means of attaining knowledge which are centered on "unswerving exclusive *yoga* in devotion to me" can also be considered in this regard.

The word *viṣṭhitam* indicates that God is situated in a special way within the heart. For meditation, *yogīs* conceive of him as seated in their hearts in a four-handed form. He also appears in the hearts of his devotees in a form that corresponds with their love for him.

Text 19

इति क्षेत्रं तथा ज्ञानं ज्ञेयं चोक्तं समासतः ।
मद्भक्त एतद्विज्ञाय मद्भावायोपपद्यते ॥१९॥

iti kṣetraṁ tathā jñānaṁ jñeyaṁ coktaṁ samāsataḥ/
mad-bhakta etad vijñāya mad-bhāvāyopapadyate//

iti—thus; *kṣetram*—the field of activities; *tathā*—also; *jñānam*—knowledge; *jñeyam*—the object of knowledge; *ca*—and; *uktam*—described; *samāsataḥ*—

briefly; *mat-bhaktaḥ*—my devotee; *etat*—this; *vijñāya*—understanding; *mat-bhāvāya*—to my love; *upapadyate*—he attains.

Thus the field of activities, knowledge, and the object of knowledge have been briefly described. Understanding this, my devotee attains love for me.

This section beginning with verse 4 is an apt description of ultimate reality in accordance with Gauḍīya Vedānta's religio-philosophical *acintya-bhedābheda-tattva.* Here we find an ultimate object of knowledge that is both one with the *jīvātmā* and matter yet different from them at the same time. This object of knowledge moves but remains still. It has no qualities but enjoys qualities. He is near yet far away. In him all contradictions are resolved.

It should be noted that only the devotee of Godhead, the *bhakti-yogī*, can realize the Bhagavān feature of Godhead. Kṛṣṇa says his devotee attains "love for me *(mad-bhāva)*," and this love is uncommon. In the very least it involves realized knowledge of Brahman and Paramātmā, and thus it has understanding and thereby transcendence of material existence and the bodily field as its ground. Though *bhakti-devī* is generous in offering herself, she is not attained cheaply. Here again, as we heard in the tenth chapter (Bg. 10.8), Kṛṣṇa informs us that attaining *bhāva* (love) requires that one take the trouble to understand its underlying *tattva* (philosophy).

Having answered Arjuna's questions regarding the bodily field, its knower, knowledge, and the object of knowledge in brief, Kṛṣṇa replies next to Arjuna's question concerning the predominating and predominated aspects of reality, *puruṣa* and *prakṛti.* In doing so, he speaks further of the bodily field, its transformations, its origin, its knower, and the potencies of the knower of the field. In this section Kṛṣṇa also reveals that the origin of the bodily field mentioned in verse 4 is the conjunction of the *puruṣa* and *prakṛti*. This discussion covers the next five verses.

Text 20

प्रकृतिं पुरुषं चैव विद्ध्यनादी उभावपि ।
विकारांश्च गुणांश्चैव विद्धि प्रकृतिसम्भवान् ॥२०॥

prakṛtiṁ puruṣaṁ caiva viddhy anādī ubhāv api/
vikārāṁś ca guṇāṁś caiva viddhi prakṛti-sambhavān//

prakṛtim—nature; *puruṣam*—person; *ca*—and; *eva*—certainly; *viddhi*—know; *anādī*—without beginning; *ubhau*—both; *api*—also; *vikārān*—transformations; *ca*—and; *guṇān*—the *guṇas*; *ca*—and; *eva*—certainly; *viddhi*—know; *prakṛti*—nature; *sambhavān*—origins.

Know that both prakṛti and puruṣa are without beginning, and know as well that the transformations and the guṇas arise from prakṛti.

The predominated reality is *prakṛti*, material nature. It represents the secondary potency of God in its totality. It is the macrocosm of the microcosmic bodily field. Kṛṣṇa's intermediate potency, although also *prakṛti* in the sense that it is predominated by him, is considered *parā-prakṛti*, a superior conscious *prakṛti*. Because the intermediate potency consists of consciousness and has the power to animate the secondary potency, in relation to that potency it is considered predominating. Thus the intermediate potency is also sometimes referred to as *puruṣa*. God is the absolute *puruṣa*, and the *jīvātmā* is a qualified *puruṣa*.

Both *prakṛti* and the qualified *puruṣa* are beginningless, being potencies *(śakti)* of God, the supreme *puruṣa*. As God has no source other than himself, and *prakṛti* and *puruṣa* are his secondary and intermediate potencies, they too are beginningless. Neither is created or destroyed. These potencies combine by God's arrangement to make the world, and thus the transformations of the senses, objects, and mind, as well as matter's threefold modus operandi, the *guṇas*, are born from the womb of *prakṛti*. While material nature is subject to such transformation, the *puruṣa* is not.

Text 21

कार्यकारणकर्तृत्वे हेतुः प्रकृतिरुच्यते ।
पुरुषः सुखदुःखानां भोक्तृत्वे हेतुरुच्यते ॥२१॥

kārya-kāraṇa-kartṛtve hetuḥ prakṛtir ucyate/
puruṣaḥ sukha-duḥkhānāṁ bhoktṛtve hetur ucyate//

kārya—effect; *kāraṇa*—cause; *kartṛtve*—in the matter of the agent; *hetuḥ*—cause; *prakṛtiḥ*—nature; *ucyate*—it is said; *puruṣaḥ*—the *puruṣa*; *sukha*—happiness; *duḥkhānām*—distress; *bhoktṛtve*—in experiencing; *hetuḥ*—the cause; *ucyate*—it is said.

Prakṛti is said to be the agent of transformation that brings about the effect of the body and its senses, which are the means to experience, whereas the puruṣa is said to be the cause of the actual experiences of happiness and distress.

In this verse the word *kārya* refers to the effect of the material body, and *kāraṇa* refers to the senses that make possible the material experiences of happiness and distress. With respect to these transformations, material nature is the agent *(kartṛtve)*. The qualified *puruṣa*, on the other hand, is the cause of the experiences of joy and sorrow. He experiences the mental modifications that happiness and distress are a manifestation of. Thus the qualified *puruṣa* is the experiencer, the enjoyer *(bhoktṛtve)*, and as Kṛṣṇa explains further in the following verse, his association with material nature is the reason behind his material experience and continued state of bewilderment.

Text 22

पुरुषः प्रकृतिस्थो हि भुंक्ते प्रकृतिजान् गुणान् ।
कारणं गुणसंगोऽस्य सदसद्योनिजन्मसु ॥२२॥

puruṣaḥ prakṛti-stho hi bhuṅkte prakṛti-jān guṇān/
kāraṇaṁ guṇa-saṅgo 'sya sad-asad-yoni-janmasu//

puruṣaḥ—the *puruṣa*; *prakṛti-sthaḥ*—situated in *prakṛti*; *hi*—certainly; *bhuṅkte*—experiences; *prakṛti-jān*—born of material nature; *guṇān*—qualities; *kāraṇam*—cause; *guṇa-saṅgaḥ*—association with qualities; *asya*—of it; *sat-asat*—good and evil; *yoni*—womb; *janmasu*—in births.

The puruṣa, situated in prakṛti, thus experiences the qualities born of material nature. Association with these qualities is the cause of his taking birth in good and evil wombs.

The individual soul as a qualified *puruṣa* takes on a particular form and corresponding nature that are a karmic product of *prakṛti*. This form is a result of his deeds, his *karma*. In this condition the soul is attached to particular experiences of material happiness and is adverse to distress—transformations of *prakṛti*. Thus the soul acts in pursuit of happiness and avoidance of distress. To fully realize his aspirations, he takes birth again and again. The duration of a particular body is a result of his previous *karma*, and each subsequent one is the result of his continued aspirations.

The words *sad-asad-yoni* imply human birth, because human life is a mixed experience of good and bad, as opposed to the life of the gods or the lower species who experience happiness (the result of good) and distress (the result of evil), respectively. They also refer to the possibility of taking birth as a god or in one of the lower species where there is less facility for enjoyment. Thus they speak of both reincarnation and transmigration.

After describing the qualified *puruṣa* and the *prakṛti*, Kṛṣṇa next discusses the position of the Paramātmā, the supreme *puruṣa*.

Text 23

उपद्रष्टानुमन्ता च भर्ता भोक्ता महेश्वरः ।
परमात्मेति चाप्युक्तो देहेऽस्मिन् पुरुषः परः ॥२३॥

upadraṣṭānumantā ca bhartā bhoktā maheśvaraḥ/
paramātmeti cāpy ukto dehe 'smin puruṣaḥ paraḥ//

upadraṣṭā—witness; *anumantā*—he who gives consent; *ca*—and; *bhartā*—maintainer; *bhoktā*—enjoyer; *mahā-īśvaraḥ*—the great controller; *parama-ātmā*—the Supreme Soul; *iti*—thus; *ca*—and; *api*—indeed; *uktaḥ*—it is said; *dehe*—in the body; *asmin*—this; *puruṣaḥ*—*puruṣa*; *paraḥ*—supreme.

The superior puruṣa in this body who witnesses, sanctions, maintains, and protects is the supreme controller and enjoyer and is called the Paramātmā.

In this verse Kṛṣṇa speaks about the *para-puruṣa*, differentiating him from the qualified *puruṣa* he speaks of in the previous verses of this section. He is the Paramātmā, described earlier as the knower of all bodily fields. He is the master of both *prakṛti* and the qualified *puruṣa*, in comparison with whom the qualified *puruṣa* is often referred to as *parā-prakṛti*, his position being so vastly different from that of the *parā-puruṣa*. In its enlightened state, the qualified *puruṣa* understands itself to be a predominated and not predominating ontological reality, a status reserved for the *parā-puruṣa*.

The *parā-puruṣa*'s consent is required for the individual soul to enjoy the fruit of its work. The soul's liberation from its delusion of being the enjoyer of matter also requires the grace of the *parā-puruṣa*. Kṛṣṇa speaks of the *parā-puruṣa* in this verse to shed light on the nature of the relationship between the Paramātmā and the individual soul. The latter is a predominated reality, albeit a sentient one and thus different from the predominated reality of *prakṛti*, and the former is the absolute predominator.

Kṛṣṇa concludes this short section with the following verse, in which the fruit of understanding these verses is stated.

Text 24

य एवं वेत्ति पुरुषं प्रकृतिं च गुणैः सह ।
सर्वथा वर्तमानोऽपि न स भूयोऽभिजायते ॥२४॥

ya evaṁ vetti puruṣaṁ prakṛtiṁ ca guṇaiḥ saha/
sarvathā vartamāno 'pi na sa bhūyo 'bhijāyate//

yaḥ—who; *evam*—thus; *vetti*—understands; *puruṣam*—*puruṣa*; *prakṛtim*—*prakṛti*; *ca*—and; *guṇaiḥ*—with the *guṇas*; *saha*—with; *sarvathā*—in all ways; *vartamānaḥ*—being situated; *api*—despite; *na*—not; *saḥ*—he; *bhūyaḥ*—again; *abhijāyate*—he is born.

One who thus understands the puruṣa and prakṛti, as well as the guṇas, is not born again, regardless of his present position.

According to Viśvanātha Cakravartī, by use of the word *ca* in this verse the *jīvātmā* is also included in that which if understood affords liberation. Here the emphasis is on actually realizing the truth about these four—the individual soul, God, *prakṛti*, and its three *guṇas*. Mention of the *guṇas* prepares us for the following chapter, where they are discussed in greater detail.

Understanding means realizing the significance of the four subjects of this verse. One who has done so attains liberation regardless of his present position with regard to his *prārabdha-karma*, even if one should transgress scriptural injunctions. The use of *api* further underscores the certainty of liberation for those who do not transgress.

Since verse 19, Kṛṣṇa has not spoken of any path to liberation other than *bhakti*. Indeed, this is the emphasis of this chapter, in which the knowledge that is concomitant to mature *bhakti* is being discussed. At this point Arjuna wonders if there are any alternative disciplines by which one can attain liberation.

Text 25

ध्यानेनात्मनि पश्यन्ति केचिदात्मानमात्मना
अन्ये सांख्येन योगेन कर्मयोगेन चापरे ॥२५॥

dhyānenātmani paśyanti kecid ātmānam ātmanā/
anye sāṅkhyena yogena karma-yogena cāpare//

dhyānena—by meditation; *ātmani*—within the self; *paśyanti*—they see; *kecit*—some; *ātmānam*—the Self; *ātmanā*—by the mind; *anye*—others;

sāṅkhyena—by introspection; *yogena*—by *yoga*; *karma-yogena*—by *karma-yoga*; *ca*—and; *apare*—others.

Some see the Self within the self through meditation. Others do so through introspection, and still others through karma-yoga.

In this verse Kṛṣṇa reiterates what he spoke of at length in the first six chapters of the *Gītā*. More than speaking of different paths, Kṛṣṇa is speaking of a development from *niṣkāma-karma-yoga* to knowledge and meditation, by which the Paramātmā is realized.

Śrīdhara Swāmī comments that while all of the above are to be practiced in sequence, they are considered different paths only with respect to differences in eligibility of the practitioner. As we have seen in the earlier chapters, all of these practices need to be mixed with *bhakti* for them to bring about liberation, and as stated in verse 19 of this chapter, love of Kṛṣṇa is attainable only by unalloyed devotion.

Text 26

अन्ये त्वेवमजानन्तः श्रुत्वान्येभ्य उपासते ।
तेऽपि चातितरन्त्येव मृत्युं श्रुतिपरायणाः ॥२६॥

anye tv evam ajānantaḥ śrutvānyebhya upāsate/
te 'pi cātitaranty eva mṛtyuṁ śruti-parāyaṇāḥ//

anye—others; *tu*—however; *evam*—thus; *ajānantaḥ*—not knowing; *śrutvā*—by hearing; *anyebhyaḥ*—from others; *upāsate*—they worship; *te*—they; *api*—also; *ca*—and; *atitaranti*—they transcend; *eva*—certainly; *mṛtyum*—death; *śruti-parāyaṇāḥ*—devoted to what they hear.

Other people, however, who do not know these things, worship having heard from others, and they, who venerate what they have heard, also transcend death.

Those who are not inclined to study these topics in depth and feel themselves unfit for meditation and even *niṣkāma-karma-yoga* can also gradually transcend death if they are inclined to hear from authorities. Through such hearing they come directly to devotion and attain liberation.

For the balance of the chapter Kṛṣṇa recapitulates what has been taught thus far stressing how the qualified *puruṣa* can disentangle itself from *prakṛti*.

Text 27

यावत्सञ्जायते किञ्चित् सत्त्वं स्थावरजंगमम् ।
क्षेत्रक्षेत्रज्ञसंयोगात् तद्विद्धि भरतर्षभ ॥२७॥

yāvat sañjāyate kiñcit sattvaṁ sthāvara-jaṅgamam/
kṣetra-kṣetrajña-saṁyogāt tad viddhi bharatarṣabha//

yāvat—inasmuch; *sañjāyate*—it comes into being; *kiñcit*—anything; *sattvam*—existence; *sthāvara*—unmoving; *jaṅgamam*—moving; *kṣetra*—field; *kṣetra-jña*—the knower of the field; *saṁyogāt*—by the union; *tat viddhi*—know this; *bharata-ṛṣabha*—O best of the Bhāratas.

Know, O descendant of Bharata, that whatever comes into being, be it moving or unmoving, is a result of the union of the field and the knower of the field.

Baladeva Vidyābhūṣaṇa comments that the union of *prakṛti* and the qualified *puruṣa* is beginningless *(anādi)*. Although the relationship between the individual soul and material nature in the form of body after body is beginningless, it is not eternal. It can be brought to an end with the intervention and subsequent knowledge of the supreme *puruṣa.*

This verse reiterates the teaching of verse 22: contact with the modes of material nature is the cause of repeated birth and death. The union of the field and its knower gives birth to the world. Following this, Kṛṣṇa explains further what he said in verse 24 by telling Arjuna once again about that which disentangles the knower from its bodily field.

Text 28

समं सर्वेषु भूतेषु तिष्ठन्तं परमेश्वरम् ।
विनश्यत्स्वविनश्यन्तं यः पश्यति स पश्यति ॥२८॥

samaṁ sarveṣu bhūteṣu tiṣṭhantaṁ parameśvaram/
vinaśyatsv avinaśyantaṁ yaḥ paśyati sa paśyati//

samam—equally; *sarveṣu*—in all; *bhūteṣu*—in beings; *tiṣṭhan-tam*—abiding; *parama-īśvaram*—the Supreme God; *vinaśyatsu*—in the perishing; *avinaśyan-tam*—not perishing; *yaḥ*—who; *paśyati*—he sees; *saḥ*—he; *paśyati*—he sees.

One who sees the Supreme God abiding equally in all beings—not perishing when they perish—truly sees.

The illusioned living entity is described here as being perishable (*vinaśyatsu*) in terms of his sense of bodily identification. This identity does not endure or exist in a real sense. It is here today and gone tomorrow. Along with the illusioned soul, the material manifestation is implied in this verse, its characteristics being the opposite of the Supreme God. One who clearly sees both the illusioned soul and the material manifestation through the eye of the scripture and similarly sees the Supreme God (*parameśvaram*), who by contrast exists (*tiṣṭhantam*) and is thus not perishable (*avinaśyantam*) and is the same (*samam*), not changing, this person sees things as they are. The result of attaining this vision is described next.

Text 29

समं पश्यन् हि सर्वत्र समवस्थितमीश्वरम् ।
न हिनस्त्यात्मनात्मानं ततो याति परां गतिम् ॥२९॥

samaṁ paśyan hi sarvatra samavasthitam īśvaram/
na hinasty ātmanātmānaṁ tato yāti parāṁ gatim//

samam—equally; *paśyan*—seeing; *hi*—certainly; *sarvatra*—everywhere; *samavasthitam*—equally situated; *īśvaram*—Lord; *na*—not; *hinasti*—he degrades; *ātmanā*—by the mind; *ātmānam*—self; *tataḥ*—then; *yāti*—he attains; *parām*—supreme; *gatim*—goal.

Seeing the Supreme God situated equally everywhere, one does not degrade oneself by the mind. Hence one attains the supreme goal.

Here *ātmā* means self as well as mind. However, it can also read "one does not degrade the self by the self," meaning that the person of enlightened vision who sees God everywhere does not out of ignorance deny the existence of the soul, either *jīvātmā* or Paramātmā. This is the opinion of Śrīdhara Swāmī.

Text 30

प्रकृत्यैव च कर्माणि क्रियमाणानि सर्वशः ।
यः पश्यति तथात्मानमकर्तारं स पश्यति ॥३०॥

prakṛtyaiva ca karmāṇi kriyamāṇāni sarvaśaḥ/
yaḥ paśyati tathātmānam akartāraṁ sa paśyati//

prakṛtyā—by material nature; *eva*—alone; *ca*—and; *karmāṇi*—actions; *kriyamāṇāni*—carried out; *sarvaśaḥ*—in all respects; *yaḥ*—who; *paśyati*—he sees; *tathā*—also; *ātmānam*—himself; *akartāram*—the nondoer; *saḥ*—he; *paśyati*—he sees.

One who sees that all actions are carried out by material nature alone, and thus that the soul is not the doer, actually sees.

Text 31

यदा भूतपृथग्भावमेकस्थमनुपश्यति ।
तत एव च विस्तारं ब्रह्म सम्पद्यते तदा ॥३१॥

yadā bhūta-pṛthag-bhāvam eka-stham anupaśyati/
tata eva ca vistāraṁ brahma sampadyate tadā//

yadā—when; *bhūta*—being; *pṛthak-bhāvam*—separated state; *eka-stham*—situated in one; *anupaśyati*—one sees; *tataḥ eva*—thereafter; *ca*—and; *vistāram*—expansion; *brahma*—Brahman; *sampadyate*—he attains; *tadā*—at that time.

At the time one sees that the various states of being rest in one thing—material nature—and that they manifest from that same material nature, one attains transcendence.

The illusion of bodily difference springs from material nature, which generates a different body for each soul in accordance with its *karma*. The underlying unity of all souls, the commonality that unifies them as units of consciousness over and above their apparent differences as men, women, animals, and so on, is masked by the appearance of difference produced by material nature. The unity of all beings is realized when one sees that all bodies are products of the one material nature from which they rise and into which they dissipate. When one understands this, one sees from the vantage point of Brahman.

Text 32

अनादित्वान्निर्गुणत्वात् परमात्मायमव्ययः ।
शरीरस्थोऽपि कौन्तेय न करोति न लिप्यते ॥३२॥

anāditvān nirguṇatvāt paramātmāyam avyayaḥ/
śarīra-stho 'pi kaunteya na karoti na lipyate//

anāditvāt—from beginningless; *nirguṇatvāt*—free from the influence of the modes of material nature; *parama*—supreme; *ātmā*—soul; *ayam*—this; *avyayaḥ*—imperishable; *śarīra-sthaḥ*—situated in the body; *api*—even; *kaunteya*—O son of Kuntī; *na*—not; *karoti*—he acts; *na*—not; *lipyate*—he is tainted.

This imperishable Supreme Soul is beginningless and free from the influence of the modes of material nature. Even though situated within the body, O son of Kuntī, he does not act, nor is he tainted.

Discussion of the Paramātmā was introduced in verse 28. While the individual soul like the Paramātmā is also imperishable, beginningless, and a nondoer who is not tainted by material nature even though situated within the body, it is not free from the influence of the material modes of nature (*nirguṇatvāt*), as is the Paramātmā. This is the difference between the two.

Kṛṣṇa next gives examples in the following two verses to help Arjuna understand how, like the Paramātmā, the *jīvātmā* does not mix with the body even though seated within it.

Text 33

यथा सर्वगतं सौक्ष्म्यादाकाशं नोपलिप्यते ।
सर्वत्रावस्थितो देहे तथात्मा नोपलिप्यते ॥३३॥

yathā sarva-gataṁ saukṣmyād ākāśaṁ nopalipyate/
sarvatrāvasthito dehe tathātmā nopalipyate//

yathā—as; *sarva-gatam*—all-pervading; *saukṣmyāt*—due to subtlety; *ākāśam*—sky; *na*—not; *upalipyate*—it mixes; *sarvatra*—everywhere; *avasthitaḥ*—situated; *dehe*—in the body; *tathā*—so; *ātmā*—self; *na*—not; *upalipyate*—it mixes.

As the all-pervading sky owing to its subtlety does not mix with anything, similarly the soul although seated in the body is not materially tainted under any circumstance.

Text 34

यथा प्रकाशयत्येकः कृत्स्नं लोकमिमं रविः ।
क्षेत्रं क्षेत्री तथा कृत्स्नं प्रकाशयति भारत ॥३४॥

yathā prakāśayaty ekaḥ kṛtsnaṁ lokam imaṁ raviḥ/
kṣetraṁ kṣetrī tathā kṛtsnaṁ prakāśayati bhārata//

yathā—as; *prakāśayati*—it illuminates; *ekaḥ*—one; *kṛtsnam*—entire; *lokam*—world; *imam*—this; *raviḥ*—sun; *kṣetram*—field; *kṣetrī*—the owner of the field; *tathā*—similarly; *kṛtsnam*—all; *prakāśayati*—it illuminates; *bhārata*—O descendant of Bharata.

As the sun alone illumines this entire world, similarly the owner of the field illumines the entire field, O descendant of Bharata.

Text 35

क्षेत्रक्षेत्रज्ञयोरेवमन्तरं ज्ञानचक्षुषा ।
भूतप्रकृतिमोक्षं च ये विदुर्यान्ति ते परम् ॥३५॥

kṣetra-kṣetrajñayor evam antaraṁ jñāna-cakṣuṣā/
bhūta-prakṛti-mokṣaṁ ca ye vidur yānti te param//

kṣetra-kṣetra-jñayoḥ—of the field and the knower of the field; *evam*—thus; *antaram*—the difference; *jñāna-cakṣuṣā*—through the eye of knowledge; *bhūta*—living entity; *prakṛti*—material nature; *mokṣam*—liberation; *ca*—and; *ye*—who; *viduḥ*—they know; *yānti*—they attain; *te*—they; *param*—supreme.

Those who see through the eye of knowledge the difference between the field and the knower of the field and thus know the means to the living entity's liberation from material nature attain the Supreme themselves.

CHAPTER FOURTEEN

गुणत्रयविभागयोगः
Guṇa-Traya-Vibhāga-yoga

YOGA OF DISTINGUISHING THE THREE MODES OF NATURE

Text 1

श्रीभगवानुवाच
परं भूयः प्रवक्ष्यामि ज्ञानानां ज्ञानमुत्तमम् ।
यज्ज्ञात्वा मुनयः सर्वे परां सिद्धिमितो गताः ॥१॥

śrī-bhagavān uvāca
paraṁ bhūyaḥ pravakṣyāmi jñānānāṁ jñānam uttamam/
yaj jñātvā munayaḥ sarve parāṁ siddhim ito gatāḥ//

śrī-bhagavān uvāca—the Lord of Śrī said; *param*—highest; *bhūyaḥ*—again; *pravakṣyāmi*—I shall explain; *jñānānām*—of knowledge; *jñānam*—knowledge; *uttamam*—highest; *yat*—which; *jñātvā*—knowing; *munayaḥ*—sages; *sarve*—all; *parām*—highest; *siddhim*—perfection; *itaḥ*—from here; *gatāḥ*—gone.

The Lord of Śrī said: I shall explain further the highest knowledge, the best knowledge, knowing which all the sages have gone from here to the highest perfection.

In the previous chapter Kṛṣṇa established that all material manifestations are a product of the interaction between the field and the knower of the field—matter and consciousness (Bg. 13.27). He also clearly explained that God pervades and dwells in every being. In this chapter Kṛṣṇa further establishes how God controls consciousness and matter and their interaction. They are not independent from God in their production of the world, as they are considered to be in Sāṅkhya philosophy. Kṛṣṇa will also speak about God's transcendent status as opposed to his immanent status in relation to material nature. Following this, Kṛṣṇa elaborates on the *guṇas* of material nature mentioned in the previous chapter (Bg. 13.20–24), explaining their nature and how they bind the soul. In mentioning the *guṇas* in chapter 13, Kṛṣṇa said that understanding them is vital to liberation. Indeed, transcending material nature's influence implies that one has understood it. Thus after discussing the modes of material nature in detail, Kṛṣṇa concludes this chapter by emphasizing devotion to himself as the means to transcend them. He explains the symptoms of one who has done so and asserts once again his supreme position, stating that even Brahman is subordinate to himself.[1]

To insure Arjuna's rapt attention, Kṛṣṇa speaks two introductory verses that glorify the knowledge that he will present in this chapter. The word *bhūyaḥ* means "again/further," and *param* can be rendered "next." Thus here Kṛṣṇa speaks further of the knowledge he has touched on elsewhere. An alternate understanding is that by use of the word *bhūyaḥ*, Kṛṣṇa is indicating that the knowledge of this chapter is that supreme *(param)* knowledge of devotion he has been discussing throughout the *Gītā*. While the knowledge itself is excellent, here Kṛṣṇa says that its fruit is also so, *jñānānāṁ jñānam uttamam*. In accordance with the emphasis of the *Gītā*'s final six chapters, this knowledge constitutes *sambandha-jñāna*, knowledge that forms the underpinning of a devotional life that leads to liberation and love of God.

Text 2

इदं ज्ञानमुपाश्रित्य मम साधर्म्यमागताः ।
सर्गेऽपि नोपजायन्ते प्रलये न व्यथन्ति च ॥२॥

idaṁ jñānam upāśritya mama sādharmyam āgatāḥ/
sarge 'pi nopajāyante pralaye na vyathanti ca//

idam—this; *jñānam*—knowledge; *upāśritya*—resorting to; *mama*—my; *sādharmyam*—similar nature; *āgatāḥ*—come to; *sarge api*—even at the time of creation; *na*—not; *upajāyante*—they are born; *pralaye*—at the time of dissolution; *na*—not; *vyathanti*—they are disturbed; *ca*—and.

Taking refuge of this knowledge and attaining a nature similar to mine, souls are neither born at the time of creation, nor disturbed at the time of dissolution.

1. Kṛṣṇa states that there is nothing higher than himself in Bg. 7.7, that he personally is the source of everything in Bg. 10.8, and that Brahman is subordinate to himself in Bg. 13.13, as he does in this chapter in verse 27.

The word *sarge* in this verse refers to the creation of the world. *Pralaye* refers to its dissolution. In between these two, the *jīvātmā* passes through innumerable incarnations. Souls who take shelter of spiritual knowledge pass beyond the individual cycle of birth and death, as well as the larger cycle of the cosmic creation and dissolution. When the world is reborn, they are not. They attain a spiritual nature like that of Kṛṣṇa. In the opinion of Śrīdhara Swāmī, whom Viśvanātha Cakravartī Ṭhākura follows in this verse, the specific language here regarding this attainment (*mama sādharmyam āgatāḥ*) refers to the liberated status known as *sārūpya-mukti*.[2] Baladeva Vidyābhūṣaṇa comments that the use of the plural case in this verse indicates that the plurality of *jīvas* is eternal.

How those who do not take shelter of spiritual knowledge and devotion are repeatedly placed within the womb of material nature, which gives them their material bodies, and how they are subsequently bound by the three *guṇas* is broached by Kṛṣṇa in the following three verses.

Text 3

मम योनिर्महद् ब्रह्म तस्मिन् गर्भं दधाम्यहम् ।
सम्भवः सर्वभूतानां ततो भवति भारत ॥३॥

mama yonir mahad brahma tasmin garbhaṁ dadhāmy aham/
sambhavaḥ sarva-bhūtānāṁ tato bhavati bhārata//

mama—my; *yoniḥ*—womb; *mahat*—great; *brahma*—nourisher; *tasmin*—in that; *garbham*—ovum; *dadhāmi*—I place; *aham*—I; *sambhavaḥ*—origin; *sarva-bhūtānām*—of all beings; *tataḥ*—thereafter; *bhavati*—it comes to exist; *bhārata*—O descendant of Bharata.

O Bhārata, the great nourisher, my material nature, is the womb that I impregnate, enabling all beings to come into existence.

The womb (*yoniḥ*) of material nature is Kṛṣṇa's secondary power. She is great (*mahat*), greater than the effect that ensues from her womb. In using the word *mahat* Kṛṣṇa differentiates his teaching from that of the Nyāya and Vaiśeṣika schools, in which it is considered that the cause is always

2. There are five types of liberation mentioned in the *Śrīmad-Bhāgavatam*. Four of them are clearly devotional in nature, the fifth is less so. Of these, *sārūpya-mukti* refers to the status of attaining a body like that of Viṣṇu. Such liberated souls attend Viṣṇu/Nārāyaṇa in Vaikuṇṭha. For more on this see ŚB. 3.15.14.

subtler and smaller than the effect. They reason that because the cause is subtler than its effect, that which is supremely great cannot be the cause of anything.

The word *brahma* is derived from the root *bṛh*, which means to expand. Material nature is described here as *brahma* because she is the great nourisher *(mahad brahma)* consisting of the three *guṇas* that nourish all created beings. She belongs to God. She is his womb for the sake of generating the world. Once she is impregnated, she is the great cause of the expansion that is the world.

Through visualization followed by will, God impregnates the womb of material nature with the seed of the living beings. God makes *saṅkalpa*, a wish, "I shall become many," endowing material nature with this resolve. God's mystic glance of consciousness fathers all beings, be they gods or goddesses, men or women, animals or plants. The universality of his fatherhood is stated next for emphasis.

Text 4

सर्वयोनिषु कौन्तेय मूर्तयः सम्भवन्ति याः ।
तासां ब्रह्म महद्योनिरहं बीजप्रदः पिता ॥४॥

sarva-yoniṣu kaunteya mūrtayaḥ sambhavanti yāḥ/
tāsāṁ brahma mahad yonir ahaṁ bīja-pradaḥ pitā//

sarva-yoniṣu—in all wombs; *kaunteya*—O son of Kuntī; *mūrtayaḥ*—the forms; *sambhavanti*—they become manifest; *yāḥ*—which; *tāsām*—of them; *brahma*—material nature; *mahat yoniḥ*—great womb; *aham*—I; *bīja-pradaḥ*—seed-giving; *pitā*—father.

O son of Kuntī, all wombs and the forms that manifest from them issue from the womb of material nature, and I am the seed-giving father.

Should Arjuna doubt that all the diverse forms of the living beings have a single origin, Kṛṣṇa stresses here that he is the only father and material nature the only mother of all beings in this world. God fathers all beings, not only in the sense of doing so at the time of creation in a macrocosmic sense, but within the creation in a microscopic sense as well. No birth would be possible without his will. This is the import of this verse.

However, Arjuna wonders about the binding agent between matter and spirit, for Kṛṣṇa has repeatedly stressed the categorical difference between the two. How does the soul remain involved with matter other than by the force of its desire? Thus Kṛṣṇa speaks in detail about that binding influence inherent in matter and activated by consciousness that ties the soul to the bodily concept of life.

Text 5

सत्त्वं रजस्तम इत गुणाः प्रकृतिसम्भवाः ।
निबध्नन्ति महाबाहो देहे देहिनमव्ययम् ॥५॥

sattvaṁ rajas tama iti guṇāḥ prakṛti-sambhavāḥ/
nibadhnanti mahā-bāho dehe dehinam avyayam//

sattvam—*sattva*; *rajaḥ*—*rajas*; *tamaḥ*—*tamas*; *iti*—thus; *guṇāḥ*—qualities; *prakṛti*—material nature; *sambhavāḥ*—born; *nibadhnanti*—they bind; *mahā-bāho*—O mighty-armed one; *dehe*—in the body; *dehinam*—the embodied; *avyayam*—imperishable.

Sattva, rajas, and tamas, the qualities born of material nature, bind the imperishable yet embodied being to the body itself, O mighty-armed one.

The word *guṇa* means "rope." The three ropes of material nature intertwined bind the embodied soul tightly. *Guṇa* also means "quality." A particular combination of the *guṇas* represents a specific strand or quality of matter and its ability to conduct enlightened thought *(sattva)*, increase material longing *(rajas)*, or immobilize *(tamas)*.

Sattva is the intelligible essence that is part of the makeup of all things. Intelligibility is a characteristic of any existing object. An object is said to exist because it manifests itself to our intelligence and thus we comprehend it. That which enables an object to do so is its *sattva*. This *sattva* is possessed of the tendency to continually manifest itself.

Objects do not merely exist or make themselves manifest. All objects act and react and thus accomplish something. They do so because they are constituted of not merely intelligible material, but an energetic essence as well. This energetic essence that gives objects the power to act is called *rajas*.

Other than intelligible essence and energetic essence, all objects also possess inertia. While the energetic essence of one object enables it to overcome others, the resistance offered by other objects is the essence of inertia inherent in those objects. All objects are partially constituted of inertia. This inertia is called *tamas*. Thus intelligible essence, energetic essence, and inertia essence, roughly analogous to mind stuff,[3] energy, and mass, are involved in the makeup of all material manifestations. These three constituents are the three *guṇas*. They govern the world of physical as well as psychic action.

In the thought world, *tamas* is represented as ignorance. Our passion to succeed and accomplish objectives is a result of *rajas*. *Sattva* represents our ability to comprehend and the state of actual clarity that gives rise to virtue and stability of character. *Sattva* begets peacefulness, *rajas* gives rise to restlessness, and *tamas* appears as lethargy.

While most systems of thought are dualistic, they often also include a third state that is the suppression, negation, or balance of two polar opposites. Freud's Eros and Thanatos are roughly analogous to the longing of *rajas* and the psychic inertia of *tamas* that represents the need to forget oneself in intoxication and other diversions. Freud teaches that the sublimation of these two influences involves harnessing them, enabling a person to accomplish positive goals. This sublimation resembles the balance that *sattva* implies. In contrast to the Gītā's culture of *sattva*, Freud's cultivation of sublimation does not result in the transcendence of passion, but it does result in deferred pleasure, which is a characteristic of *sattva* mentioned in chapter 18 (Bg. 18.37).

Taoism's *yin* and *yang* parallel the Gītā's *tamas* and *rajas* with the exception that in Taoism *yin* is cast in a somewhat more positive light than the Gītā's *tamas*. *Yin* is the period of rest that gives rise to new creativity. However, it is worth noting that there is a place for and thus a positive side to *tamas* as well. The Taoist *yang* eventually turns into *yin*, just as *rajas* often degenerates into *tamas*. When *rajas* predominates, as it does in our goal-oriented culture, it often results in destruction of the very society it created. Industrialization may end up destroying ecosystems and species, including our own.

The ideal in Taoist thinking is the state of equilibrium between *yin* and *yang*. This closely resembles the Gītā's *sattva*, which is predominated over by Viṣṇu, who maintains the world by keeping the forces of passion (creation) and ignorance (destruction) in check.

The Gītā's *sattva* is not transcendental. It is the mode of material nature that best facilitates the pursuit of transcendence. Thus the need to culture *sattva* is stressed later in this chapter and in subsequent chapters as well.

3. This is a term coined by Eddington in his *Nature of the Physical World*.

The *Gītā* teaches that a psychologically well-adjusted person is aware of the particular influence the *guṇas* exert on his psyche and thus acts in consideration of these influences. This basic awareness is itself the influence of *sattva*, which subtly governs the *Gītā's* *varṇāśrama* social system. In the *Gītā's* vision, the essential first step of goodness is to be situated in one's prescribed duty, a duty that corresponds with one's psychology. By being properly placed, one finds a sense of harmony with one's materially conditioned self that makes the cultivation of other aspects of goodness possible. One whose actions are not determined in consideration of one's psychology will be out of balance and thus more easily fall prey to the influences of passion and ignorance. At the same time, *sattva* itself must also be transcended because it keeps us from ultimate freedom in loving union with God. Under its influence, one often remains a prisoner to tradition, rather than realizing the spiritual tradition's essential message.

Those whose psyche is predominated by *sattva* can to that extent directly and naturally pursue transcendental life, whereas those dominated by *rajas* and *tamas* will find this course more difficult. Although to the extent that persons do practice they will be benefited, their ability to practice properly is often impeded by psychological dysfunctions resulting from being out of balance. This notion of the *guṇas* and their relation to spiritual culture and psychological well-being fits well with the model of transpersonal psychology, in which the necessity of being a psychologically well-adjusted person or developing along these lines is considered a prerequisite or parallel discipline intended to compliment spiritual culture proper.

In this verse Kṛṣṇa says that the *guṇas* arise from material nature. They constitute its very fabric. However, because the *guṇas* are not different from material nature, the question arises as to how they are born (*prakṛti-sambhavāḥ*) of it. Prior to the manifestation of the world, the *guṇas* of *prakṛti* exist within God in a state of equilibrium. Each of the *guṇas* holds the others in check as God rests figuratively on the causal ocean (*kāraṇa-samudra*) on the eve of creation. As he awakens, the cosmic mind of the Paramātmā is at first still. Then thought commences like a seed that first roots itself. This is followed by the sprouting of actual thought, visualization of that thought, and finally the will to enact the thought. The flowering of the first thought of the Paramātmā is the will to expand, "I shall become many." (Ch. Up. 6.2.3) This thought disturbs the equilibrium of the *guṇas* and thus causes their birth. Material nature begins to manifest along with the *jīvas*, and the desire of the *jīvas* meets with the binding agent of the three *guṇas*.

The creation of the world is more of an expansion than it is a creation in the strict sense. As we learned in the previous chapter, both the secondary and intermediate powers of God, the ingredients of the world, are beginningless. They are never created or destroyed. The two come together through the above-mentioned process, and after some time this process is reversed. The material manifestation returns to an unmanifest condition. This reversal is the inevitable result of disturbing the original state of equilibrium. Once disturbed, all that evolves from the state of equilibrium tends ultimately toward returning from instability to stability. Returning to the state of equilibrium, the *guṇas* rest. The gross material manifestation returns to its subtlest state of equilibrium. The notion of a universe that plays itself out until it reverses its outward motion and returns to an unmanifest condition is roughly analogous to the modern scientific principle of entropy.

The individual units of consciousness also return to their source, and the desires of the *jīvas* become dormant, their individuality obscured, as the heterogeneous multiplicity returns to a homogeneous rest. God rests during the cosmic night of creation, presumably tired of the love affair of the world. When he awakens, he again sets it in motion out of compassion for the *jīva* souls, who once again are afforded the opportunity to love him.

It is out of love for the *jīvas* that God wills to become many again *(lokavat tu līlā-kaivalyam*, Vs. 2.1.33), and thus the *jīvas* evolve from a plane of undifferentiated consciousness in which their individuality is dormant into an individual unit of will, a reflection *(cid-abhāsa)* of God's image with the stamp of his consciousness. From homogeneity, heterogeneity emerges again. The *jīvas*, units of will, meet material nature and express themselves in relation to her. This creates a problem for them, for these individual units of will, unlike their source, are weak in relation to material nature. Their likeness to God is qualitative, their difference quantitative. They cannot control material nature as God can.

To facilitate the *jīvas*, God himself manifests within the world along with revealed knowledge. With the help of this knowledge, the *jīvas* can deal with material nature such that they ultimately rise above the *guṇas'* influence to know the love of God and share in that love with him. Although this is the plan of God, father of all souls, each soul, being an imprint of God, is constituted of will, and this will can be misused. Compared to material nature, the *jīva* is small. It can become overwhelmed by material nature's influence. If the *jīva* does not take guidance from scripture, it is lost to bondage. As God is motivated from the start by love, the need for his intervention arises, and thus his descent as the *avatāra*. To this end the *Bhagavad-gītā* is spoken, that the *jīvas* might know the love of their divine source.

The material predicament can be viewed as an unavoidable consequence of God's love. The Paramātmā who presides over material nature manifests the *jīvas* out of love. The consequence of this act of love is the activation of the material nature and the *guṇas*, which in turn driven by time *(kāla)* provide a field of activity for the *jīvas*. This field, however, is insufficient to fulfill the *jīvas'* search for love, nor are the *jīvas* competent to deal with her influence alone, yet they are often unwilling to take help. To realize their potential for love, they must meet their maker. Helplessly searching the field, they cannot find themselves or their source. Bound by the three *guṇas*, the *jīvas'* only hope lies in God's act of salvation.

Over the next three verses, Kṛṣṇa discusses each of the *guṇas* and the nature of their influence.

Text 6

तत्र सत्त्वं निर्मलत्वात् प्रकाशकमनामयम् ।
सुखसङ्गेन बध्नाति ज्ञानसङ्गेन चानघ ॥६॥

tatra sattvaṁ nirmalatvāt prakāśakam anāmayam/
sukha-saṅgena badhnāti jñāna-saṅgena cānagha//

tatra—there; *sattvam*—*sattva*; *nirmalatvāt*—free from impurity; *prakāśakam*—illuminating; *anāmayam*—without sorrow; *sukha*—happiness; *saṅgena*—through attachment; *badhnāti*—it binds; *jñāna*—knowledge; *saṅgena*—through attachment; *ca*—and; *anagha*—O sinless one.

Of these, sattva is free of impurity. It is illuminating and without sorrow. O sinless one, it binds through attachment to happiness and knowledge.

The unadulterated influence of *sattva* on the soul is purification, illumination, and happiness. *Sattva* is transparent and luminous like a crystal. It is free from impurity and thus produces purity, and it is free from sorrow and thus gives rise to happiness. *Anāmayam* also means freedom from disease. Under *sattva*'s influence one does not engage in activities that cause distress or ignorance. The illuminating effects of *sattva* are such that under its influence the *jīvātmā* can observe the transformations occurring from *rajas* and *tamas*. *Sattva* effects a sense of detachment, and its influence is conducive to spiritual practice.

However, in spite of *sattva*'s virtue, it is nonetheless binding for the soul. It too must be transcended, for it produces attachment to the mental modifications that cause knowledge and happiness to manifest. It thus gives rise to a sense of complacency and mental serenity; however, because it produces attachment to happiness and knowledge, it also causes one to be attached to the means of producing them. Although *sattva* is useful for spiritual pursuit, when not channeled toward transcendence itself, one becomes susceptible to the influences of *rajas* and *tamas*, which are not conducive to spiritual practice.

When the *jīvātmā* identifies itself with the material body, the influence of *sattva* causes it to think "I am happy" and "I know," when in fact the qualities of happiness and knowledge are products of material nature, as described in the seventh verse of the previous chapter. Characteristics of the object (material nature) cannot be characteristics of the subject (the soul). Thus the identification and attachment resulting from *sattva* amounts to ignorance. Attachment to happiness and knowledge causes pride and the descent into *rajas*. Here Kṛṣṇa implores sinless Arjuna *(anagha)* not to be bound even by *sattva*, much less come under the influence of the two lower *guṇas*.

Text 7

रजो रागात्मकं विद्धि तृष्णासङ्गसमुद्भवम् ।
तन्निबध्नाति कौन्तेय कर्मसङ्गेन देहिनम् ॥७॥

rajo rāgātmakaṁ viddhi tṛṣṇā-saṅga-samudbhavam/
tan nibadhnāti kaunteya karma-saṅgena dehinam//

rajaḥ—*rajas*; *rāga-ātmakam*—characterized by passion; *viddhi*—know; *tṛṣṇā*—hankering; *saṅga*—attachment; *samudbhavam*—born of; *tat*—that; *nibadhnāti*—it binds; *kaunteya*—O son of Kuntī; *karma-saṅgena*—by attachment to action; *dehinam*—the embodied.

Know that the nature of rajas is passion born of hankering and attachment. This binds the embodied, O son of Kuntī, by attachment to action.

The root word *rañj* from which *rajas* is derived means to color. *Rajas* colors the clear crystal *(nirmala)* of the sattvic heart with longing *(tṛṣṇa)* and attachment *(rāga)* to action in pursuit of such longings. Under the influence of *rajas* one hankers for what one does not have and experiences attachment for what one possesses. It causes attachment to the fruits of one's work and to work itself (*karma-saṅgena*).

Rajas is the birthplace of sense desires (*kāma*). In the third chapter (Bg. 3.37), Kṛṣṇa describes *kāma* born of *rajas* to be the greatest enemy of the soul. When we try to attain sense objects we are attached to, we also become attached to the means of acquiring them. This in turn gives birth to more desires and more work in a never-ending, ever-increasing spiral. Under the influence of *rajas*, the soul, although not the agent of action, thinks, "I shall do this; I shall enjoy the fruit of my work."

Text 8

तमस्त्वज्ञानजं विद्धि मोहनं सर्वदेहिनाम् ।
प्रमादालस्यनिद्राभिस्तन्निबध्नाति भारत ॥८॥

tamas tv ajñāna-jaṁ viddhi mohanaṁ sarva-dehinām/
pramādālasya-nidrābhis tan nibadhnāti bhārata//

tamaḥ—*tamas*; *tu*—however; *ajñāna-jam*—born of ignorance; *viddhi*—know; *mohanam*—delusion; *sarva-dehinām*—of all embodied beings; *pramāda-ālasya-nidrābhiḥ*—through madness, lethargy, and sleep; *tat*—that; *nibadhnāti*—it binds; *bhārata*—O descendant of Bharata.

On the other hand, know that tamas is born of the ignorance that deludes all embodied beings. O descendant of Bharata, it binds through madness, lethargy, and sleep.

Kṛṣṇa differentiates *tamas* from *rajas* and *sattva* here by the word *tu* (however). The qualities of *tamas* are the antithesis of *sattva* and *rajas*. Madness (*pramāda*) is the opposite of *sattva*'s illuminating influence that produces accurate understanding. Lethargy (*ālasya*) opposes the tendency to act that is characteristic of *rajas*. Sleep (*nidrā*) opposes both *sattva* and *rajas*. *Tamas*, born of ignorance, has the power to cover the soul and thus produce a delusion (*mohanam*).

Text 9

सत्त्वं सुखे सञ्जयति रजः कर्मणि भारत ।
ज्ञानमावृत्य तु तमः प्रमादे सञ्जयत्युत ॥९॥

sattvaṁ sukhe sañjayati rajaḥ karmaṇi bhārata/
jñānam āvṛtya tu tamaḥ pramāde sañjayaty uta//

sattvam—*sattva*; *sukhe*—in happiness; *sañjayati*—it causes attachment; *rajaḥ*—*rajas*; *karmaṇi*—in action; *bhārata*—O descendant of Bharata; *jñānam*—knowledge; *āvṛtya*—covering; *tu*—but; *tamaḥ*—*tamas*; *pramāde*—in delusion; *sañjayati*—it causes attachment; *uta*—indeed.

O descendant of Bharata, wheras sattva causes attachment to happiness and rajas attachment to action, tamas, covering knowledge, leads to delusion.

Sattva causes attachment to happiness, while *rajas* causes attachment to action. *Tamas* often covers actual knowledge, even as one is on the verge of understanding. In this way it produces misunderstanding, engendering attachment to acts contrary to one's moral obligations and spiritual pursuit. These are the most important effects of the three *guṇas*.

Text 10

रजस्तमश्चाभिभूय सत्त्वं भवति भारत ।
रजः सत्त्वं तमश्चैव तमः सत्त्वं रजस्तथा ॥१०॥

rajas tamaś cābhibhūya sattvaṁ bhavati bhārata/
rajaḥ sattvaṁ tamaś caiva tamaḥ sattvaṁ rajas tathā//

rajaḥ—*rajas*; *tamaḥ*—*tamas*; *ca*—and; *abhibhūya*—overpowering; *sattvam*—*sattva*; *bhavati*—becomes; *bhārata*—O descendant of Bharata; *rajaḥ*—*rajas*; *sattvam*—*sattva*; *tamaḥ*—*tamas*; *ca*—and; *eva*—similarly; *tamaḥ*—*tamas*; *sattvam*—*sattva*; *rajaḥ*—*rajas*; *tathā*—thus.

O descendant of Bharata, sattva increases by subduing rajas and tamas; rajas increases by overpowering sattva and tamas; similarly, tamas increases by overpowering sattva and rajas.

Each of the *guṇas* is characterized by mutually contradictory effects, and they are all present at the same time. However, they never fully cancel one another out. They influence the soul with varying potency resulting from past *karma*. Each *guṇa* succeeds in influencing a person by temporarily overpowering the other *guṇas*. The three *guṇas* are in constant flux, vying for dominance, and *prārabdha-karma* is the driving force of this apparent competition. The dominant influence of a particular *guṇa* is observable through external symptoms. Kṛṣṇa speaks of these symptoms in the following three verses.

Text 11

सर्वद्वारेषु देहेऽस्मिन् प्रकाश उपजायते ।
ज्ञानं यदा तदा विद्याद् विवृद्धं सत्त्वमित्युत ॥११॥

sarva-dvāreṣu dehe 'smin prakāśa upajāyate/
jñānaṁ yadā tadā vidyād vivṛddhaṁ sattvam ity uta//

sarva-dvāreṣu—in all the gates; *dehe asmin*—in this body; *prakāśaḥ*—light; *upajāyate*—it is born; *jñānam*—knowledge; *yadā*—when; *tadā*—at that time; *vidyāt*—may it be known; *vivṛddham*—dominant; *sattvam*—*sattva*; *iti*—thus; *uta*—etcetera.

When the light of knowledge shines through all the gates of the body, it should be understood that sattva is dominant.

Knowledge occurs when the bodily gates of the senses in touch with sense objects are combined with proper discrimination resulting in intellectual illumination. Detachment brought about by *sattva* affords one the ability to be objective and thus know a thing for what it is without coloring it by attachment, which results in loss of objectivity.

The word *uta* (etcetera) implies that when happiness appears through the senses, this too is indicative of *sattva*'s influence. Baladeva Vidyābhūṣaṇa says, "The word *uta* should be taken in the sense of *api* (also), that one should also know [that *sattva* is predominant] by other signs, such as happiness [appearing in the gates of the body]." Viśvanātha Cakravartī Ṭhākura says that the word *uta* indicates that the happiness of *sattva* is generated by the soul. *Sattva* sheds light on the soul.

Text 12

लोभः प्रवृत्तिरारम्भः कर्मणामशमः स्पृहा ।
रजस्येतानि जायन्ते विवृद्धे भरतर्षभ ॥१२॥

lobhaḥ pravṛttir ārambhaḥ karmaṇām aśamaḥ spṛhā/
rajasy etāni jāyante vivṛddhe bharatarṣabha//

lobhaḥ—greed; *pravṛttiḥ*—activity; *ārambhaḥ*—endeavor; *karmaṇām*—of actions; *aśamaḥ*—restlessness; *spṛhā*—hankering; *rajasi*—in *rajas*; *etāni*—these; *jāyante*—they arise; *vivṛddhe*—in the dominance; *bharata-ṛṣabha*—O best of the Bharatas.

Greed, constant endeavor, ambitious undertakings, restlessness, and hankering are born when the influence of rajas is dominant, O best of the Bharatas.

Lobha refers to insatiable desire that increases constantly, even after the object of one's desire is attained. A person influenced by this product of *rajas* is unable to part with his money enough to donate a portion of it for spiritual or other beneficial causes. If he does come to part with it, he does not entirely let go of it, attaching to it his particular desire as to how he would like it spent.

Text 13

अप्रकाशोऽप्रवृत्तिश्च प्रमादो मोह एव च ।
तमस्येतानि जायन्ते विवृद्धे कुरुनन्दन ॥१३॥

aprakāśo 'pravṛttiś ca pramādo moha eva ca/
tamasy etāni jāyante vivṛddhe kuru-nandana//

aprakāśaḥ—darkness; *apravṛttiḥ*—inactivity; *ca*—and; *pramādaḥ*—bewilderment; *mohaḥ*—delusion; *eva*—certainly; *ca*—and; *tamasi*—in *tamas*; *etāni*—these; *jāyante*—they arise; *vivṛddhe*—in the dominance; *kuru-nandana*—O descendant of Kuru.

O descendant of the Kuru dynasty, when tamas predominates surely darkness, inactivity, bewilderment, and delusion are born.

Aprakāśa refers to the condition in which proper understanding does not arise despite good instruction. It also refers to the lack of discrimination that leads one to accept conclusions that are opposed to the scriptural canon. *Apravṛtti* indicates unwillingness to engage in any undertaking whatsoever or not caring about anything. *Pramāda* is the unwillingness to accept as true something that is staring one in the face. By use of the word *ca* in conjunction with *moha*, sleep and other characteristics of ignorance are implied. The emphasis expressed through the word *eva* implies that *moha* (illusion) illustrates the complete manifestation of ignorance.

It is important that the spiritual practitioner be aware of the external symptoms of the three *guṇas*. Such awareness better enables him to cultivate the influence of *sattva* for the sake of spiritual progress. Rising above *rajas* and *tamas* enables one to think clearly and pursue transcendence of the *guṇas* altogether.

The extent to which one is influenced by any of these *guṇas* at the time of death determines one's next birth. Kṛṣṇa speaks about this in the following two verses.

Text 14

यदा सत्त्वे प्रवृद्धे तु प्रलयं याति देहभृत् ।
तदोत्तमविदां लोकानमलान् प्रतिपद्यते ॥१४॥

yadā sattve pravṛddhe tu pralayaṁ yāti deha-bhṛt/
tadottama-vidāṁ lokān amalān pratipadyate//

yadā—when; *sattve*—in *sattva*; *pravṛddhe*—in the dominance; *tu*—but; *pralayam*—death; *yāti*—he goes; *deha-bhṛt*—the embodied; *tadā*—at that time; *uttama-vidām*—of those who know the ultimate; *lokān*—the worlds; *amalān*—pure; *pratipadyate*—he attains.

When the embodied being dies under the influence of sattva, he attains the pure worlds of those who adore the ultimate.

The word *uttama-vidām* indicates those who adore *(vidām)* the ultimate/highest *(uttamam)*. The pure worlds *(lokān amalān)* are the heavenly realms of religious pleasure and beyond where happiness and spiritual pursuit predominate, respectively. According to Hindu cosmology, beyond material heaven attained by the pious, planets of spiritual practice exist where God is perpetually worshipped and meditated on with a view to attain him. One who dies under the influence of *sattva* attains such destinations.

Text 15

रजसि प्रलयं गत्वा कर्मसङ्गिषु जायते ।
तथा प्रलीनस्तमसि मूढयोनिषु जायते ॥१५॥

rajasi pralayaṁ gatvā karma-saṅgiṣu jāyate/
tathā pralīnas tamasi mūḍha-yoniṣu jāyate//

rajasi—in *rajas*; *pralayam*—death; *gatvā*—going; *karma-saṅgiṣu*—among those attached to fruitive activities; *jāyate*—he is born; *tathā*—similarly; *pralīnaḥ*—dying; *tamasi*—in *tamas*; *mūḍha-yoniṣu*—in the womb of the deluded; *jāyate*—he is born.

When one dies under the influence of rajas, he is born among those attached to fruitive activity. Similarly, when one dies under the influence of tamas, he takes birth from the wombs of deluded fools.

Those attached to fruitive activity *(karma-saṅgiṣu)* are human beings. The deluded fools *(mūḍha)* are animals and humans who act like them, as well as still lower species of life.

Text 16

कर्मणः सुकृतस्याहुः सात्त्विकं निर्मलं फलम् ।
रजसस्तु फलं दुःखमज्ञानं तमसः फलम् ॥१६॥

karmaṇaḥ sukṛtasyāhuḥ sāttvikaṁ nirmalaṁ phalam/
rajasas tu phalaṁ duḥkham ajñānaṁ tamasaḥ phalam//

karmaṇaḥ—of work; *su-kṛtasya*—virtuous action; *āhuḥ*—they say; *sāttvikam*—sattvic; *nirmalam*—pure; *phalam*—result; *rajasaḥ*—of *rajas*; *tu*—but; *phalam*—result; *duḥkham*—sorrow; *ajñānam*—ignorance; *tamasaḥ*—of *tamas*; *phalam*—result.

It is said that the result of virtuous action is pure and accomplished through sattva. The result of work in rajas is sorrow, and the result of work in tamas, ignorance.

The result of action performed under the influence of *sattva* is pure *(nirmalam)*. It is happiness that is not colored by *rajas* or *tamas*. In *rajas*, action brings predominantly unhappy results. Whatever happiness is derived from action under the influence of *rajas* is eventually transformed into sorrow. Action performed under the influence of *tamas* produces ignorance. Such activity is synonymous with vice.

A detailed explanation of the characteristics of activities that are performed under the influence of the different *guṇas* is found in chapter 18 (Bg. 18.23–25). Regarding the reason for the various results of actions performed under the *guṇas'* influence, Kṛṣṇa reiterates in the next verse what he discussed in verses 11 through 13.

Text 17

सत्त्वात्सञ्जायते ज्ञानं रजसो लोभ एव च ।
प्रमादमोहौ तमसो भवतोऽज्ञानमेव च ॥१७॥

sattvāt sañjāyate jñānaṁ rajaso lobha eva ca/
pramāda-mohau tamaso bhavato 'jñānam eva ca//

sattvāt—from *sattva*; *sañjāyate*—it is born; *jñānam*—knowledge; *rajasaḥ*—from *rajas*; *lobhaḥ*—longing; *eva*—certainly; *ca*—and; *pramāda-mohau*—error and illus ion; *tamasaḥ*—from *tamas*; *bhavataḥ*—they arise; *ajñānam*— ignorance; *eva*—certainly; *ca*—and.

From sattva knowledge is born, and from rajas avarice is born. From tamas error, delusion, as well as ignorance are born.

The effects of sattvic work are purity and happiness because from it knowledge is born. The effect of *rajas* is sorrow because from *rajas* hankering without end is born. Working under the influence of *tamas* produces ignorance because from *tamas* ignorance is born. Ignorance produces more ignorance, whereas according to earlier verses (Bg. 2.62–3, 3.37), *rajas* tends to degrade into ignorance over time. Later in chapter 16 (Bg. 16.19) this is also indicated. *Rajas* can be transformed directly into *tamas* or *sattva*.

Text 18

ऊर्ध्वं गच्छन्ति सत्त्वस्था मध्ये तिष्ठन्ति राजसाः ।
जघन्यगुणवृत्तिस्था अधो गच्छन्ति तामसाः ॥१८॥

ūrdhvaṁ gacchanti sattva-sthā madhye tiṣṭhanti rājasāḥ/
jaghanya-guṇa-vṛtti-sthā adho gacchanti tāmasāḥ//

ūrdhvam—upwards; *gacchanti*—they go; *sattva-sthāḥ*—those established in *sattva*; *madhye*—in the middle; *tiṣṭhanti*—they remain; *rājasāḥ*—those in *rajas*; *jaghanya*—lowest; *guṇa*—quality; *vṛtti-sthāḥ*—in the condition; *adhaḥ*—downwards; *gacchanti*—they go; *tāmasāḥ*—those in *tamas*.

Those established in sattva go upwards; those in rajas remain mediocre; those in tamas, the lowest quality, go downwards.

In verse 15 Kṛṣṇa spoke of dying in a particular *guṇa* and the birth that results from it. In this verse he speaks of one's lifestyle, which generally determines one's consciousness at the time of death.

Those whose lives are established in *sattva* go upwards in their next life to take birth in planets of the pious and spiritually inclined. Those established in *rajas* remain in the middle planetary system, which includes earth. Those established in *tamas* go down, taking lower births. This verse may also apply to one's social status within this life. Unbridled passion is not enough for material advancement. Sense control, the influence of *sattva*, must harness rajasic energy. If it does not, this energy will degrade into *tamas*.

Thus far in this chapter Kṛṣṇa has spoken of God's position as the seed-giving father of material existence, as well as of the *guṇas* and how they bind the soul. In the next two verses, he turns Arjuna's attention to the means to transcend the *guṇas* and attain a spiritual nature like that of God.

Text 19

नान्यं गुणेभ्यः कर्तारं यदा द्रष्टानुपश्यति ।
गुणेभ्यश्च परं वेत्ति मद्भावं सोऽधिगच्छति ॥१९॥

nānyaṁ guṇebhyaḥ kartāraṁ yadā draṣṭānupaśyati/
guṇebhyaś ca paraṁ vetti mad-bhāvaṁ so 'dhigacchati//

na—not; *anyam*—other; *guṇebhyaḥ*—than the *guṇas*; *kartāram*—agent; *yadā*—when; *draṣṭā*—perceiver; *anupaśyati*—sees; *guṇebhyaḥ*—than the *guṇas*; *ca*—and; *param*—higher; *vetti*—he knows; *mat-bhāvam*—my nature; *saḥ*—he; *adhigacchati*—he attains.

When the perceiver sees no other agent of action than the guṇas and knows what is beyond the guṇas, he attains a nature like my own.

In the word *anupaśyati* the prefix *anu* implies that the seer *(draṣṭā)* sees *(paśyati)* with the help of God *(anu)*. He is not independent in the act of perceiving. When by the grace of God a person develops acute power of discrimination and thus sees that the *guṇas* are the agents of all actions and that he is only the witness, he attains self-realization. Such a person sees that all of the bodily organs are but transformations of the *guṇas* and thus different from himself. When he sees further that not only he himself is above the *guṇas*, but that God is above them and never comes under their influence, he attains God-realization *(mad-bhāvam)*. Baladeva Vidyābhūṣaṇa says that *mad-bhāvam* indicates the quality of Kṛṣṇa that is eternally liberated or the qualification to enter into the highest devotion. Viśvanātha Cakravartī refers to verse 26 of this chapter to further explain the meaning of *mad-bhāvam*—post-liberated *bhakti*.

Text 20

गुणानेतानतीत्य त्रीन् देही देहसमुद्भवान् ।
जन्ममृत्युजरादुःखैर्विमुक्तोऽमृतमश्नुते ॥२०॥

guṇān etān atītya trīn dehī deha-samudbhavān/
janma-mṛtyu-jarā-duḥkhair vimukto 'mṛtam aśnute//

guṇān—*guṇas*; *etān*—these; *atītya*—transcending; *trīn*—three; *dehī*—the embodied; *deha*—body; *samudbhavān*—produced of; *janma*—birth; *mṛtyu*—death; *jarā*—old age; *duḥkhaiḥ*—by the distresses; *vimuktaḥ*—released; *amṛtam*—nectar; *aśnute*—he attains.

When the embodied being transcends these three guṇas from which the body originates, released from birth, death, old age, and their distress, he attains the nectar of immortality.

Text 21

अर्जुन उवाच
कैर्लिङ्गैस्त्रीन् गुणानेतानतीतो भवति प्रभो ।
किमाचारः कथं चैतांस्त्रीन् गुणानतिवर्तते ॥२१॥

arjuna uvāca
kair liṅgais trīn guṇān etān atīto bhavati prabho/
kim ācāraḥ kathaṁ caitāṁs trīn guṇān ativartate//

arjunaḥ uvāca—Arjuna said; *kaiḥ*—by which; *liṅgaiḥ*—by symptoms; *trīn*—three; *guṇān*—*guṇas*; *etān*—these; *atītaḥ*—transcended; *bhavati*—he is; *prabho*—O Lord; *kim*—what; *ācāraḥ*—conduct; *katham*—how; *ca*—and; *etān*—these; *trīn*—three; *guṇān*—*guṇas*; *ativartate*—he transcends.

Arjuna said: O Lord, by what symptoms is one who has transcended these three guṇas recognized? How does he conduct himself, and how does he transcend the three guṇas?

In verses 19 and 20 Kṛṣṇa speaks of the *jīvanmukta*, one who is liberated while still embodied. In this verse Arjuna asks further about such persons. Although his questions are similar to those asked in chapter 2 (Bg. 2.54), here Arjuna's inquiry is primarily concerned with the means by which one transcends the *guṇas*. Arjuna also wants to know if the liberated soul is independent of scriptural guidelines or enjoined to follow them. Kṛṣṇa answers in the following five verses.

Texts 22–25

श्रीभगवानुवाच
प्रकाशं च प्रवृत्तिं च मोहमेव च पाण्डव ।
न द्वेष्टि सम्प्रवृत्तानि न निवृत्तानि काङ्क्षति ॥२२॥
उदासीनवदासीनो गुणैर्यो न विचाल्यते ।
गुणा वर्तन्त इत्येवं योऽवतिष्ठति नेङ्गते ॥२३॥
समदुःखसुखः स्वस्थः समलोष्टाश्मकाञ्चनः ।
तुल्यप्रियाप्रियो धीरस्तुल्यनिन्दात्मसंस्तुतिः ॥२४॥
मानापमानयोस्तुल्यस्तुल्यो मित्रारिपक्षयोः ।
सर्वारम्भपरित्यागी गुणातीतः स उच्यते ॥२५॥

śrī-bhagavān uvāca
prakāśaṁ ca pravṛttiṁ ca moham eva ca pāṇḍava/
na dveṣṭi sampravṛttāni na nivṛttāni kāṅkṣati//
udāsīna-vad āsīno guṇair yo na vicālyate/
guṇā vartanta ity evaṁ yo 'vatiṣṭhati neṅgate//
sama-duḥkha-sukhaḥ sva-sthaḥ sama-loṣṭāśma-kāñcanaḥ/
tulya-priyāpriyo dhīras tulya-nindātma-saṁstutiḥ//
mānāpamānayos tulyas tulyo mitrāri-pakṣayoḥ/
sarvārambha-parityāgī guṇātītaḥ sa ucyate//

śrī-bhagavān uvāca—the Lord of Śrī said; *prakāśam*—illumination; *ca*—and; *pravṛttim*—activity; *ca*—and; *moham*—delusion; *eva ca*—and; *pāṇḍava*—O son of Pāṇḍu; *na*—not; *dveṣṭi*—dislikes; *sampravṛttāni*—presences; *na*—not; *nivṛttāni*—absences; *kāṅkṣati*—he desires; *udāsīna-vat*—as if neutral; *āsīnaḥ*—seated; *guṇaiḥ*—by the *guṇas*; *yaḥ*—who; *na*—not; *vicālyate*—he is disturbed; *guṇāḥ*—the *guṇas*; *vartante*—they are operative; *iti evam*—thus; *yaḥ*—who; *avatiṣṭhati*—he remains; *na*—not; *iṅgate*—he flickers; *sama*—equal; *duḥkha*—sorrow; *sukhaḥ*—happiness; *sva-sthaḥ*—situated in himself; *sama*—equally; *loṣṭa*—a lump of earth; *aśma*—stone; *kāñcanaḥ*—gold; *tulya*—equally disposed; *priya*—dear; *apriyaḥ*—not dear; *dhīraḥ*—steady; *tulya*—equal; *nindā*—blame; *ātma-saṁstutiḥ*—praise of himself; *māna-apamānayoḥ*—in honor and dishonor; *tulyaḥ*—equal; *tulyaḥ*—equal; *mitra*—friend; *ari*—enemy; *pakṣayoḥ*—to the parties; *sarva*—all; *ārambha*—undertaking; *parityāgī*—renouncer; *guṇa-atītaḥ*—gone beyond the *guṇas*; *saḥ*—he; *ucyate*—is said.

The Lord of Śrī said: O son of Pāṇḍu, one who does not like or dislike the presence or absence of illumination, activity, or delusion, who is seated as though indifferent, undisturbed by the guṇas, thinking "only the guṇas are operative," who thus remains steady, to whom happiness and sorrow are equal, who dwells in the self, to whom a lump of earth, a stone, and gold are the same, who regards equally the desirable and undesirable, who is steadfast, to whom blame and praise are equal, to whom honor and dishonor are the same, who treats alike friend and foe, and who has renounced all material undertakings—such a person is said to have transcended the guṇas.

The symptoms mentioned in verse 22 are perceivable only to oneself. Others cannot observe them. They are internal symptoms of liberated souls, as opposed to their outward conduct, which is discussed in the subsequent verses.

The influx of the *guṇas* in the form of illumination *(sattva)*, activity *(rajas)*, and delusion *(tamas)* is experienced by the *jīvanmukta*, as is its absence. In either condition he remains aloof, knowing these influences to be merely the interaction of the *guṇas*. He may be illuminated with knowledge or deluded by sensual information, mistaking a rope for a snake, but all of this has no bearing on his self, and he remains acutely aware of this.

The conduct of the self-realized is observable criterion. Their conduct is to be emulated in practice, whereas it is second nature for them. Next Kṛṣṇa describes how they arrive at this status.

Text 26

मां च योऽव्यभिचारेण भक्तियोगेन सेवते ।
स गुणान् समतीत्यैतान् ब्रह्मभूयाय कल्पते ॥२६॥

māṁ ca yo 'vyabhicāreṇa bhakti-yogena sevate/
sa guṇān samatītyaitān brahma-bhūyāya kalpate//

mām—me; *ca*—and; *yaḥ*—who; *avyabhicāreṇa*—exclusively; *bhakti-yogena*—by devotional *yoga*; *sevate*—he serves; *saḥ*—he; *guṇān*—the *guṇas*; *samatītya*—transcending; *etān*—these; *brahma-bhūyāya*—to absorption in Brahman; *kalpate*—he is fit.

One who serves me exclusively with the yoga of constant devotion, having transcended the guṇas, is fit for liberation.

Here Kṛṣṇa answers Arjuna's third question regarding the means of liberation. Viśvanātha Cakravartī comments that the word *ca* in this verse is used for the sake of emphasizing that devotion is the only means to attain transcendence.

Those who are able by the grace of God to perceive the difference between themselves and the *guṇas* will attain liberation, should they engage in constant devotion to Kṛṣṇa. Others who do not take to devotion will not. Those who attain Brahman realization do so by combining their power of discrimination with devotion to the one who is beyond the *guṇas* (God). Regarding the unalloyed devotees, they are already situated in Brahman merely by their devotion to Kṛṣṇa, for as we shall see in the final verse of this chapter, Brahman realization is subordinate to God (Paramātmā/Bhagavān) realization.

Should Arjuna wonder how Kṛṣṇa's devotees will attain Brahman, Kṛṣṇa speaks the concluding verse of this chapter. Should anyone else wonder how devotion to Kṛṣṇa, who to the philosophically untrained, nondevotional eye appears to be a mere human, can bear the fruit of Brahman realization, Kṛṣṇa next states, as he did in the previous chapter (Bg. 13.13), that Brahman itself is subordinate to him.

Text 27

ब्रह्मणो हि प्रतिष्ठाहममृतस्याव्ययस्य च ।
शाश्वतस्य च धर्मस्य सुखस्यैकान्तिकस्य च ॥२७॥

brahmaṇo hi pratiṣṭhāham amṛtasyāvyayasya ca/
śāśvatasya ca dharmasya sukhasyaikāntikasya ca//

brahmaṇaḥ—of Brahman; *hi*—certainly; *pratiṣṭhā*—the basis; *aham*—I; *amṛtasya*—of the immortal; *avyayasya*—of the imperishable; *ca*—and; *śāśvatasya*—of the everlasting; *ca*—and; *dharmasya*—of *dharma; sukhasya*—of happiness; *aikāntikasya*—of absolute; *ca*—and.

For I am the basis of Brahman, the immortal, the imperishable, everlasting dharma, and absolute bliss.

Here Kṛṣṇa informs Arjuna that his unalloyed devotees, who approach him with devotion from the very beginning of their spiritual practice, upon attaining him automatically attain Brahman. Brahman, Kṛṣṇa says here, is subordinate to himself. It rests on him. He is its foundation. Who knows Kṛṣṇa, Bhagavān, knows Brahman in full. The reverse, however, is not necessarily true.

As Kṛṣṇa is the support of Brahman, so too is he the support of the immortal, the imperishable, everlasting *dharma*, and absolute bliss. One may ask, "What is everlasting *dharma* (*śāśvatasya ca dharmasya*)?" The Vaiṣṇavas reply that all paths other than *bhakti* terminate on delivering their result. *Bhakti* alone manifests both in practice and perfection. Its *sādhana* and *sādhya* are the same. The only difference is that one is unripe *bhakti*, the other ripe.

From this chapter it is clear that relative material existence resulting from attachment to the *guṇas* is easily transcended by devotion to Kṛṣṇa, either unalloyed or mixed with *jñāna*. Indeed, Kṛṣṇa never really speaks of any means other than *bhakti*.

CHAPTER FIFTEEN

पुरुषोत्तमयोगः
Puruṣottama-yoga

YOGA OF THE HIGHEST PERSON

Text 1

श्रीभगवानुवाच
ऊर्ध्वमूलमधःशाखमश्वत्थं प्राहुरव्ययम् ।
छन्दांसि यस्य पर्णानि यस्तं वेद स वेदवित् ॥१॥

śrī-bhagavān uvāca
ūrdhva-mūlam adhaḥ-śākham aśvatthaṁ prāhur avyayam/
chandāṁsi yasya parṇāni yas taṁ veda sa veda-vit//

śrī-bhagavān uvāca—the Lord of Śrī said; *ūrdhva-mūlam*—with roots above; *adhaḥ*—downwards; *śākham*—branch; *aśvattham*—*aśvattha* tree; *prāhuḥ*—they say; *avyayam*—imperishable; *chandāṁsi*—the Vedic hymns; *yasya*—of which; *parṇāni*—leaves; *yaḥ*—who; *tam*—that; *veda*—he knows; *saḥ*—he; *veda-vit*—knower of the *Vedas*.

The Lord of Śrī said: It is said that there is an imperishable aśvattha tree with its roots above and branches below, and whose leaves are the Vedic hymns. One who knows this tree knows all there is to be known.

Kṛṣṇa concluded the previous chapter by stating that Brahman is subordinate to himself. He is the Supreme Person. He also taught Arjuna that devotion to himself is the means to transcend the *guṇas*. His devotees attain Brahman realization in the course of their devotion to him. After having so clearly stated his supremely exalted position, Kṛṣṇa finds Arjuna wonder struck as the present chapter commences. In this chapter he elaborates on the position of the Supreme Being and thus clarifies how it is that one who becomes his devotee realizes Brahman. In the course of doing so, he also speaks further about the nature of the material world and the need for renunciation.

In the first four verses that introduce this chapter, Kṛṣṇa compares the material world to an *aśvattha* tree. The sacred *aśvattha* tree is sometimes considered to be the banyan, pippala, or fig tree, all of which are from the same family. From the further description of it in the following verse, it appears that the banyan tree with its branches that extend downward forming new roots, and subsequently becoming a veritable forest of its own, most closely resembles the tree Kṛṣṇa is referring to.

The word *aśvattha*, derived from the words *aśva* and *stha*, first appears in the *Vedas*, where it refers to that which a horse *(aśva)* is tethered to *(stha)*. The material world is strong like this post and capable of tying down the unbridled spirit of the soul.

Several commentators have brought out another meaning of *aśvattha*. The Sanskrit word *śvas* means tomorrow. That which lasts until tomorrow is *śvattha*. *Aśvattha* is thus that which will not last until tomorrow.

Although Kṛṣṇa also describes this tree as imperishable *(avyayam)*, this is in relation to its bewildering potency for those who do not seek to cut it down. Such persons remain in *saṁsāra*, chasing the *aśvattha* tree of material existence, which, while perpetual in an overall sense, is at the same time here today and gone tomorrow in terms of its varied manifestations. While it remains for those intent on material life, it has no tomorrow for the liberated.

In Kṛṣṇa's *aśvattha* metaphor, he has turned the sacred tree upside down. Bhaktivedanta Swami Prabhupāda comments that we all have experience of an upside-down tree when we visit the bank of a river and see one reflected in the water. Similarly the upside-down *aśvattha* tree of this verse represents the material world, where the priorities have been turned upside down. This is the nature of the material world compared here to the *aśvattha* tree.

The metaphorical *aśvattha*'s roots extend upwards *(ūrdhva-mūlam)*, as the material world is rooted *(mūlam)* in the Supreme Being, who is the highest *(ūrdhva)* cause of all causes. Śrīdhara Swāmī comments that this Supreme Person is superior to both the perishable material manifestation and the imperishable soul. Kṛṣṇa states this himself later in this chapter. Indeed, this is the import of the entire chapter.

The *aśvattha*'s branches extend downward and represent the variegated, many-branched material experience, the various forms of material life. The real life within the tree of material experience is its leaves, representing the Vedic hymns, from which the world is said to manifest. *Kaṭha Upaniṣad* says that a tree is beautified by its leaves. The leaves of the Gītā's *aśvattha* tree beautify it because from the Vedic rites the karmic world of material prospect expands. From these leaves one can achieve the four goals of human life: righteousness *(dharma)*, wealth *(artha)*, material desire *(kāma)*, and liberation *(mokṣa)*. Because the *aśvattha* tree provides facility for attaining these goals, it is the best of trees, and Kṛṣṇa himself has said in the tenth chapter of the Gītā, "Of trees I am the *aśvattha*." (Bg. 10.26)

However, in spite of its virtue, the *aśvattha* tree must be cut down if one is to succeed in human life by attaining love of God. The word *vṛkṣa* (tree) is related with the verbal root *bṛh* (to uproot). One who knows this tree knows the import of the *Vedas* and thus endeavors to cut it down. To this end, the present chapter stresses renunciation, without which liberation is not possible. Renunciation is the ax by which the *aśvattha* tree is cut down. While discrimination between matter and consciousness has been discussed in the previous two chapters, the renunciation that gives rise to proper discrimination is highlighted in this chapter. Detachment from an object affords the objectivity required to understand its nature. Preliminary discrimination leads to renunciation, and this renunciation begets mature discrimination. Both of these can be helpful to one beginning the path of devotion,[1] while devotion itself also brings about knowledge and detachment.

Text 2

अधश्चोर्ध्वं प्रसृतास्तस्य शाखा
गुणप्रवृद्धा विषयप्रवालाः ।
अधश्च मूलान्यनुसन्ततानि
कर्मानुबन्धीनि मनुष्यलोके ॥२॥

adhaś cordhvaṁ prasṛtās tasya śākhā
guṇa-pravṛddhā viṣaya-pravālāḥ/
adhaś ca mūlāny anusantatāni
karmānubandhīni manuṣya-loke//

adhaḥ—downward; *ca*—and; *ūrdhvam*—upward; *prasṛtāḥ*—spread; *tasya*—its; *śākhāḥ*—branches; *guṇa-pravṛddhāḥ*—nourished by the *guṇas*; *viṣaya*—sense object; *pravālāḥ*—twigs; *adhaḥ*—downward; *ca*—and; *mūlāni*—roots; *anusantatāni*—extended; *karma-anubandhīni*—engendering action; *manuṣya-loke*—in human society.

1. See Brs. 1.2.248.

This tree's branches, nourished by the guṇas, spread above and below and have sense objects as its twigs. It also has roots of karmic reaction that reach downward in human society.

The figurative *aśvattha* tree has branches that grow downward and take root in the ground of material existence. These are its secondary roots (*mūlāni*). Normally they would grow upwards toward the principal roots of this upside-down tree, but here they are described as growing downward as well, indicating further the bewildering nature of the tree of material existence. Indeed, the word *ca* (*adhaś ca mūlāni*) indicates that the secondary roots of this tree are spread in all directions. These secondary roots symbolize desires that cause work and take humanity to different branches of the tree, thus entangling everyone in karmic reactions (*karmānubandhīni*). The perpetuation of *karma* springs from the human form of life.

The branches of the *aśvattha* tree extend up and down and represent higher and lower forms of life, respectively. They are nourished by the *guṇas*. The tender twigs and buds represent sense objects that first catch one's attention. As buds appear on the ends of branches, so do the sense objects connect with the external extremities of the body, the senses.

Texts 3–4

न रूपमस्येह तथोपलभ्यते
नान्तो न चादिर्न च सम्प्रतिष्ठा ।
अश्वत्थमेनं सुविरूढमूल-
मसङ्गशस्त्रेण दृढेन छित्त्वा ॥३॥
ततः पदं तत्परिमार्गितव्यं
यस्मिन् गता न निवर्तन्ति भूयः ।
तमेव चाद्यं पुरुषं प्रपद्ये
यतः प्रवृत्तिः प्रसृता पुराणी ॥४॥

na rūpam asyeha tathopalabhyate
nānto na cādir na ca sampratiṣṭhā/
aśvattham enaṁ su-virūḍha-mūlam
asaṅga-śastreṇa dṛḍhena chittvā//
tataḥ padaṁ tat parimārgitavyaṁ
yasmin gatā na nivartanti bhūyaḥ/
tam eva cādyaṁ puruṣaṁ prapadye
yataḥ pravṛttiḥ prasṛtā purāṇī//

na—not; *rūpam*—form; *asya*—of it; *iha*—in this world; *tathā*—also; *upalabhyate*—it can be perceived; *na*—not; *antaḥ*—end; *na*—not; *ca*—also; *ādiḥ*—beginning; *na*—not; *ca*—also; *sampratiṣṭhā*—foundation; *aśvattham*—*aśvattha* tree; *enam*—this; *su-virūḍha*—fully grown; *mūlam*—root; *asaṅga-śastreṇa*—by the weapon of detachment; *dṛḍhena*—by strong; *chittvā*—cutting; *tataḥ*—thereafter; *padam*—goal; *tat*—that; *parimārgitavyam*—to be pursued; *yasmin*—where; *gatāḥ*—gone; *na*—not; *nivartanti*—they return; *bhūyaḥ*—again; *tam*—that; *eva*—certainly; *ca*—also; *ādyam*—original; *puruṣam*—person; *prapadye*—I surrender; *yataḥ*—from whom; *pravṛttiḥ*—activity; *prasṛtā*—extended; *purāṇi*—old.

This tree's form is not perceptible in this world—not its beginning, end, or foundation. Cut down this deeply rooted aśvattha tree with the ax of detachment and pursue that place which having attained one never returns, thinking, "I surrender to the original person from whom the primordial activities of creation expand."

The *aśvattha* tree of this world is imperceptible for one entangled in its branches. Although it is difficult to see it *(upalabhyate na)* for what it is, and although its secondary roots of our desires are deeply rooted *(suvirūḍha)*, it should nonetheless be cut down with the weapon of detachment *(asaṅga-śastreṇa)*. Detachment is the proper ax to use on this imperceptible tree, for its imperceptibility stems from our entanglement within it. If we draw back from it to gaze upon it with an eye of detachment, we can see it objectively and know its true nature. The extent to which one is attached to an object is as much as one's eye of objectivity is obscured. Thus detachment reveals the nature of the world and the necessity to uproot ourselves from it.

After cutting ourselves free from the roots of material desire, we must search out the primary root of the tree of material existence, the Supreme Being, and take shelter of him. When we cut the roots of material attachment, we cannot hold on to any of the branches of the tree of material existence. Empty-handed, weightlessly drifting on the air of detachment, we must grab on to the primary root of this tree and become grounded in surrender and devotion to the Supreme Person, thus entering the land of no return. Kṛṣṇa next describes the characteristics of those who enter his abode.

Text 5

निर्मानमोहा जितसङ्गदोषा
   अध्यात्मनित्या विनिवृत्तकामाः ।
द्वन्द्वैर्विमुक्ताः सुखदुःखसंज्ञै-
   र्गच्छन्त्यमूढाः पदमव्ययं तत् ॥५॥

nirmāna-mohā jita-saṅga-doṣā
adhyātma-nityā vinivṛtta-kāmāḥ/
dvandvair vimuktāḥ sukha-duḥkha-saṁjñair
gacchanty amūḍhāḥ padam avyayaṁ tat//

niḥ—without; *māna*—pride; *mohāḥ*—illusions; *jita*—conquered; *saṅga*—attachment; *doṣāḥ*—faults; *adhyātma*—spirituality; *nityāḥ*—eternal; *vinivṛtta*—turned away; *kāmāḥ*—desires; *dvandvaiḥ*—from the dualities; *vimuktāḥ*—freed; *sukha-duḥkha*—pleasure and pain; *saṁjñaiḥ*—by those recognized as; *gacchanti*—they attain; *amūḍhāḥ*—unbewildered; *padam*—abode; *avyayam*—imperishable; *tat*—that.

The undeluded who are free from pride, illusion, and the fault of attachment, who are ever devoted to spirituality, have turned away from material desire, and are free from the dualities of pleasure and pain attain that imperishable abode.

Text 6

न तद् भासयते सूर्यो न शशाङ्को न पावकः ।
   यद् गत्वा न निवर्तन्ते तद्धाम परमं मम ॥६॥

na tad bhāsayate sūryo na śaśāṅko na pāvakaḥ/
yad gatvā na nivartante tad dhāma paramaṁ mama//

na—not; *tat*—that; *bhāsayate*—it illumines; *sūryaḥ*—sun; *na*—not; *śaśāṅkaḥ*—moon; *na*—not; *pāvakaḥ*—fire; *yat*—which; *gatvā*—going; *na*—not; *nivartante*—they come back; *tat dhāma*—that abode; *paramam*—supreme; *mama*—my.

That supreme abode of mine is not illumined by the sun, the moon, or fire. Having gone there, no one returns.

The abode of God is self-luminous. This implies that only if he wants to reveal it to someone can one understand it, otherwise not. Kṛṣṇa's abode is made of consciousness and thus it is not perceptible to inert things, such as the senses and mind.

Kṛṣṇa says that the light of the sun cannot reveal it. The sun is the predominating deity of the eyes. This implies that the eyes as well as all of the physical senses are not suitable instruments for perceiving God's abode. Fire is the predominating deity of speech. Thus speech is not capable of fully describing the nature of God's abode. In other words, one can never say enough about it—its glory is unlimited.

As the physical senses are limited in their capacity to perceive the nature of God's abode, so too is the psychic sense, the mind. The moon is the predominating deity of the mind, and here Kṛṣṇa says that it cannot illumine his abode. Going there requires going beyond the mind, and once there one never returns to the petty world of the mind.

Viśvanātha Cakravartī Ṭhākura comments that the sun and moon also represent heat and cold, and thus Kṛṣṇa's abode, being constructed out of nondual consciousness, is beyond these dualities. Consciousness is the principal ingredient of his abode. This verse clearly elaborates on Kṛṣṇa's concluding statement of the previous chapter, where he declared Brahman, nondual consciousness, to be subordinate to himself.

After alluding to his primary potency, Kṛṣṇa next describes his intermediate potency in terms of its becoming subordinate to his secondary potency. While the individual soul has the potential of attaining Kṛṣṇa's abode, it is under the influence of material illusion and thus bound by the mind and senses.

Text 7

ममैवांशो जीवलोके जीवभूतः सनातनः ।
मनःषष्ठानीन्द्रियाणि प्रकृतिस्थानि कर्षति ॥७॥

mamaivāṁśo jīva-loke jīva-bhūtaḥ sanātanaḥ/
manaḥ-ṣaṣṭhānīndriyāṇi prakṛti-sthāni karṣati//

mama—my; *eva*—certainly; *aṁśaḥ*—fragment; *jīva-loke*—in the world of beings; *jīva-bhūtaḥ*—the individual soul; *sanātanaḥ*—eternal; *manaḥ*—mind; *ṣaṣṭhāni*—six; *indriyāṇi*—senses; *prakṛti*—material nature; *sthāni*—situated; *karṣati*—it drags.

In this world the individual soul, who is an eternal fragment of myself, drags with him the senses and the mind, which belong to material nature.

The pure soul can enter the abode of God and never return to the material world. However, a person who has not realized his actual position in relation to the material mind and senses can never enter the land of no return, Kṛṣṇa's abode. The reason for this is stated in the present verse. He is shackled by his identification with the mind and senses and thus returns or takes birth again and again.

Here Kṛṣṇa stresses the eternal individuality *(jīva-bhūtaḥ sanātanaḥ)* of the *jīva* soul. Although it is eternal, because it is a mere fragment of God *(mamaivāṁśo)*, it struggles in connection with material nature. Unlike God, it is not capable of fully controlling material nature. What is the nature of its struggle? The *jīva* soul drags with it the burden of the mind and senses owing to misidentification with them. As a prisoner drags his shackles with him wherever he goes, so the deluded *jīva*, although essentially different from matter, drags the ball and chain of his material mind and senses with him life after life. The *jīva*'s struggle is ultimately not with anything external to itself. Its burden is its own mind and senses alone, which prevent it from seeing things as they are.

In this verse, the senses Kṛṣṇa speaks of are those that, along with the sixth sense, the mind, make up the subtle body. What we perceive as senses, the openings on the physical body, are in fact outlets for our actual senses. It is in this subtle body that the *jīva* soul moves from one physical body to another, carrying misconceptions about who and what it is. Kṛṣṇa gives an analogy in the next verse to describe how this takes place.

Text 8

शरीरं यदवाप्नोति यच्चाप्युत्क्रामतीश्वरः ।
गृहीत्वैतानि संयाति वायुर्गन्धानिवाशयात् ॥८॥

śarīraṁ yad avāpnoti yac cāpy utkrāmatīśvaraḥ/
gṛhītvaitāni saṁyāti vāyur gandhān ivāśayāt//

śarīram—body; *yat*—as; *avāpnoti*—he gets; *yat*—as; *ca api*—also; *utkrāmati*—he departs; *īśvaraḥ*—master; *gṛhītvā*—acquiring; *etāni*—these; *saṁyāti*—he goes; *vāyuḥ*—wind; *gandhān*—aromas; *iva*—like; *āśayāt*—from source.

When acquiring a body, its master, the soul, takes these senses and mind with him from the body he leaves, just as the wind carries aromas from their source. In this way he attains a new body.

The word *īśvara* in this verse refers to the soul, who considers himself the master of his body, rather than a servant of God. Here it is used almost sarcastically, for the soul gives up and takes new bodies without any control. However, should the embodied soul change his disposition and think himself the servant of God, he actually becomes the master of his mind and body. Otherwise in illusion he thinks himself the master, even while he is forced to move from one body to another, life after life.

The illusioned soul's movement is like the wind, which has no choice in the matter of which fragrance it will carry, nor in where it blows—making the word *īśvara* even more poignant. Like the wind, the soul moves along with his subtle body to another physical body. What he does in the physical body he inhabits is described next.

Text 9

श्रोत्रं चक्षुः स्पर्शनं च रसनं घ्राणमेव च ।
अधिष्ठाय मनश्चायं विषयानुपसेवते ॥९॥

śrotraṁ cakṣuḥ sparśanaṁ ca rasanaṁ ghrāṇam eva ca/
adhiṣṭhāya manaś cāyaṁ viṣayān upasevate//

śrotram—hearing; *cakṣuḥ*—sight; *sparśanam*—touch; *ca*—also; *rasanam*—taste; *ghrāṇam*—smell; *eva*—also; *ca*—and; *adhiṣṭhāya*—presiding over; *manaḥ*—mind; *ca*—also; *ayam*—he; *viṣayān*—sense objects; *upasevate*—he enjoys.

Presiding over the ears, eyes, the organs of touch, taste, and smell, as well as the mind, the soul enjoys sense objects.

Once within the physical body the presiding soul enjoys sense objects by the medium of mind through the external senses. The external senses of the physical body contact sense objects and thus relay messages to the mind. The mind in turn likes or dislikes them, and the world of material duality is born. The above interactions are imperceptible to the deluded soul, whose vision, or lack of it, is next contrasted with that of the wise.

Text 10

उत्क्रामन्तं स्थितं वापि भुञ्जानं वा गुणान्वितम् ।
विमूढा नानुपश्यन्ति पश्यन्ति ज्ञानचक्षुषः ॥१०॥

utkrāmantaṁ sthitaṁ vāpi bhuñjānaṁ vā guṇānvitam/
vimūḍhā nānupaśyanti paśyanti jñāna-cakṣuṣaḥ//

utkrāmantam—departing; *sthitam*—situated; *vā api*—either; *bhuñjānam*—enjoying; *vā*—or; *guṇa-anvitam*—in association with the *guṇas*; *vimūḍhāḥ*—the deluded; *na*—not; *anupaśyanti*—they see; *paśyanti*—they see; *jñāna-cakṣuṣaḥ*—those who have the eyes of knowledge.

The deluded can neither see that the soul is transmigrating, nor understand the nature of its experience under the influence of the guṇas. The wise can see all of this with eyes of knowledge.

Text 11

यतन्तो योगिनश्चैनं पश्यन्त्यात्मन्यवस्थितम् ।
यतन्तोऽप्यकृतात्मानो नैनं पश्यन्त्यचेतसः ॥११॥

yatanto yoginaś cainaṁ paśyanty ātmany avasthitam/
yatanto 'py akṛtātmāno nainaṁ paśyanty acetasaḥ//

yatantaḥ—striving; *yoginaḥ*—*yogīs; ca*—also; *enam*—this; *paśyanti*—they see; *ātmani*—in the self; *avasthitam*—situated; *yatantaḥ*—trying; *api*—although; *akṛta-ātmānaḥ*—those lacking discrimination; *na*—not; *enam*—this; *paśyanti*—they see; *acetasaḥ*—the thoughtless.

Yogīs striving to see the soul situated within themselves can do so, but those lacking discrimination, whose minds are not pure, cannot, even though they try.

In verse 10 Kṛṣṇa explains that only those with eyes of knowledge can understand the position of the soul. In this verse he explains why this is so: their minds are pure. This is the implication of *jñāna-cakṣuḥ* (eyes of knowledge) mentioned in verse 10. The pure mind sees with eyes of knowledge.

Having described why the *jīva* associated with matter returns to the darkness of birth and death rather than enter his self-luminous abode, Kṛṣṇa speaks in the next four verses about his position as the Supreme Being to whom even Brahman is subordinate. Devotion to him enables the *jīva* to leave the world of birth and death (*saṁsāra*).

Text 12

यदादित्यगतं तेजो जगद्भासयतेऽखिलम् ।
यच्चन्द्रमसि यच्चाग्नौ तत्तेजो विद्धि मामकम् ॥१२॥

yad āditya-gataṁ tejo jagad bhāsayate 'khilam/
yac candramasi yac cāgnau tat tejo viddhi māmakam//

yat—which; *āditya-gatam*—proceeding from the sun; *tejaḥ*—splendor; *jagat*—world; *bhāsayate*—it illuminates; *akhilam*—entirely; *yat*—which; *candramasi*—in the moon; *yat*—which; *ca*—also; *agnau*—in fire; *tat*—that; *tejaḥ*—splendor; *viddhi*—know; *māmakam*—mine.

Know that I am the light in the sun, moon, and fire that illumines the world.

In verse 6 Kṛṣṇa says that his abode is self-luminous. Here he says further that the material world is not so. It is he who illumines it through the sun, moon, and fire. Neither he nor his abode are dependent on these material manifestations. They shed light on his nature if we think of them in the terms they are described here.

If we understand that the sun is illumined by God, we can understand something about the position of God by contemplating the sun. As he is the light in the sun, so also is he the light in the moon and fire, by which food is nourished and prepared, respectively. Through these material manifestations—sun, moon, and fire—the world is made livable.

Text 13

गामाविश्य च भूतानि धारयाम्यहमोजसा ।
पुष्णामि चौषधीः सर्वाः सोमो भूत्वा रसात्मकः ॥१३॥

gām āviśya ca bhūtāni dhārayāmy aham ojasā/
puṣṇāmi cauṣadhīḥ sarvāḥ somo bhūtvā rasātmakaḥ//

gām—the earth; *āviśya*—entering; *ca*—also; *bhūtāni*—the beings; *dhārayāmi*—I sustain; *aham*—I; *ojasā*—by energy; *puṣṇāmi*—I cause to flourish; *ca*—and; *auṣadhīḥ*—plants; *sarvāḥ*—all; *somaḥ*—moon; *bhūtvā*—becoming; *rasa-ātmakaḥ*—palatable.

I also enter the world through my power and sustain all beings. Becoming the moon, the source of flavor, I cause all plants to flourish.

Text 14

अहं वैश्वानरो भूत्वा प्राणिनां देहमाश्रितः ।
प्राणापानसमायुक्तः पचाम्यन्नं चतुर्विधम् ॥१४॥

ahaṁ vaiśvānaro bhūtvā prāṇināṁ deham āśritaḥ/
prāṇāpāna-samāyuktaḥ pacāmy annaṁ catur-vidham//

aham—I; *vaiśvānaraḥ*—digesting fire; *bhūtvā*—becoming; *prāṇinām*—of the beings; *deham*—body; *āśritaḥ*—situated; *prāṇa-apāna*—inhalation and exhalation; *samāyuktaḥ*—joined with; *pacāmi*—I digest; *annam*—food; *catuḥ-vidham*—of four kinds.

Becoming the fire of digestion, I reside in the bodies of all living entities; then, in conjunction with the life airs, both incoming and outgoing, I digest the four kinds of food.

Having spoken about his position from a macrocosmic *(samaṣṭi)* orientation in the previous two verses, Kṛṣṇa explains in this and the following verse how we are dependent on him from the microcosmic *(vyaṣṭi)* perspective as well. Not only is he the light in the sun by which we see, the moon by which plants are nourished and made succulent, and fire by which they are prepared, he is also present within every being as the digestive fire by which food is assimilated and its energy distributed throughout the body.

The fire in the stomach is increased by *prāṇa* and *apāna*, two of the five life airs located in the heart and intestines, respectively. The four kinds of food mentioned here are those that are chewed *(bhakṣya)*, such as bread, those drunk *(bhojya)*, such as soup, those licked *(lehya)*, such as honey, and those sucked *(coṣya)*, such as sugarcane.

Text 15

सर्वस्य चाहं हृदि सन्निविष्टो
मत्तः स्मृतिर्ज्ञानमपोहनं च ।
वेदैश्च सर्वैरहमेव वेद्यो
वेदान्तकृद् वेदविदेव चाहम् ॥१५॥

sarvasya cāhaṁ hṛdi sanniviṣṭo
mattaḥ smṛtir jñānam apohanaṁ ca/
vedaiś ca sarvair aham eva vedyo
vedānta-kṛd veda-vid eva cāham//

sarvasya—of all; *ca*—and; *aham*—I; *hṛdi*—in the heart; *sanniviṣṭaḥ*—situated; *mattaḥ*—from me; *smṛtiḥ*—remembrance; *jñānam*—knowledge; *apohanam*—forgetfulness; *ca*—and; *vedaiḥ*—by the Vedas; *ca*—also; *sarvaiḥ*—by all; *aham*—I; *eva*—certainly; *vedyaḥ*—knowable; *vedānta-kṛt*—the compiler of the Vedānta; *veda-vit*—the knower of the *Vedas*; *eva*—certainly; *ca*—and; *aham*—I.

I am seated in the hearts of all; from me come knowledge, remembrance, and forgetfulness. I alone am to be known by the Vedas. Indeed, I am the compiler of the Vedānta and the knower of the Vedas as well.

In verses 12 through 14, Kṛṣṇa explained how the living beings are physically dependent on him. In this verse, he explains that we are dependent on him for our intellectual life as well. He enters the heart of all beings, the vital center from which every human function proceeds and without which no activity can be performed. From this strategic position he provides the knowledge we need to proceed in any endeavor. He gives us remembrance of our *saṁskara* and thus prompts us to act accordingly. He also gives rise to the living beings' forgetfulness, which allows them to continue in ignorance in accordance with their desire.

In the second half of this verse Kṛṣṇa instructs Arjuna regarding his role in the lives of those concerned with liberation from material existence. He tells Arjuna that he is that which is to be known from the study of the *Vedas*, which ultimately teach about liberation and love of God. The *Vedas* exist for the purpose of guiding souls within the world so that they will ultimately come to realize their own nature and thus transcend material existence. Although the *Vedas* appear to deal with many subjects and the propitiation of many gods for many purposes, careful study of the Vedic texts in consideration of their underlying unity reveals that the *Vedas* posit one object of knowledge, Kṛṣṇa. Bhaktivedanta Swami Prabhupāda implies in his commentary that they do so in a threefold manner by giving knowledge of our relationship with God and matter *(sambandha-tattva)*, the means to disentangle ourselves from matter *(abhidheya-tattva)*, and the fruit of this in the form of love of God *(prayojana-tattva)*.

The first attempt to demonstrate the concordance of the *Upaniṣads*, the concluding portion of the *Vedas*, is the *Vedānta-sūtra*. Here Kṛṣṇa says that he in the form of Veda Vyāsa is the compiler of the *sūtras*. It is well known that the legendary Vyāsa, who is said to have compiled the *Vedas*, is an *avatāra* of Kṛṣṇa.

Although previously Kṛṣṇa said that one who knows the tree of material existence knows the *Vedas*, this knowing is dependent on Kṛṣṇa, and thus he is the only independent knower.

Hearing Kṛṣṇa assert his position as the knower of the *Vedas*, Arjuna wants to ask Kṛṣṇa about their import. He takes the natural and direct approach to understanding this complex body of *mantras* and texts, inquiring from one who understands it. In response to his friend's mental inquiry, Kṛṣṇa further stresses his supreme authority in the next three texts, shedding light on the nature of the *jīva* soul's relationship with him *(sambandha-tattva)*. Kṛṣṇa then discusses the Vedic means for attaining him *(abhidheya-tattva)* and the goal of the *Vedas (prayojana-tattva)* in the final two verses of this chapter.

Text 16

द्वाविमौ पुरुषौ लोके क्षरश्चाक्षर एव च ।
क्षरः सर्वाणि भूतानि कूटस्थोऽक्षर उच्यते ॥१६॥

dvāv imau puruṣau loke kṣaraś cākṣara eva ca/
kṣaraḥ sarvāṇi bhūtāni kūṭa-stho 'kṣara ucyate//

dvau—two; *imau*—these; *puruṣau*—*puruṣas*; *loke*—in the *Vedas; kṣaraḥ*—fallible; *ca*—and; *akṣaraḥ*—infallible; *eva*—certainly; *ca*—and; *kṣaraḥ*—fallible; *sarvāṇi*—all; *bhūtāni*—beings; *kūṭa-sthaḥ*—unchanging; *akṣaraḥ*—infallible; *ucyate*—it is said.

In the Vedas there are two types of puruṣas, the fallible and the infallible. The fallible are all beings; the unchanging is called infallible.

Baladeva Vidyābhūṣaṇa suggests an alternative meaning to the word *loke* in this verse. He says that it does not refer to the world, but rather to the *Vedas*. The *Vedas* are that by which we see the truth, and the word *loke* here is derived from the Sanskrit verbal root *lok* (to see). Thus, referring to the *Vedas* mentioned in the previous verse, Kṛṣṇa says, "Two types of *puruṣas* are discussed in the *Vedas*. One of these classes of *puruṣa* is fallible, the other is infallible." Viśvanātha Cakravartī renders *loke* as "the fourteen planetary systems," in which two types of *puruṣas* are famous.

The fallible or perishable *(kṣara) puruṣa* is the fallen soul deluded by material existence. This *puruṣa* is fallible because of its identification with the perishable material body. This sense of identity will not endure. According to Vaiṣṇava commentators other than Viśvanātha Cakravartī, the infallible *(akṣara) puruṣa* is the liberated soul, who has transcended material existence. This soul identifies with itself, imperishable consciousness, and is thus *kūṭastha*, unchanging. His position is fixed, unlike the fallible *puruṣa* whose position in identification with the material body is always changing. This understanding makes sense in the context of this chapter and in relation to the conclusion of the previous chapter, where the liberated and materially conditioned souls are contrasted.

Viśvanātha Cakravartī Ṭhākura understands the *akṣara* in this verse to be the Brahman feature of the Absolute. According to the Ṭhākura, Kṛṣṇa says, "Because I am the knower of the *Vedas*, I will give you (Arjuna) the essence of the *Vedas* in three verses. In this world there are two *puruṣas*. One is the *jīva* soul, whose position in relation to matter is perishable, the other is Brahman, who is known throughout the *Vedas* by the word *akṣara*, the imperishable."

Viśvanātha Cakravartī's interpretation is based on Kṛṣṇa's statement in chapter 8 (Bg. 8.3), where he identifies *akṣara* with Brahman. The *Chāndogya Upaniṣad* supports this as well. However, in this verse the word *akṣara* is an adjective that qualifies one of the two kinds of *puruṣas* mentioned. *Akṣara* is not the subject of the verse, *puruṣa* is. This *puruṣa* is further qualified as *kūṭastha* (unchanging). Thus, according to the Sanskrit grammar, the *akṣara puruṣa* is the *kūṭastha puruṣa*. Furthermore, Brahman is generally not identified with the *puruṣa* because *puruṣa* indicates personal consciousness, whereas Brahman does not. Through this interpretation, Viśvanātha Cakravartī wants to point out that the Paramātmā feature of Godhead discussed in verse 17 is a more complete manifestation of the Absolute than its Brahman feature. According to Viśvanātha Cakravartī, while the *akṣara puruṣa* mentioned in verse 16 is the Brahman feature of the Absolute, the Paramātmā discussed in verse 17 is a second *akṣara puruṣa*. Following this line of reasoning, Viśvanātha Cakravartī in his commentary on verse 18 brings out the superiority of the Bhagavān feature of the Absolute over Brahman and Paramātmā. However, in this commentary he acknowledges that his interpretation of the present verse is controversial. Those who will find it to be controversial are the Adwaitins. To them Viśvanātha Cakravartī politely offers his obeisances thus: *namo'stu kevala-vidbhyaḥ*. At the same time, he stands firm in his explanation. While his explanation is controversial, it is not incorrect to conclude that Brahman, Paramātmā, and Bhagavān are all *akṣara*. Furthermore, Brahman is a partial manifestation of the Supreme Person—his aura.

The fallible *puruṣa* mentioned in this verse is the class of souls that appear in the world as all living beings *(sarva-bhūtāni)*. The status of the souls in this class as *puruṣas* is perishable because when liberated these souls function as predominated aspects of reality. The word *puruṣa*, like *īśvara*, carries the sense of being the predominator, but *jīva* souls are predominators only in relation to matter. In their normal position in relation to God, the supreme *puruṣa*, they are predominated. Thus they are sometimes called *parā prakṛti* rather than *puruṣa*. This is how they were introduced in the *Gītā* in chapter 7 (Bg. 7.5).

Text 17

उत्तमः पुरुषस्त्वन्यः परमात्मेत्युदाहृतः ।
यो लोकत्रयमाविश्य बिभर्त्यव्यय ईश्वरः ॥१७॥

uttamaḥ puruṣas tv anyaḥ paramātmety udāhṛtaḥ/
yo loka-trayam āviśya bibharty avyaya īśvaraḥ//

uttamaḥ—the highest; *puruṣaḥ*—*puruṣa*; *tu*—but; *anyaḥ*—another; *parama*—supreme; *ātmā*—soul; *iti*—thus; *udāhṛtaḥ*—he is called; *yaḥ*—who; *loka*—world; *trayam*—three; *āviśya*—entering; *bibharti*—he supports; *avyayaḥ*—imperishable; *īśvaraḥ*—Lord.

However, there is another higher puruṣa called the Supreme Soul, who is the imperishable God that enters the world and supports it.

Here we find clarification of verses 12 through 15. He who maintains us is a personal being. Everything is ultimately directed by a conscious being. This is a refutation once again of Sāṅkhya and its non-Vedic counterpart, Jainism, which see only a multiplicity of *puruṣas*, some of whom are bound by nature and others that are liberated. Here Kṛṣṇa refers to the Paramātmā feature of the Absolute. This feature is a more complete expression of the Godhead than Brahman, for in this feature the personality of the Godhead is more manifest. As Paramātmā, God enters the world and supports it. He is different from the materially conditioned living beings and the liberated souls.

Viśvanātha Cakravartī Ṭhākura says that "a flame, a lamp, and a big fire are all luminous objects and in this sense nondifferent. However, a big fire is more effective in removing the miseries of those suffering from cold. Superior to a big fire is the sun itself (the source of all illumination). Similarly, Bhagavān Śrī Kṛṣṇa is the topmost Absolute reality." It could be said that Brahman is like a flame, Paramātmā a lamp, Bhagavān a big fire, and Puruṣottama Kṛṣṇa, who is the subject of the next verse, the sun itself.

Text 18

यस्मात्क्षरमतीतोऽहमक्षरादपि चोत्तमः ।
अतोऽस्मि लोके वेदे च प्रथितः पुरुषोत्तमः ॥१८॥

yasmāt kṣaram atīto 'ham akṣarād api cottamaḥ/
ato 'smi loke vede ca prathitaḥ puruṣottamaḥ//

yasmāt—since; *kṣaram*—fallible; *atītaḥ*—transcendental; *aham*—I; *akṣarāt*—than the infallible; *api*—also; *ca*—and; *uttamaḥ*—best; *ataḥ*—therefore; *asmi*—I; *loke*—in the world; *vede*—in the *Vedas; ca*—and; *prathitaḥ*—celebrated; *puruṣa-uttamaḥ*—as the Supreme Person.

Because I am transcendental to the fallible and am most excellent even when compared with the infallible, I am therefore celebrated in the world and the Vedas as the Supreme Person.

Kṛṣṇa is superior to both the illusioned and liberated soul. Furthermore, as Bhagavān himself he exhibits greater transcendental excellence than he does in his appearance as Paramātmā. Here he distinguishes himself from his Paramātmā feature, describing himself as Puruṣottama, the Supreme Person.

Kṛṣṇa has been explaining his position as the one who is to be known from study of the *Vedas*. Here he says that the position he ascribes to himself is declared with joy throughout the *Vedas*, as well as in the world by his blissful devotees.

Text 19

यो मामेवमसम्मूढो जानाति पुरुषोत्तमम् ।
स सर्वविद् भजति मां सर्वभावेन भारत ॥१९॥

yo mām evam asammūḍho jānāti puruṣottamam/
sa sarva-vid bhajati māṁ sarva-bhāvena bhārata//

yaḥ—who; *mām*—me; *evam*—thus; *asammūḍhaḥ*—undeluded; *jānāti*—he knows; *puruṣa-uttamam*—the Supreme Person; *saḥ*—he; *sarva-vit*—the knower of everything; *bhajati*—he worships; *mām*—me; *sarva-bhāvena*—with one's being; *bhārata*—O descendant of Bharata.

O descendant of Bharata, one who is undeluded knows me as the Supreme Person. He knows everything and thus worships me with his entire being.

That which follows a proper conceptual orientation to life *(sambandha-tattva)* is worship *(abhidheya-tattva)*. Proper knowledge leads to devotion. In verses 16 through 18, Kṛṣṇa gave Arjuna knowledge of the interrelation between matter, consciousness, and God. Material manifestations are ephemeral, and thus souls identifying with them are considered fallible. However, in reality the soul is superior to matter. Thus liberated souls who have transcended identification with matter are considered infallible. Both materially illusioned and liberated souls are subordinate to God. Furthermore, God has three features—Brahman, Paramātmā, and Bhagavān, in order of spiritual excellence. Those who know this are undeluded *(asammūḍhaḥ)*. They are not bewildered about who to worship among the many deities of the *Vedas* because they have understood the context in which these deities are mentioned and have thus realized the conclusion of the *Vedas* as to the ultimacy of *bhakti* and Bhagavān Śrī Kṛṣṇa.

Baladeva Vidyābhūṣaṇa comments that Kṛṣṇa says in this verse, "One who knows me as I have described myself in the previous three verses, as the Supreme Person, is all-knowing *(sarva-vit)*." Viśvanātha Cakravartī clearly explains that such souls are all-knowing in the sense that they know the actual meaning and *tattva* of all the scriptures. They are not omniscient in every respect. Baladeva Vidyābhūṣaṇa says further that those who do not know Kṛṣṇa in this way, even if they worship him, are not his devotees, and if they know everything else in the *Vedas* but do not understand this point they gain nothing.

Madhusūdana Saraswatī comments that the undeluded are those who know that Kṛṣṇa is not merely a human being. They know that he is the Supreme Person himself. Such undeluded persons are all-knowing *(sarva-vit)* because they know Kṛṣṇa, who is all-pervasive and thus all-knowing. Madhusūdana Saraswatī says that such persons adore Kṛṣṇa in every way through *bhakti*, which is characterized by love. Thus he sees this verse as a substantiation of the last two verses of the previous chapter. He concludes his commentary on this verse with the following advice: "O you who are conversant with good works, worship again and again the light which is by nature consciousness and bliss, which has the color of the rain cloud, which is the quintessence of the Vedic utterances, the necklace of the women of Vraja, the shore of the sea of the wise, and who repeatedly incarnates to remove the burden of the earth!" The fruit of this worship *(prayojana-tattva)* is the subject of the concluding verse of this chapter.

Text 20

इति गुह्यतमं शास्त्रमिदमुक्तं मयानघ ।
एतद् बुद्ध्वा बुद्धिमान् स्यात् कृतकृत्यश्च भारत ॥२०॥

iti guhyatamaṁ śāstram idam uktaṁ mayānagha/
etad buddhvā buddhimān syāt kṛta-kṛtyaś ca bhārata//

iti—thus; *guhyatamam*—most secret; *śāstram*—scripture; *idam*—this; *uktam*—explained; *mayā*—by me; *anagha*—O sinless one; *etat*—this; *buddhvā*—understanding; *buddhi-mān*—wise; *syāt*—one should be; *kṛta-kṛtyaḥ*—fulfilled all duties; *ca*—and; *bhārata*—O son of Bharata.

Thus I have taught you this most secret doctrine of the scripture, O sinless one. Understanding this, a person becomes wise and his actions know perfection.

One who understands the confidential doctrine of the Supreme Person detailed in this chapter becomes enlightened, and thus his actions in devotion bear the fruit of perfection in love of God *(prayojana-tattva)*. Such persons have no duty to perform. They have fulfilled all obligations. Kṛṣṇa implies here that short of this, something remains to be accomplished for anyone on any other path.

Thus in the concluding five verses of this chapter, Kṛṣṇa has discussed the three principal subjects of the *Vedas*: *sambandha*, *abhidheya*, and *prayojana*. He does this in the course of explaining how he is that which is to be known in the *Vedas* and the fact that he alone knows the *Vedas*, both of which he asserted in text 15.

In this verse Kṛṣṇa tells Arjuna that the knowledge and *yoga* of the Supreme Person is not for everyone. It is confidential, and only pure *(anagha)* persons can know its mystery. Such sinless persons can cut down the ephemeral *aśvattha* tree of this world with the ax of detachment and subsequent discrimination and thus become fit for devotion proper by which they can enter Kṛṣṇa's abode.

The great Adwaitin, Madhusūdana Saraswatī, concludes his commentary on this chapter with the following remark: "I do not know any other reality than Kṛṣṇa, whose hands are adorned with a flute, whose luster is like that of a new rain cloud, who wears a yellow cloth, whose lips are reddish like the bimba fruit, whose face is beautiful like the full moon, and whose eyes are like lotuses. . . . Those fools who cannot tolerate the wonderful glory of Kṛṣṇa go to hell."

CHAPTER SIXTEEN

दैवासुरसम्पद्योगः

Daivāsura-Sampada-yoga

YOGA OF DISCERNING GODLY AND UNGODLY NATURES

Texts 1–3

श्रीभगवानुवाच
अभयं सत्त्वसंशुद्धिर्ज्ञानयोगव्यवस्थितिः ।
दानं दमश्च यज्ञश्च स्वाध्यायस्तप आर्जवम् ॥१॥
अहिंसा सत्यमक्रोधस्त्यागः शान्तिरपैशुनम् ।
दया भूतेष्वलोलुप्त्वं मार्दवं ह्रीरचापलम् ॥२॥
तेजः क्षमा धृतिः शौचमद्रोहो नातिमानिता ।
भवन्ति सम्पदं दैवीमभिजातस्य भारत ॥३॥

śrī-bhagavān uvāca
abhayaṁ sattva-saṁśuddhir jñāna-yoga-vyavasthitiḥ/
dānaṁ damaś ca yajñaś ca svādhyāyas tapa ārjavam//
ahiṁsā satyam akrodhas tyāgaḥ śāntir apaiśunam/
dayā bhūteṣv aloluptvaṁ mārdavaṁ hrīr acāpalam//
tejaḥ kṣamā dhṛtiḥ śaucam adroho nāti-mānitā/
bhavanti sampadaṁ daivīm abhijātasya bhārata//

śrī-bhagavān uvāca—the Lord of Śrī said; *abhayam*—fearlessness; *sattva-saṁśuddhiḥ*—purity of heart; *jñāna*—knowledge; *yoga*—*yoga*; *vyava-sthitiḥ*—consistency; *dānam*—charity; *damaḥ*—sense control; *ca*—and; *yajñaḥ*—sacrifice; *ca*—and; *svādhyāyaḥ*—study of scripture; *tapaḥ*—austerity; *ārjavam*—righteousness; *ahiṁsā*—nonviolence; *satyam*—truthfulness; *akrodhaḥ*—absence of anger; *tyāgaḥ*—renunciation; *śāntiḥ*—peacefulness; *apaiśunam*—aversion to criticizing; *dayā*—compassion; *bhūteṣu*—toward beings; *aloluptvam*—freedom from covetousness; *mārdavam*—gentleness; *hrīḥ*—modesty; *acāpalam*—freedom from restlessness; *tejaḥ*—courage; *kṣamā*—forgiveness; *dhṛtiḥ*—fortitude; *śaucam*—cleanliness; *adrohaḥ*—freedom from malice; *na*—not; *ati-mānitā*—excessive pride; *bhavanti*—they are;

sampadam—endowment; *daivīm*—divine; *abhijātasya*—of one who is born; *bhārata*—O descendant of Bharata.

The Lord of Śrī said: Fearlessness, purity of heart, consistency in knowledge and yoga, charity, sense control, sacrifice, study of the scripture, austerity, righteousness, nonviolence, truthfulness, absence of anger, renunciation, peacefulness, aversion to criticizing others, compassion, freedom from covetousness, gentleness, modesty, steadiness, courage, forgiveness, fortitude, cleanliness, freedom from malice, and pridelessness—those born of divine nature are endowed with these, O descendant of Bharata.

In the previous chapter Kṛṣṇa described the Supreme Person, knowing whom one becomes truly wise such that one's actions know perfection. In this chapter he describes who is qualified to tread the path of perfection and who is not, the godly and ungodly natures. First one must ascertain the weight of an object, and only then can one decide who can lift it. Śrīdhara Swāmī, citing Kumarila Bhaṭṭa, sees this as the relationship between chapters 15 and 16.[1]

Chapters 16 through 18 involve a shift in focus from the previous three chapters. While chapters 13, 14, and 15 deal with the metaphysics of the *Gītā* in depth, the final three chapters focus more on the practical tenets of the text. From the metaphysics of the Supreme Person in the previous chapter, we shift in the present chapter to a discussion of socioreligious structure, scriptural adherence, and morality (good versus evil).

In the last five verses of the previous chapter, Kṛṣṇa explains precisely how he is that which is to be known from the study of the *Vedas*. In this chapter he explains how those eligible to know him must live in accordance with the *Vedas*. They are of a godly nature. Those who are ungodly are those who do not live their lives in this way. The underlying purpose of this discussion is to stress that the entire teaching of the *Gītā* is reinforced by the scriptural canon.

This chapter begins with a list of the virtues that qualify one to pursue the godly path. As we shall see, this description implies that the godly have abiding faith in scripture, and thus the qualities Kṛṣṇa mentions here have been explained by both Baladeva Vidyābhūṣaṇa and Madhusūdana

1. Kumarila Bhaṭṭa is a famous Mīmāṁsaka.

Saraswatī in relation to *varṇāśrama-dharma*. This scripturally enjoined socioreligious structure consisting of four social and four religious orders has been mentioned earlier in chapter 4 (Bg. 4.13).

The first two lines of verse 1 describe the qualities of the renunciates (*sannyāsīs*). They extend fearlessness to all living beings by their own example, because they are not fearful as to where they will get their next meal or under which roof they will sleep at night. They know that God is maintaining them. Their minds are pure (*sattva-saṁśuddhiḥ*). This purity results from knowledge and constant *yoga* practice (*jñāna-yoga-vyavasthitiḥ*). Madhusūdana Saraswatī comments that since perfect purity is not possible without devotion to God, which is by far the best means, *bhakti* is implied in this verse. Indeed, he says that the godly nature itself is synonymous with devotion to God. Madhusūdana Saraswatī supports his insight with a reference to the thirteenth verse of chapter 9, where Kṛṣṇa describes those of divine nature thus: "Those great souls who take refuge in the divine nature worship me with undeviated minds, knowing me to be the origin of all beings and imperishable."

The second half of the first verse describes the godliness of the other religious orders of life: the householders (*gṛhasthas*), celibate students (*brahmacārīs*), and persons retired from family obligations (*vānaprasthas*). Householders should give in charity (*dānam*), for in the ideal society they alone have money and are thus expected to support others who are directly engaged in spiritual culture without the distractions of family life. The householders should also practice control of their senses (*damaḥ*), especially the regulation of sex desire, which the other sectors abstain from. Their lives should involve sacrifice (*yajñaḥ*) and religious ritual such that their worldly orientation is brought in touch with spiritual pursuit. Celibate students should be engaged in study of the scriptures (*svādhyāya*). Śrīdhara Swāmī comments that this also refers to chanting God's name. Austerity (*tapaḥ*) is for those who are retired and are preparing to leave the world.

Following the description of the godly nature and activities of the four religious orders of society, Kṛṣṇa describes the godly nature of the four social/occupational divisions of society: the priests (*brāhmaṇas*), the warriors/administrators (*kṣatriyas*), the farmers/merchants (*vaiśyas*), and the laborers (*śūdras*). The qualities beginning with righteousness (*ārjavam*) and ending with absence of restlessness (*acāpalam*) belong to the godly nature of the priests. They must have these qualities. The warriors of godly nature exhibit courage and the other qualities up to and including fortitude (*dhṛtiḥ*).

The godliness of the merchants involves freedom from malice, and for the laborers absence of pride.

Viśvanātha Cakravartī Ṭhākura considers this list of twenty-six godly qualities to indicate a sattvic disposition. He understands these godly qualities and the ungodly qualities described next to be the previously unmentioned fruits of the *aśvattha* tree of material existence that introduced chapter 15.

Text 4

दम्भो दर्पोऽभिमानश्च क्रोधः पारुष्यमेव च ।
अज्ञानं चाभिजातस्य पार्थ सम्पदमासुरीम् ॥४॥

dambho darpo 'bhimānaś ca krodhaḥ pāruṣyam eva ca/
ajñānaṁ cābhijātasya pārtha sampadam āsurīm//

dambhaḥ—hypocrisy; *darpaḥ*—arrogance; *abhimānaḥ*—conceit; *ca*—and; *krodhaḥ*—anger; *pāruṣyam*—harshness; *eva*—certainly; *ca*—and; *ajñānam*—ignorance; *ca*—and; *abhijātasya*—of one who is born; *pārtha*—O son of Pṛthā; *sampadam*—endowment; *āsurīm*—ungodly.

Hypocrisy, arrogance, conceit, anger, harsh speech, and ignorance are the qualities of those born of ungodly natures.

Ancient sages who spoke Sanskrit often used invented etymologies as didactic tools and mnemonic devices. While these etymologies are not the actual sources of a particular word's formation, they are often instructive. An example of this practice is the idea that the word *asura* in this verse is derived from two the words, *asu* and *ramate*. *Asu* means life breath and *ramate* means to enjoy. To enjoy one's life breath, one's body, at the cost of spiritual emancipation is thus the preoccupation of an *asura*.

One's nature, godly or ungodly, is a product of one's *karma*. This is what is implied by the word *abhijāta* (born of).

Text 5

दैवी सम्पद् विमोक्षाय निबन्धायासुरी मता ।
मा शुचः सम्पदं दैवीमभिजातोऽसि पाण्डव ॥५॥

daivī sampad vimokṣāya nibandhāyāsurī matā/
mā śucaḥ sampadaṁ daivīm abhijāto 'si pāṇḍava//

daivī—divine; *sampat*—quality; *vimokṣāya*—meant for liberation; *nibandhāya*—for bondage; *āsurī*—ungodly; *matā*—considered; *mā*—never; *śucaḥ*—

you lament; *sampadam*—nature; *daivīm*—divine; *abhijātaḥ*—born; *asi*—you are; *pāṇḍava*—O son of Pāṇḍu.

The divine nature is considered to lead to liberation, the ungodly nature to bondage. Do not lament, O son of Pāṇḍu! You are born of the divine nature.

According to scripture the divine nature leads to liberation. The ungodly nature leads to bondage. The word *matā* (is considered) in this verse refers to the *Vedas*. The *Vedas* opine that the activities prescribed for the different religious and social sectors of society bear the fruit of liberation when they are performed in a spirit of duty and scriptural adherence without attachment to the results. As one moves through the religious stages of life arriving at *sannyāsa*, the qualities of fearlessness, constant practice of *yoga*, and the culture of knowledge and devotion lead one to liberation.

After describing the qualities of the ungodly to Arjuna, Kṛṣṇa assures his disciple that he should not worry *(mā śucaḥ)*, for his nature is not ungodly. With these two words Kṛṣṇa sums up the *Gītā*'s entire message, *mā śucaḥ*: "don't worry." The spirit of this expression is that we should depend on Kṛṣṇa and not on our own strength, be it physical, mental, or intellectual. This is underscored in Kṛṣṇa's concluding words to Arjuna, *sarva-dharmān parityajya*: "give up all separate endeavor," and *mokṣayiṣyāmi mā śucaḥ*, "depend on me, do not worry." (Bg. 18.66) To depend on one's own strength without acknowledging that it comes from God is ungodly.

Here Arjuna is concerned that he is of the ungodly nature. This is the spirit of the devotees. They do not think that they are godly. First Kṛṣṇa described the divine qualities to Arjuna. After hearing the demoniac qualities, such as arrogance, anger, and harshness, Arjuna naturally assumed that he was ungodly, for these are qualities that warriors often exhibit in battle. Kṛṣṇa's assuring Arjuna otherwise is significant. It informs us that one may exhibit such qualities and not be ungodly. The converse is equally applicable. Outward displays of humility, self-control, sacrifice, modesty, cleanliness, study of the *Vedas*, austerity, renunciation, and the host of other divine qualities may be outer expressions of an inner ungodly spirit. Thus Kṛṣṇa implies that we must look beneath the surface in determining who is godly and who is ungodly. In his commentary on the previous verse, Viśvanātha Cakravartī Ṭhākura says that hypocrites *(dambhaḥ)* are those who present themselves as being religious while actually being irreligious.

The qualities that Arjuna is concerned with are appropriate for a warrior doing battle. That which is righteous is to some extent relative to the performer, time, and circumstance of any action. Had Arjuna been known for exhibiting arrogance, conceit, and speaking harshly off the battlefield, then this would have been indicative of an ungodly nature. However, he was a perfect gentleman off the battlefield. Indeed, he exhibited this in his reluctance to fight. Bhaktivedanta Swami Prabhupāda comments that Arjuna sincerely considered the pros and cons of the war and was thus not acting out of anger or arrogance in contemplating the battle.

Kṛṣṇa next elaborates on the ungodly nature to further allay Arjuna's apprehension about himself. Thus he addresses Arjuna by referring to his saintly mother.

Text 6

द्वौ भूतसर्गौ लोकेऽस्मिन् दैव आसुर एव च ।
दैवो विस्तरशः प्रोक्त आसुरं पार्थ मे शृणु ॥६॥

dvau bhūta-sargau loke 'smin daiva āsura eva ca/
daivo vistaraśaḥ prokta āsuraṁ pārtha me śṛṇu//

dvau—two; *bhūta-sargau*—created beings; *loke*—in the world; *asmin*—this; *daivaḥ*—godly; *āsuraḥ*—ungodly; *eva*—certainly; *ca*—and; *daivaḥ*—godly; *vistaraśaḥ*—at length; *proktaḥ*—said; *āsuram*—ungodly; *pārtha*—O son of Pṛthā; *me*—from me; *śṛṇu*—listen.

In this world there are two types of created beings, the godly and the ungodly. Thus far I have discussed the godly at length. Now, O son of Pṛthā, hear from me about the ungodly.

Kṛṣṇa has discussed the qualities of the divine nature in earlier chapters. In chapter 2 he discusses those of steady intelligence (Bg. 2.55–71). In chapter 12 he describes qualities of devotees (Bg. 12.13–20). In chapter 13 he describes the qualities of those in knowledge (Bg. 13.8–12), and in chapter 14 he describes the godly qualities of those who have transcended the *guṇas* (Bg. 14.22–26). Other than a brief reference to the ungodly nature in chapter 9 (Bg. 9.12) and the first three verses of this chapter, Kṛṣṇa has not elaborated on it. He will do so for the bulk of this chapter, starting with this verse and continuing for the next twelve verses.

Here the words *loke 'smin* refer to the earth, where we find both of these natures, not to heaven or hell where the godly and ungodly reside, respectively. Although previously in chapter 9 Kṛṣṇa mentioned two divisions of the ungodly *(rākṣasīm* and *āsurīm)*, here he merges them into one category. The ungodly are those dominated by *rajo-guṇa* and *tamo-guṇa*, whereas the godly are influenced by *sattva*.

In this verse Kṛṣṇa tells Arjuna to hear from him about the ungodly nature so that he can avoid it. An elaboration on the disposition of the ungodly is essential. When one's knowledge of this disposition is complete, only then can one fully reject it. Although this verse says that the godly and ungodly natures are found in two types of created beings *(dvau bhūta-sargau)*, this does not imply that one has no choice in the matter of being godly or ungodly. Creation refers to our material birth, which is a product of our previous actions. While this predisposes us toward a godly or ungodly nature, it does not do away with our free will.

The doctrine of *karma* is not one of absolute determinism. It is not merely effect, but cause as well. The just, stern, moral law of *karma* rewards us with the fruits of the seeds we sow. Our past *karma* determines the bodily field of our present life. We in turn are obliged to make what we can of this life and in this way determine our future. While suffering may be the effect of our past life, how we react to that past—what we do about it—in this life is our privilege, our freedom to create our future. In this chapter Kṛṣṇa emphasizes choosing to change any ungodliness in our nature to godliness.

Text 7

प्रवृत्तिं च निवृत्तिं च जना न विदुरासुराः ।
न शौचं नापि चाचारो न सत्यं तेषु विद्यते ॥७॥

pravṛttiṁ ca nivṛttiṁ ca janā na vidur āsurāḥ/
na śaucaṁ nāpi cācāro na satyaṁ teṣu vidyate//

pravṛttim—action; *ca*—also; *nivṛttim*—inaction; *ca*—and; *janāḥ*—persons; *na*—not; *viduḥ*—they know; *āsurāḥ*—the ungodly; *na*—not; *śaucam*—cleanliness; *na*—not; *api*—also; *ca*—and; *ācāraḥ*—behavior; *na*—not; *satyam*—truth; *teṣu*—in them; *vidyate*—there is.

The ungodly do not know when to act and when to refrain from action. Neither cleanliness, good behavior, nor truth is found in them.

The ungodly do not know what religion is and what irreligion is. They do not know what to do and what not to do because they do not follow scriptural directives for human society. To be truthful is to be concerned about the truth of the self. The ungodly are concerned only with their bodily demands.

At this point Arjuna wonders how one can be ignorant with regard to what is to be done and what is not to be done, when the scripture makes this abundantly clear and is well known for being of divine origin. In response Kṛṣṇa reveals further the thoughts of the ungodly with regard to scripture and God.

Text 8

असत्यमप्रतिष्ठं ते जगदाहुरनीश्वरम् ।
अपरस्परसम्भूतं किमन्यत्कामहैतुकम् ॥८॥

asatyam apratiṣṭhaṁ te jagad āhur anīśvaram/
aparaspara-sambhūtaṁ kim anyat kāma-haitukam//

asatyam—unreal; *apratiṣṭham*—without basis; *te*—they; *jagat*—world; *āhuḥ*—they say; *anīśvaram*—without a God; *aparaspara*—without cause (other than mutual union); *sambhūtam*—arisen; *kim anyat*—what else; *kāma-haitukam*—caused by sense desire.

They describe the world as being without truth, without a basis, without a God, brought about by mutual union—nothing more—caused by desire for sense gratification.

The ungodly do not acknowledge the scriptural canon to be truth. They attribute its authorship to ordinary persons. Thus they often conclude that the world has no moral basis and that there is no God who gives directives to human society or creates the world. They think that the world is spontaneously generated without any ultimate controller, and if anything, the cause of its manifestation is the union between the sexes that is a manifestation of sense desire.

Here the truth *(satyam)*, basis *(pratiṣṭhā)*, and God himself *(īśvara)* that the ungodly do not acknowledge can be thought of in terms of the three levels of divine involvement in the world—Brahman, Paramātmā, and Bhagavān. Brahman is the truth *(sat)* of the world with which we are identified as units of consciousness. Paramātmā is the basis of the world, from whom the world expands and by whom it is pervaded. Bhagavān is God himself, who appears in the world to enact his *līlā* and grace his creation. We are accustomed to hearing the argument that the religious do not accept the reality of the material world and thus manufacture another so-called spiritual one. Here Kṛṣṇa argues that unless one recognizes the different levels of divine involvement in the world—Brahman, Paramātmā, and Bhagavān—one does not live in the real world and is thus unaware of its deeper meaning and value.

Rāmānujācārya comments that the words *aparaspara-sambhūtam* in this verse can be understood to mean that the ungodly do not accept the fact that the world is a result of the combination of matter and consciousness *(prakṛti* and *puruṣa)* and erroneously conclude that it is a product of nothing other than the desire to satisfy one's senses *(kim anyat kāma-haitukam)*. This point of view of the ungodly should be rejected by those desirous of godly life, as Kṛṣṇa implies in the following verse.

Text 9

एतां दृष्टिमवष्टभ्य नष्टात्मानोऽल्पबुद्धयः ।
प्रभवन्त्युग्रकर्माणः क्षयाय जगतोऽहिताः ॥९॥

etāṁ dṛṣṭim avaṣṭabhya naṣṭātmāno 'lpa-buddhayaḥ/
prabhavanty ugra-karmāṇaḥ kṣayāya jagato 'hitāḥ//

etām—this; *dṛṣṭim*—view; *avaṣṭabhya*—holding; *naṣṭa*—lost; *ātmānaḥ*—souls; *alpa-buddhayaḥ*—of meager intelligence; *prabhavanti*—they come forth; *ugra-karmāṇaḥ*—engaged in horrible acts; *kṣayāya*—for destruction; *jagataḥ*—of the world; *ahitāḥ*—enemies.

Holding this view, these lost souls of meager intelligence and cruel actions come forth as enemies of the world engaging in destructive acts.

Baladeva Vidyābhūṣaṇa comments that "destruction of the world" *(kṣayāya jagataḥ)* means that which "leads people away from the spiritual purpose of life."

While it may be true that in today's world those who do not believe in God are sometimes nonviolent, peaceful, clean, and champions of moral life in general, this does not stand in contradiction to this section of the *Gītā*. Here Krsna is speaking of those who are almost entirely dominated by *rajo-guṇa* and *tamo-guṇa*, with very little influence of *sattva-guṇa*. These persons do not have a developed sense of morality and are thus considered immoral by most standards. Yet it is the influence of *sattva*, however slight, to which the honesty among thieves is indebted.

The extent to which a person is influenced by *sattva* determines his sense of the need for a moral life, even when that moral imperative is motivated by worldly desires. The influence of *sattva* may not be dominant enough to shed light on the reality of God, but it will nonetheless exert itself, resulting in a semblance of godly behavior. Thus humanistic morality is itself a product of *sattva*, whereas the humanist's endeavor for material progress and atheism are products of *rajo-guṇa* and *tamo-guṇa*.

Text 10

काममाश्रित्य दुष्पूरं दम्भमानमदान्विताः ।
मोहाद् गृहीत्वासद्ग्राहान् प्रवर्तन्तेऽशुचिव्रताः ॥१०॥

kāmam āśritya duṣpūraṁ dambha-māna-madānvitāḥ/
mohād gṛhītvāsad-grāhān pravartante 'śuci-vratāḥ//

kāmam—desire; *āśritya*—attached to; *duṣpūram*—insatiable; *dambha*—hypocrisy; *māna*—arrogance; *mada-anvitāḥ*—absorbed in; *mohāt*—by illusion; *gṛhītvā*—embracing; *asat*—false; *grāhān*—ideas; *pravartante*—they act; *aśuci*—unclean; *vratāḥ*—vows.

Attached to insatiable desires, vain, arrogant, proud, and embracing false ideas due to lack of discrimination, they adopt impure vows and act accordingly.

Baladeva Vidyābhūṣaṇa understands impure vows *(aśuci-vratāḥ)* to refer to the "left-handed" tantric practices, all of which involve impure practices, often including liquor, flesh, and sex. His understanding is an elaboration on Śrīdhara Swāmī's comments *(madya-maṁsādīni viṣayīṇi)*.

Texts 11–12

चिन्तामपरिमेयां च प्रलयान्तामुपाश्रिताः ।
कामोपभोगपरमा एतावदिति निश्चिताः ॥११॥
आशापाशशतैर्बद्धाः कामक्रोधपरायणाः ।
ईहन्ते कामभोगार्थमन्यायेनार्थसञ्चयान् ॥१२॥

cintām aparimeyāṁ ca pralayāntām upāśritāḥ/
kāmopabhoga-paramā etāvad iti niścitāḥ//

āśā-pāśa-śatair baddhāḥ kāma-krodha-parāyaṇāḥ/
īhante kāma-bhogārtham anyāyenārtha-sañcayān//

cintām—anxiety; *aparimeyām*—immeasurable; *ca*—and; *pralaya-antām*—ending in death; *upāśritāḥ*—beset; *kāma-upabhoga-paramāḥ*—having the gratification of their desires as the highest goal of life; *etāvat*—so much; *iti*—thus; *niścitāḥ*—convinced; *āśā-pāśa*—network of hopes; *śataiḥ*—by hundreds; *baddhāḥ*—bound; *kāma*—lust; *krodha*—anger; *parāyaṇāḥ*—absorbed; *īhante*—they desire; *kāma-bhoga-artham*—for the fulfillment of desires; *anyāyena*—illegally; *artha*—wealth; *sañcayān*—hoards.

Beset with worry beyond measure that ends only with death, engrossed in gratifying their desires, seeing this as the ultimate goal of life, convinced that this is all in all, bound by a network of hundreds of hopes, absorbed in lust and anger, they try to secure money by illegal means for the fulfillment of their desires.

Texts 13–15

इदमद्य मया लब्धमिमं प्राप्स्ये मनोरथम् ।
इदमस्तीदमपि मे भविष्यति पुनर्धनम् ॥१३॥
असौ मया हतः शत्रुर्हनिष्ये चापरानपि ।
ईश्वरोऽहमहं भोगी सिद्धोऽहं बलवान् सुखी ॥१४॥
आढ्योऽभिजनवानस्मि कोऽन्योऽस्ति सदृशो मया ।
यक्ष्ये दास्यामि मोदिष्य इत्यज्ञानविमोहिताः ॥१५॥

idam adya mayā labdham imaṁ prāpsye manoratham/
idam astīdam api me bhaviṣyati punar dhanam//
asau mayā hataḥ śatrur haniṣye cāparān api/
īśvaro 'ham ahaṁ bhogī siddho 'haṁ balavān sukhī//
āḍhyo 'bhijanavān asmi ko 'nyo 'sti sadṛśo mayā/
yakṣye dāsyāmi modiṣya ity ajñāna-vimohitāḥ//

idam—this; *adya*—today; *mayā*—by me; *labdham*—gained; *imam*—this; *prāpsye*—I shall gain; *manaḥ-ratham*—desire; *idam*—this; *asti*—there is; *idam*—this; *api*—also; *me*—mine; *bhaviṣyati*—it will increase; *punaḥ*—again; *dhanam*—wealth; *asau*—that; *mayā*—by me; *hataḥ*—slain; *śatruḥ*—enemy; *haniṣye*—I shall slay; *ca*—also; *aparān*—others; *api*—certainly; *īśvaraḥ*—lord; *aham*—I; *aham*—I; *bhogī*—enjoyer; *siddhaḥ*—successful; *aham*—I; *balavān*—powerful; *sukhī*—happy; *āḍhyaḥ*—wealthy; *abhijana-vān*—aristocratic;

asmi—I am; *kaḥ*—who; *anyaḥ*—other; *asti*—there is; *sadṛśaḥ*—like; *mayā*—(by) me; *yakṣye*—I shall sacrifice; *dāsyāmi*—I shall give charity; *modiṣye*—I shall rejoice; *iti*—thus; *ajñāna*—ignorance; *vimohitāḥ*—deluded.

They think, "I have gained this today. This desire I shall attain fulfillment of next. This is mine, and it will increase in the future. That enemy has been slain by me, and I shall slay others as well. I am the lord. I am the enjoyer. I am successful, powerful, and happy. I am wealthy and of high birth. Who is equal to me? I shall sacrifice, give charity, and rejoice." Thus they are deluded by ignorance.

Text 16

अनेकचित्तविभ्रान्ता मोहजालसमावृताः ।
प्रसक्ताः कामभोगेषु पतन्ति नरकेऽशुचौ ॥१६॥

aneka-citta-vibhrāntā moha-jāla-samāvṛtāḥ/
prasaktāḥ kāma-bhogeṣu patanti narake 'śucau//

aneka—many; *citta*—thought; *vibhrāntāḥ*—bewildered; *moha*—delusion; *jāla*—network; *samāvṛtāḥ*—enveloped; *prasaktāḥ*—attached; *kāma-bhogeṣu*—to sense gratification; *patanti*—they fall; *narake*—into hell; *aśucau*—impure.

Bewildered by many thoughts as a result of being caught in a network of delusion and engrossed in enjoying objects they desire, they fall into an impure hell.

Text 17

आत्मसम्भाविताः स्तब्धा धनमानमदान्विताः ।
यजन्ते नामयज्ञैस्ते दम्भेनाविधिपूर्वकम् ॥१७॥

ātma-sambhāvitāḥ stabdhā dhana-māna-madānvitāḥ/
yajante nāma-yajñais te dambhenāvidhi-pūrvakam//

ātma-sambhāvitāḥ—self-conceited; *stabdhāḥ*—stubborn; *dhana-māna-mada-anvitāḥ*—accompanied by the pride and arrogance of wealth; *yajante*—they perform sacrifice; *nāma*—in name; *yajñaiḥ*—with sacrifices; *te*—they; *dambhena*—hypocritically; *avidhi-pūrvakam*—without following the injunctions.

Self-conceited, stubborn, full of pride and the intoxication of wealth, they hypocritically perform sacrifices in name only that are not in accordance with Vedic injunctions.

Text 18

अहंकारं बलं दर्पं कामं क्रोधं च संश्रिताः ।
मामात्मपरदेहेषु प्रद्विषन्तोऽभ्यसूयकाः ॥१८॥

ahaṅkāraṁ balaṁ darpaṁ kāmaṁ krodhaṁ ca saṁśritāḥ/
mām ātma-para-deheṣu pradviṣanto 'bhyasūyakāḥ//

ahaṅkāram—egotism; *balam*—power; *darpam*—arrogance; *kāmam*—lust; *krodham*—anger; *ca*—also; *saṁśritāḥ*—resorting to; *mām*—me; *ātma*—own; *para*—other; *deheṣu*—in bodies; *pradviṣantaḥ*—hating; *abhyasūyakāḥ*—envious.

Resorting to egotism, power, arrogance, lust, and anger, such envious people hate me who am situated in their own bodies and the bodies of others.

What Kṛṣṇa means here when he says that the ungodly "hate me who am situated in their own bodies and the bodies of others" has been explained differently by commentators. Baladeva Vidyābhūṣaṇa says such persons hate God and the scripture that glorifies him. Viśvanātha Cakravartī says *ātma-para* refers to "devotees of the Paramātmā," indicating that the ungodly vilify the saintly devotees. Madhusūdana Saraswatī offers three possible explanations for what Kṛṣṇa means here, the most interesting of which is "They hate me... on account of mistaking me for a human being." He says the ungodly "hate Kṛṣṇa's own body *(ātma-deha)* which is not a body in which a *jīva* soul resides, but is a body created through divine play and called Vāsudeva, etc." He supports his interpretation by citing Kṛṣṇa's words elsewhere in the *Gītā* (Bg. 7.24, 9.10–11). He also explains *para-deheṣu pradviṣanto 'bhyasūyakāḥ* (the envious who hate me in the bodies of others) as hating the bodies of devotees like Prahlāda where God is always present.

Text 19

तानहं द्विषतः क्रूरान् संसारेषु नराधमान् ।
क्षिपाम्यजस्रमशुभानासुरीष्वेव योनिषु ॥१९॥

tān ahaṁ dviṣataḥ krūrān saṁsāreṣu narādhamān/
kṣipāmy ajasram aśubhān āsurīṣv eva yoniṣu//

tān—those; *aham*—I; *dviṣataḥ*—envious; *krūrān*—cruel; *saṁsāreṣu*—in the cycle of rebirth; *nara-adhamān*—the lowest of humanity; *kṣipāmi*—I cast; *ajasram*—repeatedly; *aśubhān*—inauspicious; *āsurīṣu*—ungodly; *eva*—certainly; *yoniṣu*—into the wombs.

I repeatedly cast those who are envious and cruel into the wombs of the ungodly life after life, for they are the worst of humanity.

Text 20

आसुरीं योनिमापन्ना मूढा जन्मनि जन्मनि ।
मामप्राप्यैव कौन्तेय ततो यान्त्यधमां गतिम् ॥२०॥

āsurīṁ yonim āpannā mūḍhā janmani janmani/
mām aprāpyaiva kaunteya tato yānty adhamāṁ gatim//

āsurīm—ungodly; *yonim*—womb; *āpannāḥ*—gaining; *mūḍhāḥ*—the deluded; *janmani janmani*—birth after birth; *mām*—me; *aprāpya*—not attaining; *eva*—certainly; *kaunteya*—O son of Kuntī; *tataḥ*—thereafter; *yānti*—they go; *adhamām*—lowest; *gatim*—destination.

Having entered the wombs of the ungodly, the deluded, not attaining me birth after birth, O son of Kuntī, go from there to the lowest destination.

Hearing of the fate of the demoniac, Arjuna considers that certainly on hearing this the ungodly will change their ways. This choice is possible with the help of good association. However, the ungodly do not care for the association of the godly, and they usually have no fear of God. Fear is the lowest level of motivation for serving him. Being devoid of this, there is little hope for them. Here Kṛṣṇa's strong words are an attempt to save human society from treading the ungodly course.

Viśvanātha Cakravartī says that Kṛṣṇa's words *mām aprāpyaiva* (not attaining me) imply that until the ungodly attain his association there is no salvation for them. It is possible to attain his association during the time of his earthly advent. This means that the appearance of Kṛṣṇa, as opposed to any of his *avatāras*, is particularly auspicious. In *Kṛṣṇa-sandarbha*, Jīva Goswāmī demonstrates from scripture that only those ungodly souls who are killed by Kṛṣṇa himself during his appearance on earth attain salvation and not those slain by other *avatāras*. The learned Uddhava has prayed in *Śrīmad-Bhāgavatam* thus: "Alas, what sane person would take shelter of anyone other than Kṛṣṇa, who granted the position of mother *(vātsalya-rasa)* to a she-demon (Pūtanā), although she was unfaithful and she prepared deadly poison to be sucked from her breast?" In this verse we find a striking contrast that illustrates the extent of Kṛṣṇa's compassion. The heinous she-demon Pūtanā, commissioned by Kaṁsa, disguised herself as a nurse, smeared poison on her breast, and attempted to kill infant Kṛṣṇa by offering her breast milk to him. Omniscient even in his apparent infanthood, Kṛṣṇa understood her purpose. Yet he sucked her breast nonetheless. Overlooking her demoniac intention, he accepted her as one of his mothers, and in slaying her by sucking her life air out of her body, he granted her the very special liberated status of *vātsalya-rasa*.

Otherwise, for the most part the salvation of the ungodly is the work of Kṛṣṇa's devotees. They live in this world for him alone. In doing so, they interact with others who may unknowingly assist them. This unconscious act makes it possible for the ungodly to gradually reverse their course.

Text 21

त्रिविधं नरकस्येदं द्वारं नाशनमात्मनः ।
कामः क्रोधस्तथा लोभस्तस्मादेतत्त्रयं त्यजेत् ॥२१॥

tri-vidhaṁ narakasyedaṁ dvāraṁ nāśanam ātmanaḥ/
kāmaḥ krodhas tathā lobhas tasmād etat trayaṁ tyajet//

tri-vidham—of three kinds; *narakasya*—of hell; *idam*—this; *dvāram*—gate; *nāśanam*—destructive; *ātmanaḥ*—of the self; *kāmaḥ*—desire; *krodhaḥ*—anger; *tathā*—as well as; *lobhaḥ*—greed; *tasmāt*—therefore; *etat*—this; *trayam*—three; *tyajet*—one should abandon.

The three gates to hell that destroy the self are lust, anger, and greed. Therefore one should abandon these three.

Among the vices described thus far, three are to be avoided above all others. Indeed, these three lead to all of the others, and thus even the godly should be on guard against them. They are the gates to hell.

Text 22

एतैर्विमुक्तः कौन्तेय तमोद्वारैस्त्रिभिर्नरः ।
आचरत्यात्मनः श्रेयस्ततो याति परां गतिम् ॥२२॥

etair vimuktaḥ kaunteya tamo-dvārais tribhir naraḥ/
ācaraty ātmanaḥ śreyas tato yāti parāṁ gatim//

etaiḥ—from these; *vimuktaḥ*—released; *kaunteya*—O son of Kuntī; *tamaḥ-dvāraiḥ*—from the gates to darkness; *tribhiḥ*—from three; *naraḥ*—a person; *ācarati*—acts; *ātmanaḥ*—of the self; *śreyaḥ*—interest; *tataḥ*—thereby; *yāti*—he goes; *parām*—highest; *gatim*—goal.

Released from these three doors to darkness, a person acts in his real self-interest, O son of Kuntī, and thereby attains the highest goal.

Release from the gates to hell is possible only by spiritual practice and the grace of God. Such practice and the means to attain God's grace are delineated in the scriptural canon. Thus Kṛṣṇa turns Arjuna's attention back to the scripture in the following verse as he concludes this chapter.

Text 23

यः शास्त्रविधिमुत्सृज्य वर्तते कामकारतः ।
न स सिद्धिमवाप्नोति न सुखं न परां गतिम् ॥२३॥

yaḥ śāstra-vidhim utsṛjya vartate kāma-kārataḥ/
na sa siddhim avāpnoti na sukhaṁ na parāṁ gatim//

yaḥ—who; *śāstra-vidhim*—scriptural injunction; *utsṛjya*—ignoring; *vartate*—he acts; *kāma-kārataḥ*—out of impulse; *na*—not; *saḥ*—he; *siddhim*—perfection; *avāpnoti*—he attains; *na*—not; *sukham*—happiness; *na*—not; *parām*—ultimate; *gatim*—goal.

One who acts out of impulse, ignoring scriptural injunctions, attains neither perfection, nor happiness, nor the ultimate goal of life.

Text 24

तस्माच्छास्त्रं प्रमाणं ते कार्याकार्यव्यवस्थितौ ।
ज्ञात्वा शास्त्रविधानोक्तं कर्म कर्तुमिहार्हसि ॥२४॥

tasmāc chāstraṁ pramāṇaṁ te kāryākārya-vyavasthitau/
jñātvā śāstra-vidhānoktaṁ karma kartum ihārhasi//

tasmāt—therefore; *śāstram*—scripture; *pramāṇam*—evidence; *te*—your; *kārya*—to be done; *akārya*—not to be done; *vyavasthitau*—in determining;

jñātvā—knowing; *śāstra*—scripture; *vidhāna*—injunction; *uktam*—prescribed; *karma*—work; *kartum*—to do; *iha*—in this world; *arhasi*—you should.

Therefore the scripture is your authority in the matter of determining what is to be done and what is not to be done. Understanding the scriptural injunctions, you should act accordingly in this world.

In summary, this chapter describes the ungodly as those who are in intellectual denial of the existence of the soul and God, and as a result of this their practical activities bring misery to themselves and others. Arjuna is encouraged by Kṛṣṇa that he is of the godly nature by virtue of his past and corresponding present birth and association, yet he is to be vigilant to avoid the ungodly nature and activities that Kṛṣṇa details. In doing so, Arjuna's actions should be guided by scripture, which expounds not only the goal of life, but the practical steps to reach it as well. Kṛṣṇa stresses that faith and adherence to scriptural injunctions preface the entire pursuit of spiritual life, while an in-depth explanation of spiritual life constitutes the central theme of the entire *Bhagavad-gītā*.

Here Kṛṣṇa underscores the importance of the scripture. Thus a word about it may be appropriate. Ultimately, the scripture represents a body of knowledge in which the supreme goal of life is described along with the means of attaining this goal. However, the scripture also seeks to direct those who are not interested in the ultimate goal of life. To this end it provides knowledge of other possible goals that humanity might achieve and how humankind can best attain these lesser goals. The scripture contains laws that govern the realization of different ideals that arise in the human psyche, and it also offers an objective means of determining the hierarchy of human values. In doing so, it is not dogmatic. It invites the complete application of reason, leaving each individual to determine in conjunction with it what is relevant to him in terms of his particular ideal. Reason is also invited to participate in one's understanding the conclusion of the *Vedas*, as well as in vindicating the scripture in the face of opposition from those who do not acknowledge its authority. The *Vedānta-sūtra* itself sets this example.

CHAPTER SEVENTEEN

श्रद्धात्रयविभागयोगः
Śraddha-Traya-Vibhāga-yoga

YOGA OF DISCERNING THREEFOLD FAITH

Text 1

अर्जुन उवाच
ये शास्त्रविधिमुत्सृज्य यजन्ते श्रद्धयान्विताः ।
तेषां निष्ठा तु का कृष्ण सत्त्वमाहो रजस्तमः ॥१॥

arjuna uvāca
ye śāstra-vidhim utsṛjya yajante śraddhayānvitāḥ/
teṣāṁ niṣṭhā tu kā kṛṣṇa sattvam āho rajas tamaḥ//

arjunaḥ uvāca—Arjuna said; *ye*—who; *śāstra-vidhim*—scriptural injunction; *utsṛjya*—ignoring; *yajante*—they worship; *śraddhayā-anvitāḥ*—possessed of faith; *teṣām*—of them; *niṣṭhā*—faith; *tu*—but; *kā*—what; *kṛṣṇa*—O Kṛṣṇa; *sattvam*—in *sattva*; *āho*—is it so; *rajaḥ*—in *rajas*; *tamaḥ*—in *tamas*.

Arjuna said: O Kṛṣṇa, what is the status of those who ignore the scripture but nonetheless worship with faith? Is their worship in sattva, rajas, or tamas?

Kṛṣṇa concluded the previous chapter by distinguishing between the godly and ungodly in terms of their adherence to scripture. The godly adhere to the scripture, whereas the ungodly do not. However, here Arjuna wonders about the status of those who for whatever reason do not take the trouble to understand the import of the scripture, yet in accordance with local tradition nonetheless worship various gods and goddesses. Such people do not disregard the scripture, but they do not take the time to understand it. They fall between those who follow the scripture properly and those who have no regard for scripture whatsoever, being both similar and dissimilar to the godly and the ungodly. Arjuna asks about the quality of their faith (*śraddhā*). Is it in *sattva, rajas*, or *tamas*? Furthermore, he wants to know the relationship between faith and scriptural adherence. Is not faith alone sufficient for spiritual progress?

After discussing different kinds of faith in relation to the *guṇas*, Kṛṣṇa goes on to discuss food, sacrifice, austerity, and charity in relation to them. He then concludes this chapter with emphasis on the *mantra oṁ tat sat*, indicating that when its utterance prefaces acts of sacrifice, austerity, and charity one's faith can be transformed from material to spiritual.

Text 2

श्रीभगवानुवाच
त्रिविधा भवति श्रद्धा देहिनां सा स्वभावजा ।
सात्त्विकी राजसी चैव तामसी चेति तां शृणु ॥२॥

śrī-bhagavān uvāca
tri-vidhā bhavati śraddhā dehināṁ sā svabhāva-jā/
sāttvikī rājasī caiva tāmasī ceti tāṁ śṛṇu//

śrī-bhagavān uvāca—the Lord of Śrī said; *tri-vidhā*—of three kinds; *bhavati*—it arises; *śraddhā*—faith; *dehinām*—of the embodied; *sā*—that; *sva-bhāva-jā*—born of one's own nature; *sāttvikī*—sattvic; *rājasī*—rajasic; *ca*—also; *eva*—certainly; *tāmasī*—tamasic; *ca*—and; *iti*—thus; *tām*—that; *śṛṇu*—hear.

The Lord of Śrī said: The faith of embodied souls that is born of their materially acquired nature is of three types: sattvic, rajasic, or tamasic. Now hear about this.

The color of one's faith is directly related to its cause. If the cause of one's faith is saintly association and deliberation on the devotional import of scripture, one's faith is enlightened, *nirguṇa-śraddhā*. Such enlightened faith is in turn the cause of one's spiritual progress, and more so, the measure of one's attainment. We live in a world of doubt, yet our highest prospect lies in entering the land of faith, all doubt removed.

Faith in general is of the nature of the material influence of *sattva*. Whatever one has faith in, that faith itself is a manifestation of *sattva*. It is the conviction behind sustained effort. Thus the sense of its being virtuous is universal. However, that in which a person places his faith is determined by the influence of his acquired nature. A person's nature acquired at birth *(svabhāva-jā)* is a product of his past *karma*. This nature is constituted of a combination of the three *guṇas*, in which one of these three predominates. The predominating influence of *sattva*, *rajas*, or *tamas* determines the object of one's faith and thus colors with shades of *rajas* and *tamas* that which is in and of itself sattvic.

The primary cause of one's faith is one's acquired nature. The material or secondary cause is the mind, to which Kṛṣṇa next turns Arjuna's attention.

Text 3

सत्त्वानुरूपा सर्वस्य श्रद्धा भवति भारत ।
श्रद्धामयोऽयं पुरुषो यो यच्छ्रद्धः स एव सः ॥३॥

sattvānurūpā sarvasya śraddhā bhavati bhārata/
śraddhā-mayo 'yaṁ puruṣo yo yac-chraddhaḥ sa eva saḥ//

sattva-anurūpā—according to truth; *sarvasya*—of everyone; *śraddhā*—faith; *bhavati*—it is; *bhārata*—O son of Bharata; *śraddhā-mayaḥ*—made of faith; *ayam*—this; *puruṣaḥ*—person; *yaḥ*—who; *yat*—which; *śraddhaḥ*—faith; *saḥ*—this; *eva*—certainly; *saḥ*—he.

One's faith corresponds with one's mind, O descendant of Bharata. A person is made of his faith. One is whatever his faith is.

The mind is indicated here by the word *sattva*. It is of the nature of illumination. Mind is a transformation of the principle of egotism *(ahaṁkāra)* influenced by the *sattva-guṇa*. Here Kṛṣṇa says that one's faith corresponds with one's mind. Because the mind is a transformation of *sattva*, faith is intrinsically sattvic. However, every individual's mind reflects his heart's condition under the influence of the three *guṇas*. Thus one's nature reflected in the mind produces a particular quality of faith, be it sattvic, rajasic, or tamasic.

Changing one's materially acquired nature is possible by deliberating on the import of the scripture and subsequently worshipping the Absolute. By this, one acquires knowledge, and through saintly association pure *sattva* takes precedence and brings about the illumination necessary for enlightened life. Otherwise, the dominant *guṇa*'s influence on the mind determines one's faith. This is the position of those whose faith causes them to worship but who do not take the time to deliberate on the import of the scripture. The quality of their particular faith is revealed through the object of their veneration.

Text 4

यजन्ते सात्त्विका देवान् यक्षरक्षांसि राजसाः ।
प्रेतान् भूतगणांश्चान्ये यजन्ते तामसा जनाः ॥४॥

yajante sāttvikā devān yakṣa-rakṣāṁsi rājasāḥ/
pretān bhūta-gaṇāṁś cānye yajante tāmasā janāḥ//

yajante—they worship; *sāttvikāḥ*—the sattvic; *devān*—gods; *yakṣa-rakṣāṁsi*—demoniac spirits; *rājasāḥ*—the rajasic; *pretān*—nature spirits; *bhūta-gaṇān*—ghosts; *ca*—and; *anye*—others; *yajante*—they worship; *tāmasāḥ*—the tamasic; *janāḥ*—people.

The sattvic worship the gods; the rajasic worship demoniac spirits; others possessed of tamas worship nature spirits and ghosts.

The *Bhagavad-gītā* teaches that the religious persuasions in the world are a product of four kinds of faith: enlightened faith of pure *sattva*, sattvic faith, rajasic faith, and tamasic faith. Only the first of these has the power to change one's nature from material to spiritual. The other three, however well-intended, cover the road of *saṁsāra* with varieties of religious pavement. If one is fortunate and by virtue of previous pious deeds one's rajasic or tamasic faith becomes dominated by *sattva*, one can become eligible for spiritual discipline enjoined in the scripture, giving birth to enlightened faith. Otherwise, under the continued influence of *rajas* and *tamas*, faith produces only misery. This condition is addressed next in verses 5 and 6.

Texts 5–6

अशास्त्रविहितं घोरं तप्यन्ते ये तपो जनाः ।
दम्भाहंकारसंयुक्ताः कामरागबलान्विताः ॥५॥
कर्षयन्त्यः शरीरस्थं भूतग्राममचेतसः ।
मां चैवान्तःशरीरस्थं तान् विद्ध्यासुरनिश्चयान् ॥६॥

aśāstra-vihitaṁ ghoraṁ tapyante ye tapo janāḥ/
dambhāhaṅkāra-saṁyuktāḥ kāma-rāga-balānvitāḥ//
karṣayantaḥ śarīra-sthaṁ bhūta-grāmam acetasaḥ/
māṁ caivāntaḥśarīra-sthaṁ tān viddhy āsura-niścayān//

aśāstra—not in the scriptures; *vihitam*—directed; *ghoram*—terrible; *tapyante*—they undergo; *ye*—who; *tapaḥ*—austerity; *janāḥ*—persons; *dambha*—hypocrisy; *ahaṅkāra*—egotism; *saṁyuktāḥ*—joined; *kāma*—lust; *rāga*—attachment; *bala*—force; *anvitāḥ*—impelled; *karṣayantaḥ*—torturing; *śarīra-stham*—situated within the body; *bhūta-grāmam*—the combination of elements; *acetasaḥ*—nondiscriminating; *mām*—me; *ca*—also; *eva*—certainly; *antaḥ*—within; *śarīra-stham*—situated in the body; *tān*—them; *viddhi*—know; *āsura-niścayān*—of ungodly conviction.

Those who completely identify with both hypocrisy and egotism, as well as lust and attachment, undergo terrible austerities that are not enjoined in the scriptures. Know that the nondiscriminating and those who torture the body, and thereby me who resides within the body, are of ungodly conviction.

The previous verse describes the activities of those whose faith is born of their acquired material nature, rather than from scripture. Because they are not against the scripture, there is the likelihood that they will rise to eligibility for spiritual discipline over time. Those described in verses 5 and 6, however, are the ungodly discussed in the previous chapter who have no regard for scripture. Kṛṣṇa mentions them here for the sake of contrast. The former class, who are the primary subject of this chapter, are further described over the next sixteen verses in terms of how the quality of their faith can be determined through external symptoms, such as the food they eat, their charity, and the type of sacrifices and austerities they perform.

Text 7

आहारस्त्वपि सर्वस्य त्रिविधो भवति प्रियः ।
यज्ञस्तपस्तथा दानं तेषां भेदमिमं शृणु ॥७॥

āhāras tv api sarvasya tri-vidho bhavati priyaḥ/
yajñas tapas tathā dānaṁ teṣāṁ bhedam imaṁ śṛṇu//

āhāraḥ—food; *tu*—but; *api*—also; *sarvasya*—of everyone; *tri-vidhaḥ*—of three kinds; *bhavati*—there is; *priyaḥ*—preferred; *yajñaḥ*—sacrifice; *tapaḥ*—austerity; *tathā*—also; *dānam*—charity; *teṣām*—of them; *bhedam*—the difference; *imam*—this; *śṛṇu*—hear.

Not only faith, but also the type of food preferred by all people is of three kinds, as are their sacrifices, austerities, and charity. Listen now to their classification.

The word *tu* (but) in this verse implies, "Not only faith but also..." It thus connects this verse to the preceding discussion of three types of faith. In accordance with the *guṇa* that predominates in their mental system and determines their faith, people choose their food, act charitably, perform sacrifice and austerity, and so on.

Text 8

आयुःसत्त्वबलारोग्यसुखप्रीतिविवर्धनाः ।
रस्याः स्निग्धाः स्थिरा हृद्या आहाराः सात्त्विकप्रियाः ॥८॥

āyuḥ-sattva-balārogya-sukha-prīti-vivardhanāḥ/
rasyāḥ snigdhāḥ sthirā hṛdyā āhārāḥ sāttvika-priyāḥ//

āyuḥ—life; *sattva*—virtue; *bala*—strength; *ārogya*—health; *sukha*—happiness; *prīti*—satisfaction; *vivardhanāḥ*—promoting; *rasyāḥ*—juicy; *snigdhāḥ*—fatty; *sthirāḥ*—wholesome; *hṛdyāḥ*—hearty; *āhārāḥ*—foods; *sāttvika*—the sattvic; *priyāḥ*—dear.

Foods that promote life, virtue, strength, health, happiness, and satisfaction, which are juicy, fatty, wholesome, and agreeable are dear to those in whom sattva predominates.

Viśvanātha Cakravartī Ṭhākura comments that the foods mentioned in this verse must be pure for them to be sattvic. He suggests that the adjective *pavitram* should be added to further qualify foods preferred by sattvic people. By pure the *ācārya* means that they must be bought with money that was earned purely, cooked purely, and served in a pure place by pure people.

Foods that increase the duration of life, produce virtue, strength, health, happiness, and satisfaction refer to foods like those derived from the cow, as well as sugar, wheat, fruits, vegetables, and rice. *Sattva* in the first line of this verse refers to virtue, which brings about steadiness of mind enabling one to remain undisturbed in the face of sorrow. Agreeable (*hṛdyāḥ*) foods are those that are hearty and agreeable both to the stomach and the eye. *Snigdha* refers to foods that are not excessively fatty, but contain some oil.

Text 9

कट्वम्ललवणात्युष्णतीक्ष्णरूक्षविदाहिनः ।
आहारा राजसस्येष्टा दुःखशोकामयप्रदाः ॥९॥

kaṭv-amla-lavaṇāty-uṣṇa-tīkṣṇa-rūkṣa-vidāhinaḥ/
āhārā rājasasyeṣṭā duḥkha-śokāmaya-pradāḥ//

kaṭu—bitter; *amla*—sour; *lavaṇa*—salty; *ati-uṣṇa*—excessively hot; *tīkṣṇa*—pungent; *rūkṣa*—dry; *vidāhinaḥ*—burning; *āhārāḥ*—foods; *rājasasya*—of the rajasic; *iṣṭāḥ*—desired; *duḥkha*—pain; *śoka*—sorrow; *āmaya*—disease; *pradāḥ*—causing.

Foods that are excessively bitter, sour, salty, hot, pungent, dry, and burning, and cause pain, sorrow, and disease are dear to those in whom rajas predominates.

The word *ati* in this verse qualifies all of the foods mentioned. They are rajasic when taken in excess *(ati)*. Such excess brings the immediate effect of pain, the aftereffect of sorrow, and the long-term effect of disease.

Text 10

यातयामं गतरसं पूति पर्युषितं च यत् ।
उच्छिष्टमपि चामेध्यं भोजनं तामसप्रियम् ॥१०॥

yāta-yāmaṁ gata-rasaṁ pūti paryuṣitaṁ ca yat/
ucchiṣṭam api cāmedhyaṁ bhojanaṁ tāmasa-priyam//

yāta-yāmam—stale; *gata-rasam*—tasteless; *pūti*—putrid; *paryuṣitam*—rotten; *ca*—also; *yat*—which; *ucchiṣṭam*—rejected by others; *api*—also; *ca*—and; *amedhyam*—unfit for sacrifice; *bhojanam*—food; *tāmasa*—to the tamasic; *priyam*—dear.

Food that is stale, tasteless, putrid, rotten, left by others, and unfit for sacrifice is dear to those in whom tamas predominates.

Madhusūdana Saraswatī comments that the foods Kṛṣṇa describes as sattvic are diametrically opposed to those in *rajas* and *tamas*. While the foods in *rajas* oppose the sattvic foods on a perceptible level, the tamasic foods do so on an imperceptible level as well. By this he means that the unbeneficial effects of rajasic food accrue in this life, whereas the unbeneficial effects of tamasic food appear in one's present life and follow one into the next life as well.

Here the word *ucchiṣṭam* does not refer to the remnants of saints.

Text 11

अफलाकाङ्क्षिभिर्यज्ञो विधिदिष्टो य इज्यते ।
यष्टव्यमेवेति मनः समाधाय स सात्त्विकः ॥११॥

aphalākāṅkṣibhir yajño vidhi-diṣṭo ya ijyate/
yaṣṭavyam eveti manaḥ samādhāya sa sāttvikaḥ//

aphala-ākāṅkṣibhiḥ—by those not desiring to enjoy the result for themselves; *yajñaḥ*—sacrifice; *vidhi-diṣṭaḥ*—according to scripture; *yaḥ*—which; *ijyate*—it is sacrificed; *yaṣṭavyam*—to be sacrificed; *eva*—certainly; *iti*—thus; *manaḥ*—mind; *samādhāya*—fixing; *saḥ*—it; *sāttvikaḥ*—sattvic.

Sacrifice performed in accordance with the scriptures by those with no desire to enjoy the result for themselves, with the attitude that it is to be performed for its own sake, is sattvic.

One's mental attitude is stressed more than any particular sacrifice. One who engages in scripturally enjoined acts of sacrifice because they should be performed and with a view to purify the mind is sattvic.

Text 12

अभिसन्धाय तु फलं दम्भार्थमपि चैव यत् ।
इज्यते भरतश्रेष्ठ तं यज्ञं विद्धि राजसम् ॥१२॥

abhisandhāya tu phalaṁ dambhārtham api caiva yat/
ijyate bharata-śreṣṭhataṁ yajñaṁ viddhi rājasam//

abhisandhāya—seeking; *tu*—but; *phalam*—result; *dambha*—hypocrisy; *artham*—purpose; *api*—also; *ca*—and; *eva*—certainly; *yat*—which; *ijyate*—it is offered; *bharata-śreṣṭha*—O best of the Bhāratas; *tam*—that; *yajñam*—sacrifice; *viddhi*—know; *rājasam*—rajasic.

However, know that sacrifice offered with a view to enjoy the result and for an outer show of religiosity, O best of the descendants of Bharata, to be rajasic.

Text 13

विधिहीनमसृष्टान्नं मन्त्रहीनमदक्षिणम् ।
श्रद्धाविरहितं यज्ञं तामसं परिचक्षते ॥१३॥

vidhi-hīnam asṛṣṭānnaṁ mantra-hīnam adakṣiṇam/
śraddhā-virahitaṁ yajñaṁ tāmasaṁ paricakṣate//

vidhi-hīnam—without scriptural direction; *asṛṣṭa-annam*—without distribution of food; *mantra-hīnam*—without chanting of *mantras*; *adakṣiṇam*—without remuneration to the priests; *śraddhā*—faith; *virahitam*—devoid; *yajñam*—sacrifice; *tāmasam*—tamasic; *paricakṣate*—they call.

They call that sacrifice tamasic which is contrary to scriptural injunction, in which no food is offered or distributed, which is performed without the appropriate mantras, in which there is no remuneration for the priests, and which is devoid of faith.

Text 14

देवद्विजगुरुप्राज्ञपूजनं शौचमार्जवम् ।
ब्रह्मचर्यमहिंसा च शारीरं तप उच्यते ॥१४॥

deva-dvija-guru-prājña-pūjanaṁ śaucam ārjavam/
brahmacaryam ahiṁsā ca śārīraṁ tapa ucyate//

deva—God; *dvija*—twice-born; *guru*—guru; *prājña*—wise; *pūjanam*—worship; *śaucam*—purity; *ārjavam*—straightforwardness; *brahmacaryam*—celibacy; *ahiṁsā*—nonviolence; *ca*—also; *śārīram*—body; *tapaḥ*—austerity; *ucyate*—it is said.

Purity, straightforwardness, celibacy, nonviolence, and worship of God, the brāhmaṇas, the guru, and the wise ones—these are considered to be physical austerities.

Here Kṛṣṇa begins to speak about austerity. Other than the physical austerity mentioned in this verse, he will speak of austerity of speech and mind. These three are progressively more difficult to perform. After explaining these three types of austerities, Kṛṣṇa describes the attitude of the performer that makes austerities of body, speech, and mind sattvic, rajasic, or tamasic.

Text 15

अनुद्वेगकरं वाक्यं सत्यं प्रियहितं च यत् ।
स्वाध्यायाभ्यसनं चैव वाङ्मयं तप उच्यते ॥१५॥

anudvega-karaṁ vākyaṁ satyaṁ priya-hitaṁ ca yat/
svādhyāyābhyasanaṁ caiva vāṅ-mayaṁ tapa ucyate//

anudvega-karam—not causing distress; *vākyam*—speech; *satyam*—truthful; *priya*—agreeable; *hitam*—beneficial; *ca*—also; *yat*—which; *svādhyāya*—reciting the scripture; *abhyasanam*—practice; *ca*—also; *eva*—certainly; *vāk-mayam*—of speech; *tapaḥ*—austerity; *ucyate*—it is said.

Speech that does not cause distress, which is truthful, agreeable, and beneficial, and which includes the practice of reciting the scripture—these are called austerities of speech.

Text 16

मनःप्रसादः सौम्यत्वं मौनमात्मविनिग्रहः ।
भावसंशुद्धिरित्येतत् तपो मानसमुच्यते ॥१६॥

manaḥ-prasādaḥ saumyatvaṁ maunam ātma-vinigrahaḥ/
bhāva-saṁśuddhir ity etat tapo mānasam ucyate//

manaḥ-prasādaḥ—peace of mind; *saumyatvam*—gentleness; *maunam*—silence; *ātma-vinigrahaḥ*—self-restraint; *bhāva-saṁśuddhiḥ*—purification of being; *iti*—thus; *etat*—this; *tapaḥ*—austerity; *mānasam*—of the mind; *ucyate*—it is said.

Peace of mind, gentleness, silence, self-restraint, purity of heart—these are austerities of the mind.

Practicing peace of mind *(manaḥ-prasādaḥ)* means to practice keeping the mind free from contemplating sense objects. Gentleness *(saumyatvam)* involves always desiring the happiness of others. Silence *(maunam)* involves controlling the mind, which is the cause of controlling speech. It implies gravity of thought. Self-restraint *(ātma-vinigrahaḥ)* means complete *(vi)* control of the modifications of the mind. Purity of heart *(bhāva-śuddhi)* is qualified here by the prefix *sam*, which indicates completeness. Thus it refers to the freedom from and nonrecurrence of lust, anger, greed, and so on. It also means freedom from duplicity in one's dealings with others.

The three kinds of austerity appear within the three *guṇas*.

Text 17

श्रद्धया परया तप्तं तपस्तत्त्रिविधं नरैः ।
अफलाकाङ्क्षिभिर्युक्तैः सात्त्विकं परिचक्षते ॥१७॥

śraddhayā parayā taptaṁ tapas tat tri-vidhaṁ naraiḥ/
aphalākāṅkṣibhir yuktaiḥ sāttvikaṁ paricakṣate//

śraddhayā—with faith; *parayā*—with the highest; *taptam*—executed; *tapaḥ*—austerity; *tat*—that; *tri-vidham*—of three kinds; *naraiḥ*—by men; *aphala-ākāṅkṣibhiḥ*—who are not attached to the result; *yuktaiḥ*—by the disciplined; *sāttvikam*—sattvic; *paricakṣate*—they call.

This threefold austerity, when performed with the highest faith by disciplined persons who are not attached to the result, is called sattvic.

Text 18

सत्कारमानपूजार्थं तपो दम्भेन चैव यत् ।
क्रियते तदिह प्रोक्तं राजसं चलमध्रुवम् ॥१८॥

satkāra-māna-pūjārthaṁ tapo dambhena caiva yat/
kriyate tad iha proktaṁ rājasaṁ calam adhruvam//

sat-kāra—reverence; *māna*—honor; *pūjā*—worship; *artham*—for the sake of; *tapaḥ*—austerity; *dambhena*—with hypocrisy; *ca*—also; *eva*—certainly; *yat*—which; *kriyate*—it is performed; *tat*—that; *iha*—in this world; *proktam*—it is said; *rājasam*—rajasic; *calam*—wavering; *adhruvam*—uncertain.

That austerity which is undertaken hypocritically for praise, honor, and worship is called rajasic. Its results are worldly, temporary, and uncertain.

Text 19

मूढग्राहेणात्मनोयत् पीडया क्रियते तपः ।
परस्योत्सादनार्थं वा तत्तामसमुदाहृतम् ॥१९॥

mūḍha-grāheṇātmano yat pīḍayā kriyate tapaḥ/
parasyotsādanārthaṁ vā tat tāmasam udāhṛtam//

mūḍha-grāheṇa—foolish intention; *ātmanaḥ*—of one's own self; *yat*—which; *pīḍayā*—by torture; *kriyate*—it is performed; *tapaḥ*—austerity; *parasya*—of another; *utsādana-artham*—for the sake of destroying; *vā*—or; *tat*—that; *tāmasam*—tamasic; *udāhṛtam*—it is said to be.

Austerity undertaken with foolish intentions, causing pain to oneself or to others, is said to be tamasic.

The selfishness that characterizes *rajo-guṇa* indirectly causes pain to oneself and others, whereas *tamo-guṇa* involves deliberate acts of violence. Those influenced by *tamo-guṇa* take pleasure in these acts of violence.

Text 20

दातव्यमिति यद्दानं दीयतेऽनुपकारिणे ।
देशे काले च पात्रे च तद्दानं सात्त्विकं स्मृतम् ॥२०॥

dātavyam iti yad dānaṁ dīyate 'nupakāriṇe/
deśe kāle ca pātre ca tad dānaṁ sāttvikaṁ smṛtam//

dātavyam—to be given; *iti*—thus; *yat*—which; *dānam*—gift; *dīyate*—it is given; *anupakāriṇe*—to a person who gives nothing in return; *deśe*—in place; *kāle*—in time; *ca*—also; *pātre*—to a suitable person; *ca*—and; *tat*—that; *dānam*—gift; *sāttvikam*—sattvic; *smṛtam*—known as.

That gift which is given at the proper time and place to a worthy person simply because it ought to be given and without expecting something in return is sattvic.

Text 21

यत्तु प्रत्युपकारार्थं फलमुद्दिश्य वा पुनः ।
दीयते च परिक्लिष्टं तद्दानं राजसं स्मृतम् ॥२१॥

yat tu pratyupakārārthaṁ phalam uddiśya vā punaḥ/
dīyate ca parikliṣṭaṁ tad dānaṁ rājasaṁ smṛtam//

yat—which; *tu*—but; *prati-upakāra-artham*—for the sake of getting some reward; *phalam*—result; *uddiśya*—aiming; *vā*—or; *punaḥ*—again; *dīyate*—it is given; *ca*—also; *parikliṣṭam*—begrudgingly; *tat*—that; *dānam*—gift; *rājasam*—rajasic; *smṛtam*—considered as.

On the other hand, that gift which is given with expectation of reward or with a desire to enjoy the result for oneself, as well as that which is given begrudgingly, is considered rajasic.

Text 22

अदेशकाले यद्दानमपात्रेभ्यश्च दीयते ।
असत्कृतमवज्ञातं तत्तामसमुदाहृतम् ॥२२॥

adeśa-kāle yad dānam apātrebhyaś ca dīyate/
asat-kṛtam avajñātaṁ tat tāmasam udāhṛtam//

adeśa-kāle—at the wrong place and time; *yat*—which; *dānam*—gift; *upātrebhyaḥ*—to unworthy persons; *ca*—also; *dīyate*—it is given; *asat-kṛtam*—without respect; *avajñātam*—with contempt; *tat*—that; *tāmasam*—tamasic; *udāhṛtam*—said to be.

That gift given at the wrong place and time to an unworthy person, without respect, or with contempt is considered tamasic.

The conclusion of this section is that in all of one's undertakings one should cultivate *sattva*, avoiding *rajas* and *tamas*. However, the intrinsic sattvic and thus virtuous nature of faith is not to be ignored even when colored by *rajas* and *tamas*. It distinguishes those who have it from the ungodly, who have no regard for scripture whatsoever.

It has already been explained that persons of faith can by virtue of the mature result of previous pious acts become virtuous themselves and gradually qualify themselves for spiritual discipline. If they are fortunate to get the association of saints, their lives can also turn in the spiritual direction. Saints are those preoccupied with God. From their lips his holy name issues. From the scripture we also learn of the efficacy of the name of God, its spiritual power. It is this sacred utterance that Kṛṣṇa next turns Arjuna's attention to.

The exercise of one's faith that is not born of scriptural study and saintly association is defective. In order that a person might make the best of his faith and overcome the defects resulting from its being less than scripturally sound, Kṛṣṇa next introduces the sacred *mantra oṁ tat sat*, stating that it should preface all acts of sacrifice, austerity, and charity. In doing so, he turns his elaboration on faith in the spiritual direction, implying that the chanting of God's name through which all acts become an offering unto him has the power to gradually elevate one from faith born of one's materially conditioned nature to the platform of enlightened faith. The following section implies that, should any defect in the execution of an auspicious act spoil its outcome, this can be counteracted by chanting *oṁ tat sat*, the name of God.

Text 23

ॐ तत्सदिति निर्देशो ब्रह्मणस्त्रिविधः स्मृतः ।
ब्राह्मणास्तेन वेदाश्च यज्ञाश्च विहिताः पुरा ॥२३॥

oṁ tat sad iti nirdeśo brahmaṇas tri-vidhaḥ smṛtaḥ/
brāhmaṇās tena vedāś ca yajñāś ca vihitāḥ purā//

oṁ—*oṁ*; *tat*—that; *sat*—eternal; *iti*—thus; *nirdeśaḥ*—designation; *brahmaṇaḥ*—of the Absolute; *tri-vidhaḥ*—threefold; *smṛtaḥ*—considered; *brāhmaṇāḥ*—the *brāhmaṇas*; *tena*—with that; *vedāḥ*—the *Vedas*; *ca*—also; *yajñāḥ*—sacrifices; *ca*—also; *vihitāḥ*—created; *purā*—formerly.

The syllables oṁ tat sat are the symbolic threefold representation of the Absolute that in ancient times gave rise to the brāhmaṇas, the Vedas, and sacrifices.

The sacred syllables *oṁ tat sat* were integral to both the religious life of material goodness and spiritual pursuit in ancient times, and its importance is no less today. Thus Kṛṣṇa stresses it to Arjuna.

In this verse the word *brāhmaṇas* refers to the priestly class that teaches both religious and spiritual values. Sacrifice is either religious when involving material assets or transcendental when involving the self. The *Vedas* deal primarily with religious life, although their conclusion is spiritual. Here Kṛṣṇa implies that the sacred syllables *oṁ tat sat* pervade both religious and spiritual life. If uttered in pursuit of subreligious ideals, they can elevate one to religious ideals governed by the *sattva-guṇa*. When uttered from a sattvic orientation, they insure the attainment of religious ideals. If they are uttered as a preface to acts in pursuit of transcendence, they also assure success despite any discrepancy.

This sacred *mantra* is one, while consisting of three aspects. It is the name of God. *Oṁ* is well known as the name or sound of God. *Tat* is also a name of God, as we find in the *Upaniṣads*, *tat tvam asi*. *Sat* is God as the cause of the world. From *sat*, the real world and the unreal world of illusion (*asat*) arise. Thus *oṁ*, *tat*, and *sat* are names of God, the chanting of which insures all success in any endeavor. The name of God should be chanted before all undertakings, rendering them an offering unto God.

Text 24

तस्माद् ॐ इत्युदाहृत्य यज्ञदानतपःक्रियाः ।
प्रवर्तन्ते विधानोक्ताः सततं ब्रह्मवादिनाम् ॥२४॥

tasmād oṁ ity udāhṛtya yajña-dāna-tapaḥ-kriyāḥ/
pravartante vidhānoktāḥ satataṁ brahma-vādinām//

tasmāt—therefore; *oṁ*—*oṁ; iti*—thus; *udāhṛtya*—uttering; *yajña*—sacrifice; *dāna*—charity; *tapaḥ*—austerity; *kriyāḥ*—acts; *pravartante*—they begin; *vidhāna-uktāḥ*—as prescribed in the scripture; *satatam*—always; *brahma-vādinām*—of the students of the *Vedas*.

Therefore, students of the Vedas always preface scripturally prescribed acts of sacrifice, austerity, and charity by uttering the syllable oṁ.

Kṛṣṇa does not elaborate on the significance of the syllable *oṁ*, as he does in the following verses on *tat* and *sat*. It is so well known that he takes for granted that Arjuna is familiar with its import. Furthermore, Kṛṣṇa has already spoken about *oṁ* previously (Bg. 7.8, 8.13, 9.17, 10.25).

Oṁ covers both religious and transcendent life in its reach. It is integral to Vedic utterances in pursuit of both, for it signifies the supreme reality, who all of the gods and goddess represent, and that which liberated life thrives in service to. Its full significance represents the supreme act of surrender to God that converts life from religious acknowledgment of God under the jurisdiction of *sattva-guṇa* into perpetual adoration of him in the transcendent *nirguṇa* reality. As Kṛṣṇa tells Arjuna next, these two aspects of the syllable *oṁ* are individually represented in the syllables *tat* and *sat*.

Text 25

तदित्यनभिसन्धाय फलं यज्ञतपःक्रियाः ।
दानक्रियाश्च विविधाः क्रियन्ते मोक्षकांक्षिभिः ॥२५॥

tad ity anabhisandhāya phalaṁ yajña-tapaḥ-kriyāḥ/
dāna-kriyāś ca vividhāḥ kriyante mokṣa-kāṅkṣibhiḥ//

tat—that; *iti*—thus; *anabhisandhāya*—without desiring; *phalam*—the result; *yajña*—sacrifice; *tapaḥ*—penance; *kriyāḥ*—acts; *dāna*—charity; *kriyāḥ*—activities; *ca*—also; *vividhāḥ*—various; *kriyante*—they are done; *mokṣa-kāṅkṣibhiḥ*—by those who desire liberation.

Those who desire liberation utter the syllable tat while performing acts of sacrifice, austerity, and charity of various sorts without desiring to enjoy the results for themselves.

The syllable *tat* is invoked for liberation in such aphorisms as *tat tvam asi.* It indicates the supreme transcendent reality. The words *brahma-vādinaḥ* in the previous verse refer to all students of the *Vedas*, whereas here Kṛṣṇa speaks of those students interested in liberation. While *oṁ* is uttered before all acts, be they religious in nature or aimed at liberation, *tat* is uttered exclusively with regard to liberation.

Text 26

सद्भावे साधुभावे च सदित्येतत् प्रयुज्यते ।
प्रशस्ते कर्मणि तथा सच्छब्दः पार्थ युज्यते ॥२६॥

sad-bhāve sādhu-bhāve ca sad ity etat prayujyate/
praśaste karmaṇi tathā sac-chabdaḥ pārtha yujyate//

sat-bhāve—in the sense of "reality"; *sādhu-bhāve*—in the sense of "goodness"; *ca*—also; *sat*—*sat; iti*—thus; *etat*—this; *prayujyate*—it is used; *praśaste*—in laudable; *karmaṇi*—in act; *tathā*—also; *sat-śabdaḥ*—the sound *sat; pārtha*—O son of Pṛthā; *yujyate*—it is used.

Sat is used to indicate both reality and goodness. The word sat is similarly used in the performance of any praiseworthy act, O son of Pṛthā.

Text 27

यज्ञे तपसि दाने च स्थितिः सदिति चोच्यते ।
कर्म चैव तदर्थीयं सदित्येवाभिधीयते ॥२७॥

yajñe tapasi dāne ca sthitiḥ sad iti cocyate/
karma caiva tad-arthīyaṁ sad ity evābhidhīyate//

yajñe—in sacrifice; *tapasi*—in austerity; *dāne*—in charity; *ca*—also; *sthitiḥ*—conviction; *sat*—*sat; iti*—thus; *ca*—and; *ucyate*—it is pronounced; *karma*—

action; *ca*—also; *eva*—certainly; *tat*—that; *arthīyam*—meant; *sat*—*sat*; *iti*—thus; *eva*—certainly; *abhidhīyate*—it is designated.

The word sat also refers to the conviction behind acts of sacrifice, austerity, and charity; acts with these purposes in mind are similarly designated as sat.

Kṛṣṇa says in verse 26 that the syllable *sat* signifies reality, God. However, he implies here that it represents God's presence in pious acts of this world. It is goodness itself and auspicious acts in *sattva-guṇa* of a religious and philanthropic nature. It is also the virtue of one's conviction in acts of sacrifice, austerity, and charity, as well as activities meant for assisting one in these acts. Thus its utterance in remembrance of God removes all discrepancy in the performance of pious acts.

As each of these two syllables are potent themselves with regard to making one's life auspicious, how much more so is the utterance of all three, *oṁ tat sat*. The import of this section is that if those who do not take the trouble to study the scripture and ascertain its conclusion, but out of some faith nonetheless worship without being inimical to the scripture by uttering this sacred *mantra* and offering their acts to God, they will eventually know perfection. Thus Kṛṣṇa speaks of the power of God's name.

Should one question the necessity of faith at all because of the power of the sacred syllables *oṁ tat sat*, Kṛṣṇa replies in the next verse.

Text 28

अश्रद्धया हुतं दत्तं तपस्तप्तं कृतं च यत् ।
असदित्युच्यते पार्थ न च तत्प्रेत्य नो इह ॥२८॥

aśraddhayā hutaṁ dattaṁ tapas taptaṁ kṛtaṁ ca yat/
asad ity ucyate pārtha na ca tat pretya no iha//

aśraddhayā—without faith; *hutam*—sacrificed; *dattam*—given; *tapaḥ*—penance; *taptam*—executed; *kṛtam*—performed; *ca*—also; *yat*—which; *asat*—false; *iti*—thus; *ucyate*—it is said; *pārtha*—O son of Pṛthā; *na*—not; *ca*—also; *tat*—that; *pretya*—having died (gone); *na u*—nor; *iha*—in this world.

O son of Pṛthā, any action performed without faith—even sacrifice, charity, and austerity—is considered impious. Such acts are fruitful neither in this world nor the next.

Kṛṣṇa ends this chapter stressing the virtue of faith by condemning sacrifice *(hutam)*, austerity *(tapas)*, and charity *(dattam)*, as well as other acts *(kṛtam)*, such as glorification of worshippable persons, performed without it. Although the chanting of *oṁ tat sat* is powerful, it manifests its power in the fertile ground of the faithful heart. Indeed, it is even said that the name of God should not be given to the faithless, and one who does so offends the holy name itself.

CHAPTER EIGHTEEN

मोक्षयोगः
Mokṣa-yoga

YOGA OF FREEDOM

Text 1

अर्जुन उवाच
सन्न्यासस्य महाबाहो तत्त्वमिच्छामि वेदितुम् ।
त्यागस्य च हृषीकेश पृथक् केशिनिषूदन ॥१॥

arjuna uvāca
sannyāsasya mahā-bāho tattvam icchāmi veditum/
tyāgasya ca hṛṣīkeśa pṛthak keśi-niṣūdana//

arjunaḥ uvāca—Arjuna said; *sannyāsasya*—of *sannyāsa*; *mahā-bāho*—O mighty-armed one; *tattvam*—truth; *icchāmi*—I want; *veditum*—to understand; *tyāgasya*—of *tyāga*; *ca*—and; *hṛṣīkeśa*—O Hṛṣīkeśa; *pṛthak*—differently; *keśi-niṣūdana*—O slayer of Keśī.

Arjuna said: O mighty-armed one, I want to understand the truth about sannyāsa and tyāga, O Hṛṣīkeśa, as well as the difference between them, O slayer of Keśī.

Arjuna's threefold address in which he refers to Kṛṣṇa as Mahābāho, Hṛṣīkeśa, and Keśi-niṣūdana implies great love on his part. At this point he has heard almost the entire gospel of the *Gītā* from the lotus lips of his dearmost friend, and he is experiencing extreme affection.

Mahā-bāho means "mighty-armed." By addressing Kṛṣṇa in this way Arjuna expresses the security he feels after hearing Kṛṣṇa's reassuring words. This epithet is also related to the next one, Keśi-niṣūdana. Kṛṣṇa of Vraja killed the horse demon Keśī by extending his mighty left arm into Keśī's mouth. This demon represents the wild horse of doubts that spring as if out of nowhere to trouble the mind of the practitioner. Here Arjuna asks

Kṛṣṇa to slay one more doubt concerning the apparent difference between *sannyāsa* and renunciation *(tyāga)*. He wants to know clearly what these two terms imply. Pure expressions of *sannyāsa* and *tyāga* involve internal control of the mind and senses. Thus Arjuna, desiring to know the truth about them, addresses Kṛṣṇa as Hṛṣīkeśa, he who has the power to remove internal disturbances.

Arjuna's doubt arises from things that Kṛṣṇa said about *sannyāsa* and *tyāga* in the first six chapters of the *Gītā*.[1] There Kṛṣṇa spoke of both ceasing from action altogether *(sannyāsa)* and foregoing only the result of action *(tyāga)*. This theme recurs throughout chapters 3 through 6. Here again Arjuna seeks clarification between *jñāna-yoga*, referred to in this verse as *sannyāsa*, and *niṣkāma-karma-yoga*, referred to as *tyāga*. Thus through his question Arjuna gives Kṛṣṇa the opportunity to begin his summary of the entire *Gītā*.

Text 2

श्रीभगवानुवाच

काम्यानां कर्मणां न्यासं सन्न्यासं कवयो विदुः ।
सर्वकर्मफलत्यागं प्राहुस्त्यागं विचक्षणाः ॥२॥

śrī-bhagavān uvāca
kāmyānāṁ karmaṇāṁ nyāsaṁ sannyāsaṁ kavayo viduḥ/
sarva-karma-phala-tyāgaṁ prāhus tyāgaṁ vicakṣaṇāḥ//

śrī-bhagavān uvāca—the Lord of Śrī said; *kāmyānām*—with desire; *karmaṇām*—of actions; *nyāsam*—renunciation; *sannyāsam*—*sannyāsa*; *kavayaḥ*—the learned; *viduḥ*—they know; *sarva*—all; *karma*—action; *phala*—result; *tyāgam*—renunciation; *prāhuḥ*—they call; *tyāgam*—*tyāga*; *vicakṣaṇāḥ*—the wise.

The Lord of Śrī said: The learned understand giving up actions performed with a desire for reward to be sannyāsa. The wise call giving up the results of all work tyāga.

Before giving his own opinion beginning with verse 4, Kṛṣṇa mentions that of others—learned persons—in this verse and the following one. In doing so, he implies that Arjuna's question is worthy, for even learned persons differ regarding the subtle meanings of *sannyāsa* and *tyāga*.

1. See Bg. 4.20 and 5.13 for examples of Kṛṣṇa's stress on *tyāga* and *sannyāsa*.

Here Kṛṣṇa says that some consider *sannyāsa* to be the renunciation of actions recommended in the scripture for fruitive gain, such as those that are aimed at acquiring a good child, a wife, and so on. Those of this opinion maintain that *sannyāsa* does, however, involve action that has no overt fruitive goal connected with it, actions that bear the fruit of purification and knowledge.

Others think that both fruitive and nonfruitive actions can be performed if one is not attached to the fruit of one's work, and this they call *tyāga*. Those mentioned in this verse are of the opinion that *sannyāsa* and *tyāga* are different from one another. There are still other opinions concerning the meaning of *tyāga*.

Text 3

त्याज्यं दोषवदित्येके कर्म प्राहुर्मनीषिणः ।
यज्ञदानतपःकर्म न त्याज्यमिति चापरे ॥३॥

tyājyaṁ doṣa-vad ity eke karma prāhur manīṣiṇaḥ/
yajña-dāna-tapaḥ-karma na tyājyam iti cāpare//

tyājyam—to be given up; *doṣa-vat*—faulty; *iti*—thus; *eke*—some; *karma*—action; *prāhuḥ*—they say; *manīṣiṇaḥ*—the thoughtful; *yajña*—sacrifice; *dāna*—charity; *tapaḥ*—austerity; *karma*—act; *na*—not; *tyājyam*—to be given up; *iti*—thus; *ca*—and; *apare*—others.

Some learned persons say that action, being inherently faulty, should be abandoned altogether, and others say that acts of sacrifice, charity, and austerity should not be abandoned.

The scholars who follow Kapila's Sāṅkhya think that all activity is inherently flawed, and thus *tyāga* involves ceasing from all action, including acts of sacrifice, charity, and austerity. They consider even enjoined sacrifices, which sometimes involve some type of violence, to be undesirable. Others, the followers of Jaimini's Karma-mīmāṁsā, differ. They recommend perpetual performance of sacrifice, charity, and austerity in spite of any perceived defect in them because these activities are enjoined in the scripture.

Having considered various opinions, Kṛṣṇa next offers his own definitive statement on the meaning of *tyāga*.

Text 4

निश्चयं शृणु मे तत्र त्यागे भरतसत्तम ।
त्यागो हि पुरुषव्याघ्र त्रिविधः सम्प्रकीर्तितः ॥४॥

niścayaṁ śṛṇu me tatra tyāge bharata-sattama/
tyāgo hi puruṣa-vyāghra tri-vidhaḥ samprakīrtitaḥ//

niścayam—conclusion; *śṛṇu*—hear; *me*—my; *tatra*—there; *tyāge*—on *tyāga*; *bharata-sat-tama*—O best of the Bhāratas; *tyāgaḥ*—*tyāga*; *hi*—certainly; *puruṣa-vyāghra*—O tiger among men; *tri-vidhaḥ*—of three kinds; *samprakīr-titaḥ*—declared to be.

O best of the descendants of Bharata, hear my conclusion on tyāga. O best of men, tyāga is declared to be of three kinds.

Kṛṣṇa's opinion addresses the implication of Arjuna's question that is carried forward from the previous chapter: although Kṛṣṇa connects renunciation with transcending the *guṇas* in chapter 2 (Bg. 2.45), Arjuna wonders if there is any relationship between some forms of renunciation and the three *guṇas*. In the course of addressing this question, Kṛṣṇa will reveal that both the terms, *sannyāsa* and *tyāga*, in essence mean the same thing and that only renunciation that is sattvic is desirable. Furthermore, it is the renunciation of the fruit of action, and not renunciation of action itself, that is at the heart of renunciation. Renunciation is an internal affair that has little to do with external actions. This is what Kṛṣṇa has stressed all along.

Text 5

यज्ञदानतपःकर्म न त्याज्यं कार्यमेव तत् ।
यज्ञो दानं तपश्चैव पावनानि मनीषिणाम् ॥५॥

yajña-dāna-tapaḥ-karma na tyājyaṁ kāryam eva tat/
yajño dānaṁ tapaś caiva pāvanāni manīṣiṇām//

yajña—sacrifice; *dāna*—charity; *tapaḥ*—austerity; *karma*—act; *na*—not; *tyājyam*—to be given up; *kāryam*—to be done; *eva*—indeed; *tat*—that; *ya-jñaḥ*—sacrifice; *dānam*—charity; *tapaḥ*—austerity; *ca*—and; *eva*—certainly; *pāvanāni*—purifying; *manīṣiṇām*—the wise.

Acts of sacrifice, charity, and austerity are not to be given up. Indeed, they should be performed, for sacrifice, charity, and austerity purify even those who are wise.

Here Kṛṣṇa says that not only are sacrifice, charity, and austerity not to be given up, one *must* engage in them. In doing so, even the wise, the *jñānīs*, purify themselves. Kṛṣṇa next describes how these three should be performed. Thus he anticipates Arjuna's doubt: are these activities not purifying in and of themselves and thus is there really any need to perform them without desiring their fruit?

Text 6

एतान्यपि तु कर्माणि सङ्गं त्यक्त्वा फलानि च ।
कर्तव्यानीति मे पार्थ निश्चितं मतमुत्तमम् ॥६॥

etāny api tu karmāṇi saṅgaṁ tyaktvā phalāni ca/
kartavyānīti me pārtha niścitaṁ matam uttamam//

etāni—these; *api*—certainly; *tu*—however; *karmāṇi*—actions; *saṅgam*—association; *tyaktvā*—renouncing; *phalāni*—results; *ca*—and; *kartavyāni*—to be performed; *iti*—thus; *me*—my; *pārtha*—O son of Pṛthā; *niścitam*— without a doubt; *matam*—opinion; *uttamam*—highest.

However, these actions are to be performed in the spirit of detachment from their results. Without a doubt this is my final opinion, O son of Pṛthā.

Śrīdhara Swāmī comments that sacrifice, charity, and austerity should be performed as acts of worship of the Lord. They should be performed without attachment to enjoying the results for oneself, without attachment to the activity itself, and without identifying oneself as the performer of these acts. This is Kṛṣṇa's final opinion. This opinion overrides those of others mentioned earlier. It is supreme *(uttamam)*, and it speaks to the heart of the spirit of renunciation.

Having established his own supreme opinion, which concurs with the opinion of those mentioned in verse 3 who advocate perpetual performance of sacrifice, charity, and austerity, Kṛṣṇa next refutes the opposite view that action itself is faulty and must be given up.

Text 7

नियतस्य तु सन्न्यासः कर्मणो नोपपद्यते ।
मोहात्तस्य परित्यागस्तामसः परिकीर्तितः ॥७॥

niyatasya tu sannyāsaḥ karmaṇo nopapadyate/
mohāt tasya parityāgas tāmasaḥ parikīrtitaḥ//

niyatasya—of prescribed; *tu*—but; *sannyāsaḥ*—renunciation; *karmaṇaḥ*—of activity; *na*—not; *upapadyate*—it is proper; *mohāt*—out of delusion; *tasya*—of it; *parityāgaḥ*—renunciation; *tāmasaḥ*—tamasic; *parikīrtitaḥ*—declared.

But renunciation of prescribed duties is improper. Abandoning them out of delusion is considered to be tamasic.

In this verse Kṛṣṇa equates *tyāga* and *sannyāsa*, using both words synonymously (*sannyāsaḥ/parityāgaḥ*). Thus he answers Arjuna's question as to the difference between the two. He also addresses the opinion of those who advocate giving up all action in the name of renunciation. Such renunciation is tamasic. It is born of delusion because prescribed duties properly performed purify the soul.

Text 8

दुःखमित्येव यत्कर्म कायक्लेशभयात्त्यजेत् ।
स कृत्वा राजसं त्यागं नैव त्यागफलं लभेत् ॥८॥

duḥkham ity eva yat karma kāya-kleśa-bhayāt tyajet/
sa kṛtvā rājasaṁ tyāgaṁ naiva tyāga-phalaṁ labhet//

duḥkham—difficult; *iti*—thus; *eva*—certainly; *yat*—which; *karma*—action; *kāya*—body; *kleśa*—trouble; *bhayāt*—out of fear; *tyajet*—he abandons; *saḥ*—he; *kṛtvā*—doing; *rājasam*—rajasic; *tyāgam*—renunciation; *na*—not; *eva*—certainly; *tyāga*—renunciation; *phalam*—fruit; *labhet*—he obtains.

One who abandons an action because it is difficult or out of fear of bodily inconvenience engages in rajasic renunciation. Such a person does not obtain the true fruit of renunciation.

The real fruits of renunciation are knowledge and steadfastness in spiritual practice. These fruits are not attained by one who renounces worldly duties because he finds them irksome. *Sannyāsa* is not about getting away from the difficulties of everyday life, but rather looking at them as a means to purification.

Text 9

कार्यमित्येव यत्कर्म नियतं क्रियतेऽर्जुन ।
सङ्गं त्यक्त्वा फलं चैव स त्यागः सात्त्विको मतः ॥९॥

kāryam ity eva yat karma niyataṁ kriyate 'rjuna/
saṅgaṁ tyaktvā phalaṁ caiva sa tyāgaḥ sāttviko mataḥ//

kāryam—to be done; *iti*—thus; *eva*—indeed; *yat*—which; *karma*—action; *niyatam*—prescribed; *kriyate*—it is performed; *arjuna*—Arjuna; *saṅgam*—attachment; *tyaktvā*—abandoning; *phalam*—fruit; *ca*—and; *eva*—certainly; *saḥ*—that; *tyāgaḥ*—renunciation; *sāttvikaḥ*—sattvic; *mataḥ*—considered.

Arjuna, when obligatory work is performed because it should be done, while abandoning attachment for it and its fruit, such renunciation is sattvic.

Here Kṛṣṇa addresses his friend as Arjuna, which, as stated earlier, means "pure," to indicate that he is pure and can thus understand the virtue of sattvic renunciation. This kind of renunciation is what is meant by *sannyāsa* and *tyāga*. Refusal to act is born of either delusion or fear of the hardships involved in performing one's duties. However, spiritual renunciation does not involve negation of activity. It involves full commitment to activity devoid of any egocentric attitude resulting from thinking oneself the doer or from personal attachment to action itself or its fruits. Renunciation belongs to the inner world, the consciousness behind action. It is freedom from self-centeredness and not freedom from work. The soul belongs to God and has duties in relation to him. Performing them dutifully eventually turns labor into love. Knowledge leading to the cessation of activity is not the goal. Love—with all of the trouble that accompanies it—is the goal of the Gītā.

Kṛṣṇa describes the symptoms of this kind of renunciation next.

Text 10

न द्वेष्ट्यकुशलं कर्म कुशले नानुषज्जते ।
त्यागी सत्त्वसमाविष्टो मेधावी छिन्नसंशयः ॥१०॥

na dveṣṭy akuśalaṁ karma kuśale nānuṣajjate/
tyāgī sattva-samāviṣṭo medhāvī chinna-saṁśayaḥ//

na—not; *dveṣṭi*—he dislikes; *akuśalam*—disagreeable; *karma*—work; *kuśale*—agreeable; *na*—not; *anuṣajjate*—he becomes attached; *tyāgī*—the renunciate; *sattva*—in *sattva*; *samāviṣṭaḥ*—absorbed; *medhāvī*—wise; *chinna*—eliminated; *saṁśayaḥ*—doubt.

Situated in sattva, the wise renunciate, who is free from doubt, does not dislike work that is disagreeable, nor is he attached to work that is agreeable.

Misery is a result of trying to be happy. How we react to misery is the key to becoming happy. A sattvic renunciate is neither attached to work that is pleasant, nor averse to that which is unpleasant.

Text 11

न हि देहभृता शक्यं त्यक्तुं कर्माण्यशेषतः ।
यस्तु कर्मफलत्यागी स त्यागीत्यभिधीयते ॥११॥

na hi deha-bhṛtā śakyaṁ tyaktuṁ karmāṇy aśeṣataḥ/
yas tu karma-phala-tyāgī sa tyāgīty abhidhīyate//

na—not; *hi*—certainly; *deha-bhṛtā*—by the embodied; *śakyam*—possible; *tyaktum*—to give up; *karmāṇi*—actions; *aśeṣataḥ*—entirely; *yaḥ*—who; *tu*—but; *karma*—action; *phala*—fruit; *tyāgī*—renouncer; *saḥ*—he; *tyāgī*—renunciate; *iti*—thus; *abhidhīyate*—he is called.

It is impossible for embodied beings to entirely give up actions. Thus one who gives up the fruit of action is called a renunciate.

Text 12

अनिष्टमिष्टं मिश्रं च त्रिविधं कर्मणः फलम् ।
भवत्यत्यागिनां प्रेत्य न तु सन्न्यासिनां क्वचित् ॥१२॥

aniṣṭam iṣṭaṁ miśraṁ ca tri-vidhaṁ karmaṇaḥ phalam/
bhavaty atyāginām pretya na tu sannyāsināṁ kvacit//

aniṣṭam—undesired; *iṣṭam*—desired; *miśram*—mixed; *ca*—and; *tri-vidham*—of three kinds; *karmaṇaḥ*—of action; *phalam*—fruit; *bhavati*—it is; *atyāginām*—for those who are not renounced; *pretya*—after dying; *na*—not; *tu*—but; *sannyāsinām*—for the renunciates; *kvacit*—whatsoever.

When those who have not adopted renunciation die, they experience three kinds of fruits from their action: evil, good, and mixed. For renunciates, however, there is no fruit whatsoever.

One who renounces the fruit of action by offering it to God does not experience this fruit after death in the form of going to heaven or hell or again taking birth on earth, where there are both heavenly and hellish conditions. The renunciate offers the fruit of his work to God and identifies himself as the agent of God through whom that work is accomplished. He is attached to serving God for the pleasure of God, rather than attached to any particular type of work. Thus he is liberated from good, bad, and mixed results of his actions. He does not take birth in heaven, hell, or in human society. Appropriate renunciation nullifies the influence of *karma.*

Thus far Kṛṣṇa has reiterated his earlier emphasis on *niṣkāma-karma-yoga*, which leads naturally to knowledge and devotion. In the first six chapters of the *Gītā*, Kṛṣṇa also discusses knowledge itself at some length, as he does more so in the final six chapters. In verses 13 through 17 of this summary chapter, Kṛṣṇa discusses the causes of action and how one can work without acquiring the fruit of work. In this section Kṛṣṇa reiterates the knowledge of Vedānta that the only real doer is God himself.

Text 13

पञ्चैतानि महाबाहो कारणानि निबोध मे ।
सांख्ये कृतान्ते प्रोक्तानि सिद्धये सर्वकर्मणाम् ॥१३॥

pañcaitāni mahā-bāho kāraṇāni nibodha me/
sāṅkhye kṛtānte proktāni siddhaye sarva-karmaṇām//

pañca—five; *etāni*—these; *mahā-bāho*—O mighty-armed one; *kāraṇāni*—factors; *nibodha*—learn; *me*—from me; *sāṅkhye*—in the Vedānta; *kṛta-ante*—in the conclusion; *proktāni*—spoken; *siddhaye*—for the accomplishment; *sarva*—all; *karmaṇām*—of activities.

Learn from me, O mighty-armed one, these five factors spoken of in the Vedānta by which all actions are accomplished.

Here the words *sāṅkhye kṛtānte* mean analysis *(sāṅkhya)*, the likes of which is found in the Vedānta, the conclusion *(kṛtānte)* of the *Vedas*. Because this subject is difficult to understand, Kṛṣṇa calls for Arjuna's rapt attention by speaking emphatically, "Learn from me *(nibodha me)*!"

Text 14–15

अधिष्ठानं तथा कर्ता करणं च पृथग्विधम् ।
विविधाश्च पृथक्चेष्टा दैवं चैवात्र पञ्चमम् ॥१४॥

शरीरवाङ्मनोभिर्यत् कर्म प्रारभते नरः ।
न्याय्यं वा विपरीतं वा पञ्चैते तस्य हेतवः ॥१८॥

adhiṣṭhānaṁ tathā kartā karaṇaṁ ca pṛthag-vidham/
vividhāś ca pṛthak ceṣṭā daivaṁ caivātra pañcamam//
śarīra-vāṅ-manobhir yat karma prārabhate naraḥ/
nyāyyaṁ vā viparītaṁ vā pañcaite tasya hetavaḥ//

adhiṣṭhānam—the seat; *tathā*—also; *kartā*—the performer; *karaṇam*—instrument; *ca*—and; *pṛthak-vidham*—of different kinds; *vividhāḥ*—various; *ca*—and; *pṛthak*—separate; *ceṣṭāḥ*—endeavors; *daivam*—fate; *ca*—and; *eva*—certainly; *atra*—here; *pañcamam*—last but not least (fifth); *śarīra-vāk-manobhiḥ*—by body, speech, and mind; *yat*—which; *karma*—action; *prārabhate*—he begins; *naraḥ*—person; *nyāyyam*—appropriate; *vā*—or; *viparītam*—opposite; *vā*—or; *pañca*—five; *ete*—these; *tasya*—of this; *hetavaḥ*—causes.

The seat of action (the body), the performer of action, the senses, the various types of endeavors, and, last but not least, God, or fate, are the five causes of whatever action, appropriate or inappropriate, a person performs in body, speech, or mind.

The body is the seat *(adhiṣṭhānam)* of activity. The soul in material consciousness under the influence of *ahaṁkāra* is the performer *(kartā)* of any action. The sense organs are the means *(karaṇam)* to accomplish any action. The various types of endeavors *(ceṣṭā)* involve the movement of the life airs, or vital energies, within the body. These four are grouped together along with the influence of God *(daivam)*, which is mentioned separately as "the fifth" *(pañcamam)* in order to distinguish it from the others. God's influence is the ultimate factor in any action, the sanction necessary for any action to be carried out, which we sometimes refer to as fate or destiny. Here the word *daivam* refers more to the Paramātmā than it does to the influence of the gods who are under the Paramātmā's control and preside over the functions of the senses. He is the source of the other four factors involved in any action. The ultimacy of the Paramātmā's influence on all action is confirmed elsewhere in the *Gītā* (Bg. 15.15, 18.61). This is also supported by *Vedānta-sūtra* 2.3.41. Rāmānujācārya describes the Paramātmā as "the most important element in determining the results of any action."

Actions in accordance with scripture are appropriate and those that are not are inappropriate. Body, speech, and mind represent the entirety of activity. Thus all action, whether good or bad, is a product of these five factors. Therefore, the soul itself in its pure identity is not involved in action. The pure soul is at best a relative doer, who acts instrumentally, having surrendered his will to God.

The apparent contradiction between God's omnipotence and the free will of the individual soul is raised by Baladeva Vidyābhūṣaṇa, Vallabha, and Rāmānujācārya in their commentaries on these verses. God provides the living being with a body, sense organs, and vital energies, all of which facilitate action. He also grants the power of initiative and thus inner moral freedom. Thus equipped, the soul expresses itself in material life. Its free will stands unimpaired, and its simultaneous dependence on God for that free will and its physical facility remains a metaphysical fact. Not a blade of grass moves without the will of God, and yet humanity is also free to act. God himself is responsible for humanity's free will. He wills our free will, and thus we are dynamically free through him and dependent on him simultaneously. We are an expression of his will, and he is the primary factor behind every act. If the living being had no freedom in making choices, there would be no need for scriptures with proscribed and recommended activities.

In the next verse Kṛṣṇa turns his attention to those who after hearing about the ultimate agency of God—the source of both our free will and our facility for action—continue to think themselves independent in action.

Text 16

तत्रैवं सति कर्तारमात्मानं केवलं तु यः ।
पश्यत्यकृतबुद्धित्वान्न स पश्यति दुर्मतिः ॥१६॥

tatraivaṁ sati kartāram ātmānaṁ kevalaṁ tu yaḥ/
paśyaty akṛta-buddhitvān na sa paśyati durmatiḥ//

tatra—there; *evam*—thus; *sati*—being; *kartāram*—doer; *ātmānam*—himself; *kevalam*—only; *tu*—but; *yaḥ*—who; *paśyati*—he sees; *akṛta-buddhitvāt*—due to imperfect understanding; *na*—not; *saḥ*—he; *paśyati*—he sees; *durmatiḥ*—foolish.

This being so, a person who sees himself as the only doer does not see things as they are. His imperfectly developed understanding renders him foolish.

One who has not deliberated properly on the import of the scripture or heard from realized souls about the nature of the self is invariably prone to imperfect understanding *(akṛta-buddhitvāt)*. As scripture and saints are reliable sources of valid evidence, those who have heard from these sources yet reject them are considered fools.

Text 17

यस्य नाहङ्कृतो भावो बुद्धिर्यस्य न लिप्यते ।
हत्वापि स इमाँल्लोकान्न हन्ति न निबध्यते ॥१७॥

yasya nāhaṅkṛto bhāvo buddhir yasya na lipyate/
hatvāpi sa imān lokān na hanti na nibadhyate//

yasya—one whose; *na*—not; *ahaṅkṛtaḥ*—egoistic; *bhāvaḥ*—nature; *buddhiḥ*—intelligence; *yasya*—one whose; *na*—not; *lipyate*—he is tinged; *hatvā*—killing; *api*—even; *saḥ*—he; *imān*—these; *lokān*—people; *na*—not; *hanti*—he kills; *na*—not; *nibadhyate*—he is bound.

A person whose mind is free from egotism and whose intellect is pure is not bound even though he slays many people, for he does not truly slay.

In this world a madman is not held accountable for killing another because he is not involved consciously in the act of killing. A soldier in war who kills on behalf of his country and superior commander is also not held accountable for killing. One's consciousness with regard to any action is the principal factor to be considered in determining accountability. Similarly, the realized soul is not bound by reaction to that which he does in the pure consciousness of being an agent of God. This pure consciousness is devoid of material egotism and intellect that has not been purified by scripture and saintly association.

The egoless action of pure intellect mentioned in this verse and how one becomes situated in it has been described at length throughout the *Bhagavad-gītā*. It is not easily attained, and it cannot be imitated. Thus abuse of this verse, which leads to antinomianism, is checked considerably by the standard of consciousness stipulated herein that one must attain before one can be considered free from karmic reactions.

While this verse returns us to the battlefield and the matter at hand, it also serves to underscore the exalted nature of the self and the God-realization that Kṛṣṇa wants Arjuna to attain. Here, just as in the first six chapters, Kṛṣṇa encourages Arjuna to fight as his agent without concern for any karmic implications resulting from the slaying of Bhīṣma, Droṇa, and other warriors. Thus for the sake of emphasizing the purity of self-realization, the contrast is made here and in the *Gītā* in general between enlightenment and the unthinkable act of killing one's relatives. Hypothetically, a person acting as a conscious agent of God in all of his actions can commit even such a heinous act yet not be held accountable for it.

Text 18

ज्ञानं ज्ञेयं परिज्ञाता त्रिविधा कर्मचोदना ।
करणं कर्म कर्तेति त्रिविधः कर्मसंग्रहः ॥१८॥

jñānaṁ jñeyaṁ parijñātā tri-vidhā karma-codanā/
karaṇaṁ karma karteti tri-vidhaḥ karma-saṅgrahaḥ//

jñānam—knowledge; *jñeyam*—the object of knowledge; *parijñātā*—the knower; *tri-vidhā*—of three kinds; *karma*—action; *codanā*—motivation; *karaṇam*—instrument; *karma*—action; *kartā*—agent; *iti*—thus; *tri-vidhaḥ*—of three kinds; *karma-saṅgrahaḥ*—basis of action.

Knowledge, the object of knowledge, and the knower make up the threefold impetus underlying action. The instrument, the object, and the agent are the three constituents of action.

With this verse, Kṛṣṇa again takes up the subject of knowledge, adding a final word to the teachings he gave in the first and last six chapters of the *Gītā*. Knowledge, the object of knowledge, and the knower were elaborately discussed in chapter 13 (Bg. 13.7–18), particularly in terms of transcending the material modes of nature. There Kṛṣṇa described knowledge to be knowledge of himself, the soul, and the bodily field of activity. He identified the object of knowledge to be himself and the knower to be both himself and the enlightened soul. Here, however, Kṛṣṇa will speak of these three aspects of knowing as they are manifest within the *guṇas*. All actions have an impetus and here Kṛṣṇa divides this impetus into three categories: those arising from knowledge, those arising from the object of knowledge, and those arising from the knower himself. Similarly, every action has three components: the instruments used in any action, the objective of one's work, and the agent who performs the work. Kṛṣṇa's analysis is made in consideration of the three predominant grammatical cases: the nominative, accusative, and instrumental, without which no action is complete. Most commentators have also pointed out that there is a correspondence between the impetuses for action and their components.

Knowledge *(jñānam)* is the understanding that is the means to accomplish action. It is the instrumental aspect of the impulse behind action. The object of knowledge *(jñeyam)* is the action itself, by which an objective is reached. It is the objective aspect of the impulse to act. The knower *(parijñātā)* is one who possesses specific knowledge with regard to action undertaken. The knower is the subjective aspect of the impulse underlying action. These three constitute the threefold impulse underlying action.

The three constituents of action include the instruments *(karaṇam)* of the senses which cause action to take place, the desired objective *(karma)*, and the agent *(kartā)* of action. These three form the constituents of action *(karma-saṅgrahaḥ)* in its instrumental, objective, and subjective aspects, respectively.

Kṛṣṇa mentions the threefold impetus for action along with the three constituents of action to further illustrate that the self, being apart from the impetus for action, its constituents, and its fruit, is not directly involved in action. Accordingly, Kṛṣṇa next elaborates on the impulse to act and the constituents of action in relation to the *guṇas*.

Text 19

ज्ञानं कर्म च कर्ता च त्रिधैव गुणभेदतः ।
प्रोच्यते गुणसंख्याने यथावच्छृणु तान्यपि ॥१९॥

jñānaṁ karma ca kartā ca tridhaiva guṇa-bhedataḥ/
procyate guṇa-saṅkhyāne yathāvac chṛṇu tāny api//

jñānam—knowledge; *karma*—action; *ca*—and; *kartā*—doer; *ca*—and; *tridhā*—of three kinds; *eva*—certainly; *guṇa-bhedataḥ*—in accordance with the *guṇas*; *procyate*—it is declared; *guṇa-saṅkhyāne*—in the scripture dealing with the *guṇas*; *yathā-vat*—respectively; *śṛṇu*—hear; *tāni*—them; *api*—also.

It is declared in the scripture dealing with the modes of nature (guṇas) that knowledge, action, and the doer are of three kinds in accordance with these modes. Hear now about these.

The words *guṇa-sāṅkhyane* in this verse refer to that scripture wherein the science of classifying things in terms of the *guṇas* is fully *(sam)* taught (*khyā*). Although Kapila has done this in his doctrine of Sāṅkhya, this verse need not be seen as a reference to his work, as other scriptures also deal with this subject. However, there is no harm in understanding Kṛṣṇa's words as a reference to Kapila's doctrine, for although his conclusions are not in harmony with Vedānta, they are correct in terms of classifying things according to the *guṇas*.

In the *Gītā* itself, the *guṇas* have been described from different angles in chapters 14 and 17. Here Kṛṣṇa further discusses them over the next twenty verses. In chapter 14 they are discussed in terms of how they bind the conditioned soul. In chapter 17 they are discussed to demonstrate the superiority of *sattva* and the need to strive for this *guṇa* and from there transcendence. Here in chapter 18 Kṛṣṇa discusses them again to stress the virtue of *sattva* and to shed light on the fact that the impetus underlying action, its constituents, and its fruit are categorically different from the self.

Text 20

सर्वभूतेषु येनैकं भावमव्ययमीक्षते ।
अविभक्तं विभक्तेषु तज्ज्ञानं विद्धि सात्त्विकम् ॥२०॥

sarva-bhūteṣu yenaikaṁ bhāvam avyayam īkṣate/
avibhaktaṁ vibhakteṣu taj jñānaṁ viddhi sāttvikam//

sarva-bhūteṣu—in all beings; *yena*—by which; *ekam*—one; *bhāvam*—situation; *avyayam*—imperishable; *īkṣate*—one sees; *avibhaktam*—undivided; *vibhakteṣu*—in the divided; *tat*—that; *jñānam*—knowledge; *viddhi*—know; *sāttvikam*—sattvic.

Know that knowledge to be sattvic in which one imperishable and unified spiritual principle is seen in all diverse beings.

Our knowledge is sattvic when we understand that, regardless of the diverse bodily circumstances souls find themselves in, all living beings are inherently spiritual and thus qualitatively the same. In this sense they are one. At the same time, they are categorically different from the bodies they inhabit.

Text 21

पृथक्त्वेन तु यज्ज्ञानं नानाभावान् पृथग्विधान् ।
वेत्ति सर्वेषु भूतेषु तज्ज्ञानं विद्धि राजसम् ॥२१॥

pṛthaktvena tu yaj jñānaṁ nānā-bhāvān pṛthag-vidhān/
vetti sarveṣu bhūteṣu taj jñānaṁ viddhi rājasam//

pṛthaktvena—because of division; *tu*—but; *yat*—which; *jñānam*—knowledge; *nānā-bhāvān*—many existences; *pṛthak-vidhān*—different; *vetti*—he knows; *sarveṣu*—in all; *bhūteṣu*—in beings; *tat*—that; *jñānam*—knowledge; *viddhi*—understand; *rājasam*—in terms of passion.

But you should understand that knowledge to be rajasic in which one sees that in every body there is a different type of living entity.

Rajasic knowledge does not recognize the unified, eternal spiritual principle in all bodies. Under its influence, one thinks that there are different types of living beings, which gives rise to sectarianism, racism, and sexism.

Text 22

यत्तु कृत्स्नवदेकस्मिन् कार्ये सक्तमहैतुकम् ।
अतत्त्वार्थवदल्पं च तत्तामसमुदाहृतम् ॥२२॥

yat tu kṛtsna-vad ekasmin kārye saktam ahaitukam/
atattvārtha-vad alpaṁ ca tat tāmasam udāhṛtam//

yat—which; *tu*—but; *kṛtsna-vat*—as all-in-all; *ekasmin*—in one; *kārye*—in course of action; *saktam*—attached; *ahaitukam*—unreasonably; *atattva-artha-vat*—not concerned with truth; *alpam*—trivial; *ca*—and; *tat*—that; *tāmasam*—tamasic; *udāhṛtam*—said to be.

However, that unreasonable knowledge which is not concerned with truth, which is trivial, and by which one is attached to one kind of physical work as though it were all-in-all is said to be tamasic.

Knowledge that is a product of *tamo-guṇa* is not at all helpful. Under its influence one does not recognize the eternal spiritual principle, thinking the body to be all-in-all.

Text 23

नियतं सङ्गरहितमरागद्वेषतः कृतम् ।
अफलप्रेप्सुना कर्म यत्तत्सात्त्विकमुच्यते ॥२३॥

niyataṁ saṅga-rahitam arāga-dveṣataḥ kṛtam/
aphala-prepsunā karma yat tat sāttvikam ucyate//

niyatam—ordained; *saṅga-rahitam*—detached; *arāga-dveṣataḥ*—without desire or aversion; *kṛtam*—done; *aphala-prepsunā*—without desire for the fruit; *karma*—action; *yat*—which; *tat*—that; *sāttvikam*—sattvic; *ucyate*—it is said.

That action which is regulated and detached, performed without desire or aversion, with no desire for its result is said to be sattvic.

Sattvic action is persistent and regulated. It is carried through to the finish. It also involves dedication and consistency with regard to the duties dictated by one's vocation in life. Such ordained (regulated) action is what should be performed by those under the influence of egoism, which creates the sense of being the doer of an action and enjoyer of its fruits. Ordained action removes this egoism and is devoid of attachment *(rāga)* and aversion *(dveṣa)*.

Text 24

यत्तु कामेप्सुना कर्म साहंकारेण वा पुनः ।
क्रियते बहुलायासं तद् राजसमुदाहृतम् ॥२४॥

yat tu kāmepsunā karma sāhaṅkāreṇa vā punaḥ/
kriyate bahulāyāsaṁ tad rājasam udāhṛtam//

yat—which; *tu*—but; *kāma-īpsunā*—by one with desires for result; *karma*—action; *sa-ahaṅkāreṇa*—with selfishness; *vā*—or; *punaḥ*—again; *kriyate*—it is performed; *bahulāyāsam*—great labor; *tat*—that; *rājasam*—rajasic; *udāhṛtam*—said to be.

An act is said to be rajasic when it requires abundant effort, is performed with an eye to enjoy its results, and is furthermore done with the conviction that one is the doer.

B. R. Śrīdhara Deva Goswāmī renders the word *bahulāyāsam* in this verse as "ambitious." When work is not a labor of love and involves the sense that one is doing something great, or work is performed with the ambition of being recognized for the effort, this work is under the influence of *rajo-guṇa*. To feel that we are ourselves accomplishing something great by our efforts and that our sacrifice is considerable takes away from the sacrifice.

Text 25

अनुबन्धं क्षयं हिंसामनपेक्ष्य च पौरुषम् ।
मोहादारभ्यते कर्म यत्तत्तामसमुच्यते ॥२५॥

anubandhaṁ kṣayaṁ hiṁsām anapekṣya ca pauruṣam/
mohād ārabhyate karma yat tat tāmasam ucyate//

anubandham—consequence; *kṣayam*—loss; *hiṁsām*—harm; *anapekṣya*—without considering; *ca*—and; *pauruṣam*—ability; *mohāt*—by illusion; *ārabhyate*—it is begun; *karma*—action; *yat*—which; *tat*—that; *tāmasam*—tamasic; *ucyate*—it is said.

That action undertaken out of delusion, without consideration of consequence, loss, harm, as well as one's own ability, is said to be tamasic.

Rāmānuja defines the word *pauruṣam* in this verse as the ability to see an action through to the end. This is absent in actions influenced by *tamo-guṇa*. Unlike Rāmānuja, Viśvanātha Cakravartī does not associate *pauruṣam* with the verb *anapekṣya*, but rather with *karma*. Thus he defines *pauruṣam* as "being concerned with minimal human activities and nothing more," *vyavahārika-puruṣa-mātra-kartavyam*. Śrīdhara Swāmī considers the word *kṣayam* (loss) to involve loss of money. One who spends foolishly is influenced by *tamo-guṇa*. Viśvanātha Cakravartī defines the same word as loss of religious principles. Baladeva Vidyābhūṣaṇa concurs, glossing *kṣayam* as *dharmādi-vināśam*, "the destruction of one's religious principles."

Text 26

मुक्तसङ्गोऽनहंवादी धृत्युत्साहसमन्वितः ।
सिद्ध्यसिद्ध्योर्निर्विकारः कर्ता सात्त्विक उच्यते ॥२६॥

mukta-saṅgo 'nahaṁ-vādī dhṛty-utsāha-samanvitaḥ/
siddhy-asiddhyor nirvikāraḥ kartā sāttvika ucyate//

mukta-saṅgaḥ—free from attachment; *anaham-vādī*—free from egotism; *dhṛti-utsāha-samanvitaḥ*—full of fortitude and diligence; *siddhi-asiddhyoḥ*—in success and failure; *nirvikāraḥ*—unperturbed; *kartā*—doer; *sāttvikaḥ*—sattvic; *ucyate*—it is said.

The doer who is free from attachment, free from egotism, full of patience and enthusiam, and unchanged in success or failure is said to be sattvic.

Text 27

रागी कर्मफलप्रेप्सुर्लुब्धो हिंसात्मकोऽशुचिः ।
हर्षशोकान्वितः कर्ता राजसः परिकीर्तितः ॥२७॥

rāgī karma-phala-prepsur lubdho hiṁsātmako 'śuciḥ/
harṣa-śokānvitaḥ kartā rājasaḥ parikīrtitaḥ//

rāgī—passionate; *karma-phala*—fruit of the action; *prepsuḥ*—desiring; *lubdhaḥ*—covetous; *hiṁsā-ātmakaḥ*—cruel-natured; *aśuciḥ*—impure; *harṣa-śoka-anvitaḥ*—concerned with joy and sorrow (moody); *kartā*—doer; *rājasaḥ*—rajasic; *parikīrtitaḥ*—declared.

Passionate, desiring the fruits of action, covetous, cruel-natured, impure, and moody—such a doer is said to be rajasic.

Text 28

अयुक्तः प्राकृतः स्तब्धः शठो नैष्कृतिकोऽलसः ।
विषादी दीर्घसूत्री च कर्ता तामस उच्यते ॥२८॥

ayuktaḥ prākṛtaḥ stabdhaḥ śaṭho naiṣkṛtiko 'lasaḥ/
viṣādī dīrgha-sūtrī ca kartā tāmasa ucyate//

ayuktaḥ—undisciplined; *prākṛtaḥ*—vulgar; *stabdhaḥ*—arrogant; *śaṭhaḥ*—deceitful; *naiṣkṛtikaḥ*—malicious; *alasaḥ*—lazy; *viṣādī*—morose; *dīrgha-sūtrī*—procrastinating; *ca*—and; *kartā*—doer; *tāmasaḥ*—tamasic; *ucyate*—it is said.

A doer who is undisciplined, vulgar, arrogant, deceitful, malicious, lazy, morose, and procrastinating is said to be tamasic.

With this verse Kṛṣṇa completes his classification of knowledge, action, and the doer according to the *guṇas*. Śrīdhara Swāmī comments that, in discussing the performer of action in verses 26 through 28 in relation to the *guṇas*, Kṛṣṇa has discussed the knower of action as well, which has not been analyzed separately here. This is so because, as we have seen earlier in verse

18, the knower and doer are one and the same, representing the subjective aspect of the impulse for action and its subjective component, respectively. Similarly, when analyzing action in verses 23 through 25, Kṛṣṇa has also described the object of knowledge. Thus Kṛṣṇa's discussion of action also implies discussion of the knowable as well, which is the objective aspect of the threefold impetus underlying action.

Remaining to be discussed in relation to the *guṇas* is the intellect that constitutes the instrumental aspect of the impulse for action, which understanding and fortitude are functions of. Discussion of the instrumental aspect of the impulse for action includes indirectly discussing the instrumental aspect (the senses) of the components of action. Kṛṣṇa turns Arjuna's attention to this next.

Text 29

बुद्धेर्भेदं धृतेश्चैव गुणतस्त्रिविधं शृणु ।
प्रोच्यमानमशेषेण पृथक्त्वेन धनञ्जय ॥२९॥

buddher bhedaṁ dhṛteś caiva guṇatas tri-vidhaṁ śṛṇu/
procyamānam aśeṣeṇa pṛthaktvena dhanañjaya//

buddheḥ—of intelligence; *bhedam*—difference; *dhṛteḥ*—of fortitude; *ca*—and; *eva*—certainly; *guṇataḥ*—in accordance with the *guṇas*; *tri-vidham*—of three kinds; *śṛṇu*—hear; *procyamānam*—described; *aśeṣeṇa*—in detail; *pṛthaktvena*—differently; *dhanañjaya*—O Dhanañjaya.

Listen, O Dhanañjaya, as I now describe completely and distinctly the threefold classification of intellect and also fortitude in accordance with the guṇas.

Intellect *(buddhi)* is considered to be one of the fourfold elements of the internal organ *(antaḥkāraṇa)*. It is characterized by the faculties of judgment and certainty. Fortitude is one of its functions. It is the firmness by which a person holds fast to his decision. Thus both intellect and fortitude are elements of the instrumental impulse to act, previously referred to as knowledge. Kṛṣṇa explains them completely by way of classifying them in accordance with the *guṇas*. The word *pṛthaktvena* implies that from his description it will be apparent which type of intellect and fortitude should be cultivated and which should be rejected.

Text 30

प्रवृत्तिं च निवृत्तिं च कार्याकार्ये भयाभये ।
बन्धं मोक्षं च या वेत्ति बुद्धिः सा पार्थ सात्त्विकी ॥३०॥

pravṛttiṁ ca nivṛttiṁ ca kāryākārye bhayābhaye/
bandhaṁ mokṣaṁ ca yā vetti buddhiḥ sā pārtha sāttvikī//

pravṛttim—activity; *ca*—and; *nivṛttim*—inactivity; *ca*—and; *kārya-akārye*—what is to be done and what is not to be done; *bhaya-abhaye*—fear and fearlessness; *bandham*—bondage; *mokṣam*—liberation; *ca*—and; *yā*—which; *vetti*—he knows; *buddhiḥ*—intellect; *sā*—that; *pārtha*—O son of Pṛthā; *sāttvikī*—sattvic.

That intellect which knows when to act and when not to act, what is to be done and what is not to be done, what is to be feared and what is not to be feared, along with knowledge of the nature of bondage and liberation, O son of Pṛthā, is sattvic.

Intellect is that by which one knows. Here it is being spoken of as if it were itself the knower, rather than the instrument of knowing. Śrīdhara Swāmī comments that Kṛṣṇa's words should be understood in the way that one understands a statement like "the fire is cooking." Kṛṣṇa's particular use of words indicates just how closely the intellect is related to the knower/doer of action.

Text 31

यया धर्ममधर्मं च कार्यं चाकार्यमेव च ।
अयथावत्प्रजानाति बुद्धिः सा पार्थ राजसी ॥३१॥

yayā dharmam adharmaṁ ca kāryaṁ cākāryam eva ca/
ayathāvat prajānāti buddhiḥ sā pārtha rājasī//

yayā—by which; *dharmam*—right; *adharmam*—wrong; *ca*—and; *kāryam*—to be done; *ca*—and; *akāryam*—not to be done; *eva*—certainly; *ca*—and; *ayathā-vat*—incorrectly; *prajānāti*—it distinguishes; *buddhiḥ*—intellect; *sā*—that; *pārtha*—O son of Pṛthā; *rājasī*—rajasic.

The intellect that cannot correctly distinguish right from wrong and what should be done from what should not be done is rajasic, O son of Pṛthā.

Text 32

अधर्मं धर्ममिति या मन्यते तमसावृता ।
सर्वार्थान् विपरीतांश्च बुद्धिः सा पार्थ तामसी ॥३२॥

adharmaṁ dharmam iti yā manyate tamasāvṛtā/
sarvārthān viparītāṁś ca buddhiḥ sā pārtha tāmasī//

adharmam—wrong; *dharmam*—right; *iti*—thus; *yā*—which; *manyate*—it thinks; *tamasā*—by ignorance; *āvṛtā*—covered; *sarva-arthān*—all things; *viparītān*—backwards; *ca*—and; *buddhiḥ*—intellect; *sā*—that; *pārtha*—O son of Pṛthā; *tāmasī*—tamasic.

The intellect that regards what is wrong to be right and, enveloped in ignorance, understands everything backwards is tamasic, O son of Pṛthā.

Text 33

धृत्या यया धारयते मनःप्राणेन्द्रियक्रियाः ।
योगेनाव्यभिचारिण्या धृतिः सा पार्थ सात्त्विकी ॥३३॥

dhṛtyā yayā dhārayate manaḥ-prāṇendriya-kriyāḥ/
yogenāvyabhicāriṇyā dhṛtiḥ sā pārtha sāttvikī//

dhṛtyā—by fortitude; *yayā*—by which; *dhārayate*—one sustains; *manaḥ*—mind; *prāṇa*—vital air; *indriya*—sense; *kriyāḥ*—functions; *yogena*—by *yoga*; *avyabhicāriṇyā*—by unswerving; *dhṛtiḥ*—fortitude; *sā*—that; *pārtha*—O son of Pṛthā; *sāttvikī*—sattvic.

The unswerving fortitude by which one controls the functions of the mind, vital air, and senses through yoga, O son of Pṛthā, is sattvic fortitude.

Text 34

यया तु धर्मकामार्थान् धृत्या धारयतेऽर्जुन ।
प्रसङ्गेन फलाकांक्षी धृतिः सा पार्थ राजसी ॥३४॥

yayā tu dharma-kāmārthān dhṛtyā dhārayate 'rjuna/
prasaṅgena phalākāṅkṣī dhṛtiḥ sā pārtha rājasī//

yayā—by which; *tu*—but; *dharma*—duty; *kāma*—sense pleasure; *arthān*—wealth; *dhṛtyā*—by fortitude; *dhārayate*—one holds; *arjuna*—O Arjuna;

prasaṅgena—with attachment; *phala-ākāṅkṣī*—desiring results; *dhṛtiḥ*—fortitude; *sā*—that; *pārtha*—O son of Pṛthā; *rājasī*—rajasic.

But that fortitude by which one maintains duty, wealth, and sense pleasure with attachment and desire for the results of action is rajasic, O son of Pṛthā.

Fortitude in *rajo-guṇa* is characterized by lack of interest in liberation. Dutiful life *(dharma)*, wealth *(artha)*, and sense pleasure *(kāma)* are the three worldly goals. All of these hold the interest of those in *rajo-guṇa*.

Text 35

यया स्वप्नं भयं शोकं विषादं मदमेव च ।
न विमुञ्चति दुर्मेधा धृतिः सा पार्थ तामसी ॥३५॥

yayā svapnaṁ bhayaṁ śokaṁ viṣādaṁ madam eva ca/
na vimuñcati durmedhā dhṛtiḥ sā pārtha tāmasī//

yayā—by which; *svapnam*—sleep; *bhayam*—fear; *śokam*—grief; *viṣādam*—depression; *madam*—conceit; *eva*—certainly; *ca*—and; *na*—not; *vimuñcati*—one gives up; *durmedhā*—unintelligent; *dhṛtiḥ*—determination; *sā*—that; *pārtha*—O son of Pṛthā; *tāmasī*—tamasic.

The fortitude of an unintelligent person who cannot overcome sleep, fear, grief, depression, and conceit is tamasic, O son of Pṛthā.

Having described action and the instrument of action in terms of their classification within the *guṇas*, Kṛṣṇa next addresses the result of action, happiness, in relation to the *guṇas*.

Text 36–37

सुखं त्विदानीं त्रिविधं शृणु मे भरतर्षभ ।
अभ्यासाद् रमते यत्र दुःखान्तं च निगच्छति ॥३६॥
यत्तदग्रे विषमिव परिणामेऽमृतोपमम् ।
तत्सुखं सात्त्विकं प्रोक्तमात्मबुद्धिप्रसादजम् ॥३७॥

sukhaṁ tv idānīṁ tri-vidhaṁ śṛṇu me bharatarṣabha/
abhyāsād ramate yatra duḥkhāntaṁ ca nigacchati//
yat tad agre viṣam iva pariṇāme 'mṛtopamam/
tat sukhaṁ sāttvikaṁ proktam ātma-buddhi-prasāda-jam//

sukham—happiness; *tu*—but; *idānīm*—now; *tri-vidham*—of three kinds; *śṛṇu*—hear; *me*—of me; *bharata-ṛṣabha*—O best amongst the Bhāratas; *abhyāsāt*—by practice; *ramate*—one enjoys; *yatra*—where; *duḥkha*—distress; *antam*—end; *ca*—and; *nigacchati*—one comes; *yat*—which; *tat*—that; *agre*—in the beginning; *viṣam iva*—like poison; *pariṇāme*—when transformed; *amṛta*—nectar; *upamam*—comparison; *tat*—that; *sukham*—happiness; *sāttvikam*—sattvic; *proktam*—said; *ātma-buddhi-prasāda-jam*—born from serenity of mind.

Now hear from me, O best of the Bhāratas, of three kinds of happiness. That happiness whose cultivation leads to the end of all suffering, which in the beginning is like poison but in the end like nectar—that happiness is said to be sattvic, being born from serenity of mind.

Sattvic happiness results from spiritual practice. It is not the immediate experience of sense pleasure that dissipates as quickly as it arises. Rather than being related to physical stimulus, it is related to the mind: it is serenity. It is purity that is unpleasant in the stage of purification and that ends suffering once and for all.

Text 38

विषयेन्द्रियसंयोगाद्यत्तदग्रेऽमृतोपमम् ।
परिणामे विषमिव तत्सुखं राजसं स्मृतम् ॥३८॥

viṣayendriya-saṁyogād yat tad agre 'mṛtopamam/
pariṇāme viṣam iva tat sukhaṁ rājasaṁ smṛtam//

viṣaya—sense object; *indriya*—sense; *saṁyogāt*—from the combination; *yat*—which; *tat*—that; *agre*—in the beginning; *amṛta-upamam*—like nectar; *pariṇāme*—when transformed; *viṣam iva*—like poison; *tat*—that; *sukham*—happiness; *rājasam*—rajasic; *smṛtam*—considered.

That happiness which at first through contact between the senses and their objects is like nectar but in the end is like poison is said to be rajasic.

Immediate pleasure that does not endure is rajasic happiness. It does not concern the self. Indeed, it obscures its clear perception. Rajasic happiness does not require that a person restrain his mind or senses to experience it.

Thus it is easy to acquire, but it does not endure. It turns to unhappiness in the long run by keeping one in *saṁsāra.*

Text 39

यदग्रे चानुबन्धे च सुखं मोहनमात्मनः ।
निद्रालस्यप्रमादोत्थं तत्तामसमुदाहृतम् ॥३९॥

yad agre cānubandhe ca sukhaṁ mohanam ātmanaḥ/
nidrālasya-pramādotthaṁ tat tāmasam udāhṛtam//

yat—which; *agre*—in the beginning; *ca*—and; *anubandhe*—at the end; *ca*—and; *sukham*—happiness; *mohanam*—deluding; *ātmanaḥ*—of the self; *nidrā*—sleep; *ālasya*—indolence; *pramāda*—neglect; *uttham*—arising from; *tat*—that; *tāmasam*—tamasic; *udāhṛtam*—said to be.

That happiness which is deluding both in the beginning and end, arising from sleep, indolence, and neglect, is said to be tamasic.

The pleasure of oversleeping is tamasic. It deludes the soul both in terms of the pursuit of itself and the pursuit of illusory material happiness. Tamasic happiness often involves merely dreaming about the happiness one will never attain, without realizing how unrealistic this is. Intoxication, the death wish, and any form of deliberate self-forgetfulness in ignorance all further characterize the happiness of *tamas.*

Text 40

न तदस्ति पृथिव्यां वा दिवि देवेषु वा पुनः ।
सत्त्वं प्रकृतिजैर्मुक्तं यदेभिः स्यात्त्रिभिर्गुणैः ॥४०॥

na tad asti pṛthivyāṁ vā divi deveṣu vā punaḥ/
sattvaṁ prakṛti-jair muktaṁ yad ebhiḥ syāt tribhir guṇaiḥ//

na—not; *tat*—that; *asti*—there is; *pṛthivyām*—on the earth; *vā*—or; *divi*—in heaven; *deveṣu*—among the gods; *vā*—or; *punaḥ*—again; *sattvam*—existence; *prakṛti-jaiḥ*—born of material nature; *muktam*—liberated; *yat*—that; *ebhiḥ*—from these; *syāt*—it may be; *tribhiḥ*—from three; *guṇaiḥ*—from the *guṇas.*

There is no being, either on earth or in heaven among the gods, that can exist independent of these three guṇas born of material nature.

Here Kṛṣṇa summarizes the previous section by stating that the entire world is under the influence of the *guṇas*. Not only that which has been described, but everything and everyone in the material world is influenced by the *guṇas*. If everything in this world is a product of the *guṇas*, one needs help from beyond the influence of the *guṇas* to transcend them. This help appears in the world but is not of it. Examples of this helping hand are the *avatāras* and *jīvanmuktas*, whom this verse does not refer to. Thus Kṛṣṇa turns Arjuna's attention to the means of liberation—his grace, the essential liberating element in both action and knowledge that fully manifests in *bhakti*. This discussion makes up the balance of the chapter.

Text 41

ब्राह्मणक्षत्रियविशां शूद्राणां च परन्तप ।
कर्माणि प्रविभक्तानि स्वभावप्रभवैर्गुणैः ॥४१॥

brāhmaṇa-kṣatriya-viśāṁ śūdrāṇāṁ ca parantapa/
karmāṇi pravibhaktāni svabhāva-prabhavair guṇaiḥ//

brāhmaṇa—*brāhmaṇa*; *kṣatriya*—*kṣatriya*; *viśām*—*vaiśya*; *śūdrāṇām*—of the *śūdras*; *ca*—and; *parantapa*—O chastiser of enemies; *karmāṇi*—activities; *pravibhaktāni*—divided; *svabhāva*—own nature; *prabhavaiḥ*—arising from; *guṇaiḥ*—by the *guṇas*.

O chastiser of enemies, the duties of the brāhmaṇas, kṣatriyas, vaiśyas, and śūdras are classified in accordance with the guṇas, arising from their natures.

Śrīdhara Swāmī comments that Kṛṣṇa explains the duties of the four social orders of life to stress that living beings attain salvation and rise above the *guṇas* by the grace of God and his worship. Thus after describing these duties in the following three verses, Kṛṣṇa tells Arjuna that the social classes originate in God, and he instructs that the duties of these social classes are to be performed for his pleasure. Following this socioreligious system within the realm of *karma*, one gradually comes to *niṣkāma-karma-yoga* and attains knowledge and salvation leading to love of God. The essential element of grace that pervades this progression is the heart of *bhakti*, which itself grants knowledge, salvation, and love of God. Without *bhakti* there is no salvation, and unalloyed *bhakti* affords the highest form of salvation, the *prema-dharma* of Vraja. In this verse Kṛṣṇa begins his summary of socioreligious life. This discussion continues through verse 48.

The division of labor as stated here is determined by the *guṇas*. It is not arbitrary, but rather a product of different physio-psychological makeups. It is the duty and natural inclination of the four classes to cultivate the qualities mentioned in the following verses.

Text 42

शमो दमस्तपः शौचं क्षान्तिरार्जवमेव च ।
ज्ञानं विज्ञानमास्तिक्यं ब्रह्मकर्मस्वभावजम् ॥४२॥

śamo damas tapaḥ śaucaṁ kṣāntir ārjavam eva ca/
jñānaṁ vijñānam āstikyaṁ brahma-karma svabhāva-jam//

śamaḥ—tranquillity; *damaḥ*—self-control; *tapaḥ*—austerity; *śaucam*—purity; *kṣāntiḥ*—forgiveness; *ārjavam*—honesty; *eva*—certainly; *ca*—and; *jñānam*—knowledge; *vijñānam*—wisdom; *āstikyam*—piety; *brahma*—of a *brāhmaṇa*; *karma*—duty; *svabhāva-jam*—born of one's own nature.

Tranquillity, self-control, austerity, purity, forgiveness, honesty, knowledge, wisdom, and faith in God are the natural qualities of the brāhmaṇas' work.

Text 43

शौर्यं तेजो धृतिर्दाक्ष्यं युद्धे चाप्यपलायनम् ।
दानमीश्वरभावश्च क्षात्रं कर्म स्वभावजम् ॥४३॥

śauryaṁ tejo dhṛtir dākṣyaṁ yuddhe cāpy apalāyanam/
dānam īśvara-bhāvaś ca kṣātraṁ karma svabhāva-jam//

śauryam—heroism; *tejaḥ*—power; *dhṛtiḥ*—determination; *dākṣyam*—resourcefulness; *yuddhe*—in battle; *ca*—and; *api*—also; *apalāyanam*—courage; *dānam*—generosity; *īśvara*—leadership; *bhāvaḥ*—nature; *ca*—and; *kṣātram*—of a *kṣatriya*; *karma*—duty; *svabhāva-jam*—born of one's own nature.

Heroism, power, determination, resourcefulness, courage in battle, generosity, and leadership are the natural qualities of the kṣatriyas' work.

Text 44

कृषिगोरक्ष्यवाणिज्यं वैश्यकर्म स्वभावजम् ।
परिचर्यात्मकं कर्म शूद्रस्यापि स्वभावजम् ॥४४॥

kṛṣi-go-rakṣya-vāṇijyaṁ vaiśya-karma svabhāva-jam/
paricaryātmakaṁ karma śūdrasyāpi svabhāva-jam//

kṛṣi—plowing; *go*—cow; *rakṣya*—protection; *vāṇijyam*—trade; *vaiśya*—of a *vaiśya*; *karma*—duty; *svabhāva-jam*—born of one's own nature; *paricaryā*—service; *ātmakam*—consisting of; *karma*—duty; *śūdrasya*—of the *śūdra*; *api*—also; *svabhāva-jam*—born of one's own nature.

Farming, cowherding, and trade are the natural duties of the vaiśyas. Service is the natural duty of the śūdras.

The laborers (*śūdras*) serve by assisting the other classes. Thus the four social orders have been described in terms of the qualities and work they are to cultivate for the pleasure of God.

Text 45

स्वे स्वे कर्मण्यभिरतः संसिद्धिं लभते नरः।
स्वकर्मनिरतः सिद्धिं यथा विन्दति तच्छृणु ॥४५॥

sve sve karmaṇy abhirataḥ saṁsiddhiṁ labhate naraḥ/
sva-karma-nirataḥ siddhiṁ yathā vindati tac chṛṇu//

sve sve—each his own; *karmaṇi*—in duty; *abhirataḥ*—contented; *saṁsiddhim*—perfection; *labhate*—one attains; *naraḥ*—man; *sva-karma*—one's own duty; *nirataḥ*—engaged; *siddhim*—perfection; *yathā*—as; *vindati*—one finds; *tat*—that; *śṛṇu*—listen.

Devoted to one's own particular duty, one attains perfection. Listen as I explain how a person can find perfection in this way.

Text 46

यतः प्रवृत्तिर्भूतानां येन सर्वमिदं ततम्।
स्वकर्मणा तमभ्यर्च्य सिद्धिं विन्दति मानवः ॥४६॥

yataḥ pravṛttir bhūtānāṁ yena sarvam idaṁ tatam/
sva-karmaṇā tam abhyarcya siddhiṁ vindati mānavaḥ//

yataḥ—from whom; *pravṛttiḥ*—the emanation; *bhūtānām*—of beings; *yena*—by whom; *sarvam*—all; *idam*—this; *tatam*—pervaded; *sva-karmaṇā*—by one's own duties; *tam*—him; *abhyarcya*—by worshipping; *siddhim*—perfection; *vindati*—one finds; *mānavaḥ*—man.

A human being attains perfection by worshipping God through his work, for the duties of life emanate from God, who pervades all things.

The healthy heart of the social body is the pleasure of God. Thus all the duties of the four classes should be performed with God's pleasure in mind. The duties are ordained by him in consideration of the *guṇas*. When performed for God's sake they gradually make one eligible for *niṣkāma-karma-yoga* leading to *bhakti*. Execution of one's prescribed duty that corresponds with one's nature frees one from evil. Kṛṣṇa next speaks of this immediate fruit of adhering to one's duty for the satisfaction of God.

Text 47

श्रेयान् स्वधर्मो विगुणः परधर्मात् स्वनुष्ठितात् ।
स्वभावनियतं कर्म कुर्वन्नाप्नोति किल्बिषम् ॥४७॥

śreyān sva-dharmo viguṇaḥ para-dharmāt sv-anuṣṭhitāt/
svabhāva-niyataṁ karma kurvan nāpnoti kilbiṣam//

śreyān—better; *sva-dharmaḥ*—one's own duty; *viguṇaḥ*—faulty; *para-dharmāt*—than another's occupation; *su-anuṣṭhitāt*—well done; *svabhāva-niyatam*—prescribed according to one's nature; *karma*—duty; *kurvan*—performing; *na*—not; *āpnoti*—one incurs; *kilbiṣam*—evil.

Performing one's own duty even when it is faulty is better than performing the duty of another without fault. Performing one's own prescribed duty in accordance with one's nature, one does not incur evil.

Here we are reminded of chapter 3, verse 35. The duty of a warrior appeared faulty to Arjuna, for in performing it so many respectable and dear persons would be slain. Should Arjuna consider putting down his bow and collecting alms like a *brāhmaṇa* to avoid this apparent fault, he would be faulty nonetheless. Thus Kṛṣṇa advises him that he would be committing a greater fault, and such a precedent would lend to the destabilization of the socioreligious order ordained by God.

Text 48

सहजं कर्म कौन्तेय सदोषमपि न त्यजेत् ।
सर्वारम्भा हि दोषेण धूमेनाग्निरिवावृताः ॥४८॥

saha-jaṁ karma kaunteya sa-doṣam api na tyajet/
sarvārambhā hi doṣeṇa dhūmenāgnir ivāvṛtāḥ//

saha-jam—inborn; *karma*—work; *kaunteya*—O son of Kuntī; *sa-doṣam*—with fault; *api*—although; *na*—not; *tyajet*—one should abandon; *sarva-ārambhāḥ*—all undertakings; *hi*—certainly; *doṣeṇa*—with fault; *dhū-mena*— with smoke; *agniḥ*—fire; *iva*—as; *āvṛtāḥ*—covered.

One should not abandon that work born of one's nature. All work is covered by some defect, just as fire is covered by smoke.

One should not stop cooking because fire produces smoke along with heat. Similarly, one should not abandon the work born of one's nature and detailed in the scripture simply because it has some defect. All work in this world is less than perfect, but if it is done with a view to satisfy God, it leads one in the direction of perfection, the criterion for which is the extent to which God is satisfied by it, *saṁsiddhir hari toṣaṇam* (ŚB. 1.2.13). As a law-abiding citizen pleases the government in a general way, so a person who acts in accordance with his nature, in terms of the duties prescribed in the scripture, pleases God. Any defect in the work is overcome to the extent that he performs his duty for duty's sake, with detachment from the work itself as well as from its fruit.

Here Kṛṣṇa points out that all work is defective in some respect, yet he does so to stress the inherent value in all work. He is not concerned with restricting people to particular duties, but rather in seeing that people are engaged according to their natures and thus find value and fulfillment in their work. This enables them to think beyond their particular work to the greater scheme of life. Should their natures be mixed, as they are in today's complex post-industrial society, people will only be engaged in accordance with their natures by engaging in a variety of duties. This inevitable crossover of duties in our complex society, as opposed to the clearly defined divisions of labor in a simple agrarian society, need not be seen as a violation of Kṛṣṇa's instruction in this verse. *Dharma* is about understanding one's nature and acting accordingly, with a view to know oneself more completely as one can do only by understanding oneself in relation to God.

After comprehensive inquiry into the nature of religious *dharma*, one is qualified to inquire into the nature of Brahman, *athāto brahma-jijñāsā* (Vs. 1.1.1). Thus Kṛṣṇa turns his summary of the means of deliverance in the direction of renunciation and the knowledge derived from selfless action.

Text 49

असक्तबुद्धिः सर्वत्र जितात्मा विगतस्पृहः ।
नैष्कर्म्यसिद्धिं परमां सन्न्यासेनाधिगच्छति ॥४९॥

asakta-buddhiḥ sarvatra jitātmā vigata-spṛhaḥ/
naiṣkarmya-siddhiṁ paramāṁ sannyāsenādhigacchati//

asakta-buddhiḥ—having detached intelligence; *sarvatra*—at all times; *jita-ātmā*—self-controlled; *vigata-spṛhaḥ*—without material desires; *naiṣkarmya-siddhim*—state of freedom from *karma; paramām*—supreme; *sannyāsena*—by renunciation; *adhigacchati*—one attains.

A person who by exercise of his intelligence is detached at all times, self-controlled, and free from material desire attains through renunciation the supreme state of freedom from karma.

By acting without attachment to the action itself or its fruits, one attains knowledge and freedom from the bondage of *karma*. This is the platform of *jñāna-yoga*. From acting with detachment, one becomes purified and any defect in one's action is overcome. On attaining knowledge of the self through such action, one attains freedom from *karma* altogether and is thus qualified to forgo karmic duties. In this way, the *jñānī* eventually attains Brahman by God's grace. Here *sannyāsa* does not mean renouncing the fruits of action, but rather renouncing action that is not conducive to meditation. This is the *yogārūḍha* mentioned in chapter 6 (Bg. 6.3).

Text 50

सिद्धिं प्राप्तो यथा ब्रह्म तथाप्नोति निबोध मे ।
समासेनैव कौन्तेय निष्ठा ज्ञानस्य या परा ॥५०॥

siddhiṁ prāpto yathā brahma tathāpnoti nibodha me/
samāsenaiva kaunteya niṣṭhā jñānasya yā parā//

siddhim—success; *prāptaḥ*—achieved; *yathā*—as; *brahma*—Brahman; *tathā*—so; *āpnoti*—one attains; *nibodha*—learn; *me*—from me; *samāsena*—briefly; *eva*—certainly; *kaunteya*—O son of Kuntī; *niṣṭhā*—state; *jñānasya*—of knowledge; *yā*—which; *parā*—supreme.

O son of Kuntī, hear from me in brief how one who has achieved success in this attains Brahman, the supreme state of knowledge.

Texts 51–53

बद्ध्या विशुद्धया युक्तो धृत्यात्मानं नियम्य च ।
शब्दादीन् विषयांस्त्यक्त्वा रागद्वेषौ व्युदस्य च ॥५१॥
विविक्तसेवी लघ्वाशी यतवाक्कायमानसः ।
ध्यानयोगपरो नित्यं वैराग्यं समुपाश्रितः ॥५२॥
अहंकारं बलं दर्पं कामं क्रोधं परिग्रहम् ।
विमुच्य निर्ममः शान्तो ब्रह्मभूयाय कल्पते ॥५३॥

buddhyā viśuddhayā yukto dhṛtyātmānaṁ niyamya ca/
śabdādīn viṣayāṁs tyaktvā rāga-dveṣau vyudasya ca//
vivikta-sevī laghv-āśī yata-vāk-kāya-mānasaḥ/
dhyāna-yoga-paro nityaṁ vairāgyaṁ samupāśritaḥ//
ahaṅkāraṁ balaṁ darpaṁ kāmaṁ krodhaṁ parigraham/
vimucya nirmamaḥ śānto brahma-bhūyāya kalpate//

buddhyā—with intellect; *viśuddhayā*—with purified; *yuktaḥ*—endowed; *dhṛtyā*—with determination; *ātmānam*—self; *niyamya*—controlling; *ca*—and; *śabda-ādīn*—sound, etc.; *viṣayān*—sense objects; *tyaktvā*—giving up; *rāga-dveṣau*—attraction and hatred; *vyudasya*—casting aside; *ca*—and; *vivikta-sevī*—dwelling in a secluded place; *laghu-āśī*—eating little; *yata*—controlled; *vāk*—speech; *kāya*—body; *mānasaḥ*—mind; *dhyāna-yoga-paraḥ*—devoted to the *yoga* of contemplation; *nityam*—constantly; *vairāgyam*—detachment; *samupāśritaḥ*—resorted to; *ahaṅkāram*—egotism; *balam*—strength; *darpam*—arrogance; *kāmam*—lust; *krodham*—anger; *parigraham*—possession; *vimucya*—giving up; *nirmamaḥ*—unselfish; *śāntaḥ*—peaceful; *brahma-bhūyāya*—for Brahman-realization; *kalpate*—one is fit.

Disciplining oneself by purified intelligence; controlling the mind with determination; abandoning the sense objects, such as sound; freeing oneself from likes and dislikes; resorting to a secluded place; eating little; controlling one's speech, body, and mind; constantly devoting oneself to the yoga of contemplation; being detached; forsaking egotism, force, arrogance, lust, anger, and possessions; being unselfish and peaceful, one is fit for Brahman realization.

In these verses Kṛṣṇa reiterates instructions he gave earlier in chapter 6.

Text 54

ब्रह्मभूतः प्रसन्नात्मा न शोचति न कांक्षति ।
समः सर्वेषु भूतेषु मद्भक्तिं लभते परम् ॥५४॥

brahma-bhūtaḥ prasannātmā na śocati na kāṅkṣati/
samaḥ sarveṣu bhūteṣu mad-bhaktiṁ labhate parām//

brahma-bhūtaḥ—one with Brahman; *prasanna-ātmā*—self-fulfilled; *na*—not; *śocati*—he laments; *na*—not; *kāṅkṣati*—he hankers; *samaḥ*—equally disposed; *sarveṣu*—to all; *bhūteṣu*—to beings; *mat-bhaktim*—devotion to me; *labhate*—one attains; *parām*—transcendental.

Once such a person has realized Brahman, he becomes self-fulfilled and no longer laments or hankers. Equally disposed to all beings, he attains transcendental devotion to me.

Having attained Brahman, the fortunate *jñānī* attains devotion proper, post-liberated *parā bhakti (mad bhaktiṁ labhate parām)*. This has also been discussed in chapter 7, where it is stated that after many, many births the *jñānī* surrenders to Kṛṣṇa, knowing him to be all in all (Bg. 7.19). According to Viśvanātha Cakravartī Ṭhākura, the element of devotion must be present to some extent in one's religious practice from *niṣkāma-karma-yoga* to *jñāna-yoga* if one is to attain Brahman. This element of *bhakti* is a partial manifestation of devotion proper, which is a function of Kṛṣṇa's primary *śakti*. However, because the *jñānī*'s goal is liberation, as opposed to *prema-bhakti*, the devotional element in his practice is not immediately perceptible. Just as small nuggets of gold are not immediately perceptible in a bag of mung dhal, but are perceptible at the bottom of the pot when the dhal is cooked; similarly, having reached the end of philosophical knowledge, the *jñānī* attains the gold of *bhakti* that was invisibly present all along. Thus this verse speaks of the knowledge born of *sattva-guṇa* (*vidyā*) that is retired with the full manifestation of *bhakti*. In his commentary on the following verse, Viśvanātha Cakravartī explains that the word *vidyā* refers to the knowledge of *sattva-guṇa*, whereas the word *jñāna* sometimes refers to the knowledge of *sattva-guṇa* and at other times the knowledge inherent in *bhakti*.

In the opinion of *Śrī Caitanya-caritāmṛta*, this verse speaks of *jñāna* mixed with *bhakti* through which liberation and then pure *bhakti* are attained (Cc. Madhya 8.65–66). This verse also shows the necessity for even the *jñānī jīvanmukta* to embrace *bhakti* to attain *videha-mukti* (Cc. Madhya 24.132) and how easily a *jñānī* attains liberation through *bhakti* (Cc. Madhya 25.155).

Here Kṛṣṇa begins to focus on the *Gītā*'s conclusion: devotion to himself is the supreme means to and end of spiritual life. Its status is post-liberated, and thus any tinge of it appearing in the path of *karma* or *jñāna* is the liberating agent in that path, for only that which is itself spiritual can grant spiritual life. Only through this *parā bhakti* can Kṛṣṇa be understood and his abode entered into.

Text 55

भक्त्या मामभिजानाति यावान् यश्चास्मि तत्त्वतः ।
ततो मां तत्त्वतो ज्ञात्वा विशते तदनन्तरम् ॥५५॥

bhaktyā mām abhijānāti yāvān yaś cāsmi tattvataḥ/
tato māṁ tattvato jñātvā viśate tad-anantaram//

bhaktyā—through devotion; *mām*—me; *abhijānāti*—one comes to experience; *yāvān*—as much as; *yaḥ ca asmi*—as I am; *tattvataḥ*—in truth; *tataḥ*—then; *mām*—me; *tattvataḥ*—in truth; *jñātvā*—knowing; *viśate*—he enters; *tat-anantaram*—thereafter.

Through devotion to me he comes to know who I am in truth. Thereafter, having understood the truth about me, he enters my abode.

In earlier chapters Kṛṣṇa explained that Brahman is subordinate to himself (Bg. 13.13, 14.27). Here he tells Arjuna that the Brahman-realized *jñānī* who engages in *parā bhakti* attains the knowledge inherent in *bhakti* and thus enters his abode. The fact that Kṛṣṇa is referring here to entrance into his abode, as opposed to *sāyujya-mukti* in which one merges with Brahman, is brought out further in the next verse. Therein, Kṛṣṇa says, "By my grace they attain the eternal imperishable abode" (*mat-prasādād avāpnoti śāśvataṁ padam avyayam*). Viśvanātha Cakravartī says in his comments to verse 56 that this refers to Kṛṣṇa's supreme abode in one of its manifestations: Dwārakā, Mathurā, or Vṛndāvana. Regarding the word *viśate* in this verse, Baladeva Vidyābhūṣaṇa says, "This entrance is like that of a person who goes into a city; he does not become the city." He notes further that *Vedānta-sūtra* (4.1.12) confirms that *bhakti* exists even after liberation: "According to the *śruti*, it is seen that even after coming to liberation, devotion remains."

However, it should also be noted that those desiring to attain *sāyujya-mukti* can do so only by the admixture of *bhakti* in their spiritual practice. Without *bhakti* the so-called liberated deceive themselves. This is confirmed in *Śrīmad-Bhāgavatam* (10.2.32) thus: "O lotus-eyed Lord, although nondevotees who accept severe austerities and penance to achieve the highest position may think themselves liberated, their intelligence is impure. They fall down from their position of imagined superiority because they have no regard for your lotus feet."

Although some persons do take the circuitous route of passing through *karma* to *jñāna* before taking to *bhakti*, in doing so they neglect the generosity of *bhakti* and the true import of the *Gītā*, to which Kṛṣṇa now turns Arjuna's attention as he comes to his final conclusion.

Text 56

सर्वकर्माण्यपि सदा कुर्वाणो मद्व्यपाश्रयः ।
मत्प्रसादादवाप्नोति शाश्वतं पदमव्ययम् ॥५६॥

sarva-karmāṇy api sadā kurvāṇo mad-vyapāśrayaḥ/
mat-prasādād avāpnoti śāśvataṁ padam avyayam//

sarva—all; *karmāṇi*—activities; *api*—even; *sadā*—always; *kurvāṇaḥ*—performing; *mat-vyapāśrayaḥ*—under my shelter; *mat-prasādāt*—by my grace; *avāpnoti*—one achieves; *śāśvatam*—eternal; *padam*—abode; *avyayam*—imperishable.

Even though engaged in any kind of work, one who always takes refuge in me attains the eternal imperishable abode by my grace.

Kṛṣṇa speaks about acting within the realm of *karma* with an admixture of *bhakti* in verse 46 of this chapter. In verse 54 he talked about the influence of *bhakti* on the *jñānī*. In this verse, having glorified the post-liberated position of pure *bhakti* and its liberating effects, as well as its influence on the liberated soul, Kṛṣṇa speaks feelingly of devotion and his devotees who are not yet liberated.

Kṛṣṇa's mention of devotion in verse 46 reiterates much of what was said in the first six chapters of the *Gītā*, and chapter 3 in particular. There he discusses *karma* mixed with *bhakti*. Here, however, the emphasis has shifted as he speaks of *bhakti* mixed with *karma*. He speaks of a person who constantly takes refuge in him alone, even though entangled in the realm of *karma*, as opposed to a person who focuses primarily on his prescribed duty offering only the result of his work to God. The strength of this approach is stressed by the use of the words *sarva-karmāṇi*. Regardless of a person's shortcomings, if he has faith that taking shelter of Kṛṣṇa is the best possible course of action, this faith itself will deliver him in due course.

The word *āśraya (vyapāśrayaḥ)* in this verse stems from the root *śrī*, which means to be radiant, bright, dazzling. Taking shelter of Kṛṣṇa, one becomes radiant and bright. As the dazzling, golden-complected Śrī (Rādhā) takes shelter of Kṛṣṇa, so too should we. She has no other shelter, not even Kṛṣṇa in any of his other forms, what to speak of other gods. If a person with faith in *bhakti* sees Kṛṣṇa as the only shelter in life, even though his devotion is imperfect owing to material desire indicated here by the prefix *apa* (not predominant), he will attain Kṛṣṇa's abode. His position is special *(vi/viśeṣa)*. This is the import of the word *vyapāśraya* according to Viśvanātha Cakravartī Ṭhākura. The word *api* in this verse indicates that he who Kṛṣṇa is describing is first and foremost his devotee, whereas secondarily *(api)* he is implicated in the realm of *karma*, be it proper action or even prohibited action. Although his devotion is not more prominent than his material desire, and thus his taking shelter of Kṛṣṇa is somewhat impaired *(apa)*, he is a devotee of Kṛṣṇa and material desire has the upper hand in his life only temporarily. Indeed, his faith in Kṛṣṇa and his taking refuge in him in all of his successes and failures will eventually enable him to rise above material desire and be delivered.

Bhakti, being independent, can enter the heart of anyone, even the most sinful person. She is constituted of God's primary *śakti* and is thus not dependent on knowledge or renunciation. Whereas knowledge requires the support of a pure heart, *bhakti* is self-supporting. Once she enters the heart, all impurities will gradually be removed by her grace. One whose heart she enters, by the desire of another whom she has so graced, need not be concerned with the details of religious duties, renunciation, or knowledge independently of *bhakti*. Paying attention to *bhakti* alone as one's primary spiritual practice, however imperfectly, is more fruitful than strict adherence to any other discipline. Indeed, knowledge and renunciation follow in the wake of *bhakti*.

Although the position of devotion and that of the devotee may insult the sensibilities of learned and cultured persons who fail to appreciate the logic of forgoing renunciation and knowledge in the pursuit of spiritual life, Viśvanātha Cakravartī Ṭhākura replies, "such is the logic of *bhakti*." She represents the inconceivable mercy *(mat-prasādāt)* of Kṛṣṇa, the logic of love. This message of the *Gītā* should give real hope to everyone, regardless of their disqualification for other spiritual practices. Indeed, careful study of the scriptural canon would result in a sense of hopelessness for anyone in this age, were it not for the generosity of *bhakti*. The implication of the word *avāpnoti* (he attains/he does) is that in the final analysis it is *bhakti* that Kṛṣṇa recommends for everyone. The position of devotion being what it is, Kṛṣṇa mandates its progressive culture in the following verse.

Text 57

चेतसा सर्वकर्माणि मयि सन्न्यस्य मत्परः ।
बुद्धियोगमुपाश्रित्य मच्चित्तः सततं भव ॥५७॥

cetasā sarva-karmāṇi mayi sannyasya mat-paraḥ/
buddhi-yogam upāśritya mac-cittaḥ satataṁ bhava//

cetasā—mentally; *sarva-karmāṇi*—all actions; *mayi*—unto me; *sannyasya*—resigning; *mat-paraḥ*—having me as the highest; *buddhi-yogam*—devotion; *upāśritya*—taking shelter of; *mat-cittaḥ*—conscious of me; *satatam*—always; *bhava*—become.

Mentally resigning all actions unto me, holding me to be the supreme object of love in devotion, taking shelter of the power of spiritual insight, always think of me.

In this verse Kṛṣṇa stresses the chastity of intelligence *(buddhi)*, mind *(cetasā/mac-cittaḥ)*, and body *(sarva-karmāṇi)* in devotion to himself. Kṛṣṇa uses the term *buddhi-yoga*, familiar to us from the second and tenth chapters (Bg. 2.39, 10.10), to instruct Arjuna to take refuge in the power of spiritual insight resulting from devotion. Kṛṣṇa supplies this insight *(dadāmi buddhi-yogam)* to the devotee who understands that he is the ultimate goal in life. Here the word *bhava* is in the imperative, indicating that it is Kṛṣṇa's mandate to Arjuna that he always think of him, the result of which he describes next along with the result of failing to do so.

Text 58

मच्चित्तः सर्वदुर्गाणि मत्प्रसादात्तरिष्यसि ।
अथ चेत्त्वमहंकारान्न श्रोष्यसि विनंक्ष्यसि ॥५८॥

mac-cittaḥ sarva-durgāṇi mat-prasādāt tariṣyasi/
atha cet tvam ahaṅkārān na śroṣyasi vinaṅkṣyasi//

mat—of me; *cittaḥ*—conscious; *sarva*—all; *durgāṇi*—difficulties; *mat-prasādāt*—by my grace; *tariṣyasi*—you will overcome; *atha*—but; *cet*—if; *tvam*—you; *ahaṅkārāt*—out of egotism; *na śroṣyasi*—you will not hear; *vinaṅkṣyasi*—you will perish.

Fixing your mind on me, you will overcome all difficulties through my grace, but if you think you know better than I, you will perish.

Here Kṛṣṇa says that one will overcome all difficulties, such as lust and anger that are so difficult to conquer, simply by his grace. Madhusūdana Saraswatī comments, "without any effort at all." Thus the uplifting power of Kṛṣṇa's grace is underscored in relation to those things that are most difficult to overcome.

Kṛṣṇa warns that should Arjuna not take shelter of him, thinking Kṛṣṇa is simply another learned person giving his own opinion, he will perish. It is not possible for Arjuna to disregard Kṛṣṇa's advice, yet Kṛṣṇa gives him this warning nonetheless. Kṛṣṇa makes clear his desire that Arjuna fight, not because it is his duty as a warrior, as he argued earlier, but as an act of surrender to him in devotion. Hypothetically speaking, Kṛṣṇa next explains what he means when he says that Arjuna will perish *(vinaṅkṣyasi)* should he decide not to fight. Arjuna's karmic warrior nature will force him to fight regardless of his present reluctance.

Text 59

यदहंकारमाश्रित्य न योत्स्य इति मन्यसे ।
मिथ्यैष व्यवसायस्ते प्रकृतिस्त्वां नियोक्ष्यति ॥५९॥

yad ahaṅkāram āśritya na yotsya iti manyase/
mithyaiṣa vyavasāyas te prakṛtis tvāṁ niyokṣyati//

yat—which; *ahaṅkāram*—egotism; *āśritya*—taking shelter; *na yotsye*—I shall not fight; *iti*—thus; *manyase*—you think; *mithyā*—vain; *eṣaḥ*—this; *vyavasāyaḥ*—decision; *te*—your; *prakṛtiḥ*—material nature; *tvām*—you; *niyokṣyati*—it will enjoin.

If owing to egotism you think, "I shall not fight," such a decision will be in vain, for your own material nature will compel you to do so.

In this verse Kṛṣṇa explains the meaning of *vinaṅkṣyasi* (you will perish) found in the previous verse. A person who does not take shelter of Kṛṣṇa will spiritually perish under the influence of his lower nature. If a person resists serving God, he will be forced to serve the demands of his body and mind—his physio-psychological karmic nature. This is unavoidable.

Here Kṛṣṇa speaks forcefully to Arjuna, as if with anger at even the slightest mental reservation on Arjuna's part. Viśvanātha Cakravartī Ṭhākura says that it is implied here that if Arjuna does not embrace Kṛṣṇa's desire that he fight out of love for him, but later fights anyway by the force of his nature, Kṛṣṇa will mock him at that time. In other words, Kṛṣṇa will not approve of Arjuna's fighting under these circumstances. This is an important footnote to the entire *Bhagavad-gītā*. Baladeva Vidyābhūṣaṇa comments that Kṛṣṇa implies any unwillingness on Arjuna's part will result in Kṛṣṇa's *māyā* in the form of *rajo-guṇa* forcing him to do so. Although Arjuna will fight in either instance, the result of this fighting will be categorically different. Fighting in devotion to Kṛṣṇa, Arjuna will flourish spiritually, whereas fighting under the influence of his lower nature, he will perish.

The use of the word *vyavasāya* in this verse indicates that the one-pointedness of mind *(vyavasāyātmikā buddhi)* advocated in chapter 2 (Bg. 2.41) can be influenced by *rajas* or *tamas* and thus be undesirable.

Text 60

स्वभावजेन कौन्तेय निबद्धः स्वेन कर्मणा ।
कर्तुं नेच्छसि यन्मोहात् करिष्यस्यवशोऽपि तत् ॥६०॥

svabhāva-jena kaunteya nibaddhaḥ svena karmaṇā/
kartuṁ necchasi yan mohāt kariṣyasy avaśo 'pi tat//

svabhāva-jena—by that which is born of your own nature; *kaunteya*—O son of Kuntī; *nibaddhaḥ*—bound; *svena*—by one's own; *karmaṇā*—by *karma; kartum*—to do; *na*—not; *icchasi*—you want; *yat*—which; *mohāt*—out of delusion; *kariṣyasi*—you will do; *avaśaḥ*—unwillingly; *api*—even; *tat*—that.

That which out of delusion you desire not to do, you will do anyway even against your will, being bound by the karma born of your own nature.

In this verse Kṛṣṇa further explains the result of not doing his bidding. If Arjuna does not follow his instructions, he will fight anyway under the influence of his karmic nature. Jīva Goswāmī comments that although it appears at first that the *Bhagavad-gītā* is about Kṛṣṇa inciting Arjuna to fight, this verse reveals otherwise. Why would Kṛṣṇa labor to convince Arjuna to fight when this will happen anyway by the force of his warrior nature born of the *guṇas*? Thus Śrī Jīva concludes the *Bhagavad-gītā* is about doing the bidding of Kṛṣṇa *(bhakti)*, as opposed to following one's acquired nature on the path of *karma*. Through it, Kṛṣṇa instructs everyone about the goal of life. This ultimate goal of life, Śrī Jīva says, is found in the sixty-fifth verse of this chapter.[2]

Having elaborated on the soul's subservience to *prakṛti* in the form of its lower nature, Kṛṣṇa next elaborates on his position as the master of *prakṛti*, the Paramātmā, whom we must serve to transcend our lower nature.

Text 61

ईश्वरः सर्वभूतानां हृद्देशेऽर्जुन तिष्ठति ।
भ्रामयन् सर्वभूतानि यन्त्रारूढानि मायया ॥६१॥

īśvaraḥ sarva-bhūtānāṁ hṛd-deśe 'rjuna tiṣṭhati/
bhrāmayan sarva-bhūtāni yantrārūḍhāni māyayā//

īśvaraḥ—God; *sarva-bhūtānām*—of all beings; *hṛt-deśe*—in the heart; *arjuna*—O Arjuna; *tiṣṭhati*—he resides; *bhrāmayan*—causing to wander; *sarva-bhūtāni*—all beings; *yantra*—machine; *ārūḍhani*—mounted on; *māyayā*—by the power of *māyā*.

O Arjuna, God resides in the hearts of all beings, directing their wanderings by the magical power of māyā, on which they are seated as if it were a machine.

Although in verse 58 Kṛṣṇa gave Arjuna the option of not following his advice, here he continues trying to convince him that he should. As in the previous verses, Kṛṣṇa speaks firmly, giving reasons why Arjuna should make the right choice. Arjuna's decision in this matter—either doing as Kṛṣṇa wants him to do or fighting under the compulsion of his lower nature—depends on the sanction of Kṛṣṇa's Paramātmā manifestation, who is behind all the movements of matter. We cannot avoid serving God. We are given the choice of either serving him in full awareness and with his guidance or unknowingly under the control of his *māyā*.

Here Kṛṣṇa says that all beings in this world experience only the illusion of freedom. They are like puppets on a string made of his illusory potency, *māyā*. Kṛṣṇa himself as the Paramātmā is the puppeteer whom they should take shelter of and thereby know real freedom. If we choose not to serve

2. See Jīva Goswāmī's *Kṛṣṇa-sandarbha*, *anuccheda* 82 and his corresponding comments on this section in his *Sarva-saṁvādinī* for all references in this chapter to Śrī Jīva's insights.

Kṛṣṇa, we must serve his *māyā* and remain in the bondage of *saṁsāra*. If we choose to serve Kṛṣṇa, we can experience the freedom of love.

Text 62

तमेव शरणं गच्छ सर्वभावेन भारत ।
तत्प्रसादात्परां शान्तिं स्थानं प्राप्स्यसि शाश्वतम् ॥६२॥

tam eva śaraṇaṁ gaccha sarva-bhāvena bhārata/
tat-prasādāt parāṁ śāntiṁ sthānaṁ prāpsyasi śāśvatam//

tam—him; *eva*—certainly; *śaraṇam gaccha*—take refuge; *sarva-bhāvena*—with all of your heart; *bhārata*—O descendant of Bharata; *tat-prasādāt*—by his grace; *parām*—supreme; *śāntim*—peace; *sthānam*—abode; *prāpsyasi*—you will attain; *śāśvatam*—eternal.

Take refuge in him alone with all of your heart, O descendant of Bharata. By his grace you will attain the supreme peace and eternal abode.

From speaking sternly to Arjuna about his own majesty, here Kṛṣṇa speaks very sweetly in concluding his fervent appeal to Arjuna. He says with certainty, "Take refuge in him, he who is the master of *māyā* and is seated in everyone's heart. That Supreme Person is me. Give your heart to me, and by my grace you will come to the end of all sorrow and attain my abode."

Although technically Kṛṣṇa speaks about surrender in relation to his Paramātmā feature in this and the previous verse, Viśvanātha Cakravartī Ṭhākura points out that the devotee's object of surrender is Bhagavān. The devotee holds his most beloved Deity (*iṣṭa-devatā*) in his heart and surrenders to him alone. Baladeva Vidyābhūṣaṇa comments that Kṛṣṇa has identified himself as the Lord of the heart in Bg. 15.15. Thus the devotee conceives of his chosen Deity residing in his heart, recognizing that Kṛṣṇa is behind the Paramātmā feature, which is only his partial manifestation.

The following verse beginning with *iti* (thus) is Kṛṣṇa's final instruction. With it Kṛṣṇa concludes his appeal to Arjuna for surrender. Thus the immortal *Bhagavad-gītā* ends. What remains is Kṛṣṇa's afterthought, in which he reiterates the *Gītā*'s deepest import.

Text 63

इति ते ज्ञानमाख्यातं गुह्याद् गुह्यतरं मया ।
विमृश्यैतदशेषेण यथेच्छसि तथा कुरु ॥६३॥

iti te jñānam ākhyātaṁ guhyād guhyataraṁ mayā/
vimṛśyaitad aśeṣeṇa yathecchasi tathā kuru//

iti—thus; *te*—to you; *jñānam*—knowledge; *ākhyātam*—explained; *guhyāt*—than confidential; *guhya-taram*—more confidential; *mayā*—by me; *vimṛśya*—deliberating; *etat*—this; *aśeṣeṇa*—fully; *yathā*—as; *icchasi*—you like; *tathā*—so; *kuru*—do.

Thus I have explained to you knowledge that is more confidential than all that is confidential. Deliberate on it fully and do as you please.

Having said this, Kṛṣṇa pauses. His divine song has been sung. In this chapter he has explained general socioreligious knowledge, confidential knowledge of the self and Brahman, the means of realizing these two kinds of knowledge, and still more confidential knowledge of his Paramātmā feature.

Jīva Goswāmī comments that the word *guhya* means confidential knowledge of Brahman, whereas *guhyatara* speaks of more confidential knowledge, that of the Paramātmā. Reiteration of *guhyatama*, the most confidential of all knowledge is yet to come. The word *guhyatama* was used to introduce the ninth chapter, which concluded with the same words found in verse 65 of this chapter. Kṛṣṇa discussed this supreme knowledge therein, as well as in chapter 10 and briefly in chapter 12. It is the knowledge of his position as *svayaṁ bhagavān* and the *prema-dharma* of Vraja.

Here Kṛṣṇa tells Arjuna to deliberate on all that he has explained thus far, imploring him to come to a decision on his own. The *Gītā* does not force us to surrender. However, the fact that we have the choice to do so, and that we are faced with this choice at every moment, is made clear. It is this choice that enables us to transcend the determinism of the *guṇas*. While we have the freedom to choose to follow Kṛṣṇa's directives or to ignore them, should we choose to ignore them, the force of nature is not negotiable. While the *Gītā* invites critical inquiry, it does not present a multitude of truths to choose from. It presents one truth throughout. However, rather than impose a dogma that dictates what an individual is to believe or do, it implores us to realize ourselves. In doing so, it concludes that we will only realize ourselves fully when we understand ourselves in relation to God.

Although Kṛṣṇa has asked Arjuna to deliberate and come to a decision, he nonetheless cannot contain himself because of his great love for him. Thus Kṛṣṇa begins to speak again before Arjuna can respond with his choice in the matter. In doing so, he reiterates the most confidential knowledge of all, thus making abundantly clear the ultimate conclusion and course of action that he recommends and expects Arjuna to arrive at.

Text 64

सर्वगुह्यतमं भूयः शृणु मे परमं वचः ।
इष्टोऽसि मे दृढमिति ततो वक्ष्यामि ते हितम् ॥६४॥

sarva-guhyatamaṁ bhūyaḥ śṛṇu me paramaṁ vacaḥ/
iṣṭo 'si me dṛḍham iti tato vakṣyāmi te hitam//

sarva-guhya-tamam—the most confidential of all; *bhūyaḥ*—again; *śṛṇu*—listen; *me*—from me; *paramam*—supreme; *vacaḥ*—instruction; *iṣṭaḥ asi*—you are dear; *me*—to me; *dṛḍham*—surely; *iti*—thus; *tataḥ*—therefore; *vakṣyāmi*—I shall say; *te*—of you; *hitam*—benefit.

Listen once again to my most important instruction, the most secret of all. You are dear to me; therefore, I shall say what is best for you.

Here Kṛṣṇa uses the words *sarva-guhyatamam*, indicating that his next instruction will be the most confidential of all, more confidential than the most secret of secrets. It is his supreme instruction *(paramaṁ vacaḥ)*. By use of the word *bhūyaḥ* (again) Kṛṣṇa indicates that he has already given this instruction earlier. He did so in the concluding verse of the ninth chapter (Bg. 9.34), which he repeats practically verbatim in the following verse. Out of great love for Arjuna, Kṛṣṇa underscores and repeats this instruction for his benefit so that there can be no uncertainty about the conclusion of his teaching. This secret knowledge is the key to unlocking the mystical treasure of the *Gītā*, its message of divine love.

Text 65

मन्मना भव मद्भक्तो मद्याजी मां नमस्कुरु ।
मामेवैष्यसि सत्यं ते प्रतिजाने प्रियोऽसि मे ॥६५॥

man-manā bhava mad-bhakto mad-yājī māṁ namaskuru/
mām evaiṣyasi satyaṁ te pratijāne priyo 'si me//

mat-manāḥ—thinking of me; *bhava*—become; *mat-bhaktaḥ*—my devotee; *mat-yājī*—sacrificing for me; *mām*—(to) me; *namaskuru*—offer obeisance; *mām*—(to) me; *eva*—certainly; *eṣyasi*—you will come; *satyam*—truly; *te*—to you; *pratijāne*—I promise; *priyaḥ*—dear; *asi*—you are; *me*—to me.

Fix your mind on me. Be my devotee! Sacrifice for me. Offer obeisance unto me. In this way you will surely come to me. I promise you this because you are my very dear friend.

At the end of chapter 9 Kṛṣṇa spoke feelingly about his devotees' love for him and the importance of cultivating this love. There he said, *mām evaiṣyasi yuktvaivam ātmānaṁ mat-parāyaṇaḥ:* "Steadfast, with me as your aim, you shall come to me." He said this in the context of telling Arjuna that which he repeats here: "Fix your mind on me. Be my devotee! Sacrifice for me. Offer obeisance unto me." In this verse, however, Kṛṣṇa says, *mām evaiṣyasi satyaṁ te pratijane priyo 'si me:* "In this way you will surely come to me. I promise you this because you are my very dear friend."

Jīva Goswāmī comments that while in chapter 9 Kṛṣṇa spoke of his devotees' love for him, here he speaks more of his love for his devotees. Out of intense love for Arjuna, Kṛṣṇa promises him, his dear friend, that he will attain him. Arjuna will attain Kṛṣṇa because Kṛṣṇa loves him, and here Kṛṣṇa begs Arjuna, "Please believe me!" Kṛṣṇa is very eager to impart the instruction in this verse to Arjuna, his eyes full of tears of love for his devotee. With folded hands, he instructs Arjuna, honestly pleading with him. By using the word *mām*, Kṛṣṇa tells Arjuna repeatedly that the promise he makes in the second half of this verse applies to those who worship him exclusively, not any other form of himself. This is his vow *(satyaṁ te)*. He can be trusted.

Not only does Kṛṣṇa want Arjuna to know his love for him, he also wants him to believe that in spite of everything he has said, one can attain perfection by simply accepting his love. After all that Kṛṣṇa has said about spiritual practice and attainment, this may seem hard to believe. Thus Kṛṣṇa feels compelled to make a solemn promise. At this point, all of his other instructions are superseded.

When instructing a disciple in spiritual life, a guru cannot tell everything at once. Sometimes he must emphasize one instruction, and at a later date that very instruction may be superseded by another seemingly contradictory instruction. It is even said that the guru may sometimes appear to lie to his disciple in the course of instructing him in the highest truth. The scripture also claims to have a license to exaggerate.[3] Great souls may deceive others

3. "Those statements of scripture promising fruitive rewards do not prescribe the ultimate good for humanity but are merely enticements for executing religious duties. They are like promises of candy spoken to induce a child to take beneficial medicine." (ŚB. 11.21.23)

in the course of enlightening them, just as a mother may cheat her son by falsely promising one thing to get him to do something that is in his higher interest. Materially speaking, it may appear that great souls cannot always be trusted. In *Śrīmad-Bhāgavatam*, Sañjaya tells Yudhiṣṭhira, *muṣito 'smi mahātmabhiḥ:* "I have been cheated by great souls." (ŚB. 1.13.37) Bhaktivedanta Swami Prabhupāda comments, "Great souls cheat others for a great cause." They can, however, be trusted to give us the ultimate truth as to the falsity of material existence and reality of love of God.

Viśvanātha Cakravartī Ṭhākura states that persons from Mathurā, the birthplace of Kṛṣṇa, are known for being deceptive. Indeed, the great and noble Vasudeva broke his word to Kaṁsa when he failed to deliver Kṛṣṇa into his hands. Kṛṣṇa himself is hardly an exception. In the greater context of the *Bhagavad-gītā*—the *Mahābhārata*—Kṛṣṇa even instructs the prince of *dharma*, Yudhiṣṭhira, to lie—and this in a book about *dharma!*

The expansion of Vraja Kṛṣṇa was born in Mathurā, and Vraja Kṛṣṇa himself is intimately connected with Mathurā, as those in a rural area are connected with the nearest city. Thus Arjuna wonders as Kṛṣṇa speaks if he can be trusted. Even in his childhood he is known for being untruthful and a thief. Of course, when he who is the proprietor of everything steals, this is merely play. It is this divine play, Kṛṣṇa *līlā*, that Kṛṣṇa encourages us to enter into in this verse. That land of Mathurā is beyond truth-seeking; it is where truth itself is folly and the crooked nature of love prevails. As Rūpa Goswāmī says, love, like a snake, does not move in a straight line: *aher iva gatiḥ premnaḥ sva-bhāva-kuṭilā bhavet* (Un., *śṛṅgāra-bheda-kathana* 102). Sometimes lovers quarrel and appear not to be in love. Sometimes they say one thing while meaning something else. In the *Gītā*, Kṛṣṇa appears to sometimes advocate one path and at other times an opposite path, while in reality he has advocated only love, either directly or indirectly. Thus Kṛṣṇa's message of love has woven its way through many religious conceptions only to fully manifest here at the conclusion of the *Bhagavad-gītā*.

Bhaktivedanta Swami Prabhupāda notes elsewhere that the transcendental position from which the activities of realized souls are enacted is called "Mathurā."[4] He writes, "Devotion to Kṛṣṇa, the son of Nanda Mahārāja, is the essence of all knowledge, and wherever such knowledge is manifested [that place] is called Mathurā. Also, when one establishes *bhakti-yoga*, excluding all other methods, one's situation is called Mathurā.

4. See Bhaktivedanta Swami Prabhupāda's purport to ŚB. 10.1.69.

Yatra nityaṁ sannihito hariḥ: 'The place where Hari, the Supreme Personality of Godhead, lives eternally is called Mathurā.' " (ŚB. 10.1.28). He cites the *Gopāla-tāpanī Upaniṣad* (2.63) in support of this: "The name Mathurā is given to the abode of Kṛṣṇa because the manifest essence of spiritual knowledge by which the entire universe has been churned appears there."

The knowledge of Brahman is called *matha*, because it churns the entire universe, extracting its essence, the person of Gopāla Kṛṣṇa himself. This Gopāla conquers Cupid who is named *man-matha*, the one who churns or bewilders the mind of everyone. He is thus called *manmatha-manmatha* or Madana-gopāla, the transcendental Cupid who conquers mundane Cupid's mind. Thus if Cupid churns the world, appearing to make it go around, then he who captivates him, the cowherd who appears in Mathurā-maṇḍala, must be the actual churner of the world. He churns away the lust of Cupid's influence and reveals the love-butter of *bhakti*—the king of knowledge *(rāja-vidyā)*. At the heart of our desire for worldly love is the soul's yearning for real love, love of Kṛṣṇa. It is by this love that the world is perfectly understood and comes to an end with regard to the false love—the cheating—of Cupid's influence.

In his commentary on *Gopāla-tāpanī Upaniṣad*, Prabhodānanda Saraswatī says that in this verse describing the import of the word Mathurā, the word *vā* (or) indicates an alternate understanding of the verse that has not been clearly mentioned. It can be taken to mean that Mathurā is the place where spiritual knowledge and *bhakti* are revealed in their most complete manifestation. Thus the apparent cheating of Mathurā has to be considered in light of the fact that the *līlā* of Kṛṣṇa is eternally manifest there.

Baladeva Vidyābhūṣaṇa comments that Kṛṣṇa tells Arjuna that although it is true that people from Mathurā cannot be trusted, it is also known that they will never deceive those they love. Here Kṛṣṇa says, "I love you, Arjuna. Trust me. Think of me always, but not like those who do so out of enmity, like Śiśupāla.[5] Think of me favorably in love. Be my devotee—not only in word, but in action as well. Therefore, worship me with flowers, incense, and other such things mentioned in the scripture. Sacrifice your life for me and offer homage unto me with your whole body prostrated, and without a doubt you will live eternally with me. Perform this drama of love on the stage of surrender, about which I shall speak next."

5. Śiśupāla thought constantly of Kṛṣṇa out of enmity. Although this led to a type of liberation, it is not *bhakti*.

Text 66

सर्वधर्मान् परित्यज्य मामेकं शरणं व्रज ।
अहं त्वां सर्वपापेभ्यो मोक्षयिष्यामि मा शुचः ॥६६॥

sarva-dharmān parityajya mām ekaṁ śaraṇaṁ vraja/
ahaṁ tvāṁ sarva-pāpebhyomokṣayiṣyāmi mā śucaḥ//

sarva-dharmān—all religious injunctions; *parityajya*—forgoing; *mām*—(to) me; *ekam*—only; *śaraṇam*—refuge; *vraja*—take; *aham*—I; *tvām*—you; *sarva*—all; *pāpebhyaḥ*—from sinful reactions; *mokṣayiṣyāmi*—I will deliver; *mā*—never; *śucaḥ*—you should grieve.

Forgoing all religious injunctions, take exclusive refuge in me. I shall deliver you from all sinful reactions. Do not fear.

This is perhaps the most frequently quoted verse of the *Bhagavad-gītā*. Together with the previous verse it constitutes Kṛṣṇa's compelling and conclusive advice for all readers of this most sacred text. After all is said about religion and spiritual pursuit, Kṛṣṇa comes to this. One should engage in devotional service to Kṛṣṇa with one's heart surrendered *(śaraṇam)*. One should be a *śaraṇāgata*, a surrendered soul. As a cow takes shelter of its herder, one should take shelter of Kṛṣṇa as if one has been bought and paid for.

In such circumstances, one need not worry for one's sustenance or protection. Accepting that which is favorable for serving Kṛṣṇa, rejecting that which is not, and surrendering one's pride in great humility, one should sacrifice oneself on the altar of loving Kṛṣṇa. This is the sixfold nature of surrender *(śaraṇāgati)*, by which all obstacles on the path to spiritual perfection are removed. The first of these six aspects of *śaraṇāgati* is clearly indicated in the word *parityajya*. One should reject everything that is not favorable for *bhakti*. Accepting what is favorable, one should proceed to embrace the other four aspects of *śaraṇāgati* as well.

How is it possible to follow Kṛṣṇa's instruction in the previous verse? How will one overcome obstacles on the path of spiritual realization and become qualified to always think of Kṛṣṇa without any other duty? What of the reactions that will come from not doing one's prescribed duties? In answer to these questions, Kṛṣṇa speaks this verse. He says, "I shall take care of any reactions that may accrue from abandoning one's superficial religious duty. I have the power to do this. I am the source of all religious injunctions,

I am eminently qualified, and on the strength of my qualifications you too will become qualified." This verse represents Kṛṣṇa's special love for his devotees that obliges him to cover for them. After thorough consideration of all that has been discussed, only a hard-hearted fool would turn away from the offer issuing from Kṛṣṇa's lotus mouth.

Jīva Goswāmī comments that some people think the *Bhagavad-gītā* suggests many different spiritual paths. To this Śrī Jīva replies that Kṛṣṇa teaches higher and lower paths in the *Gītā* to help persons distinguish one from the other but that the concluding portion of a book represents its essence. Overcoming fear and becoming free from worry is the subject of the *Gītā*'s opening lines. Here Kṛṣṇa says, "Don't worry," echoing his first words to Arjuna, where he admonished him and told him not to lament (Bg. 2.11).

In his concluding words, Kṛṣṇa stresses exclusive worship in surrender unto himself. By this spiritual practice one will overcome all fear. One whose heart is saturated with faith in this instruction, and more, one who is eager to attain that which Kṛṣṇa alludes to in this verse need not be concerned with religious duties, nor any other means of qualifying oneself for spiritual culture and attainment. One should not worry, being motivated by fear of reprisal for neglecting anything else in spiritual culture. Any such fear should be replaced with a sense of the love in Kṛṣṇa's voice as he speaks this verse. Trust in love requires no reasoning and vanquishes all fear.

Here Kṛṣṇa's mind drifts once and for all from the battlefield. Rejecting *dharma* and appearing to advise *adharma*, he speaks of *prema-dharma*. Thus as B. R. Śrīdhara Deva Goswāmī points out, the word *vraja* in this verse suggests its most common meaning: Vraja. Although here it is a verb in the imperative, meaning "take refuge, surrender!" it also brings Kṛṣṇa's homeland of Vraja to his mind. That homeland within the *maṇḍala* of Mathurā is the refuge of all souls. It is that place in which we find "all things appropriate."[6] In Vraja, love resolves all contradictions, and all things are possible. Everything has its place when properly adjusted—centered on Kṛṣṇa.

This realm exists *because* of the Kṛṣṇa conception of the Absolute. He alone is *akhila rasāmṛta-murtiḥ* (Brs. 1.1.1), the form of loving reciprocation in sacred aesthetic rapture. Under scrutiny, no other conception of the Absolute facilitates the extent of loving exchange that is possible when one's notion of divinity is Kṛṣṇa, the all-attractive irresistible Absolute.

6. This is the unique sense given to the word Vraja in Jīva Goswāmī's *Gopāla Campū*.

There are many noble manifestations of Godhead, but Kṛṣṇa is the heart of divinity. Other manifestations of divinity are no doubt motivated by love, but Kṛṣṇa is the very act of love itself personified in selfless purity, giving himself like no other.

This verse is not merely about the renunciation *(parityajya)* of religious rites and duties and entering into monasticism to sit in silence forever. When Rāya Rāmānanda suggested to Śrī Caitanya that the goal of life is accomplished by giving up the duties of *varṇāśrama-dharma*, he cited this verse as evidence.[7] Śrī Caitanya rejected this suggestion, considering it to be superficial. Mere acceptance of *sannyāsa* and forgoing one's socioreligious duties is not the heart of life's goal. Indeed, Kṛṣṇa would hardly recommend this to Arjuna when at the same time ordering him to fight. Nor is Kṛṣṇa speaking to Arjuna alone in this verse; he speaks to all gentle souls. His message is not that they must take *sannyāsa* and thereby attain salvation. They must give up any pursuit other than taking shelter of him. The full import of this verse is not what one should reject, but in whom one should take exclusive shelter.

The prefix *pari* in the word *parityajya* in this verse implies complete renunciation of religious injunctions *(dharma)* and any path mentioned thus far other than *bhakti*. In Vraja, the *gopīs* abandoned *dharma* and ran in the night toward the sound of Kṛṣṇa's flute. Here in this verse Kṛṣṇa's mind runs to the Vraja *gopīs* and their love for him. This is the clarion call of the *Gītā*, the flute sound of Kṛṣṇa calling all souls to join him in the eternal love that he himself is lost in and conquered by. This is the secret of the *Gītā* that Kṛṣṇa has confided in Arjuna, even though Arjuna himself is not suited for this kind of love. Although after hearing it Arjuna wants to run and tell it everywhere, Kṛṣṇa catches himself long enough to caution him, lest he be disappointed that everyone does not share his enthusiasm. While love seeks to share itself with everyone, in doing so it also realizes the necessity for secrecy, lest it be misunderstood.

Text 67

इदं ते नातपस्काय नाभक्ताय कदाचन ।
न चाशुश्रूषवे वाच्यं न च मां योऽभ्यसूयति ॥६७॥

7. Cc. Madhya 8.63. This verse is also cited in Madhya 9.265 in reference to unalloyed devotion being transcendental to *varṇāśrama*. It is also cited in Madhya 22.94 in reference to rejecting *varṇāśrama* in favor of unalloyed devotion.

idaṁ te nātapaskāya nābhaktāya kadācana/
na cāśuśrūṣave vācyaṁ na ca māṁ yo 'bhyasūyati//

idam—this; *te*—by you; *na*—not; *atapaskāya*—to one who is not austere; *na*—not; *abhaktāya*—to one who is not a devotee; *kadācana*—at any time; *na*—not; *ca*—and; *aśuśrūṣave*—to one who does not wish to hear; *vācyam*—to be spoken; *na*—not; *ca*—and; *mām*—(toward) me; *yaḥ*—who; *abhyasūyati*—he is envious.

This should never be explained to one who is devoid of austerity, is not a devotee, does not wish to hear it, or is envious of me.

Kṛṣṇa has now ended the *Gītā* twice, after verse 63 and again in the previous verse. At this point his teaching is complete. However, with this verse Kṛṣṇa again resumes his speech, this time for the purpose of establishing guidelines with regard to the dissemination of his teaching.

This *(idam)* secret meaning of all the revealed scripture, known as the *Bhagavad-gītā* and spoken by the Supreme God himself, should not under any circumstances *(kadācana)* be taught to four types of people: those who practice no austerity in their lives, those who are not devoted to Kṛṣṇa, those who are not interested in this wondrous teaching, and those who are envious of Kṛṣṇa. Even if a person is austere, nonenvious of Kṛṣṇa, and interested in the message of the *Gītā*, he should not be given this teaching if he is not a devotee. A person who is a devotee of Kṛṣṇa is naturally austere, interested in the *Gītā*'s sublime message, and nonenvious. Those envious of Kṛṣṇa are known by their characteristics of considering him to be an ordinary mortal and finding fault in him.

One might ask what scope there is for innocent persons to become devotees, if explaining the *Gītā* to those who are nondevotees is prohibited. In answer to this, it can be said that this prohibition extends only to the most confidential knowledge mentioned in the *Gītā*'s conclusion. This is meant only for his devotees. Others who are not yet devotees can be taught the *Bhagavad-gītā* in general, as long as they are not devoid of devotion altogether, even though they are not yet devotees of Kṛṣṇa per se. They will become devotees of Kṛṣṇa by studying the *Gītā* under the direction of a qualified guru and thus qualifying themselves for understanding its deepest import. One cannot understand this import, nor can one draw it from the text, without being a devotee of Kṛṣṇa.

If one argues further that the most confidential knowledge of the *Gītā* is that one should become Kṛṣṇa's devotee *(bhava mad bhaktaḥ)*, and thus it is meaningless to say that its confidential message is reserved for Kṛṣṇa devotees, I reply as follows. The most confidential knowledge of the *Gītā* is not merely that one become Kṛṣṇa's devotee. Go back and read again. The most confidential knowledge of the *Gītā* is that one follow in the footsteps of the inhabitants of Vraja and become *that* kind of devotee.

Furthermore, although Kṛṣṇa has restricted the dissemination of this secret inner doctrine of the *Gītā* in this verse, in his appearance as Śrī Caitanya he has adjusted this stance, giving it to everyone, albeit in a gradual progression and not all at once.[8] Only Kṛṣṇa himself has the power to override his own instruction. The fact that he has done so is truly remarkable. It is no wonder that as Śrī Caitanya he is referred to as *mahā-vadānya-avatāra*, the most munificent incarnation of God.

It is not surprising that in Kṛṣṇa's encore appearance as Śrī Caitanya, Arjuna demonstrated that he had personally understood the most confidential message of the *Gītā*. Notably, a parallel of this conversation between Kṛṣṇa and Arjuna occurs within the *līlā* of Śrī Caitanya in the form of Rāmānanda Saṁvāda, Śrī Caitanya's conversation with Rāya Rāmānanda (Cc. Madhya 8), through whom Arjuna tasted the highest reach of Vraja *bhakti*.[9] In this sacred conversation Kṛṣṇa tested Arjuna's understanding of the *Gītā*, making him the teacher and becoming the student himself. There the commonly accepted understanding of the *Gītā*'s climactic verse is rejected by Śrī Caitanya. This understanding, by which one concludes the essence of the *Gītā* to be renunciation of *dharma* and acceptance of dry monasticism, is replaced with Vraja *bhakti*. Arjuna as Rāya Rāmānanda embraces Kṛṣṇa's submission to Śrī Rādhā as the zenith of spiritual culture.

Having described those to whom the confidential knowledge of the *Gītā* should not be disclosed, Kṛṣṇa goes on in two verses to discuss the fruit of teaching it to the devoted.

8. Śrī Caitanya teaches a progression of practice requiring that one attain eligibility before advancing from one step to the next. While the practitioner begins with *bhakti*, and thus dispenses with the *Gītā*'s progression, within the culture of *bhakti* a similar progression is found. Beginners are not encouraged to meditate on Kṛṣṇa *līlā* day and night, as advanced devotees are expected to do. They are encouraged to chant God's name and engage in ritualistic worship with a view to attain eligibility for such meditation.

9. In Cc. Ādi 10.132, Śrī Caitanya says that Bhavānanda Rāya is an incarnation of Pāṇḍu and his five sons are the Pāṇḍavas. It is implied that the dearest among them, Rāmānanda Rāya, was Arjuna. This is confirmed in *Gaura-gaṇoddeśa-dīpikā* (120–24).

Text 68

य इदं परमं गुह्यं मद्भक्तेष्वभिधास्यति ।
भक्तिं मयि परां कृत्वा मामेवैष्यत्यसंशयः ॥६८॥

ya idaṁ paramaṁ guhyaṁ mad-bhakteṣv abhidhāsyati/
bhaktiṁ mayi parāṁ kṛtvā mām evaiṣyaty asaṁśayaḥ//

yaḥ—who; *idam*—this; *paramam*—supreme; *guhyam*—secret; *mat*—my; *bhakteṣu*—to devotees; *abhidhāsyati*—he explains; *bhaktim*—devotion; *mayi*—in me; *parām*—highest; *kṛtvā*—doing; *mām*—(to) me; *eva*—certainly; *eṣyati*—he will come; *asaṁśayaḥ*—without doubt.

One who explains this supreme secret to my devotees engages in the highest devotion to me. He will undoubtedly come to me.

Here the word *abhidhāsyati* implies a thorough explanation of the *Gītā*. Such an explanation involves establishing its purport in every way by analyzing its words and drawing out its deepest meaning. One who does this in devotion to Kṛṣṇa and then explains the *Gītā* in a way that it can be readily understood renders the highest service. As it was first spoken for the devotees, it should be explained to them, for only those with devotion can lend a receptive ear.

Explaining the *Gītā* should be undertaken as an act of devotion. It should be explained by one who, devoid of any ulterior motive, thinks, "I am doing this for the pleasure of Kṛṣṇa." One who thinks like this and explains the secret of the *Gītā* to devoted persons will both overcome all doubts and undoubtedly attain Kṛṣṇa and Kṛṣṇa alone *(mām eva)*. Such a person will not attain any other god by this practice, even though all the gods will be pleased with him. Kṛṣṇa will not allow a person who has endeared himself to him to go to anyone else.

Text 69

न च तस्मान्मनुष्येषु कश्चिन्मे प्रियकृत्तमः ।
भविता न च मे तस्मादन्यः प्रियतरो भुवि ॥६९॥

na ca tasmān manuṣyeṣu kaścin me priya-kṛttamaḥ/
bhavitā na ca me tasmād anyaḥ priyataro bhuvi//

na—not; *ca*—and; *tasmāt*—than he; *manuṣyeṣu*—among men; *kaścit*—anyone; *me*—to me; *priya-kṛt-tamaḥ*—more dear; *bhavitā*—he will become;

na—nor; *ca*—and; *me*—to me; *tasmāt*—than him; *anyaḥ*—other; *priya-taraḥ*—dearer; *bhuvi*—in this world.

No one in this world is more dear to me than he is, nor will there ever be anyone on earth more dear to me.

Text 70

अध्येष्यते च य इमं धर्म्यं संवादमावयोः ।
ज्ञानयज्ञेन तेनाहमिष्टः स्यामिति मे मतिः ॥७०॥

adhyeṣyate ca ya imaṁ dharmyaṁ saṁvādam āvayoḥ/
jñāna-yajñena tenāham iṣṭaḥ syām iti me matiḥ//

adhyeṣyate—he will study; *ca*—and; *yaḥ*—who; *imam*—this; *dharmyam*—sacred; *saṁvādam*—dialogue; *āvayoḥ*—of us two; *jñāna*—knowledge; *yajñena*—by the sacrifice; *tena*—by him; *aham*—I; *iṣṭaḥ*—worshipped; *syām*—might I be; *iti*—thus; *me*—my; *matiḥ*—opinion.

It is my conviction that whoever studies this sacred dialogue of ours worships me by the sacrifice of intellect.

Madhusūdana Saraswatī comments that *adhyeṣyate* (study) implies reading the *Gītā* as though one is repeating a *mantra*. Thus from the mere repetition of the text, even without understanding its meaning, one attains liberation. How is this possible? Kṛṣṇa, hearing that someone is singing about his glories, understands what he is saying and delivers him, even though that person may be ignorant.

Text 71

श्रद्धावाननसूयश्च शृणुयादपि यो नरः ।
सोऽपि मुक्तः शुभाँल्लोकान् प्राप्नुयात्पुण्यकर्मणाम् ॥७१॥

śraddhāvān anasūyaś ca śṛṇuyād api yo naraḥ/
so 'pi muktaḥ śubhāl lokān prāpnuyāt puṇya-karmaṇām//

śraddhā-vān—faithful; *anasūyaḥ*—not envious; *ca*—and; *śṛṇuyāt*—he should hear; *api*—certainly; *yaḥ*—who; *naraḥ*—man; *saḥ*—he; *api*—also; *muktaḥ*—liberated; *śubhān*—auspicious; *lokān*—worlds; *prāpnuyāt*—he should attain; *puṇya-karmaṇām*—of the pious.

Even one who merely listens to this conversation with faith, free from envy, will become free and attain the auspicious worlds of the virtuous.

With this verse Kṛṣṇa concludes his description of the fruits of properly explaining the *Gītā*. He underscores the value of studying and disseminating the *Gītā* by mentioning the fruits of merely hearing it with faith, free of envy. If merely by hearing the *Gītā* faithfully one achieves wonderful results, how much more beneficial it is to study the *Gītā* and teach it.

Here the words *muktaḥ* and *puṇya-karmaṇām* can be taken as references to liberation and attainment of heaven, respectively. However, this rendering does not take into consideration the order in which they appear in the verse. Liberation normally occurs after attaining heaven, not before. In consideration of this, it is necessary to understand *muktaḥ* as referring to freedom from impiety, the result of which is attainment of heaven, which follows the sequence both of the words in the verse as well as the actual sequence involved in attaining heaven. However, this understanding limits the fruit of faithfully hearing the *Gītā* to material existence. If, however, we understand *muktaḥ* to refer to liberation from material existence and *puṇya-karmaṇām* as a reference to those of virtuous deeds who reside in the most auspicious *(śubhān)*, eternally liberated planets *(lokān)* of God known as Vaikuṇṭha that lie beyond material heaven, the word sequence concurs with the order of spiritual progress from liberation to Vaikuṇṭha and the fruit of merely hearing the transcendental message of the *Gītā* is itself transcendental.

In the following verse, Kṛṣṇa utters his last word, setting the appropriate example for the guru with regard to instructing his disciple.

Text 72

कच्चिदेतच्छ्रुतं पार्थ त्वयैकाग्रेण चेतसा ।
कच्चिदज्ञानसम्मोहः प्रणष्टस्ते धनञ्जय ॥७२॥

kaccid etac chrutaṁ pārtha tvayaikāgreṇa cetasā/
kaccid ajñāna-sammohaḥ praṇaṣṭas te dhanañjaya//

kaccit—whether; *etat*—this; *śrutam*—heard; *pārtha*—O son of Pṛthā; *tvayā*—by you; *eka-agreṇa*—with full attention; *cetasā*—by the mind; *kaccit*—whether; *ajñāna*—ignorance; *sammohaḥ*—delusion; *praṇaṣṭaḥ*—dispelled; *te*—of you; *dhanañjaya*—O Dhanañjaya.

O Pārtha, have you listened to this with undivided attention? O Dhanañjaya, have your ignorance and delusion been removed?

The *guru* must be prepared to explain the spiritual reality to his disciple until he has understood, even if this involves repeating his instruction again and again. Although Kṛṣṇa is omniscient, he asks this question, setting an ideal example. Implied here is both Kṛṣṇa's willingness to repeat the entire *Gītā* again should Arjuna not yet fully understand it, as well as the suggestion on Kṛṣṇa's part that such repetition will not be necessary. Kṛṣṇa addresses Arjuna as both Pārtha, demonstrating his deep affection for Arjuna and willingness to speak further if necessary, and Dhanañjaya, indicating that he knows that his dear disciple is now filled with the wealth of spiritual understanding.

Text 73

अर्जुन उवाच
नष्टो मोहः स्मृतिर्लब्धा त्वत्प्रसादान्मयाच्युत ।
स्थितोऽस्मि गतसन्देहः करिष्ये वचनं तव ॥७३॥

arjuna uvāca
naṣṭo mohaḥ smṛtir labdhā tvat-prasādān mayācyuta/
sthito 'smi gata-sandehaḥ kariṣye vacanaṁ tava//

arjunaḥ uvāca—Arjuna said; *naṣṭaḥ*—destroyed; *mohaḥ*—delusion; *smṛtiḥ*—memory; *labdhā*—restored; *tvat-prasādāt*—by your grace; *mayā*—by me; *acyuta*—O Acyuta; *sthitaḥ*—situated; *asmi*—I am; *gata*—removed; *sandehaḥ*—doubt; *kariṣye*—I shall execute; *vacanam*—order; *tava*—your.

Arjuna said: O Acyuta, my delusion is destroyed and my memory restored by your grace. I now stand free from doubt and shall do as you command.

By Kṛṣṇa's grace all ignorance can be destroyed. Now Arjuna's delusion, which was created by Kṛṣṇa himself for the purpose of teaching the *Bhagavad-gītā*, stands removed. His memory restored and free from doubt, he is prepared to do as Kṛṣṇa wishes.

At this point in his manifest earthly *līlā*, Kṛṣṇa has returned to Vraja, and in his nearly complete *purṇa-kalpa-prakāśa* manifestation he has entered along with his Vraja devotees into the unmanifest eternal *līlā*, mitigating their pangs of separation from him. In his most complete *pūrṇatama- prakāśa* manifestation he has remained and does so perpetually in earthly Vraja, invisible to material eyes. In yet another plenary manifestation (*pūrṇa-prakāśa*), he mounted his chariot and returned alone to Dwārakā. Here in

Kurukṣetra this Kṛṣṇa wants Arjuna to assist him in the final stage of removing the burden of impiety from the earth and thereby establishing *dharma.*

Remaining visible on earth in his *pūrṇa-prakāśa* expansion, the sober *dhīra-praśānta* Kṛṣṇa of Dwārakā, the chariot driver of Arjuna, focuses on his mission of establishing *dharma.* Yet remembering the Vraja *līlā*, Kṛṣṇa has lost heart for fighting and he turns to Arjuna, asking for his assistance. The principal purpose of Kṛṣṇa's move to Dwārakā and the battles he engaged in was to protect the cowherds of Vraja. Otherwise, he would have never left the village life. Establishing *dharma* is a by-product of protecting his devotees. Now that the Vraja devotees are no longer in need of such protection, Kṛṣṇa's principal impetus for slaying the enemies of *dharma* is removed. He has put down his weapons. His competent elder brother Balarāma has been dispatched to the south where he will slay Romaharṣana and Balvala, and Kṛṣṇa himself has sworn not to fight in the Battle of Kurukṣetra. Thus he must do so through Arjuna. Through Arjuna he will now establish religious principles of *dharma*, and through Arjuna he has made clear the ideal of *prema-dharma* that transcends religious law. At the same time, Arjuna's willingness to surrender to Kṛṣṇa's will and rise above religious *dharma* insures that *dharma* itself will also be established.

Thus the *Bhagavad-gītā* teaches that we should first understand the ideal of *prema-dharma* and hold it in our hearts as our ideal in life. By aspiring for this ideal through the proper means—the culture of unalloyed *bhakti* in spontaneous love—one will pass through and understand every other progressive stage taught in the *Gītā*. These stages include religious life, purification of the heart, knowledge of the self, and liberation itself. These are all by-products of the culture of unalloyed *bhakti*. As practitioners, we should look for these developments, considering them to be signs that our devotional culture is authentic. In time, the primary fruit of the culture of unalloyed *bhakti*, love of Kṛṣṇa, will manifest in our hearts. As this awakens, we will join Kṛṣṇa wherever he enacts his *līlā* in this world, pay our deepest respects to Arjuna, and then return with Kṛṣṇa and the Vraja devotees to the unmanifest eternal *līlā* once and for all. Tribute to Arjuna whose greatness lies in his surrender to the will of the infallible *(acyuta)*—Kṛṣṇa!

Text 74

सञ्जय उवाच
इत्यहं वासुदेवस्य पार्थस्य च महात्मनः ।
संवादमिममश्रौषमद्भुतं रोमहर्षणम् ॥७४॥

sañjaya uvāca
ity ahaṁ vāsudevasya pārthasya ca mahātmanaḥ/
saṁvādam imam aśrauṣam adbhutaṁ roma-harṣaṇam//

sañjayaḥ uvāca—Sañjaya said; *iti*—thus; *aham*—I; *vāsudevasya*—of Vāsudeva; *pārthasya*—of Arjuna; *ca*—and; *mahā-ātmanaḥ*—of the great soul; *saṁvādam*—conversation; *imam*—this; *aśrauṣam*—I have heard; *adbhutam*—wondrous; *roma-harṣaṇam*—making the hair stand on end.

Sañjaya said: Thus I have heard this conversation between the son of Vāsudeva and that great soul, Pārtha. Wondrous, it causes one's hair to stand on end.

Being wondrous and miraculous *(adbhutam)* in every respect, the sacred conversation between Kṛṣṇa and Arjuna, the immortal *Bhagavad-gītā*, causes Sañjaya, who merely heard it from a distance, to exhibit ecstatic symptoms such as horripilation *(roma-harṣaṇam)*.

Text 75

व्यासप्रसादाच्छ्रुतवानेतद् गुह्यमहं परम् ।
योगं योगेश्वरात्कृष्णात्साक्षात्कथयतः स्वयम् ॥७५॥

vyāsa-prasādāc chrutavān etad guhyam ahaṁ param/
yogaṁ yogeśvarāt kṛṣṇāt sākṣāt kathayataḥ svayam//

vyāsa-prasādāt—by the grace of Vyāsa; *śrutavān*—hearing; *etat*—this; *guhyam*—confidential; *aham*—I; *param*—highest; *yogam*—*yoga; yoga-īśvarāt*—from the master of *yoga; kṛṣṇāt*—from Kṛṣṇa; *sākṣāt*—directly; *kathayataḥ*—speaking; *svayam*—personally.

By the grace of Vyāsa I have directly heard about this highest and most confidential yoga, which Kṛṣṇa, the master of yoga, has himself spoken of!

As mentioned in chapter 1, Sañjaya received the blessing of Vyāsa that he could know everything, even the minds of the assembled warriors on the battlefield of Kurukṣetra. Thus through mystic power he witnessed the conversation between Kṛṣṇa and Arjuna. In this conversation, Kṛṣṇa, the master of all mysticism *(yogeśvara)*, has revealed the highest and most secret *yoga* of devotion. Having heard about the most secret and supreme form of *yoga* from the greatest authority on the subject, Sañjaya rejoices here in this verse.

Text 76

राजन् संस्मृत्य संस्मृत्य संवादमिममद्भुतम् ।
केशवार्जुनयोः पुण्यं हृष्यामि च मुहुर्मुहुः ॥७६॥

rājan saṁsmṛtya saṁsmṛtya saṁvādam imam adbhutam/
keśavārjunayoḥ puṇyaṁ hṛṣyāmi ca muhur muhuḥ//

rājan—O King; *saṁsmṛtya*—remembering; *saṁsmṛtya*—remembering; *saṁvādam*—conversation; *imam*—this; *adbhutam*—wonderful; *keśava-arjunayoḥ*—of Keśava and Arjuna; *puṇyam*—sacred; *hṛṣyāmi*—I rejoice; *ca*—and; *muhuḥ muhuḥ*—repeatedly.

O King, recalling again and again this wonderful and sacred conversation between Keśava and Arjuna, I am thrilled at every moment.

Text 77

तच्च संस्मृत्य संस्मृत्य रूपमत्यद्भुतं हरेः ।
विस्मयो मे महान् राजन् हृष्यामि च पुनः पुनः ॥७७॥

tac ca saṁsmṛtya saṁsmṛtya rūpam aty-adbhutaṁ hareḥ/
vismayo me mahān rājan hṛṣyāmi ca punaḥ punaḥ//

tat—that; *ca*—and; *saṁsmṛtya*—remembering; *saṁsmṛtya*—remembering; *rūpam*—form; *ati*—greatly; *adbhutam*—amazing; *hareḥ*—of Kṛṣṇa; *vismayaḥ*—wonder; *me*—my; *mahān*—great; *rājan*—O King; *hṛṣyāmi*—I rejoice; *ca*—and; *punaḥ punaḥ*—again and again.

And remembering repeatedly that amazing form of Kṛṣṇa I am struck with wonder, and I rejoice again and again.

Text 78

यत्र योगेश्वरः कृष्णो यत्र पार्थो धनुर्धरः ।
तत्र श्रीर्विजयो भूतिर्ध्रुवा नीतिर्मतिर्मम ॥७८॥

yatra yogeśvaraḥ kṛṣṇo yatra pārtho dhanur-dharaḥ/
tatra śrīr vijayo bhūtir dhruvā nītir matir mama//

yatra—where; *yoga-īśvaraḥ*—the master of *yoga*; *kṛṣṇaḥ*—Kṛṣṇa; *yatra*—where; *pārthaḥ*—Pārtha; *dhanuḥ-dharaḥ*—archer; *tatra*—there; *śrīḥ*—good fortune; *vijayaḥ*—victory; *bhūtiḥ*—wealth; *dhruvā*—sure; *nītiḥ*—righteousness; *matiḥ mama*—my opinion.

Wherever Kṛṣṇa, the master of yoga, and the archer Pārtha are, there will always be good fortune, victory, wealth, well-being, and righteousness. This is my conviction.

Here Sañjaya advises the blind king Dhṛtarāṣṭra to give up any hope of his sons being victorious in battle. All that he might be concerned with—good fortune, victory, wealth, well-being, and righteousness—is on the side of the Pāṇḍavas, for on their side stand Kṛṣṇa and Arjuna. Thus Sañjaya encourages the king to take refuge of Kṛṣṇa, satisfy the Pāṇḍavas, and give everything to them. Only one blind to his real self-interest would refuse to do so.

Concluding words

On the auspicious advent day of Adwaita Ācārya in the year 2000, I end this commentary on the *Bhagavad-gītā: Its Feeling and Philosophy*. May he who mystically learned the devotional import to every verse of the *Gītā* from Śrī Caitanya himself be merciful to me.

He is Adwaita because he is nondifferent from Kṛṣṇa, being his incarnation, and he is known as Ācārya because he taught the *bhāgavata prema-dharma* inculcated in the *Bhagavad-gītā*. He is also known as Mahā-Viṣṇu because he is both Mahādeva (Śiva) and Viṣṇu combined. Thus he is the spark of the splendor of Śrī Kṛṣṇa from whom the entire world issues, and by his willful glance of compassionate love the multitude of souls gain the opportunity to meet their maker and know his love for them.

Adwaita Ācārya called Śrī Caitanya to this world, without whom the deepest import of Śrī Kṛṣṇa's speech to Arjuna would not have been revealed. No one can fathom his glory, and he cannot fathom the glory of Śrī Caitanya, who is Kṛṣṇa himself in every way, imbued with the love of Rādhā.

Glossary

acintya-bhedābheda—the metaphysic of Gauḍīya Vedānta describing the energetic source of all existence (God/Kṛṣṇa) to be inconceivably, simultaneously one and different from his energy.

aiśvarya—"opulence"; the Godly manifestation of Kṛṣṇa as Viṣṇu/ Nārāyaṇa.

avatāra—God's descent into human society.

avyakta—"unmanifest"; refers to the night of Brahmā at which time the material manifestation becomes partially unmanifest, as well as to Viṣṇu in whom the entire material manifestation rests at the end of Brahmā's life.

Bhagavān—the personality of Godhead.

bhakti-yoga—discipline of love and devotion to God.

bhāva—spiritual emotion.

Brahman—all-pervasive manifestation of Godhead.

dharma—"righteousness"; the inherent characteristic of anything.

dhīra-lalita—the hero who is both sober and playful.

dhīra-praśānta—the hero who is sober and peaceful.

dhyāna—meditation.

Dwārakā—the place of Kṛṣṇa's aristocratic *līlā* where reverence for him prevails over intimacy.

gopī—milkmaid of Kṛṣṇa.

guṇa—threefold influence of material nature: *sattva*, *rajas*, and *tamas*.

jīva—individual soul.

jñāna-yoga—discipline of culturing spiritual knowledge.

Kali-yuga—age of hypocrisy.

karma—reactionary work.

māyā—illusion.

nirvāṇa—cessation of material existence.

niṣkāma-karma-yoga—discipline of acting with detachment from the fruits of one's work with a view to attain self-realization and God-realization.

parā-prakṛti—individual souls.

Paramātmā—indwelling manifestation of Godhead.

paramparā—succession of gurus.

prakṛti—material nature.

prārabdha-karma—reactions from previous lives that are now bearing fruit.

prema—love of God.

puruṣa—the Supreme Person; sometimes used to describe the individual soul.

rāgānuga—the path of spontaneous love following the ideal of Vraja *bhakti*.

rajas—passion, movement of matter.

rasa—sacred aesthetic rapture in which the individual soul unites with God in a transcendental relationship.

śakti—potency or energy of God.

sannyāsa—renounced order of life in which obligatory work is transcended.

sattva—goodness, clarity, intelligibility of matter.

saṁskāra—a subtle impression made on the soul that impels it to act in a particular way.

sāṅkhya—analytical study of material nature.

Sāṅkhya—one of the six *darśanas* of Indian philosophy founded by sage Kapila.

śruti—the *Upaniṣads*.

tamas—ignorance, inertia.

taṭastha—potency of God of which the individual souls are constituted.

tyāga—renunciation of the fruits of one's actions.

varṇāśrama—the socioreligious system in which persons are classified in terms of their psychosomatic nature and religious status and thus assigned corresponding duties.

viśva-rūpa—the form of the universe, a divine manifestation in which God is seen to pervade the entire universe.

Vraja—the intimate pastoral setting of Kṛṣṇa's *līlā* with the *gopīs*.

yuga—cosmic time cycle.

Index of Verses

A

abhayaṁ sattva-saṁśuddhir 16.1
abhisandhāya tu phalaṁ 17.12
abhito brahma-nirvāṇaṁ 5.26
abhyāsād ramate yatra 18.36
abhyāsa-yoga-yuktena 8.8

abhyāsa-yogena tato 12.9
abhyāsena tu kaunteya 6.35
abhyāse 'py asamartho 'si 12.10
abhyutthānam adharmasya 4.7
ā-brahma-bhuvanāl lokāḥ 8.16

ācaraty ātmanaḥ śreyas 16.22
ācāryāḥ pitaraḥ putrās 1.33
ācāryam upasaṅgamya 1.2
ācāryān mātulān bhrātṝn 1.26
ācāryopāsanaṁ śaucaṁ 13.8

acchedyo 'yam adāhyo 2.24
adeśa-kāle yad dānam 17.22
adharmābhibhavāt kṛṣṇa 1.40
adharmaṁ dharmam 18.32
adhaś ca mūlāny 15.2

adhaś cordhvaṁ prasṛtās 15.2
adhibhūtaṁ ca kiṁ proktam 8.1
adhibhūtaṁ kṣaro bhāvaḥ 8.4
adhiṣṭhānaṁ tathā kartā 18.14
adhiṣṭhāya manaś cāyaṁ 15.9

adhiyajñaḥ kathaṁ ko 'tra 8.2
adhiyajño 'ham evātra 8.4
adhyātma-jñāna 13.12
adhyātma-vidyā 10.32
adhyeṣyate ca ya imaṁ 18.70

āḍhyo 'bhijanavān asmi 16.15
ādityānām ahaṁ viṣṇur 10.21
adṛṣṭa-pūrvaṁ hṛṣito 11.45
adveṣṭā sarva-bhūtānāṁ 12.13
ādy-antavantaḥ kaunteya 5.22

āgamāpāyino 'nityās 2.14
aghāyur indriyārāmo 3.16
agnir jyotir ahaḥ śuklaḥ 8.24
aham ādir hi devānāṁ 10.2
aham ādiś ca madhyaṁ ca 10.20

aham ātmā guḍākeśa 10.20
aham evākṣayaḥ kālo 10.33
ahaṁ hi sarva-yajñānāṁ 9.24
ahaṁ kratur ahaṁ yajñaḥ 9.16
ahaṁ kṛtsnasya jagataḥ 7.6

ahaṁ sarvasya prabhavo 10.8
ahaṁ tvāṁ sarva 18.66
ahaṁ vaiśvānaro bhūtvā 15.14
ahaṅkāra itīyaṁ me 7.4
ahaṅkāraṁ balaṁ darpaṁ 16.18

ahaṅkāraṁ balaṁ darpaṁ 18.53
ahaṅkāra-vimūḍhātmā 3.27
āhārā rājasasyeṣṭā 17.9
āhāras tv api sarvasya 17.7
ahiṁsā samatā tuṣṭis 10.5

ahiṁsā satyam akrodhas 16.2
aho bata mahat pāpaṁ 1.44
āhus tvām ṛṣayaḥ sarve 10.13
airāvataṁ gajendrāṇāṁ 10.27
ajānatā mahimānaṁ 11.41

ajñānaṁ cābhijātasya 16.4
ajñānenāvṛtaṁ jñānaṁ 5.15
ajñaś cāśraddadhānaś ca 4.40
ajo nityaḥ śāśvato 'yaṁ 2.20
ajo 'pi sann avyayātmā 4.6

akarmaṇaś ca boddhavyaṁ 4.17
ākhyāhi me ko bhavān 11.31
akīrtiṁ cāpi bhūtāni 2.34
akṣaram brahma paramaṁ 8.3
akṣarāṇām a-kāro 'smi 10.33

amānitvam adambhitvam 13.8

amī ca tvāṁ dhṛtarāṣṭrasya 11.26
amī hi tvāṁ sura-saṅghā 11.21
amṛtaṁ caiva mṛtyuś ca 9.19
anādi-madhyāntam ananta 11.19

anādi mat-paraṁ brahma 13.13
anāditvān nirguṇatvāt 13.32
ananta deveśa jagan 11.37
anantaś cāsmi nāgānāṁ 10.29
anantavijayaṁ rājā 1.16

ananta-vīryāmita-vikramas 11.40
ananya-cetāḥ satataṁ 8.14
ananyāś cintayanto māṁ 9.22
ananyenaiva yogena 12.6
anapekṣaḥ śucir dakṣa 12.16

anārya-juṣṭam asvargyam 2.2
anāśino 'prameyasya 2.18
anāśritaḥ karma-phalaṁ 6.1
anātmanas tu śatrutve 6.6
aneka-bāhūdara-vaktra 11.16

aneka-citta-vibhrāntā 16.16
aneka-divyābharaṇaṁ 11.10
aneka-janma-saṁsiddhas 6.45
aneka-vaktra-nayanam 11.10
anena prasaviṣyadhvam 3.10

anicchann api vārṣṇeya 3.36
aniketaḥ sthira-matir 12.19
aniṣṭam iṣṭaṁ miśraṁ ca 18.12
anityam asukhaṁ lokam 9.33
annād bhavanti bhūtāni 3.14

anta-kāle ca mām eva 8.5
antavanta ime dehā 2.18
antavat tu phalaṁ teṣāṁ 7.23
anubandhaṁ kṣayaṁ 18.25
anudvega-karaṁ vākyaṁ 17.15

anye ca bahavaḥ śūrā 1.9
anye sāṅkhyena yogena 13.25

anye tv evam ajānantaḥ 13.26
apāne juhvati prāṇaṁ 4.29
aparaṁ bhavato janma 4.4

aparaspara-sambhūtaṁ 16.8
apare niyatāhārāḥ 4.29
apareyam itas tv anyāṁ 7.5
aparyāptaṁ tad asmākaṁ 1.10
apaśyad deva-devasya 11.13

aphalākāṅkṣibhir yajño 17.11
aphalākāṅkṣibhir yuktaiḥ 17.17
aphala-prepsunā karma 18.23
api ced asi pāpebhyaḥ 4.36
api cet su-durācāro 9.30

api trailokya-rājyasya 1.35
aprakāśo 'pravṛttiś ca 14.13
aprāpya māṁ nivartante 9.3
aprāpya yoga-saṁsiddhiṁ 6.37
apratiṣṭho mahā-bāho 6.38

āpūryamāṇam acala 2.70
ārto jijñāsur arthārthī 7.16
ārurukṣor muner yogaṁ 6.3
asad ity ucyate pārtha 17.28
asakta-buddhiḥ sarvatra 18.49

asaktaṁ sarva-bhṛc caiva 13.15
asaktir anabhiṣvaṅgaḥ 13.10
asakto hy ācaran karma 3.19
asaṁmūḍhaḥ sa martyeṣu 10.3
asaṁśayaṁ mahā-bāho 6.35

asaṁśayaṁ samagraṁ māṁ 7.1
asaṁyatātmanā yogo 6.36
āśā-pāśa-śatair baddhāḥ 16.12
aśāstra-vihitaṁ ghoraṁ 17.5
asat-kṛtam avajñātaṁ 17.22

asatyam apratiṣṭhaṁ te 16.8
asau mayā hataḥ śatrur 16.14
āścarya-vac cainam anyaḥ 2.29
āścarya-vat paśyati kaścid 2.29
asito devalo vyāsaḥ 10.13

asmākaṁ tu viśiṣṭā ye 1.7
aśocyān anvaśocas tvaṁ 2.11

aśraddadhānāḥ puruṣā 9.3
aśraddhayā hutaṁ dattaṁ 17.28
āsthitaḥ sa hi yuktātmā 7.18

āsurīṁ yonim āpannā 16.20
āśvāsayām āsa ca bhītam 11.50
aśvatthaḥ sarva-vṛkṣāṇāṁ 10.26
aśvatthāmā vikarṇaś ca 1.8
aśvattham enaṁ su-virūḍha 15.3

atattvārtha-vad alpaṁ ca 18.22
atha cainaṁ nitya-jātaṁ 2.26
atha cet tvam ahaṅkārān 18.58
atha cet tvam imaṁ 2.33
atha cittaṁ samādhātuṁ 12.9

athaitad apy aśakto 'si 12.11
atha kena prayukto 'yaṁ 3.36
atha vā bahunaitena 10.42
athavā yoginām eva 6.42
atha vyavasthitān dṛṣṭvā 1.20

ātmaiva hy ātmano bandhur 6.5
ātmany eva ca santuṣṭas 3.17
ātmany evātmanā tuṣṭaḥ 2.55
ātma-sambhāvitāḥ 16.17
ātma-saṁsthaṁ manaḥ 6.25

ātma-saṁyama-yogāgnau 4.27
ātmaupamyena sarvatra 6.32
ātmavantaṁ na karmāṇi 4.41
ātma-vaśyair vidheyātmā 2.64
ato 'smi loke vede ca 15.18

atra śūrā maheṣv-āsā 1.4
atyeti tat sarvam idaṁ 8.28
avācya-vādāṁś ca bahūn 2.36
avajānanti māṁ mūḍhā 9.11
avāpya bhūmāv asapatnam 2.8

avibhaktaṁ ca bhūteṣu 13.17
avibhaktaṁ vibhakteṣu 18.20
avināśi tu tad viddhi 2.17
āvṛtaṁ jñānam etena 3.39
avyaktādīni bhūtāni 2.28

avyaktād vyaktayaḥ sarvāḥ 8.18
avyaktā hi gatir duḥkhaṁ 12.5

avyaktaṁ vyaktim 7.24
avyakta-nidhanāny eva 2.28
avyakto 'kṣara ity uktas 8.21

avyakto 'yam acintyo 'yam 2.25
ayaneṣu ca sarveṣu 1.11
ayathāvat prajānāti 18.31
ayatiḥ śraddhayopeto 6.37
āyudhānām ahaṁ vajraṁ 10.28

āyuḥ-sattva-balārogya 17.8
ayuktaḥ kāma-kāreṇa 5.12
ayuktaḥ prākṛtaḥ 18.28

B

bahavo jñāna-tapasā 4.10
bahir antaś ca bhūtānām 13.16
bahūdaraṁ bahu-daṁṣṭrā 11.23
bahūnāṁ janmanām ante 7.19
bahūni me vyatītāni 4.5

bahūny adṛṣṭa-pūrvāṇi 11.6
bahu-śākhā hy anantāś ca 2.41
bāhya-sparśeṣv asaktātmā 5.21
balaṁ balavatāṁ cāhaṁ 7.11
bandhaṁ mokṣaṁ ca 18.30

bandhur ātmātmanas tasya 6.6
bhajanty ananya-manaso 9.13
bhaktiṁ mayi parāṁ kṛtvā 18.68
bhakto 'si me sakhā ceti 4.3
bhaktyā mām abhijānāti 18.55

bhaktyā tv ananyayā 11.54
bhavāmi na cirāt pārtha 12.7
bhavān bhīṣmaś ca karṇaś ca 1.8
bhavanti bhāvā bhūtānāṁ 10.5
bhavanti sampadaṁ daivīm 16.3

bhavāpyayau hi bhūtānāṁ 11.2
bhāva-saṁśuddhir ity etat 17.16
bhavaty atyāginām pretya 18.12
bhaviṣyāṇi ca bhūtāni 7.26
bhavitā na ca me tasmād 18.69

bhayād raṇād uparataṁ 2.35
bhīṣma-droṇa-pramukhataḥ 1.25
bhīṣmam evābhirakṣantu 1.11

bhīṣmo droṇaḥ sūta-putras 11.26
bhogaiśvarya-prasaktānāṁ 2.44

bhoktāraṁ yajña-tapasāṁ 5.29
bhrāmayan sarva-bhūtāni 18.61
bhruvor madhye prāṇam 8.10
bhūmir āpo 'nalo vāyuḥ 7.4
bhuñjate te tv aghaṁ pāpā 3.13

bhūta-bhartṛ ca taj 13.17
bhūta-bhāvana bhūteśa 10.15
bhūta-bhāvodbhava-karo 8.3
bhūta-grāmaḥ sa evāyaṁ 8.19
bhūta-grāmam imaṁ 9.8

bhūta-bhṛn na ca bhūta-stho 9.5
bhūta-prakṛti-mokṣaṁ ca 13.35
bhūtāni yānti bhūtejyā 9.25
bhūya eva mahā-bāho 10.1
bhūyaḥ kathaya tṛptir hi 10.18

bījaṁ māṁ sarva 7.10
brahma-bhūtaḥ 18.54
brahmacaryam ahiṁsā ca 17.14
brahmāgnāv apare yajñaṁ 4.25
brahmaiva tena gantavyaṁ 4.24

brāhmaṇa-kṣatriya-viśāṁ 18.41
brahmāṇam īśaṁ 11.15
brāhmaṇās tena vedāś ca 17.23
brahmaṇo hi pratiṣṭhāham 14.27
brahmaṇy ādhāya karmāṇi 5.10

brahmārpaṇaṁ brahma 4.24
brahma-sūtra-padaiś caiva 13.5
bṛhat-sāma tathā sāmnāṁ 10.35
buddhau śaraṇam anviccha 2.49
buddher bhedaṁ dhṛteś 18.29

buddhir buddhimatām asmi 7.10
buddhir jñānam 10.4
buddhi-yogam upāśritya 18.57
buddhi-yukto jahātīha 2.50
buddhyā viśuddhayā 18.51
buddhyā yukto yayā pārtha 2.39

C

cañcalaṁ hi manaḥ kṛṣṇa 6.34
cātur-varṇyaṁ mayā 4.13
catur-vidhā bhajante māṁ 7.16
cetasā sarva-karmāṇi 18.57
chandāṁsi yasya parṇāni 15.1

chinna-dvaidhā yatātmānaḥ 5.25
chittvainaṁ saṁśayaṁ 4.42
cintām aparimeyāṁ ca 16.11

D

dadāmi buddhi-yogaṁ 10.10
daivam evāpare yajñaṁ 4.25
daivī hy eṣā guṇa-mayī 7.14
daivī sampad vimokṣāya 16.5
daivo vistaraśaḥ prokta 16.6

dambhāhaṅkāra-saṁyuktāḥ 17.5
dambho darpo 'bhimānaś 16.4
daṁṣṭrā-karālāni ca te 11.25
dāna-kriyāś ca vividhāḥ 17.25
dānaṁ damaś ca yajñaś ca 16.1

dānam īśvara-bhāvaś ca 18.43
daṇḍo damayatām asmi 10.38
darśayām āsa pārthāya 11.9
dātavyam iti yad dānaṁ 17.20
dayā bhūteṣv aloluptvaṁ 16.2

dehī nityam avadhyo 'yaṁ 2.30
dehino 'smin yathā dehe 2.13
deśe kāle ca pātre ca 17.20
devā apy asya rūpasya 11.52
deva-dvija-guru-prājña 17.14

devān bhāvayatānena 3.11
devān deva-yajo yānti 7.23
dharma-kṣetre kuru-kṣetre 1.1
dharma-saṁsthāpanārthāya 4.8
dharmāviruddho bhūteṣu 7.11

dharme naṣṭe kulaṁ 1.39
dharmyād dhi yuddhāc 2.31
dhārtarāṣṭrā raṇe hanyus 1.45
dhārtarāṣṭrasya durbuddher 1.23
dhṛṣṭadyumno virāṭaś ca 1.17

dhṛṣṭaketuś cekitānaḥ 1.5
dhṛtyā yayā dhārayate 18.33
dhūmenāvriyate vahnir 3.38
dhūmo rātris tathā kṛṣṇaḥ 8.25
dhyānāt karma-phala 12.12

dhyāna-yoga-paro nityaṁ 18.52
dhyānenātmani paśyanti 13.25
dhyāyato viṣayān puṁsaḥ 2.62
diśo na jāne na labhe 11.25
divi sūrya-sahasrasya 11.12

divya-mālyāmbara 11.11
divyaṁ dadāmi te cakṣuḥ 11.8
dīyate ca parikliṣṭaṁ 17.21
doṣair etaiḥ kula-ghnānāṁ 1.42
draṣṭum icchāmi te rūpam 11.3

dravya-yajñās tapo-yajñā 4.28
droṇaṁ ca bhīṣmaṁ ca 11.34
dṛṣṭvādbhutaṁ rūpam 11.20
dṛṣṭvā hi tvāṁ 11.24
dṛṣṭvā tu pāṇḍavānīkaṁ 1.2

dṛṣṭvedaṁ mānuṣaṁ 11.51
dṛṣṭvemaṁ sva-janaṁ 1.28
drupado draupadeyāś ca 1.18
duḥkham ity eva yat karma 18.8
duḥkheṣv anudvigna 2.56

dūreṇa hy avaraṁ karma 2.49
dvandvair vimuktāḥ sukha 15.5
dvau bhūta-sargau loke 16.6
dvāv imau puruṣau loke 15.16
dyāv ā-pṛthivyor idam 11.20

dyūtaṁ chalayatām asmi 10.36

E

ekākī yata-cittātmā 6.10
ekam apy āsthitaḥ samyag 5.4
ekaṁ sāṅkhyaṁ ca yogaṁ ca 5.5
ekatvena pṛthaktvena 9.15
ekayā yāty anāvṛttim 8.26

eko 'tha vāpy acyuta 11.42
eṣā brāhmī sthitiḥ pārtha 2.72
eṣā te 'bhihitā sāṅkhye 2.39
eṣa tūddeśataḥ prokto 10.40
etac chrutvā vacanaṁ 11.35

etad buddhvā buddhimān 15.20
etad dhi durlabhataraṁ 6.42
etad veditum icchāmi 13.1
etad-yonīni bhūtāni 7.6
etad yo vetti taṁ prāhuḥ 13.2

etair vimohayaty eṣa 3.40
etair vimuktaḥ kaunteya 16.22
etaj jñānam iti proktam 13.12
etāṁ dṛṣṭim avaṣṭabhya 16.9
etāṁ vibhūtiṁ yogaṁ ca 10.7

etan me saṁśayaṁ kṛṣṇa 6.39
etān na hantum icchāmi 1.34
etāny api tu karmāṇi 18.6
etasyāhaṁ na paśyāmi 6.33
etat kṣetraṁ samāsena 13.7

evaṁ bahu-vidhā yajñā 4.32
evaṁ buddheḥ paraṁ 3.43
evam etad yathāttha tvam 11.3
evaṁ jñātvā kṛtaṁ karma 4.15
evaṁ paramparā-prāptam 4.2

evaṁ pravartitaṁ cakraṁ 3.16
evaṁ-rūpaḥ śakya ahaṁ 11.48
evaṁ satata-yuktā ye 12.1
evaṁ trayī-dharmam 9.21
evam ukto hṛṣīkeśo 1.24

evam uktvā hṛṣīkeśaṁ 2.9
evam uktvārjunaḥ saṅkhye 1.46
evam uktvā tato rājan 11.9

G

gacchanty apunar-āvṛttiṁ 5.17
gām āviśya ca bhūtāni 15.13
gandharvāṇāṁ citrarathaḥ 10.26
gandharva-yakṣāsura 11.22
gāṇḍīvaṁ sraṁsate hastāt 1.29

gata-saṅgasya muktasya 4.23
gatāsūn agatāsūṁś ca 2.11
gatir bhartā prabhuḥ sākṣī 9.18
gṛhītvaitāni saṁyāti 15.8
guṇā guṇeṣu vartanta 3.28

guṇān etān atītya trīn 14.20
guṇā vartanta ity evaṁ 14.23
guṇebhyaś ca paraṁ vetti 14.19
gurūn ahatvā hi mahānubhāvān 2.5

H

hanta te kathayiṣyāmi 10.19
harṣāmarṣa-bhayodvegair 12.15
harṣa-śokānvitaḥ kartā 18.27
hato vā prāpsyasi svargaṁ 2.37
hatvāpi sa imāl lokān 18.17

hatvārtha-kāmāṁs tu 2.5
hetunānena kaunteya 9.10
hṛṣīkeśaṁ tadā vākyam 1.20

I

icchā dveṣaḥ sukhaṁ 13.7
icchā-dveṣa-samutthena 7.27
idam adya mayā labdham 16.13
idam astīdam api me 16.13
idaṁ jñānam upāśritya 14.2

idaṁ śarīraṁ kaunteya 13.2
idaṁ te nātapaskāya 18.67
idaṁ tu te guhyatamaṁ 9.1
idānīm asmi saṁvṛttaḥ 11.51
ihaika-sthaṁ jagat kṛtsnaṁ 11.7

ihaiva tair jitaḥ sargo 5.19
īhante kāma-bhogārtham 16.12
ijyate bharata-śreṣṭha 17.12
īkṣate yoga-yuktātmā 6.29
imaṁ vivasvate yogaṁ 4.1

indriyāṇāṁ hi caratāṁ 2.67
indriyāṇāṁ manaś cāsmi 10.22
indriyāṇi daśaikaṁ ca 13.6
indriyāṇi mano buddhir 3.40
indriyāṇīndriyārthebhyas 2.58

indriyāṇīndriyārthebhyas 2.68
indriyāṇīndriyārtheṣu 5.9
indriyāṇi parāṇy āhur 3.42
indriyāṇi pramāthīni 2.60
indriyārthān vimūḍhātmā 3.6

indriyārtheṣu vairāgyam 13.9
indriyasyendriyasyārthe 3.34
iṣṭān bhogān hi vo devā 3.12
iṣṭo 'si me dṛḍham iti 18.64
iṣubhiḥ pratiyotsyāmi 2.4

īśvaraḥ sarva-bhūtānāṁ 18.61
īśvaro 'ham ahaṁ bhogī 16.14
iti guhyatamaṁ śāstram 15.20
iti kṣetraṁ tathā jñānaṁ 13.19
iti māṁ yo 'bhijānāti 4.14

iti matvā bhajante māṁ 10.8
iti te jñānam ākhyātaṁ 18.63
ity ahaṁ vāsudevasya 18.74
ity arjunaṁ vāsudevas 11.50

J

jaghanya-guṇa-vṛtti-sthā 14.18
jahi śatruṁ mahā-bāho 3.43
janma-bandha-vinirmuktāḥ 2.51
janma karma ca me divyam 4.9
janma-mṛtyu-jarā 14.20

janma-mṛtyu-jarā-vyādhi- 13.9
jarā-maraṇa-mokṣāya 7.29
jātasya hi dhruvo mṛtyur 2.27
jayo 'smi vyavasāyo 'smi 10.36
jhaṣāṇāṁ makaraś cāsmi 10.31

jijñāsur api yogasya 6.44
jitātmanaḥ praśāntasya 6.7
jīva-bhūtāṁ mahā-bāho 7.5
jīvanaṁ sarva-bhūteṣu 7.9
jñānāgni-dagdha 4.19

jñānāgniḥ sarva-karmāṇi 4.37
jñānam āvṛtya tu tamaḥ 14.9
jñānaṁ jñeyaṁ jñāna 13.18
jñānaṁ jñeyaṁ parijñātā 18.18
jñānaṁ karma ca kartā ca 18.19

jñānaṁ labdhvā parāṁ 4.39
jñānaṁ te 'haṁ sa-vijñānam 7.2
jñānaṁ vijñānam 18.42
jñānaṁ vijñāna-sahitaṁ 9.1
jñānaṁ yadā tadā vidyād 14.11

jñāna-vijñāna-tṛptātmā 6.8
jñāna-yajñena cāpy anye 9.15

jñāna-yajñena tenāham 18.70
jñāna-yogena sāṅkhyānāṁ 3.3
jñānena tu tad ajñānaṁ 5.16

jñātuṁ draṣṭuṁ ca 11.54
jñātvā śāstra-vidhānoktaṁ 16.24
jñeyaḥ sa nitya-sannyāsī 5.3
jñeyaṁ yat tat 13.13
joṣayet sarva-karmāṇi 3.26

jyāyasī cet karmaṇas te 3.1
jyotiṣām api taj jyotis 13.18

K

kaccid ajñāna 18.72
kaccid etac chrutaṁ 18.72
kaccin nobhaya-vibhraṣṭaś 6.38
kair liṅgais trīn guṇān 14.21
kair mayā saha 1.22

kālo 'smi loka-kṣaya-kṛt 11.32
kalpa-kṣaye punas tāni 9.7
kāma eṣa krodha eṣa 3.37
kāmaḥ krodhas tathā 16.21
kāmais tais tair hṛta-jñānāḥ 7.20

kāma-krodha-vimuktānāṁ 5.26
kāma-krodhodbhavaṁ 5.23
kāmam āśritya duṣpūraṁ 16.10
kāma-rūpeṇa kaunteya 3.39
kāmātmānaḥ svarga-parā 2.43

kāmopabhoga-paramā 16.11
kāmyānāṁ karmaṇāṁ 18.2
kāṅkṣantaḥ karmaṇāṁ 4.12
kāraṇaṁ guṇa-saṅgo 'sya 13.22
karaṇaṁ karma karteti 18.18

karma brahmodbhavaṁ 3.15
karma caiva tad-arthīyaṁ 17.27
karma-jaṁ buddhi-yuktā hi 2.51
karma-jān viddhi tān 4.32
karmaṇaḥ sukṛtasyāhuḥ 14.16

karmaṇaiva hi saṁsiddhim 3.20
karmāṇi pravibhaktāni 18.41
karmaṇo hy api 4.17
karmaṇy abhipravṛtto 'pi 4.20

karmaṇy akarma yaḥ 4.18

karmaṇy evādhikāras te 2.47
karmendriyaiḥ karma-yogam 3.7
karmendriyāṇi saṁyamya 3.6
karmibhyaś cādhiko yogī 6.46
kārpaṇya-doṣopahata 2.7

karṣayantaḥ śarīra-sthaṁ 17.6
kartavyānīti me pārtha 18.6
kartuṁ necchasi yan 18.60
kārya-kāraṇa-kartṛtve 13.21
kāryam ity eva yat karma 18.9

kāryate hy avaśaḥ karma 3.5
kasmāc ca te na nameran 11.37
kāśyaś ca parameṣv-āsaḥ 1.17
kathaṁ bhīṣmam ahaṁ 2.4
katham etad vijānīyāṁ 4.4

kathaṁ na jñeyam 1.38
kathaṁ sa puruṣaḥ pārtha 2.21
kathaṁ vidyām ahaṁ 10.17
kathayantaś ca māṁ 10.9
kaṭv-amla-lavaṇāty-uṣṇa 17.9

kaunteya pratijānīhi 9.31
kaviṁ purāṇam 8.9
kāyena manasā buddhyā 5.11
kecid vilagnā 11.27
keśavārjunayoḥ puṇyaṁ 18.76

keṣu keṣu ca bhāveṣu 10.17
kim ācāraḥ kathaṁ 14.21
kiṁ karma kim akarmeti 4.16
kiṁ no rājyena govinda 1.32
kiṁ punar brāhmaṇāḥ 9.33

kiṁ tad brahma kim 8.1
kīrtiḥ śrīr vāk ca nārīṇāṁ 10.34
kirīṭinaṁ gadinaṁ cakra 11.46
kirīṭinaṁ gadinaṁ 11.17
klaibyaṁ mā sma gamaḥ 2.3

kleśo 'dhikataras teṣām 12.5
kriyate bahulāyāsaṁ 18.24
kriyate tad iha proktaṁ 17.18
kriyā-viśeṣa-bahulāṁ 2.43

krodhād bhavati sammohaḥ 2.63

kṛpayā parayāviṣṭo 1.27
kṛṣi-go-rakṣya-vāṇijyaṁ 18.44
kṣaraḥ sarvāṇi bhūtāni 15.16
kṣetra-jñaṁ cāpi māṁ 13.3
kṣetra-kṣetrajña-saṁyogāt 13.27

kṣetra-kṣetrajñayor evam 13.35
kṣetra-kṣetrajñayor jñānaṁ 13.3
kṣetraṁ kṣetrī tathā 13.34
kṣipāmy ajasram aśubhān 16.19
kṣipraṁ bhavati 9.31

kṣipraṁ hi mānuṣe loke 4.12
kṣudraṁ hṛdaya-daurbalyaṁ 2.3
kula-kṣaya-kṛtaṁ doṣaṁ 1.38
kula-kṣaya-kṛtaṁ doṣaṁ 1.37
kula-kṣaye praṇaśyanti 1.39

kuru karmaiva tasmāt tvaṁ 4.15
kuryād vidvāṁs tathāsaktaś 3.25
kutas tvā kaśmalam idaṁ 2.2

L

labhante brahma-nirvāṇam 5.25
labhate ca tataḥ kāmān 7.22
lelihyase grasamānaḥ 11.30
lipyate na sa pāpena 5.10
lobhaḥ pravṛttir ārambhaḥ 14.12

loka-saṅgraham evāpi 3.20
loke 'smin dvi-vidhā niṣṭhā 3.3

M

mac-cittaḥ sarva-durgāṇi 18.58
mac-cittā mad-gata-prāṇā 10.9
mad-anugrahāya paramaṁ 11.1
mad-artham api karmāṇi 12.10
mad-bhakta etad vijñāya 13.19

mad-bhāvā mānasā jātā 10.6
mādhavaḥ pāṇḍavaś caiva 1.14
mahā-bhūtāny ahaṅkāro 13.6
maharṣayaḥ sapta pūrve 10.6
maharṣīṇāṁ bhṛgur ahaṁ 10.25

mahāśano mahā-pāpmā 3.37

mahātmānas tu māṁ 9.13
mā karma-phala-hetur bhūr 2.47
mama dehe guḍākeśa 11.7
mamaivāṁśo jīva-loke 15.7

māmakāḥ pāṇḍavāś caiva 1.1
mām aprāpyaiva 16.20
mām ātma-para-deheṣu 16.18
mama vartmānuvartante 3.23
mama vartmānuvartante 4.11

mama yonir mahad brahma 14.3
māṁ caivāntaḥ śarīra 17.6
māṁ ca yo 'vyabhicāreṇa 14.26
mām evaiṣyasi satyaṁ te 18.65
mām evaiṣyasi yuktvaivam 9.34

mām eva ye prapadyante 7.14
māṁ hi pārtha vyapāśritya 9.32
mām upetya punar janma 8.15
mām upetya tu kaunteya 8.16
manaḥ-prasādaḥ 17.16

manaḥ saṁyamya mac 6.14
manaḥ-ṣaṣṭhānīndriyāṇi 15.7
mānāpamānayos tulyas 14.25
manasaivendriya-grāmaṁ 6.24
manasas tu parā buddhir 3.42

man-manā bhava mad 9.34
man-manā bhava mad 18.65
mantro 'ham aham 9.16
manuṣyāṇāṁ sahasreṣu 7.3
manyase yadi tac chakyaṁ 11.4

marīcir marutām asmi 10.21
māsānāṁ mārga-śīrṣo 10.35
mā śucaḥ sampadaṁ 16.5
mā te vyathā mā ca 11.49
mat-karma-kṛn mat 11.55

mat-prasādād avāpnoti 18.56
mātrā-sparśās tu kaunteya 2.14
mat-sthāni sarva-bhūtāni 9.4
matta eveti tān viddhi 7.12
mattaḥ parataraṁ nānyat 7.7

mātulāḥ śvaśurāḥ pautrāḥ 1.34

maunaṁ caivāsmi 10.38
mayādhyakṣeṇa prakṛtiḥ 9.10
mayā hatāṁs tvaṁ jahi 11.34
mayaivaite nihatāḥ pūrvam 11.33

mayā prasannena 11.47
mayā tatam idaṁ sarvaṁ 9.4
māyayāpahṛta-jñānā 7.15
mayi cānanya-yogena 13.11
mayi sarvam idaṁ protaṁ 7.7

mayi sarvāṇi karmāṇi 3.30
mayy arpita-mano-buddhir 8.7
mayy arpita-mano 12.14
mayy āsakta-manāḥ pārtha 7.1
mayy āveśya mano ye māṁ 12.2

mayy eva mana ādhatsva 12.8
mithyaiṣa vyavasāyas te 18.59
moghāśā mogha-karmāṇo 9.12
mohād ārabhyate karma 18.25
mohād gṛhītvāsad-grāhān 16.10

mohāt tasya parityāgas 18.7
mohitaṁ nābhijānāti 7.13
mṛgāṇāṁ ca mṛgendro 10.30
mṛtyuḥ sarva-haraś 10.34
mūḍha-grāheṇātmano yat 17.19

mūḍho 'yaṁ nābhijānāti 7.25
mukta-saṅgo 'nahaṁ-vādī 18.26
munīnām apy ahaṁ 10.37
mūrdhny ādhāyātmanaḥ 8.12

N

nabhaḥ-spṛśaṁ dīptam 11.24
nabhaś ca pṛthivīṁ caiva 1.19
nābhinandati na dveṣṭi 2.57
na buddhi-bhedaṁ janayed 3.26
na cābhāvayataḥ śāntir 2.66

na cainaṁ kledayanty āpo 2.23
na caitad vidmaḥ kataran 2.6
na caiva na bhaviṣyāmaḥ 2.12
na ca māṁ tāni karmāṇi 9.9
na ca mat-sthāni bhūtāni 9.5

na ca śaknomy avasthātuṁ 1.30

na ca sannyasanād eva 3.4
na ca śreyo 'nupaśyāmi 1.31
na cāśuśrūṣave vācyaṁ 18.67
na cāsya sarva-bhūteṣu 3.18

na ca tasmān manuṣyeṣu 18.69
na cāti-svapna-śīlasya 6.16
nādatte kasyacit pāpaṁ 5.15
na dveṣṭi sampravṛttāni 14.22
na dveṣṭy akuśalaṁ 18.10

nāhaṁ prakāśaḥ sarvasya 7.25
nāhaṁ vedair na tapasā 11.53
na hi deha-bhṛtā śakyaṁ 18.11
na hi jñānena sadṛśaṁ 4.38
na hi kalyāṇa-kṛt kaścid 6.40

na hi kaścit kṣaṇam api 3.5
na hinasty 13.29
na hi prapaśyāmi 2.8
na hi te bhagavan vyaktiṁ 10.14
na hy asannyasta-saṅkalpo 6.2

nainaṁ chindanti śastrāṇi 2.23
naiṣkarmya-siddhiṁ 18.49
naite sṛtī pārtha jānan 8.27
naiva kiñcit karomīti 5.8
naiva tasya kṛtenārtho 3.18

na jāyate mriyate vā 2.20
na kāṅkṣe vijayaṁ kṛṣṇa 1.31
na karmaṇām anārambhān 3.4
na karma-phala-saṁyogaṁ 5.14
na kartṛtvaṁ na karmāṇi 5.14

nakulaḥ sahadevaś ca 1.16
namaḥ purastād atha 11.40
na māṁ duṣkṛtino mūḍhāḥ 7.15
na māṁ karmāṇi limpanti 4.14
namaskṛtvā bhūya evāha 11.35

namasyantaś ca māṁ 9.14
na me pārthāsti kartavyaṁ 3.22
na me viduḥ sura-gaṇāḥ 10.2
namo namas te 'stu sahasra 11.39
nānā-śastra-praharaṇāḥ 1.9

nānavāptam avāptavyaṁ 3.22

nānā-vidhāni divyāni 11.5
nāntaṁ na madhyaṁ na 11.16
nānto 'sti mama 10.40
nānyaṁ guṇebhyaḥ 14.19

nāpnuvanti mahātmānaḥ 8.15
na prahṛṣyet priyaṁ prāpya 5.20
narake niyataṁ vāso 1.43
na rūpam asyeha 15.3
na sa siddhim avāpnoti 16.23

nāsato vidyate bhāvo 2.16
na śaucaṁ nāpi cācāro 16.7
nāśayāmy ātma-bhāva 10.11
nāsti buddhir ayuktasya 2.66
naṣṭo mohaḥ smṛtir labdhā 18.73

na tad asti pṛthivyāṁ vā 18.40
na tad asti vinā yat syān 10.39
na tad bhāsayate sūryo 15.6
na tu māṁ abhijānanti 9.24
na tu māṁ śakyase 11.8

na tvat-samo 'sty 11.43
na tv evāhaṁ jātu nāsaṁ 2.12
nāty-aśnatas tu yogo 'sti 6.16
nāty-ucchritaṁ nāti-nīcaṁ 6.11
nava-dvāre pure dehī 5.13

na veda-yajñādhyayanair na 11.48
na vimuñcati durmedhā 18.35
nāyakā mama sainyasya 1.7
nāyaṁ loko 'sti na paro 4.40
nāyaṁ loko 'sty ayajñasya 4.31

na yotsya iti govindam 2.9
nehābhikrama-nāśo 'sti 2.40
nibadhnanti mahā-bāho 14.5
nidrālasya-pramādotthaṁ 18.39
nihatya dhārtarāṣṭrān naḥ 1.35

nimittāni ca paśyāmi 1.30
nindantas tava sāmarthyaṁ 2.36
nirāśīr nirmamo bhūtvā 3.30
nirāśīr yata-cittātmā 4.21
nirdoṣaṁ hi samaṁ brahma 5.19

nirdvandvo hi mahā-bāho 5.3
nirdvandvo nitya-sattva 2.45
nirmamo nirahaṅkāraḥ 2.71
nirmamo nirahaṅkāraḥ 12.13
nirmāna-mohā jita-saṅga 15.5

nirvairaḥ sarva-bhūteṣu 11.55
niścayaṁ śṛṇu me tatra 18.4
nispṛhaḥ sarva-kāmebhyo 6.18
nityaḥ sarva-gataḥ sthāṇur 2.24
nityaṁ ca sama-cittatvam 13.10

nivasiṣyasi mayy eva 12.8
niyataṁ kuru karma tvaṁ 3.8
niyataṁ saṅga-rahitam 18.23
niyatasya tu sannyāsaḥ 18.7
nyāyyaṁ vā viparītaṁ vā 18.15

O

oṁ ity ekākṣaraṁ brahma 8.13
oṁ tat sad iti nirdeśo 17.23

P

pañcaitāni mahā-bāho 18.13
pāñcajanyaṁ hṛṣīkeśo 1.15
pāpam evāśrayed asmān 1.36
pāpmānaṁ prajahi hy enaṁ 3.41
paramaṁ puruṣaṁ divyaṁ 8.8

paramātmeti cāpy ukto 13.23
paraṁ bhāvam ajānanto 7.24
paraṁ bhāvam ajānanto 9.11
paraṁ bhūyaḥ pravakṣyāmi 14.1
paraṁ brahma paraṁ 10.12

parasparaṁ bhāvayantaḥ 3.11
paras tasmāt tu bhāvo 'nyo 8.20
parasyotsādanārthaṁ vā 17.19
paricaryātmakaṁ karma 18.44
pariṇāme viṣam iva 18.38

paritrāṇāya sādhūnāṁ 4.8
pārtha naiveha nāmutra 6.40
paryāptaṁ tv idam eteṣāṁ 1.10
paśyādityān vasūn rudrān 11.6
paśyaitāṁ pāṇḍu-putrāṇām 1.3

paśya me pārtha rūpāṇi 11.5
paśyāmi devāṁs tava 11.15
paśyāmi tvāṁ dīpta-hutāśa 11.19
paśyāmi tvāṁ durnirīkṣyaṁ 11.17
paśyañ śṛṇvan spṛśañ 5.8

paśyaty akṛta-buddhitvān 18.16
patanti pitaro hy eṣāṁ 1.41
patraṁ puṣpaṁ phalaṁ 9.26
pauṇḍraṁ dadhmau mahā 1.15
pavanaḥ pavatām asmi 10.31

pitāham asya jagato 9.17
pitāsi lokasya carācarasya 11.43
piteva putrasya sakheva 11.44
pitṝṇām aryamā cāsmi 10.29
prabhavaḥ pralayaḥ 9.18

prabhavanty ugra 16.9
prādhānyataḥ kuru10.19
prahlādaś cāsmi 10.30
prajahāti yadā kāmān 2.55
prajanaś cāsmi kandarpaḥ 10.28

prakāśaṁ ca pravṛttiṁ ca 14.22
prakṛteḥ kriyamāṇāni 3.27
prakṛter guṇa-sammūḍhāḥ 3.29
prakṛtiṁ puruṣaṁ caiva 13.1
prakṛtiṁ puruṣaṁ caiva 13.20

prakṛtiṁ svām adhiṣṭhāya 4.6
prakṛtiṁ svām avaṣṭabhya 9.8
prakṛtiṁ yānti bhūtāni 3.33
prakṛtyaiva ca karmāṇi 13.30
pralapan visṛjan gṛhṇann 5.9

pramādālasya-nidrābhis 14.8
pramāda-mohau tamaso 14.17
praṇamya śirasā devaṁ 11.14
prāṇāpāna-gatī ruddhvā 4.29
prāṇāpāna-samāyuktaḥ 15.14

prāṇāpānau samau kṛtvā 5.27
praṇavaḥ sarva-vedeṣu 7.8
prāpya puṇya-kṛtāṁ lokān 6.41
prasāde sarva-duḥkhānāṁ 2.65
prasaktāḥ kāma-bhogeṣu 16.16

prasaṅgena phalākāṅkṣī 18.34
prasanna-cetaso hy āśu 2.65

praśānta-manasaṁ hy 6.27
praśāntātmā vigata-bhīr 6.14
praśaste karmaṇi tathā 17.26

pratyakṣāvagamaṁ 9.2
pravartante vidhānoktāḥ 17.24
pravṛtte śastra-sampāte 1.20
pravṛttiṁ ca nivṛttiṁ ca 16.7
pravṛttiṁ ca nivṛttiṁ ca 18.30

prayāṇa-kāle ca kathaṁ 8.2
prayāṇa-kāle manasācalena 8.10
prayāṇa-kāle 'pi ca māṁ 7.30
prayātā yānti taṁ kālaṁ 8.23
prayatnād yatamānas tu 6.45

pretān bhūta-gaṇāṁś cānye 17.4
priyo hi jñānino 'tyartham 7.17
procyamānam aśeṣeṇa 18.29
procyate guṇa-saṅkhyāne 18.19
pṛthaktvena tu yaj jñānaṁ 18.21

puṇyo gandhaḥ pṛthivyāṁ ca 7.9
purodhasāṁ ca mukhyaṁ 10.24
purujit kuntibhojaś ca 1.5
puruṣaḥ prakṛti-stho hi 13.22
puruṣaḥ sa paraḥ pārtha 8.22

puruṣaḥ sukha 13.21
puruṣaṁ śāśvataṁ 10.12
pūrvābhyāsena tenaiva 6.44
puṣṇāmi cauṣadhīḥ sarvāḥ 15.13

R

rāga-dveṣa-vimuktais tu 2.64
rāgī karma-phala-prepsur 18.27
rajaḥ sattvaṁ tamaś caiva 14.10
rājan saṁsmṛtya 18.76
rajasas tu phalaṁ 14.16

rajasi pralayaṁ gatvā 14.15
rajas tamaś cābhibhūya 14.10
rajasy etāni jāyante 14.12
rāja-vidyā rāja-guhyaṁ 9.2
rajo rāgātmakaṁ viddhi 14.7

rakṣāṁsi bhītāni diśo 11.36
rākṣasīm āsurīṁ caiva 9.12

rasa-varjaṁ raso 'py asya 2.59
raso 'ham apsu kaunteya 7.8
rasyāḥ snigdhāḥ sthirā 17.8

rātriṁ yuga-sahasrāntāṁ 8.17
rātry-āgame pralīyante 8.18
rātry-āgame 'vaśaḥ pārtha 8.19
ṛṣibhir bahudhā gītaṁ 13.5
ṛte 'pi tvāṁ na bhaviṣyanti 11.32

rudrādityā vasavo ye ca 11.22
rudrāṇāṁ śaṅkaraś cāsmi 10.23
rūpaṁ mahat te bahu-vaktra 11.23

S

śabdādīn viṣayāṁs tyaktvā 18.51
śabdādīn viṣayān anya 4.26
sa brahma-yoga-yuktātmā 5.21
sa buddhimān manuṣyeṣu 4.18
sa ca yo yat-prabhāvaś ca 13.4

sad-bhāve sādhu-bhāve ca 17.26
sādhibhūtādhidaivaṁ māṁ 7.30
sādhur eva sa mantavyaḥ 9.30
sādhuṣv api ca pāpeṣu 6.9
sadṛśaṁ ceṣṭate svasyāḥ 3.33

sa evāyaṁ mayā te 'dya 4.3
sa ghoṣo dhārtarāṣṭrāṇāṁ 1.19
sa guṇān samatītyaitān 14.26
saha-jaṁ karma kaunteya 18.48
sahasaivābhyahanyanta 1.13

sahasra-yuga-paryantam 8.17
saha-yajñāḥ prajāḥ sṛṣṭvā 3.10
sa kāleneha mahatā 4.2
sakheti matvā prasabhaṁ yad 11.41
śaknotīhaiva yaḥ soḍhuṁ 5.23

sa kṛtvā rājasaṁ tyāgaṁ 18.8
saktāḥ karmaṇy avidvāṁso 3.25
śakya evaṁ-vidho draṣṭuṁ 11.53
samādhāv acalā buddhis 2.53
sama-duḥkha-sukhaḥ sva 14.24

sama-duḥkha-sukhaṁ dhīraṁ 2.15
samaḥ sarveṣu bhūteṣu 18.54
samaḥ śatrau ca mitre ca 12.18

samaḥ siddhāv asiddhau ca 4.22
samaṁ kāya-śiro-grīvaṁ 6.13

samaṁ paśyan hi sarvatra 13.29
samaṁ sarveṣu bhūteṣu 13.28
samāsenaiva kaunteya 18.50
sambhavaḥ sarva-bhūtānāṁ 14.3
sambhāvitasya cākīrtir 2.34

śamo damas tapaḥ śaucaṁ 18.42
samo 'haṁ sarva-bhūteṣu 9.29
samprekṣya nāsikāgraṁ svaṁ 6.13
saṁvādam imam aśrauṣam 18.74
śanaiḥ śanair uparamed 6.25

saṅgaṁ tyaktvā phalaṁ caiva 18.9
saṅgāt sañjāyate kāmaḥ 2.62
sa niścayena yoktavyo 6.24
saṅkalpa-prabhavān kāmāṁs 6.24
saṅkarasya ca kartā syām 3.24

saṅkaro narakāyaiva 1.41
sāṅkhya-yogau pṛthag bālāḥ 5.4
sāṅkhye kṛtānte proktāni 18.13
sanniyamyendriya-grāmaṁ 12.4
sannyāsaḥ karma-yogaś ca 5.2

sannyāsaṁ karmaṇāṁ kṛṣṇa 5.1
sannyāsas tu mahā-bāho 5.6
sannyāsasya mahā-bāho 18.1
sannyāsa-yoga-yuktātmā 9.28
śāntiṁ nirvāṇa-paramāṁ 6.15

santuṣṭaḥ satataṁ yogī 12.14
sargāṇām ādir antaś ca 10.32
sarge 'pi nopajāyante 14.2
śārīraṁ kevalaṁ karma 4.21
śarīraṁ yad avāpnoti 15.8

śarīra-stho 'pi kaunteya 13.32
śarīra-vāṅ-manobhir yat 18.15
śarīra-yātrāpi ca te 3.8
sarva-bhūtāni kaunteya 9.7
sarva-bhūtāni sammohaṁ 7.27

sarva-bhūta-stham ātmānaṁ 6.29
sarva-bhūta-sthitaṁ yo māṁ 6.31
sarva-bhūtātma-bhūtātmā 5.7

sarva-bhūteṣu yenaikaṁ 18.20
sarva-dharmān parityajya 18.66

sarva-dvārāṇi saṁyamya 8.12
sarva-dvāreṣu dehe 'smin 14.11
sarva-guhyatamaṁ bhūyaḥ 18.64
sarva-jñāna-vimūḍhāṁs tān 3.32
sarva-karmāṇi manasā 5.13

sarva-karmāṇy api sadā 18.56
sarva-karma-phala-tyāgaṁ 18.2
sarva-karma-phala-tyāgaṁ 12.11
sarvam etad ṛtaṁ manye 10.14
sarvaṁ jñāna-plavenaiva 4.36

sarvaṁ karmākhilaṁ pārtha 4.33
sarvāṇīndriya-karmāṇi 4.27
sarvārambhā hi doṣeṇa 18.48
sarvārambha-parityāgī 12.16
sarvārambha-parityāgī 14.25

sarvārthān viparītāṁś ca 18.32
sarva-saṅkalpa-sannyāsī 6.4
sarvāścarya-mayaṁ devam 11.11
sarvasya cāhaṁ hṛdi 15.15
sarvasya dhātāram acintya 8.9

sarvataḥ pāṇi-pādaṁ tat 13.14
sarvataḥ śrutimal loke 13.14
sarvathā vartamāno 'pi 13.24
sarvathā vartamāno 'pi 6.31
sarvatra-gam acintyaṁ ca 12.3

sarvatrāvasthito dehe 13.33
sarva-yoniṣu kaunteya 14.4
sarvendriya-guṇābhāsam 13.15
sarve 'py ete yajña-vido 4.30
sa sannyāsī ca yogī ca 6.1

sa sarva-vid bhajati māṁ 15.19
śāśvatasya ca dharmasya 14.27
satataṁ kīrtayanto māṁ 9.14
sa tayā śraddhayā yuktas 7.22
satkāra-māna-pūjārthaṁ 17.18

sattvaṁ prakṛti-jair 18.40
sattvaṁ rajas tama iti 14.5
sattvaṁ sukhe sañjayati 14.9

sattvānurūpā sarvasya 17.3
sattvāt sañjāyate jñānaṁ 14.17

sāttvikī rājasī caiva 17.2
saubhadraś ca mahā-bāhuḥ 1.18
saubhadro draupadeyāś ca 1.6
śauryaṁ tejo dhṛtir 18.43
sa yat pramāṇaṁ kurute 3.21

sa yogī brahma-nirvāṇaṁ 5.24
senānīnām ahaṁ skandaḥ 10.24
senayor ubhayor madhye 1.21
senayor ubhayor madhye 1.24
senayor ubhayor madhye 2.10

sīdanti mama gātrāṇi 1.28
siddhiṁ prāpto yathā 18.50
siddhy-asiddhyor 18.26
siddhy-asiddhyoḥ samo 2.48
siṁha-nādaṁ vinadyoccaiḥ 1.12

śītoṣṇa-sukha-duḥkheṣu 6.7
śītoṣṇa-sukha-duḥkheṣu 12.18
smṛti-bhraṁśād buddhi 2.63
so 'pi muktaḥ śubhāl 18.71
so 'vikalpena yogena 10.7

sparśān kṛtvā bahir 5.27
śraddadhānā mat-paramā 12.20
śraddhā-mayo 'yaṁ puruṣo 17.3
śraddhāvāl labhate jñānaṁ 4.39
śraddhāvān anasūyaś ca 18.71

śraddhāvān bhajate yo 6.47
śraddhāvanto 'nasūyanto 3.31
śraddhā-virahitaṁ yajñaṁ 17.13
śraddhayā parayā taptaṁ 17.17
śraddhayā parayopetās 12.2

śreyān dravya-mayād 4.33
śreyān sva-dharmo 18.47
śreyān sva-dharmo viguṇaḥ 3.35
śreyo hi jñānam abhyāsāj 12.12
śrotrādīnīndriyāṇy anye 4.26

śrotraṁ cakṣuḥ sparśanaṁ 15.9
śruti-vipratipannā te 2.53
sthāne hṛṣīkeśa tava 11.36

sthira-buddhir asammūḍho 5.20
sthita-dhīḥ kiṁ prabhāṣeta 2.54

sthita-prajñasya kā bhāṣā 2.54
sthito 'smi gata-sandehaḥ 18.73
sthitvāsyām anta-kāle 'pi 2.72
strīṣu duṣṭāsu vārṣṇeya 1.40
striyo vaiśyās tathā śūdrās 9.32

śubhāśubha-parityāgī 12.17
śubhāśubha-phalair evaṁ 9.28
śucau deśe pratiṣṭhāpya 6.11
śucīnāṁ śrīmatāṁ gehe 6.41
su-durdarśam idaṁ 11.52

suhṛdaṁ sarva-bhūtānāṁ 5.29
suhṛn-mitrāry-udāsīna 6.9
sukha-duḥkhe same kṛtvā 2.38
sukham ātyantikaṁ yat tad 6.21
sukhaṁ duḥkhaṁ bhavo 10.4

sukhaṁ tv idānīṁ tri 18.36
sukhaṁ vā yadi vā 6.32
sukha-saṅgena badhnāti 14.6
sukhena brahma 6.28
sukhinaḥ kṣatriyāḥ pārtha 2.32

śukla-kṛṣṇe gatī hy ete 8.26
sūkṣmatvāt tad avijñeyaṁ 13.16
śuni caiva śva-pāke ca 5.18
svabhāva-jena kaunteya 18.60
svabhāva-niyataṁ karma 18.47

sva-dharmam api cāvekṣya 2.31
sva-dharme nidhanaṁ 3.35
svādhyāyābhyasanaṁ 17.15
svādhyāya-jñāna-yajñāś ca 4.28
sva-janaṁ hi kathaṁ hatvā 1.36

sva-karmaṇā tam 18.46
sva-karma-nirataḥ 18.45
sv-alpam apy asya 2.40
svastīty uktvā maharṣi-siddha 11.21
śvaśurān suhṛdaś caiva 1.26

svayam evātmanātmānaṁ 10.15
sve sve karmaṇy abhirataḥ 18.45

T

tac ca saṁsmṛtya 18. 77

tadā gantāsi nirvedaṁ 2.52
tad ahaṁ bhakty-upahṛtam 9.26
tad-arthaṁ karma kaunteya 3.9
tad asya harati prajñāṁ 2.67

tad-buddhayas tad-ātmānas 5.17
tad ekaṁ vada niścitya 3.2
tad eva me darśaya 11.45
tad ity anabhisandhāya 17.25
tadottama-vidāṁ lokān 14.14

tadvat kāmā yaṁ praviśanti 2.70
tad viddhi praṇipātena 4.34
ta ime 'vasthitā yuddhe 1.33
tair dattān apradāyaibhyo 3.12
tamas tv ajñāna-jaṁ viddhi 14.8

tamasy etāni jāyante 14.13
tam eva cādyaṁ puruṣaṁ 15.4
tam eva śaraṇaṁ gaccha 18.62
taṁ tam evaiti kaunteya 8.6
taṁ taṁ niyamam āsthāya 7.20

taṁ tathā kṛpayāviṣṭam 2.1
tam uvāca hṛṣīkeśaḥ 2.10
taṁ vidyād duḥkha 6.23
tān ahaṁ dviṣataḥ krūrān 16.19
tān akṛtsna-vido mandān 3.29

tāni sarvāṇi saṁyamya 2.61
tan nibadhnāti kaunteya 14.7
tān samīkṣya sa kaunteyaḥ 1.27
tāny ahaṁ veda sarvāṇi 4.5
tapāmy aham ahaṁ varṣaṁ 9.19

tapasvibhyo 'dhiko yogī 6.46
tāsāṁ brahma mahad yonir 14.4
tasmāc chāstraṁ pramāṇaṁ 16.24
tasmād ajñāna-sambhūtaṁ 4.42
tasmād aparihārye 'rthe 2.27

tasmād asaktaḥ satataṁ 3.19
tasmād evaṁ viditvainaṁ 2.25
tasmād oṁ ity udāhṛtya 17.24
tasmād uttiṣṭha kaunteya 2.37
tasmād yasya mahā-bāho 2.68

tasmād yogāya yujyasva 2.50

tasmān nārhā vayaṁ 1.36
tasmāt praṇamya 11.44
tasmāt sarva-gataṁ 3.15
tasmāt sarvāṇi bhūtāni 2.30

tasmāt sarveṣu kāleṣu 8.7
tasmāt sarveṣu kāleṣu 8.27
tasmāt tvam indriyāṇy 3.41
tasmāt tvam uttiṣṭha 11.33
tasyāhaṁ na praṇaśyāmi 6.30

tasyāhaṁ nigrahaṁ manye 6.34
tasyāhaṁ sulabhaḥ pārtha 8.14
tasya kartāram api māṁ 4.13
tasya sañjanayan harṣaṁ 1.12
tasya tasyācalāṁ śraddhāṁ 7.21

tata eva ca vistāraṁ 13.31
tataḥ padaṁ tat 15.4
tataḥ śaṅkhāś ca bheryaś ca 1.13
tataḥ sa vismayāviṣṭo 11.14
tataḥ sva-dharmaṁ 2.33

tataḥ śvetair hayair yukte 1.14
tatas tato niyamyaitad 6.26
tathā dehāntara-prāptir 2.13
tathaiva nāśāya viśanti 11.29
tathāpi tvaṁ mahā-bāho 2.26

tathā pralīnas tamasi 14.15
tathā śarīrāṇi vihāya 2.22
tathā sarvāṇi bhūtāni 9.6
tathā tavāmī nara-loka 11.28
tat kiṁ karmaṇi ghore māṁ 3.1

tat kṣetraṁ yac ca yādṛk ca 13.4
tato māṁ tattvato jñātvā 18.55
tato yuddhāya yujyasva 2.38
tat-prasādāt parāṁ 18.62
tatra cāndramasaṁ jyotir 8.25

tatraikāgraṁ manaḥ kṛtvā 6.12
tatraika-sthaṁ jagat 11.13
tatraivaṁ sati kartāram 18.16
tatrāpaśyat sthitān pārthaḥ 1.26
tatra prayātā gacchanti 8.24

tatra sattvaṁ nirmalatvāt 14.6

tatra śrīr vijayo bhūtir 18.78
tatra taṁ buddhi 6.43
tat sukhaṁ sāttvikaṁ 18.37
tat svayaṁ yoga 4.38

tat tad evāvagaccha tvaṁ 10.41
tat te karma pravakṣyāmi 4.16
tattva-vit tu mahā-bāho 3.28
tāvān sarveṣu vedeṣu 2.46
tayor na vaśam āgacchet 3.34

tayos tu karma-sannyāsāt 5.2
te brahma tad viduḥ 7.29
te dvandva-moha-nirmuktā 7.28
tejaḥ kṣamā dhṛtiḥ śaucam 16.3
tejobhir āpūrya jagat 11.30

tejo-mayaṁ viśvam 11.47
tenaiva rūpeṇa catur 11.46
te 'pi cātitaranty eva 13.26
te 'pi mām eva kaunteya 9.23
te prāpnuvanti mām eva 12.4

te puṇyam āsādya surendra 9.20
teṣām āditya-vaj jñānaṁ 5.16
teṣām ahaṁ samuddhartā 12.7
teṣām evānukampārtham 10.11
teṣāṁ jñānī nitya-yukta 7.17

teṣāṁ niṣṭhā tu kā kṛṣṇa 17.1
teṣāṁ nityābhiyuktānāṁ 9.22
teṣāṁ satata-yuktānāṁ 10.10
te taṁ bhuktvā svarga 9.21
trai-guṇya-viṣayā vedā 2.45

trai-vidyā māṁ soma-pāḥ 9.20
tribhir guṇa-mayair bhāvair 7.13
tri-vidhā bhavati śraddhā 17.2
tri-vidhaṁ narakasyedaṁ 16.21
tulya-nindā-stutir maunī 12.19

tulya-priyāpriyo dhīras 14.24
tvad-anyaḥ saṁśayasyāsya 6.39
tvam ādi-devaḥ puruṣaḥ 11.38
tvam akṣaraṁ paramaṁ 11.18
tvam avyayaḥ śāśvata 11.18

tvattaḥ kamala-patrākṣa 11.2

tyāgasya ca hṛṣīkeśa 18.1
tyāgī sattva-samāviṣṭo 18.10
tyāgo hi puruṣa-vyāghra 18.4
tyājyaṁ doṣa-vad ity eke 18.3

tyaktvā dehaṁ punar janma 4.9
tyaktvā karma 4.20

U

ubhau tau na vijānīto 2.19
ubhayor api dṛṣṭo 'ntas 2.16
uccaiḥśravasam aśvānāṁ 10.27
ucchiṣṭam api cāmedhyaṁ 17.10
udārāḥ sarva evaite 7.18

udāsīna-vad āsīno 14.23
udāsīna-vad āsīnam 9.9
uddhared ātmanātmānaṁ 6.5
upadekṣyanti te jñānaṁ 4.34
upadraṣṭānumantā ca 13.23

upaiti śānta-rajasaṁ 6.27
upaviśyāsane yuñjyād 6.12
ūrdhvaṁ gacchanti sattva 14.18
ūrdhva-mūlam adhaḥ 15.1
utkrāmantaṁ sthitaṁ vāpi 15.10

utsādyante jāti-dharmāḥ 1.42
utsanna-kula-dharmāṇāṁ 1.43
utsīdeyur ime lokā 3.24
uttamaḥ puruṣas tv anyaḥ 15.17
uvāca pārtha paśyaitān 1.25

V

vaktrāṇi te tvaramāṇā 11.27
vaktum arhasy aśeṣeṇa 10.16
vāsāṁsi jīrṇāni yathā 2.22
vaśe hi yasyendriyāṇi 2.61
vāsudevaḥ sarvam iti 7.19

vasūnāṁ pāvakaś cāsmi 10.23
vaśyātmanā tu yatatā 6.36
vāyur yamo 'gnir varuṇaḥ 11.39
vedāhaṁ samatītāni 7.26
vedaiś ca sarvair aham 15.15

vedānāṁ sāma-vedo 'smi 10.22
veda-vāda-ratāḥ pārtha 2.42

vedāvināśinaṁ nityaṁ 2.21
vedeṣu yajñeṣu tapaḥsu 8.28
vedyaṁ pavitram oṁkāra 9.17

vepathuś ca śarīre me 1.29
vettāsi vedyaṁ ca paraṁ 11.38
vetti sarveṣu bhūteṣu 18.21
vetti yatra na caivāyaṁ 6.21
vidhi-hīnam asṛṣṭānnaṁ 17.13

vidyā-vinaya-sampanne 5.18
vigatecchā-bhaya-krodho 5.28
vihāya kāmān yaḥ sarvān 2.71
vijñātum icchāmi 11.31
vikārāṁś ca guṇāṁś caiva 13.20

vimṛśyaitad aśeṣeṇa 18.63
vimucya nirmamaḥ śānto 18.53
vimūḍhā nānupaśyanti 15.10
vināśam avyayasyāsya 2.17
vinaśyatsv avinaśyantaṁ 13.28

viṣādī dīrgha-sūtrī ca 18.28
viṣayā vinivartante 2.59
viṣayendriya-saṁyogād 18.38
viṣīdantam idaṁ vākyam 2.1
vismayo me mahān rājan 18. 77

visṛjya sa-śaraṁ cāpaṁ 1.46
viṣṭabhyāham idaṁ 10.42
vistareṇātmano yogaṁ 10.18
vīta-rāga-bhaya-krodhā 4.10
vīta-rāga-bhaya-krodhaḥ 2.56

vivasvān manave prāha 4.1
vividhāś ca pṛthak ceṣṭā 18.14
vivikta-deśa-sevitvam 13.11
vivikta-sevī laghv-āśī 18.52
vṛṣṇīnāṁ vāsudevo 'smi 10.37

vyāmiśreṇeva vākyena 3.2
vyapeta-bhīḥ prīta-manāḥ 11.49
vyāsa-prasādāc chrutavān 18.75
vyavasāyātmikā buddhir 2.41
vyavasāyātmikā buddhiḥ 2.44

vyūḍhāṁ drupada-putreṇa 1.3

Y

yābhir vibhūtibhir lokān 10.16
yac candramasi yac 15.12
yac cāpi sarva-bhūtānāṁ 10.39
yac cāvahāsārtham asat 11.42
yac chreya etayor ekaṁ 5.1

yac chreyaḥ syān niścitaṁ 2.7
yadā bhūta-pṛthag 13.31
yad āditya-gataṁ tejo 15.12
yad agre cānubandhe ca 18.39
yad ahaṅkāram āśritya 18.59

yadā hi nendriyārtheṣu 6.4
yad akṣaraṁ veda-vido 8.11
yadā saṁharate cāyaṁ 2.58
yadā sattve pravṛddhe tu 14.14
yadā te moha-kalilaṁ 2.52

yadā viniyataṁ cittam 6.18
yadā yadā hi dharmasya 4.7
yad gatvā na nivartante 15.6
yadi bhāḥ sadṛśī sā syād 11.12
yad icchanto brahmacaryaṁ 8.11

yadi hy ahaṁ na varteyaṁ 3.23
yadi mām apratīkāram 1.45
yad rājya-sukha-lobhena 1.44
yadṛcchā-lābha-santuṣṭo 4.22
yadṛcchayā copapannaṁ 2.32

yad yad ācarati śreṣṭhas 3.21
yad yad vibhūtimat 10.41
yady apy ete na paśyanti 1.37
ya enaṁ vetti hantāraṁ 2.19
ya evaṁ vetti puruṣaṁ 13.24

yaḥ paśyati tathātmānam 13.30
yaḥ prayāti sa mad-bhāvaṁ 8.5
yaḥ prayāti tyajan dehaṁ 8.13
yaḥ sarvatrānabhisnehas 2.57
yaḥ sa sarveṣu bhūteṣu 8.20

yaḥ śāstra-vidhim utsṛjya 16.23
ya idaṁ paramaṁ 18.68
yajante nāma-yajñais te 16.17
yajante sāttvikā devān 17.4
yaj jñātvā munayaḥ sarve 14.1

yaj jñātvā na punar moham 4.35
yaj jñātvā neha bhūyo 'nyaj 7.2
yajña-dāna-tapaḥ-karma 18.3
yajña-dāna-tapaḥ-karma 18.5
yajñād bhavati parjanyo 3.14

yajñānāṁ japa-yajño 'smi 10.25
yajñārthāt karmaṇo 'nyatra 3.9
yajña-śiṣṭāmṛta-bhujo 4.30
yajña-śiṣṭāśinaḥ santo 3.13
yajñas tapas tathā dānaṁ 17.7

yajñāyācarataḥ karma 4.23
yajñe tapasi dāne ca 17.27
yajño dānaṁ tapaś caiva 18.5
yakṣye dāsyāmi modiṣya 16.15
yaṁ hi na vyathayanty ete 2.15

yām imāṁ puṣpitāṁ vācaṁ 2.42
yaṁ labdhvā cāparaṁ 6.22
yaṁ prāpya na nivartante 8.21
yaṁ sannyāsam iti prāhur 6.2
yaṁ yaṁ vāpi smaran 8.6

yān eva hatvā na jijīviṣāmas 2.6
yā niśā sarva-bhūtānāṁ 2.69
yānti deva-vratā devān 9.25
yasmān nodvijate loko 12.15
yasmāt kṣaram atīto 'ham 15.18

yasmin sthito na duḥkhena 6.22
yaṣṭavyam eveti manaḥ 17.11
yas tu karma-phala-tyāgī 18.11
yas tv ātma-ratir eva syād 3.17
yas tv indriyāṇi manasā 3.7

yasyāṁ jāgrati bhūtāni 2.69
yasya nāhaṅkṛto bhāvo 18.17
yasyāntaḥ-sthāni bhūtāni 8.22
yasya sarve samārambhāḥ 4.19
yataḥ pravṛttir bhūtānāṁ 18.46

yatanto 'py akṛtātmāno 15.11
yatanto yoginaś cainaṁ 15.11
yatatām api siddhānāṁ 7.3
yatate ca tato bhūyaḥ 6.43
yatato hy api kaunteya 2.60
yāta-yāmaṁ gata-rasaṁ 17.10

yatendriya-mano-buddhir 5.28
yathā dīpo nivāta-stho 6.19
yathaidhāṁsi samiddho 4.37
yathākāśa-sthito nityaṁ 9.6
yathā nadīnāṁ bahavo 11.28

yathā pradīptaṁ jvalanaṁ 11.29
yathā prakāśayaty ekaḥ 13.34
yathā sarva-gataṁ 13.33
yatholbenāvṛto garbhas 3.38
yat karoṣi yad aśnāsi 9.27

yato yato niścalati 6.26
yatra caivātmanātmānaṁ 6.20
yatra kāle tv anāvṛttim 8.23
yatra yogeśvaraḥ kṛṣṇo 18.78
yatroparamate cittaṁ 6.20

yat sāṅkhyaiḥ prāpyate 5.5
yat tad agre viṣam iva 18.37
yat tapasyasi kaunteya 9.27
yat te 'haṁ prīyamāṇāya 10.1
yat tu kāmepsunā karma 18.24

yat tu kṛtsna-vad ekasmin 18.22
yat tu pratyupakārārthaṁ 17.21
yat tvayoktaṁ vacas tena 11.1
yāvad etān nirīkṣe 'haṁ 1.21
yāvān artha udapāne 2.46

yāvat sañjāyate kiñcit 13.27
yayā dharmam adharmaṁ 18.31
yayā svapnaṁ bhayaṁ 18.35
yayā tu dharma 18.34
ye bhajanti tu māṁ 9.29

ye caiva sāttvikā bhāvā 7.12
ye cāpy akṣaram avyaktaṁ 12.1
ye hi saṁsparśa-jā bhogā 5.22
ye me matam idaṁ nityam 3.31
yena bhūtāny aśeṣāṇi 4.35

ye 'py anya-devatā-bhaktā 9.23
yeṣām arthe kāṅkṣitaṁ no 1.32
yeṣāṁ ca tvaṁ bahu-mato 2.35
yeṣāṁ tv anta-gataṁ 7.28
ye śāstra-vidhim utsṛjya 17.1
ye tu dharmāmṛtam idaṁ 12.20

ye tu sarvāṇi karmāṇi 12.6
ye tv akṣaram anirdeśyam 12.3
ye tv etad abhyasūyanto 3.32
ye yathā māṁ prapadyante 4.11
yogaṁ yogeśvarāt kṛṣṇāt 18.75

yogārūḍhasya tasyaiva 6.3
yoga-sannyasta-karmāṇaṁ 4.41
yoga-sthaḥ kuru karmāṇi 2.48
yoga-yukto munir brahma 5.6
yoga-yukto viśuddhātmā 5.7

yogenāvyabhicāriṇyā 18.33
yogeśvara tato me tvaṁ 11.4
yoginaḥ karma kurvanti 5.11
yogīnām api sarveṣāṁ 6.47
yogino yata-cittasya 6.19

yogī yuñjīta satatam 6.10
yo loka-trayam āviśya 15.17
yo mām ajam anādiṁ ca 10.3
yo mām evam 15.19
yo māṁ paśyati sarvatra 6.30

yo na hṛṣyati na dveṣṭi 12.17
yo 'ntaḥ-sukho 'ntar 5.24
yotsyamānān avekṣe 'haṁ 1.23
yo 'yaṁ yogas tvayā 6.33
yo yo yāṁ yāṁ tanuṁ 7.21

yudhāmanyuś ca vikrānta 1.6
yuktāhāra-vihārasya 6.17
yuktaḥ karma-phalaṁ 5.12
yukta ity ucyate yogī 6.8
yukta-svapnāvabodhasya 6.17

yuñjann evaṁ sadātmānaṁ 6.15
yuñjann evaṁ sadātmānaṁ 6.28
yuyudhāno virāṭaś ca 1.4

INDEX

abhidheya-tattva, 482
Absolute, the
  Kṛṣṇa as the love life of, *xix*
  as *param brahman*, 32
  potencies of, 32–33
  and sacred aesthetic rapture, 568–569
  spiritual need of, 243
  three features of, 426–427
acintya-bhedābheda
  reconciles contradictions, 289
  as ultimate reality, 420–430
  as Vedānta of Gauḍīya Vaiṣṇavism, 286
action
  causes of, 529–534
  and the *guṇas*, 533–540
  renouncing, 169–170, 528
  selfless, 169–171
  and spirit of sacrifice, 153
  See also karma
Acyuta (Kṛṣṇa addressed as), 17–18
adhikāra
  for approaching a guru, 37
  of Arjuna, 69–70, 284, 343–344, 360
  of less qualified persons, 345
  and liberation, different paths to, 435
  for *niṣkāma-karma-yoga*, 70–71
  in *Śrīmad-Bhāgavatam*, 70
  truth revealed according to, 113–114
Adwaita Ācārya, 427, 579
ahiṁsā, 328
aparā prakṛti, 417–419
  See also matter; māyā; māyā-śakti; nature; *prakṛti*
Arjuna
  addressed as Bhārata, 45, 113
  addressed as Dhanañjaya, 14, 72, 365, 575
  addressed as Guḍākeśa, 19, 40, 345
  addressed as Kaunteya, 45, 216, 261
  addressed as Kirīṭī, 378
  addressed as Mahābāho, 88
  addressed as Parantapa, 133, 135
  addressed as Pārtha, 109, 575
  addressed as Savyasācin, 377
  addresses Kṛṣṇa as Kamala-patrākṣa, 359
  adhikāra of, 69–70, 284, 343, 360
  decision to fight, 558–559, 575–576
  dharma as warrior, 57–64
  doubts of, 17, 21–29
  eagerness to hear, 343–344
  ecstatic symptoms, 365, 378–379
  as ideal person, 77–92
  Kṛṣṇa establishes *dharma* through, 576–577
  love for Kṛṣṇa of, *xv–xvi*, 357–358
  name of, meaning, 33, 135, 527
  offers obeisances to Kṛṣṇa, 381–387
  and *prāṇāyāma yoga*, 214
  relationship with Kṛṣṇa, 259, 261, 324, 379, 384, 390
  trembling causes metrical irregularity, 357
  as ungodly in his own estimation, 489
  and universal form, vision of, 362–363
  willingness to be God's instrument, 377–378, 579
artha-śāstra, 24, 57
aśvattha tree, 465–469, 488
ātmā, 257–258, 419
austerity, 511–514, 525
avatāra
  God enters the world as, for *līlā*, 292
  and *guru-paramparā*, 130–132
  surrender to, versus surrender to Kṛṣṇa, 238
  and transcending the *guṇas*, 546
Baladeva Vidyābhūṣaṇa
  on Arjuna
    relationship with Kṛṣṇa, 384
    reluctance to fight, 559
    seeing the universal form, 374–375

Bhagavad-gītā commentary of, *xxiii–xxiv*
challenges Adwaitin reading of *ātmā*, 419
on destruction of Bhīṣma and Droṇa, 374
on destruction of the world, 493
on Duryodhana's army, 10
on fruits of activities, 150
gives example of king's servant, 320
on glance of devotees, 251
Govinda-bhāṣya of, *xxi–xxii*
on impartiality of inner renunciation, 183
on impure vows, 494
on knowledge and action, 167–168
on knowledge and meditation, 408
on knowledge as gateway to devotion, 416
on Kṛṣṇa,
abode, 554
all-pervasiveness, 382–383
carries devotee's burden, 307
freedom from partiality, 147
as *gāyatrī*, 352
as Lord of the heart, 561
punishment of unrighteous, 139
as *saguṇa* or *nirguṇa*, 232
as the Supreme Person, 482
on meanings of
"all things abiding in me," 161
Bg. 18.25, 538
brahmaṇi in verse 5.10, 177
mad-bhāvam, 260, 458
Mathurā, 566
samādhi, 67
on pious persons, 242
on the plurality of *jīvas* as eternal, 443
on *prārabdha-karma* of devotee, 79
on *puruṣas*, two types of, 478
on *rākṣasas*, 296
on renunciation, 171–172, 196
on *sattva*'s influence, 453
on soul as one of several factors in action, 114–115
on soul's union with nature as beginningless, 436
Śvetāśvatara Upaniṣad, cites, 140
on *svabhāva*, 257–258
on ungodly persons, 497
on Viṣṇu as progenitor, 101
on worshipping with honestly acquired goods, 100
on *yoga*, 130
banyan tree. *See aśvattha* tree
Bhagavad-gītā
bhakti as essence of, 284, 310–321, 527, 555–557, 559–560, 563–569
commentaries on, *xxiii–xxiv*, *xxvi–xxvii*
conclusive advice of, 567–570
disseminating teachings of, 570–572
"don't worry" as message of, 489, 568
explaining, results of, *xii*, 572–574
four essential verses of, 330–338
Gauḍīyas' writings on, *xxi–xxii*
generosity of *bhakti* as message of, 555–557
gopīs' path as secret message of, 569
higher and lower paths in, 568
justification for this edition of, *xix*
and *Mahābhārata*, 1
metaphysics of, 486
meter in, 36
mystical treasure of, 563–569
parallelism between verse 18.66 and
verse 2.11, 42
verse 3.35, 120–121
practical tenets of, 486
presents one truth, 562
and Rāmānanda Saṁvāda, 571
as song of God, 41
studying and hearing, 573–574
summary of, 31–91
and the *Upaniṣads*, *xxii*
Bhagavān, 33
and *bhakti-yoga*, 430
as feature of Godhead, 225–253
as joyful aspect of the Absolute, 426
līlā of, 226
and *nirviśeṣa brahman*, 32
opulence and sweetness of, 227–228
opulences, six, 33
as *paraṁ brahman*, 32
as partial to his devotees, 313

and Śrī, 32–33
as superior to Paramātmā and Brahman, 426, 479–482
See also Kṛṣṇa; Vraja Kṛṣṇa

bhakti
Absolute rendered humanlike by, 276
benefit of, never lost, 65, 315–318
and *dharma*, 258
as eternal function of the soul, 120
as fruit of *Vedas*, 69
generosity of, 555–557
and hearing and chanting, 113
indirect advocacy of, 61, 120–121
as ingress of *svarūpa-śakti*, 297
and *karma* and *yoga* as a continuum, 62
as king of knowledge, 284
loving Kṛṣṇa in, 262
mixed with *karma*, 555–556
and moral lapses of devotees, 315–318, 556
parā bhakti as post-liberated form of, 553–554
practice of, as easy, 403
and *prārabdha-karma*, 78–79
pure heart is not a prerequisite for, 113
rāgānugā, 317, 576
as real meaning of *Bhagavad-gītā*, 559–560
and *śraddhā*, 287
two glories of, 63–64, 312, 416
two types of, 404, 405–406
unalloyed, 576
union in love in, 313
as wise existence and wise love, 333
See also bhakti-yoga; devotion; devotional service; *prema-dharma* of Vraja; *rāgānugā-bhakti*; Vraja *bhakti*

Bhaktivedanta Swami Prabhupāda
on Arjuna, 490
on *aśvattha* tree, 466
on *ātman* referring to Kṛṣṇa himself, 210
on "beginningless Brahman," 425–426
on Bg. 10.10, 335
on bodily suffering and distress, 180
on cheating of great souls, 565–566
on Kṛṣṇa's descent, 138–139
on material nature, 230
on offering food to Kṛṣṇa, 103
on soul's individuality, 43
on transcendental knowledge, 163
on the *Vedas*, 477
on writing books, *xvi–xvii*

Bhaktivinoda Ṭhākura
on *bhakti* and moral lapses of devotees, 317–318
and Gauḍīya tradition, revival of, *xxvi*
on *gopīs*' violation of socioreligious codes, 318
on Kṛṣṇa's name and revelation of one's spiritual form, 406
on philanthropic work, 400

bhakti-yoga, 395–414, 404–407
as both means and end, 64, 463
frees one from concern for acquisition and comfort, 68
jīvanmuktas on path of, 242–243
and *karma-yoga* and *jñāna-yoga*, 167, 358
and ladder of *yoga*, 62–63
love of Kṛṣṇa as result of, 143
three stages of, 226–227
as wavering or unwavering, 329–330
See also bhakti; devotion; devotional service; *prema-dharma* of Vraja; *rāgānugā-bhakti*; Vraja *bhakti*

bhāva
attaining, requires understanding of *tattva*, 430
dawning of, 297
of Gauḍīya commentators on *Gītā*, *xxvi*
nature of those possessing, 333
as product of grace, 295
See also prema-dharma of Vraja; *rāgānugā-bhakti*

birth, 54, 137

body, 55, 114
cannot be maintained without action, 99
change of, 44, 50–51, 472–473
contrasted to the soul, 417
death of, 260–262
devotee's, as transcendental, 79–80

ephemeral, 319–320
interaction with mind and soul, 472–473
nine gates of, 178, 266
as seat of activity, 530
Brahmā, 101, 269, 331
brahma-jijñāsā, 41, 160–161
Brahman
attaining, 551–553
"beginningless" in 13.13, 425–426
existential aspect of the Absolute, 426
as the halo of God, 76
infallible and supreme, 257
jīvas are of the nature of, 185
Kṛṣṇa superior to, 232, 330, 339, 396, 403, 425–426, 442, 462–463, 471, 480–482
realization, 400–402
saguṇa and *nirguṇa*, 232–233, 401–402
śaktis of, as innumerable, 32–33
Śaṅkara's view of Kṛṣṇa and, 396–398
seeing from the vantage point of, 438
and syllable *tat*, 140
and *Vedas* in verse 4.32, 157
brāhmaṇas, 327, 547
brahma-nirvāṇam. *See nirvāṇa*
Brahma-sūtras, 421
Bṛhad-āraṅyaka Upaniṣad, 163
B. R. Śrīdhara Deva Goswāmī
on actions and indwelling Lord, 117
on ambitious work as rajasic, 537
on "beginningless Brahman" in 13.13, 425–426
on *bhakti* as soul's eternal function, 120
on *jñāna* of *gopīs* and Bg. 10.10, 337–338
on Kṛṣṇa as the guru, 332
on worship of Śrī Caitanya, 333
Buddhism, 54, 90–91
See also nirvāṇa
buddhi-yoga, 85
as devotee's power of discrimination, 335–336
as spiritual insight resulting from devotion, 557
as wisdom in *yoga*, 62
Caitanya. *See* Śrī Caitanya
Caitanya Bhāgavata, 427
Caitanya-caritāmṛta
Bhagavad-gītā cited in, *xxii*
on descent of Kṛṣṇa as Śrī Caitanya, 108
on *jñāna* mixed with *bhakti*, 553
Carvaka Muni, materialism of, 49, 54
Chandogya Upaniṣad, 421
chanting, 333
efficacy of, 267, 515–520
as *mahātmā*'s principal expression of devotion, 298–299
one's spiritual form revealed by, 406
in *vaidhī-bhakti* leads to *rāgānugā-bhakti*, 406–407
and vulture story, 197–198
See also Kṛṣṇa: name of; *mantra*
charity, 514–515, 524–525
consciousness
and accountability for actions, 532–533
and attachment, 290
as foundation of existence, 34
interaction of, with matter, 436, 441
as "knower of the field," 441
death
and birth as unavoidable, 54
remembering Kṛṣṇa at time of, 260–262
two paths taken by *yogī* at time of, 277–281
desire
conquering, 122–127
and *karma*, 468
living beings disposed to material action by, 181
material, 98
and the self, 77
for sense objects, 188
soul is bound to the body by, 257–258
Śrīmad-Bhāgavatam cited on, 122
detachment, 469, 525
devotees
accompany Kṛṣṇa through birth in his *līlā*, 268
aspire only to serve Kṛṣṇa, 403
chanting of, 212

dark night of the soul of, 138
external and internal characteristics, 297–299
falling away of, 218–222
God's partiality toward, 181, 313–314
influence of *svarūpa-śakti* on, 297
as instruments and ingredients of worship, 144
as integrated persons, 223, 321
and *jñāna-yogīs*, 396
Kṛṣṇa cares for and maintains, 306–307, 568–569
Kṛṣṇa conquered by love of, 338
Kṛṣṇa delivers, 403
Kṛṣṇa's love for, 564
minds of, are fixed on Kṛṣṇa, 320–321
moral lapses, 316–317
offer their food to Kṛṣṇa, 103
oneness with Kṛṣṇa, 242–244
rāgātmikā, and Bg. 10.10, 336
and sacred literature, 337
sorrow and happiness of, 78, 138
spiritual nature of the body of, 79–80
steady insight of, 76–91, 411–414
symptoms of, 409–414, 489, 570
vision of, 210–211
of Vraja exist only for Kṛṣṇa, 334
worship by, 333
wrongdoing of, 314–318
See also jīvanmukta; mahātmā

devotion
benefit of, is never lost, 314–318
buddhi-yoga in relation to, 61, 334–336, 557
and control of mind, 96
as freedom, 311–312
jñānī attains, if fortunate, 553
and knowledge of the self, 96
Kṛṣṇa speaks feelingly of, 555–556
mixed, 263, 278–280, 312
niṣṭhā as steadiness in, 96
power of, 283–321
pure, can clear *prārabdha-karma*, 286
results of, 334–336, 398
as soul's natural function, 120
as *yoga*, highest type of, 223, 395
See also bhakti; bhakti-yoga; devotional service; *prema-dharma* of Vraja; *rāgānugā-bhakti*; Vraja *bhakti*

devotional service, 108
See also bhakti; bhakti-yoga; devotion; *prema-dharma* of Vraja; *rāgānugā-bhakti*; Vraja *bhakti*

dharma, 4–5, 550
and *bhakti*, 258
everlasting, 463
gopīs cross over, 110–111, 212, 569
Kṛṣṇa descends to establish, *xx*, 138, 576
Kṛṣṇa only secondarily concerned with, 378, 567–569, 576
and Kurukṣetra, 4–5
of love, 1
of one's own nature, 120–121
performance of, as purifying, 48
practice of, 60
righteousness of practicing, 57–65
service is, of the soul, 413
See also prema-dharma of Vraja

dharma-jijñāsā, 41, 160–161

dharma-śāstra
contrasted with *artha-śāstra*, 24, 57
contravened by killing guru of elders, 24
refuted by *Upaniṣads*, 42

Dhṛtarāṣṭra, 1–2

dhyāna-yoga, 63, 191–192
in *Gītā* chapter six, 193–223
Kṛṣṇa as highest object of, 203–204

Duryodhana
army of, 9–11
and Droṇa, relationship, 6
name of, meaning, 2
on opposite side of Yudhiṣṭhira in battle, 2

elements, gross and subtle, 229–230, 422

evidence. *See pramāṇa*

faith
acquired nature as cause of, 504–505

and eligibility for *bhakti*, 252
and knowledge, 165
logical proof not required for, 140
mind as secondary cause of, 505–506
three types of, 504–508
of the ungodly, 507
yoga of, 503–520
family, 25–27, 110–112
Gauḍīya Vedānta, *xxi*, 33
Gautama, Nyāya school of, 49
Gītā. *See Bhagavad-gītā*
God
as both just and merciful, 293
experiences world of the senses through the *jīvātmā*, 427
impregnates nature, 443–444
as Kṛṣṇa gives himself to devotee, 295
is motivated by love, 448–449
as *nirguṇa*, 428
offending, 296
only real doer of action, 529–531
qualities of, 327
senses of living beings are manifested by, 427–428
See also Bhagavān; Kṛṣṇa; *puruṣa*
Gopāla-tāpanī Upaniṣad, 566
gopīs
and Bg. 10.10, 336
grew fonder of Kṛṣṇa in his absence, 3, 334
and *jñāna*, 337–338
Kṛṣṇa's reciprocation with, 142–143
at Kurukṣetra, 331–332
love of, for Kṛṣṇa, 4, 110–111, 143, 211–212, 243, 331–332
violated socioreligious codes, 212, 318, 569
as *yogīs*, 212
Govardhana, *xxv*, 331, 358
Govinda (Kṛṣṇa addressed as), 23, 40
guṇas, 441–463
and action, 98, 114–116, 145–146, 533–540
animals and persons in relation to, 184
austerities in relation to, 511–514
characteristics of action in each, 456–458, 537–538
charity in relation to, 514–516
determinism of, transcending, 562
duties in relation to, 546–550
faith in relation to, 504–508
food in relation to, 508–510
fortitude in, 542–543
God is above, 428
happiness in relation to, 544–545
intellect in relation to, 540–542
intelligence covered by, 123
knowledge manifest within, 533–540
means "rope" or "quality," 445
mutually contradictory effects of, 452
perform all actions, 179
pradhāna as unmanifest condition of, 422
and *prakṛti*, 431
renunciation in, 526–527
sacrifice in relation to, 510–511
transcending, 237–239, 458–459
and transpersonal psychology, 447
types of worship in, 309, 503–504, 506
world is under the influence of, 545–546
See also rajo-guṇa; sattva-guṇa; tamo-guṇa
guru
approaching, 159–161
disciple's relationship with, 40, 133, 564, 575
embracing practices given by, 216–217
instructing, 335
knowledge received from, 161–164
Kṛṣṇa as, 160
paramparā, 130–132, 263
plurality of, 160
as representation of Rādhā, 332
happiness
and controlling the senses, 87
in relation to the *guṇas*, 544–545
and virtue, 422
from within, 188–189
heaven, 304–306
hell, 499
Hṛṣīkeśa (Kṛṣṇa addressed as), 16, 40, 379

awakens Arjuna from illusion, 19
as controller of the senses, 14
ignorance, 313
Indra, 305
intellect
and the *guṇas*, 540–542
and mind and senses, 88, 125–127
rajasic, 541
sattvic, 541
situated just beneath the soul, 271
tamasic, 542
Jaimini, Karma-mīmāṁsā of, 523
Jainism, 480
Janārdana (Kṛṣṇa addressed as), 25, 27
as caretaker and killer of everyone, 23
gives his friends painful orders, 94
is petitioned by all souls, 94
is prayed to by all people, 343
Jīva Goswāmī
on the Absolute, 327
acintya-bhedābheda terminology and, 286
on Adwaitin reading of *ātmā*, 419
on Bg. 2.11 and 18.66, 42
on *Bhagavad-gītā*, 568
on Bhagavān, 33
on *bhakti*
and moral lapses of devotees, 316–317
as real meaning of the *Bhagavad-gītā*, 559–560
what to avoid in cultivation of, 240
on *dharma* and *bhakti*, 258
on *jīvas* being of the nature of Brahman, 185
on knowledge, 562
on Kṛṣṇa
birth and activities, 140
first visit to Kurukṣetra, 3–4
as incarnation, 249
love for his devotees, 564
superiority over Paramātmā, 253
on meanings of
"beginningless Brahman," 425–426
prakṛti in verse 4.6, 136
soul as *sarva-gataḥ*, 53
on offerings to the gods, 258
on *rāgānugā-bhakti*, 317
on *sārūpya-mukti*, 258
on ŚB. 1.7.10 and Bg. 2.53, 75
on soul's knowledge being covered, 180
on *Śrīmad-Bhāgavatam* and evidence, 132
on ungodly persons, 498–499
on Vāsudeva as Balarāma, 353
on Vraja, 568
jīvanmukta
characteristics of, 76–91, 184–185, 210–211, 458–461
helps one transcend the *guṇas*, 546
prārabdha-karma of, 163
and *rati*, 142
steady insight of, 76–91, 411–414
two types of, 242–243
See also devotees; *jīvanmukti; mahātmā*
jīvanmukti, 77
jīva-śakti, 230–231, 257
as intermediate potency of the Absolute, 33
See also jivātmā; parā prakṛti; puruṣa (qualified); self; soul
jīvātmā
does not mix with the body, 439–440
eternal individuality of, 472
as Kṛṣṇa's eternal servant, 120, 258
as qualified *puruṣa*, 431
and self's inherent nature, 257–258
as unit of will, 448
See also jīva-śakti; parā prakṛti; puruṣa (qualified); self; soul
jñāna
associated with *sāṅkhya*, 62
and *gopīs*, 337–338
and *vijñāna*, 227–228, 394
See also jñāna-yoga; knowledge
jñāna-śāstra, 42
jñāna-yoga, 129
and devotion, 244–245, 553–554
and freedom from bondage of *karma*, 551
in Gītā chapter four, 129–168
jīvanmuktas on path of, 242–243, 553

and *karma-yoga*, 95–99
and *niṣkāma-karma-yoga*, 522
result of, 143, 398
as *sannyāsa*, 522
worshippers on path of, 300, 304
See also jñāna; knowledge
kalpas, 291–293
See also yugas
karma
and antinomianism, 532
and *bhakti* and *yoga* as continuum, 62
bhakti mixed with, 555–556
defects, always covered by, 550
demonstrates that God is just, 293
doctrine of, 491
gives birth to the world, 258
godly and ungodly natures as product of, 488
and *guṇas*, 114–116
human form of life perpetuates, 468
inaction within, 95
intricacies of, 148–152
liberation from, 312–313, 551
as religious sacrifice, 258
and renunciation, 528–529
soul takes on body according to, 432
stages of, 78–79
stored in seed form, 286
in *Vedānta-sūtra*, 180–181
See also action; *prārabdha-karma*
Karma-mīmāṁsā of Jaimini, 523
karma-yoga
and *jñāna-yoga*, 96–100
knowledge within, 171–172
performed by great persons, 108
practice and results of, 166–167
psychology of, 175–176
and purification, 97
and renunciation, 170–171, 174–178
and Vedic sacrifice, 153
warriors who attained success through, 107–108
worshippers on path of, 305–306
See also niṣkāma-karma-yoga
Kaṭha Upaniṣad, 49
Keśava (Kṛṣṇa addressed as)
as killer of Keśī demon, 21
as supreme over Brahmā and Śiva, 94, 340
knowledge, 422–429
of Bhagavān, 228
confidential and most confidential, 283–284, 562–571
and faith, 164–166
in the *guṇas*, 533–540
in *karma-yoga*, 171–172
of Kṛṣṇa, 141–142
nature of God and self revealed by, 182
as *niṣkāma-karma-yoga*'s initial fruit, 415
object of, 425–430
practices leading to, 423–424
rajasic, 536
sattvic, 535, 553
of soul is covered by ignorance, 180
tamasic, 536
transcendental, 161–164, 337–338
as *vidyā* and *jñāna*, 553
See also jñāna; jñāna-yoga
Kṛṣṇa
abode of, 274–276, 282, 470–471, 555–557, 565–566
and *acintya-bhedābheda*, 289–290
on action versus renunciation, 524–525
all-pervasiveness of, 382–383
appearance of, 134–140, 325–326
attained only by devotion, 276
and Brahman, 339, 396–403, 462, 480–482
compassion for Pūtanā demon, 499
conch of, 15
and creation and destruction, 291–292
as Cupid, 566
detachment of, 146–147
devotees aspire for relationship with, 298–299
and devotees' love for him, 18, 307, 337
and devotees' sorrow, 21, 22
disappearance of, 575–576
of Dwārakā, *xxiv–xxv*, 3–4, 331–332, 576

eternality of, 136–137
everything rests on, 232–233, 303–304
as example for others, 109–112
as father and mother of universe, 302, 444
form of, 248, 265, 288
  four-armed, 386–387
  humanlike, 294–295, 342, 363, 387, 389–393, 396
  saguṇa and *nirguṇa*, 232–233, 396–398
and the *guṇas*, 236–237
as the guru, 332
heart of, stolen by love of his devotees, 310
as heart of divinity, 245
instruction of, to fix mind on him, 321–322, 558, 564–566
līlā of,
  eating dirt as a child, 275
  entering, 142, 565, 576
  meditating on, 113
and living beings, 288–291, 474–477
as Lord of the world, 326–329
as master of all mysticism, 577
name of, 267
  conquers the mind, 215
  devotee's faults removed by, 215
  See also chanting; *mantra*
not attained by *varṇāśrama*, 145–146
offerings to, 310–312
as *oṁ*, 233, 302
omniscience of, 135–136, 250, 340, 359–360
oneness with, in devotion, 242–244
ontology of, 401
opulence and majesty of, 288–295, 325–326, 339, 341–342, 344–355, 357–358, 384, 387–388
as origin of Kumāras and Manus, 328–329
and Paramātmā, 355
as Parameśvara, 359–360
as partial and impartial, 292–294, 313–314
Rādhā has no shelter other than, 556
reciprocation of, 142–143
relationship with, aspiring for, 267–268
as reservoir of loving reciprocation, 332
and sacred aesthetic rapture, 568–569
as *Sāma Veda*, 346
subdues senses, 83
surrender to, persons who do not, 239–240
as *svayaṁ bhagavān*, 143, 330–331
as true object of worship, 308–309
universal representations of, 233–236, 301–304, 344–355 *See also* universal form
as Vedic ritual and sacrifice, 301–302
Vraja *līlā* of, *xvi–xvii*
worship of, in pursuit of material goals, 247
worshippers of, 240–242
See also Bhagavān; Vraja Kṛṣṇa
Kṛṣṇadāsa Kavirāja Goswāmī, 108, 335
kṣatriyas, 547
Kurukṣetra
  battle of, background to, 1–3
  devotion to Rādhā at, 4
  as *dharma-kṣetra*, 5
  Rādhā and Kṛṣṇa's meeting at, *xxv–xxvi*, 3–5, 331–332
  sacredness of, 2–3
lamentation, 41–42, 54, 78
liberation
  as fruit of hearing *Bhagavad-gītā*, 574
  paths to, 435
  prārabdha-karma does not prevent, 434
  qualities leading to, 489
  renunciation is required for, 467
  in *sāyujya-mukti*, 139, 554–555
  and syllable *tat*, 518
love
  does not move in a straight line, 565
  esoteric mystery of divine, 284
  five expressions of devotional, *xix–xx*
  as goal of *Bhagavad-gītā*, 527
  of the *gopīs* for Kṛṣṇa, 3–4, 211–212, 243, 331–332
  jīvas can realize their potential for, 449
  Kṛṣṇa as ultimate object of, 402
  and sacrifice, 104, 320
  transcends scripture, 236

Mādhava (Kṛṣṇa addressed as), 13, 24
Madhusūdana (Kṛṣṇa addressed as)
  and Arisūdana, 35
  as reinstater of the Vedic path, 24
  as slayer of Arjuna's doubts, 32
  as slayer of the illusion of material happiness, 23
Madhusūdana Saraswatī
  on addressing Arjuna as Parantapa, 135
  Bhagavad-gītā commentary of, *xxiii–xxiv*
  on desire and motivation, 149
  on Kṛṣṇa as *saguṇa* or *nirguṇa*, 232–233
  on Kṛṣṇa's form, 238, 483–484, 497
  on meanings of
    Bg. 13.13, 425
    name "Kṛṣṇa," 21
    prakṛti in verse 4.6, 136
  on *rati*, 142
  on *samādhi* and *prārabdha-karma*, 77
  on those surrendered to Kṛṣṇa, 238
mahātmā
  Arjuna addresses Kṛṣṇa as, 380
  aspires for devotional union with God, 298
  chanting of, 298–299
  at death, 280
  Kṛṣṇa reserves this term for his devotees, 211, 244, 268–269, 297–298
  sees God everywhere, 211
  See also devotees; *jīvanmukta*
Mahā-Viṣṇu, 291–292, 579
  See also Viṣṇu
mantra
  gāyatrī, 352
  gopāla-mantra, 280
  oṁ, 266, 517
  oṁ tat sat, 515–520
  See also chanting; Kṛṣṇa: name of
Mathurā
  cheating of those from, 566
  Kṛṣṇa's return to, *xxiv–xxv*
matter, 436, 441
  See also aparā prakṛti; māyā; māyā-śakti; nature; *prakṛti*
māyā
  influence of, 249–251
  jīvas deluded by, 250–251
  meaning of, 48, 136–137, 249
  See also aparā prakṛti; matter; *māyā-śakti;* nature; *prakṛti*
māyā-śakti, 229–230
  Kṛṣṇa's explanation of, 135
  pradhāna represents totality of, 422
  as *prakṛti*, 136–137
  as secondary potency of the Absolute, 33
  See also aparā-prakṛti; matter; *māyā;* nature; *prakṛti*
mind
  of artificial renunciate, 98
  austerites of, 512–513
  and body and soul, 472–473
  concentration of, and meditation, 202
  and egotism, 532–533
  and faith, 505–506
  fixing, on Kṛṣṇa, 320–321, 557–558, 564–566
  and intellect and senses, 87–88, 125–127
  as *jīva*'s burden, 471–472
  Kṛṣṇa's name conquers, 215
  one-pointedness of, 65–66, 559
  practices to restrain, 216–217
  as self's friend and enemy, 197–198
  small world of, 45
  subduing, 215
  symptoms of one who has controlled, 76–90
moderation, 205–206
Nārada, 339
nature
  as creation's agency, 292
  as God's womb, 443–444
  personification of, 102
  worship of, 301
  See also aparā prakṛti; matter; *māyā; māyā-śakti; prakṛti*
nirvāṇa
  brahma-nirvāṇa conception of Gītā, 91, 188–190, 204, 398

cessation of suffering as meaning of, 90–91
See also Buddhism
nirviśeṣa brahman
Adwaitin notion of ultimate reality, 425
as spiritual halo of Bhagavān, 32
See also Brahman
niṣkāma-karma-yoga
buddhi-yoga as, 336
distinguished from *jñāna-yoga*, 522
efficacy of, 94
eligibility for, 70
emphasis on, in relation to renunciation, 528–529
knowledge of Brahman as fruit of, 63, 415
Kṛṣṇa recommends, 116–117, 407
leads to *bhakti*, 63, 415
liberation as positive result of, 117–118
mature stage of, 63
purifies heart, 63, 97
referred to as *tyāga*, 522
as scripturally enjoined detached action, 97
selfless action as spirit of, 71
social activism as rudimentary form of, 99
and *varnāśrama*, 70–71, 549
See also action; *karma*; *karma-yoga*
niṣṭhā, 65–66, 96
Nyāya school of Gautama, 49
obeisances, 299
Padma Purāṇa
on *namaḥ*, 299
on stages of *karma*, 78
pantheism, 300–304
Paramātmā
and *aṣṭāṅga-yogī*, 198
and Brahman, 480
as cognitive aspect of the Absolute, 426
and *dhyāna-yogī*, 63
and *guṇas*, 439, 447
as impartial witness, 313
as indwelling guide, 76
jīvas are manifested by his love, 448–449
Kapiladeva on, 213
Kṛṣṇa superior to, 253, 344–345, 561
master of *prakṛti* and qualified *puruṣa*, 433
material world presided over by, 331
as plenary portion of Kṛṣṇa, 355
as puppeteer, 560
as *sarva-loka maheśvaram*, 192
as superior *puruṣa*, 433
as supersubjective reality, 417–419
as ultimate factor in action, 530–531, 560
will of, 447–448
parā prakṛti, 431
as "knower of the field," 417–419
as qualified *puruṣa*, 431, 433
See also *jīva-śakti*; *jivātmā*; self; soul
Prabhodānanda Saraswatī, 566
prakṛti, 431–434
See also *aparā prakṛti*; matter; *māyā*; *māyā-śakti*; nature
pramāṇa, 82
prārabdha-karma, 78–80
destroyed by knowledge, 163
distribution of, 79
expressed as lamentation, 42
and the *guṇas*, 452
liberation regardless of, 434
prayojana-tattva, 483
prema-bhakti, 287
prema-dharma of Vraja
as essence of *dharma*, 121
faith in, 287–288
as height of *dharma*, 4
and the *Mahābhārata*, 1
as most confidential knowledge, 562
rāgānugā-bhakti as means of attaining, 576
as secret of the *Upaniṣads*, xxi
transcends religious mandates, 317, 576
See also *bhāva*; *rāgānugā-bhakti*
puruṣa, 275
Paramātmā as superior, 433
and *prakṛti*, 431–433
two types of, 478–481
See also Bhagavān; God; Kṛṣṇa
Puruṣa-bodhinī Upaniṣad, 140
puruṣa (qualified), 432
as *parā prakṛti*, 431, 433

as predominated reality, 433
See also *jīva-śakti; jivātmā; parā prakṛti;* self; soul
Puruṣottama (Kṛṣṇa addressed as), 256, 341
yoga of, 465–484
rāgānugā-bhakti
chanting in *vaidhi-bhakti* leads to, 406
culture of, 576
deepest import of, 337
devotees on path of, 317
Kṛṣṇa *nāma* reveals one's spiritual form in, 406
path of, 333–334, 404
See also bhāva; prema-dharma of Vraja
rajo-guṇa
action in, 537, 539
austerities in, 513
avarice born from, 457
charity in, 515
dying under influence of, 456
effects and symptoms of, 450–451, 454
as energetic essence of things, 445–446
faith and worship in, 506
fear in, 328
food in, 509
fortitude in, 543
Freud's Eros and Thanatos comparable to, 446
happiness in, 544–545
increases material longing, 445
intellect in, 541
knowledge in, 536
lifestyles in, 457–458
and material progress, 494
renunciation in, 526
sacrifice in, 510
and Taoism, 446
work in, 456
Rāmānuja
on Adwaitin reading of *ātmā*, 419
Bhagavad-gītā commentary of, *xxii–xxiv*
on Brahman, 396–398, 400
on *karma-yoga* and *bhakti*, 413–414
on meaning of
"beginningless Brahman," 425–426
Bg. 18.25, 538
brahmaṇi in verse 5.10, 177
prakṛti in verse 4.6, 136
on Paramātmā, 530
on *samādhi*, 77
on ungodly view of world, 493
rāsa-līlā, 338
Rāya Rāmānanda, 569, 571
reality, 420–430
religious duty. *See dharma*
renunciation
of action, 169–192
artificial, 98
discrimination as result of, 467
of fruit of action, 524–525
inner, 183
of prescribed duties, 526–527
purification required for, 97–98
See also sannyāsa
Rūpa Goswāmī
on the Absolute as the perfect lover, *xxi*
on *bhāva*, 333
on dawning of *bhāva*, 297
on how love moves, 565
on Kṛṣṇa of Dwārakā, *xxv*
on *niṣṭhā*, 96
sacrifice
as heart of worship and basis of love, 320
with honestly acquired goods, 100
of inner attachments, 158
and inner wisdom, 158
and *karma-yoga*, 100–105
in modes of material nature, 510–511
not to be given up, 524–525
recommended, 100–105
religious versus transcendental, 516
results of, 156–157
types of, 152–156
and *Vedas*, 157
Viṣṇu as, 259
sādhana, 216–217
in *bhakti-yoga*, 226–227

and knowledge, 423–424
and *sādhya*, 158
śakti, 32–33
See also jīva-śakti; māyā-śakti; svarūpa-śakti
samādhi, 67, 198–199, 208, 405
and begging for alms, 151
of Brahman realization, 76–91, 152–153,188–189, 204
of Paramātmā realization, 198–199
practices to steady the mind in, 216–217
and ŚB. 1.7.10, 75
stages of, 77
sambandha-jñāna
as *bhakti*, 429, 441–442
as knowledge of *tattva*, 288–294
sambandha-tattva, 478–482
Sanātana Goswāmī, *xxv*, 79
Sañjaya, 2, 41, 579
Śaṅkara
on Brahman and Kṛṣṇa, 232–233, 396–398, 401–402
on goal of *yoga*, 130
sāṅkhya (analytical study), 61–62, 173, 529, 534–535
Sāṅkhya, Kapila's doctrine of, 62, 114, 441, 480, 523
sannyāsa, 551
and *jñāna-yoga*, 522
not goal of life, 569
purification required for, 97
qualities of, 487
of Śaṅkara school, 175
and *tyāga*, 522–529
as understood by the learned, 522–523
of Vaiṣṇava school, 175
yoga of, 312
See also renunciation; *tyāga*
sattva-guṇa, 327
action in, 537
austerities in, 513
charity in, 328, 514
dying under the influence of, 455
effects and symptoms of, 449–450, 453
faith in, 504–506
fame in, 328
fear in, 328
food in, 508
fortitude in, 542
happiness in, 544
humanistic morality as a result of, 494
intellect in, 541
as intelligible essence of things, 445–446
knowledge in, 98, 449–450, 457, 535
lifestyles in, 457–458
renunciation in, 527–528
sacrifice in, 510
and syllable *sat*, 519
and Taoism, 446
and *varnāśrama*, 447
work in, 456
scripture, 119
authority of, 501
license to exaggerate of, 564
See also Vedas
self
according to Carvaka Muni's materialism, 49, 54
according to Nyāya school of Gautama, 49
distinguished from mental/emotional body, 45
as God's eternal servant, 182
identifies with material objects, 47
of the nature of consciousness, 47
qualities of, 52–53
superior to senses, mind, and intelligence, 127
See also jīva-śakti; jīvātmā; parā prakṛti; puruṣa (qualified); self; soul
self-realization, 46
sense objects, 422
interaction with, by enlightened soul, 85–86
withdrawal from, 88–89
senses, 422
controlling, 83–84, 87, 284
jīva soul burdened by, 472
as means to accomplish action, 530
and mind and intellect, 87–88, 125–127

pleasures of, critiqued, 186–187
and sense objects, 84–86
serenity, 85–86
sincerity, 219
Śiva, 331
Skanda Purāṇa, 15
soul, 432
and body and senses, 473
as changeless, 50
creative power of, 258
enlightened, 89–91
as eternal fragment of God, 471–472
as eternal servant of Kṛṣṇa, 120
as fallible *puruṣa*, 479–480
free will of, 180–181, 530–533
and *guṇas*, 439
as indestructible, 47
individuality of, 43, 180
measurement of, 48
misidentification of, with the body, 257–258
nature of, 47–53
never materially tainted, 439
origin of, 448
as performer of action, 114–115, 530–531
reincarnation and transmigration of, 44, 433, 473–474
as self-satisfied, 106–107
service as *dharma* of, 413
See also jīva-śakti; jivātmā; parā prakṛti; puruṣa (qualified); self
spiritual life, experiential 82
in concluding portion of *Vedas*, 68
as fruit of faith in scripture, 69
and self-surrender of devotion, 68
in *Upaniṣads*, 42
and *yoga*, 62–63
śraddhā, 116–118, 287
Śrī, 32–33
Śrī Caitanya
on goal of life, 571
on *jīva* soul as eternal servant of Kṛṣṇa, 120, 258
as Kṛṣṇa himself, 108
magnanimity of, 287, 571
mind of, as Vṛndāvana, *xxv*
as Rādhā and Kṛṣṇa combined, 333
Śrīdhara Swāmī, 486
on action, 539–540
Bhagavad-gītā commentary of, *xxiii*
on moral lapses of devotees, 315–316
on *brahmacārīs* and chanting God's name, 487
on complete sensual withdrawal, 89
on detached action, 525
on liberation, 435
on meaning of
Bg. 18.25, 538
brahmaṇi in verse 5.10, 176–177
prakṛti in verse 4.6, 136
samādhi, 67
on rarity of knowing Kṛṣṇa in truth, 228
on *sārūpya-mukti*, 443
on seeing God everywhere, 437
on the Supreme Person, 466
on work that pleases God, 550
Śrīmad-Bhāgavatam
on approaching Kṛṣṇa with desire for wealth, 241
on being cheated by great souls, 564–565
on desire, 122
on spiritual quality of devotee's body, 80
four essential verses of, 330
on four Kumāras, 244
on great souls' apparent character flaws, 36
on Kṛṣṇa
form of, 342
as the guru, 160
returning to Vraja, *xxvi–xxv*
on pantheism, 301
on pleasing God, 111
on *sāyujya-mukti*, 554–555
on scripture's license to exaggerate, 564
opening stanza of, 325
Uddhava's prayer in, 499
verse 1.7.10 of, and *Gītā* verse 2.53, 75
on virtue and eligibility, 70
śūdras, 548

suffering
nirvāṇa as cessation of, 91
three types of, 78
Śukadeva Goswāmī, 228–229
sukṛti, 241, 251–252
surrender, 567–569
svarūpa-śakti
ingress of, in the individual soul, 297
and Kṛṣṇa's abode, 471
and Kṛṣṇa līlā, 260
and prakṛti, 136–137
as the primary potency of the Absolute, 33
See also yoga-māyā
Śvetāśvatara Upaniṣad, 48, 140, 418–419, 426, 427–428
Swāmī B. R. Śrīdhara. See B. R. Śrīdhara Deva Goswāmī
Taittirīya Upaniṣad, xxi, 397
tamo-guṇa
action in, 538
atheism as a result of, 494
austerities in, 514
charity in, 515
dying under the influence of, 456
effects of, 451
error, delusion, and ignorance are born from, 457
faith and worship in, 506
fear in, 328
food in, 509–510
fortitude in, 543
happiness in, 545
as immobility of matter, 445
inertia of things as, 445–446
intellect in, 542
knowledge in, 536
lifestyles in, 457–458
renunciation in, 526
sacrifice in, 511
symptoms of, 454
and Taoism, 446
work in, 456
taṭastha-śakti, 33
tat tvam asi
knowledge and, 329
meaning "you are his," 225
and oṁ tat sat, 516–518
Ṭhākura Bhaktivinoda (See Bhaktivinoda Ṭhākura)
tolerance, 45–46
truth
indicates Brahman, 140
revealed in installments, 113, 121
tyāga, 524–525
distinguished from sannyāsa, 522–529
and niṣkāma-karma-yoga, 522
as understood by the learned, 522–523
universal form, 360–375, 376–378
Upaniṣadic language
tat tvam asi explained as, 225
used by Kṛṣṇa, 46–47, 264–265, 418–419
Upaniṣads
Bhagavad-gītā based on, 293
on Bhagavān's śaktis, 32–33, 41
and language of aesthetics, xxi
on measurement of the soul, 48–49
prema-dharma of Vraja as secret of, xxi
restrictions on the study of, 113
and Vedānta-sūtra, 477
Vaikuṇṭha, 74
vaiśyas, 548
varṇāśrama, 145–146, 486–488, 546–550
and eligibility for niṣkāma-karma-yoga, 549
Kṛṣṇa created, 145–146
as pleasing God in a general sense, 112
and sattva, 447
and social order today, 70–71, 111–112, 146, 550
and well-adjusted persons, 447
See also brāhmaṇas; kṣatriyas; śūdras; vaiśyas
Vedānta
as conclusion of Vedas, 529
qualification to hear, 41
Vedānta-sūtra
on beginningless karma, 180–181
on bhakti remaining after liberation, 554

cited, 202, 264, 397, 402, 420–421, 501, 530, 550
"I shall become many," 447–448
and *Upaniṣads*, 477
Vedas, 69, 477–478
authority of, 501
and Brahman as used in verse 4.32, 157
karma-kāṇḍa doctrine of, 75
letter of, not all in all, 66, 69
living in accordance with, 486
rituals of, 69, 467
sacrifice in accordance with, 153
Viṣṇu
as the progenitor, 101
See also Mahā-Viṣṇu
Viśvanātha Cakravartī Ṭhākura
on *acintya-bhedābheda*, 290
on Adwaitin reading of *ātmā*, 419
on Arjuna's reluctance to fight, 559
on attainment in paths with and without *bhakti*, 241
on Bg. 5.18, 184
on Bg. 10.8–10.11, 330, 399
Bhagavad-gītā commentary of, *xxii–xxiv*
on Bhagavān, 227–228, 480, 561
on *bhakti* as fruit of knowledge and action, 416
on *bhakti*'s superiority over *jñāna* and *karma*, 68
on Brahmā as the progenitor, 101
on *brahma-nirvāṇa*, 190
on confidential knowledge, 324
on devotees
bodies as spiritual, 80
and fruitive workers and *jñānīs*, 296
moral lapses, 315–316
response to erroneous understanding of God, 141
take shelter of Kṛṣṇa, 556–557
on devotion in lower religious practices, 553
on *dharma* and *bhakti*, 258
on direct experience of God, 82
on Duryodhana's army, 10–11
esoteric explanations of Kṛṣṇa's *līlās* with *gopīs*, *xxii*
on form of God, 237, 297,
on generosity of *bhakti*, 556–557
on intelligence fixed in spiritual pursuit, 65–66
on *jñāna* and Bg. 10.10, 337–338
on *karma-yoga*, 175, 408–409, 414
on knowledge that is concomitant to *bhakti*, 429
on Kṛṣṇa
abode of, 471, 554
demonstrating universe in his mouth, 295
and *gopīs*, *xxii*
personal form of, 342, 399, 404
punishment of the unrighteous, 139
remaining invisibly in earthly Vraja, *xxiv–xxv*
as Supreme Person, 482
on liberation, 434, 443
on *mahātmā*'s devotional union with God, 298
on Mathurā, 565
on meanings of
"all things abiding in me," 161
Bg. 18.25, 538
brahmaṇi in verse 5.10, 176
Janārdana (name of Kṛṣṇa), 94, 343
mad-bhāvam, 141, 458
sāṅkhya, 61
vidyā and *jñāna*, 553
on the mind, 215
on *niṣkāma-karma-yoga*, 407
on paying homage in devotion, 299
on practices outlined by the guru, 216
on *puruṣas*, two types of, 478–479
on religious hypocrisy, 489
on *samādhi*, 208
on *sattva*, 453, 488
on sattvic foods, 508
on ungodly persons, 497, 498
on worship by Monists, 300

on *yoga* implying *bhakti*, 64
Vraja *bhakti*
aspirants for, 334
and Bg. 10.10, 337–338
and esoteric meaning of *catuḥ-ślokī*, 330–338
hearing and chanting on path of, 238
nature of, 288, 358
Śrī Caitanya's descent and, 108
Vraja Kṛṣṇa
as acme of God's incarnation, *xxi*
and *dharma*, 110–111, 569, 576
as Godhead and playful Casanova, 331
Godhood of, is concealed, 288
and Kṛṣṇa's Dwārakā *līlā*, *xxv*
and Mathurā, 565
and *rāsa* dance, 211
as speaker of *Gītā*, *xx–xxi*, *xxiv*, 110–111
Śyāmasundara form of, 399
unmanifest *līlā* of, *xxiv–xxv*, 576
Vyāsa, 477
worlds
creation and dissolution of, 443
as planes of experience, 269–273
worship, 310
of oneness, gods, and nature, 300–301, 304
on path of *karma*, 304–306
in unalloyed devotion, 306–307
Yamunā, *xxi*, 331, 336
yoga, 73
of breath control, 156, 214
and compassion, 213
devotion as highest type of, 195, 223, 276, 298, 395
eating and sleeping habits in, 205
eightfold mystic, 154–156
as equanimity of mind, 71
failure in, 218–222
of freedom, 521–579
grace and effort required for success in, 216
ladder of, 62–63
and *māyā*, overlap of meaning with, 249
mental planes in, 201
Paramātmā as object of meditation in, 192
of Patañjali, 62
as positive union, 62
and selflessness, 62–63, 194–195
sitting arrangements in, 200–203
sutras, 155, 176, 187
symptoms of attainment, 196–200, 213
techniques of, 190–191, 264–266
See also dhyāna-yoga
yoga-māyā, 249–251, 342
Yudhiṣṭhira, 2, 14, 565
yugas, 270–273
See also kalpas